W9-BNK-739

Fun and Games

Fun and Games

A Text on Game Theory

Ken Binmore
University of Michigan
Ann Arbor

D. C. Heath and Company
Lexington, Massachusetts *Toronto*

Address editorial correspondence to:
D. C. Heath
125 Spring Street
Lexington, MA 02173

Cover Photograph: Eric S. Fordham

The John Tenniel illustrations on pages v, vii, 1, 23, 65, 93, 127, 167, 217, 275, 345, 391, 443, 499, and 571, and the "Ocean Chart" on page xv by Henry Holiday are taken from *The Complete Illustrated Works of Lewis Carroll*, published by Chancellor Press, London, 1982.

Technical art by Tech-Graphics, Woburn, Mass.

Published simultaneously in Canada.

Printed in the United States of America.

International Standard Book Number: 0-669-24603-4

Library of Congress Catalog Number: 90-83786

789-QF-00 99 98 97

I dedicate
Fun and Games
to my wife
Josephine.

Preface

Game theory is an activity like skiing or tennis that is only fun if you try to do it well. But learning to do something well is seldom quick and easy, and game theory is no exception. Moreover, unlike skiing or tennis, it really matters that we learn to use game theory well. Its aim is to investigate the manner in which rational people should interact when they have conflicting interests. So far, it provides answers only in simple situations, but these answers have already led to a fundamental restructuring of the way in which economic theorists think about the world, and the time is perhaps not too far distant when the same will be true for all the social sciences.

Thus, although I have tried to develop the theory with a light touch, this is a serious book about a serious subject.

Above all, *Fun and Games* is a how-to-do-it book. It is not like one of those television programs in which you look over an artist's shoulder while he briskly applies ready-mixed paints to an already-prepared canvas using techniques that are never fully explained lest the viewer lose interest and switch to another channel. Encouraging people to appreciate art is doubtless a worthy activity, but I am not interested in trying to do the same thing for game theory. My aims are more ambitious. I hope that, after reading this book, you will be able to do more than admire how other people have used game theory. My hope is that you will be able to apply game-theoretic skills to simple problems *all by yourself*.

Fun and Games is intended to be a serious book on game theory that is suitable for teaching both undergraduate and graduate students. I know that the book works for both purposes because I have been using it and its less-polished predecessors for more than fifteen years at various institutions both in the United States and in Europe. I also know that other approaches that seem as though they might work do not. The practicalities of running a serious course in game theory for undergraduates impose severe limitations on what it is wise to attempt both in terms of content, and in terms of presentation. To these I have added two further constraints. The first is that the focus of the book is on *noncooperative* game theory. Very little is said about *cooperative* game theory. This is partly because of the second constraint, which may be less popular. I have to confess to being squeamish about teaching things to undergraduates that might turn out to be wrong. I know that it is fun for the teacher to weigh the pros and cons of new ideas, but undergraduates tend to treat anything said in class as though Moses had brought it down from the mountain engraved on tablets of stone. Where intellectual honesty allows, I have therefore tried very hard to exclude controversial theoretical ideas altogether.[1]

The book is suitable for teaching students from a number of disciplines. However, the binding practical constraint is that of attracting and holding an audience large enough to merit a case for game theory being retained on the list of undergraduate courses offered by an economics department. Perhaps the increasing recognition of the importance of game

---

[1]Game theory is still being developed at a very fast rate. In such circumstances, it is inevitable that many of the new ideas being tried out will be found wanting and discarded after enjoying a brief period in the limelight. I have adopted the very conservative policy of including only those ideas that I believe are sure to survive. This still leaves more than enough material to fill a semester course for undergraduates twice over.

theory will change things in the future, but as things stand at present, one cannot realistically ask for much in the way of mathematical prerequisites from the students; nor can one restrict entry to economics majors—unless one is to abandon the ambition of teaching a serious how-to-do-it course in favor of a superficial romp through a collection of oversimplified applications whose significance the students will have no way of evaluating. The Teaching Guide that follows this Preface explains the implications in detail. In brief, there is a limit to how much mathematical technique can be taught along the way, and there is a need to respect the wide interests of your audience in choosing the examples used to illustrate the theory.

This is not a scholarly work. It contains no references and, with a few exceptions, mention is made only of the great pioneers in game theory. This would be standard in a book at this level in more established disciplines. Apologies need to be made on this count in a book on game theory only because much of the work is recent and those who contributed are mostly still alive and kicking. All I can say to those who feel that they should have been cited explicitly is that they are in very good company. However, I do want to express my thanks to some individuals whose efforts helped to shape this book, either directly, or indirectly through their published work.

First, there is the Victorian artist John Tenniel, whose magnificent illustrations from Lewis Carroll's *Alice Through the Looking Glass* and elsewhere I have shamelessly stolen. Second, my thanks go to Donald Knuth and to Leslie Lamport for providing the LaTeX typesetting program in which the text was written. Third, I want to thank my publisher D. C. Heath for tolerating such idiosyncracies as punctuating "like this", instead of "like this." George Lobell and Jennifer Brett were particularly helpful in getting the book on the road. Fourth, Pat O'Connell-Young deserves thanks for typing most of the current version, and Mimi Bell for typing a previous version of the book. Fifth, there are D. C. Heath's reviewers: James Bergin, Engelbert Dockner, Ray Farrow, Chris Harris, David Levine, George Mailath, Andrew McLennan, Michael Meurer and Max Stinchcombe. Finally, there is a long list of other economists and mathematicians to whom I owe a debt of gratitude: Steve Alpern, Bob Aumann, Pierpaolo Battigalli, Ted Bergstrom, Adam Brandenburger, James Friedman, Drew Fudenberg, David Gale, John Harsanyi, David Kreps, Hervé Moulin, Roger Myerson, Barry O'Neill, Adam Ostaszewski, Barry Nalebuff, John Nash, Andy Postelwaite, Phil Reny, Bob Rosenthal, Ariel Rubinstein, Larry Samuelson, Reinhard

Selten, Avner Shaked, John Sutton, Jean Tirole, Hal Varian and Robert Wilson.

Finally, on the subject of what pass for jokes in the text, let me say that I feel entitled to the same immunity from criticism as the musician in the Western saloon whose piano was reported by Oscar Wilde to carry a notice saying, "Please do not shoot the pianist. He is doing his best". It isn't easy to sustain a light-hearted atmosphere in a work of this kind. Perhaps it was over-ambitious to promise both *Fun* and *Games*. Certainly, I thought it wise to write in a more deadpan style in the earlier chapters. However, I hope that some readers at least will agree that I did eventually try to live up to my title.

K. B.

Contents

Teaching Guide

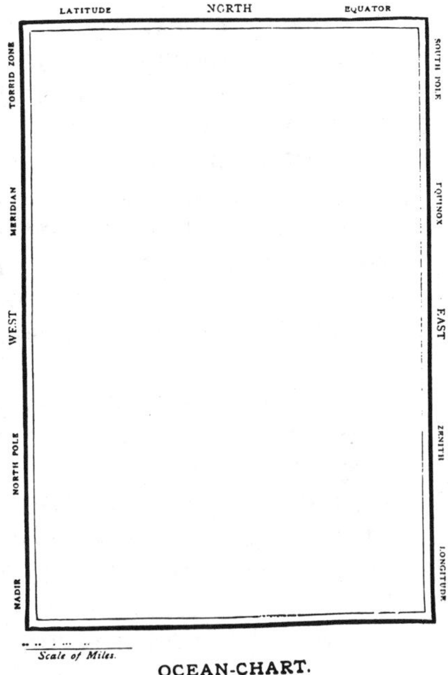

OCEAN-CHART.

Charting a Course

Fun and Games is aimed at two distinct groups of students, and is therefore written on two distinct levels. Teachers therefore need to chart a careful course through the material since things could go awry if there is a mismatch between the students and the topics chosen for study. Or, to say the same thing more colorfully, in seeking to reveal the nature of the snark to your students, beware lest you show them a boojum by mistake. As Lewis Carroll put it, your audience will then "softly and suddenly vanish away", like the Bellman's crew in the *Hunting of the Snark*. However, the Bellman had only the Ocean Chart shown above to guide him.

One aim of *Fun and Games* is to provide a semester course in game theory for undergraduates. The undergraduates do not need to have much prior knowledge of anything, but they will have to be well motivated. Note, in particular, that the undergraduates do not need to be economics majors. This latter point is quite important, since, in many institutions, an undergraduate course in game theory at the level of this book may not be viable if aimed exclusively at economists. However, my experience is that one attracts a respectable audience[1] if one is willing to admit students from all disciplines, and to teach material that takes account of their wide range of interests.

Another aim is to provide "pre-med" material in game theory for graduate students in economics. In this role, the book is not intended as a competitor to the excellent books written by Fudenburg and Tirole and by Myerson. It is intended to serve only as an easy way into the serious stuff for those who do not feel the urge to plunge in immediately at the deep end.

The two aims frequently dovetail very neatly, and the join between the two levels of exposition would not always be easy to spot if it were not pointed out explicitly. Teachers must decide for themselves how often to cross this boundary line. I certainly cross it myself when the idiosyncracies of my audience seem to call for it. However, it is unwise to cross the line too often, since the risk of frightening off one audience and boring the other is considerable. Of course, nothing will or should prevent enthusiastic undergraduates from reading the more advanced material on the side. At the same time, graduate students will need to skim the more elementary material in order to make sense of the topics written specifically for them. In class, however, I recommend keeping on the appropriate side of the demarcation line nearly all the time.

Material that is a candidate for being skipped when teaching a semester course to undergraduates is indicated by a stylized version of John Tenniel's Mad Hatter in the margin. When the Mad Hatter is running away, consider very carefully whether the material following his appearance is suitable for your undergraduates. If not, then skip the material and go to the section number indicated beneath the fleeing Mad Hatter. When I teach economics undergraduates, for example, my instructions are that the Mad Hatter is to be

[1]Last term I taught game theory at the University of Michigan to 46 undergraduates taking the course for credit, and an indeterminate number of auditors of various types.

followed wherever he goes, except when he is skipping some economics. When I teach mathematics undergraduates, my instructions are more complicated.

Nothing whatever in the book is too hard for graduate students. They should certainly *not* follow the Mad Hatter anywhere at all. On the contrary, his appearance should signal the fact that the material that follows contains something that merits their close attention.

Sometimes the Mad Hatter in the margin is not running away. Instead he is shown somewhat apprehensively hanging around to see what happens next. Usually what happens next is something mathematical. Such passages may be difficult for some undergraduates, but cannot be skipped without disrupting the continuity of the exposition.

Review

Math

Econ

As in the examples given above, all the marginal Mad Hatters are equipped with a label indicating the type of material to which they refer. The five labels used are

Review **Math** **Econ** **Phil** **Fun**

The same labeling is used to categorize many of the exercises that appear at the end of each chapter. What do these labels mean?

Review. My experience is that one cannot run a viable course for undergraduates if the mathematical prerequisites are set too high. The most one can realistically do is to restrict entry to students who have passed a serious freshman calculus course. Many of the students will know more than this. The others will have to pick up what extra mathematics they need along the way. Students seem ready to put in the necessary work on the side provided that what is required of them is made very clear. This explains the presence of the REVIEW sections. The chief topics covered in these sections are probability, matrices and vectors, and convexity. Calculus does not get the same treatment, since students are assumed to know what little is needed already. However, reminders about how to do various things sometimes appear as footnotes.[2]

[2]Although I know that those who need such reminders do not read such things as footnotes, appendices and introductions.

Do not think for one moment of teaching the review material at the blackboard. I have already pulled the rug out from under such a project by using the label REVIEW. It seems a universal knee-jerk reaction in the human species to switch off as soon as this word is mentioned in the classroom. What I do myself is to point out those mathematical ideas in the REVIEW sections that are indispensable, and then sneak some discussion of them into the hours devoted to going over the exercises.

Actually, there is a lot more in these REVIEW sections than undergraduate students are going to need to study *Fun and Games*. When writing them, I also had graduate students in mind. If my experience is anything to go by, many graduate students would be advised to skim these mathematical REVIEW sections very slowly.

Math. When teaching undergraduates, you will probably wish to skip nearly all the MATH sections that the Mad Hatter is shown running away from, unless your audience consists primarily of mathematics majors. However, mathematicians should not take this to imply that the MATH sections are written in a formal style. None of the arguments offered come anywhere near meeting the standards of a mathematical proof. Mostly, I follow the Bellman and use the principle that what I tell you three times is true. On the other hand, I have tried hard to be intellectually honest. All the arguments offered can be fleshed out into formal proofs without calling for mathematical techniques that would be beyond the understanding of an average undergraduate willing to take some time and trouble. I hope that these proof schemata will be particularly useful to graduate students who are too often shortchanged with a list of cookbook techniques whose validity they are expected to take on trust.

Econ. I have taught game theory in numerous institutions. The undergraduate classes consist mostly of economists, but there is always a substantial number of students majoring in other disciplines whose presence livens things up a fair amount. The disciplines include mathematics, engineering, philosophy and political science. Some of the ECON sections are intended to acquaint such students with relevant elementary ideas from economics. These sections are intended to be read on the side. Later ECON sections indicate some of the more straightforward applications of game theory to economics. Although the Mad Hatter is shown running away from these sections because they are not usually strictly necessary to the flow of the exposition, economists will want to teach this material unless it has been adequately covered in other economics courses. My experience with majors in other disciplines is that they welcome the opportunity to learn a little economics.

If *Fun and Games* proceeds to a second edition, I plan to include an organized supplement on simple applications of game theory in economics and elsewhere. In the meantime, three things should be noted. First, those applications covered in the text are not covered in a superficial way. That is, the text provides enough detail to make it possible for the students to work problems on the material. Second, many of the ECON exercises at the end of each chapter are very instructive. (I hope that graduate students will not neglect to attempt as many of these as time allows.) My own preference is to encourage students to teach themselves how to apply game theory to economics via these exercises. Finally, remember that some of your audience will not be economics majors.

Phil. It is not wise to try to teach the foundations of game theory to undergraduates in a formal way. On the other hand, your more adventurous students are not going to be fobbed off with easy answers. Somehow it is necessary to satisfy the sceptics without bewildering the rest of the class. I try to do this with the PHIL sections. My recommendation is to soft-pedal this material when teaching undergraduates. Personally, I find the issues fascinating. However, trying to discuss them seriously with undergraduates can sometimes be very frustrating. Fortunately, most undergraduates are only too happy to leave philosophical questions to the philosophers.

Graduate students, on the other hand, cannot dispense with a view on these issues. But a fully rounded view will have to be obtained from some other source since I have tried hard in writing this book to steer clear of controversial matters. However, perhaps the PHIL sections will make it clear what some of the issues are on which a view is needed. Perhaps they will also serve to instill a little scepticism about some of the views that are currently fashionable.

Fun. I hope that you will not skip all the FUN sections. Some of them are very instructive.

How Far to Go

My advice to graduate students is simple. I advocate reading everything (including the final chapter on Poker) as much for the mathematical techniques that will be encountered as for the content. As a focus for your studies, I suggest that you make it your objective to get to Chapters 7, 8, 10 and 11 as soon as possible. Otherwise there is nothing more that needs to be said to a graduate student except that it is a waste of time to read anything at all without planning to work at least some of the exercises. However, the position for undergraduates is more complicated.

Even if the Mad Hatter is followed wherever he goes, *Fun and Games* still contains a lot more material than it would be wise to try and teach to undergraduates in a one-semester course. Given that adequate time is set aside for discussion of the exercises, there is a choice to be made about what topics to cover. To a large extent, this is a judgment call. However, if this book is to be used, I do not recommend changing the *order* in which topics are introduced, even when the order I have chosen may seem curious. I have been experimenting with various approaches for more than fifteen years, and my reasons for doing it my way may not always be immediately obvious. For example, why does the chapter on bargaining precede the chapter on zero-sum games? The reason is that the chapter on zero-sum games is more technically demanding for undergraduates than you might think. In particular, whatever their background, you cannot always rely on your students' knowing anything useful about convexity at all. However, after the chapter on bargaining, they will no longer think of a convex set as being some mysterious and incomprehensible mathematical object. Why is the notion of a Nash equilibrium introduced in Chapter 1 and then kept simmering all the way up to Chapter 7 before it is discussed comprehensively? This is because undergraduates can become overwhelmed if you try to tell them everything at once. They often need time to build up some confidence in their ability to cope before you hit them with too much. Why so much fuss about Hex in Chapter 1? Because it is going to get used in Chapter 7 in a discussion of fixed point theorems.[3] Such a litany of questions and answers could be continued indefinitely. In brief, some of the later material depends on earlier material in ways that may not be immediately apparent.

The list of chapters given next indicates what each chapter is intended to achieve. Three routes through the material are

[3]However, if you follow the Mad Hatter, you will skip most of the fuss about Hex and all the discussion of fixed point theorems—although I have taught both topics successfully to undergraduates.

then proposed, of which I would advocate the first if you are teaching game theory to undergraduates for the first time.

Introduction. The introduction provides some ammunition for a preliminary pep-talk if this seems necessary. It is about where game theory came from and where it is going to, what it can do and why it matters.

1. **Winning Out.** The formal definition of a game is not introduced all at once. This chapter introduces two-player games of perfect information with no chance moves. A few results about the strictly competitive case are proved carefully to indicate the flavor of what is to come. The ideas of Nash and subgame-perfect equilibrium make a first tentative appearance.
2. **Taking Chances.** Chance moves and lotteries are introduced. Elementary probability ideas are reviewed and put to use.
3. **Accounting for Tastes.** A review of elementary utility theory is followed by an extended example that touches upon the modeling of imperfect information and emphasizes that rational behavior may depend on the players' attitudes to taking risks. Von Neumann and Morgenstern utility theory is then discussed.
4. **Getting Paid Off.** The notion of a Von Neumann and Morgenstern payoff is systematically exploited. After an extended review of vectors and matrices, the idea of successively deleting dominated strategies is explained. Common knowledge is mentioned briefly, and the distinction between Nash and subgame-perfect equilibrium is stressed.
5. **Making Deals.** This chapter is about bargaining. After reviewing convexity, it introduces the Nash bargaining solution. (This is the only use of cooperative game theory in the book.) The remainder of the chapter uses the Rubinstein bargaining model to press home the idea of a subgame-perfect equilibrium.
6. **Mixing Things Up.** Mixed strategies are introduced as a preliminary to a conventional analysis of zero-sum games. (Note that mixed strategies are needed in all later chapters, and minimax ideas are relevant in studying repeated games.)
7. **Keeping Your Balance.** Now that Nash equilibrium is familiar, its properties are studied in some detail. Here is where the Prisoners' Dilemma is first discussed. Reaction curves, applications to oligopoly, equilibrium selection and existence are all in this long chapter. Even the mathematics of fixed point methods is not neglected.

8. **Repeating Yourself.** This chapter is about repeated games. It begins with an example intended to emphasize how complicated strategies can get in this context. This example motivates the chapter's use of finite automata in describing strategies. A simple version of the folk theorem is given together with some philosophizing about social contracts.
9. **Adjusting to Circumstances.** This chapter describes some simple trial-and-error adjustment processes. It includes an introduction to the use of game theory in evolutionary biology and a discussion of the "evolution of cooperation".
10. **Knowing Your Place.** This chapter contains an unusually careful account of the role of the theory of knowledge in game theory. Information sets are finally tied down properly, and signaling is introduced. Common knowledge gets a thorough airing, and some foundational issues are raised.
11. **Knowing Who to Believe.** Incomplete information is discussed in detail. The chapter includes material on signaling, auctions, the revelation principle and mechanism design. The reasons why refinement theory is controversial are mentioned.
12. **Bluffing It Out.** This chapter is ostensibly about Poker, but is really an extended exercise in the use of the techniques the book has introduced.

There are at least three viable routes through the book for a one-semester course for undergraduates. Whether you wish to prefix any of these routes with some propaganda about the importance of game theory drawn from the Introduction is a matter of taste. I find that there is time for a few excursions off the main routes. What diversions I make depend on whom I am teaching. When teaching mostly economists, for example, I do not always follow the Mad Hatter past the economics sections.

- **Route 1.** Begin at Chapter 1 and follow the Mad Hatter all the way through to the end of Chapter 7.
- **Route 2.** Follow the first route until the end of Chapter 4, and then skip forward to Chapter 7 and follow the Mad Hatter onwards from there (perhaps omitting Chapter 9 and looking instead at some of the more advanced material in Chapters 10 and 11). You will need to do some patching on the subject of mixed strategies in Chapter 7.
- **Route 3.** Spend as little time as possible on Chapters 1, 2 and 3, and then follow the Mad Hatter from Chapter 4

onwards (perhaps omitting some of Chapters 5, 6 or 9 to leave more time for Chapters 10 and 11).

If the third and most ambitious route is followed, some cautionary remarks may be helpful. Chapters 2 and 3 can be telescoped into discussions of the games Duel and Russian Roulette. You will not be able to evade saying something about lotteries and expected utility, but what you say can be kept very brief.[4] However, Chapter 1 does not compress so readily. You will need at least to cover the extensive and strategic forms of a game, some version of Zermelo's algorithm, the notion of the value of a strictly competitive game like Chess, and the ideas of Nash and subgame-perfect equilibrium. However, I have two reasons for suggesting that this chapter not be taken quite so swiftly. The first is that it is never wise to hurry the first few lectures of any course. The second is that Chapter 1 is partly designed to fulfill a *screening* role. Some of the arguments offered are therefore more closely reasoned than is perhaps strictly necessary so as not to give a false impression about what is coming later.

Questions and Answers

I attach very great importance to the working of exercises in whatever course I teach. For this reason, *Fun and Games* contains large numbers of exercises for students to work by themselves. Normally, I insist on written answers being handed in to about five exercises a week. If you do this, it is important to explain that you understand that your class is only human, and that you are not so unreasonable as to expect perfect answers to every problem. Some of the problems are, and ought to be, challenging. What you want from the students is their best shot. However, this includes being careful about the presentation of their answers. Students learn astonishingly quickly that it is not acceptable to embed a correct answer in a few lines of indecipherable scrawl, or to submerge the answer in several pages of irrelevant waffle. My impression is that they *like* being made to do things right.

The students will, of course, be worried about your grading policy, so make it clear from the outset that you understand

[4] Provided that your students are confident about their ability to cope with simple probabilistic problems. Personally, I think it a great pity to skip the Von Neumann and Morgenstern theory of decision-making under risk. All sorts of misunderstandings are commonly made because this theory is not understood. However, I recognize that this is a judgment call.

that they are not a randomly drawn sample from the student population. They are a highly self-selected group and your grades will reflect this reality. After setting some demanding exercises, you can reinforce this piece of propaganda by complimenting them on how cleverly the class as a whole approached the difficulties, even though few of them may have been able to see their way through to a triumphant conclusion. Usually, this will be nothing less than the plain truth. Things will be going well if, after some time, you find the students arguing among themselves about last week's problems when you enter the classroom. As for examinations, I think it reasonable to tell the students that you plan to ask them questions that are similar to those that they have been asked to do for homework, or else are even more similar to other exercises of comparable difficulty that appear in the book.

The exercises at the end of each chapter are a mixed bunch. They range from questions that require little more than repeating a definition to problems that might stump Von Neumann himself. A little care is therefore necessary in selecting problems for your students to answer. The list below is a set of possible weekly assignments. The starred items are suitable

Assignment	Exercise section	Questions				
1	1.10	2	3	7	10	20
2†	1.10	21	22	23	24	25
3	2.6	5	7	11	21	23
4	3.7	5	9	11	14	22
5	4.8	2	16	21	24	25
6	5.9	13	15	21	23	25
7	6.10	4	14	15	18	19
8	6.10	27	29	34	36	41
9	7.9	1	11	13	14	18
10†	7.9	27	29	34	35	40
11	8.6	5	8	10	21	23
12*	9.8	2	7	15	17	23
13	10.9	1	11	12	15	17
14*†	10.9	20	23	30	31	35
15	11.10	1	2	3	4	11
16*†	11.10	22	23	24	27	29
17*†	11.10	38	41	42	43	44

only for graduate students. Those marked with a dagger cover topics that you may prefer to incorporate into the main body of your course.

I am grateful to Bruce Linster for providing outline answers to a selection of ten questions from each chapter at the end of the book. For the earlier chapters, the answers are mostly to questions that one might reasonably ask undergraduates to attempt. These mainstream answers are supplemented with a few hints on how to solve the occasional brainteaser with which the exercises have been salted. There is no overlap between the questions to which answers are provided and those that appear in the suggested assignments. Teachers can obtain a full set of answers from the publisher.

Why Teach This Way?

Intro ⟶

Notice the Mad Hatter in the margin inviting you to escape the philosophical remarks coming up by skipping forward to the Introduction. The philosophical question to be considered is why I chose to write a book like this, rather than a romp through some undemanding "applications" of the theory in easily described economic models.

Early this morning, one of the more talented students in my undergraduate Intermediate Microeconomics class at the University of Michigan asked me when he was going to be taught something with some substance: something that he could get his teeth into. I had to tell him that Intermediate Microeconomics is about as challenging as regular undergraduate courses in economics get. Later this morning, I have to teach a graduate class, Microeconomic Theory II. The content of this graduate course is not intrinsically difficult and the students are intelligent, but many of them have to work very hard to keep abreast of things. They are very ready to work hard, but such effort would not be necessary in an ideal world. In such a world, a person at the end of his or her undergraduate career would have been equipped with the learning skills needed to cope comfortably with serious material presented seriously. I am not talking here about a lack of technical skills, although this is certainly part of the problem. What holds the students back is their lack of self-confidence. Before many of them can begin to learn in earnest, they first have to learn that they really are able to learn. Such confidence comes only through studying at least one challenging subject *in depth*. Nobody can be confident about their learning skills if they have never been offered the opportunity to do more than skim the surface of the subjects they are taught.

However, too many undergraduates are never offered such an opportunity.

Much of what passes for an undergraduate education, both in the United States and in Europe, seems to me little more than an unwitting conspiracy between the teacher and the student to defraud whoever is paying the fees. The teacher pretends to teach, and the student pretends to learn, material that both know in their hearts is so emasculated that it cannot possibly be properly understood in the form in which it is presented. Even the weaker students grow tired of such a diet of predigested pap. They understand perfectly well that "appreciating the concepts" is getting them nowhere except nearer to a piece of paper that entitles them to write letters after their names. But most students want more than this. They want to learn things *properly* so that they are in a position to feel that they can defend what they have been taught without having to resort to the authority of their teachers or the textbook. Of course, learning things properly can be hard work. But my experience is that students seldom protest at being worked hard provided that their program of study is organized so that they quickly see that their efforts are producing tangible dividends.

However, it is one thing to see that our system of education could be improved, but quite another to do something about it. When teaching traditional courses in economics and the other social sciences, one tends to get trapped by the system. It is particularly hard to organize a serious course in a way that allows students to see their efforts being quickly rewarded. Teachers of introductory courses will typically already have skimmed the cream from the material that you are supposed to teach by discussing most of the intellectually exciting ideas in some diluted form. But you will seldom be able to rely on students' knowing what is taught in such introductory courses sufficiently well that you can make use of their knowledge. Indeed, what lodges in the minds of students when they are "appreciating the concepts" in introductory courses is sometimes so confused that they need to be "untaught" before further progress is possible. A great deal of what students will despise as "review material" is therefore inevitable unless you are willing to be innovative about the syllabus. But monkeying around with the syllabus is seldom a practical option unless your colleagues teaching companion courses are unusually tolerant.

Teaching game theory provides an opportunity to break free from some of these constraints, because traditions about how it should be taught have yet to evolve. In particular, it usually gets only a passing mention in introductory courses. Most students who sign up for game theory therefore come with an open mind in the hope of being taught something new and interesting. They sometimes even think that the material may be fun to learn. They also know that the subject does not depend too heavily on material that should have been mastered in earlier courses but is now water long gone under the bridge. In none of these expectations will they be disappointed. It is also true that game theory has assumed a central role in much of economic theory, and so students who are contemplating graduate work can congratulate themselves on doing something that will certainly be useful to them. At the same time, you can truthfully tell students that the role of game theory is bound to expand in the future, not only within economics, but also in the other social sciences. It already has, for example, firm footholds in biology and political science.

All of this means that someone teaching game theory can afford to be more ambitious than the teacher of a more traditional subject. The students come with a positive attitude, and you can carry them forward quickly into areas that will seem new and exciting to them. An opportunity therefore exists to provide some genuine education—to train some minds in how to think about serious problems seriously. I believe that, although the substantive content of game theory is certainly of great importance, it is this opportunity that should excite us most. That is to say, in teaching game theory, it really is true that the medium is at least as important as the message.

Other Books

Robert Aumann, *Lectures on Game Theory*, Westview Press (Underground Classics in Economics), 1989. These are the classroom notes of one of the great game theorists.

Robert Aumann and Sergio Hart, *Handbook of Game Theory.* This will be a comprehensive collection of survey articles on game theory and its applications for research workers in the field.

Elwyn Berlekamp, John Conway and Richard Guy, *Winning Ways for Your Mathematical Plays,* Academic Press, 1982. This is a witty and incredibly inventive book about combinatorial game theory. The authors try very hard to make their ideas accessible to the layman, but I suspect one needs mathematical training for it to hold the attention.

Ken Binmore, *Essays on the Foundations of Game Theory,* Blackwell, 1990. Some of these essays grapple with the controversial issues that *Fun and Games* avoids, but don't expect any definitive answers. (Readers of *Fun and Games* will be able to skip Chapters 2, 3 and 4.)

Steven Brams, *Superior Beings*, Springer-Verlag, 1983. If you thought game theory had no applications in theology—think again!

Avinash Dixit and Barry Nalebuff, *Thinking Strategically*, Norton, 1991. This is a delightful collection of stories and anecdotes drawn from real life that illustrate game theory in action. Its accessibility is attested to by its appearance on the Book-of-the-Month Club list.

James Friedman, *Game Theory with Applications to Economics*, second edition, MIT Press, 1990. James Friedman pioneered the application of repeated games to problems in industrial organization. Here you can learn the tricks of the trade.

Drew Fudenberg and Jean Tirole, *Game Theory*, MIT Press, 1991. This is the book to read if you want to be published in *Econometrica*. It is remarkable how much ground they manage to cover.

Josef Hofbauer and Karl Sigmund, *The Theory of Evolution and Dynamical Systems,* Cambridge University Press, 1988. This is a highly accessible and unfussy introduction to the mathematics of evolutionary systems.

Tashiro Ichiishi, *Game Theory for Economic Analysis*, Academic Press, 1983. This is a formal book that concentrates on cooperative game theory. The mathematical exposition is admirably clear and unfussy.

David Kreps, *A Course in Microeconomic Theory,* Princeton University Press, 1990. This big book takes it for granted that game theory is part of microeconomic theory. It is a must for those planning to make a career in economics. The problems are often very instructive indeed.

David Kreps, *Game Theory and Economic Modelling*, Oxford University Press, 1990. Listen to what daddy says on economic modeling and you won't go far wrong!

Duncan Luce and Howard Raiffa, *Games and Decisions*, Wiley, 1957. This evergreen classic is a model for how a book should be written.

John Maynard Smith, *Evolution and the Theory of Games*, Cambridge University Press, 1982. Everyone should at least dip into this beautiful book.

Hervé Moulin, *Game Theory for the Social Sciences*, second revised edition, New York University Press, 1986. This is an elementary introduction to game theory in which the mathematics is allowed to speak for itself. It is particularly valuable as a source of instructive problems. (You want *both* volumes.)

Roger Myerson, *Game Theory: Analysis of Conflict*, Harvard University Press, 1991. Roger Myerson is the prime mover in the subject of mechanism design. His book is an encyclopedic introduction to game theory in which each brick is carefully laid precisely where it belongs. This is a book for those who feel that things should be done properly.

Peter Ordeshook, *Game Theory and Political Theory*, Cambridge University Press, 1986. This is the place to look for applications in political science.

Martin Osborne and Ariel Rubinstein, *Bargaining and Markets*, Academic Press, 1990. If you want more on bargaining than Chapter 5 of *Fun and Games* has to offer, this is an excellent place to begin.

Guillermo Owen, *Game Theory*, second edition, Academic Press, 1982. This elegant book is particularly strong on cooperative game theory.

Eric Rasmusen, *Games and Information,* Blackwell, 1989. This is a book for those who want to get straight to the economic applications without having to fiddle around with the theory first.

Thomas Schelling, *The Strategy of Conflict,* Harvard University Press, 1960. This is a classic that will remain on everybody's reading list for many years to come.

Martin Shubik, *Game Theory in the Social Sciences,* MIT Press, 1984. Martin Shubik is one of the great pioneers in applying game theory to economics. The second volume of this monumental work is where he gives us the benefit of his wide experience.

Jean Tirole, *The Theory of Industrial Organization*, MIT Press, 1988. This beautiful book is a model of its kind. Those who want a quick introduction to game theory will find their needs catered to in a magnificently concise appendix.

John Von Neumann and Oskar Morgenstern, *The Theory of Games and Economic Behavior*, Princeton University Press, 1944. I have read the great classic of game theory from cover to cover, but I do not recommend the experience to others! Its current interest is largely historical.

Herbert Yardley, *The Education of a Poker Player*, Jonathan Cape, 1959. Don't waste time on Chapter 12 of *Fun and Games* if what you care about is how to make money playing Poker.

Introduction

The poet Horace advised his young disciples to begin *in media res*. I think he was right. The way to learn game theory is to turn straight to the first chapter and plunge into the *middle of things*. This introduction is for the faint-hearted and the middle-aged who want some questions answered before making a commitment.

- What is game theory about?
- Where is it coming from?
- Where is it going to?
- What can it do for us?

These are big questions to which there are no neat and tidy answers. An introduction can only give some flavor of the answers that game theorists offer.[1] But perhaps this will be enough to whet your appetite.

0.1 What Is Game Theory About?

A game is being played whenever people interact with each other. If you drive a car in a busy city street, you are playing a game with the drivers of the other cars. When you make a bid at an auction, you are playing a game with the other bidders. When a supermarket manager decides the price at which she will try to sell cans of beans, she is playing a game with her customers and with the managers of rival supermarkets. When a firm and a union negotiate next year's wage contract, they are playing a game. The prosecuting and defending attorneys are playing a game when each decides what arguments to put before the jury. Napoleon and Wellington were playing a game at the Battle of Waterloo, and so were Khrushchev and Kennedy during the Cuban missile crisis.

If all these situations are games, then game theory is clearly something important. Indeed, one could argue that all the social sciences are nothing more than subdisciplines of game theory. However, this doesn't mean that game theorists are the people to ask for answers to all the world's problems. This is because game theory, as currently developed, is mostly about what happens when people interact in a *rational* manner. If this observation tempts you to return *Fun and Games*

[1] Chapter 1 of my *Essays on the Foundations of Game Theory* (Blackwell, 1990) is a longer introduction to the subject. Dixit and Nalebuff's *Thinking Strategically* (Norton, 1991) is a delightful collection of stories and anecdotes showing game theory in action in real-life situations. Kreps' *Game Theory and Economic Modelling* (Oxford University Press, 1990) is an introduction that emphasizes the uses of game theory in economics.

to the bookstore in the hope of getting your money refunded, think again. Nobody is saying that people *always* behave rationally. But neither is it true that people always act *irrationally.* Most of us try at least to spend our money sensibly, and most of the time we don't do too badly. Otherwise, economic theory wouldn't work at all. Even when we are not actively thinking things out in advance, it does not necessarily follow that we are behaving irrationally. In fact, game theory has had some notable successes in analyzing the behavior of insects and plants, neither of which can be said to think at all. Their behavior is rational because those insects and plants whose genes programmed them to behave irrationally are now extinct. Evolution removed them. And, just as biological evolution acts to remove biologically unfit behavior, so other kinds of evolution can act to remove socially or economically unfit behavior. For example, firms that manage their affairs stupidly tend to go bankrupt and so disappear from the scene.

Perhaps you will agree that rational interaction between groups of people is an exciting area to study, but why call it *game theory?* Do we not trivialize the problems that people face by calling them *games?* Worse still, do we not devalue our humanity by reducing our struggle for fulfillment to the status of mere *play* in a game?

The proper answers to these questions stand them on their heads. The more deeply we feel about issues, the more important it is that we do not allow ourselves to be misled by wishful thinking. Game theory makes a virtue out of using the language of parlor games like Chess or Poker to discuss the *logic* of strategic interaction. I know that Bridge players sometimes shoot their partners. I have sometimes felt the urge myself. Nevertheless, most of the time, people are able to think about the strategic issues that arise in parlor games *dispassionately.* That is to say, they are willing to follow the logic wherever it goes without throwing their hands up in horror if it leads to an unwelcome destination. In insisting on using the language of parlor games, game theorists are therefore not revealing themselves to be cold-hearted followers of Machiavelli who care nothing for the sorrows of the world. They are simply attempting to separate those features of a problem that are susceptible to uncontroversial rational analysis from those that are not.

Human beings are not naturally very good at thinking about problems of strategic interaction. We become distressed when confronted with circular reasoning. But circular reasoning cannot be evaded in considering strategic issues. If John and

Mary are playing a game, then John's choice of strategy will depend on what he predicts Mary's choice of strategy will be. But she is simultaneously choosing a strategy, using her prediction of John's strategy choice. Given that it is necessarily based on such involuted logic, it is perhaps not surprising that game theory abounds with surprises and paradoxes.

- Is it possible, do you think, that someone at a committee meeting might find it optimal to vote for the alternative they *like the least*?
- Could it be be a good idea for a general to *toss a coin* to decide whether to attack today or tomorrow?
- Can it be optimal for a Poker player always to bet the maximum when dealt the *worst possible hand*?
- Could it ever make sense for someone with goods to trade to begin by *throwing some of them away*?
- Might it ever be rational for someone with a house to sell to use an auction in which the highest bidder gets the house, but only has to pay the bid made by the *second-highest* bidder?

You will have guessed, of course, that the seemingly crazy answer is correct in each case. Let us look at the first and last questions to try and understand why our intuitions are so unhelpful. This will simultaneously provide some feel for the whole book, since problems of the first kind are discussed in Chapter 1 at the beginning of the book, and problems of the last kind are discussed in Chapter 11 towards its end.

0.1.1 Strategic Voting

Boris, Horace and Maurice are the membership committee of the very exclusive Dead Poets Society. The final item on their agenda one morning is a proposal that Alice should be admitted as a new member. No mention is made of another possible candidate called Bob, and so an amendment to the final item is proposed. The amendment states that Alice's name should be replaced by Bob's. The rules for voting in committees call for amendments to be voted on in the order in which they are proposed. The committee therefore begins by voting on whether Bob should replace Alice. If Alice wins, they then vote on whether Alice or Nobody should be made a new member. If Bob wins, they then vote on whether Bob or Nobody should be made a new member. Figure 0.1(a) is a diagrammatic representation of the order in which the voting takes place. Figure 0.1(b) shows how the three committee members rank the three possible outcomes.

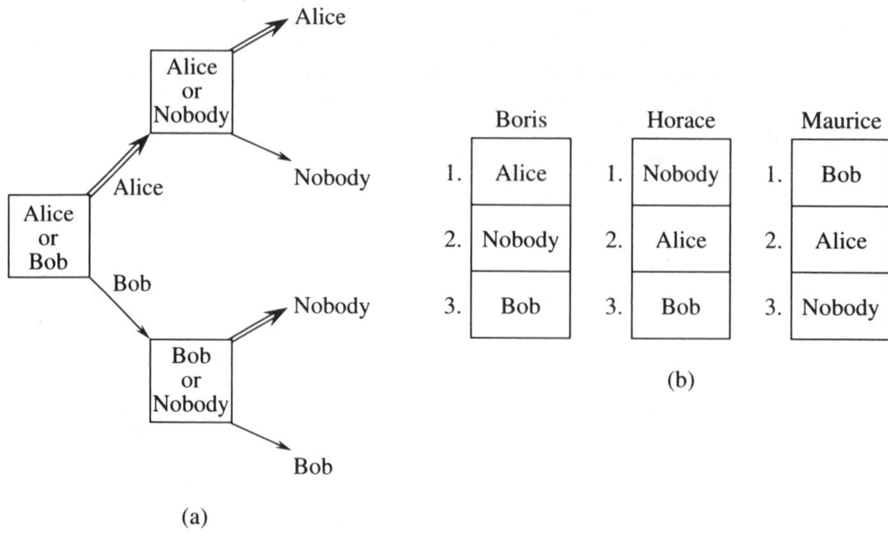

Figure 0.1 Strategic voting.

The doubled lines in Figure 0.1(a) show who would win the vote if everybody just voted according to their rankings. For example, in a vote between Alice and Bob, Alice would win because both Boris and Horace rank Alice above Bob and so Maurice would be outvoted. Thus, if there is no strategic voting, Alice will be elected to the club because she will also win when she is matched against Nobody.

However, if Horace looks ahead, he will see that there is no point in voting against Bob at the first vote. If Bob wins the first vote, then Nobody will triumph at the second vote,[2] and Nobody is Horace's first preference. Thus, Horace should switch his vote from Alice at the first vote, and cast his vote instead for Bob, who is the candidate *he likes the least.* If Boris and Maurice do not also vote strategically, the result will be that Nobody is elected.

But this is not the end of the story. Maurice may anticipate that Horace will vote strategically. If so, Maurice will also vote strategically by switching his vote from Bob to Alice. Maurice will then fail to vote for the candidate he likes the most. His reason for doing so is that he thereby ensures that Alice is elected rather than Nobody.

The reasoning used by Horace and Maurice in this story is called *backwards induction.* They predict what would happen in the future and then reason backwards to the present. The mathematician Zermelo applied the same type of reasoning

[2]Why is there no point in anyone voting strategically at the second vote?

to Chess as long ago as 1912. For this reason, the process is called *Zermelo's algorithm* in Section 1.4 of the text.

Game theorists care about what happens when everybody reasons optimally. Here this means that everybody uses Zermelo's algorithm, and hence everybody votes strategically. Does this mean that Alice gets elected? You will be able to work this out for sure after reading Chapter 1!

0.1.2 Auctions

Econ 0.1.3 ⟶

Mad Hatters, like the little guy who has just appeared in the margin, are designed to help you find your way around the text. The Teaching Guide explains their significance in detail. Here he is rushing on to Section 0.1.3 to avoid learning some economics. Mathematical folk may think him wise. As Lewis Carroll put it:

> And what mean all these mysteries to me
> Whose life is full of indices and surds?
>
> $$x^2 + 7x + 53$$
> $$= \cdots \tfrac{11}{3}$$

However, you won't get much from this book if you just read the mathematical bits.

Alice wants to get the best price she can for her very fancy house. There are two potential buyers, Horace and Maurice. If she knew the maximum each would be willing to pay, her problem would be easy. However, although she doesn't know their reservation prices, she is not entirely ignorant. It is common knowledge that each potential buyer has a reservation price of either three million or four million dollars, and that each value is equally likely. Moreover, the two reservation prices are independent of each other (Section 2.1.2).

An auctioneer advises her to run a "second-price auction". In such an auction, each bidder secretly seals his bid in an envelope. The envelopes are then publicly opened, and the house is sold to the highest bidder,[3] but not at the price he bid. Instead it is sold to him at the highest price *bid by a loser*. The advantage of such an arrangement, the auctioneer explains, is that it induces rational people to bid their *true* reservation prices. Horace, for example, would reason like this. Suppose that Maurice's bid is for *less* than my reservation price. Then I want to win the auction, and I can do so just by bidding my own reservation price truthfully. On

[3] If there is a tie, it is broken at random.

the other hand, if Maurice's bid is for *more* than my reservation price, then I don't want to win, and I can guarantee not doing so by bidding my own reservation price truthfully. Thus, in a second-price auction, telling the truth about your reservation price is a heads-I-win-tails-you-lose proposition. Game theorists say that bidding truthfully is a strategy that *dominates* all its alternatives.

Alice understands all this, but she doesn't much like what she hears. It seems obvious to her that she must do better by selling the house for the highest price that gets bid rather than for the second highest price. So she fires the first auctioneer and hires instead a second auctioneer who tells her what she wants to hear. He organizes a sealed-bid auction just like the first auctioneer's, except that the house is now sold to the highest bidder at whatever price he bids.

Math 0.1.3 ⟶

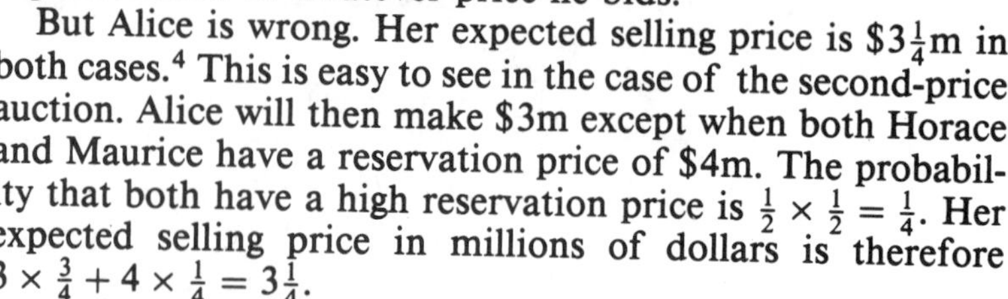

But Alice is wrong. Her expected selling price is $\$3\frac{1}{4}$m in both cases.[4] This is easy to see in the case of the second-price auction. Alice will then make \$3m except when both Horace and Maurice have a reservation price of \$4m. The probability that both have a high reservation price is $\frac{1}{2} \times \frac{1}{2} = \frac{1}{4}$. Her expected selling price in millions of dollars is therefore $3 \times \frac{3}{4} + 4 \times \frac{1}{4} = 3\frac{1}{4}$.

Perhaps this mention of probabilities and expected values makes you feel apprehensive. If so, take careful note of the Mad Hatter who has appeared in the margin, and follow him by rushing on to the next section. What you need to know about probabilities and expected values (which isn't much) will be reviewed in Chapter 2. As for the piece of mathematics that the Mad Hatter is rushing on to avoid, you might use this as a test for how suitable *Fun and Games* is for someone with your background. At the end of the book, I hope that such an argument will seem transparently clear. However, if you get more than a general impression about what is going on right now, then you should perhaps be thinking of reading a more advanced book[5] than this!

To figure out what selling price Alice can expect in a "first-price" sealed-bid auction, we need to solve the bidding problem such an auction poses for Horace and Maurice. A consultant game theorist will see no reason to advise someone with a reservation price of \$3m to do anything but bid this truthfully. However, if Horace has a *high* reservation price of

---

[4]Provided that Horace and Maurice bid rationally and are risk-neutral (Section 3.4.3).

[5]Like Fudenberg and Tirole's *Game Theory* (MIT Press, 1991) or Myerson's *Game Theory: Analysis of Conflict* (Harvard University Press, 1991).

\$4m, he may get some curious advice from the game theorist. The game theorist will explain that, whatever bid Horace may think of sealing in his envelope, there is a risk that Maurice will predict it. If he does, Maurice will then win the auction by bidding one penny more on those occasions when he also has a high reservation price. The only way that Horace can be sure of keeping Maurice guessing is by using a *mixed strategy*. What this means is that Horace should *randomize* over the bids that it is sensible for him to make.

If Horace is still listening, the game theorist will now start getting serious about *how* Horace should randomize. The advice might go like this. Never bid less than \$3m or more than \$$3\frac{1}{2}$m. Randomize over all the bids between \$3m and \$$3\frac{1}{2}$m in such a way that the probability of your bidding less than \$$b$ is precisely $(b-3)/(4-b)$.

If Maurice is also getting exactly the same advice from another game theorist, how much should Horace expect to make when his randomizing device tells him to seal \$$b$m in his envelope? If he outbids Maurice, he will make \$$(4-b)$m, because this is the difference between what he pays and what the house is worth to him. If he loses, he makes nothing. How often will Horace win? Half the time he will win for certain because Maurice's reservation price will be only \$3m. The other half of the time, Horace will win with probability $(b-3)/(4-b)$, because this is the probability that Maurice will bid less than \$$b$m when his reservation price is \$4m. Thus, the total probability that Horace wins when he bids \$$b$m is

$$\frac{1}{2}+\frac{1}{2}\left(\frac{b-3}{4-b}\right)=\frac{1}{2(4-b)}.$$

His expected gain is obtained by multiplying this probability by \$$(4-b)$m, which is what he gets when he wins. His expected gain is therefore always \$$\frac{1}{2}$m whatever bid \$$b$m between \$3m and \$$3\frac{1}{2}$m he may make.

The reason that game theorists will offer such complicated advice to Horace and Maurice is that, if they follow it, then each will be responding *optimally* to the strategy choice of the other. In particular, there is nothing that Horace can do to improve on \$$\frac{1}{2}$m. He will certainly never want to bid \$$B$m when $B > 3\frac{1}{2}$ because, although this guarantees his winning the auction, his victory will be hollow since he will make only \$$(4-B)$ from his triumph.[6]

It will be clear that Alice was premature in thinking that

---

[6]Assuming that his reservation price is high. If his reservation price is low, he will never want to bid more than \$3m.

anything in this situation is "obvious". Much of the time, Horace and Maurice will be bidding far below their true reservation prices. Alice therefore needs to calculate quite hard before she is entitled to an opinion on the relative merits of first and second price auctions. If she assumes that Horace and Maurice follow the advice of their tame game theorists, she will find that her expected selling price will be *exactly the same* in a first-price auction as in a second-price auction—namely $\$3\frac{1}{4}$m. It will also be the same in various other types of auction. In particular, the expected selling price is exactly the same in the familiar type of auction in which the buyers keep raising each other's bids until only one contender is left bidding.

Should we conclude that Alice is wasting her time in looking for a better auction? Far from it! If Alice reads *Fun and Games* as far as Section 11.7.4, she will discover that, if she is clever, she can design an auctioning mechanism that raises her expected selling price to a magnificent $\$3\frac{1}{2}$m.

0.1.3 What Is the Moral?

The two preceding examples are intended to make it clear that game theory is good for something. Our untutored intuition is not very reliable in strategic situations. We need to *train* our strategic intuition by considering instructive examples. These need not be realistic. On the contrary, there are often substantial advantages in studying *toy games*, if these are carefully chosen. In such toy games, all the irrelevant clutter that typifies real-world problems can be swept away so that attention can be focused entirely on the strategic questions for which game theory exists to provide answers.

Often, game theorists introduce their toy games with silly stories. It is a little silly, for example, that the committee members in the strategic voting example were called Boris, Horace and Maurice.[7] But even such silliness is not without its value. Here, it allows us to disengage our emotions from the problem. Nobody can get worked up about fictions like Boris, Horace and Maurice. However, if they were recognizable as real people, we might let our indignation at the fact that the chairman has "rigged the agenda", or that Horace is planning to "vote dishonestly", distract our attention from the underlying strategic realities. For a game theorist, this would be an error comparable to a mathematician's fudging on the laws of arithmetic because he dislikes the answers he is coming up with.

[7]Those whose native language is not the Queen's English may be surprised to learn that these names rhyme.

0.2 Where Is Game Theory Coming From?

Phil 0.4 ⟶ Game theory was created by Von Neumann and Morgenstern in their classic book *The Theory of Games and Economic Behavior*, published in 1944. Others had anticipated some of the ideas. The economists Cournot and Edgeworth were particularly innovative in the nineteenth century. Later contributions mentioned in this book were made by the mathematicians Borel and Zermelo. Von Neumann himself had already laid the groundwork in a paper published in 1928. However, it was not until Von Neumann and Morgenstern's book appeared that the world realized what a powerful tool for studying human interaction had been discovered.

When the penny dropped, people went overboard in their enthusiasm. The social sciences, so it was thought, would be revolutionized overnight. But this was not to be. Von Neumann and Morgenstern's book proved to be just the first step on a long road. However, there is no mind more closed than that of a disappointed convert, and once it became clear that *The Theory of Games and Economic Behavior* was not be compared with the tablets of stone that Moses brought down from the mountain, game theory languished in the doldrums. One can still find old men who will explain that game theory is useless because life is not a "zero-sum game", or because one can get any result one likes by selecting an appropriate "cooperative solution concept".

Fortunately, things have moved on very rapidly in the last twenty years, and this and other modern books on game theory are no longer hampered by some of the restrictive assumptions that Von Neumann and Morgenstern found necessary to make progress. As a consequence, the early promise of game theory is beginning to be realized. Its impact on economic theory in recent years has been nothing less than explosive. However, it is still necessary to know a little about game theory's short history, if only to understand why some of the terminology is used.

Von Neumann and Morgenstern investigated two distinct possible approaches to the theory of games. The first of these is the *strategic* or *noncooperative* approach. This requires specifying in close detail what the players can and cannot do during the game, and then searching for a strategy for each player that is *optimal*. At first sight, it is not even clear what optimal might mean in this context. What is best for one player depends on what the other players are planning to do, and this in turn depends on what they think the first player will do. Von Neumann and Morgenstern solved this problem for the particular case of two-player games in which the players' interests are diametrically opposed. Such games are called *strictly competitive* or *zero-sum* because any gain by one player is always exactly balanced by a corresponding loss by the other. Chess, Backgammon and Poker are games that usually get treated as zero-sum.

In the second part of their book, Von Neumann and Morgenstern developed their *coalitional* or *cooperative* approach, in which they sought to describe optimal behavior in games with many players. Since this is a much more difficult problem, it is not surprising that their results were much less sharp than for the two-player, zero-sum case. In particular, they abandoned the attempt to specify optimal strategies for individual players. Instead, they aimed at classifying the patterns of coalition formation that are consistent with rational behavior. Bargaining, as such, had no explicit role in this theory. In fact, they endorsed a view that had held sway among economists since at least the time of Edgeworth, namely that two-person bargaining problems are inherently *indeterminate.*

In a sequence of remarkable papers in the early fifties, the mathematician John Nash broke open two of the barriers that Von Neumann and Morgenstern had erected for themselves. On the noncooperative front, they seem to have felt that the idea of an *equilibrium* in strategies, as introduced by Cournot in 1832, was not an adequate notion in itself on which to build a theory—and hence their restriction to zero-sum games. However, Nash's general formulation of the equilibrium idea made it clear that no such restriction is necessary. Nowadays the notion of a *Nash equilibrium*[8] is perhaps the most important of the tools that game theorists have at their disposal. Nash also contributed to Von Neumann and Morgenstern's cooperative approach. He disagreed with the view that game theorists must regard two-person bargaining problems as indeterminate, and proceeded to offer arguments for determining them. His views on this subject were widely misunderstood and, perhaps in consequence, game theory's years in the doldrums were largely spent pursuing Von Neumann and Morgenstern's cooperative approach along lines that ultimately turned out to be unproductive.

---

[8]This arises when each player's strategy choice is a best reply to the strategy choices of the other players. Horace and Maurice were advised to use a Nash equilibrium by their consultant game theorist when wondering how to bid in the first-price auction of Section 0.1.2.

The history of game theory in the last twenty years is too packed with incident to be chronicled here. However, there are some names that cannot pass unmentioned. The acronym NASH may assist in remembering who they are. Nash himself gets the letter N; A is for Aumann; S is for both Shapley and Selten; and H is for Harsanyi. By the end of the book, you won't be needing an acronym!

What is perhaps most important about the last twenty years in game theory is that all the major advances have been made in *noncooperative* theory. For this reason, *Fun and Games* confines its attention almost entirely to this branch of the subject. This is not because I believe that no insights are to be found in *cooperative* game theory, but simply because I share with many others the belief that one cannot sensibly discuss the cooperative branch of the subject without first having mastered the noncooperative branch.

0.3 Where Is Game Theory Going To?

It is hard to explain where game theory is going to an audience that doesn't know where it's at. So these remarks are for people who know some game theory already.

Phil 0.4 →

I have some very firm views on where game theory ought to be going, and it is encouraging to see that things seem to be moving in the right direction. However, I have kept these views out of the text nearly everywhere, because I think a book written at this level should contain a minimum of controversial material. However, it is only right that I should lay my cards on the table somewhere. So let me say that I think most of the literature on "refinements of Nash equilibrium" belongs on the same shelf with the works of the medieval scholastics. Even more controversially, let me say that attempts to make Bayesianism the foundation stone for game theory should be likened not so much to building houses upon the sand, but to the building of castles in the air. In retrospect, the current elevation of Bayesian decision theory to something more than a convenient analytical tool will seem very odd indeed.[9]

My gesture to the future is Chapter 9, which some may feel is an idiosyncratic inclusion. It is about how equilibrium may be achieved by evolutionary trial-and-error processes when the players are not fully rational. The appearance of finite automata in Chapter 8 is also partly motivated by the

[9]Chapters 4, 5 and 6 of my *Essays on the Foundations of Game Theory* (Blackwell, 1990) summarize my views on these issues.

importance I attach to getting some sort of handle on the problem of bounded rationality in game theory. Of course, those who disagree about the way ahead are free to skip this material.

0.4 What Can Game Theory Do for Us?

This section gives some indications of how game theory can be applied. Economics is the biggest customer for the ideas churned out by game theorists, and so this is the discipline with which to begin.

0.4.1 Applications in Economics

It should not be surprising that game theory has found ready application in economics. The dismal science is supposedly about the allocation of scarce resources. If resources are scarce, it is because more people want them than can have them. Such a scenario creates all the necessary ingredients for a game. Moreover, neoclassical economists proceed on the assumption that people will act rationally in this game. In a sense, neoclassical economics is therefore nothing other than a branch of game theory. Economists who do not realize this are like M. Jourdain in Molière's *Le Bourgeois Gentilhomme* who was astonished to learn that he had been speaking prose all his life without knowing it. However, although economists may always have been closet game theorists, their progress was hampered by the fact that they did not have access to the tools provided by Von Neumann and Morgenstern. As a consequence, they could only analyze particularly simple games. This explains why *monopoly* and *perfect competition* are well-understood, while all the varieties of imperfect competition that lie between these two extremes are only now beginning to get the detailed treatment they deserve.

The reason that monopoly is simple from a game-theoretic perspective is that it can be treated as a game with only one player. The reason that perfect competition is simple is that the number of players is effectively infinite, so that each individual agent can have no effect on market aggregates if he or she acts alone. A toy model may help to clarify this point. It will also indicate why game theory is so intimately connected with the problem of imperfect competition.[10]

[10]Section 7.2 covers the same ideas in more detail.

Cournot Oligopoly. An industry contains N firms who all have constant unit cost c. Each firm simultaneously decides on an output q_i. When the total output $q = q_1 + q_2 + \cdots + q_N$ gets unloaded on the market, the price at which it sells is given by the demand equation $p = D(q)$. The ith firm's profit is then

$$\pi_i = pq_i - cq_i = (D(q) - c)q_i \,,$$

which is its revenue minus its cost.

A game theorist sees such a Cournot oligopoly problem as a game with N players, each of whom chooses a strategy q_i with the purpose of maximizing profit π_i. At a Nash equilibrium, each player's choice of strategy will be optimal given the strategy choices of the others.

To make a best reply to the strategy choices of the other firms, the ith firm will choose its own strategy q_i so that

$$\frac{\partial \pi_i}{\partial q_i} = D'(q)q_i + D(q) - c = 0 \,.$$

If all the firms behave like this, they will all choose the same output. Thus $q_i = q/N$, where

$$D'(q)\frac{q}{N} + D(q) - c = 0 \,.$$

Consider the special case in which the price elasticity of demand is constant. This just means that $p = D(q) = kq^{-\varepsilon}$, where k and ε are positive constants. The equation then simplifies to

$$\frac{p}{c} = \left(1 - \frac{\varepsilon}{N}\right)^{-1}$$

This formula will be familiar to economists in the case $N = 1$ as the profit-maximizing mark-up for a monopolist. When $N \to \infty$, we obtain that $p = c$. This is the classic result of perfect competition that says that the equilibrium price must equal marginal cost. For intermediate values of N, we have a result about equilibrium behavior in a model with imperfect competition.

Such calculations require no special knowledge of game theory. However, as soon as one turns to models in which *timing* or *risk* is important, or in which the handling of *information* matters, then one is helpless without the conceptual scaffolding that game theory provides. Auctions, insurance markets, patent races, entry deterrence and bargaining are just some of the topics on which we can now speak with some authority where previously little or nothing could usefully be said. Some of these topics are studied in a preliminary way in *Fun and Games*. However, you will have to look elsewhere for a systematic exploitation of game theory ideas in economics.[11] If such a task were attempted here, no room would be left to describe the theory itself.

0.4.2 Applications in Political Science

Game theory has not had the same impact in political science as in economics. Perhaps this is because people behave less rationally when their ideas are at stake rather than their money. Nevertheless, it has become an important tool for clarifying the underlying logic of a number of paradigmatic problems. Strategic voting was mentioned in Section 0.1.1. Here a simple model will be studied that seeks to cast some light on how parties choose their political platforms. It bears a family resemblance to economic models in which the incumbent firms in an industry distort their behavior in an attempt to deter new firms from entering the industry.

Choosing a Platform. This toy game begins with two political parties: the Formalists and the Idealists. Neither cares anything for matters of principle. They care only about power, and so choose a platform with the sole aim of maximizing their vote at the next election. The voters, on the other hand, care only about matters of principle and hence are devoid of party loyalties. For simplicity, the opinions a voter might hold are identified with the real numbers x in the interval $[0, 1]$.[12] One can imagine that this interval represents the left-right political spectrum. Thus, someone with the opinion $x = 0$ believes society should be organized like an anthill, while someone with the opinion $x = 1$ thinks it should be organized like a pool of sharks.

Each party chooses its platform somewhere along the political spectrum and is not able to shift its position later. The voters then cast their votes for the party whose position is nearest to their own. Since the voters are assumed to be uniformly distributed[13] over the political spectrum, it is easy to see how many votes each party will get once both have chosen their platforms. The secret is to look for the *median*

---

[11] Perhaps Tirole's *Theory of Industrial Organization* (MIT Press, 1988) or, at a more advanced level, Fudenburg and Tirole's *Game Theory* (MIT Press, 1991).

[12] The interval $[0, 1]$ is the set of values of x satisfying $0 \leq x \leq 1$.

[13] This just means that a fraction l of the population have views lying in any interval of length l.

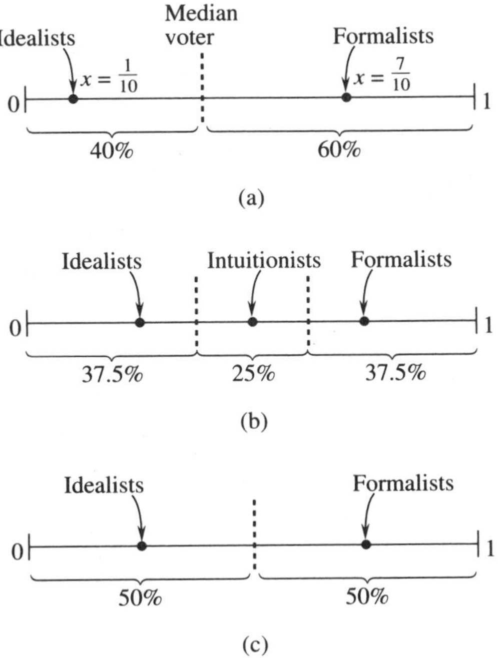

Figure 0.2 Choosing a political platform.

voter amongst those whose opinions lie between the two party platforms. The median voter is located halfway between the political positions of the two parties. Hence those to the right of the median voter cast their votes for one party, and those to the left cast their votes for the other. Figure 0.2(a) provides an example.

Suppose that the parties enter the political arena one by one. First the Idealists choose a platform and then the Formalists. Where should each locate? Such problems can be solved by backwards induction, as explained in Section 0.1.1. For each possible platform x, the Idealists ask what would happen if they located at x. If $x < \frac{1}{2}$, the Formalists would respond by locating just to the right of x. The Idealists would then pick up a fraction x of the voters and the Formalists would pick up $1 - x$. The Idealists would then receive less than half the vote. The same is true if the Idealists locate at $x > \frac{1}{2}$, except that now the Formalists will respond by locating just to their left. It is therefore best for the Idealists to locate at the center of the political spectrum. The Formalists will then also locate at $x = \frac{1}{2}$, and the vote will split fifty-fifty.

Such a model may make sense for the American political scene. Certainly Europeans find it hard to discern any significant difference between Democrats and Republicans. However, the model clearly bears little resemblance to the European political scene. Should Americans therefore deduce that European political parties actually care about the principles that they espouse? Such a conclusion would be premature because it is doubtful whether the European situation can be sensibly analyzed with a two-party model, even in countries like Britain where only two of the parties get a sizable number of votes at most elections. To explore this observation, let us consider how things would change if there were a third party to be taken into account.

In this model, the Intuitionist party chooses a platform after the Idealists and the Formalists. This changes things a great deal. The Idealists and the Formalists will now certainly not locate at the center of the political spectrum. If they were to do so, the Intuitionists could locate immediately to their left or right. They would then take half the vote, leaving the original parties to split the other half. A backwards induction argument[14] shows that the Idealists and the Formalists will locate at $x = \frac{1}{4}$ and $x = \frac{3}{4}$, leaving the Intuitionists to take up the centralist position $x = \frac{1}{2}$ as shown in Figure 0.2(b). Each of the original parties will then receive $\frac{3}{8}$ of the vote, and the Intuitionists will pick up only $\frac{1}{4}$.

But why should the Intuitionists bother to enter the political arena at all if they are doomed to the role of Cinderella, with the original parties playing the Ugly Sisters? Let us therefore modify the model so that the Intuitionists think it worthwhile forming a party only if they anticipate receiving more than 26% of the vote. The Idealists will then shift a little towards the center, but not enough to allow the Intuitionists to enter by outflanking them to the left. They will therefore shift only from $x = 0.25$ to $x = 0.26$. Similarly the Formalists will shift from $x = 0.75$ to $x = 0.74$. The result will be a two-party election as in Figure 0.2(c). In this election, the Idealists and the Formalists split the vote equally, and the Intuitionists stay out.

A political commentator who was unaware of the threat of entry by the Intuitionists might easily misunderstand the reasons for the platforms chosen by the Idealists and the Formalists. The commentator might even assume that each was deterred from an attempt to seize the middle ground by

[14]There are some subtleties that arise from the fact that an infinite number of political views are available. Here and later, these can be evaded by imagining that the Idealists and the Formalists take up positions that are slightly more extreme than those described.

considerations of principle. It is only after a strategic analysis, that the behavior of the two parties can be properly assessed. Note, in particular, that their behavior is determined by something that did not actually happen. As Sherlock Holmes explained, it is often the fact that the dog *didn't* bark in the night that is significant.

0.4.3 Applications in Biology

One cannot hope to match the elan with which evolutionary biologists who use game theory tell stories about animal behavior.[15] I don't know whether they choose indelicate stories deliberately to spice their performance with a little sexual innuendo, or whether these really are the best examples with which to illustrate how game theory is relevant. In any case, here is what biologists say about the bluegill sunfish.

The male of the species comes in two types. The first is a regular homebody who takes seven years to grow to maturity. Once he is grown, he builds a nest which attracts egg-laying females. When the eggs are laid, he not only fertilizes them, but defends the resulting family as best he can while the female gets on with her life elsewhere. The other type of male is a rogue. As biologists tell it, he is physically little more than a self-propelled sexual organ. This gives him an advantage over a regular male in that he grows to maturity in only two years. However, he is not capable of caring for a family. Instead, he lurks in hiding until a female has laid her eggs in response to the signals of a regular male, and then rushes out to fertilize the eggs before the regular male has an opportunity to do so. If the rogue is successful, the regular male then defends a family who are not related to him at all, but carry instead the genes of the rogue.

Game theory helps to explain how the two types of male can co-exist together in fixed proportions. Imagine a lake that supports N males of the species, where N is large. One can then think in terms of a game with N players. Each player's aim is to maximize his expected number of offspring. A player's possible strategies in the game are *homebody* and *rogue*. The payoff a player gets from choosing one of these strategies depends on the strategy choices made by the other players. If enough of the other players choose *homebody*, the best strategy is to choose *rogue* because there will be an ample supply of potential cuckolds to exploit. If enough of the other

[15] See, for example, Maynard Smith's *Evolution and the Theory of Games* (Cambridge University Press, 1982).

players choose *rogue*, the best strategy to choose is *homebody* because of the difficulty of finding someone to cuckold. When *homebody* is sufficiently popular as a strategy choice, there is therefore an incentive to buck the trend by choosing *rogue*. Similarly, when *rogue* is sufficiently popular, there is an incentive to switch to *homebody*.

A Nash equilibrium in this N-player game occurs when the proportion of players who choose *homebody* and the proportion who choose *rogue* is so finely balanced that each player finds himself just *indifferent* between using his current strategy and switching to its alternative. Once this is understood, it becomes easy to understand why the two types of male both survive, and why their population frequencies remain stable—or rather, it *would* become easy to understand if fish *were* rational optimizers able to make choices about what genes they should carry.

For a game-theoretic story to hold together in this context, we need an explanation of how the distribution of genes came to be just what was needed to ensure that each fish would be optimizing, given the current population mix of homebodies and rogues. It is not enough to say that Nature "red in tooth and claw" will act so that only the fit survive. Such a reply evades the question of how and why it sometimes turns out that being fit entails acting rationally. This seems to be one of those big questions that have no easy answers. Chapter 9 does no more than point out some of the directions in which answers may lie. Perhaps current research will result in a breakthrough in this area. If so, game theory will really hit the big-time!

0.4.4 Applications in Social Philosophy

This fashionable area of application certainly is a great deal of fun. Was it really the toy game called the Prisoners' Dilemma (Section 7.5.4) that Thomas Hobbes had in mind in his *Leviathan* of 1654, when he categorized man's state of nature as the "war of all against all" in which life is "solitary, poor, nasty, brutish and short"? Or did he mean the game Chicken? Does Immanuel Kant's *categorical imperative* tell us to cooperate in the Prisoners' Dilemma or should it be seen only as an equilibrium selection criterion? Was Karl Marx talking about a game when he wrote about the exploitation of the working class? How do real people play the Stag-Hunt Game of Jean-Jacques Rousseau? Is it really rational to use the maximin principle in the "original position" as postulated by John Rawls in his celebrated *Theory of Justice*?

I am too irreverent a person to be entitled to an opinion on such weighty questions. However, for what it is worth, I think that the works of the great philosophers are usually more valuable for the questions they raise than for the answers they offer. Even more irreverently, I believe that there is a whole category of questions to which the great philosophers of the past could not be expected to provide answers because this would involve their having anticipated at least some of the insights that game theory has brought to modern social philosophy.

However, the philosopher David Hume is a very notable exception to this judgment. Game theorists believe that they can demonstrate formally how even the most selfish individuals will often find it in their own enlightened self-interest to cooperate with their neighbors in a long-term relationship. For this purpose, they study the equilibria of *repeated* games—games that the same players play with each other over and over again. Little of what they have discovered in this area so far would have come as a surprise to David Hume who had already articulated the essential mechanisms some two hundred years before. However, these insights are now firmly grounded in formal models. Future advances will have to await progress on the problem of selecting equilibria in games that have many equilibria. When such progress comes, I suspect that social philosophy without game theory will be regarded as something inconceivable—and that David Hume will be universally regarded as its true founding father.

0.5 Conclusion

If you have read this far, you are probably hooked. But don't swallow the line and sinker as well. Listen to what this and other game books say, and then make up your own mind. A great deal of nonsense has been written about game theory, and who is to say that this book is not more of the same? It is true, as Bertrand Russell said of philosophy, that reading game theory is like reading a fairy tale—you must suspend disbelief while the tale is being told if you are to appreciate what is going on. But don't forget to resume your skeptical mode when the story is over!

CHAPTER

1

Winning Out

1.1 Introduction

The formal definition of a game is quite simple from a mathematical point of view, but it is not so simple to appreciate what the formal definition means. The necessary ideas will therefore be introduced bit by bit in the next few chapters. In the current chapter, only two-player games of perfect information without chance moves will be considered. Moreover, attention will be largely restricted to strictly competitive games. This simply means that the players' aims are diametrically opposed.

Tictactoe (or Noughts and Crosses) is a simple example of such a game. Chess is a much more complex example. These are games of perfect information because, whenever a player has to move, he knows everything that he might wish to know about what has happened in the game so far. Parcheesi (or Ludo) is a two-player, strictly competitive game with chance moves. What a player can do when it is his turn to move depends on the roll of a dice. Poker is a game of imperfect information. When deciding how to bet in Poker, everyone would like to know the hands that the other players are holding, but this information is concealed from them.

1.2 The Rules of the Game

The rules of a game must tell us *who* can do *what* and *when* they can do it. They must also indicate who gets *how much* when the game is over. The structure used to convey such information in game theory is called a tree. This is a special case of what is called a graph in combinatorial mathematics. A graph in this sense is simply a set of nodes (or vertices) some of which are linked by edges. A tree is a connected graph with no cycles, as illustrated in Figure 1.1.

When? The first move of a game is identified with a distinguished node of the game tree. This is often called the *root* of the tree.

A *play* of the game consists of a connected chain of edges starting at the root of the tree and ending, if the game is finite, at a terminal node. The terminal nodes of the tree correspond to the possible outcomes of the game. The tree of a game G is shown in Figure 1.2(a). (Ignore Figure 1.2(b) for the moment.) The root of the tree is labeled with the letter a. A possible play of the game is indicated by thickening appropriate edges.

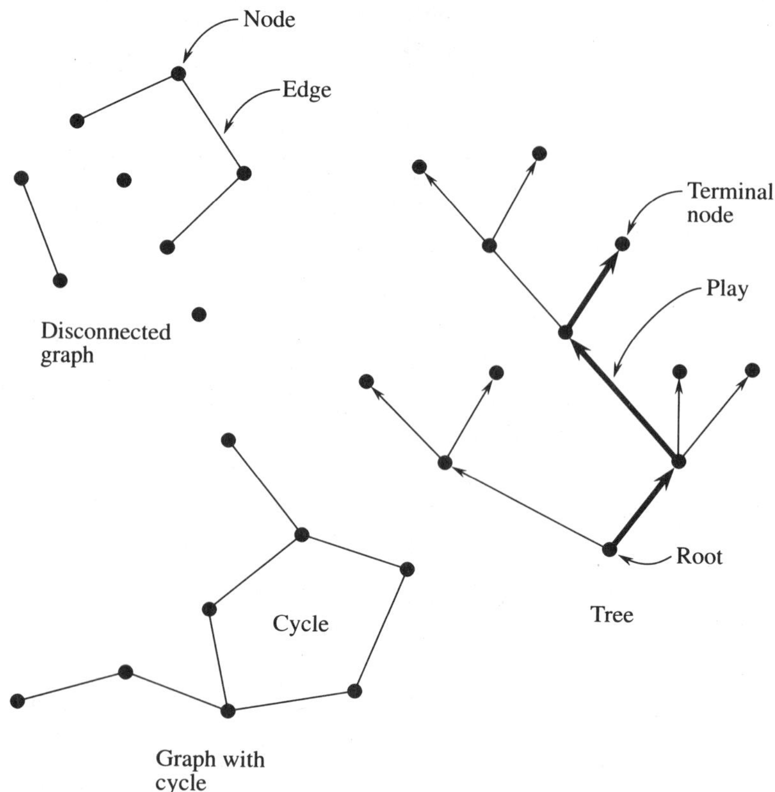

Figure 1.1 Some graphs.

What? The nodes in the tree represent the possible moves in the game. The edges leading away from a node represent the choices or actions available at that move. Thus there are two choices available at the first move in the game tree of Figure 1.2(a). These have been labeled l and r.

Who? Each node other than a terminal node is assigned a player's name or number so that it is known who makes the choice at that move. In the game tree of Figure 1.2(a), it is player I who chooses at the first move. If he chooses action r, then it will be player II who makes the next move. She has three choices labeled L, M and R. If she chooses action R, then the game is over. If she chooses action L, then she gets to move again.

(Some games have chance moves. For example, in Parcheesi, what the players can do depends on how large a number they score when a dice is thrown. Such situations are dealt with by assigning some moves to a mythical player called

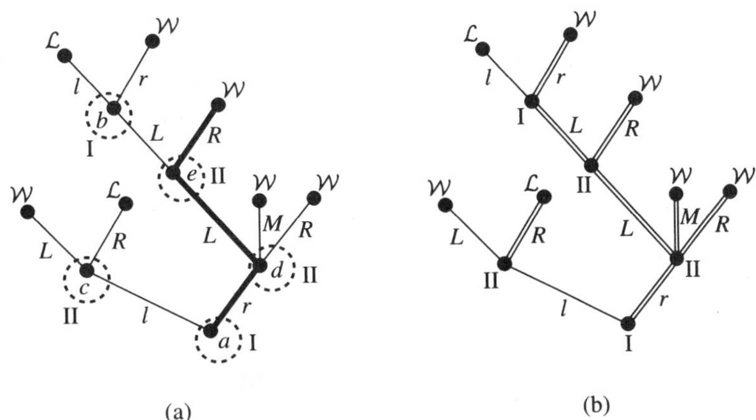

Figure 1.2 The game tree of G.

Chance. Each action at a chance move is labeled with the probability that it will be chosen. This issue will be discussed in the next chapter.)

How Much? Each terminal node must be labeled with the consequences for each player if the game ends in the outcome corresponding to that terminal node. For the moment, attention will be restricted to examples of games that can only be lost or won. Each terminal node may then be labeled either with $\mathcal{W}$ (to mean a win for player I and a loss for player II), or with $\mathcal{L}$ (to mean a loss for player I and a win for player II). The game G of Figure 1.2(a) is an example. It will be taken for granted that neither player is motivated by a perverse desire to lose. The aim of both players is to win the game if they can.

1.2.1 Two Examples

Tictactoe. Everybody knows how to play this game. Its game tree is very large in spite of the simplicity of the game. Figure 1.3 therefore just shows part of the tree. Only three of its many terminal nodes are shown. These are labeled with the letters $\mathcal{W}$, $\mathcal{L}$ and $\mathcal{D}$ to indicate a win, loss and a draw respectively for player I.

Nim. This is a simple game that people sometimes play. It begins with several piles of matches. Two players take alternate moves. On his or her move, a player selects one of the piles and removes at least one match from that pile. The last player to remove a match wins. The game tree is shown

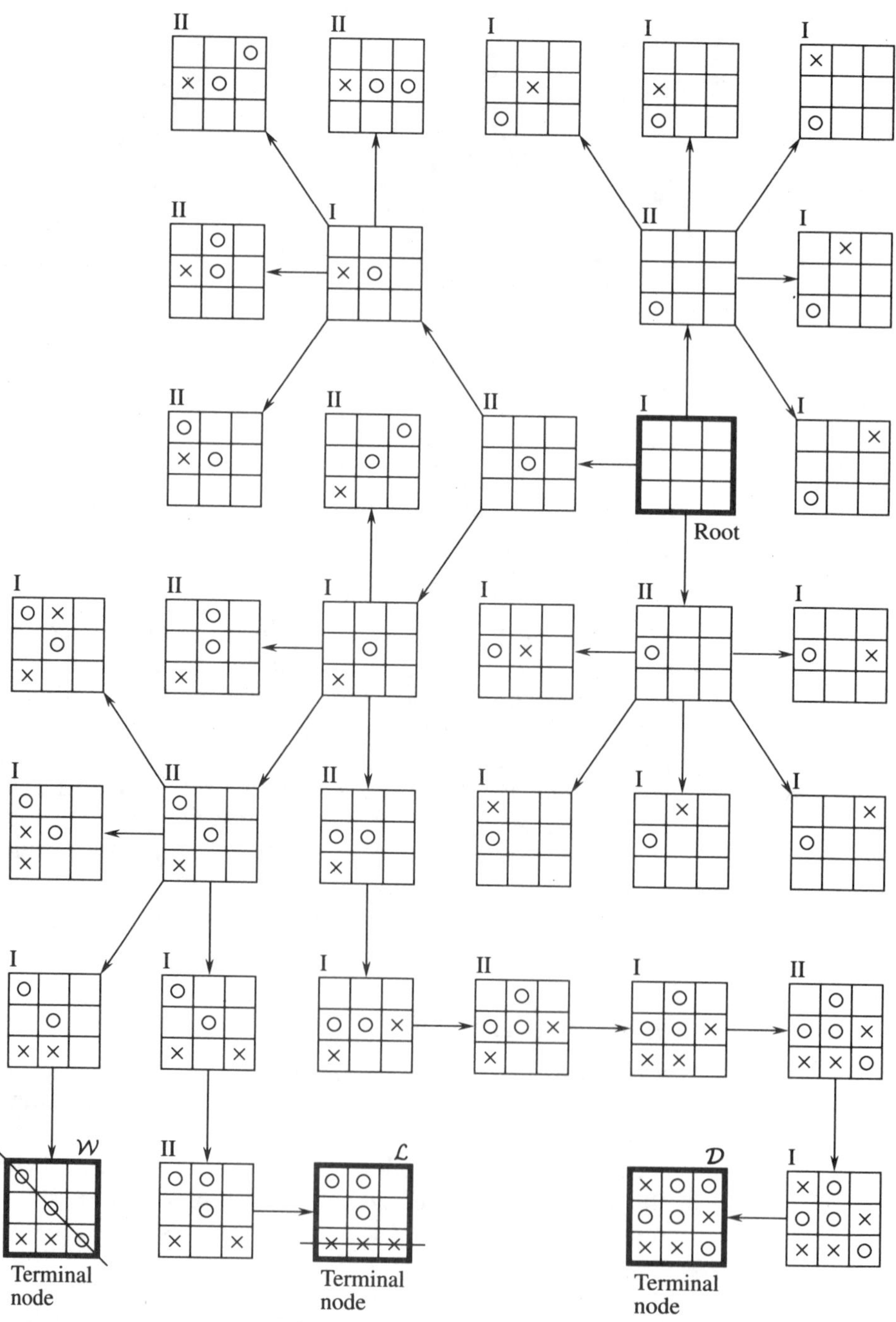

Figure 1.3 Tictactoe.

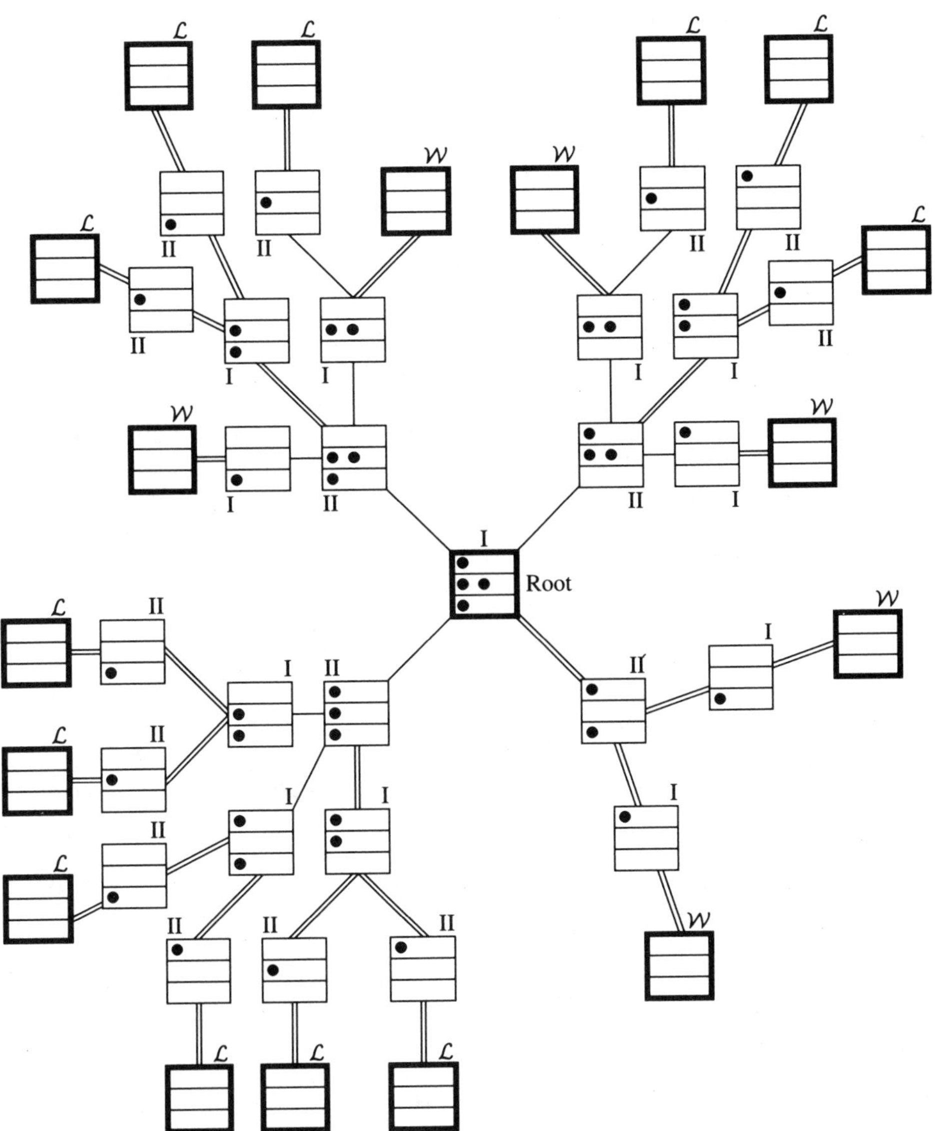

Figure 1.4 The game of Nim.

in Figure 1.4 for the case when the game begins with three piles of matches, two containing only one match and the other containing two matches. (Ignore for the moment the fact that some of the edges in the tree have been doubled.) The terminal nodes are all labeled with either $\mathcal{W}$ or $\mathcal{L}$. Unlike Tictactoe, Nim cannot end in a draw. One player or the other must win. Only games of this type will be considered until Section 1.7, when Chess will be studied.

1.3 Strategies

At this point only *pure* strategies need to be discussed.[1] A pure strategy for player i in the games considered in this chapter[2] is a statement that specifies an action at *each* of the decision nodes at which it would be player i's duty to make a decision if that node were actually reached. If all the players in a game select a pure strategy and stick with it, then this totally determines how a game without chance moves will be played.

Consider the game G of Figure 1.2(a). The nodes at which it would be up to player I to make a decision are labeled a and b. A pure strategy for player I must therefore specify an action for player I at node a and an action for player I at node b. Since there are 2 available actions for player I at node a and 2 available actions at node b, it follows that player I has a total of $2 \times 2 = 4$ pure strategies. These can be labeled as follows:

$$ll, \quad lr, \quad rl, \quad rr.$$

The pure strategy labeled lr means that action l is to be used if node a is reached and action r is to be used if node b is reached. The pure strategy rr means that action r is to be used at both node a and node b. (Notice that, if player I uses pure strategy lr, then it is *impossible* that node b will be reached whatever player II may do. However, the formal definition of a strategy still requires the specification of an action at node b even though the action specified at node b will never have any affect on how the game gets played.)

The nodes at which it would be up to player II to make a decision are labeled c, d and e for the game G of Figure 1.2(a). A pure strategy for player II must therefore specify an action for player II at node c, an action for player II at node d, and an action for player II at node e. Since there are 2 available actions for player II at node c, 3 available actions at node d and 2 available actions at node e, it follows that player II has a total of $2 \times 3 \times 2 = 12$ pure strategies. These can be labeled as follows:

$$\begin{array}{cccccc} LLL, & LLR, & LML, & LMR, & LRL, & LRR, \\ RLL, & RLR, & RML, & RMR, & RRL, & RRR. \end{array}$$

[1]A *mixed* strategy requires a player to randomize between his pure strategies.

[2]In games of imperfect information, the definition of a strategy has to be modified so that one asks only for a specification of an action for each *information set* at which it would be up to player i to choose an action if that information set were reached.

	LLL	*LLR*	*LML*	*LMR*	*LRL*	*LRR*	*RLL*	*RLR*	*RML*	*RMR*	*RRL*	*RRR*
ll	$\mathcal{W}$	$\mathcal{W}$	$\mathcal{W}$	$\mathcal{W}$	$\mathcal{W}$	$\mathcal{W}$	$\mathcal{L}$	$\mathcal{L}$	$\mathcal{L}$	$\mathcal{L}$	$\mathcal{L}$	$\mathcal{L}$
lr	$\mathcal{W}$	$\mathcal{W}$	$\mathcal{W}$	$\mathcal{W}$	$\mathcal{W}$	$\mathcal{W}$	$\mathcal{L}$	$\mathcal{L}$	$\mathcal{L}$	$\mathcal{L}$	$\mathcal{L}$	$\mathcal{L}$
rl	$\mathcal{L}$	$\mathcal{W}$	$\mathcal{W}$	$\mathcal{W}$	$\mathcal{W}$	$\mathcal{W}$	$\mathcal{L}$	$\mathcal{W}$	$\mathcal{W}$	$\mathcal{W}$	$\mathcal{W}$	$\mathcal{W}$
rr	$\mathcal{W}$	$\mathcal{W}$	$\mathcal{W}$	$\mathcal{W}$	$\mathcal{W}$	$\mathcal{W}$	$\mathcal{W}$	$\mathcal{W}$	$\mathcal{W}$	$\mathcal{W}$	$\mathcal{W}$	$\mathcal{W}$

Figure 1.5 The strategic form of the game G.

The pure strategy labeled LMR means that action L is to be used if node c is reached, action M is to be used if node d is reached and action R is to be used if node e is reached.

The play of the game G in Figure 1.2(a) begins at the root node a with player I choosing action r. This leads to node d at which player II chooses action L. This in turn takes the game to node e, where player II chooses action R. The game is thereby brought to an end at a terminal node labeled with $\mathcal{W}$ to indicate a win for player I. Such a play of the game will be denoted by the sequence $[rLR]$ of actions that generates it. (The square parentheses are intended to emphasize that a play is not at all the same thing as a pure strategy.)

What are the strategies that result in the play $[rLR]$ of G? The pair of strategies chosen by the players must be of the form (rx, XLR), where rx stands for any strategy for player I in which r is chosen at node a. There are 2 such strategies, namely rl and rr. Similarly, XLR stands for any strategy for player II at which L is chosen at node d and R is chosen at node e. There are 2 such strategies, namely LLR and RLR. Hence the total number of strategy pairs that result in the play $[rLR]$ is $2 \times 2 = 4$.

Figure 1.5 shows the *strategic form*[3] of the game G of Figure 1.2(a). The game tree representation of G in Figure 1.2(a) is called the *extensive form* of G. The strategic form indicates, for each pair of strategies, what the outcome of the game will

[3]Game theory as a discipline began with the publication of Von Neumann and Morgenstern's book, *The Theory of Games and Economic Behavior,* in 1944. The book begins by discussing the *extensive form* of a game. This is based on the notion of a game tree as described in Section 1.2. It continues by defining the *normal form* of a game. As their terminology indicates, Von Neumann and Morgenstern felt that the "normal" procedure in analyzing a game should always be to discard the extensive form in favor of the normal form. However, it turns out that this would often be unwise. To signal this fact, I follow those game theorists who prefer to speak of the *strategic form* of a game rather than the normal form. However, it is necessary to bear in mind that the normal form and the strategic form of a game are exactly the same thing.

be if that pair of strategies is used. The rows of the matrix represent player I's pure strategies, and the columns represent player II's pure strategies. Thus, the cell in row *rl* and column *LLR* contains the letter $\mathcal{W}$. This indicates that player I will win the game if he uses pure strategy *rl* and player II uses pure strategy *LLR*. This fact was checked out in the previous paragraph by tracing the play [*rLR*] that results from the use of strategy pairs of the form (rx, XLR).

1.4 Zermelo's Algorithm

Zermelo used this method way back in 1912 to analyze Chess. It requires starting from the end of the game and then working backwards to its beginning. For this reason, the technique is sometimes called "backwards induction". In Operations Research essentially the same notion goes by the name of "dynamic programming". The very simple idea is illustrated using the game G of Figure 1.2(a). What will be proved is that player I has a strategy for G that guarantees him victory no matter what strategy player II may employ. The method used will be one that can be applied in general to such games.

1.4.1 Analyzing the Game G

Figure 1.6 shows all the *subgames* of G. In the case of the games considered in this chapter, each node x other than a terminal node determines a subgame.[4] The subgame consists simply of node x together with all of the game tree that follows x. (Notice that the definition makes G a subgame of itself.)

Let us say that the *value* $v(H)$ of a subgame H of G is $\mathcal{W}$ if player I has a strategy for H that wins the game H whatever strategy player II may use. Similarly, let the value $v(H)$ of the subgame H be $\mathcal{L}$ if player II has a strategy that wins the game H whatever strategy player I may use. Notice that there is no *a priori* reason why either of these statements should be true, and so it is conceivable that a subgame H might not have a value at all according to our definition. It turns out that all the subgames do in fact have a value, but this is not something that should be taken for granted. (It is, in fact, a feature special to strictly competitive games.)

Consider first the one-player subgames G_0 and G_3 of Figure 1.6. Player II wins G_0 by choosing action R. (Recall that an

[4]For games of imperfect information, like Poker, this is false and a more careful definition that takes into account what people know or don't know at each stage of the game must be employed.

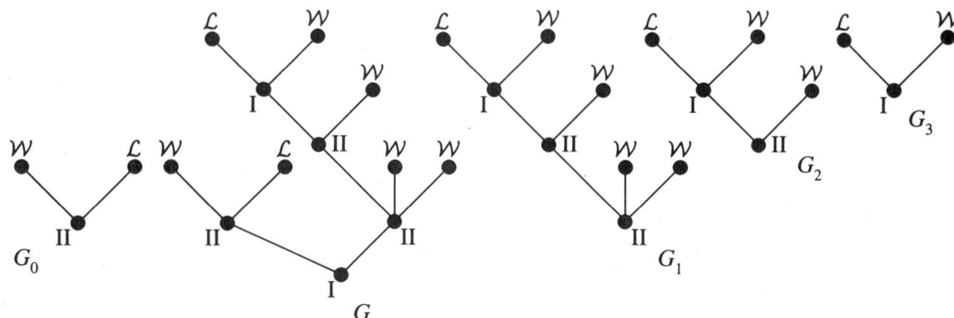

Figure 1.6 The game G and its subgames.

outcome is labeled with an $\mathcal{L}$ when player II *wins*.) Thus $v(G_0) = \mathcal{L}$. Similarly, player I wins G_3 by choosing action r. Thus $v(G_3) = \mathcal{W}$.

Next consider the game G' of Figure 1.7. This is obtained from G by replacing the subgame G_0 with a terminal node labeled with the value $\mathcal{L}$ of G_0, and replacing the subgame G_3 with a terminal node labeled with the value $\mathcal{W}$ of G_3. If player I has a strategy s' that always wins in game G', then he has a strategy s that always wins in G. Why is this?

Whatever the strategy used by player II, player I's use of the strategy s' in G' will result in a play of G' that leads to a terminal node x of G' labeled with $\mathcal{W}$. Such a terminal node x may correspond to a subgame G_x of G. If so, then $v(G_x) = \mathcal{W}$. Hence player I has a winning strategy s_x in G_x. It follows that player I has a winning strategy s in G. This consists of playing according to s' until one of the subgames G_x is reached and then playing according to s_x.

A very similar argument shows that, if player II has a strategy t' that always wins in game G', then she has a strategy t that always wins in G. It follows that, if G' has a value, then so does G and $v(G') = v(G)$.

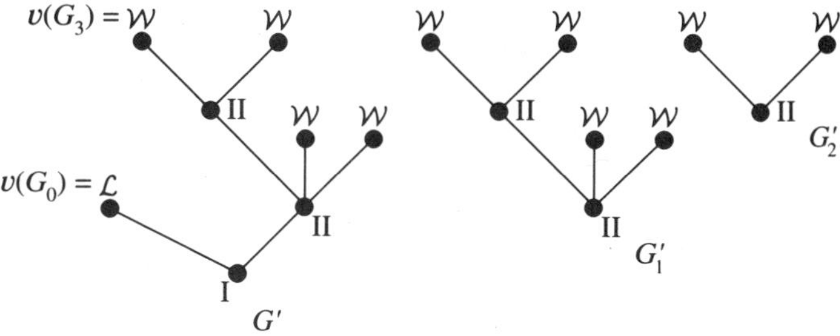

Figure 1.7 The game G' and its subgames.

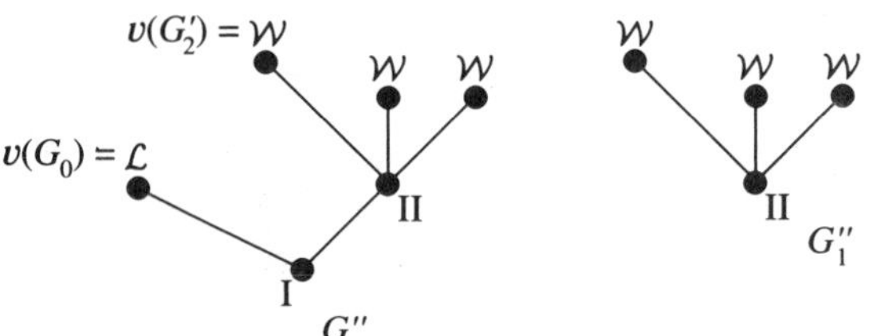

Figure 1.8 The game G'' and its subgames.

Next consider the game G'' of Figure 1.8. This is obtained from G' by replacing the subgame G_2' by a single terminal node labeled with the value $\mathcal{W}$ of G_2'. The reason why $v(G_2') = \mathcal{W}$ is that player II loses in the one-player game G_2', no matter which of the actions L or R she chooses. By the reasoning used before, if G'' has a value, then so does G' and $v(G'') = v(G')$.

Finally, consider the game G''' of Figure 1.9. This is obtained from G'' by replacing the subgame G_1'' by a single terminal node labeled with the value of G_1''. As previously, if G''' has a value, then so does G'' and $v(G''') = v(G'')$.

But G''' is a one-player game that player I can win by choosing r. Thus G''' has a value and $v(G''') = \mathcal{W}$. It follows that G also has a value, and $v(G) = v(G') = v(G'') = v(G''') = \mathcal{W}$. Hence, player I has a strategy that wins in G whatever strategy is used by player II.

1.4.2 What Is a Winning Strategy in G?

One way of finding a winning strategy for player I in G is to read it off from the strategic form of the game as given in Figure 1.5. Notice that the row corresponding to player I's pure strategy rr contains only $\mathcal{W}$'s. This means that, if player I uses pure strategy rr, then he will win no matter what pure strategy is chosen by player II. Thus rr is a winning strategy. (In G, no other strategy for player I is a winning strategy, but often games will have many winning strategies.) However, except in very simple cases, this is not a sensible way of locating a winning strategy because the heavy labor involved in constructing the strategic form makes the method impractical.

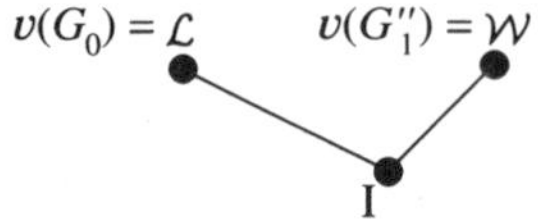

Figure 1.9 The game G'''.

A better way of finding a winning strategy is to mimic the method by means of which it was proved that a winning strategy exists for G. Begin by looking at the smallest subgames of G (those with no subgames of their own). In each such subgame, double the edges that correspond to optimal choices in the subgame. Now pretend that the *undoubled* edges in these subgames do not exist. This creates a new game G^*. Now repeat the procedure with G^* and continue in this way until there is nothing left to do. At the end of the procedure there will be at least one play of G whose edges have all been doubled. These are the only plays that can be followed if it is common knowledge between the players that each will always try to win under all circumstances.

This procedure has been carried through for the game G in Figure 1.2(b). Only one play of the game has all its edges doubled and this leads to a win for player I, thus confirming that it is player I who has a winning strategy. A winning pure strategy can be read off directly from the diagram by choosing one of the doubled edges at each node where it would be up to player I to make a decision if the node were reached. In the case of G, only the r edge is doubled at each of these nodes. Hence player I has only one winning pure strategy, and this is rr.

1.5 Nim

The procedure just described has also been carried through for the version of Nim given in Figure 1.4. Observe that, in order to guarantee victory, player I must take all the matches in the pile containing two matches. This is all player I really needs to know. Notice, however, that he does not have a *unique* winning strategy because, at some of the nodes at which he would have the move if they were reached, more than one edge is doubled. Notice also that, if he does not use a winning strategy, it is not *guaranteed* that he will lose. If he fails to take the winning action at the first move, then a subgame is reached in which player II has a winning strategy. But player II may fail to use her winning strategy in this subgame.

This procedure for finding winning strategies is easy to use when the game tree is given explicitly. But usually one has to construct the game tree from a set of rules that are given only verbally. This may involve much labor. Moreover the game tree, once constructed, may be very large. This is true even of simple games like Tictactoe or Nim (unless the numbers of matches in each pile are very small). One therefore has to

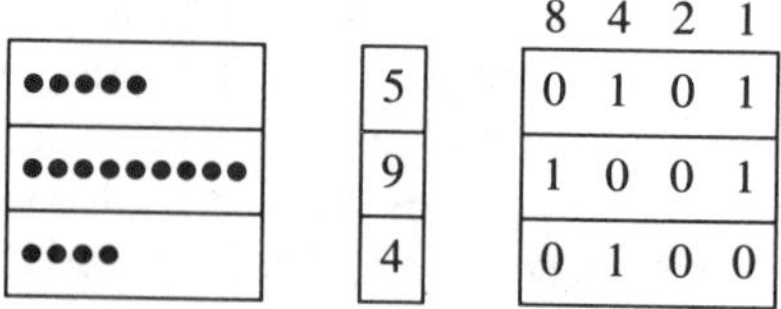

Figure 1.10 Nim with many matches.

look around for less mechanical ways of discovering things about the winning strategies.

For Nim, there is an elegant way of proceeding that avoids the necessity of constructing a game tree. This will be illustrated using the version of Nim given in Figure 1.10. In this figure, the numbers of matches in each pile have first been converted into decimal notation and then into binary notation.[5]

Call a game of Nim *balanced* if each column of the binary representation has an even number of 1s, and *unbalanced* otherwise. The example of Figure 1.10 is unbalanced because the eights column has an odd number of 1s. It is easy to verify that *any* admissible move in Nim converts a balanced game into an unbalanced game.[6]

The player who moves first in a balanced game cannot win on his first move. The reason is that a balanced game must have matches in at least two piles. The player moving therefore cannot pick up the last match immediately because he or she is allowed to take matches from only one pile at a time. It follows that one of the players has a winning strategy of which the crucial feature is that an unbalanced situation should always be converted into a balanced situation.[7] The reason such a strategy wins is that it ensures that the opponent cannot win on the next move. Since this is true at every stage in the game, it follows that the opponent cannot win at all. But, someone must pick up the last match. If it is not my opponent, it must be me. Hence I must be using a winning strategy.

Notice that it is not always player I who has a winning strategy. If the original configuration of matches is unbalanced, then it will be player I who has a winning strategy. If the original configuration is balanced, it will be player II who has the winning strategy.

---

[5]For example, the number whose decimal notation is 9 comprises 1 eight, 0 fours, 0 twos and 1 one. Hence its representation in binary form is 1001.

[6]At least one 1 in the binary representation of the pile from which matches are taken will necessarily be changed to a 0. If the column in which this occurs had $2n$ 1s, it will then have $2n - 1$ afterwards.

[7]Why is this always possible?

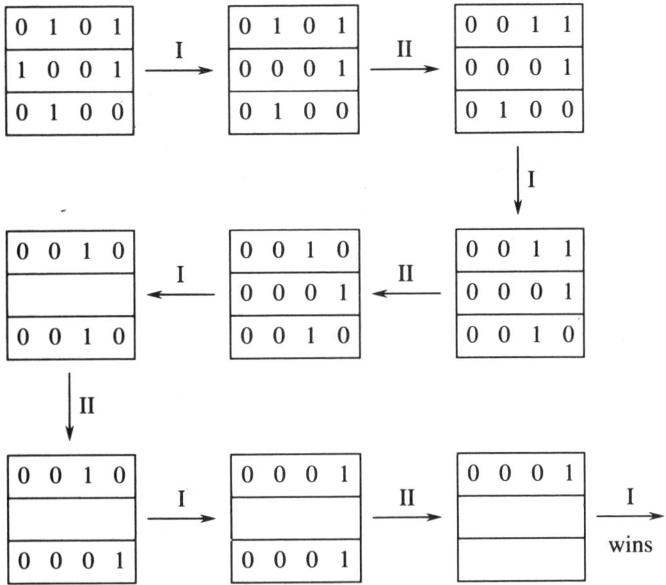

Figure 1.11 Player I uses a winning strategy in Nim.

A possible play of the version of Nim given in Figure 1.10 is shown in Figure 1.11. Player I is using a winning strategy. It is worth noticing that, once player I is faced with only two piles of matches with equal numbers of matches in each, then he can win by "strategy-stealing". All he need do is to take as many matches from one pile as player II took from the other.

1.6 Hex

The game of Hex is played on a board consisting of n^2 hexagons arranged in a parallelogram as illustrated in Figure 1.12(a). The players move alternately. A move consists of labeling a vacant hexagon on the board with a circle (for player I) or a cross (for player II). The hexagon then becomes part of the territory of the player who labeled it. At the beginning, each player's territory consists of two opposite sides of the board. The winner is the first to link their two sides of the board by a continuous chain of hexagons labeled with their emblem. In the game that has just concluded in Figure 1.12(b), it is Cross who was the winner. Hex is interesting for a number of reasons. First, it was investigated by John Nash of whom much more will be heard later. Second, it turns out to be significant that the game cannot end in a draw, but a conclusive proof of this fact requires some close thinking. Third, although the arguments given in Section 1.4 show that one of

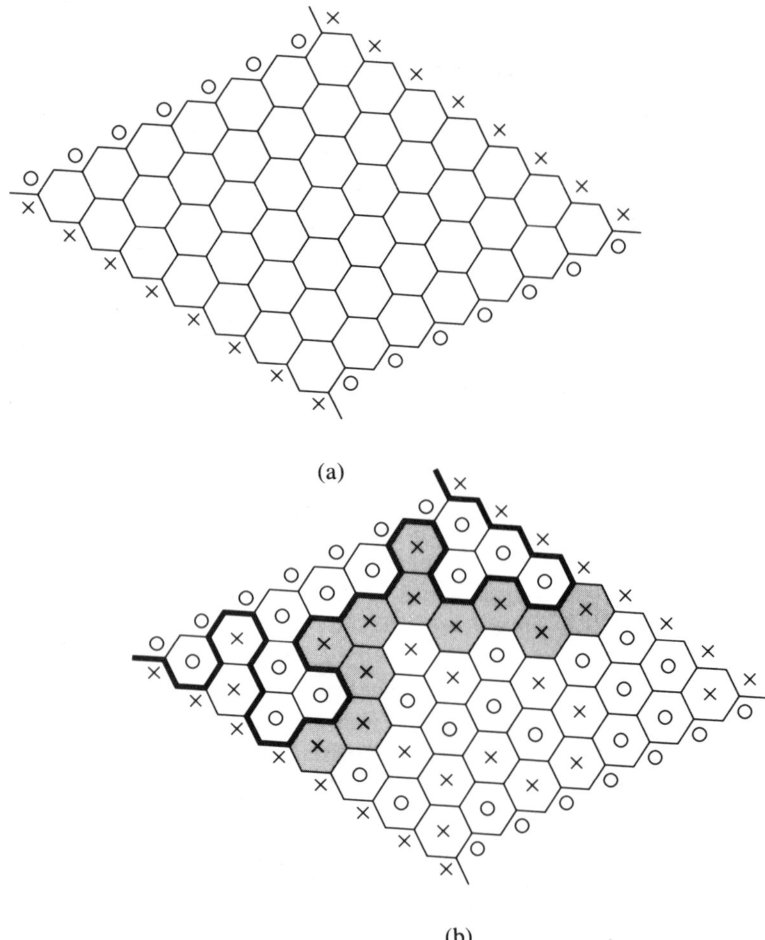

(a)

(b)

Figure 1.12 Hex.

the players has a winning strategy for Hex, it is not known what the winning strategies are unless n is quite small. Nevertheless, it is possible to prove that it must be the first player to move who has a winning strategy.

1.6.1 Why Hex Cannot End in a Draw

There is one sense in which it is "obvious" that Hex cannot end in a draw. If the circles are thought of as water and the crosses as land, then, when *all* the hexagons have been labeled, either water will flow between the two oceans originally belonging to Circle, or else the channel will be dammed. In the first case, Circle wins. In the second case, Cross wins.

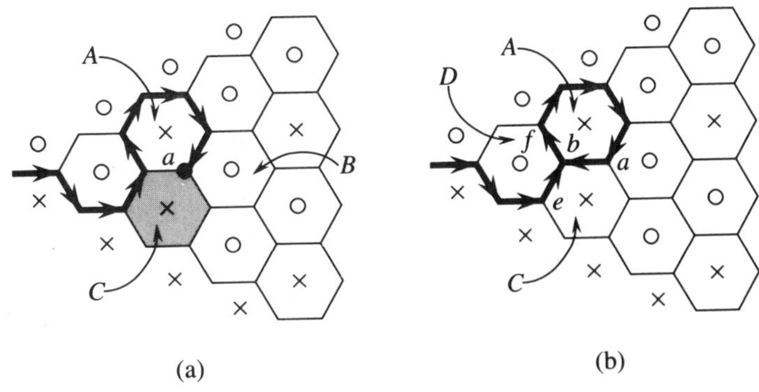

Figure 1.13 Gale's algorithm for Hex.

Math 1.7 ⟶

To *prove* such a result requires some mathematical reasoning, as the appearance of a Mad Hatter in the margin indicates. The Teaching Guide explains in detail how such Mad Hatters should be used to help find one's way around in the text. Here you are invited to skip forward to Section 1.7 unless you are a mathematical enthusiast. If reading this book is your first experience of game theory, you may want to consider simply following the Mad Hatter wherever he goes.

The following algorithm of David Gale shows that, if every hexagon is labeled with a circle or a cross, then one of the two opposite pairs of sides must be linked. Start from a corner, as indicated in Figure 1.13(a), and trace out a path using the principle that the next segment of the path is always chosen so that a circled hexagon lies on one side and a crossed hexagon on the other.[8]

Such a path can never terminate on the board. Nor can it return to a point it has visited before. The two diagrams of Figure 1.13 are meant to indicate why these assertions are true.

Figure 1.13(a) shows a path that has reached the point a in the interior of the board. To get to a it has to have just passed between a crossed hexagon A and a circled hexagon B. There must be a third hexagon C for which a is a vertex. If this is crossed, as in Figure 1.13(a), then the path can be continued by passing between B and C. If it is circled, then the path can be continued by passing between A and C. If a is on the edge of the board, the argument has to be adapted slightly, but still holds. Only if a is one of the four points off

[8]This could be done by immediately going back the way you just came, but this is understood not to be allowed.

the corners of the board does the argument fail. These are the only points where the path can terminate.

Figure 1.13(b) shows a path that has returned to a point b that it has visited before. But to do this, the path has had to violate the requirement that it keep a crossed hexagon on one side and a circled hexagon on the other. To check that a path can never loop back on itself without violating this requirement, suppose that b is the *first* point the path revisits. For it to be possible for b to have been visited the first time, the three hexagons A, C and D with a common vertex at b cannot all be labeled the same. Suppose, as in Figure 1.13(b), that D is circled and the other two hexagons are crossed. Then the path must have passed between D and C and between D and A on the first visit. Since b is the *first* revisited point on the path, then the path cannot have got back to b via e or f. It must have got back to b from a. But A and C are both crossed and so this is impossible. As before, the argument has to be modified slightly for a point on the edge of the board, but it still holds.

Since the Hex board is finite and the path cannot stop on the board or return to where it has been before, it must terminate at one of the points off the corners of the board other than that from which it began. It follows, as illustrated in Figure 1.12(b), that one of the two opposite sides of the board must be linked. Thus Hex cannot end in a draw.

1.6.2 Why Player I Has a Winning Strategy

The argument is by contradiction. The structure of such arguments can sometimes be confusing and so the logic will be outlined in advance. Let P be the proposition that player II has a winning strategy. It will be shown that $P \Rightarrow (\text{not}\, P)$.[9] Thus, if P were true, then $(\text{not}\, P)$ would be true as well. But it is contradictory for both P and $(\text{not}\, P)$ to be true simultaneously. Therefore P cannot be true. Hence $(\text{not}\, P)$ must be correct. Thus player II does not have a winning strategy. But we know from Section 1.4 that *someone* has a winning strategy. Since it is not player II, it must be player I. Thus player I has a winning strategy for Hex.

To prove that $P \Rightarrow (\text{not}\, P)$, we have to show that, if player II has a winning strategy, then player I must have a winning

[9]The notation $P \Rightarrow Q$ means that P implies Q. That is to say, if P is true, then Q is true.

strategy as well. Nash gave a "strategy-stealing" argument that demonstrates this fact.

If player II has a winning strategy, then player I can steal it by obeying the following instructions:

1. At the first move, choose a hexagon at random and label it with a circle.
2. At any later move, pretend that the last hexagon you labeled with a circle is unlabeled. Next pretend that the remaining circled hexagons are all crossed, and the crossed hexagons are all circled. You have now imagined yourself into a position to which player II's winning strategy applies. Pick the hexagon that player II would choose in this position if she were to use her winning strategy. Label this with a circle. The only possible snag is that this hexagon may be the hexagon you are only pretending is unlabeled. If so, then you do not need to steal player II's winning move for the position because you have *already* stolen it. Just choose a free hexagon at random to label with a circle.

This strategy must win for player I because he is simply doing what supposedly guarantees player II a win. Not only this, he does everything one move sooner than player II would do it. The fact that he has an extra hexagon labeled with his emblem does not hurt him at all. On the contrary, its presence may serve to provide him with a victory sooner than would otherwise have been the case.

1.7 Chess

Except for Tictactoe, the games considered so far have necessarily ended in a victory for one player or the other. However, Chess may end in one of three possible ways. To the possibilities that White might win or lose, we have to add the possibility that the game might end in a draw. These three possibilities will be labeled $\mathcal{W}$, $\mathcal{L}$ and $\mathcal{D}$ respectively. Player I's preferences over these outcomes are indicated by writing

$$\mathcal{L} \prec_1 \mathcal{D} \prec_1 \mathcal{W}.$$

Player II's preferences are given by

$$\mathcal{L} \succ_2 \mathcal{D} \succ_2 \mathcal{W}.$$

In general, the notation $a \preceq_i b$ means that player i likes outcome b at least as much as a. The notation $a \prec_i b$ means that player i strictly prefers b to a. That is to say, he or she will never choose a when b is available. The notation $a \sim_i b$ means that player i is indifferent between a and b. To write $a \preceq_i b$ is therefore equivalent to saying that either $a \prec_i b$ or else $a \sim_i b$.

The properties of such preference relations will be discussed more carefully in Chapter 3. For the moment, it will be enough to observe that the preferences attributed to players I and II make Chess a *strictly competitive* game. In terms of preference relations, this means[10] that, for each outcome a and b,

$$a \prec_1 b \quad \Leftrightarrow \quad b \prec_2 a \,.$$

Math 1.7.1 ⟶ The players' aims are therefore diametrically opposed. Whatever is good for one is bad for the other.

The principal result in this section is that Chess has a value. This will be deduced from a more general theorem whose proof is little more than a tidying up of the account of Zermelo's algorithm given in Section 1.4. In the statement of the theorem, the assertion that player i can *force* an outcome in a set S means that player i has a strategy that guarantees that the outcome will be in the set S whatever strategy is used by the opponent. The notation $\sim S$ is used for the *complement*[11] of a set S. In the theorem, for example, $\sim T$ consists of all outcomes of the game that are not in the set T.

Theorem 1.7.1 (Zermelo) Let T be any set of outcomes in a finite[12] two-player game of perfect information without chance moves. Then, either player I can force an outcome in T, or player II can force an outcome in $\sim T$.

Proof. Label all outcomes in T with the letter $\mathcal{W}$, and all outcomes in $\sim T$ with the letter $\mathcal{L}$. In the rest of the proof attention

---

[10]The notation $P \Leftrightarrow Q$ means that P is true if and only if Q is true. That is to say, $P \Leftrightarrow Q$ means that both $P \Rightarrow Q$ and $Q \Rightarrow P$ are true. To express the fact that $P \Rightarrow Q$ one can say that P is a *sufficient* condition for Q. Similarly, $Q \Rightarrow P$ means that P is a *necessary* condition for Q. Thus, $P \Leftrightarrow Q$ may also be translated as P is a necessary and sufficient condition for Q.

[11]The notation $x \in S$ means that x is an element (or a member) of the set S. The notation $x \notin S$ means that x is not an element of S. The complement $\sim S$ of a set S can therefore be defined symbolically as $\sim S = \{x : x \notin S\}$. For the definition to be meaningful, it is necessary to know the range of the variable x in advance. In the text, the range is understood to be the set U of all outcomes of the game under study.

[12]This just means that the game tree has a finite number of nodes.

may then be restricted to finite, two-player games whose terminal nodes are all labeled with $\mathcal{W}$ or $\mathcal{L}$. As in Section 1.4, define the value $v(H)$ of such a game H to be $\mathcal{W}$ if player I can force a win in H and $\mathcal{L}$ if player II can force a win in H. The theorem will be proved if it can be shown that any game H of the type under study has a value. Clearly, the argument of Section 1.4 can be used for this purpose. However, since this is to be the proof of a formal theorem, the argument ought to be given reasonably carefully.

Let the rank of a game be the number of edges in its longest possible play. It is certainly true that any game of rank 1 has a value. Such a game consists of a root and some terminal nodes. If player I chooses at the root, then he can win immediately if one of the terminal nodes is labeled with $\mathcal{W}$. Otherwise all the terminal nodes are labeled with $\mathcal{L}$ and hence player II can force a win without doing anything at all. Similar reasoning shows that a game of rank 1 has a value if it is player II who chooses at its root.

Next suppose that, for some value of n, all games of rank n have a value. It will be shown that all games of rank $n+1$ must then have a value also.

Let G be a game of rank $n+1$. On each play of length $n+1$ in G, locate the last nonterminal node x on the play. Construct a new game G' by deleting everything that follows each such node x in G. The nodes x then become terminal nodes of G'. Label each such terminal node x with the value $v(G_x)$ of the subgame G_x whose root is x. Such subgames are of rank 1 and hence have a value.

Since the game G' is of rank n, it has a value. Suppose it is player I who has a strategy s' that wins the game G' against any strategy that player II might use. The use of s' guarantees that G' will end at a terminal node of G' labeled with $\mathcal{W}$. If this terminal node corresponds to a subgame G_x of G, then $v(G_x) = \mathcal{W}$ and so player I has a winning strategy s_x in G_x. Thus player I can force a win in G by playing s' in G' and s_x in each subgame G_x for which he has a winning strategy. The same reasoning applies if it is player II who has a winning strategy in G'. Thus one of the players can force a win in G and so G has a value.

It has been shown that games of rank 1 have a value. It has also been shown that, *if* all games of rank n have a value, *then* so do all games of rank $n+1$. It follows that *all* games have a value. To see why this is the case, begin by taking $n = 1$. Since games of rank 1 have a value, we can deduce that games of rank 2 have a value. Now take $n = 2$. This allows us to deduce

Player II can force an outcome in here.

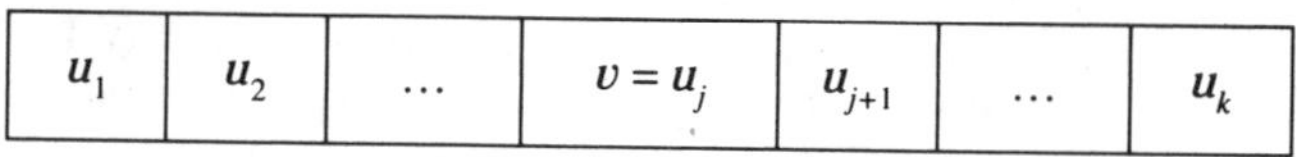

Player I can force an outcome in here.

Figure 1.14 The value v of a strictly competitive game.

that games of rank 3 have a value. This allows us to deduce that games of rank 4 have a value, and so on.[13]

It has been shown that all the games under study have a value. Thus, either player I can force an outcome in T, or else player II can force an outcome in $\sim T$. □

1.7.1 Values of Strictly Competitive Games

Math

Notice first that a Mad Hatter has appeared in the margin. The Teaching Guide explains in detail what his appearance signifies. Usually, he is running away to some other section, and beginners would be advised to follow him. Here he is *not* running away, although he looks as though he would like to. This means that something a little tougher than usual is coming up, but that the temptation to rush on by should be resisted.

An outcome v will be said to be a value of a finite, strictly competitive game G if and only if player I can force an outcome in the set $W_v = \{u : u \succeq_1 v\}$ *and* player II can force an outcome in the set $L_v = \{u : u \succeq_2 v\}$. Without loss of generality in what follows, it will be assumed that player I is not indifferent between any pair of outcomes of G. Thus the outcomes in the set $U = \{u_1, u_2, \ldots, u_k\}$ of all possible outcomes of G can be labeled so that

$$u_1 \prec_1 u_2 \prec_1 \cdots \prec_1 u_k .$$

Player II's preferences then satisfy $u_1 \succ_2 u_2 \succ_2 \cdots \succ_2 u_k$. Figure 1.14 illustrates what it means for such a game to have a value v.

Corollary 1.7.1 Any finite, strictly competitive game of perfect information without chance moves has a value.

[13] The general statement of this mode of reasoning is called the *Principle of Induction.* It asserts that, if $P(n)$ is a proposition that is defined for each $n = 1, 2, \ldots,$ and

1. $P(1)$ is true;
2. For each n, $P(n) \Rightarrow P(n+1)$ is true;

then $P(n)$ is true for all values of n.

Proof. Player I can certainly force an outcome in the set W_{u_1} because this contains all outcomes of the game. He certainly cannot force an outcome in a set smaller than W_{u_k} because this set contains only the single element u_k. Hence there is a *smallest* set W_v in which player I can force the outcome to lie. Thus, if $v = u_j$, player I *cannot* force the outcome to be in $W_{u_{j+1}}$. From Zermelo's theorem, it follows that player II *can* force an outcome in $\sim W_{u_{j+1}} = L_v$. This completes the proof. □

Corollary 1.7.2 Chess has a value.

Proof. This follows immediately from Corollary 1.7.1. □

1.7.2 Saddle Points

A strategy pair (s, t) is a saddle point of the strategic form of a strictly competitive game if, from the point of view of player I, the outcome v that results from the use of (s, t) is no worse than any outcome in the column corresponding to t and no better than any outcome in the row corresponding to s.

Corollary 1.7.3 The strategic form of a finite, strictly competitive game of perfect information without chance moves has a saddle point (s, t).

Proof. Suppose the game has value v. Let s be a strategy that guarantees player I an outcome $u \succeq_1 v$. Then each entry in row s of the strategic form must be no worse than v for player I. Let t be a strategy that guarantees player II an outcome $u \succeq_2 v$. Then each entry in column t must be no worse than v for player II. Because the game is strictly competitive, each entry in column t is therefore no better than v for player I. The actual outcome that results from the play of (s, t) must therefore be no worse and no better for player I than v. Since players are assumed not to be indifferent between outcomes in this section, it follows that the result of playing (s, t) must be v. The corollary then follows. □

A converse of this result will also be useful.

Theorem 1.7.2 Suppose that the strategic form of any strictly competitive game G has a saddle point (s, t) for which the corresponding outcome is v. Then G has value v.

Proof. Since v is the worst outcome in its row for player I, he can force an outcome at least as good for him as v by playing

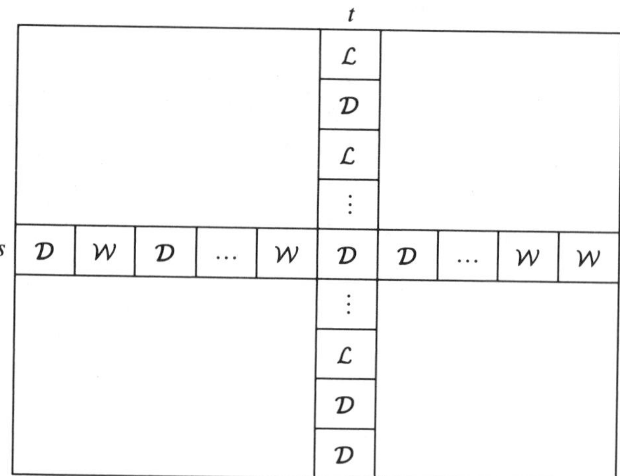

Figure 1.15 The strategic form of Chess.

s. Since v is the best outcome in its column for player I, it is the worst in its column for player II. Hence player II can force an outcome at least as good for her as v by playing t. □

These results are illustrated in Figure 1.15, which is a notional strategic form for Chess. Chess is so complicated that its actual value v may never be known. If $v = \mathcal{W}$, then White can force a win. If $v = \mathcal{L}$, then Black can force a win. If $v = \mathcal{D}$, then both players can force a draw. Figure 1.15 is drawn on the assumption that this third possibility is correct. The strategy s represents a pure strategy that guarantees a draw or better for player I and t represents a pure strategy that guarantees a draw or better for player II. By Corollary 1.7.3, the pair (s, t) is then a saddle point of the strategic form of Chess.

1.8 Rational Play?

What advice should a game theory book give to each of two players who are about to play a strictly competitive game G of perfect information without chance moves? If the game has value v, the answer may seem easy. Surely each player should simply choose pure strategies that guarantee each an outcome no worse than v. If such a pair (s, t) of pure strategies is used, then the outcome of the game will be v.[14] However, a little

[14]Assuming, as in the preceding section, that the players are not indifferent between any of the outcomes. If they are sometimes indifferent between two outcomes, then the result of the play of (s, t) might be an outcome w that is not the same as v, but which both players regard as equivalent to v.

care is necessary before accepting the pair (s, t) as a solution to the game. The rest of this section is devoted to a discussion of some of the relevant issues.

1.8.1 Nash Equilibrium

The pair (s, t) certainly satisfies one of the criteria that must be satisfied if it is to be proposed by a game theory book for general adoption as the solution of a game. The criterion is that (s, t) be a *Nash equilibrium*. This simply means that s must be an optimal choice for a player I who knows that player II will choose t: simultaneously, t must be an optimal choice for a player II who knows that player I will choose s. In other words, each of the pure strategies in the pair (s, t) must be a best reply to the other.

In a strictly competitive game, the condition for a pair (s, t) to be a Nash equilibrium is that it be a saddle point of the strategic form of the game. The fact that v is best in its row makes s a best reply to t for player I. In a strictly competitive game, if v is worst in its row for player I, then it must be best in its row for player II. Thus t is a best reply to s for player II.

Consider, for example, the strategic form of Figure 1.5. This has many Nash equilibria. All pure strategy pairs in which player I uses rr are Nash equilibria. That is to say, *every* outcome along the bottom row of the matrix corresponds to a saddle point.

It would be self-defeating for a game theorist to publish a recommendation for each player that was not a Nash equilibrium. If the advice were generally adopted, then it would be common knowledge how the game would be played. But if it is known that any player II will actually carry out the book's advice by playing t, no rational player I will carry out the book's advice to play s unless s is a best reply to t. Similarly, if it is known that any player I will actually carry out the book's advice by playing s, then no rational player II will carry out the book's advice to play t unless t is a best reply to s.

1.8.2 Subgame-Perfect Equilibrium

In the strategic form of Figure 1.5, (rr, LLL) is a Nash equilibrium. It is not, however, a strategy pair that will be selected by Zermelo's algorithm. As we know from Section 1.4, Zermelo's algorithm always selects rr for player I. The pure strategies it selects for player II can be read off from Figure 1.2(b). They correspond to edges that are doubled in this diagram. That is to say, they are the pure strategies of the form RXY. The pure strategy LLL is not one of these.

The reason that Zermelo's algorithm does not select LLL is that this pure strategy calls upon player II to plan to make the *irrational* choice of L at node c. The choice is said to be irrational because, if node c *were* reached, then player II could win by playing R, whereas playing L leads to her losing. The fact that the strategy LLL incorporates such an irrational plan is not detected by the definition of a Nash equilibrium because, if player I uses his Nash equilibrium strategy of rr, then node c will not be reached. Hence player II will never be called upon to use her irrational plan of action at node c. The point here is that restricting attention to Nash equilibrium strategies only ensures that players will behave rationally at nodes *on the equilibrium path*. This is the play of the game that is followed when the equilibrium strategies are used. Off the equilibrium path, Nash equilibrium strategies may call for all sorts of crazy behavior.

Consider, for example, the game of Chess. If the value of Chess is $\mathcal{D}$, then player I can guarantee a draw or better by playing a pure strategy s. But he cannot do any better if player II uses a pure strategy t that guarantees her a draw or better. But perhaps player II might make a momentary error that results in a subgame being reached that would not have been reached if player II had not deviated from t by mistake. The use of strategy s will still guarantee a draw or better for player I because s guarantees such a result whether player II plays well or badly. However, after player II has made a mistake, it may be that player I can do better than forcing a draw. In the subgame reached as a result of player II's blunder, it may be that player I has a winning strategy. If so, then he may not wish to stick with pure strategy s. If s guarantees only a draw in the subgame, but there is another strategy s' that guarantees victory, then player I will wish to switch from s to s'.

It is therefore clear that a game theorist would be failing in his duty if he were content to recommend *any* Nash equilibrium of Chess as its solution. A theorist must offer more refined advice. In particular, the strategy pairs (s, t) selected by Zermelo's algorithm are not only Nash equilibria in the whole game: they also induce Nash equilibria in *every* subgame. Following Reinhard Selten, a pair of strategies with this property is said to be a *subgame-perfect equilibrium*.

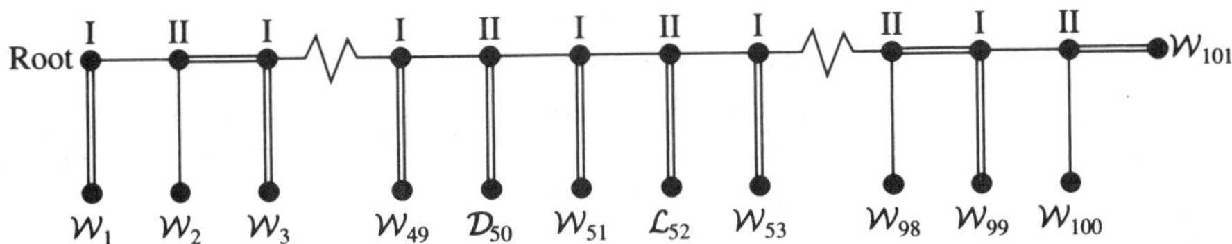

Figure 1.16 A Chess-like game.

1.8.3 Exploiting Bad Play

Phil 1.9 → Would a game theorist be safe in recommending a subgame-perfect equilibrium as the solution of Chess? Consider the example of Figure 1.16, which is like Chess to the extent that players I and II move alternately and the labels $\mathcal{W}$, $\mathcal{L}$ or $\mathcal{D}$ refer to a win, draw or loss for player I. However, unlike Chess, the players are assumed to care about how long the game lasts. Player I's preferences are given by

$$\mathcal{W}_1 \succ_1 \mathcal{W}_2 \succ_1 \cdots \succ_1 \mathcal{W}_{101} \succ_1 \mathcal{D}_{50} \succ_1 \mathcal{L}_{52}\,.$$

Player II is assumed to hold opposing preferences. This makes the game strictly competitive. The doubled edges in Figure 1.16 show the result of applying Zermelo's algorithm.

Since only one edge is doubled at every node, there is only one subgame-perfect equilibrium. This requires player II to play "down" at node 50. Is this good advice? The answer is that it all depends on what is known about the opponent. It is sound advice if player II is so sure that player I is rational that no evidence to the contrary will change her mind. A rational player I would certainly play "down" if he found himself at node 51 because this results in an immediate victory for him. Hence player II had best not let node 51 be reached. Instead she should settle for a draw by playing "down" at node 50.

But, in order for the game to reach node 50, player I must have played "across" on 25 consecutive occasions when it was rational to play "down". This evidence is not consistent with player II's hypothesis that player I is rational. She may, however, argue that even players who are rational nearly all the time sometimes make mistakes. If so, then she can attribute player I's behavior in always playing "across" to 25 independent random errors. Each time, she can argue, he *meant* to play "down", but fate intervened by jogging his elbow or by distracting his attention at a crucial moment so that he finished up playing "across". She will agree that only a very small probability p should be attached to his making each mistake, and hence the probability p^{25} of his making 25 independent mistakes will be an incredibly small number.[15] Nevertheless, it is logically coherent for her to believe that this unlikely event has occurred rather than give up the hypothesis that her opponent can be expected to play rationally with high probability in the future even though he has not done so in the past.

Of course, in real life, nobody is that sure of the rationality of an opponent. In particular, nobody seeking to explain the behavior of an opponent in Chess who has just made 25 consecutive bad moves would think it plausible that he really meant to make a good move every time but inadvertently moved the wrong piece each time. The natural conclusion to draw from observing bad play is that the opponent is a weak player. The question then arises as to how to take advantage of his weakness.[16]

In the game of Figure 1.16, player I's weakness seems to consist of a fixation on playing "across" no matter what. A player II at node 50 who thinks that this explanation of his behavior is very likely may care to risk playing "across" herself. The risk is that player I may deviate from his pattern of behavior in the past by playing "down" at node 51. If so, then player II has passed up the chance for a draw to no avail. However, if player I continues to play "across" at node 52, then player II can win at node 52 by playing "down".

What is important here is that game theory does not pretend to tell you how to make judgments about the shortcomings of an opponent. In making such judgments, you would be better advised to consult a psychologist than a game theorist. Game theory is about what players will do when it is understood that both are rational in some sense. Sometimes, as in the case of the Chess-like game of Figure 1.16, this means that an orthodox game-theoretic analysis is not necessarily a very helpful guide on how to play against real people. Perhaps this is just as well for those games that are played mostly for fun. Watching two people play Poker optimally would be about as interesting as watching paint dry: and nobody would play Chess at all if it were known how to play it optimally.

Does this mean that game theory is useless? Obviously I do

---

[15]If there is less than one chance in ten of making one mistake, then there is less than one chance in one billion, billion, billion of making 25 such mistakes.

[16]In general, one may be taking a risk in doing so. The opponent could conceivably be a hustler who is setting you up for a sting. However, this is not possible in the game of Figure 1.16. No possible advantage can accrue to player I from playing "across" 25 times in a row when he can win immediately on each occasion just by playing "down".

not think so or I would not devote my time to it. It is however true that, unless there are good reasons for supposing that the people involved will behave rationally, game theory cannot realistically be used in a naive way to make predictions about what real people will do. As a consequence, a player would often be unwise to use the strategy that a game theory book may label as "optimal" because this will usually only be optimal if *everyone* plans to play optimally. Of course, there are circumstances in which it *is* reasonable to work on the hypothesis that people will behave in a reasonably rational manner. Economics is somewhat shakily founded on the assumption that this will typically be the case in commercial and business transactions. However, it would be skating on very thin ice to use game theory for predictive purposes if none of the following criteria were satisfied:

- The game is simple.
- The players have played the game many times before[17] and hence have had much opportunity for trial-and-error learning.
- The incentives for playing well are adequate.

The second and third criteria are satisfied, for example, when Poker is played by experts at the "World Poker Championships". Moreover, while Poker is not as simple as Tictactoe or Nim, it is simple when compared to Chess. That is to say, it can be analyzed successfully. Thus, the first criterion is also satisfied to some degree. It is therefore reassuring that play at these championships is much closer to what game theory predicts for rational players than is the case for nickel-and-dime neighborhood games.[18] However, even when all three criteria are satisfied, game-theoretic predictions can only realistically be applied with great caution.

1.9 Conflict and Cooperation

Phil 1.10 ⟶

So far this chapter has been concerned with strictly competitive games in which what is good for one player is bad for the other. The theory of such games is very much better

[17] Against different opponents each time. If you are to play a particular game against the same opponent many times, one must model the repeated situation as a single "super-game".

[18] For example, game theory recommends much bluffing on very bad hands.

developed than for games in general. As a consequence, game theory books tended to concentrate on such games until comparatively recently. This has led some critics in the past to the erroneous conclusion that game theory is *only* about strictly competitive games. If such a conclusion were correct, they would certainly be right to reject game theory as having little practical significance. It is seldom the case that the games we have to play in real life present us with no opportunities at all to cooperate with the other players.

Real-life games typically offer opportunities both for conflict and for cooperation, and many of the really interesting questions are concerned with when it is or is not rational to cooperate with other rational players. However, a serious look at these issues is delayed until Chapter 5, which considers some bargaining games. In contrast to strictly competitive games, it is always rational in these bargaining games for the players to cooperate by coming to an agreement. But they are not free from conflict altogether because the players' views on what agreement should be chosen will not necessarily coincide.

In the current section, attention will be restricted to some simple examples of games that are not strictly competitive. They are chosen largely to make it clear that most of the pleasant properties of strictly competitive games that have been studied in this chapter so far do not carry over to more general games. In each example, outcomes will be labeled with a pair $(\$x, \$y)$ of dollar amounts. The interpretation is that, if the game ends in an outcome labeled $(\$x, \$y)$, then player I gets a payment of $\$x$ and player II gets a payment of $\$y$. Each player is assumed to prefer more money to less and to care about nothing in the game except how much money he or she is paid at the end. In diagrams, the outcome $(\$x, \$y)$ will be represented by a box with player I's payment of $\$x$ in the southwest corner and Player II's payoff of $\$y$ in the northeast corner.

1.9.1 A Team Game

A team game is as far from a strictly competitive game as it is possible to get. In team games, the players' interests coincide. Whatever is good for one player is also good for the others. Figure 1.17(a) provides a very simple example. Zermelo's algorithm has been applied by doubling appropriate edges. There is a unique subgame-perfect equilibrium (l, L) which leads to the outcome $(\$2, \$2)$. One can check that this is

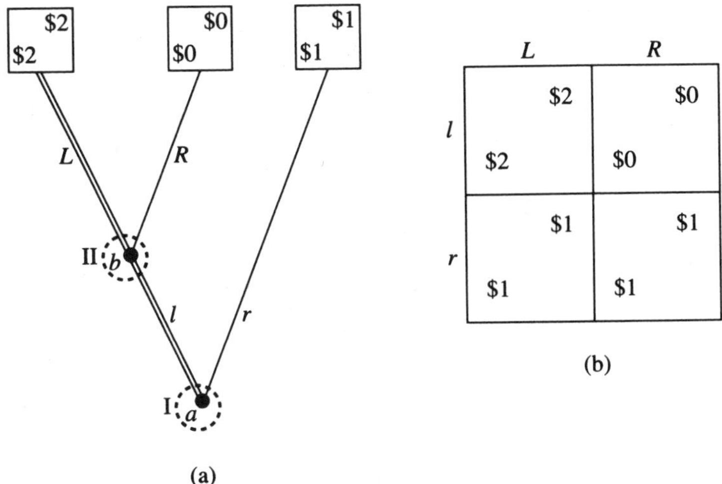

Figure 1.17 A team game.

a Nash equilibrium in the strategic form shown in Figure 1.17(b) by noting that player I's payment of \$2 is the largest of his payments in the column corresponding to L. Thus l is a best reply to L. At the same time, \$2 is the largest of player II's payments in the row corresponding to l. Thus L is a best reply to l.

Team games of perfect information are not very interesting because one might as well analyze them as one-player games.[19] But the current example will serve to make one important point: namely that games that are not strictly competitive do not necessarily have a value v in the sense that this was defined in Section 1.7.1.

One might wish to argue that the outcome (\$2, \$2) should be regarded as the value of the game, but it is false that player I has a strategy s that guarantees him a payment of \$2 or better whatever player II does. Player I has to play pure strategy l and to rely on player II choosing pure strategy L in order to get a payment of \$2. But if player II were irrationally to choose pure strategy R, player I would get only a payment of \$0. The largest payment that player I can *guarantee* is \$1. He guarantees this by choosing pure strategy r. The largest payment that player II can *guarantee* is also \$1. She

[19]When information is imperfect, however, team games can be very interesting indeed. For example, their study can teach us things about optimal ways of transmitting information within organizations whose members share a common goal.

guarantees this by playing pure strategy L. (This choice will yield a payment of \$2 if player I chooses l, but only \$1 if player I chooses r.)

In a later chapter, we shall say that pure strategy r is player I's *security strategy* and that the payment \$1 that this secures is player I's *security level*. Similarly, player II's security strategy is L and her security level is \$1. In a strictly competitive game, both players secure the value of the game by playing one of their security strategies. All that will be noted here, is that security strategies are only of secondary importance to an analysis of the game. In particular, player I would be unwise to be overconcerned about what he can *guarantee*. He has actively to predict player II's prospective behavior if he is to make a sensible decision about what to do.

1.9.2 Multiple Equilibria

In the strictly competitive games studied in this chapter, the existence of multiple equilibria is not a problem. A pure strategy pair (s, t) is a subgame-perfect equilibrium for such a game if and only if s guarantees that player I will get no worse an outcome in any subgame than its value and t does the same for player II. Thus, if (s, t) and (s', t') are two subgame-perfect equilibria, player I does not have to worry about whether player II will use t or t' in deciding which of s or s' to choose. Either will do equally well. If player I chooses s and player II chooses t' then (s, t') is still a subgame-perfect equilibrium whose use in any subgame will yield an outcome equivalent to the value of the subgame. (Technically, (s, t) and (s', t') are said to be equivalent and interchangeable as explained in Section 7.3.1.) However, for games in general, the problems raised by multiple equilibria can be very troublesome.

The game of Figure 1.18 has two Nash equilibria, namely (l, L) and (r, R). Both of these are subgame-perfect equilibria. One can check this using Zermelo's algorithm. However, in games that are not strictly competitive, it is necessary to take more care about what happens when a player has more than one optimal choice of action at a node. In strictly competitive games, one may simply work with a single game tree and double *all* the edges corresponding to optimal choices. For games that are not strictly competitive, one must usually draw a separate diagram for each optimal choice at a node.

Figure 1.18 illustrates this point. If node b is reached, then player II is indifferent between playing L and R because both

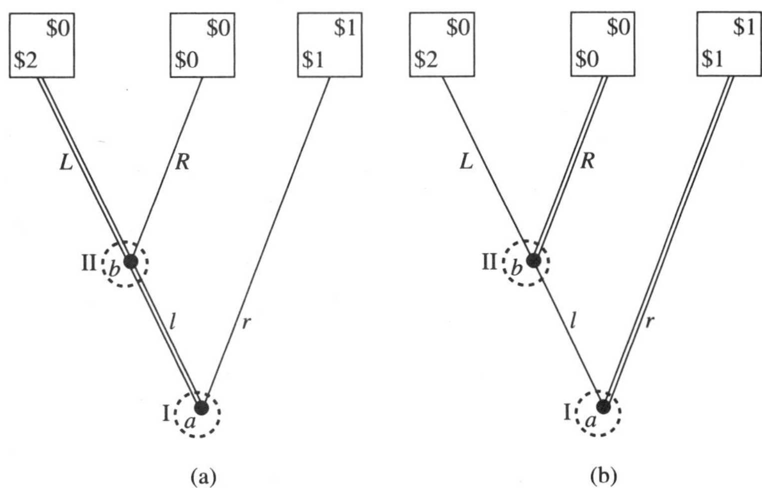

Figure 1.18 A game with noninterchangeable equilibrium strategies.

choices result in her being paid $0. Thus it is necessary to draw *two* diagrams: Figure 1.18(a) in which the edge corresponding to L is doubled, and Figure 1.18(b) in which the edge corresponding to R is doubled. In Figure 1.18(a), it is then optimal for player I to choose l. In Figure 1.18(b), it is optimal for player I to choose r. What is best for player I at node a therefore depends very strongly on what he predicts player II would do at node b if it were reached.

What advice can a game theorist give about which of these two equilibria should be selected? When strictly competitive games are studied, this problem does not have to be faced. But here (l, L) and (r, R) are neither equivalent nor interchangeable. They are not equivalent because the payment pair ($2, $0) resulting from the use of (l, L) is not the same as the payment pair ($1, $1) resulting from the use of (r, R). They are not interchangeable because, for example, if player I plays l (thinking that player II will play L) and player II plays R, the resulting pair (l, R) is not an equilibrium.

It might be argued that a game theory book should recommend the equilibrium (l, L) as the "solution" of the game on the grounds that there is no reason why player II should be advised "selfishly" to deny player I a payment of $2 if node b is reached. Against this it might be argued that it would be "selfish" of player I to allow b to have been reached in the first place. The players themselves are assumed not to care in the least about whether their behavior is or is not selfish.

By hypothesis, they care only about how much money they make. A game theorist who wishes to propose one equilibrium rather than another on ethical grounds will therefore have to impose his own value judgments or prejudices on the situation.

In any case, there are other arguments. One might argue in favor of the equilibrium (r, R) on the grounds that player I "ought" to believe a threat from player II that she plans to play R. The reason is that she has nothing to lose by carrying through the threat if node b is reached. Against this is the undeniable fact that neither would she have anything to gain. One might argue that she will wish to carry out the threat to "teach player I a lesson". But, by hypothesis, she is not interested in teaching anyone a lesson: she is interested only in how much money she makes. If one wishes to take account of other factors that may motivate players, one should alter the players' preferences over the outcomes to reflect this fact.

Not all game theorists share this opinion, but I believe the appropriate attitude to the equilibrium selection problem is the same as that a mathematician takes to a quadratic equation. If you ask him which of the two roots should be recommended as the "correct" solution, he will think the question stupid. It is not a question that makes any sense in the abstract. When a quadratic equation arises in a mathematical model constructed to represent some aspect of the real world, one computes both its roots and then asks which of them makes sense for the concrete phenomenon in the real world that the model is intended to describe. Often, for example, one of the roots is positive and the other is negative, and the latter can be rejected because it would not have a meaningful interpretation in the real world. Similarly, the question of which equilibrium in a game should be selected is often meaningless until one considers the context to which the game is to be applied.[20] Sometimes, a close examination of the context will suggest a study of a more complicated game that has a *unique* equilibrium. More often, one is left to exercise one's modeling judgment in making a selection from the available equilibria.

[20]Cognoscenti should not read this as asserting that there is nothing to be gained from the study of refinements of Nash equilibria. All that is being said is that the question of which refinement, if any, should be employed is a matter that usually calls for more information than is encoded in the formal definition of a game.

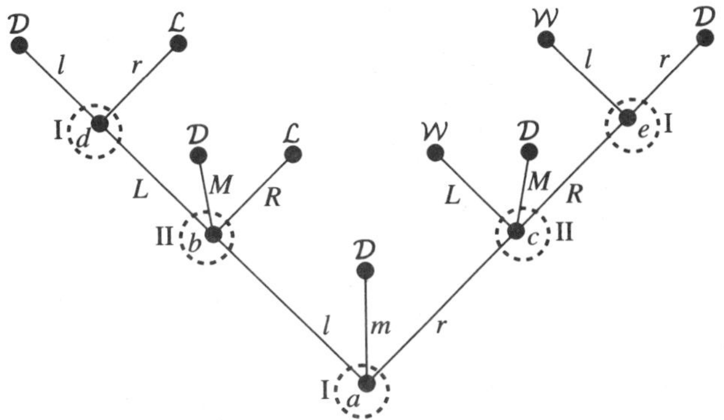

Figure 1.19 The game for Exercise 1.10.1.

1.10 Exercises

1. Figure 1.19 illustrates the tree of a strictly competitive game G of perfect information without chance moves.
   (a) How many pure strategies does each player have?
   (b) List each player's pure strategies using the notation of Section 1.3.
   (c) What play results from the use of the pure strategy pair (rll, LM)?
   (d) Find all pure strategy pairs that result in the play $[rRl]$.
   (e) Write down the strategic form of G.
   (f) Find all the saddle points.
2. Dominoes can be placed on an $m \times n$ board so as to cover two squares exactly. Two players alternate in doing this. The first to be unable to place a domino is the loser. Draw the game tree for the case $m = 2$ and $n = 3$.
3. Figure 1.20 is a skeleton for the tree of a game called Blackball. A committee of three club members (I, II and III) has to select one from a list of four candidates (A, B, C and D) as a new member of the club. Each committee member is allowed to blackball (veto) one candidate. This right is exercised in rotation, beginning with player I and ending with player III.

   Label each nonterminal node on a copy of Figure 1.20 with the numeral of the player who decides at that node. The edges representing choices at the node should be labeled with the candidates who have yet to be blackballed. Each terminal node should be labeled with the letter of the candidate elected to the club if the game ends there.

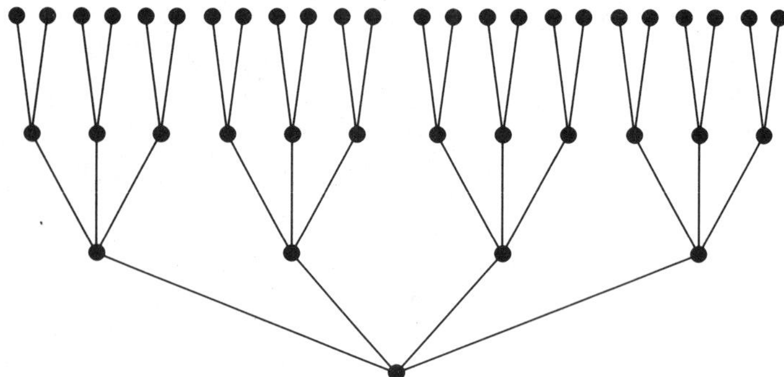

Figure 1.20 A skeleton for the tree of Blackball.

How many pure strategies does each player have? What information has not been supplied that is necessary to analyze the game?

4. Begin to draw the game tree for Chess. Include at least one complete play of the game in your diagram.

Math

5. Two players alternately choose either 0 or 1 forever. A play of this *infinite* game can therefore be identified with a sequence of 0s and 1s. For example, the play 101000... began with player I choosing 1. Then player II chose 0, after which player I chose 1 again. Thereafter both players always chose 0. A sequence of 0s and 1s can be interpreted[21] as the binary expansion of a real number x satisfying $0 \leq x \leq 1$. For a given set of E of real numbers, player I wins if $x \in E$ but loses if $x \in {\sim}E$.

   Begin to draw the game tree.

6. Apply Zermelo's algorithm to the game G of Exercise 1.10.1. What is the value of G? What is the value of the subgame starting at node b? What is the value of the subgame starting at node c? Show that the pure strategy rrr guarantees that player I gets the value of G or better. Why is this pure strategy not selected by Zermelo's algorithm?

Fun

7. Apply Zermelo's algorithm to the 2×3 version of the domino-placing game of Exercise 1.10.2. Find the value of the game and determine a winning strategy for one of the players.

Fun

8. Who would win a game of Nim with $n \geq 2$ piles of matches of which the kth pile contains 2^{k-1} matches?[22]

[21] For example, $\frac{5}{8} = .101000\ldots$, because $\frac{5}{8} = 1(\frac{1}{2}) + 0(\frac{1}{2})^2 + 1(\frac{1}{2})^3 + \cdots$.

[22] Try this with particular values of n to begin with. For example, $n = 3$.

Describe a play of the game in which $n = 3$ and the winner plays optimally while the loser always takes one match from a pile with the median number of matches. (The median pile is the middle-sized pile).

Fun 9. Repeat the previous exercise for $2^n - 1$ piles of which the kth pile contains k matches.

Fun 10. Who has a winning strategy in the domino-placing game of Exercise 1.10.2 when:
(a) m and n are even;
(b) m is even and n is odd;
(c) $m = n = 3$?
Justify your answers.

Fun 11. What are the winning opening moves in 3×3, 4×4 and 5×5 Hex?

Fun 12. On an $n \times (n + 1)$ Hex board, with the first player having to link the more distant sides, show that the second player has a winning strategy.

Math 13. The game board of Figure 1.21 represents the downtown street plan of a city. Players I and II represent groups of gangsters. Player I controls the areas to the north and to the south of the city. Player II controls the areas to the east and west. The nodes in the street plan represent street intersections. The players take turns in labeling nodes that have not already been labeled. Player I uses a circle as his label. Player II uses a cross. A player who manages to label both ends of a street controls the street.

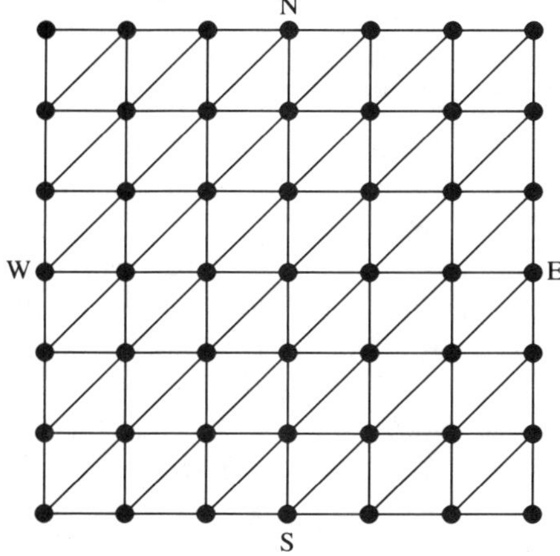

Figure 1.21 A city street plan.

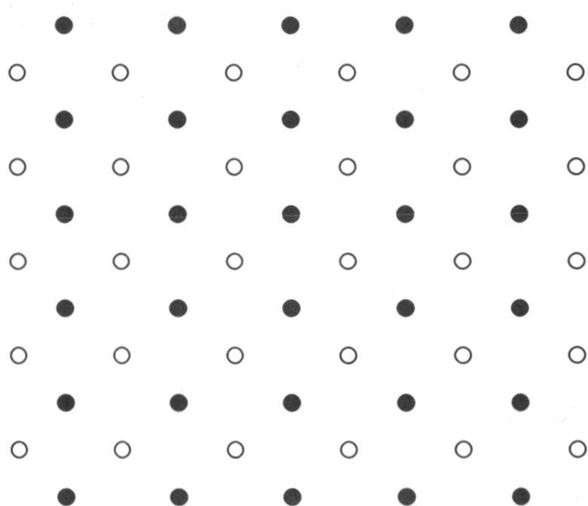

Figure 1.22 The board for Bridgit.

Player I wins if he links the north and south with a route that he controls. Player II wins if she links the east and west.

Why is this game entirely equivalent to Hex?

Math

14. The game of Bridgit was invented by David Gale. It is played on a board like that shown in Figure 1.22. Black tries to link top and bottom by joining neighboring black nodes horizontally or vertically. White tries to link left and right by joining neighboring white nodes horizontally or vertically. Neither player is allowed to cross a linkage made by the other.
    (a) Find an argument, like that used for Hex, which shows that the game cannot end in a draw.
    (b) Why does it follow that someone can force a win?
    (c) Why is it the first player who has a winning strategy?
    (d) What is a winning strategy?[23]

Math

15. Two players alternately remove nodes from a connected graph $\mathcal{G}$. Except in the case of the first move, a player may only remove a node if it is joined by an edge to the node removed by the previous player. The player left with no legitimate vertex to remove loses.

    Explain why the second player has a winning strategy if there exists a set E of edges with no endpoint in common such that each node is the endpoint of an edge in the set E. Show that no such set E exists for the graph of Figure 1.23. Find a winning strategy for the first player.

[23]Don't feel bad if you cannot answer this last question. It is difficult!

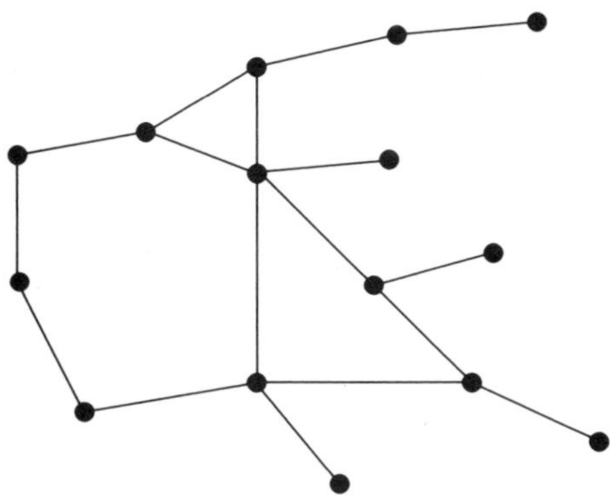

Figure 1.23 A graph $\mathcal{G}$ for Exercise 1.10.15.

Math

16. The value of Chess is unknown. It may be $\mathcal{W}$, $\mathcal{D}$ or $\mathcal{L}$. Explain why a simple strategy-stealing argument cannot be used to eliminate the possibility that the value of Chess is $\mathcal{L}$.

Math

17. Explain why player I has a winning strategy in the number construction game of Exercise 1.10.5 when $E = \{x : x > \frac{1}{2}\}$. What is player I's winning strategy when $E = \{x : x \geq \frac{2}{3}\}$? What is player II's winning strategy when $E = \{x : x > \frac{2}{3}\}$? Explain why player II has a winning strategy when E is the set of all rational numbers.[24] (A rational number is the same thing as a fraction.)
18. Let (s, t) and (s', t') be two different saddle points for a strictly competitive game. Prove that (s, t') and (s', t) are also saddle points.
19. Find all Nash equilibria in the game G of Exercise 1.10.1. Which of these are subgame-perfect?
20. Find the subgame-perfect equilibria for Blackball of Exercise 1.10.3 in the case when the players preferences satisfy:

$$A \succ_1 B \succ_1 C \succ_1 D\,,$$
$$B \succ_2 C \succ_2 D \succ_2 A\,,$$
$$C \succ_3 D \succ_3 A \succ_3 B\,.$$

[24] One may ask whether this infinite game always has a value whatever the set E may be. The answer is abstruse. If one assumes a set-theoretic principle called the Axiom of Choice, then there are sets E for which the game has no value. But some mathematicians have proposed replacing the Axiom of Choice with an axiom that would imply that the game has a value for every set E.

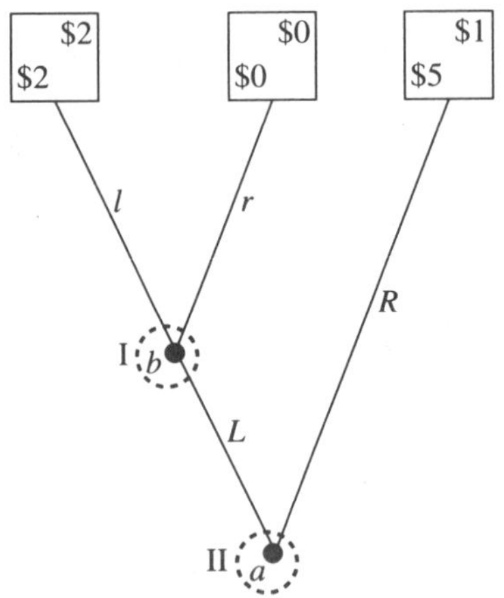

Figure 1.24 Selten's Chain-store Game.

Who gets elected to the club if a subgame-perfect equilibrium is used? Find at least one Nash equilibrium that is not subgame-perfect.

Econ 21. In the Chain-store Game of Figure 1.24, find:

(a) The strategic form.
(b) The players' security strategies.
(c) The players' security levels.
(d) All Nash equilibria.
(e) All subgame-perfect equilibria.

Econ 22. The Chain-store Game studied in Exercise 1.10.21 is often used to illustrate the logic of "entry deterrence". Player I is an incumbent monopolist in an industry, who makes \$5m if left to enjoy his privileged position undisturbed. Player II is a firm that could enter the industry, but earns \$1m if it chooses not to enter. If the potential entrant decides to enter, then the monopolist can do one of two things: he can fight by flooding the market with his product so as to force down the price, or he can acquiesce and split the market with the entrant. A fight is damaging to both players. They then make only \$0m each. If they split the market, each will make \$2m.

(a) Explain how the actions l, r, L and R in Figure 1.24 should be interpreted for the Chain-store Game to fit the preceding story.
(b) The incumbent monopolist will threaten the potential entrant that he will fight if she disregards his warning to keep out of the industry. Why will she not find his threat credible?
(c) What will happen if both players act rationally?

Econ 23. How would matters change in Exercise 1.10.22 if, before the game, the incumbent monopolist could prove to the potential entrant that he had made an irrevocable commitment to fight if she were to enter?

(a) Write down a new game tree that represents the story of Exercise 1.10.22 preceded by a preliminary move at which player I decides whether or not to make a commitment to fight if player II should enter.

(b) Find a subgame-perfect equilibrium of the new game.

(c) Can you think of ways in which player I could make an irrevocable commitment to fighting? If so, how would he convince player II of the fact that he was committed?

Econ 24. The point of the last item in Exercise 1.10.23 is that it is very hard in real life to commit yourself to a plan of action for the future that will not be in your interests should certain contingencies actually arise. Just *saying* that you are committed will not convince anyone who believes that you are rational. However, sometimes it is possible to find irreversible actions that have the same effect as making a commitment. As in the story that follows, such actions usually need to be costly so that the other players can see that you are putting your money where your mouth is.

Suppose that the incumbent monopolist in Exercise 1.10.22 can decide, before anything else happens, to make an irreversible investment in extra capacity. This will involve a dead loss of \$2m if he makes no use of the capacity, and the only time that the extra capacity would get used is if the monopolist decides to fight the entrant. He will then make \$1m (inclusive of the cost of the extra capacity) instead of \$0m because the existence of the extra capacity will make it cheaper for him to flood the market. Player II's payoffs remain unchanged.

(a) Draw a new game tree illustrating the changed situation. This will have five nodes of which the first represents player I's investment decision. If he invests, the payoffs resulting from later actions in the game will need to be modified to take into account the costs and benefits of the extra capacity.

(b) Determine the unique subgame-perfect equilibrium.

(c) Someone who knows no game theory might say that it is necessarily irrational to invest in extra capacity that you do not believe you will ever use. How might a game theorist reply?

Econon

25. Find all subgame-perfect equilibria in the game of Figure 1.25. Which equilibrium would you recommend if the players sought your advice?

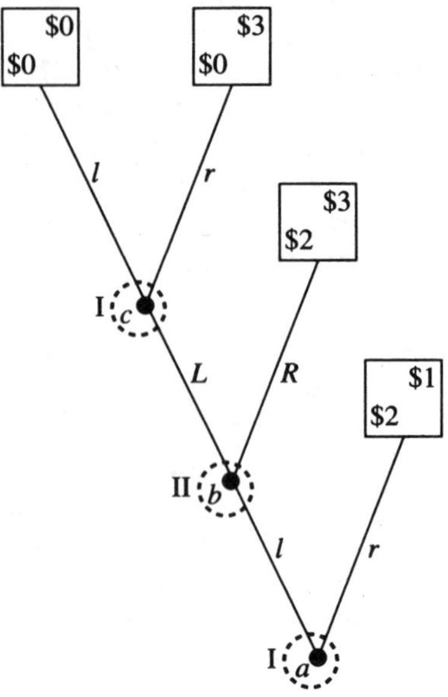

Figure 1.25 The game for Exercise 1.10.25.

CHAPTER

2

Taking Chances

2.1 Introduction

Most of the preceding chapter is about two-player, strictly competitive games of perfect information. This chapter continues their study with the innovation that chance moves are now to be admitted. Attention will be restricted to the case when the only possible outcomes are $\mathcal{W}$ or $\mathcal{L}$. In such games, the motivation of a rational player is to maximize the *probability* of winning. The chapter is therefore largely concerned with how to use probabilities in a game context.

2.1.1 Probability Measures

Review 2.2.3 ⟶

Suppose a dice is rolled. When it comes to rest, it will show one of the numbers 1, 2, 3, 4, 5 or 6. Statisticians call the set

$$\Omega = \{1, 2, 3, 4, 5, 6\}$$

a *sample space*. They identify possible *events* that can result from rolling the dice with the subsets of Ω. Thus the event that the dice shows an even number may be identified with the set $E = \{2, 4, 6\}$. Let S denote the set of all possible events. (Thus S is the set of all subsets of Ω.)

A *probability measure* is a function[1]

$$\text{prob} : S \to [0, 1]$$

such that

$$\begin{aligned} &\text{(i) } \text{prob}(\emptyset) = 0; \quad \text{prob}(\Omega) = 1 \\ &\text{(ii) } \text{prob}(E \cup F) = \text{prob}(E) + \text{prob}(F), \\ &\quad\ \text{whenever } E \cap F = \emptyset. \end{aligned}$$

The number $\text{prob}(E)$ is to be interpreted as the probability of the event E. The empty set $\emptyset$ is defined to be the set with no elements. To write $\text{prob}(\emptyset) = 0$, as in item (i), is therefore to assert that the probability of the impossible event that nothing at all will happen is zero. To write $\text{prob}(\Omega) = 1$ means that the probability of the certain event that something will happen is 1.

Item (ii) in the definition of a probability measure has more substance than item (i). If E and F are events, then $E \cap F$ represents the event that both E and F occur. To

[1] A function $f : A \to B$ is a rule that assigns to each $a \in A$ a unique $b \in B$. The object b assigned to a is denoted by $f(a)$. It is said to be the value of the function at the point a. The notation $[a, b]$ represents the set $\{x : a \leq x \leq b\}$ of real numbers. The function $\text{prob} : S \to [0, 1]$ therefore assigns to each event $E \in S$ a unique real number $x = \text{prob}(E)$ satisfying $0 \leq x \leq 1$.

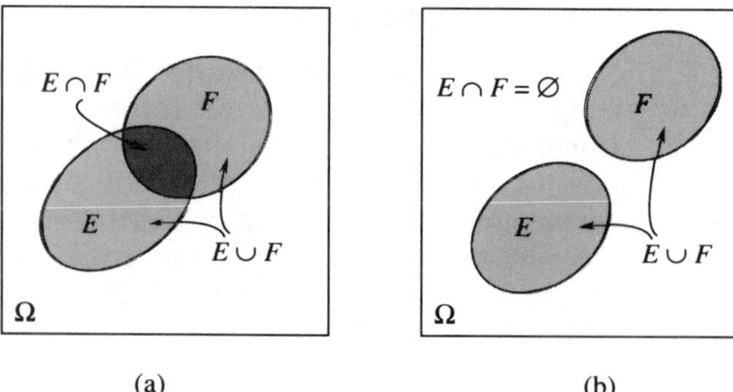

(a) (b)

Figure 2.1 Venn diagrams of $E \cup F$.

write $E \cap F = \emptyset$ therefore means that E and F cannot both occur simultaneously. The events E and F are then said to be *disjoint*. The situation is illustrated in the "Venn diagram" of Figure 2.1(b). The set $E \cup F$ represents the event that at least one of E or F occurs. Item (ii) therefore says that, if two events cannot occur together, then the probability that one or the other will occur is the *sum* of their separate probabilities.

Suppose, for example, that the dice is "fair". Then it will be true that $\text{prob}(\{1\}) = \text{prob}(\{2\}) = \cdots = \text{prob}(\{6\}) = \frac{1}{6}$. The probability that an even number will appear is therefore

$$\begin{aligned}\text{prob}(E) &= \text{prob}(\{2,4,6\}) \\ &= \text{prob}(\{2\}) + \text{prob}(\{4\}) + \text{prob}(\{6\}) \\ &= \tfrac{1}{6} + \tfrac{1}{6} + \tfrac{1}{6} = \tfrac{1}{2}\,.\end{aligned}$$

The proper interpretation of probabilities is a subject for philosophers. For the purposes of game theory, it is usually enough to say that a statement like $\text{prob}(E) = \frac{1}{2}$ means that there is one chance in two that E will occur. To write $\text{prob}(\{4\}) = \frac{1}{6}$ means that there is one chance in six of 4 being rolled.

In gambling terminology, to say that $\text{prob}(\{4\}) = \frac{1}{6}$ is the same as saying that the odds are 5:1 against rolling 4. In general, if the odds against an event in a "fair" bet are $a : b$, then its probability is $b/(a+b)$.

2.1.2 Independent Events

If A and B are sets, the set $A \times B$ consists of all the pairs[2] (a, b) with $a \in A$ and $b \in B$. Figure 2.2(a) shows the sample

[2]The notation (a, b) here means the pair of real numbers a and b with a taken first. If the order of the numbers were irrelevant, one would simply use the notation $\{a, b\}$ for the set containing a and b. It is worth noting

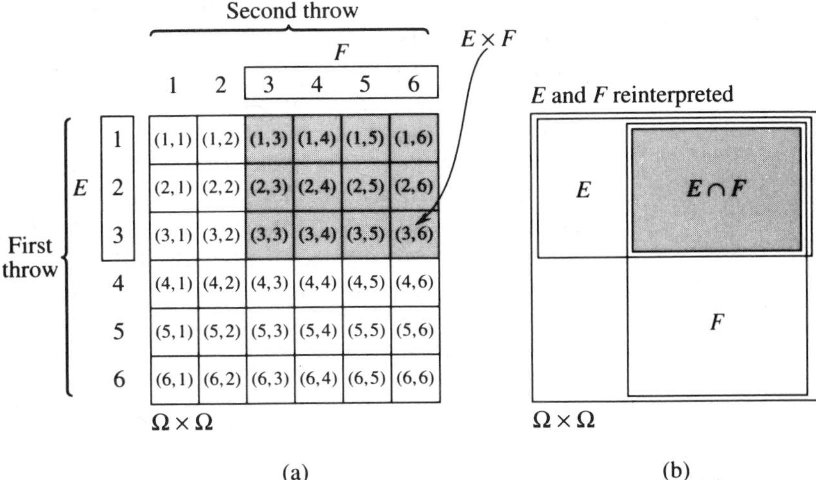

Figure 2.2 The sample space $\Omega \times \Omega$ for two independent rolls of the dice.

space $\Omega^2 = \Omega \times \Omega$ obtained when two *independent* rolls of the dice are observed. In this diagram, $(5,4)$ represents the event that 5 is rolled with the first dice and 4 with the second. This is not the same event as (4,5) which means that 4 is rolled with the first dice and 5 with the second. The event $E \times F$ has been shaded. It is the event that a 3 or less is thrown with the first dice and a 3 or more with the second dice.

There are $36 = 6 \times 6$ entries in the square representing $\Omega \times \Omega$. With the independence assumption, each of these is equally likely. The probability of each is therefore $\frac{1}{36}$. This means that the probability of $E \times F$ must be

$$\text{prob}(E \times F) = \tfrac{12}{36} = \tfrac{1}{3}.$$

Notice that $\text{prob}(E) = \frac{1}{2}$ and $\text{prob}(F) = \frac{2}{3}$. Thus

$$\text{prob}(E \times F) = \text{prob}(E) \times \text{prob}(F).$$

This identity holds whenever E and F are *independent* events.

Usually this conclusion is expressed by saying that

$$\text{prob}(E \cap F) = \text{prob}(E)\,\text{prob}(F)$$

when E and F are independent. That is, the probability that both of two independent events will occur simultaneously is

that mathematicians use the notation (a, b) ambiguously. It also means the open interval $\{x : a < x < b\}$ of real numbers (as opposed to the closed interval $[a, b] = \{x : a \le x \le b\}$). One has to deduce from the context how (a, b) is being used.

the *product* of their separate probabilities. Strictly speaking, this requires reinterpreting E and F as events in $\Omega \times \Omega$ as indicated in Figure 2.2(b). In this diagram, E is no longer the event that the first dice will show 1, 2 or 3. Such an event is a subset of Ω. It is instead the subset of $\Omega \times \Omega$ corresponding to the event in which the first dice shows 1, 2 or 3 and the second dice shows anything. Similarly F becomes the subset of $\Omega \times \Omega$ corresponding to the event that the first dice shows anything and the second dice shows 3, 4, 5 or 6. Such care in interpreting E and F is admittedly pedantic, but a failure to exercise such care can often lead to much confusion.

2.1.3 Paying Off the Mafia

A man needs \$1,000 to pay off the Mafia tomorrow, but only has a total of \$2. He therefore buys two lottery tickets costing \$1 each in two independent lotteries. The winner in each lottery gets a prize of \$1,000 (and there are no second prizes). If the probability of winning in each lottery is $q = 0.0001$, what is the probability that the man will win enough money to pay off the Mafia tomorrow?

Let $\mathcal{W}_1$ and $\mathcal{L}_1$ be the events that the man wins or loses in the first lottery. Let $\mathcal{W}_2$ and $\mathcal{L}_2$ be defined similarly. Then

$$\begin{aligned} \text{prob}(\mathcal{W}_1) &= q\,; \quad \text{prob}(\mathcal{L}_1) = 1 - \text{prob}(\mathcal{W}_1) = 1 - q\,; \\ \text{prob}(\mathcal{W}_2) &= q\,; \quad \text{prob}(\mathcal{L}_2) = 1 - \text{prob}(\mathcal{W}_2) = 1 - q\,. \end{aligned}$$

What we require is $\text{prob}(\mathcal{W}_1 \cup \mathcal{W}_2)$. But this is *not* equal to $\text{prob}(\mathcal{W}_1) + \text{prob}(\mathcal{W}_2)$ because $\mathcal{W}_1$ and $\mathcal{W}_2$ are not disjoint events. They can occur simultaneously. The man might win both lotteries.

However, $\mathcal{W}_1 \cap \mathcal{W}_2$, $\mathcal{W}_1 \cap \mathcal{L}_2$ and $\mathcal{L}_1 \cap \mathcal{W}_2$ are disjoint events, and so

$$\begin{aligned} \text{prob}(\mathcal{W}_1 \cup \mathcal{W}_2) &= \text{prob}(\mathcal{W}_1 \cap \mathcal{W}_2) + \text{prob}(\mathcal{W}_1 \cap \mathcal{L}_2) \\ &\qquad + \text{prob}(\mathcal{L}_1 \cap \mathcal{W}_2) \\ &= \text{prob}(\mathcal{W}_1)\,\text{prob}(\mathcal{W}_2) + \text{prob}(\mathcal{W}_1)\,\text{prob}(\mathcal{L}_2) \\ &\qquad + \text{prob}(\mathcal{L}_1)\,\text{prob}(\mathcal{W}_2) \\ &= q^2 + q(1-q) + (1-q)q \;=\; 0.00019998\,. \end{aligned}$$

Our hero's prospects with the Mafia are therefore not good. He has less than two chances in ten thousand of coming up with the money.

In such problems, it is often easier to work out the probability that the event will *not* happen. Here this is the event

$\mathcal{L}_1 \cap \mathcal{L}_2$ that he loses in both lotteries. The required answer is then simply

$$1 - \text{prob}(\mathcal{L}_1 \cap \mathcal{L}_2) = 1 - (1-q)^2 = 0.00019998$$

as before.

2.1.4 Conditional Probability

What of the probability of $E \cap F$ when the events E and F are not independent? In this case, the appropriate formula is

$$\text{prob}(E \cap F) = \text{prob}(E)\,\text{prob}(F|E)\,,$$

where $\text{prob}(F|E)$ is the *conditional* probability of F given E. That is to say, $\text{prob}(F|E)$ is the probability that one would attach to the event F if one knew that E had already occurred.

For example, suppose someone rolls a dice and tells you that the outcome is the event E that the result is even. What is the conditional probability that the dice is actually showing 3? Obviously, $\text{prob}(\{3\}|E) = 0$, because it is impossible that the dice can show 3 if an even number was rolled. What is the conditional probability that the dice is showing 2? Given that the outcome is even, there are only three possibilities: 2, 4 and 6. Each of these is equally likely. Hence the probability of each must be $\frac{1}{3}$. Thus $\text{prob}(\{2\}|E) = \frac{1}{3}$.

The principle being used in making these calculations is embodied in the formula

$$\text{prob}(F|E) = \text{prob}(E \cap F)/\text{prob}(E)\,.$$

For example, $\text{prob}(\{2\}|E) = \text{prob}(E \cap \{2\})/\text{prob}(E)$. Since $E \cap \{2\} = \{2\}$, it follows that $\text{prob}(E \cap \{2\}) = \text{prob}(\{2\}) = \frac{1}{6}$. Also $\text{prob}(E) = \frac{1}{6} + \frac{1}{6} + \frac{1}{6} = \frac{1}{2}$. Hence $\text{prob}(\{2\}|E) = \frac{1}{6}/\frac{1}{2} = \frac{1}{3}$.

Sometimes the calculations can be eased by appealing to Bayes' Rule. This asserts that

$$\text{prob}(F|E) = \frac{\text{prob}(E|F)\,\text{prob}(F)}{\text{prob}(E)}\,.$$

Although a lot of fuss is made of this result, it is far from being deep. It follows immediately from the fact that

$$\text{prob}(F|E)\,\text{prob}(E) = \text{prob}(E \cap F) = \text{prob}(E|F)\,\text{prob}(F)\,.$$

Its use is best illustrated with an example.

2.1.5 Guessing in Examinations

In a multiple choice test, a candidate has to choose among m answers. Each candidate is either entirely ignorant and simply chooses an answer at random, or else is omniscient and knows the right answer for sure. If the proportion of omniscient candidates is p, what is the probability that a candidate who got the answer right was guessing?

With notation that is intended to be self-explanatory, we are asked to compute prob(ignorant|right). Bayes' Rule tells us that this probability is given by

$$\text{prob}(\text{ignorant}|\text{right}) = \frac{\text{prob}(\text{right}|\text{ignorant})\text{prob}(\text{ignorant})}{\text{prob}(\text{right})}.$$

An ignorant candidate chooses at random, and so prob(right| ignorant) $= 1/m$. We are given that prob(ignorant) $= 1 - p$. What of the denominator prob(right)?

It is often wise to avoid calculating the denominator by using the following trick. Write $c = 1/\text{prob}(\text{right})$. Then

$$\text{prob}(\text{ignorant}|\text{right}) = c(1-p)/m.$$

The same mode of reasoning also shows that

$$\text{prob}(\text{omniscient}|\text{right}) = cp,$$

because prob(right|omniscient) $= 1$ and prob(omniscient) $= p$.

However, a candidate who got the answer right must either be ignorant or omniscient and cannot be both. Hence

$$\text{prob}(\text{ignorant}|\text{right}) + \text{prob}(\text{omniscient}|\text{right}) = 1.$$

It follows that $c(1-p)/m + cp = 1$ and thus $c = m/(1-p+pm)$. This concludes the calculation. The final result is that

$$\text{prob}(\text{ignorant}|\text{right}) = \frac{1-p}{1-p+pm}.$$

For example, if there are three answers to choose from and only one person in a class of 100 is not ignorant, then $m = 3$ and $p = 0.01$. The probability that a person who got the answer right was guessing is then 0.971.

2.2 Lotteries

2.2.1 Random Variables

Formally, a *random variable* is a function[3] $X : \Omega \to \mathbb{R}$. For example, you would probably want to bet with someone who maintains that the odds are more than 3 : 2 against an even

[3]The letter $\mathbb{R}$ denotes the set of all real numbers. Thus, for any $\omega \in \Omega$, $X(\omega)$ is a real number.

number being rolled with a fair dice.[4] A bookie who quotes such odds would be willing to take a bet in which you pay him \$2 if an odd number appears and he pays you \$3 if an even number appears. The sample space in this case is $\Omega = \{1, 2, 3, 4, 5, 6\}$ and the random variable X that describes the bet is defined by

$$X(\omega) = \begin{cases} 3, \text{ if } \omega = 2, 4 \text{ or } 6, \\ -2, \text{ if } \omega = 1, 3 \text{ or } 5. \end{cases}$$

Thus $X = 3$ when you win \$3 because the dice shows an even number, and $X = -2$ when you lose \$2 because the dice shows an odd number. The probability that $X = 3$ is then given by $\text{prob}(\{2, 4, 6\}) = \frac{1}{2}$. Similarly, the probability that $X = -2$ is given by $\text{prob}(\{1, 3, 5\}) = \frac{1}{2}$.

2.2.2 Expectation

The *expectation* or *expected value* $\mathcal{E}X$ of a random variable X is defined by

$$\mathcal{E}X = \sum k \,\text{prob}(X = k),$$

where the summation extends over all values of k for which $\text{prob}(X = k)$ is not zero.[5] If many independent observations of the value of X are averaged, then the probability that this "long-run average" will differ from $\mathcal{E}X$ will be small.

For example, your expected dollar winnings in the bet described above are given by

$$\begin{aligned} \mathcal{E}X &= \sum k \,\text{prob}(X = k) \\ &= 3 \times \tfrac{1}{2} + (-2) \times \tfrac{1}{2} \\ &= \tfrac{1}{2}. \end{aligned}$$

This tells you that, if you bet over and over again on the outcome of the roll of a fair dice, winning \$3 when the outcome was even and losing \$2 when the outcome was odd, then you would make an average of 50 cents per bet in the long-run.

2.2.3 Lotteries

Usually reference will be made to *lotteries* rather than to random variables. For example, accepting the bet described above can be thought of as choosing the lottery **L** illustrated

[4]This is the same as saying that the probability of getting an even number when rolling a fair dice is less than $\frac{2}{5}$.

[5]It is assumed implicitly here that the set of all such k is finite. If not, a more sophisticated definition needs to be used.

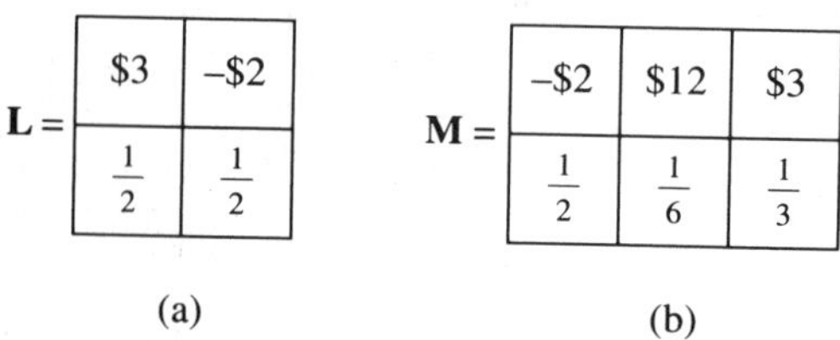

Figure 2.3 Two lotteries.

in Figure 2.3(a). The top row shows the possible final outcomes or *prizes*, and the bottom row shows the respective probabilities with which these occur. The lottery **M** in Figure 2.3(b) is a little more complicated in that it has three prizes. The big prize of $12, for example, occurs with probability $\frac{1}{6}$.

In mathematical expressions, **L** is identified with the random variable which is equal to the prize that results when the lottery is used. If the prizes have numerical values, the expectation of **L** can be calculated. To compute $\mathcal{E}\mathbf{L}$, simply multiply the numerical value of each prize by the probability with which it occurs, and then sum the resulting products.

For the examples of Figure 2.3, we already know that the expectation in dollars of the lottery **L** is $\mathcal{E}\mathbf{L} = \frac{1}{2}$. The expected dollar value of the lottery **M** is

$$\mathcal{E}\mathbf{M} = (-2) \times \tfrac{1}{2} + 1 \times \tfrac{1}{3} + 12 \times \tfrac{1}{6} = 2\,.$$

2.2.4 Compound Lotteries

A compound lottery is a lottery in which the prizes are themselves lotteries. What you win is then a chance of winning in a second lottery. Unless otherwise stated, it should always be assumed that all the lotteries involved are *independent*.

Figure 2.4 illustrates the compound lottery $p\mathbf{L} + (1 - p)\mathbf{M}$. The notation means that you get the lottery **L** with probability p and the lottery **M** with probability $1 - p$.

A compound lottery can always be reduced to a simple lottery by computing the total probability of each final outcome. In the example of Figure 2.4:

$$\begin{aligned} q_1 &= p \times \tfrac{1}{2} + (1-p) \times \tfrac{1}{2} = \tfrac{1}{2} \\ q_2 &= (1-p) \times \tfrac{1}{6} = \tfrac{1}{6} - \tfrac{1}{6}p \\ q_3 &= p \times \tfrac{1}{2} + (1-p) \times \tfrac{1}{3} = \tfrac{1}{3} + \tfrac{1}{6}p. \end{aligned}$$

The value of q_3, for example, may be calculated as follows. The probability of winning the prize **L** in the compound lottery is p. The probability of winning $3 in the lottery **L** is $\frac{1}{2}$. These events are independent and hence the probability

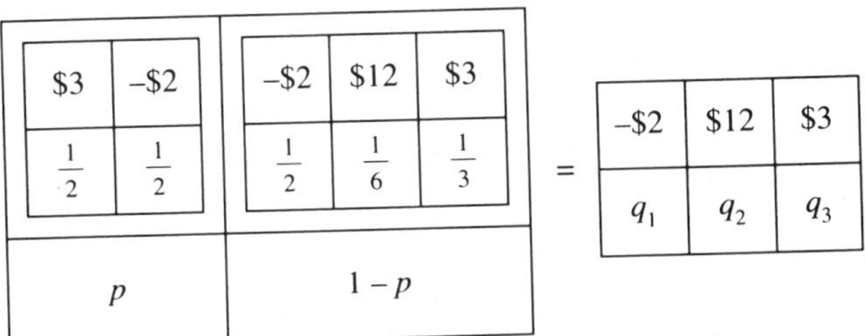

Figure 2.4 The compound lottery $p\mathbf{L} + (1 - p)\mathbf{M}$.

of the event E that they both occur is $p \times \frac{1}{2}$. Similarly, the event F that **M** is won in the compound lottery and that $3 is won in the lottery **M** has probability $(1 - p) \times \frac{1}{3}$. Since E and F cannot both happen, they are disjoint events and so the event $E \cup F$ that the final outcome is $3 has probability $q_3 = p \times \frac{1}{2} + (1 - p) \times \frac{1}{3}$.

2.3 Game Values

In Chapter 1, it was shown that every two-player, strictly competitive game of perfect information without chance moves has a value v. That is, player I has a pure strategy s that guarantees him an outcome that is at least as good for him as v, while player II has a pure strategy t that guarantees her an outcome that is at least as good for her as v. For games with chance moves, neither player will usually be able to guarantee doing at least as well as some particular final outcome v every time that the game is played. If luck is against a player, he may lose no matter how cleverly he plays. We therefore have to cease thinking about what can be achieved for certain. After each player has chosen a pure strategy, all that will be determined is the probability with which each final outcome occurs. A pure strategy pair therefore determines only a lottery over the final outcomes. Instead of asking what final outcomes can be achieved for certain, we should therefore be asking what *lotteries* over the final outcomes can be achieved for certain. Thus, one must anticipate that the value of a strictly competitive game with chance moves will be a lottery.

Matters are considerably simplified in the current chapter by confining attention to games in which the only possible final outcomes are $\mathcal{W}$ or $\mathcal{L}$. A lottery then takes the form illustrated in Figure 2.5. As always in strictly competitive games, the label $\mathcal{W}$ indicates a win for player I and a loss for player II. Similarly, $\mathcal{L}$ represents a loss for player I and a win for player II.

	$\mathcal{W}$	$\mathcal{L}$
$\mathbf{p} =$	p	$1-p$

Figure 2.5 A lottery in a winning or losing game.

It will be assumed that, in games for which the only possible final outcomes are $\mathcal{W}$ or $\mathcal{L}$, a rational player will seek to maximize the probability of winning. Player I's preferences can then be described by saying that he likes the lottery $\mathbf{p}$ at least as much as the lottery $\mathbf{q}$ if and only if $p \geq q$. The lottery $\mathbf{p}$ assigns player II a probability of $1 - p$ of winning. She therefore likes the lottery $\mathbf{p}$ at least as much as the lottery $\mathbf{q}$ if and only if $p \leq q$. When only the two final outcomes $\mathcal{W}$ and $\mathcal{L}$ have to be considered, it follows that a game is necessarily strictly competitive even if it has chance moves. That is to say,

$$\mathbf{p} \preceq_1 \mathbf{q} \quad \Leftrightarrow \quad \mathbf{p} \succeq_2 \mathbf{q}\,.$$

2.4 Duel

Two duelists approach one another. In the interests of realism, both are assumed to be male in this example. Each is armed with a pistol loaded with one bullet. The probability of hitting the opponent increases the closer the two approach. How close should a duelist get to his opponent before firing? This is literally a question of life and death because, if one duelist fires and misses, the other will be able to advance to point-blank range with fatal consequences for the duelist who fired first.

Math

2.4.1 An Extensive Form for Duel

One way of modeling the situation is as follows. Take the initial distance between the players to be D. Then select points $d_0, d_1, \ldots, d_n$ so that

$$0 = d_0 < d_1 < \cdots < d_n = D\,.$$

These serve as decision nodes for player I and player II in the finite game of Figure 2.6(a). In this figure, $\mathcal{W}$ indicates player I's survival and player II's demise. Similarly, $\mathcal{L}$ indicates player II's survival and player I's demise.

The square nodes are chance moves. At these nodes, Chance decides whether a player will hit or miss the opponent when he fires his pistol. The probability of player I hitting when he fires

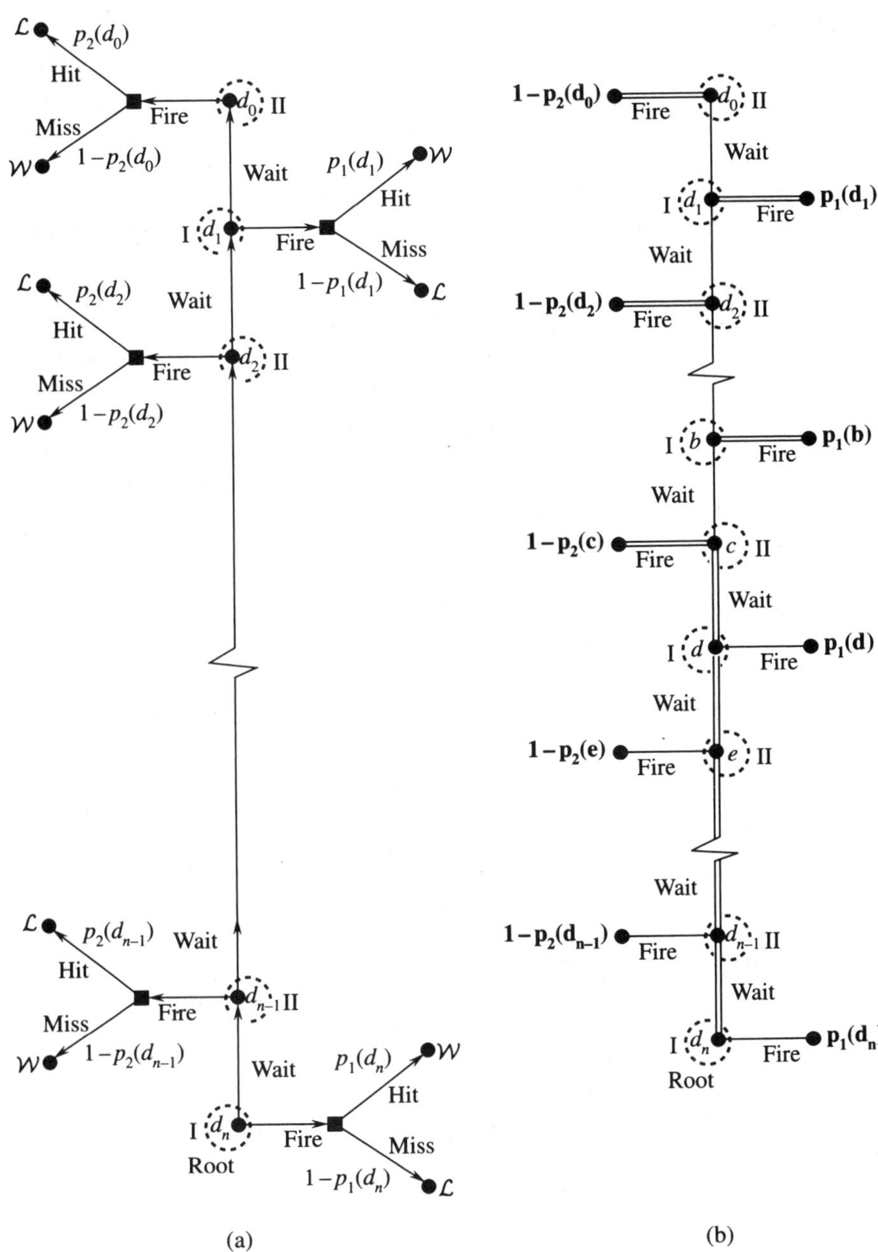

Figure 2.6 Extensive forms for Duel.

at distance d is $p_i(d)$. Hence the probability of his missing is $1 - p_i(d)$.

The first step in analyzing the game is to recognize that a subgame rooted at a chance move is simply a lottery. If player I survives in the subgame with probability p, the subgame is equivalent to the lottery $\mathbf{p}$. When Zermelo's algorithm is applied, each such subgame may therefore be replaced with a terminal node labeled with the symbol $\mathbf{p}$. This first step has been carried through in Figure 2.6(b).

This reduced game has no chance moves at all, and so it can be analyzed just as in the previous chapter. In particular, it has a value. This will be a lottery $\mathbf{v}$. Player I has a strategy s that guarantees him $\mathbf{v}$ or better and player II has a strategy t that guarantees him $\mathbf{v}$ or better. What this means is that s guarantees that player I will survive with probability v or more, and t guarantees that player II will survive with probability $1 - v$ or more.

To continue using Zermelo's algorithm, look next at node d_1 in Figure 2.6(b). Player I can secure the lottery $\mathbf{p_1(d_1)}$ by firing. If he waits, he will get the lottery $\mathbf{1 - p_2(d_0)}$. He will therefore fire if

$$p_1(d_1) > 1 - p_2(d_0),$$
$$p_1(d_1) + p_2(d_0) > 1.$$

In order to know whether such an inequality holds, it is necessary to make some assumptions about the functions $p_i : [0, D] \to [0, 1]$. It will be assumed that these are continuous and strictly decreasing[6] on $[0, D]$, with $p_i(0) = 1$ and $p_i(D) = 0$, as illustrated in Figure 2.7(a). It is also necessary to be informed about the location of the points $d_0, d_1, \ldots, d_n$. The interesting assumption to make is that there are a very large number of such points and that the distance between each pair of neighboring points is very small.

With these assumptions, $p_1(d_1) + p_2(d_0)$ will be nearly equal to 2. Thus $p_1(d_1) + p_2(d_0) > 1$, and so player I will fire at node d_1. The edge that represents this choice has therefore been doubled in Figure 2.6(b).

At node d_2, player II secures the lottery $\mathbf{1 - p_2(d_2)}$ by firing and gets the lottery $\mathbf{p_1(d_1)}$ by waiting. Player II will therefore fire if

$$1 - p_2(d_2) < p_1(d_1)$$
$$p_1(d_1) + p_2(d_2) > 1.$$

[6] A real-valued function f is continuous on an interval if its graph above the interval can be drawn without lifting the pen from the paper. It is strictly decreasing if, for each x and y in the interval, $x < y \Rightarrow f(x) > f(y)$.

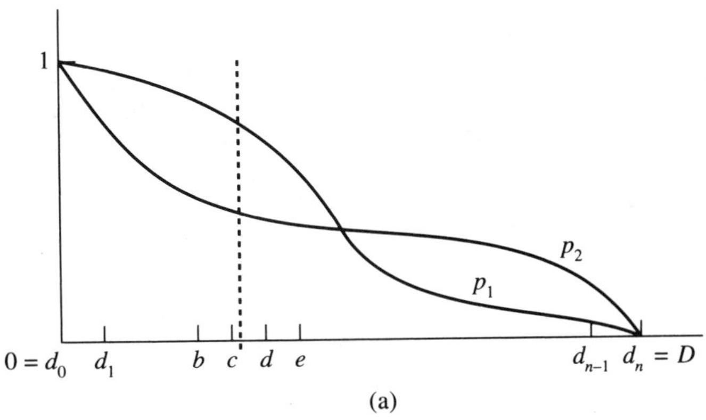

(a)

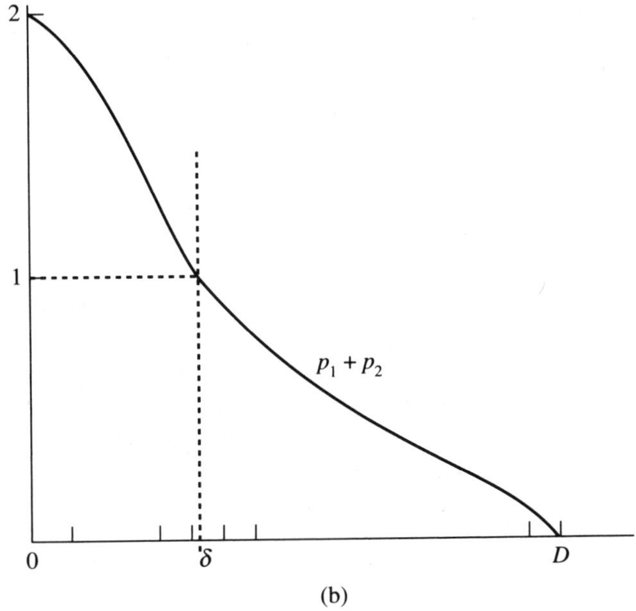

(b)

Figure 2.7 Hitting probabilities for Duel.

Since $p_1(d_1) + p_2(d_2)$ is only slightly less than $p_1(d_1) + p_2(d_0)$, this last inequality will be satisfied. Hence player II will fire at node d_2.

Continuing in this way, all the firing edges will be doubled until the *first* time that neighboring nodes c and d are reached with the property that

$$p_1(d) + p_2(c) \leq 1 .$$

This must happen eventually because $p_1(d_n) + p_2(d_{n-1})$ is nearly 0. To keep things simple, only the case when $c < d$ and $p_1(d) + p_2(c) < 1$ is considered in detail. This case is illustrated in Figure 2.6(b). At node d, player I can secure the lottery $\mathbf{p_1(d)}$ by firing. If he waits, he gets the lottery $\mathbf{1 - p_2(c)}$. Since $p_1(d) + p_2(c) < 1$, he prefers the latter. Thus player I waits at node d, and hence the waiting edge at d has been doubled.

At the smallest node e larger than d, player II can secure the lottery $\mathbf{1 - p_2(e)}$ by firing. If he waits, he gets the lottery $\mathbf{1 - p_2(c)}$. He prefers the latter because $p_2(c) > p_2(e)$. Thus player II waits at node e. In fact, similar reasoning shows that both players wait whenever they are more than d apart.[7] All the waiting edges at such nodes are therefore doubled.

Since c and d are the first pair of neighboring nodes for which $p_1(d) + p_2(c) \le 1$, it must be true that $p_1(b) + p_2(c) > 1$. But b, c and d are assumed to be close together. Moreover, p_1 and p_2 are continuous. It follows that b, c and d must all be close to the point δ at which

$$p_1(\delta) + p_2(\delta) = 1 ,$$

as illustrated in Figure 2.7(b).

Zermelo's algorithm therefore selects a pure strategy s for player I that consists of waiting until the opponent is approximately δ away and then planning to fire at all subsequent opportunities.[8] The pure strategy t selected for player II is approximately the same. The value of the game is approximately $\mathbf{v}$, where $v = p_1(\delta) = 1 - p_2(\delta)$. Thus, if the pure strategy pair (s, t) is used, player I will survive with probability about v and player II will survive with probability about $1 - v$.

If, for example, $p_1(d) = 1 - (d/D)$ and $p_2(d) = 1 - (d/D)^2$, then you should plan to wait until your opponent is about distance δ away, where

$$1 - (\delta/D) + 1 - (\delta/D)^2 = 1 .$$

Taking the positive root of this quadratic equation, we obtain that the duelists should open fire when approximately distance $\frac{1}{2}D(\sqrt{5} - 1)$ apart. Player II will have the greatest probability of surviving because the probability of his

[7] A formal argument is not really necessary. If you plan to fire before the other guy, it is obvious that you should plan to fire *just* before he plans to do so in order to maximize the probability of a hit.

[8] Of course, if you *do* fire at your first opportunity, you will not be able to fire at subsequent opportunities because your pistol contains only one bullet. Your plan to fire at a subsequent opportunity is therefore contingent on your not having fired earlier for some reason.

$\mathcal{W}$	$\mathcal{L}$	$\mathcal{W}$	$\mathcal{L}$
q	$1-q$	r	$1-r$
p		$1-p$	

=

$\mathcal{W}$	$\mathcal{L}$
$pq + (1-p)r$	$p(1-q) + (1-p)(1-r)$

Figure 2.8 The identity $p\mathbf{q} + (1-p)\mathbf{r} = \mathbf{pq} + (\mathbf{1}-\mathbf{p})\mathbf{r}$.

scoring a hit at any given distance is always greater than player I's.

2.5 Parcheesi

A much simplified version of Parcheesi (or Ludo) will now be studied. Its analysis requires the use of compound lotteries. This is particularly easy when the only prizes available

Fun 2.6 ⟶ are $\mathcal{W}$ or $\mathcal{L}$. As illustrated in Figure 2.5, the notation $\mathbf{p}$ can then be used for the lottery in which the prize $\mathcal{W}$ occurs with probability p and the prize $\mathcal{L}$ with probability $1-p$. Figure 2.8 shows the compound lottery $p\mathbf{q} + (1-p)\mathbf{r}$. It is easy to check that this is equivalent to the simple lottery $\mathbf{pq} + (\mathbf{1}-\mathbf{p})\mathbf{r}$.

Parcheesi is strictly an infinite game in that the rules allow it to continue forever. However, such an eventuality occurs with zero probability[9] and so is irrelevant to an analysis of the game. In any case, this and other technical issues will be ignored in the discussion. It will simply be taken for granted that Parcheesi and all its subgames have values, and attention will be concentrated on determining what these values are.

2.5.1 The Rules of Simplified Parcheesi

The game is played between Player I (White) and Player II (Black) on the board indicated in Figure 2.9. The winner is the first to reach the shaded square following the routes indicated. The players alternate in taking turns starting with player I. Before each of their turns, a fair coin is tossed. The player concerned may then choose to move his or her counter, or leave it where it is. If the counter is moved, it must be moved *one* square if tails is thrown. If heads is thrown, the counter must be moved *two* squares. The last

[9] A zero probability event need not be impossible. For example, it is possible that, if a fair coin is tossed an infinite number of times, the result will always be heads. But this event has zero probability.

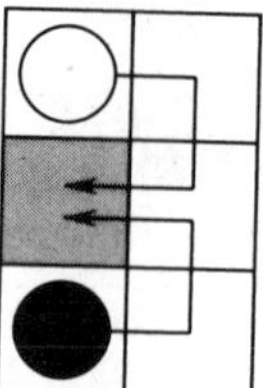

Figure 2.9 The board for simplified Parcheesi.

rule has an exception. If the winning square can be reached in one move, the winning move is allowed even when heads has been thrown.

If a player's counter finishes on the same square as the opponent's, then the opponent's counter is sent back to its starting place.

If both players choose not to move their counters on consecutive turns, the game ends and the winner is determined simply by tossing the coin.

2.5.2 Possible Positions in Simplified Parcheesi

Figure 2.10 lists the eight possible positions in which player I might find himself when it is his turn to move. It is taken for granted that each subgame of Parcheesi that begins from

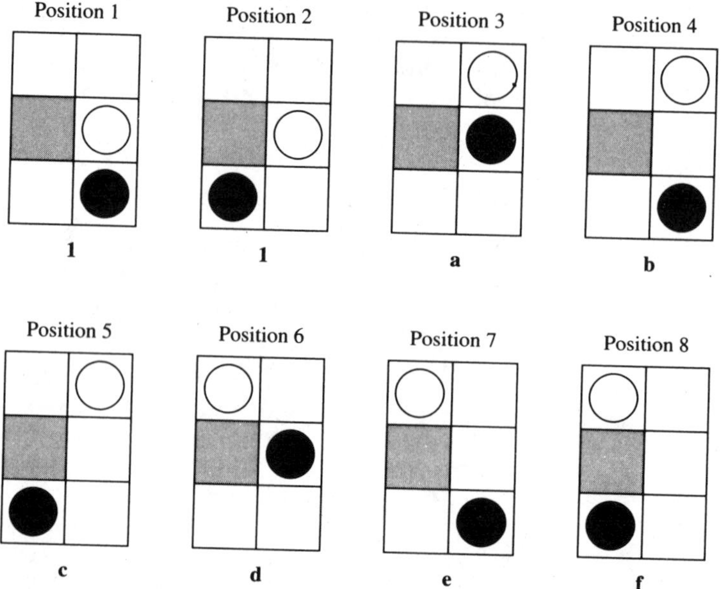

Figure 2.10 Possible positions when it is White's turn in Parcheesi.

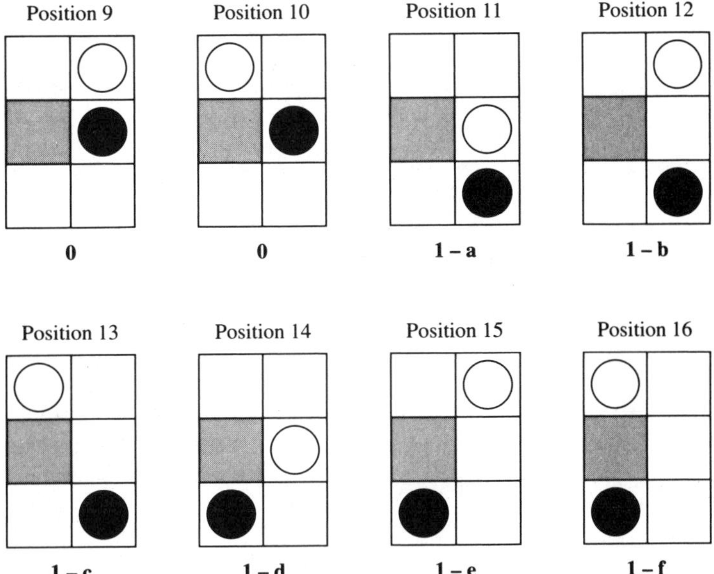

Figure 2.11 Possible positions when it is Black's turn in Parcheesi.

one of these positions has a value. The value corresponding to a position is written beneath it. Thus positions 1 and 2 have the lottery **1** written beneath them because player I can win for certain if these positions are reached when it is his turn to move.

It is also necessary to consider eight possible positions when it is player II's turn to move. These are listed in Figure 2.11. Their values can be determined from Figure 2.10. For example, position 11 looks the same to Black as position 3 looks to White. Hence the value for position 11 is **1 – a**.

The value for simplified Parcheesi is **f** since the game starts in this position with White to take the first turn. But to compute f using a version of Zermelo's algorithm, it is necessary to calculate a thru e simultaneously.

2.5.3 Analyzing the Game

Step 1. The diagram for a subgame rooted at position 3 in Figure 2.12 shows the optimal actions for player I after the coin is tossed. It follows that $\mathbf{a} = \frac{1}{2}\mathbf{1} + \frac{1}{2}(\mathbf{1} - \mathbf{d})$. Hence

$$a = \tfrac{1}{2}(1) + \tfrac{1}{2}(1 - d)$$
$$a + \tfrac{1}{2}d = 1\,. \qquad (2.1)$$

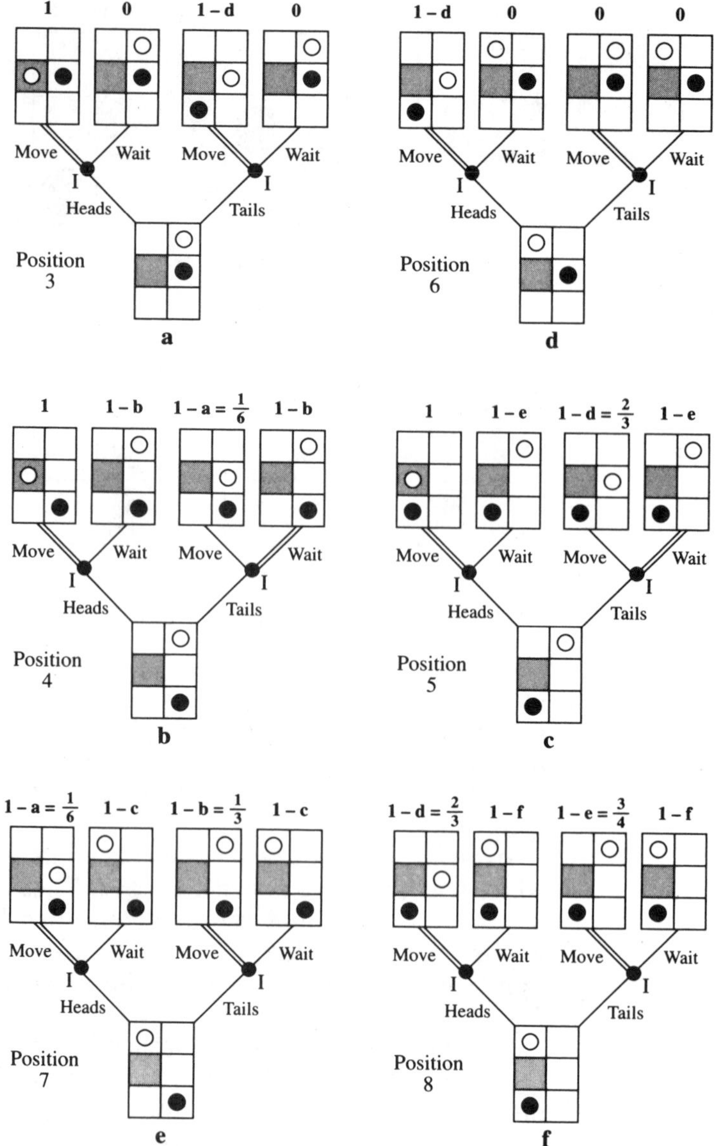

Figure 2.12 Reaching one Parcheesi position from another.

Step 2. Now look at position 6 in Figure 2.12. Proceeding as before, we obtain that

$$d = \tfrac{1}{2}(1 - d) + \tfrac{1}{2}(0)$$
$$d = \tfrac{1}{3},$$

and hence, from equation (2.1),

$$a = \tfrac{5}{6}.$$

Step 3. Next consider position 4 in Figure 2.12. It is not immediately obvious whether player I should move his counter after a tail appears. If $1 - b \leq \frac{1}{6}$ and so $b \geq \frac{5}{6}$, it is optimal to move after a tail. But then

$$\begin{aligned} b &= \tfrac{1}{2}(1) + \tfrac{1}{2}(1-a) \\ &= \tfrac{1}{2}(1) + \tfrac{1}{2}(\tfrac{1}{6}) \\ b &= \tfrac{7}{12}, \end{aligned}$$

which is a contradiction. Hence it is optimal *not* to move, and

$$\begin{aligned} b &= \tfrac{1}{2}(1) + \tfrac{1}{2}(1-b) \\ b &= \tfrac{2}{3}. \end{aligned}$$

Step 4. Positions 5 and 7 in Figure 2.12 are taken together. If it were the case that $1 - e \geq \frac{2}{3}$ and so $e \leq \frac{1}{3}$, then an examination of position 5 shows that

$$\begin{aligned} c &= \tfrac{1}{2}(1) + \tfrac{1}{2}(1-e) \\ c + \tfrac{1}{2}e &= 1. \end{aligned} \tag{2.2}$$

But then $1 - c = \frac{1}{2}e \leq \frac{1}{6}$, and hence, from position 7,

$$\begin{aligned} e &= \tfrac{1}{2}(1-a) + \tfrac{1}{2}(1-b) \\ &= \tfrac{1}{2}(\tfrac{1}{6}) + \tfrac{1}{2}(\tfrac{1}{3}) \\ e &= \tfrac{1}{4}. \end{aligned} \tag{2.3}$$

It follows from equation (2.2) that

$$c = \tfrac{7}{8}. \tag{2.4}$$

Equation (2.4) was obtained on the assumption that $e \leq \frac{1}{3}$. Suppose, on the other hand, that $e > \frac{1}{3}$. Then, from position 5,

$$\begin{aligned} c &= \tfrac{1}{2}(1) + \tfrac{1}{2}(1-d) \\ &= \tfrac{1}{2}(1) + \tfrac{1}{2}(\tfrac{2}{3}) = \tfrac{5}{6}, \end{aligned}$$

and so, from position 7,

$$e = \tfrac{1}{2}(\tfrac{1}{6}) + \tfrac{1}{2}(\tfrac{1}{3}) = \tfrac{1}{4},$$

which contradicts the fact that $e > \frac{1}{3}$. Thus equations (2.3) and (2.4) hold.

Step 5. A strategy-stealing argument shows that $f \geq \frac{1}{2}$. Hence $1 - f \leq \frac{1}{2}$ and thus, from position 8,

$$\begin{aligned} f &= \tfrac{1}{2}(1-d) + \tfrac{1}{2}(1-e) \\ &= \tfrac{1}{2}(\tfrac{2}{3}) + \tfrac{1}{2}(\tfrac{3}{4}) \\ f &= \tfrac{17}{24}. \end{aligned}$$

This concludes the analysis. The value of the game is $\frac{17}{24}$. Player I can guarantee that he will win with probability at least $\frac{17}{24}$. To do this, he always moves his counter *unless* a tail is thrown in positions 4, 5 or 6. In positions 4 and 5 he should not move his counter if a tail is thrown. In position 6, his decision is irrelevant. Player II's optimal strategy is a mirror image of player I's. Her play of this strategy guarantees that she will win with probability at least $\frac{7}{24}$.

2.6 Exercises

Review

1. Explain why the number of distinct possible hands in Straight Poker is

$$\binom{52}{5} = \frac{52!}{5!47!} = \frac{52 \times 51 \times 50 \times 49 \times 48}{5 \times 4 \times 3 \times 2 \times 1}.$$

(A deck of cards contains 52 cards. A Straight Poker hand contains 5 cards. You are therefore asked how many ways there are of selecting 5 cards from 52 cards when the order in which they are selected is irrelevant.)

What is the probability of being dealt a royal flush in Straight Poker? (A royal flush consists of the A, K, Q, J and 10 of the same suit.)

Review

2. Suppose that you are dealt the A, K, Q and 10 of hearts and the 2 of clubs. In Draw Poker, you get to change some of your cards after the first round of betting. If you discard the 2 of clubs, hoping to draw the J of hearts, what is the probability that you will be successful?

What is the probability of drawing a straight?[10] (Any J will suffice for this purpose.)

Review

3. A man is prepared to make a bet that Punter's Folly will win the first race when the odds are 2:1 against. He is prepared to make a bet that Gambler's Ruin will win the second race when the odds are 3:1 against. He is not prepared to bet that both horses will win when the odds for this event offered are 15:1 against. If the two races are independent, is the man consistent in his betting behavior?

Review

4. A bookie offers odds of a_k:1 against the kth horse in a race being the winner. If there are n horses in the race

[10]This is the classic act of folly: drawing to an inside straight. However, it is only an act of folly if you make a substantial bet at the first round of betting in order to be able to make the draw.

and

$$\frac{1}{a_1+1}+\frac{1}{a_2+1}+\cdots+\frac{1}{a_n+1}<1,$$

how should you bet if you want to be certain of winning?

5. John believes that the Democrat will be elected in a presidential election with probability $\frac{5}{8}$. Mary believes the Republican will be elected with probability $\frac{3}{4}$. Neither gives third party candidates any chance at all. They agree to bet \$10 on the outcome at even odds. (Thus John will pay Mary \$10 if the Republican wins, and she will pay him \$10 if the Democrat wins.) What is John's expected dollar gain? What is Mary's?

   How would you be able to make money *for sure* by betting with John and Mary if they are both always ready to accept any bet that they believe has a nonnegative dollar expectation?

6. What is the expected value in dollars of the compound lottery of Figure 2.4 in the case when $p = \frac{1}{2}$?

7. Figure 2.13 illustrates a game with only chance moves. Each chance move represents the independent toss of a fair coin. Express the situation as a simple lottery. Also express the situation as a simple lottery in the case when the chance moves are *not* independent, but all refer to a single toss of the same coin.

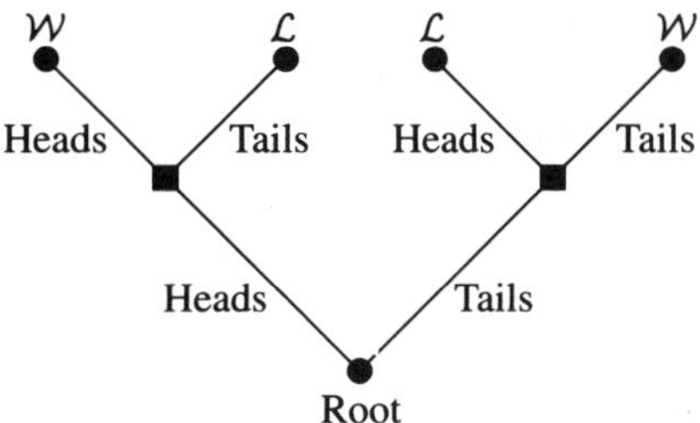

Figure 2.13 A game with only chance moves.

Review

8. A box contains one gold and two silver coins. Two coins are drawn at random from the box. A man looks at the coins that have been drawn without your being able to see. He then selects one of the coins and shows it to you. It is silver. At what odds will you bet with him that the other is gold?

   At what odds will you bet if the coin that you are shown is selected at random from the drawn pair?

	c	d
a	0.01	0.09
b	0	0.9

Figure 2.14 The table for Exercise 2.6.9.

Review

9. The table of Figure 2.14 shows the probabilities of the four pairs (a, c), (a, d), (b, c) and (b, d). The random variable x can take either of the values a or b. The random variable y can take either of the values c or d. Calculate the following probabilities:
   (a) $\text{prob}(x = a)$ (b) $\text{prob}(y = c)$
   (c) $\text{prob}(x = a \text{ and } y = c)$ (d) $\text{prob}(x = a \text{ or } y = c)$
   (e) $\text{prob}(x = a \mid y = c)$ (f) $\text{prob}(y = c \mid x = a)$

Review

10. The n countries of the world have populations $M_1, M_2, \ldots, M_n$. The number of left-handed people in each country is $L_1, L_2, \ldots, L_n$. What is the probability that a left-handed person chosen at random from the world population comes from the first country?
11. Player I can choose l or r at the first move in a game G. If he chooses l, a chance move selects L with probability p or R with probability $1 - p$. If L is chosen, the game ends in the outcome $\mathcal{L}$. If R is chosen, a subgame identical in structure to G is played. If player I chooses r, then a chance move selects L with probability q or R with probability $1 - q$. If L is chosen, the game ends in the outcome $\mathcal{W}$. If R is chosen, a subgame is played that is identical to G *except* that the outcomes $\mathcal{W}$ and $\mathcal{L}$ are interchanged together with the roles of players I and II.
    (a) Begin the game tree.
    (b) Why is this an infinite game?
    (c) With what probability will the game continue forever if player I always chooses l?
    (d) If the value of G is **v**, show that $v = q + (1 - q)(1 - v)$, and hence work out the probability v that player I will win if both players use optimal strategies.
    (e) What is v when $q = \frac{1}{2}$?
12. Analyze Nim when the players do not alternate in moving but always toss a fair coin to decide who moves next.
13. How close to the opponent before firing should one get in Duel when $p_1(d) = p_2(d) = 1 - (d/D)^2$?

Math 14. The analysis of Duel of Section 2.4.1 looks in detail only at the case when $c < d$ and $p_1(d) + p_2(c) < 1$. How do things change if $p_1(c) + p_2(d) < 1$? What happens when $c < d$ and $p_1(d) + p_2(c) = 1$?

15. How does the analysis of Duel change if $p_1(D) + p_2(D) > 1$? What if $p_1(0) + p_2(0) < 1$? What if $p_1(d) + p_2(d) = 1$ for all d satisfying $\frac{1}{3}D \leq d \leq \frac{2}{3}D$?

Math 16. How does the analysis of Duel change if extra nodes are introduced between d_k and d_{k+1}, all of which are assigned to the player who decides at node d_k?

Math 17. What will optimal play look like in Duel if the players do not alternate in having the opportunity to fire, but the player who gets to fire at each node is decided by a chance move that assigns equal probabilities to both players?

Fun 18. What is the probability that the simplified Parcheesi of Section 2.5 will continue for five moves or more if both players always move their counters the maximum number of squares consistent with the rules?

Fun 19. What is the strategy-stealing argument appealed to at step 5 in Section 2.5.3 during the analysis of simplified Parcheesi? What strategy-stealing argument shortens the argument at step 3?

Fun 20. No mention is made in Section 2.5.3 of the possibility that neither player may choose to move at all on consecutive turns. Why does this possibility not affect the analysis?

Fun 21. Analyze the simplified Parcheesi game of Section 2.5 with the modification that, when a head is thrown, a player may move 0, 1 or 2 squares at his or her discretion. Assume that the other rules remain unchanged.

Fun 22. Analyze the simplified Parcheesi game of Section 2.5 with the modification that, when a counter is exactly one square from the winning square, then only the throw of a tail permits it to be advanced.[11] Assume that the other rules remain unchanged.

23. When a "roulette wheel" from Figure 2.15 is spun, each number on it is equally likely to result. In Gale's Roulette,

[11]This modification makes the game more like real Parcheesi. The new version can be solved by the same method as the original version, but the algebra is a little harder. In particular, positions 1 and 2 of Figure 2.10 no longer have value **1**. If their values are taken to be **g** and **h** respectively, you will be able to show that a contradiction follows unless $d < g < h$.

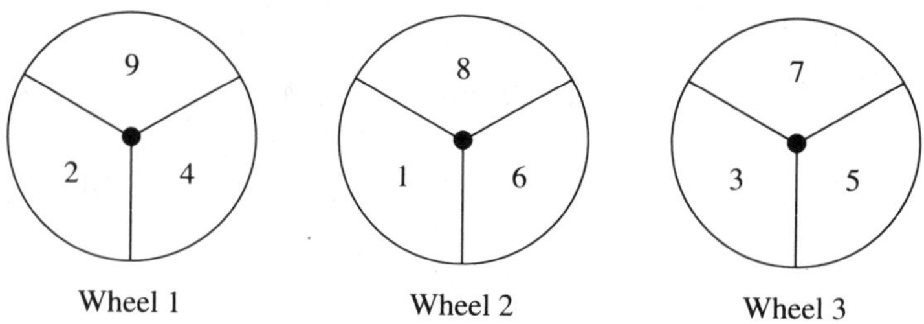

Figure 2.15 Gale's Roulette wheels.

player I begins by choosing a wheel and spinning it. While player I's wheel is still spinning, player II chooses one of the remaining wheels and spins it. The player whose wheel stops on the larger number wins and the other player loses.

(a) If player I chooses wheel 1 and player II chooses wheel 2, the result is a lottery **p**. What is the value of p? (Assume that the Roulette wheels are independent.)

(b) Draw a game tree for Gale's Roulette.

(c) Reduce the game tree to one without chance moves, as was done for Duel in Section 2.4.

(d) If both players choose optimally, show that player II will win with probability $\frac{5}{9}$.

(e) A superficial analysis of Gale's Roulette argues that player I should choose the best wheel. Player II will then have to be content with the second-best wheel. But this cannot be right because player I would then win more often than player II. What is the fallacy in the argument?[12]

24. Let $\Omega = \{1, 2, 3, \ldots, 9\}$. If player I chooses wheel 2 in Gale's Roulette of Exercise 2.6.23, he is selecting a lottery $\mathbf{L}_2$ with prizes in Ω. Express this lottery as a table of the type given in Figure 2.3. Show that

$$\mathcal{E}\mathbf{L}_1 = \mathcal{E}\mathbf{L}_2 = \mathcal{E}\mathbf{L}_3 = 5\,.$$

Let $\mathbf{L}_1 - \mathbf{L}_2$ denote the lottery in which the winning prize is $\omega_1 - \omega_2$ if the outcome of lottery $\mathbf{L}_1$ is ω_1 and the outcome of lottery $\mathbf{L}_2$ is ω_2. What is the probability of the prize $-2 = 4 - 6$ in the lottery $\mathbf{L}_1 - \mathbf{L}_2$? Why is it true that $\mathcal{E}(\mathbf{L}_1 - \mathbf{L}_2) = \mathcal{E}\mathbf{L}_1 - \mathcal{E}\mathbf{L}_2$? Deduce that

$$\mathcal{E}(\mathbf{L}_1 - \mathbf{L}_2) = \mathcal{E}(\mathbf{L}_2 - \mathbf{L}_3) = \mathcal{E}(\mathbf{L}_1 - \mathbf{L}_3) = 0\,.$$

[12]This exercise provides an advance example of an *intransitive* relation (Section 3.1).

25. In an alternative version of Gale's Roulette, each of the three roulette wheels is labeled with *four* equally likely numbers. The numbers on the first wheel are 2, 4, 6 and 9; those on the second wheel are 1, 5, 6 and 8; and those on the third wheel are 3, 4, 5 and 7. If the two wheels chosen by the players stop on the same number, the wheels are spun again and again until someone is a clear winner.
   (a) If player I chooses the first wheel and player II chooses the second wheel, show that the probability p that player I will win satisfies $p = \frac{1}{2} + \frac{1}{16}p$.
   (b) What is the probability that player I will win the whole game if both players choose optimally?

Fun

26. In a popular television quiz game, contestants are offered the opportunity of choosing one of three doors. One of the doors conceals a prize. The others have nothing behind them. The contestant has no reason to believe that any particular door is more likely to conceal the prize than any other.

    The quizmaster knows which door conceals the prize. After the contestant has provisionally chosen a door, he *must* open one of the other doors. The contestant then has the opportunity to change her mind about which door to select. Assume that the contestant wishes to maximize her probability of getting the prize, and that the quizmaster wishes to minimize her probability.
   (a) Describe an optimal strategy for the quizmaster. Assume from now on that he plays according to the strategy you have described.
   (b) If the contestant never switches her original choice, explain why her probability of winning *before* the quizmaster opens a door is $\frac{1}{3}$. Why does her probability of winning remain $\frac{1}{3}$ even *after* the quizmaster has opened a door? Why might a naive person think the latter probability would be $\frac{1}{2}$?
   (c) If the contestant *always* switches her choice after the quizmaster has opened a door, explain why her probability of winning is now $\frac{2}{3}$, if she and the quizmaster play optimally. Why might a naive person think the probability would be $\frac{1}{2}$?
   (d) Discuss how the situation would alter if the quizmaster was not forbidden to open the door provisionally chosen by the contestant, but was free to open any of the three doors.

C H A P T E R

3

Accounting for Tastes

3.1 Rational Preferences

The most primitive way of describing preferences is with a preference relation $\preceq$ defined on the set Ω of outcomes. The idea was introduced in Section 1.7, but without any discussion of the properties that the preferences of a rational individual should satisfy. The necessary assumptions taken for granted previously are that:

$$a \preceq b \quad \text{or} \quad b \preceq a \qquad\qquad \text{(totality)}$$
$$a \preceq b \quad \text{and} \quad b \preceq c \quad \Rightarrow \quad a \preceq c \qquad \text{(transitivity)}$$

for all a, b and c in Ω.

It is only transitivity that is genuinely a rationality requirement. Totality only ensures that the individual is always able to express a preference between any two outcomes.[1]

3.1.1 The Money Pump

Why should a rational person have transitive preferences? Suppose instead that a man's preferences over a, b and c were to satisfy

$$a \preceq b \preceq c \prec a.$$

If a, b and c are objects that can be traded, then he could be pumped dry of money in the following way.

Suppose that the victim begins by possessing a. Since he likes b at least as much as a, he should be ready to trade a for b. Similarly, he should be ready to trade b for c. But he *strictly* prefers a to c. Hence he should be willing to pay a small sum of money, say one penny, to trade c for a. But, if he makes these trades, then the victim will end up holding a again but with one penny less. To extract all his money, simply repeat the process until his wallet is empty.

3.1.2 Indifference and Strict Preference

A preference relation $\preceq$ should not be confused with the order relation $\leq$ used to indicate which of two real numbers is larger. The latter satisfies an extra condition:

$$a \leq b \quad \text{and} \quad b \leq a \quad \Leftrightarrow \quad a = b$$

---

[1]In mathematics, a relation satisfying totality and transitivity is called a (total) pre-ordering. If totality is replaced by $a \preceq a$ (reflexivity), then $\preceq$ becomes a *partial* pre-ordering.

that we definitely do not want to hold for preference relations in general. Instead the indifference relation $\sim$ is defined by:

$$a \preceq b \quad \text{and} \quad b \preceq a \quad \Leftrightarrow \quad a \sim b.$$

The strict preference relation $\prec$ is defined by:

$$a \preceq b \quad \text{and} \quad \text{not}(a \sim b) \quad \Leftrightarrow \quad a \prec b.$$

3.2 Utility Functions

Decision problems reduce to finding the outcome ω in a subset S of Ω that the decision-maker most prefers.[2]

Such a problem looks easy when stated in this abstract way but, in practice, it can be hard to resolve if the objects in Ω are complicated and so the preference relation $\preceq$ is difficult to describe. Utility functions are a mathematical device intended to simplify the situation.

A function $u : \Omega \to \mathbb{R}$ is a utility function representing the preference relation $\preceq$ if and only if

$$u(a) \leq u(b) \quad \Leftrightarrow \quad a \preceq b.$$

If the utility function u represents the preference relation $\preceq$, then the problem of finding an optimal ω in S reduces to the more tractable problem of finding a value of ω in S for which

$$u(\omega) = \max_{s \in S} u(s).$$

3.2.1 Optimizing Consumption

Pandora regards alcohol as desirable. For her, gin and vodka are perfect substitutes. She is always willing to trade these at a rate of 5 bottles of gin for 3 bottles of vodka.

Econ 3.3 ⟶ Let (g, v) represent the commodity bundle consisting of g bottles of gin and v bottles of vodka. Let Ω denote the set of all such bundles. One can express Pandora's preferences over Ω in terms of a preference relation $\preceq$. Such a preference relation is often represented graphically as in Figure 3.1 by drawing its indifference curves.[3]

[2]Such an ω may not exist if S is infinite. There is, for example, *no* largest number in the *open* interval (0,1). However, such difficulties are evaded in the text.

[3]An indifference set for $\preceq$ consists of all $s \in \Omega$ that satisfy $s \sim \omega$ for some given ω. Such a set is usually a curve in the examples commonly considered by economists.

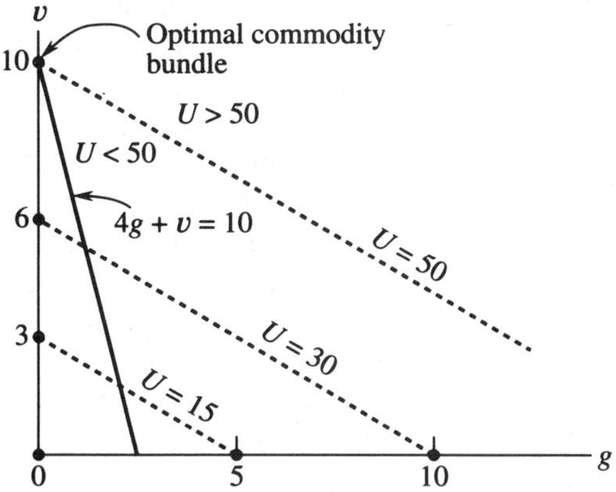

Figure 3.1 Optimizing alcohol consumption.

Pandora's preference relation can be represented by the utility function $U : \Omega \to \mathbb{R}$ defined by:

$$U(g, v) = 3g + 5v.$$

Thus, for example, the fact that she is indifferent between the commodity bundles $(5, 0)$ and $(0, 3)$ is reflected in the fact that

$$U(5, 0) = U(0, 3) = 15.$$

Pandora lived long ago when the price of a bottle of gin was \$4 and the price of a bottle of vodka was \$1. If she has \$10 to spend on gin or vodka, then she can buy any bundle (g, v) on her budget line $4g + v = 10$. What bundle should she buy if she spends all \$10?

Figure 3.1 shows how this question can be answered graphically. To solve the problem using the utility function U, observe that the utility of a bundle (g, v) on her budget line is given by

$$U(g, 10 - 4g) = 3g + 5(10 - g) = 50 - 17g.$$

This is obviously maximized when g is smallest: namely when $g = 0$. It follows that her optimal consumption bundle is $(0, 10)$. That is, she should buy 10 bottles of vodka and no bottles of gin.

3.2.2 A Fallacy

Once utility functions have become familiar, it is easy to fall into the habit of saying that a decision-maker prefers a to b *because* the utility of a exceeds that of b. This is harmless if not taken too literally. However, it is as well to be aware that, in the approach to utility theory being discussed here, it is *fallacious* to argue that a person's preference for a over b is *caused* by the fact that the utility of a exceeds that of b. On the contrary, it is because $a \succ b$ that a utility function satisfying $u(a) > u(b)$ is chosen.

Economists are very careful *not* to claim that people *really* have utility generators inside their heads. It is true that the brain contains pleasure and pain centers, but what is known about these is too slender to form the basis of a viable theory. When economists discuss utility maximization, they therefore only claim that rational individuals will behave *as though* their aim were to maximize a utility function. The reason for introducing utility functions is to simplify the mathematics, not to provide an explanation of why people do what they do. In consumer theory, people's choice behavior is taken as *given* and no attempt to explain it is offered at all.

3.2.3 Constructing Utility Functions

Suppose that Pandora has five commodity bundles, a, b, c, d and e to consider. If her preferences are rational, then the five bundles can be ranked in terms of increasing preference. To be specific, suppose that

$$b \prec c \sim d \prec a \prec e.$$

Thus, if Pandora has to make a choice from the set $\{b, c, d\}$, she will definitely not choose b, but she might choose either c or d.

To find a utility function $U : \{a, b, c, d, e\} \to \mathbb{R}$ that represents her preferences is very easy. She regards the bundle b as being the worst available. We therefore define $U(b) = 0$. She regards e as the best bundle. Therefore define $U(e) = 1$.

Next choose any bundle intermediate between the worst bundle b and the best bundle e and define its utility to be $\frac{1}{2}$. In Pandora's case, d is a convenient bundle intermediate between b and e and so we define $U(d) = \frac{1}{2}$. Since $c \sim d$, we then have no choice but to define $U(c) = \frac{1}{2}$ also. Only the bundle a is now left. This is intermediate between d and e and so we define its utility to be $\frac{3}{4}$, because $\frac{3}{4}$ is intermediate between $U(d) = \frac{1}{2}$ and $U(e) = 1$. Thus $U(a)$ is defined to be $\frac{3}{4}$.

As the table of Figure 3.2 shows, the utilities assigned to the bundles are ranked in the same way as the bundles

x	b	c	d	a	e
$U(x)$	0	$\frac{1}{2}$	$\frac{1}{2}$	$\frac{3}{4}$	1
$V(x)$	−100	20	20	21	1,000

Figure 3.2 Constructing utility functions.

themselves. Hence in making choices, Pandora behaves *as though* she were maximizing the value of U.

Notice that the construction would work no matter how many bundles there are, because, between any pair of real numbers, there is always another real number. Notice also that there are *many* ways in which we could have assigned utilities to the bundles in a manner consistent with Pandora's preferences. The third row of the table of Figure 3.2 gives an example of a utility function V that represents Pandora's preferences just as well as U. The only criterion that is relevant when deciding which of the many utility function representations of a preference relation to use is that of mathematical convenience.

3.3 Russian Roulette

This game is introduced to indicate some of the modeling difficulties that need to be resolved in analyzing games more complicated than those of the previous chapters. We shall meet some important ideas for the first time in studying the game. The idea of an information set in a game of imperfect information will be particularly valuable. However, we shall find that we can get by perfectly well until Chapter 10 without making any fuss about the formal properties of information sets.

The story that goes with Russian Roulette involves two officers in the army of the Czar who have been competing for the affections of a Muscovite maiden. They agree that it is not rational that both should press their claims simultaneously, but cannot agree on who should withdraw from the competition. Eventually they decide to settle the matter with a game of Russian Roulette. In this game, a bullet is loaded at random into one of the chambers of a six-shooter. The two players then alternate in taking turns. When it is his turn, a player may chicken out or point the gun at his own head and pull the trigger. Chickening out or death disqualify a player from further pursuit of the lady.

Neither player cares about the welfare of the other, and so each distinguishes only three alternatives, $\mathcal{L}$, $\mathcal{D}$ or $\mathcal{W}$. The alternative $\mathcal{L}$ means that a player shoots himself. The alternative $\mathcal{D}$ means that he chickens out and so has to sit alone in the officers' club while his rival devotes his time to winning the maiden's heart. The alternative $\mathcal{W}$ means that a player is left to woo the lady undisturbed. The preferences for player i over the set $\{\mathcal{L}, \mathcal{D}, \mathcal{W}\}$ are assumed to satisfy

$$\mathcal{L} \prec_i \mathcal{D} \prec_i \mathcal{W}.$$

3.3.1 Version 1 of Russian Roulette

Figure 3.3 shows one way of drawing the game tree for Russian Roulette. The act of loading the gun is represented by a single chance move at the beginning of the game. Chance has six choices at this node, corresponding to the six chambers of a six-shooter. The chambers are labeled 1 through 6 according to the order in which they will be reached as the trigger is pulled. Chance chooses each of these chambers with equal probability, and so the probability that the bullet is in any particular chamber is $\frac{1}{6}$.

The edges at nodes where a player decides what to do are labeled A (for across) and D (for down). Playing "down" corresponds to chickening out. Playing "across" corresponds to a player pointing the gun at his own head and pulling the trigger.

Information Sets. The nodes at which a player chooses between A or D are labeled with the number of the chamber that contains the bullet. However, the players do not know this item of information when they decide whether or not to chicken out. The fact that a player will not know at which of several nodes he may be located when he makes a decision is indicated by enclosing the nodes in a broken line in Figure 3.3. The set of nodes enclosed by such a broken line is called an *information set*.

Perfect and Imperfect Information. A game is said to be of *perfect information* if every information set contains only a single node. No player will then ever be in any doubt about what has happened in the game so far. The version of

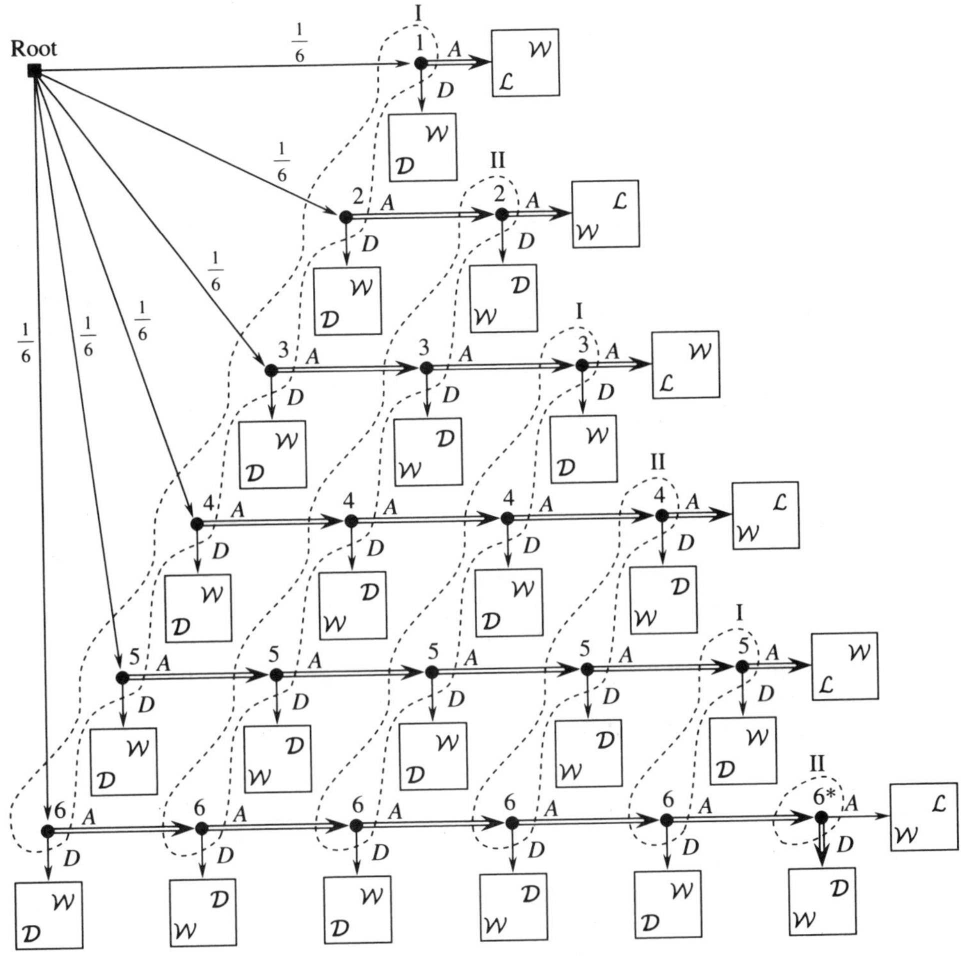

Figure 3.3 Russian Roulette—version 1.

Russian Roulette illustrated in Figure 3.3 is therefore a game of *imperfect information.*

Strategies with Imperfect Information. In a game of imperfect information, a pure strategy for a player does not consist of a choice of action at every *node* at which the player's decision determines what happens. A pure strategy in a game of imperfect information specifies an action only at each of the player's *information sets.*

The pure strategy pair (AAA, AAD) for the first version of Russian Roulette has been indicated in Figure 3.3 by doubling edges. Notice that all six "across" edges at player I's first information set have been doubled. It is impossible for him to plan to play differently at different nodes in the same information set, because he will not be able to tell the nodes apart when he makes his decision.

A Play. Once player I has chosen pure strategy AAA and player II has chosen pure strategy AAD, the course of the game is entirely determined except for the initial decision made by Chance. Suppose that Chance places the bullet in chamber 6. The action in the game will then start at the root and proceed vertically downward to the first node labeled with a 6. It is now player I's move. His pure strategy tells him to choose action A. That is to say, he pulls the trigger. This shifts the action horizontally to the second node labeled with a 6. Here it is player II's move. His pure strategy tells him to play A also, and so the action shifts horizontally again to the third node labeled with a 6. This continues until node 6* is reached at the bottom right of Figure 3.3. Here it is player II's move. Since player II is using pure strategy AAD, he now plays D. This action concludes the game by taking it vertically downward to a payoff box in which player I gets the outcome $\mathcal{W}$ (because player II just chickened out), and player II gets the outcome $\mathcal{D}$ (which is better than the outcome $\mathcal{L}$ that player II would have got if he had chosen to pull the trigger at node 6*).

There is a lot to keep in mind when working with a complicated game tree. But, when working with a game of imperfect information, it is vital not to lose track of who knows what as you trace a play through the tree. In the play just considered, you and I knew the chamber in which Chance had placed the bullet. But the players were in suspense until node 6* was reached. In particular, when player I chose to pull the trigger at his first move, he did not know he was about to pull the trigger on an empty chamber. Although *we* knew that the game had reached the node labeled 6 in his first information set, *he* thought it just as likely that the game had reached any of the other nodes in the information set. He therefore thought he was taking a risk when he pulled the trigger. To be precise, he thought the probability that he would shoot himself when he pulled the trigger was $\frac{1}{6}$, because this is the probability with which Chance places the bullet in chamber 1.

Subgames. Version 1 of Russian Roulette has only one proper subgame. The root of this subgame is the node labeled 6*.

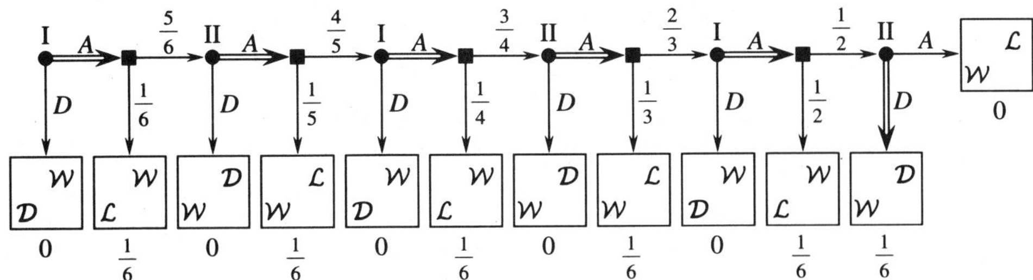

Figure 3.4 Russian Roulette—version 2.

No other nonterminal node, except for the opening chance move, can serve as the root of a subgame. Each such node is enclosed with other nodes in an information set and one cannot disentangle it from its companions without making nonsense of the informational assumptions of the problem.[4] It follows that Zermelo's algorithm will not take us very far in analyzing this version of Russian Roulette.

3.3.2 Version 2 of Russian Roulette

Figure 3.4 shows a second way of drawing a game tree for Russian Roulette that dispenses with the need to indicate information sets because the new version is a game of perfect information. The price paid for this simplification is that six chance moves have to be included: one for each chamber of the six-shooter.

[4]After a game is over, one has to be able to say which play of the game actually occurred. Otherwise nobody would know what the result of the game was! But if the game began with an information set containing more than one node, one would not even know what the first node in the play of the game had been. This is why the definition of a game insists that it begin with a *unique* root. (Sometimes one could get away with a weaker definition. It would be possible to allow a game to begin with an information set containing more than one node if, for some reason, it were possible to assign unambiguous probabilities to each of the nodes in the information set proposed as the "first move" of the game. One could then imagine that, before the game began, a suppressed opening chance move had selected one of the nodes in the information set being regarded as the "first move". As it happens, such a more relaxed definition of a game would allow each information set in version 1 of Russian Roulette to be seen as the "first move" of a "subgame". If this were not the case, it would be impossible to produce a remodeled version 2 of Russian Roulette that is a game of perfect information. However, the rewards from using a more relaxed definition are not worth the effort of formulating it carefully.)

Once both players have chosen their pure strategies, the entire course of the game is determined, *except* for the chance moves. Consider, for example, the strategy pair (AAA, AAD), which has been indicated by doubling edges in Figure 3.4. Its use results in the various terminal nodes being reached with the probabilities written beneath them. Thus, if the strategy pair (AAA, AAD) is used, then player I will end up with the outcome $\mathcal{W}$ half the time and with the outcome $\mathcal{L}$ the remainder of the time. On the other hand, if the strategy pair (DDD, AAD) is used, then player I will get $\mathcal{D}$ for certain. If player I knows or guesses that player II will choose AAD, which of his pure strategies AAA or DDD should he prefer?

The question is unanswerable with the information we have so far about player I's preferences. It is not enough to know that $\mathcal{L} \prec_1 \mathcal{D} \prec_1 \mathcal{W}$. We need to know whether or not he prefers the outcome $\mathcal{D}$ to the lottery in which $\mathcal{W}$ occurs with probability $\frac{1}{2}$ and $\mathcal{L}$ with probability $\frac{1}{2}$. This will depend on his attitude to taking risks. If player I were especially young and romantic, he might perhaps prefer the lottery. Middle-aged gentlemen like myself will not see the potential rewards as being worth much of a risk. However, both of us will agree in seeing $\mathcal{D}$ as an outcome intermediate between $\mathcal{W}$ and $\mathcal{L}$.

3.4 Making Risky Choices

The problem raised at the end of the previous section is that of finding a mathematically tractable way of describing a player's preferences over lotteries that involve more than two prizes.

A naive response to this problem is to replace each prize in a lottery by its monetary equivalent[5] and then to compute the expected value in dollars of the new lottery. Would a rational person then not simply prefer whichever of two lotteries has the largest dollar expectation?

The inadequacy of such an approach is usually pointed out with the aid of a story, which, like that accompanying Russian Roulette, is set in the last days of the Czars.

[5]The smallest amount in dollars for which the player would be willing to forgo enjoying the prize.

Prize	\$2	\$4	\$8	\$16	...	$\$2^k$	...
Coin sequence	H	TH	TTH	$TTTH$	...	$TT \dots TH$	...
Probability	$\frac{1}{2}$	$\frac{1}{4}$	$\frac{1}{8}$	$\frac{1}{16}$	...	$\left(\frac{1}{2}\right)^k$	...

Figure 3.5 The St. Petersburg lottery.

3.4.1 The St. Petersburg Paradox

A casino in St. Petersburg,[6] so the story goes, was willing to run any lottery whatever, provided that the management could set the price of a ticket to participate.

Consider the lottery illustrated in Figure 3.5. This can be realized by tossing a fair coin repeatedly until it shows heads for the first time. If this occurs on the kth trial, you win $\$2^k$. How much should you be willing to pay in order to participate in this lottery?

Assuming that each toss of the coin is independent, the probabilities are calculated as indicated below for the case $k = 4$:

$$\begin{aligned} \text{prob}(TTTH) &= \text{prob}(T)\,\text{prob}(T)\,\text{prob}(T)\,\text{prob}(H) \\ &= \left(\tfrac{1}{2}\right)^4 = \tfrac{1}{16}. \end{aligned}$$

The expectation in dollars of the St. Petersburg lottery $\mathbf{L}$ is therefore

$$\begin{aligned} \mathcal{E}(\mathbf{L}) &= 2\,\text{prob}(H) + 4\,\text{prob}(TH) + 8\,\text{prob}(TTH) + \cdots \\ &= 2 \times \tfrac{1}{2} + 4 \times \tfrac{1}{4} + 8 \times \tfrac{1}{8} + \cdots \\ &= 1 + 1 + 1 + 1 + \cdots, \end{aligned}$$

which means that the expected dollar value of the lottery is "infinite". Should you therefore be willing to liquidate your entire worldly wealth in order to buy a ticket to participate in the lottery? Few people would be willing to do so, especially after noting that the probability of ending up with more than \$8 is only $\frac{1}{8}$.

This is not to argue that always choosing the lottery with the largest expectation in dollars is irrational. All that is being said is that a theory that claims that *only* such behavior is rational will not suffice. Nor will *any* theory that purports

[6]Renamed Leningrad by the Bolsheviks.

to be able to *deduce* people's attitudes to taking risks from their attitudes in nonrisky situations. Something more subtle is required. An adequate theory needs to recognize that the extent to which people are willing to bear risk is as much part of their preference profile as their willingness to eat ice cream or to listen to Beethoven.

3.4.2 Von Neumann and Morgenstern Utility

Although the St. Petersburg paradox shows that a rational person would not necessarily wish to maximize the expected *monetary* value of a lottery, Von Neumann and Morgenstern gave a list of rationality postulates about preferences in risky situations that imply that a rational person will behave as though maximizing *something*. What is this "something"?

A clue to what is required is already present in Chapter 2. Attention was there restricted to the case of lotteries in which the only prizes are drawn from the set $\Omega = \{\mathcal{L}, \mathcal{W}\}$. As before, it will be assumed that $\mathcal{W} \succ \mathcal{L}$. If a utility function $u : \Omega \to \mathbb{R}$ represents this preference, it must be that $u(\mathcal{L}) = a$ and $u(\mathcal{W}) = b$, where $a < b$.

Recall that $\mathbf{p}$ denotes the lottery in which $\mathcal{W}$ occurs with probability p and $\mathcal{L}$ with probability $1 - p$. The set of lotteries with prizes drawn from the set Ω will be denoted by lott(Ω). Thus $\mathbf{p}$ is a member of the set lott $(\{\mathcal{W}, \mathcal{L}\})$. The expected utility derived from the lottery $\mathbf{p}$ is given by

$$
\begin{aligned}
\mathcal{E}u(\mathbf{p}) &= p\,u(\mathcal{W}) + (1-p)\,u(\mathcal{L}) \\
&= pb + (1-p)a \\
&= a + p(b-a)\,. \qquad (3.1)
\end{aligned}
$$

Since $b - a > 0$, it follows that $\mathcal{E}u(\mathbf{p})$ is largest when the probability p of winning is largest.

The first of Von Neumann and Morgenstern's assumptions about rational preferences is now required. It is the assumption that, of two lotteries whose prizes consist only of $\mathcal{W}$ and $\mathcal{L}$, a rational player will always prefer whichever attaches the larger probability to $\mathcal{W}$. When this assumption is satisfied, equation (3.1) tells us that $\mathcal{E}u$ is necessarily a utility function for a rational player's preferences over lott $(\{\mathcal{W}, \mathcal{L}\})$. That is, a rational player acts as though maximizing expected utility when making decisions involving those lotteries with prizes drawn from the set $\Omega = \{\mathcal{W}, \mathcal{L}\}$.

Matters become more complicated when prizes intermediate between $\mathcal{W}$ and $\mathcal{L}$ have to be considered as well, so that Ω

becomes a larger set. Extra rationality assumptions must be made, and it ceases to be true that $\mathcal{E}u$ is a utility function for a rational player's preferences over lotteries whenever u is a utility function for his or her preferences over prizes. If $\mathcal{E}u$ is to represent a rational player's preferences over *lotteries*, it is generally necessary to select the utility function $u : \Omega \to \mathbb{R}$ very carefully from the large class of utility functions that represent a player's preferences over *prizes*. A utility function $u : \Omega \to \mathbb{R}$ selected in this careful way is called a *Von Neumann and Morgenstern utility function.*

The second of Von Neumann and Morgenstern's assumptions about rational preferences is that each prize ω intermediate between the best prize $\mathcal{W}$ and the worst prize $\mathcal{L}$ is equivalent to some lottery involving only $\mathcal{W}$ and $\mathcal{L}$. That is to say, for each prize ω in the set Ω, there is a probability q such that

$$\omega \sim \mathbf{q}\,.$$

For example, if $\mathcal{W} = \$100$ and $\mathcal{L} = \$0$, what would be your value of q when $\omega = \$10$? It is unlikely that you would pay \$10 to participate in the lottery $\mathbf{q}$ if $q = 0.01$. But you might be willing to pay \$10 to participate when $q = 0.25$. If so, then somewhere between 0.01 and 0.25, there is a value of q that will make you just indifferent between participating at a cost of \$10 and not participating at all.

It is now possible to construct a Von Neumann and Morgenstern utility function $u : \Omega \to \mathbb{R}$. This is defined so that the value of $u(\omega)$ is the probability q in the above discussion. Thus $q = u(\omega)$ is defined so as to make it true that the rational player under consideration is indifferent between getting ω for certain and getting the lottery in which $\mathcal{W}$ occurs with probability $u(\omega)$ and $\mathcal{L}$ with probability $1 - u(\omega)$.

To check that u is a Von Neumann and Morgenstern utility function, it is necessary to confirm that $\mathcal{E}u$ is a utility function for the rational player's preferences over lotteries. Figure 3.6 illustrates the two steps in the argument that justifies this conclusion. Each step requires a further assumption.

The first step requires the assumption that rational players will not care if a prize in a lottery is replaced by another prize that they regard as equivalent to the prize it replaces.[7]

[7]Critics of the theory often forget that, if one of the prizes is itself a lottery, then it is implicitly assumed that this lottery is independent of all other lotteries involved.

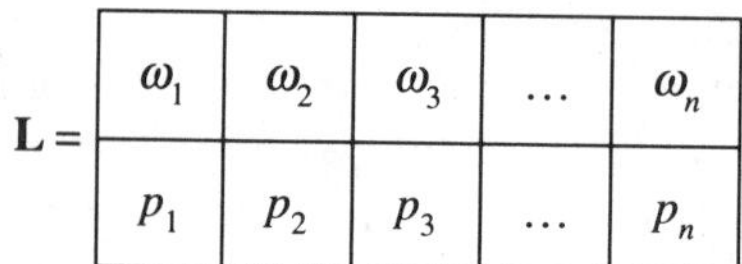

$\mathbf{L} =$

ω_1	ω_2	ω_3	$\cdots$	ω_n
p_1	p_2	p_3	$\cdots$	p_n

$\sim$

$\mathcal{W}$ / $\mathcal{L}$ — q_1 / $1-q_1$	$\mathcal{W}$ / $\mathcal{L}$ — q_2 / $1-q_2$	$\mathcal{W}$ / $\mathcal{L}$ — q_3 / $1-q_3$	$\cdots$	$\mathcal{W}$ / $\mathcal{L}$ — q_n / $1-q_n$
p_1	p_2	p_3	$\cdots$	p_n

$\sim$

$\mathcal{W}$	$\mathcal{L}$
$p_1q_1 + p_2q_2 + \cdots + p_nq_n$	$1 - (p_1q_1 + p_2q_2 + \cdots + p_nq_n)$

Figure 3.6 Von Neumann and Morgenstern's argument.

In Figure 3.6, the prizes available in an arbitrary lottery **L** are $\omega_1, \omega_2, \ldots, \omega_n$. Each prize ω_k is then replaced by a lottery $\mathbf{q_k}$ that the player regards as being equivalent to ω_k. That is, q_k is chosen so that $\omega_k \sim \mathbf{q_k}$. In the compound lottery that results, the total probability that the outcome will be $\mathcal{W}$ is $r = p_1q_1 + p_2q_2 + \cdots + p_nq_n$. (Recall Figure 2.9.) The final assumption needed is that a rational player will not care if the compound lottery is replaced by the simple lottery **r**.[8] It will then be true that original lottery **L** is equivalent to a compound lottery that is in turn equivalent to **r**.

The argument shows that, given two lotteries like **L**, rational players will prefer that which corresponds to the larger value of r. Thus they behave as though they are seeking to maximize

$$\begin{aligned} r &= p_1q_1 + p_2q_2 + \cdots + p_nq_n \\ &= p_1u(\omega_1) + p_2u(\omega_2) + \cdots + p_nu(\omega_n) \\ &= \mathcal{E}u(\mathbf{L}). \end{aligned}$$

It follows that $\mathcal{E}u : \text{lott}(\Omega) \to \mathbb{R}$ is a utility function that rep-

[8]Sometimes Von Neumann and Morgenstern utility functions are said to measure how much fun people get from gambling. However, this assumption about reducing compound lotteries to simple lotteries makes it clear that this is not the case. Players who enjoyed the *process* of gambling for its own sake would presumably prefer the compound lottery to its simple equivalent.

resents the player's preferences over lotteries. Thus $u : \Omega \to \mathbb{R}$ is a Von Neumann and Morgenstern utility function for the player's preferences over prizes.

3.4.3 Risk-Aversion

How does the Von Neumann and Morgenstern theory deal with the St. Petersburg paradox?

Consider a rational person whose utility for money is given by the Von Neumann and Morgenstern utility function[9] $u : \mathbb{R}_+ \to \mathbb{R}$ defined by

$$u(x) = 4\sqrt{x}\,. \tag{3.2}$$

His or her expected utility for the St. Petersburg lottery **L** of Figure 3.5 is

$$\begin{aligned}\mathcal{E}u(\mathbf{L}) &= \tfrac{1}{2}u(2) + (\tfrac{1}{2})^2u(2^2) + (\tfrac{1}{2})^3u(2^3) + \cdots \\ &= 4\left\{\tfrac{1}{2}\sqrt{2} + (\tfrac{1}{2})^2\sqrt{2^2} + (\tfrac{1}{2})^3\sqrt{2^3} + \cdots\right\} \\ &= 4\left\{\left(\tfrac{1}{\sqrt{2}}\right) + \left(\tfrac{1}{\sqrt{2}}\right)^2 + \left(\tfrac{1}{\sqrt{2}}\right)^3 + \cdots\right\} \\ &= \frac{4}{1 - \frac{1}{\sqrt{2}}} \\ &= \frac{4\sqrt{2}}{\sqrt{2} - 1} \approx 4 \times 3.42\,.\end{aligned}$$

The player will be indifferent between the lottery **L** and a sum of money X if and only if their utilities are the same. Thus, $\$X$ is the dollar equivalent of the lottery if and only if

$$\begin{aligned}u(X) &= \mathcal{E}u(\mathbf{L}) \\ 4\sqrt{X} &\approx 4 \times 3.42 \\ X &\approx (3.42)^2 = 11.70\end{aligned}$$

Thus \$11.70 is the most that the player will pay to participate in the St. Petersburg lottery.

---

[9]The set $\mathbb{R}_+ = \{x : x \geq 0\}$ is the set of all nonnegative real numbers. The following observations will be helpful in the argument that follows:

1. $\sqrt{a^n} = (a^n)^{1/2} = a^{n/2} = (\sqrt{a})^n$;
2. $\sqrt{b}/b = 1/\sqrt{b}$;
3. If $|r| < 1$, then the geometric series $1 + r + r^2 + \cdots$ adds up to something finite. Its sum s satisfies $s = 1 + r + r^2 + \cdots = 1 + r(1 + r + \cdots) = 1 + rs$, and hence $s = 1/(1 - r)$.

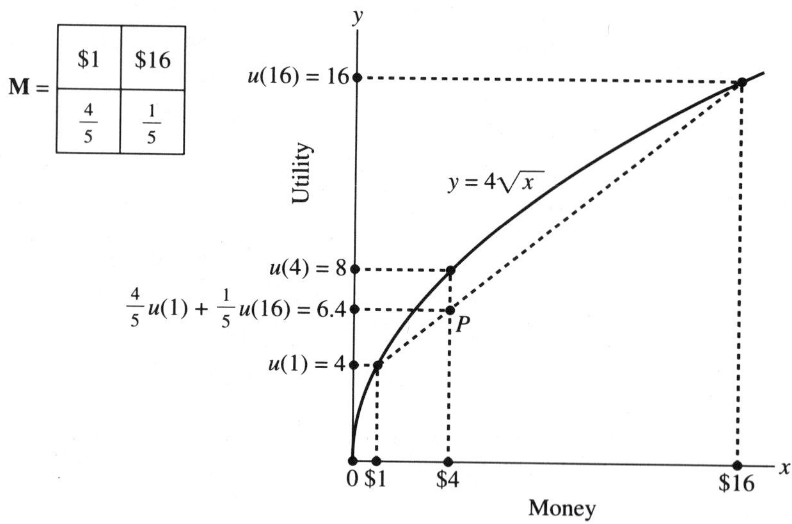

Figure 3.7 A lottery with dollar expectation equal to $4.

The lottery **M** of Figure 3.7 is simpler than the St. Petersburg lottery. A player whose preferences are represented by the square root utility function of (3.2) will assign this lottery a utility of

$$\begin{aligned}\mathcal{E}u(\mathbf{M}) &= \tfrac{4}{5}u(1) + \tfrac{1}{5}u(16) \\ &= \tfrac{4}{5} \times 4\sqrt{1} + \tfrac{1}{5} \times 4\sqrt{16} \\ &= \tfrac{16}{5} + \tfrac{16}{5} = 6.4.\end{aligned}$$

The expectation of the lottery **M** *in dollars* is

$$\mathcal{E}\mathbf{M} = \tfrac{4}{5} \times 1 + \tfrac{1}{5} \times 16 = 4.$$

The graph on the right of Figure 3.7 illustrates the fact that the player prefers getting $4 for certain to participating in the lottery **M**. In algebraic terms, the requirement is that $u(4) > \mathcal{E}u(\mathbf{M})$. This inequality is satisfied because $u(4) = 4\sqrt{4} = 8$ and $\mathcal{E}u(\mathbf{M}) = 6.4$.

A person who would always be prepared to sell the opportunity to participate in a lottery with money prizes for an amount equal to its expected value in dollars is said to be *risk-averse* over money. A person who would always be prepared to buy the opportunity to participate in a lottery for an amount equal to its expected value in dollars is said to be *risk-loving*. A person who is always indifferent between buying and selling is said to be *risk-neutral*.

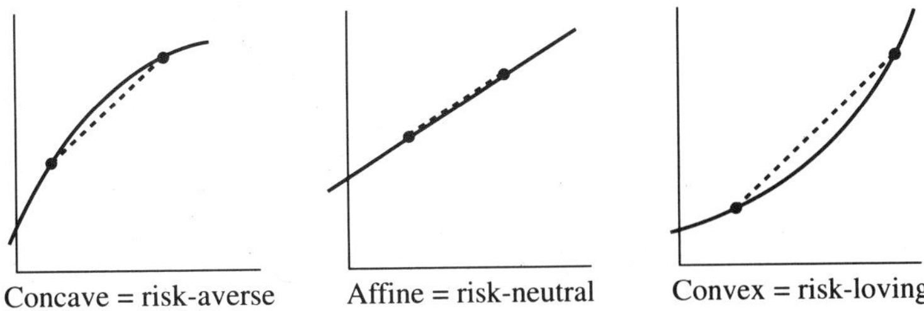

Figure 3.8 How the shape of a utility function determines attitudes to risk.

Figure 3.8 illustrates the graphs of utility functions that respectively represent risk-averse, risk-neutral and risk-loving preferences. As we saw in Figure 3.7, chords drawn to the graph of the utility function of a risk-averse person lie on or below the graph. Mathematicians call a function with this property *concave*.[10] They refer to a function whose chords lie on or above its graph as *convex*. A person with a convex Von Neumann and Morgenstern utility function is risk-loving.

A function with a straight-line graph is said to be affine. An affine function is therefore simultaneously convex and concave (but not *strictly* convex nor *strictly* concave). A person with an affine Von Neumann and Morgenstern utility function is therefore risk-neutral.[11] He or she is always indifferent between buying or selling a lottery for a dollar amount equal to its expected value in dollars, and hence is simultaneously risk-loving and risk-averse. As explained in the next section, one would normally wish to choose the utility scale of a risk-neutral player so that his or her preferences

[10]A differentiable function u is concave on an interval I if and only if its derivative u' is decreasing inside I. Economists refer to $u'(x)$ as a *marginal utility*. Thus a risk-averse player has decreasing marginal utility for money. Each extra dollar is worth less than its predecessor to such a player.

A differentiable function is decreasing on I if and only if $u'(x) \leq 0$ when x is inside I. Thus, if u can be differentiated twice, it is concave on I if and only if $u''(x) \leq 0$ when x is inside I. In the case $u(x) = \sqrt{x}$, $u'(x) = \frac{1}{2}x^{-1/2} > 0$ for $x > 0$, and so u is (strictly) increasing on $\mathbb{R}_+$. Also $u''(x) = -\frac{1}{4}x^{-3/2} < 0$ for $x > 0$, and so u is (strictly) concave on $\mathbb{R}_+$.

A function u is convex on I if and only if $-u$ is concave on I. Thus a criterion for a function u to be convex on I is that $u''(x) \geq 0$ when x is inside I.

[11]Because affine functions have a straight-line graph, they are often said to be "linear". Thus risk-neutral players are sometimes said to have preferences that are "linear in money".

over money are represented by the simple utility function $u : \mathbb{R}_+ \to \mathbb{R}$ defined by

$$u(x) = x.$$

The fallacy that makes the St. Petersburg story seem paradoxical is that a rational person must necessarily be risk-neutral. This may or may not be the case. A rational person who happens to be risk-neutral (or risk-loving) will indeed be prepared to pay anything whatever to be allowed to participate in the St. Petersburg lottery. However, as we have seen, a rational person who is sufficiently risk-averse will not be so reckless. In particular, a person with the square root utility function will only pay \$11.70 to participate.[12]

3.5 Utility Scales

Math 3.5.2 →

The requirement for $u : \Omega \to \mathbb{R}$ to be a utility function representing the preference relation $\preceq$ defined on the set Ω is that $a \preceq b \Leftrightarrow u(a) \leq u(b)$ for each a and b in Ω. Since $u(a) \leq u(b) \Leftrightarrow (u(a))^3 \leq (u(b))^3$, it follows that the function $v : \Omega \to \mathbb{R}$ defined by $v(s) = (u(s))^3$ is also a utility function for $\preceq$.

Similarly, $u(a) \leq u(b) \Leftrightarrow 2u(a) + 5 \leq 2u(b) + 5$. Thus the function $w : \Omega \to \mathbb{R}$ defined by $w(s) = 2u(s) + 5$ is another utility function for $\preceq$. Any of these utility functions and innumerable others are equally good representations of the preference relation $\preceq$ on Ω.

The same freedom is not available when choosing a Von Neumann and Morgenstern utility function $u : \Omega \to \mathbb{R}$. It is true that $(\mathcal{E}u)^3$ and $2(\mathcal{E}u) + 5$ represent a rational player's preferences over lotteries just as well as $\mathcal{E}u$ when u is a Von Neumann and Morgenstern utility function. It is also true that u^3 represents the rational player's preferences over *prizes* just as well as u. But it is generally false that u^3 is a Von Neumann and Morgenstern utility function. That is to say, it is generally not true that $\mathcal{E}(u^3)$ represents the rational player's preferences over *lotteries*.

But it is true that $2u + 5$ is necessarily a Von Neumann and Morgenstern utility function whenever u is. The reason is

---

[12]This demolishes only one form of the St. Petersburg paradox. Others can be constructed if *unbounded* Von Neumann and Morgenstern utility functions are allowed (Exercise 3.7.21). However, such recondite forms of the paradox need not concern us since we shall nearly always be working only with a *finite* number of possible prizes.

that, for any constants $A > 0$ and B, it is always the case that $\mathcal{E}(Au + B) = A\mathcal{E}u + B$. Hence, maximizing $\mathcal{E}u$ is the same as maximizing $\mathcal{E}(Au + B)$ when $A > 0$.

3.5.1 Affine Transformations

The function $Au + B$ is said to be a strictly increasing affine transformation[13] of u. The next theorem says that *only* strictly increasing affine transformations of a Von Neumann and Morgenstern utility function can also be Von Neumann and Morgenstern utility functions for the same preference relation.

Theorem 3.5.1 Suppose that $u_1 : \Omega \to \mathbb{R}$ and $u_2 : \Omega \to \mathbb{R}$ are both Von Neumann and Morgenstern utility functions for the preference relation $\preceq$ defined on lott(Ω). Then there exist constants $A > 0$ and B such that

$$u_2 = Au_1 + B.$$

Proof. Choose constants $A_i > 0$ and B_i so that the Von Neumann and Morgenstern utility functions $U_i = A_i u_i + B_i$ satisfy $U_i(\mathcal{L}) = 0$ and $U_i(\mathcal{W}) = 1$. Consider any prize ω in Ω and choose q so that $\omega \sim \mathbf{q}$. Then

$$U_i(\omega) = \mathcal{E}U_i(\mathbf{q}) = qU_i(\mathcal{W}) + (1 - q)U_i(\mathcal{L}) = q.$$

Thus $A_1 u_1(\omega) + B_1 = A_2 u_2(\omega) + B_2$. The conclusion of the theorem follows on solving this equation for $u_2(\omega)$. □

3.5.2 Temperature Scales

Theorem 3.5.1 shows that the origin and unit of a Von Neumann and Morgenstern utility scale can be chosen in an arbitrary fashion, but then there is no more room for maneuver. In

[13]The terminology used in this context can often be confusing. As noted earlier, some authors refer to the affine function $f : \mathbb{R} \to \mathbb{R}$ defined by $f(x) = Ax + B$ as "linear" because it has a straight-line graph. But this usage is inconsistent with the way mathematicians use the word linear in linear algebra. This requires that a linear function $f : \mathbb{R} \to \mathbb{R}$ satisfy $f(x) = Ax$. Sometimes f is said to be a "positive" affine function (because $A > 0$). However, the natural definition of a positive function simply requires that it take only positive values. Other authors insist on referring to Von Neumann and Morgenstern utility functions $u : \Omega \to \mathbb{R}$ in general as "linear". They do not mean that u necessarily has a straight-line graph. They mean that $\mathcal{E}u$ is obtained from u using the linear operator $\mathcal{E}$. It is true that $\mathcal{E}$ is a linear operator in the strict mathematical sense, but this does not seem an adequate excuse for introducing such a misleading piece of terminology.

introducing the idea, Von Neumann and Morgenstern made a useful analogy with the measurement of temperature.

The Centigrade or Celsius scale assigns 0°C to the freezing point of water at a stated atmospheric pressure and 100°C to its boiling point. Once these choices have been made, the Centigrade value for all other temperatures is determined. The Fahrenheit scale assigns 32°F to the freezing point of water and 212°F to its boiling point. Again, once these choices have been made, the Fahrenheit value for all other temperatures is determined. Observe that the Fahrenheit temperature f is a strictly increasing affine function of the Centigrade temperature c. In fact,

$$f = \tfrac{9}{5}c + 32.$$

One may establish a Von Neumann and Morgenstern utility scale in a similar way. Having found one Von Neumann and Morgenstern utility function $u : \Omega \to \mathbb{R}$, one may recalibrate the scale it defines as follows. Choose an outcome ω_0 in Ω to correspond to the origin of the new utility scale. Choose another outcome ω_1 in Ω with $\omega_1 \succ \omega_0$ to define the unit of the new scale. Now look for a Von Neumann and Morgenstern utility function $U : \Omega \to \mathbb{R}$ for which $U(\omega_0) = 0$ and $U(\omega_1) = 1$.

By Theorem 3.5.1, $U = Au + B$. Thus, A and B must be chosen to satisfy the equations:

$$\begin{aligned} 0 &= Au(\omega_0) + B \\ 1 &= Au(\omega_1) + B. \end{aligned}$$

The values of A and B that solve this pair of linear equations are not important. All that matters is that the equations have a solution and so a new Von Neumann and Morgenstern utility scale with an arbitrary origin and unit can always be established.[14]

---

[14]An *ordinal* property of a function $u : \Omega \to \mathbb{R}$ is one that is invariant under strictly increasing transformations. That is, for any strictly increasing $f : \mathbb{R} \to \mathbb{R}$, the composite function $f \circ u : \Omega \to \mathbb{R}$ must retain the same property. The composite function $f \circ u$ is defined by $f \circ u(s) = f(u(s))$.

A *cardinal* property is one that is invariant under strictly increasing *affine* transformations. That is, for any $A > 0$ and any B, the function $Au + B$ must retain the same property. The property of defining a temperature scale is therefore cardinal as is that of being a Von Neumann and Morgenstern utility function that represents a given preference relation $\preceq$. The property of being any utility function at all that represents $\preceq$ is ordinal.

The interest in these terms is largely historical, dating from a time when economists believed the idea of a cardinal utility function to be intrinsically meaningless.

3.5.3 Comparing Utils

The unit on a Von Neumann and Morgenstern utility scale is sometimes called a *util* just as the unit on a temperature scale is called a degree. In using this terminology, various fallacies have to be avoided of which the most important for game theory purposes is that which assumes that player I's utils can be directly compared with player II's.

Since the choice of origin and unit on a Von Neumann and Morgenstern utility scale is arbitrary, it will be clear that to take for granted that one player's util is "worth" the same as another's makes as much sense as arguing that two rooms are equally warm because their temperatures are the same without first checking that the thermometers in the two rooms both use the same temperature scale.

This is not to say that comparing utils is *intrinsically* nonsensical, only that the Von Neumann and Morgenstern theory provides no basis for doing so.

3.6 The Noble Savage

This section is not about noble savages à la Rousseau. It briefly discusses how the statistician Savage elaborated the Von Neumann and Morgenstern theory to include a description of how a person who makes rational decisions must organize his or her beliefs in situations when objective probabilities are not specified.

3.6.1 Allais' Paradox

Econ 3.7 ⟶

First it needs to be said that the Von Neumann and Morgenstern theory is not without critics. The economist Allais has been particularly vocal. His intervention during a talk given by Savage is much quoted.

Allais asked for Savage's preferences between some lotteries, and then demonstrated that the preferences that Savage expressed are inconsistent with the Von Neumann and Morgenstern rationality principles. The moral meant to be drawn is that, if an arch-advocate of the theory like Savage does not honor the rationality principles, why should anyone else?

Allais' point can be illustrated with the four lotteries of Figure 3.9. The prizes in the set $\Omega = \{\$0\text{m}, \$1\text{m}, \$5\text{m}\}$ have been given in millions of dollars to dramatize the situation.

Like Savage, most people express the preference $\mathbf{J} \succ \mathbf{K}$ because **J** guarantees \$1m for sure, while **K** seems comparatively

J =

\$0m	\$1m	\$5m
0	1	0

K =

\$0m	\$1m	\$5m
.01	.89	.10

L =

\$0m	\$1m	\$5m
.89	.11	0

M =

\$0m	\$1m	\$5m
.9	0	.1

Figure 3.9 Lotteries for Allais' paradox.

unattractive because of the risk of getting nothing at all. Again like Savage, most people express the preference $\mathbf{M} \succ \mathbf{L}$. Here the risk of ending up with nothing at all cannot be avoided. On the contrary, the risk of this final outcome is high in both cases. However, if the probability .89 in **L** is rounded up to .9 and .11 is rounded down to .1, then anyone who understands what is going on would prefer **M** to the new **L**. If one thinks that the new **L** is essentially the same as the old **L**, one therefore has a reason for preferring **M** to the old **L**.

The preferences $\mathbf{J} \succ \mathbf{K}$ and $\mathbf{M} \succ \mathbf{L}$ are inconsistent with the Von Neumann and Morgenstern rationality assumptions. Otherwise they could be described with a Von Neumann and Morgenstern utility function $u : \Omega \to \mathbb{R}$. But the following argument shows that this is impossible.

Two points on a utility scale can be fixed in an arbitrary manner. In this case, it is convenient to fix $u(0) = 0$ and $u(5) = 1$. What can then be said about Savage's value for $x = u(1)$? Observe that

$$\mathcal{E}u(\mathbf{J}) = u(0) \times 0.0 + u(1) \times 1.0 + u(5) \times 0.0 = x$$
$$\mathcal{E}u(\mathbf{K}) = u(0) \times .01 + u(1) \times .89 + u(5) \times .10 = .89x + .10.$$

Since $\mathbf{J} \succ \mathbf{K}$, it must therefore be true that

$$x > .89x + .10$$
$$x > \tfrac{10}{11}.$$

On the other hand,

$$\mathcal{E}u(\mathbf{L}) = u(0) \times .89 + u(1) \times .11 + u(5) \times 0.0 = .11x$$
$$\mathcal{E}u(\mathbf{M}) = u(0) \times .9 + u(1) \times 0 + u(5) \times .10 \quad = .10$$

Since $\mathbf{L} \prec \mathbf{M}$, it must therefore be true that

$$.11x < .10$$
$$x < \tfrac{10}{11}.$$

But it cannot be true simultaneously that $x > \frac{10}{11}$ and $x < \frac{10}{11}$. Savage's preferences are therefore inconsistent with the Von Neumann and Morgenstern rationality postulates.

Should we conclude from such examples that the Von Neumann and Morgenstern postulates are not acceptable as rationality principles? One might as well conclude from the fact that great mathematicians are famous for making elementary arithmetical errors that there is something wrong with the laws of arithmetic. In essence, this was Savage's response to Allais. Once his inconsistencies had been pointed out, Savage confessed to having made a mistake and hastened to correct the preferences he was willing to express.

3.6.2 Bayesian Rationality

In the lotteries that have been discussed so far, the probabilities were given in advance. The implicit understanding has been that these were objective probabilities.

Phil 3.7 ⟶

For example, if one suspects that a pair of dice is weighted, one could roll them perhaps 3,600 times. If the dice were fair, snake eyes (a pair of ones) should appear about 100 times, because the probability of snake eyes in a single roll is 1/36. However, if snake eyes appears only 10 times in 3,600 rolls, then one would have to be very trusting indeed not to reject the hypothesis that the dice are fair. Indeed, the evidence suggests that the probability of rolling snake eyes in a single throw is about 1/360.

When a large amount of data is available, as in the preceding example, one is entitled to speak of *objective* probabilities. However, one would often like to make use of the Von Neumann and Morgenstern theory in situations where objective probabilities are not available.

Suppose, for example, that John has a date with Mary, but she does not turn up at the appointed time. How long should John wait before deciding that he has been stood up? If this is their first date, he will have no data. Nevertheless, he still has a decision to make.

One might simplify John's decision by distinguishing only two events that he need consider. The first event E is that Mary will turn up eventually if he waits for her. The second event F is that she has stood him up, and so he will wait for her in vain. If he waits, and she does turn up eventually, he gets a prize $\mathcal{W}$. If he waits, and she does not turn up, his prize is $\mathcal{L}$. He also has the option of abandoning his vigil and just going home. This option will be identified with another prize $\mathcal{D}$. Does he prefer the prize $\mathcal{D}$ or does he prefer the "lottery" in which he gets $\mathcal{W}$ if the event E occurs, and $\mathcal{L}$ if the event F occurs?

Savage gave a list of postulates about the preferences a rational person might be anticipated to hold in such circumstances. He showed that a person who satisfies these postulates will make decisions *as though* maximizing a Von Neumann utility function $u : \Omega \to \mathbb{R}$ relative to some probability measure $\text{prob} : \Omega \to \mathbb{R}$. Thus, if John is rational, he will behave as though he were choosing the larger of $u(\mathcal{D})$ and

$$u(\mathcal{W})\text{prob}(E) + u(\mathcal{L})\text{prob}(F).$$

The beauty of Savage's theory is that it allows a rational decision-maker to be characterized simply in terms of his or her *tastes* and *beliefs*. John's tastes are summarized by the utility function $u : \Omega \to \mathbb{R}$. His beliefs are summarized by the probability measure $\text{prob} : \Omega \to \mathbb{R}$. The numbers $\text{prob}(E)$ and $\text{prob}(F)$ are called *subjective* probabilities. This is to emphasize that nobody is claiming that John's probabilities necessarily reflect any objective data about the world. All that is claimed is that, unless John behaves as though he had beliefs summarized by such subjective probabilities, he would necessarily be inconsistent in the way he makes decisions. In particular, he would be vulnerable to having a *Dutch book* made against him. This means that someone could propose a system of bets to which John would willingly agree, but which ensures that he would be bound to lose overall no matter what happens. A Dutch book is therefore the betting equivalent of the money pump with which the idea of transitive preferences was defended in Section 3.1.1.

Of course, there is a lot more to being rational than simply being consistent in how one makes decisions. For this reason, a person who does not violate Savage's postulates when making decisions is said to be *Bayesian* rational. This is something of a misnomer. The theory itself certainly has nothing to do with Thomas Bayes, whose rule was mentioned in Section 2.1.4. However, it is true that a Bayesian-rational person will often find Bayes' rule useful, and so the terminology is not entirely off the wall.

Savage emphasized that one should only anticipate his rationality postulates being satisfied under certain conditions. Roughly speaking, he argued that it only makes sense for a rational person to be consistent if he or she has had the opportunity to consider what his or her attitudes would be under *all* possible contingencies that might arise. He called this restriction on the range of applicability of his theory the *small world* assumption. Only when the range of possibilities is sufficiently small will it be practical for someone to evaluate in advance the implications of anything that might conceivably happen.

Even with this proviso, not everyone would agree that Savage's postulates make sense. Allais is among those who take issue with Savage's *sure-thing principle*. In John's problem, for example, suppose that John likes the outcome $\mathcal{D}$ at least as much as the outcome $\mathcal{L}$. Then the sure-thing principle implies that, if the prize $\mathcal{L}$ in the "lottery" that he gets by deciding to wait is replaced by the prize $\mathcal{D}$, then he will necessarily prefer the new lottery to the old.[15] It may seem hard to dispute such a rationality principle. However, as we saw in Section 3.6.1, things become more problematic when the prizes are themselves lotteries.

In choosing material for this book, my aim has been to avoid including material that is controversial. However, there is no way that a book on game theory can be written if Bayesian rationality cannot be assumed. My own view is that criticisms like those made by Allais should be directed not at the plausibility of Savage's rationality assumptions, but at the plausibility of treating ordinary people as though they make decisions in a consistent way when faced by situations that make them feel uncertain. On the other hand, those critics who attack the rationality assumptions as rationality assumptions, are usually responding to some of the wilder assertions of "naive Bayesians" who do not think it necessary to honor Savage's small world restriction.

Game theorists can fortunately steer a middle course. They can agree with Allais that real people are often not Bayesian-rational, but explain that game theory is about those situations when they behave as though they are. Nor need they feel any reason to sympathize with naive Bayesians. Savage's small world assumption is automatically satisfied

[15]It may be helpful to look over Section 3.4.2 again with a view to locating where an equivalent of the sure-thing principle is used in deriving Von Neumann and Morgenstern utility functions.

within the narrow confines of a game. The use that game theorists make of the theory is therefore not easy to attack successfully so long as they resist the temptation to stray outside their bailiwick.

3.7 Exercises

Math

1. If $\preceq$ is a rational preference relation in the sense of Section 3.1, show that one and only one of

$$a \prec b, \quad a \sim b, \quad a \succ b$$

holds.

Math

2. Show that any rational preference relation $\preceq$ is reflexive. That is, for any a in the set Ω, $a \preceq a$.

Math

3. If $\preceq$ is a rational preference relation and $\sim$ is the associated indifference relation, show that $\sim$ satisfies totality and transitivity. Show that the associated strict preference relation $\prec$ satisfies only transitivity.

Math

4. If $\preceq$ is a rational preference relation, show that

$$a \prec b \text{ and } b \preceq c \quad \Rightarrow \quad a \prec c\,.$$

5. A club committee with three members (I, II and III) determines its collective preferences over three candidates (A, B and C) for membership in the club by voting. The individual preferences of the committee members are $A \prec_1 B \prec_1 C$, $B \prec_2 C \prec_2 A$ and $C \prec_3 A \prec_3 B$. Thus, in a vote on who of A and B is to be preferred, B will win because he gets two votes and A gets only one vote. Show that a collective preference for the committee obtained in this way is not transitive.[16]

Econ

6. Solve Pandora's optimization problem of Section 3.2.1 in the case when $U : \Omega \to \mathbb{R}$ is defined by:
(a) $U(g,v) = gv$ (b) $U(g,v) = g^2 + v^2$

Econ

7. Construct two different utility functions that represent the preferences

$$a \sim b \prec c \prec d \prec e \sim f.$$

Econ

8. Pandora can buy gin and vodka in only one of the four following packages: $A = (1,2)$, $B = (8,4)$, $C = (2,16)$ or $D = (4,8)$. When purchasing, she always has precisely \$24

[16]This apparent breakdown of "collective rationality" is sometimes referred to as the "paradox of voting".

to spend. If gin and vodka are both sold at \$2 a bottle, she sometimes buys bundle B and sometimes bundle D. If gin sells for \$4 a bottle and vodka for \$1 a bottle, then she always buys C. Find a utility function $U : \{A, B, C, D\} \to \mathbb{R}$ that is consistent with this behavior.

9. The preferences of a rational person satisfy $\mathcal{L} \prec \mathcal{D}_1 \prec \mathcal{D}_2 \prec \mathcal{W}$. The person regards $\mathcal{D}_1$ and $\mathcal{D}_2$ as being equivalent to certain lotteries whose only prizes are $\mathcal{W}$ or $\mathcal{L}$. The appropriate lotteries are given in Figure 3.10. Find a Von Neumann and Morgenstern utility function that represents these preferences. Use this to determine the person's preferences between the lotteries **L** and **M** of Figure 3.10.

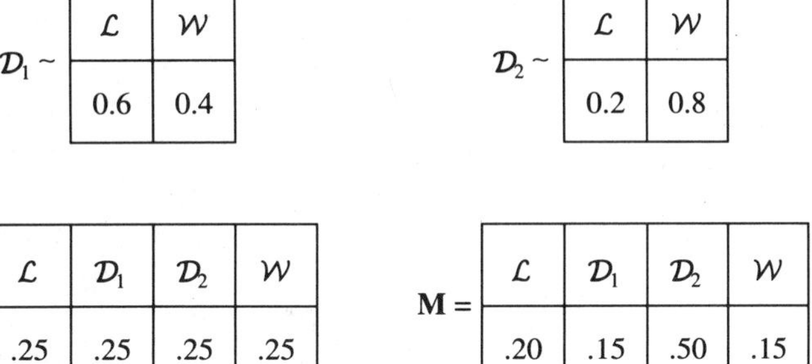

$\mathcal{D}_1 \sim$

$\mathcal{L}$	$\mathcal{W}$
0.6	0.4

$\mathcal{D}_2 \sim$

$\mathcal{L}$	$\mathcal{W}$
0.2	0.8

L =

$\mathcal{L}$	$\mathcal{D}_1$	$\mathcal{D}_2$	$\mathcal{W}$
.25	.25	.25	.25

M =

$\mathcal{L}$	$\mathcal{D}_1$	$\mathcal{D}_2$	$\mathcal{W}$
.20	.15	.50	.15

Figure 3.10 Lotteries for Exercise 3.7.9.

10. A person's preferences over money are represented by a Von Neumann and Morgenstern utility function $u : \mathbb{R}_+ \to \mathbb{R}$ defined by $u(x) = x^a$. What would be implied about his or her preferences if $a < 0$? What if $a = 0$? Explain why the person is risk-averse if $0 \leq a \leq 1$ and risk-loving if $a \geq 1$.

    If $a = 2$, explain why the person would pay \$1m for the opportunity to participate in the lottery **K** of Figure 3.9. What is the person's dollar equivalent for the lottery **K**?

11. Pandora's Von Neumann and Morgenstern utility function is chosen so that $u(\$0) = 0$ and $u(\$10) = 1$.
    (a) If Pandora is risk-averse, explain why $u(\$1) \geq 0.1$ and $u(\$9) \geq 0.9$.
    (b) In one lottery **L**, the prizes \$0, \$1, \$9 and \$10 are available with respective probabilities 0.4, 0.3, 0.2 and 0.1. In a second lottery **M**, the same prizes are available with respective probabilities 0.5, 0.2, 0.1

and 0.2. Explain why a risk-averse Pandora would violate the Von Neumann and Morgenstern rationality axioms if she expressed the preference $\mathbf{L} \prec \mathbf{M}$.

Math

12. If $u : \Omega \to \mathbb{R}$ is a Von Neumann and Morgenstern utility function and $\mathbf{L}$ is a lottery, explain why it is true that

$$\mathcal{E}\,(Au(\mathbf{L}) + B) = A\mathcal{E}u(\mathbf{L}) + B.$$

13. What is the Fahrenheit temperature when it is 20°C? What is the Centigrade temperature when it is −10°F?

Econ

14. Reverse the prizes \$0m and \$5m in the lotteries of Figure 3.9. Are Savage's original preferences still inconsistent?

15. The rules of Gale's Roulette of Exercise 2.6.23 are changed so that the loser must pay the winner an amount in dollars equal to the difference in their scores. If both players are risk-neutral over money, explain why they will not care which choices they make in the game. (See Exercise 2.6.24.)

16. In the version of Gale's Roulette of Exercise 3.7.15, player I's preferences are altered so that his utility for money is described by the Von Neumann and Morgenstern utility function $\phi_1 : \mathbb{R} \to \mathbb{R}$ given by $\phi_1(x) = 3^x$. Denote the event that player I chooses wheel i and player II chooses wheel j by $(\mathbf{L}_i, \mathbf{L}_j)$. List the six possible events of this type. For each such event, find player I's dollar expectation and the utility that he assigns to getting a dollar amount equal to this expectation. Also find player I's expected utility for each of the six events.

Is player I risk-averse? Assume that player II's utility for money is described by the Von Neumann and Morgenstern utility function $\phi_2 : \mathbb{R} \to \mathbb{R}$ given by $\phi_2(x) = -3^{-x}$. Is she risk-averse?

Econ

17. A charity is to run a garden party to raise money, but the organizer is anxious about the possibility of rain, which will occur on the day chosen for the event with probability p. She therefore considers insuring against rain. Her Von Neumann and Morgenstern utility for money $u : \mathbb{R} \to \mathbb{R}$ satisfies $u'(x) > 0$ and $u''(x) < 0$ for all x. Why does she like more money rather than less? Why is she strictly risk-averse? Why is the function u' strictly decreasing?

If it is sunny on the day of the event, the charity will make \$$y$. If it rains, the charity will make only \$$z$. The insurance company offers full insurance against the potential loss of $\$(y-z)$ from rain at a premium of $\$M$, but the organizer may elect against full coverage by paying only a fraction f of the full premium. This means that she pays $\$Mf$ before the event, and the insurance company repays $\$0$ if it is sunny and $\$(y-z)f$ if it rains. (Keep things simple by *not* making the realistic assumption that f is restricted to the range $0 \le f \le 1$.)

(a) What is the insurance company's dollar expectation if she buys full insurance? Why does it make sense to call the insurance contract (actuarially) "fair" if $M = p(y-z)$?

(b) Why does the organizer choose f so as to maximize $(1-p)u(y-Mf) + pu(z+(y-z)f - Mf)$? What do you get when this expression is differentiated with respect to f?

(c) Show that the organizer buys full insurance ($f = 1$) if the insurance contract is "fair".

(d) Show that the insurance contract is "fair" if the organizer buys full insurance.

(e) If the insurance contract is "unfair" with $M > p(y-z)$, show that the organizer definitely buys less than full insurance ($f < 1$).

(f) How would the organizer feel about taking out a "fair" insurance contract if she were risk-neutral?

Fun

18. A misanthropic billionaire enjoys seeing people make mistakes. Claiming to be a philanthropist, he shows Pandora two closed boxes containing money. Pandora is to keep the money in whichever box she chooses to open. The billionaire explains that, however much she finds in the box she opens, the probability that the other box will contain twice as much is $\frac{1}{2}$. Since the boxes are identical in appearance, Pandora opens one at random. It contains $\$n$. Being risk-neutral, she now calculates the expected dollar value of the other box as $\frac{1}{2}(\frac{1}{2}n) + \frac{1}{2}(2n) = 5n/4$. When she laments at having chosen wrongly, the misanthropic billionaire departs chuckling with glee.

(a) Could Pandora have chosen better?

(b) What is paradoxical about this story?

(c) Did Pandora calculate the expected dollar value of the other box correctly?

(d) Suppose that the billionaire actually chose the boxes so that the probability of one containing $\$2^k$ and the other containing $\$2^{k+1}$ is p_k ($k = 0, \pm 1, \pm 2, \ldots$). If Pandora knew this, and opened a box containing $\$n = 2^k$, explain why her conditional probability that the other box contains \$$2n$ would be $p_k/(p_k + p_{k-1})$. What would her conditional probability be for the event that the other box contains \$$\frac{1}{2}n$?

(e) Continuing (d), which law of probability would the probabilities p_k fail to satisfy if what the billionaire said to Pandora were correct?

19. The billionaire of the previous exercise is displeased at being exposed as a liar, and so he proposes another choice problem for Pandora. He chooses a natural number k with probability $p_k > 0$ ($k = 1, 2, \ldots$) and then puts \$$M_k$ in one box and \$$M_{k+1}$ in the other. Pandora again selects a box at random. If the billionaire arranges matters so that $M_2 > M_1$ and

$$M_{k+1}p_k + M_{k-1}p_{k-1} > M_k p_k + M_k p_{k-1} \qquad (k = 1, 2, \ldots),$$

explain why Pandora will always regret not having chosen the other box. Check that the choices $M_k = 3^k$ and $p_k = (\frac{1}{2})^k$ suffice to make the billionaire's plan work.

Math 20. Suppose that Pandora is no longer risk-neutral in the previous exercise. Instead M_k now represents a Von Neumann and Morgenstern utility for whatever the billionaire puts in a box. Explain why her expected utility *before* she looks in a box is given by

$$\tfrac{1}{2}p_1 M_1 + \sum_{k=2}^{\infty} \tfrac{1}{2}(p_k + p_{k-1})M_k.$$

If this expected utility is *finite*, show how summing the displayed inequality of the previous exercise between appropriate limits leads to the conclusion that $M_{k-1} > M_k$ ($k = 2, 3, \ldots$).

Explain why it follows that the billionaire cannot play his trick on Pandora unless her intitial expected utility is infinite. Relate this conclusion to the St. Petersburg paradox of Section 3.4.1.

Math 21. Continuing the last exercise, explain why Pandora will only be immune to the billionaire's trick if her Von Neumann and Morgenstern utility for money is *bounded*. If she is immune, why does it follow that she cannot always be risk-loving when choosing among lotteries whose prizes are monetary amounts?

Econ 22. Critics of Von Neumann and Morgenstern's utility theory sometimes sharpen up Allais' paradox (Section 3.6.1) by proposing the following variant. A rich man is forced to play a version of Russian Roulette that is quite different from that of Section 3.3. The cylinder of a six-shooter revolver containing *two* bullets is spun and the barrel is then pointed at his head. He is now offered the opportunity of paying money to have the two bullets removed before the trigger is fired. It turns out that the payment can be made as high as $10,000,000 before he becomes indifferent between paying and taking the risk of getting shot.

(a) Why would the rich man also be indifferent between having the trigger pulled when the revolver contains *four* bullets and paying $10,000,000 to have *one* of the bullets removed before the trigger is pulled? (Assume that he is rational in the sense of Von Neumann and Morgenstern.)

(b) Why would the rich man not be willing to pay as much as $10,000,000 to have *one* bullet removed from a revolver containing only one bullet?

(c) Would *you* be willing to pay more to have one bullet removed from a revolver containing four bullets than to have one bullet removed from a revolver containing only one bullet? If you answer *yes*, then you are not rational in the sense of Von Neumann and Morgenstern. But perhaps you would prefer not to be![17]

---

[17]My own reaction to this and similar examples is not what critics of the Von Neumann and Morgenstern theory would wish. I have no gut feelings about whether I would rather pay more to get one bullet removed from a revolver containing only one bullet than to get one bullet removed from a revolver containing four bullets. You might as well ask me whether I would prefer to have $11 \times 17 \times 29$ dollars or $13 \times 19 \times 23$ dollars. In both cases, I feel the need to calculate before I can answer the question. As for the gut feelings that other people seemingly have that contradict what the Von Neumann and Morgenstern theory prescribes, would such folk also be willing to pay more to get one bullet removed from a revolver containing one bullet than to get one bullet removed from a revolver containing *six* bullets? I suspect not. But getting one bullet removed when there are six bullets is not so different from getting one bullet removed when there are five bullets. This, in turn, is not so different from getting one bullet removed when there are four bullets. *How* different is the difference between each of these cases? This is a question that gut feelings do not seem very well adapted to answer.

CHAPTER

4

Getting Paid Off

4.1 Payoffs

In Chapter 1, strategic forms of various games were constructed. For example, Figure 1.5 shows the outcome, $\mathcal{W}$ or $\mathcal{L}$, that would result for each possible pure strategy choice the players might make in the game G of Sections 1.3 and 1.4. Figure 1.17 shows a strategic form of a game in which the outcomes are money payments. In more complicated situations, the outcomes may be more difficult to describe. Chapter 2, for example, makes it clear that it would sometimes be necessary to include lotteries as possible outcomes.

Things would often get very messy if it were not possible to appeal to the work of Chapter 3. We learned there to identify each outcome in a game with a list of *payoffs*, one for every player. Each player i is assumed to be rational in the sense of Von Neumann and Morgenstern. He or she therefore acts as though seeking to maximize the expected value of a Von Neumann and Morgenstern utility function $u_i : \Omega \to \mathbb{R}$ defined on the set Ω of final outcomes of the game. Player i's *payoff* at an outcome ω is then simply the Von Neumann and Morgenstern utility $u_i(\omega)$.

4.1.1 Payoff Functions

Let S be the set of player I's pure strategies in a two-player game and let T be the set of player II's pure strategies. If player I chooses pure strategy s and player II chooses pure strategy t, then the course that the game then takes is entirely determined, except for the chance moves. Thus the pair (s, t) determines a *lottery* $\mathbf{L}$ over the set Ω of final outcomes of the game. The payoff $\pi_i(s, t)$ that player i gets when the pair (s, t) is used is the expected utility of the lottery $\mathbf{L}$. That is,

$$\pi_i(s, t) = \mathcal{E} u_i(\mathbf{L}) .$$

4.1.2 A Strategic Form for Duel

As an example of the use of payoff functions, consider the game Duel introduced in Section 2.4. Recall that $\mathcal{W}$ denotes the outcome in which player II gets shot and $\mathcal{L}$ denotes the outcome in which player I gets shot. The lottery in which $\mathcal{W}$ occurs with probability q and $\mathcal{L}$ occurs with probability $1 - q$ is denoted by $\mathbf{q}$.

What matters about a pure strategy in Duel is how close it permits the opponent to get before the trigger is pulled. A pure strategy that calls for a player to wait until a particular node d has been reached, and then to plan to fire at d will be denoted by d.[1]

If player I uses pure strategy d and player II uses pure strategy e, then the outcome of the game depends on who fires first. If $d > e$, so that player I fires first, the result is the lottery $\mathbf{p}_1(\mathbf{d})$. This is the lottery in which player I survives with probability $p_1(d)$ and player II survives with probability $1 - p_1(d)$. If $d < e$, so that player II fires first, the result is the lottery $\mathbf{1} - \mathbf{p}_2(\mathbf{e})$.

The payoff $\pi_1(d, e)$ that player I gets if he uses pure strategy d and player II uses pure strategy e is therefore given by

$$\pi_1(d, e) = \begin{cases} p_1(d), \text{ if } d > e, \\ 1 - p_2(e), \text{ if } d < e, \end{cases} \tag{4.1}$$

provided that player I's Von Neumann and Morgenstern utility function $u_1 : \{\mathcal{L}, \mathcal{W}\} \to \mathbb{R}$ is chosen, as in Section 3.4.2, so that $u_1(\mathcal{L}) = 0$ and $u_1(\mathcal{W}) = 1$.

Similarly, the payoff $\pi_2(d, e)$ that player II gets if he uses pure strategy e and player II uses pure strategy d is given by

$$\pi_2(d, e) = \begin{cases} 1 - p_1(d), \text{ if } d > e, \\ p_2(e), \text{ if } d < e, \end{cases} \tag{4.2}$$

provided that player II's Von Neumann and Morgenstern utility function $u_2 : \{\mathcal{L}, \mathcal{W}\} \to \mathbb{R}$ is chosen so that $u_2(\mathcal{L}) = 1$ and $u_2(\mathcal{W}) = 0$.

In the rest of the example, take $D = 1$ and let $d_0 = 0$, $d_1 = 0.1$, $d_2 = 0.2$ and so on. Thus $d_{10} = 1$ is the root of the game tree of Figure 2.6. The probability $p_1(d)$ is taken to be $1 - d$, and $p_2(d)$ to be $1 - d^2$. These are the choices for $p_1(d)$ and $p_2(d)$ used in the final paragraph of Section 2.4.1 for the case when $D = 1$.

It is now possible to construct a table showing the payoffs for each pair of pure strategies (d, e) under consideration.

---

[1] In fact, there will be many such pure strategies. Recall from Section 1.3 that a pure strategy must specify what a player will do at *every* decision node at which he makes the move, including those that will not be reached if he follows his own plan. To do things properly, we should therefore also specify what a player would do even at a node $e < d$ that will only be reached if he fails to carry out his plan of firing at node d. The simplest such pure strategy calls for him to plan to fire not only at d, but at any subsequent node if some misadventure should result in its being reached. The reason that we need not distinguish between the different pure strategies that are to be labeled with the letter d is that any two pure strategies of this type never lead to different outcomes. This is because they specify different behavior only at nodes that will never be reached. Two such pure strategies would therefore be indistinguishable if both were included in the strategic form of Duel.

	$d_9 = 0.9$	$d_7 = 0.7$	$d_5 = 0.5$	$d_3 = 0.3$	$d_1 = 0.1$
$d_{10} = 1.0$	1.00 0.00	1.00 0.00	1.00 0.00	1.00 0.00	1.00 0.00
$d_8 = 0.8$	0.19 0.81	0.80 0.20	0.80 0.20	0.80 0.20	0.80 0.20
$d_6 = 0.6$	0.19 0.81	0.51 0.49	0.60 0.40	0.60 0.40	0.60 0.40
$d_4 = 0.4$	0.19 0.81	0.51 0.49	0.75 0.25	0.40 0.60	0.40 0.60
$d_2 = 0.2$	0.19 0.81	0.51 0.49	0.75 0.25	0.91 0.09	0.20 0.80
$d_0 = 0.0$	0.19 0.81	0.51 0.49	0.75 0.25	0.91 0.09	0.99 0.01

Figure 4.1 A reduced strategic form for Duel.

Consider, for example, the pair $(d_2, d_5) = (0.2, 0.5)$. Since $d_2 < d_5$,

$$\pi_1(d_2, d_5) = 1 - p_2(d_5) = 1 - (1 - d_5^2) = d_5^2 = (0.5)^2 = 0.25;$$
$$\pi_2(d_2, d_5) = p_2(d_5) = 1 - d_5^2 = 1 - 0.25 = 0.75.$$

These payoffs belong in the cell of Figure 4.1 that lies in row d_2 and column d_5. Player I's payoff goes in the southwest corner of this cell and player II's payoff goes in the northeast corner.

4.1.3 Nash Equilibrium

The idea of a Nash equilibrium can be expressed particularly easily in terms of payoff functions. Recall from Section 1.8.1 that a pair (σ, τ) of strategies is a Nash equilibrium in a two-player game if σ is a best reply to τ, and τ is simultaneously a best reply to σ. This is the same as requiring that the inequalities

$$\left.\begin{array}{l} \pi_1(\sigma, \tau) \geq \pi_1(s, \tau) \\ \pi_2(\sigma, \tau) \geq \pi_2(\sigma, t) \end{array}\right\} \tag{4.3}$$

hold for all pure strategies s and t. The first inequality says that player I cannot improve on σ if player II does not deviate from τ. The second inequality says that player II cannot improve on τ if player I does not deviate from σ.

A reduced strategic form for Duel is given in Figure 4.1. The best payoff for player I in each column has been circled. For example, 0.40 has been circled in column d_5. Since 0.40 lies in row d_6, this tells us that pure strategy d_6 is player I's best reply to a choice of pure strategy d_5 by player II. Often there will be many best replies. For example, any pure strategy except d_{10} is a best reply for player I to a choice of pure strategy d_9 by player II.

The best payoff for player II in each row has also been circled. For example, 0.60 has been circled three times in row d_6. Pure strategies d_5, d_3 and d_1 are therefore best replies for player II to a choice of pure strategy d_6 by player I.

Notice that the only cell in Figure 4.1 that has *both* payoffs circled is that which lies in row d_6 and column d_5. Thus the only pure strategy pair that constitutes a Nash equilibrium is (d_6, d_5). Each pure strategy in this pair is a best reply to the other.[2]

How does this conclusion compare with the analysis of Duel offered in Section 2.4.1? In Section 2.4.1, Zermelo's algorithm was used to determine a subgame-perfect equilibrium for Duel. The method used in the current section is less refined in that it finds the set of *all* Nash equilibria.[3] The subgame-perfect equilibria lie in this set because any subgame-perfect equilibrium is also a Nash equilibrium (Section 1.8). But the set may also contain Nash equilibria that are not subgame-perfect. Fortunately, this difficulty does not arise here because only one Nash equilibrium exists and so this must be the subgame-perfect equilibrium that an application of Zermelo's algorithm would reveal.

The final paragraph of Section 2.4.1 observes that rational players will open fire when they are distance $\delta = (\sqrt{5} - 1)/2 = 0.62$ apart, provided that the nodes $d_0, d_1, \ldots, d_n$ are very

[2]Notice that (d_6, d_5) is a saddle point in Figure 4.1. As explained in Section 1.7.2, this means that the outcome $\pi_1(d_6, d_5) = 0.4$ is best for player I in its column, and worst for player I in its row. However, it is only in strictly competitive games like Duel that a Nash equilibrium is necessarily the same as a saddle point. In strictly competitive games, the second inequality of (4.3) is equivalent to $\pi_1(\sigma, \tau) \leq \pi_1(\sigma, t)$ because what is good for player II in such games is bad for player I. However, in more general games there need be no relationship at all between what is good for player II and what is bad for player I.

[3]That is, the set of all *pure* strategy Nash equilibria. There may also be *mixed* strategy Nash equilibria. (See Chapter 6.)

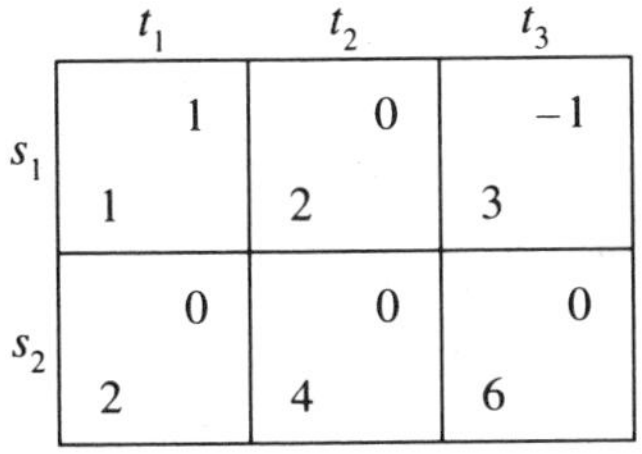

	t_1	t_2	t_3
s_1	1 (SW), 1 (NE)	2 (SW), 0 (NE)	3 (SW), −1 (NE)
s_2	2 (SW), 0 (NE)	4 (SW), 0 (NE)	6 (SW), 0 (NE)

Figure 4.2 A bimatrix game.

closely spaced. In the version of Duel studied here, the spacing between nodes is 0.1. This is not very small when compared with $D = 1$. Nevertheless, player I opens fire at distance $d_6 = 0.60$, which is quite close to δ.

4.2 Bimatrix Games

The payoff functions $\pi_i : S \times T \to \mathbb{R}$ are nothing more than a symbolic representation of the strategic form of a game. For example, suppose that player I has two pure strategies, s_1 and s_2, while player II has three pure strategies, t_1, t_2 and t_3. The players' payoff functions are defined by

$$\pi_1(s_i, t_j) = ij$$
$$\pi_2(s_i, t_j) = (i-2)(j-2).$$

The situation is illustrated by Figure 4.2. In this figure, row s represents player I's pure strategy s and column t represents player II's pure strategy t. Player I's payoff $\pi_1(s, t)$ is placed in the southwest corner of the cell in row s and column t. Player II's payoff $\pi_2(s, t)$ is placed in the northeast corner.

Sometimes such a strategic form representation is called a *bimatrix game* because it is determined by two *payoff matrices*.[4] In Figure 4.2, player I's payoff matrix is A and player II's payoff matrix is B, where

$$A = \begin{bmatrix} 1 & 2 & 3 \\ 2 & 4 & 6 \end{bmatrix}; \qquad B = \begin{bmatrix} 1 & 0 & -1 \\ 0 & 0 & 0 \end{bmatrix}.$$

4.2.1 Simultaneous-Move Games

In passing from the extensive form of a game to the strategic form, one makes things simpler from a mathematical point

[4]Matrices are briefly discussed in Section 4.3.

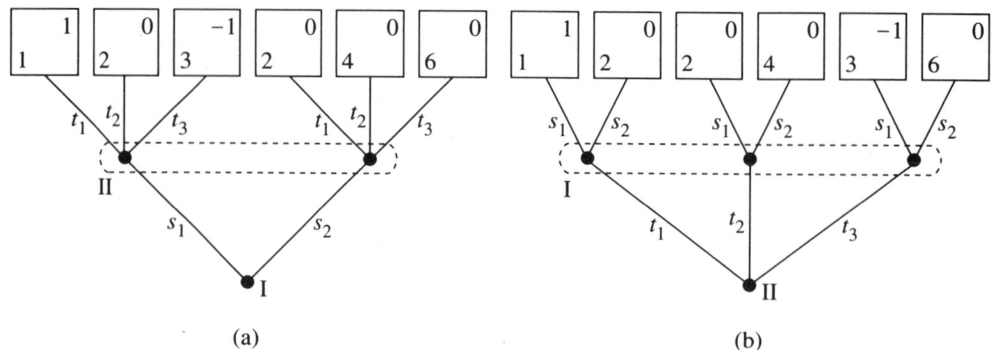

Figure 4.3 Simultaneous-move games.

of view. A game tree is a complicated mathematical object, whereas two matrices are easy to describe. Sometimes the gain in simplicity is achieved without any price having to be paid. For example, our study of a strategic form of Duel in Section 4.1.2 led to the same conclusion as our study of its extensive form in Section 2.4.1. However, as we shall see, matters are not always so satisfactory.

There is one class of games for which it is *guaranteed* that nothing is lost in passing to the strategic form. This is the class of simultaneous-move games. At first sight, it might be thought impossible to model such games as extensive forms, since a game tree, by its very nature, imposes a sequential order on the times at which events take place. However, consider the two games illustrated in Figure 4.3.

In the game of Figure 4.3(a), player I moves first, but the information set enclosing player II's two decision nodes ensures that she does not know player I's decision when she makes her own choice. Thus the two players might as well be moving simultaneously. The same is true in the game of Figure 4.3(b). Although player II moves first in this game, the fact that player I is ignorant of her choice when he decides on his own move means that both might as well be moving simultaneously.

Everything that matters about the two extensive forms of Figure 4.3 is therefore embodied in their common strategic form. This is the bimatrix game of Figure 4.2.

We have seen that nothing is lost in confining attention to the strategic form of a simultaneous-move game. The same is sometimes argued of games in general. The argument is that rational players can condense all their considerations into a

Phil 4.3 ⟶ single instant before the play of the game. In this instant, they simultaneously choose a pure strategy. Since rational players make optimal choices, the need for reconsideration will never arise. Thus, so the argument goes, *all* games can be regarded as simultaneous-move games, and therefore any extensive form can be replaced without loss by its strategic form.

This argument is not sound.[5] However, it is true that much can often be learned by examining only the strategic form of a game. Sometimes, as in Duel, one can learn everything that one wants to know.

4.3 Matrices

It is not necessary to know much about matrices to study bimatrix games. Even the material that follows is more than is really essential.

Review 4.5 ⟶ An $m \times n$ *matrix* is a rectangular array of numbers with m rows and n columns. Some examples are

$$A = \begin{bmatrix} 0 & 1 & 3 \\ -1 & 0 & 2 \end{bmatrix}; \qquad B = \begin{bmatrix} 1 & 2 \\ 0 & -1 \\ 3 & 0 \end{bmatrix}.$$

Note that A is a 2×3 matrix and B is a 3×2 matrix. Sometimes the notation used invites confusion between a matrix and a number. For example, the *zero matrix*, of whatever dimensions, is always denoted by 0. One writes

$$0 = \begin{bmatrix} 0 & 0 & 0 \\ 0 & 0 & 0 \end{bmatrix}; \qquad 0 = \begin{bmatrix} 0 & 0 \\ 0 & 0 \\ 0 & 0 \end{bmatrix}$$

and leaves the reader to deduce from the context whether 0 is the zero number or a zero matrix. However, it is always important to be quite clear about what is a number and what is a matrix. Often the difference is emphasized by referring to numbers as *scalars*.

---

[5]Even though it was proposed by Von Neumann and Morgenstern and continues to be defended by some eminent game theorists. The reason the argument is not sound is that an analysis of a game that takes for granted that suboptimal strategies are literally impossible cannot be adequate. For example, if suboptimal play were *literally* impossible in Duel, then the strategic form of Figure 4.1 would consist only of the single cell (d_6, d_5). To explain why strategies are optimal, it is necessary to consider the consequences of alternative strategies being played so that their suboptimality can be demonstrated. However, this rebuttal would not be adequate in the face of more sophisticated versions of the argument.

4.3.1 Matrix Arithmetic

Transposition. The *transpose*[6] $M^\top$ of a matrix M is obtained by taking the rows of $M^\top$ to be the columns of M. For example,

$$A^\top = \begin{bmatrix} 0 & -1 \\ 1 & 0 \\ 3 & 2 \end{bmatrix}; \qquad B^\top = \begin{bmatrix} 1 & 0 & 3 \\ 2 & -1 & 0 \end{bmatrix}.$$

Three simple facts are worth noting. First, it is always true that $(M^\top)^\top = M$. Second, if M is a 1×1 matrix, then $M = M^\top$. Third, if M is an $m \times n$ matrix, then $M = M^\top$ can only hold if $m = n$, which means that M is a *square* matrix. If $M = M^\top$ does hold, then M is called a *symmetric* matrix.

Matrix Addition. Two matrices can be added if and only if they have the same dimensions. Simply add the corresponding entries. For example,

$$A + B^\top = \begin{bmatrix} 0 & 1 & 3 \\ -1 & 0 & 2 \end{bmatrix} + \begin{bmatrix} 1 & 0 & 3 \\ 2 & -1 & 0 \end{bmatrix} = \begin{bmatrix} 1 & 1 & 6 \\ 1 & -1 & 2 \end{bmatrix};$$

$$B + 0 = \begin{bmatrix} 1 & 2 \\ 0 & -1 \\ 3 & 0 \end{bmatrix} + \begin{bmatrix} 0 & 0 \\ 0 & 0 \\ 0 & 0 \end{bmatrix} = \begin{bmatrix} 1 & 2 \\ 0 & -1 \\ 3 & 0 \end{bmatrix}.$$

One has to assume that the 0 in $B + 0$ represents the 3×2 zero matrix to make the expression meaningful. Notice, however that there is no way in which the expression

$$A + B = \begin{bmatrix} 0 & 1 & 3 \\ -1 & 0 & 2 \end{bmatrix} + \begin{bmatrix} 1 & 2 \\ 0 & -1 \\ 3 & 0 \end{bmatrix}$$

can be rendered meaningful.

Scalar Multiplication. Any matrix can be multiplied by any scalar. Simply multiply each matrix entry by the given scalar. For example,

$$4A = 4\begin{bmatrix} 0 & 1 & 3 \\ -1 & 0 & 2 \end{bmatrix} = \begin{bmatrix} 0 & 4 & 12 \\ -4 & 0 & 8 \end{bmatrix}$$

$$B - A^\top = \begin{bmatrix} 1 & 2 \\ 0 & -1 \\ 3 & 0 \end{bmatrix} + (-1)\begin{bmatrix} 0 & -1 \\ 1 & 0 \\ 3 & 2 \end{bmatrix} = \begin{bmatrix} 1 & 3 \\ -1 & -1 \\ 0 & -2 \end{bmatrix}.$$

[6]Often the notation M' is used for the transpose of M.

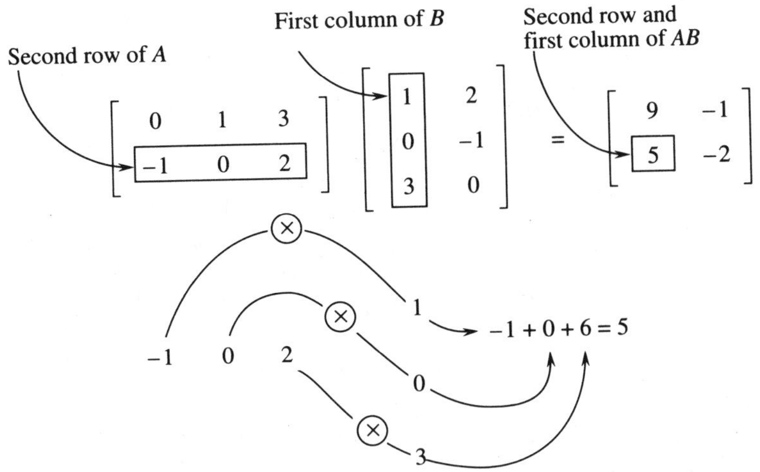

Figure 4.4 Multiplying matrices.

Matrix Multiplication. The matrix product CD is meaningful if C has the same number of columns as D has rows: *but not otherwise*. If C is an $m \times n$ matrix and D is an $n \times p$ matrix, then CD is an $m \times p$ matrix.

For example, if A is a 2×3 matrix and B is a 3×2 matrix, then the product AB is meaningful. It is the 2×2 matrix given by

$$AB = \begin{bmatrix} 0 & 1 & 3 \\ -1 & 0 & 2 \end{bmatrix} \begin{bmatrix} 1 & 2 \\ 0 & -1 \\ 3 & 0 \end{bmatrix} = \begin{bmatrix} 9 & -1 \\ 5 & -2 \end{bmatrix}.$$

The entries of AB are calculated as follows:

$$9 = \ \ 0 \times 1 + 1 \times 0 + 3 \times 3; \quad -1 = \ \ 0 \times 2 + 1 \times -1 + 3 \times 0;$$
$$5 = -1 \times 1 + 0 \times 0 + 2 \times 3; \quad -2 = -1 \times 2 + 0 \times -1 + 2 \times 0.$$

Consider the entry 5. This is in the *second* row and *first* column of AB. It is therefore computed using the *second* row of A and the *first* column of B. Simply multiply corresponding entries in the second row of A and the first column of B and sum the results as illustrated in Figure 4.4.

Some more examples of matrix products are

$$BA = \begin{bmatrix} 1 & 2 \\ 0 & -1 \\ 3 & 0 \end{bmatrix} \begin{bmatrix} 0 & 1 & 3 \\ -1 & 0 & 2 \end{bmatrix} = \begin{bmatrix} -2 & 1 & 7 \\ 1 & 0 & -2 \\ 0 & 3 & 9 \end{bmatrix}$$

$$B^{\top}A^{\top} = \begin{bmatrix} 1 & 0 & 3 \\ 2 & -1 & 0 \end{bmatrix} \begin{bmatrix} 0 & -1 \\ 1 & 0 \\ 3 & 2 \end{bmatrix} = \begin{bmatrix} 9 & 5 \\ -1 & -2 \end{bmatrix}.$$

Notice that $(AB)^\top = B^\top A^\top$. This useful identity is true whenever the product AB is meaningful.

It is necessary to be more than a little cautious when multiplying matrices. There is no guarantee that the product of two arbitrary matrices is meaningful. For example, one cannot multiply a 2×3 matrix by another 2×3 matrix, and so it is not meaningful to write $AB^\top$. Even when all the matrix products involved make sense, only some of the usual laws of multiplication are valid. For example, it is always true that $(LM)N = L(MN)$ when all the products are meaningful, but it need not be true that $LM = ML$, even when both sides make sense. Notice, for example, that $AB \neq BA$. The two matrices do not even have the same dimensions. The matrix AB is 2×2, whereas BA is 3×3.

4.4 Vectors

An n-dimensional vector can be thought of as a list of n real numbers $x_1, x_2, \ldots, x_n$. This list can be specified with the aid of the $n \times 1$ matrix

$$x = \begin{bmatrix} x_1 \\ x_2 \\ \vdots \\ x_n \end{bmatrix}.$$

The entries x_1, x_2, ..., x_n in this matrix are called the *coordinates* of the *column vector* x. Such a representation of a vector as a column is convenient when matrix algebra is to be used. Otherwise, it is more convenient to represent a vector as the $1 \times n$ matrix

$$x^\top = [x_1 \quad x_2 \quad \cdots \quad x_n],$$

since this consumes less space on a page. This notation for a *row vector* will be used interchangeably with the more common $x^\top = (x_1, x_2, \ldots, x_n)$.

The set of all n-dimensional vectors is denoted by $\mathbb{R}^n = \mathbb{R} \times \mathbb{R} \times \cdots \times \mathbb{R}$. A vector in $\mathbb{R}^2$ is usually interpreted as the location of a point in a plane referred to Cartesian axes. The zero vector $0 = (0, 0)$ serves as the origin for the pair of axes. Figure 4.5(a) shows the location of $x = (x_1, x_2)$ when this is thought of as specifying a point.

Figure 4.5(b) shows an alternative interpretation of a vector x as a displacement. With this interpretation, x means "move everything x_1 units to the right and x_2 units up". This displacement can be represented with an arrow whose blunt

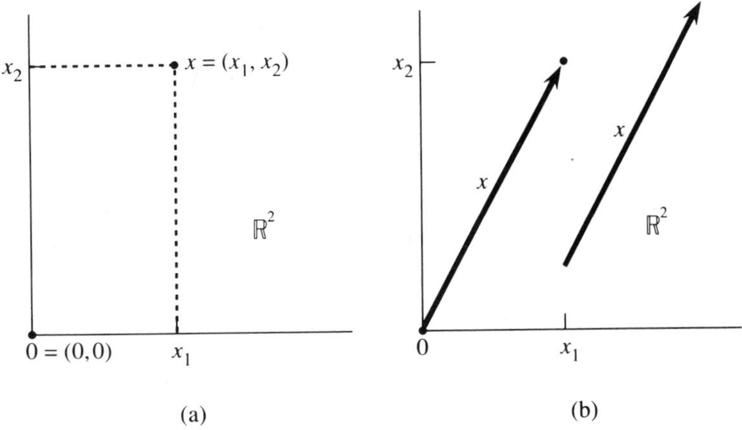

Figure 4.5 Vectors as points or displacements.

end is at 0 and whose sharp end lies at the location x. However, the same displacement can be represented by any arrow with the same length and direction.

4.4.1 Vector Arithmetic

Since vectors can be represented as matrices, they can be added together and multiplied by a scalar in the same way as matrices. If α and β are scalars, and x and y are vectors in $\mathbb{R}^2$, then the *linear combination* $\alpha x + \beta y$ is defined by

$$\alpha x + \beta y = \alpha(x_1, x_2) + \beta(y_1, y_2) = (\alpha x_1 + \beta y_1, \alpha x_2 + \beta y_2).$$

(Notice that a row vector representation has been chosen so that the definition will fit on just one line.)

The geometric significance of such expressions is very important. More on this will appear in Chapter 5. For the moment, simply observe that $x + y$ can be interpreted as the displacement that results from first using the displacement x and then using the displacement y. Figure 4.6(a) illustrates the idea. (It also clarifies why the rule for adding vectors x and y is called the *parallelogram law*.)

4.4.2 Orthogonal Vectors

Suppose that x and y are n-dimensional column vectors. One cannot simply multiply x and y because the product of two $n \times 1$ matrices is not meaningful (unless $n = 1$). However, the product $x^\top y$ *is* meaningful because $x^\top$ is a $1 \times n$ matrix

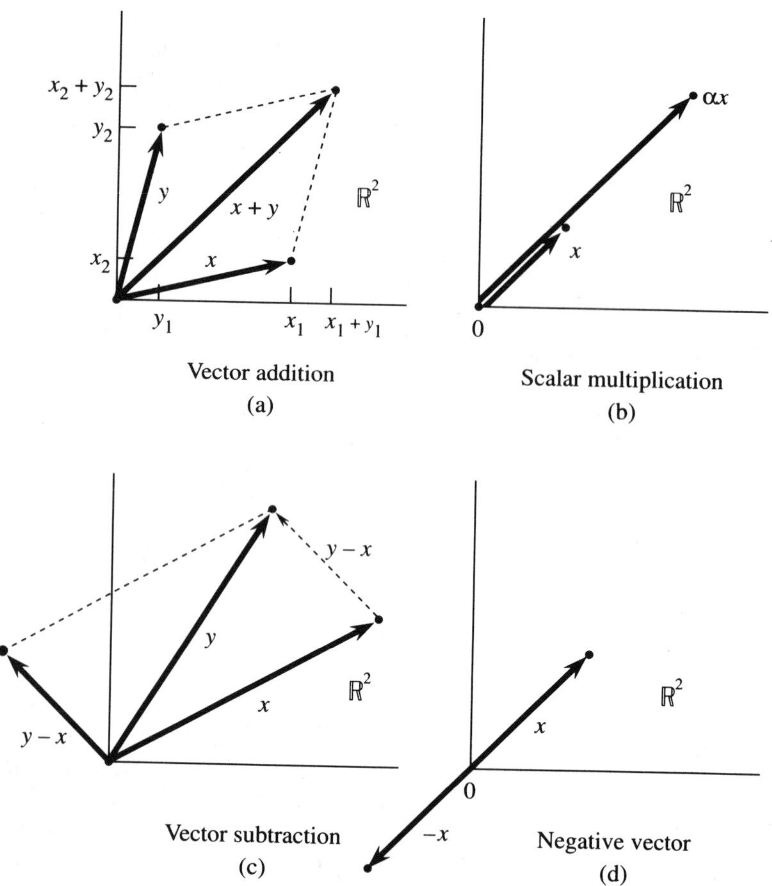

Figure 4.6 Vector addition and scalar multiplication.

and y is an $n \times 1$ matrix. The product of two such matrices is a 1×1 matrix. Thus $x^\top y$ is the scalar given by

$$x^\top y = [x_1 \quad x_2 \quad \cdots \quad x_n] \begin{bmatrix} y_1 \\ y_2 \\ \vdots \\ y_n \end{bmatrix} = x_1 y_1 + x_2 y_2 + \cdots + x_n y_n .$$

Mathematicians usually refer to $x^\top y$ as the *inner product* [7] of the vectors x and y.

As in the previous section, the geometric significance of the idea is important. To see why, it is necessary to introduce

[7]Often the notation $(x, y) = x^\top y$ is used in spite of the risk of confusion with the other uses of (x, y). Sometimes $x^\top y$ is called a *scalar product.* Sometimes it is written as $x \cdot y$ and called the *dot product.*

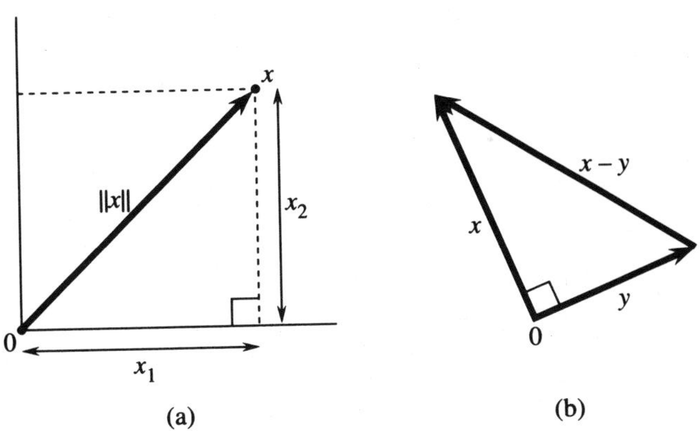

Figure 4.7 Pythagoras' theorem.

the notion of the *length* $\|x\|$ of a vector x. This is defined by

$$\|x\|^2 = x^\top x = x_1^2 + x_2^2 + \cdots + x_n^2 .$$

The case $n = 2$ is illustrated in Figure 4.7(a). Pythagoras' theorem then tells us that $\|x\|$ is simply the length of the arrow that represents x when thought of as a displacement.

Now apply Pythagoras' theorem in the right-angled triangle of Figure 4.7(b). Then, because[8] $y^\top x = x^\top y$,

$$\begin{aligned} \|x - y\|^2 &= \|x\|^2 + \|y\|^2 \\ (x - y)^\top(x - y) &= x^\top x + y^\top y \\ x^\top x - y^\top x - x^\top y + y^\top y &= x^\top x + y^\top y \\ x^\top y &= 0 . \end{aligned}$$

The important lesson to be learned from this piece of algebra is that a necessary and sufficient condition for two vectors x and y to be *orthogonal* (or perpendicular, or "at right angles") is that their inner product $x^\top y$ be zero.

4.4.3 Ordering Vectors

If x and y are n-dimensional vectors, then $x \leq y$ means that $x_1 \leq y_1,\ x_2 \leq y_2,\ \ldots,\ x_n \leq y_n$. For example,

$$(4, -1, 2, 0) \leq (4, 0, 3, 1); \qquad \begin{bmatrix} 2 \\ -1 \\ 1 \end{bmatrix} \leq \begin{bmatrix} 2 \\ 0 \\ 1 \end{bmatrix} \tag{4.4}$$

[8]Both sides of the equation are equal to $x_1y_1 + x_2y_2 + \cdots + x_ny_n$. Or, more elegantly, since $y^\top x$ is a scalar, it is equal to its own transpose. Thus $y^\top x = (y^\top x)^\top = x^\top(y^\top)^\top = x^\top y$.

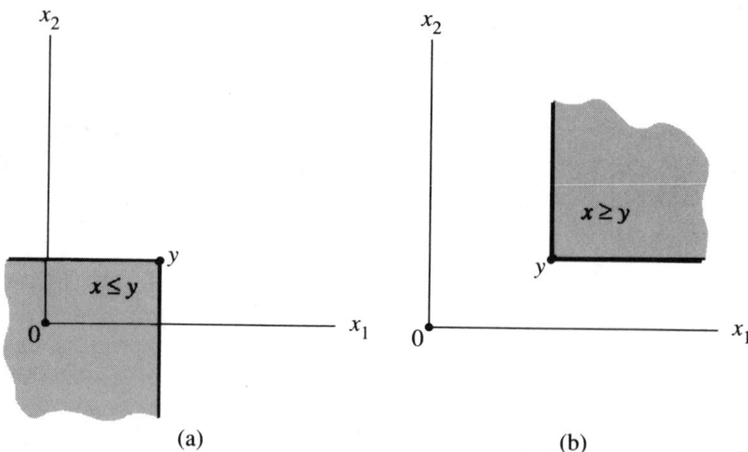

Figure 4.8 Ordering vectors in $\mathbb{R}^2$.

Figure 4.8(a) shows the set of all x in $\mathbb{R}^2$ such that $x \leq y$. Figure 4.8(b) shows the set of all x in $\mathbb{R}^2$ such that $x \geq y$. Notice that these two sets do not make up the whole of $\mathbb{R}^2$. That is, for some x and y, it is neither true that $x \leq y$ nor true that $x \geq y$. For example, it is false that $(1, 2) \geq (2, 1)$ and false that $(1, 2) \leq (2, 1)$.

The notation $x < y$ will be used to mean that $x \leq y$ but $x \neq y$. One may therefore replace both the $\leq$ symbols in (4.4) by $<$ symbols. The notation $x \ll y$ will be used to mean that $x_1 < y_1, x_2 < y_2, \ldots, x_n < y_n$. It would therefore be incorrect to replace the $\leq$ symbols in (4.4) by $\ll$ symbols. Some correct statements are

$$(4, -1, 2, 0) \ll (5, 0, 4, 1); \qquad \begin{bmatrix} 2 \\ -1 \\ 1 \end{bmatrix} \ll \begin{bmatrix} 4 \\ 5 \\ 7 \end{bmatrix}.$$

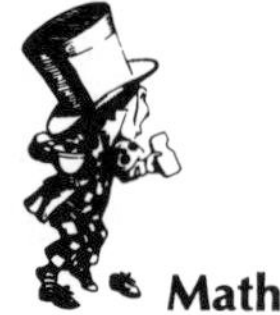
Math

4.5 Hyperplanes

What is the equation of a plane in $\mathbb{R}^3$? More precisely, what is the equation of the plane that passes through the point $y = (1, 2, 3)^\top$ and is orthogonal to the vector $p = (2, 2, 8)^\top$?

The diagram of Figure 4.9(a) will help in answering this question. If the point $x = (x_1, x_2, x_3)^\top$ lies in the plane, it must be that p is orthogonal to the vector $x - y$. The inner product of the vectors p and $x - y$ is therefore zero. That is,

$$p^\top(x - y) = 0.$$

Thus the equation of the plane is

$$p^\top x = c,$$

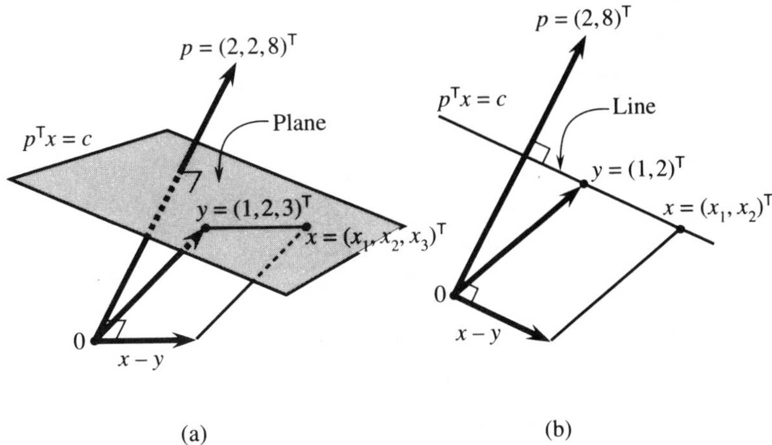

Figure 4.9 Hyperplanes.

where $c = p^\top y = 2 \times 1 + 2 \times 2 + 8 \times 3 = 30$. Alternatively, the equation can be written as

$$2x_1 + 2x_2 + 8x_3 = 30. \tag{4.5}$$

One might similarly ask for the equation of the line in $\mathbb{R}^2$ that passes through the point $y = (1,2)^\top$ and is orthogonal to the vector $p = (2,8)^\top$. This line is illustrated in Figure 4.9(b). The same reasoning as before shows the line to be $p^\top x = c$, where $c = p^\top y = 2 \times 1 + 8 \times 2 = 18$. This can be written as

$$2x_1 + 8x_2 = 18.$$

In general, if $p \neq 0$, the set of all x in $\mathbb{R}^n$ that satisfies the equation $p^\top x = c$ is called a *hyperplane*.[9] The vector p is a *normal* to the hyperplane. This simply means that it is orthogonal to the hyperplane. We have seen that the hyperplane $2x_1 + 8x_2 = 18$ in $\mathbb{R}^2$ is a line that has $(2,8)^\top$ as a normal. The hyperplane $2x_1 + 2x_2 + 8x_3 = 30$ in $\mathbb{R}^3$ is a regular plane with $(2,2,8)^\top$ as a normal. In $\mathbb{R}^n$, the linear equation

$$p_1 x_1 + p_2 x_2 + \cdots + p_n x_n = c$$

defines a hyperplane with $p = (p_1, p_2, \ldots, p_n)^\top$ as a normal.[10]

[9]The prefix "hyper" signifies an n-dimensional analog of some familiar three-dimensional object. Its use will be familiar from shows like Star Trek.

[10]A hyperplane does not have a *unique* normal. If p is a normal and $\lambda \neq 0$ is a scalar, then λp is also a normal. For example, $(1,1,4)^\top$ is a second normal to the plane defined by (4.5) since this equation can be rewritten as $x_1 + x_2 + 4x_3 = 15$.

Math 4.6 ⟶

4.5.1 Gradient Vectors

Calculus texts introduce the idea of the *gradient* of a differentiable function $f : \mathbb{R}^n \to \mathbb{R}$. The gradient vector $\nabla f(y)$ of f at the point y is

$$\nabla f(y) = (f_{x_1}(y), f_{x_2}(y), \ldots, f_{x_n}(y))^\top.$$

In this expression, $f_{x_i}(y)$ denotes the partial derivative $\partial f/\partial x_i$ evaluated at the point y.

For example, if $g : \mathbb{R}^2 \to \mathbb{R}$ is defined by $g(x_1, x_2) = x_1^2 x_2^3$, then

$$g_{x_1} = \frac{\partial g}{\partial x_1} = 2x_1 x_2^3 ; \qquad g_{x_2} = \frac{\partial g}{\partial x_2} = 3x_1^2 x_2^2 .$$

In the case when $y = (2, 1)^\top$,

$$\nabla g(y) = (g_{x_1}(2,1),\ g_{x_2}(2,1)) = (4, 12)^\top.$$

If the point y lies on the surface[11]

$$f(x) = c\,,$$

then $\nabla f(y)$ is a normal vector to the surface at the point y. This fact will be taken for granted here. It follows that the hyperplane

$$\nabla f(y)^\top (x - y) = 0$$

must be tangent to the surface $f(x) = c$ at the point y.

The diagram of Figure 4.10(a) shows the situation for the curve $x_1^2 x_2^3 = 4$. Since $y = (2, 1)^\top$ lies on the curve $g(x_1, x_2) = 4$, the vector $\nabla g(y) = (4, 12)^\top$ is normal to the curve $x_1^2 x_2^3 = 4$ at the point $(2, 1)^\top$. The tangent line[12] to the curve $x_1^2 x_2^3 = 4$ at the point $(2, 1)^\top$ is given by $4(x_1 - 2) + 12(x_2 - 1) = 0$.

Econ 4.6 ⟶

4.5.2 Price Vectors

Vectors are used in economics for many purposes. For example, in Section 3.2.1, Pandora was considering how much gin and vodka to buy with the \$10 in her pocket. Gin sold at \$4 a bottle and vodka at \$1 a bottle. She was therefore

[11]Some authors prefer to say "hypersurface".

[12]A more familiar derivation requires expressing the curve in the form $x_2 = h(x_1) = (4x_1^{-2})^{1/3}$. The slope of the required tangent line is then $h'(2) = -4^{1/3} \times \frac{2}{3} \times 2^{-5/3} = -2^{2/3} \times \frac{2}{3} \times 2^{-5/3} = -\frac{1}{3}$. To relate this to the discussion in the text, recall that

$$\frac{dx_2}{dx_1} = -\frac{\partial g/\partial x_1}{\partial g/\partial x_2}.$$

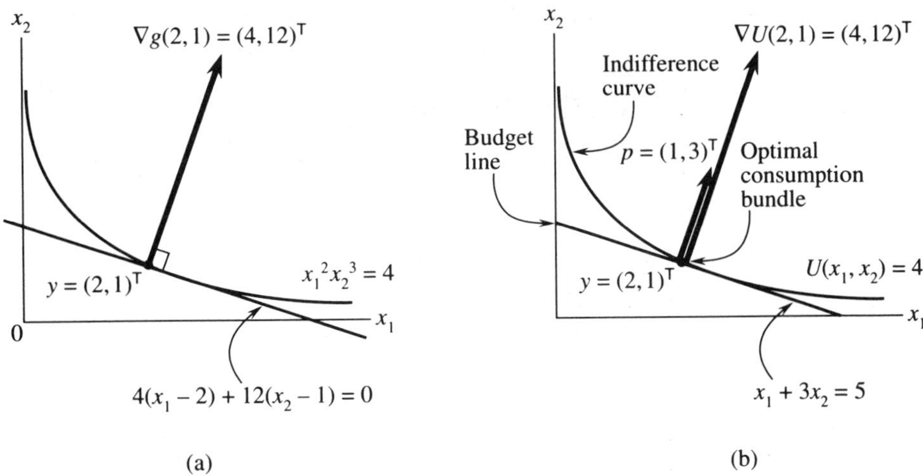

Figure 4.10 Normals and tangents.

able to buy any commodity bundle (g, v) on her budget line $4g + v = 10$. The immediate point is simply that the commodity bundle (g, v) is a two-dimensional vector.

In a more complicated situation, Pandora may have n commodities to consider. She would then have to choose an n-dimensional vector x from those she can afford. To determine which commodity bundles x she can afford, she needs an n-dimensional *price vector* p. The kth coordinate p_k of the price vector p is the price at which the kth commodity is traded. Thus the value of the commodity bundle x is $p_1x_1 + p_2x_2 + \cdots + p_nx_n$. If she has \$$I$ in her pocket and spends it all, the commodity bundle x that she buys will therefore satisfy $p_1x_1 + p_2x_2 + \cdots + p_nx_n = I$. Treating p and x as column vectors, we obtain the conclusion that a commodity bundle x purchased at prices p for an amount I lies on Pandora's *budget hyperplane*

$$p^\top x = I\,.$$

Figure 4.10(b) shows the case when $n = 2$. Pandora's utility function $U : \mathbb{R}^2_+ \to \mathbb{R}$ is defined by $U(x_1, x_2) = x_1^2 x_2^3$. The price vector p is given by $p = (1,3)^\top$. Thus the first commodity (gin) costs \$1 per unit and the second commodity (vodka) costs \$3 per unit. She has \$5 to spend. Her problem is to choose the optimal consumption bundle x subject to the constraint that x lie on her budget line $x_1 + 3x_2 = 5$.

The optimal bundle y must be located at a point where an indifference curve $U(x) = c$ touches the budget line $p^\top x = I$. At such a point, normals to $U(x) = c$ and $p^\top x = I$ must point in the same (or opposite) direction, as illustrated in Figure 4.10(b). Two vectors u and v point in the same (or opposite[13]) direction if and only if there is a scalar $\lambda \neq 0$ such that $u = \lambda v$. Since p is a normal to $U(x) = c$ at y, a necessary condition that y be optimal is that there exist a scalar $\lambda \neq 0$ such that

$$p = \lambda \nabla U(y) . \tag{4.6}$$

(Those who know about such things will recognize λ as a "Lagrangian multiplier" or "shadow price".)

In Pandora's case, (4.6) reduces to

$$\begin{bmatrix} 1 \\ 3 \end{bmatrix} = p = \lambda \nabla U(y) = \lambda \begin{bmatrix} U_{x_1}(y) \\ U_{x_2}(y) \end{bmatrix} = \begin{bmatrix} 2\lambda y_1 y_2^3 \\ 3\lambda y_1^2 y_2^2 \end{bmatrix} .$$

This vector equation can be written as the two scalar equations

$$1 = 2\lambda y_1 y_2^3 ,$$
$$3 = 3\lambda y_1^2 y_2^2 .$$

On dividing these equations, we obtain that

$$1 = \frac{2y_2}{y_1} .$$

This has to be solved along with the equation

$$y_1 + 3y_2 = 5 ,$$

which says that y lies on the budget line. The solutions are $y_1 = 2$ and $y_2 = 1$. Thus the optimal consumption bundle is $y = (2, 1)^\top$.

4.6 Domination

In the bimatrix game of Figure 4.2, player I has two pure strategies, s_1 and s_2. Pure strategy s_2 *strongly dominates* pure strategy s_1. This means that it is better for player I to use s_2 rather than s_1, *whatever* player II may do. The criterion in algebraic terms is that

$$\pi_1(s_2, t) > \pi_1(s_1, t) ,$$

for all three values of player II's pure strategy t. Row s_1 of player I's payoff matrix is $(1, 2, 3)$. Row s_2 is $(2, 4, 6)$. The criterion for s_2 to strongly dominate s_1 can be expressed in terms of these rows by writing

$$[2 \quad 4 \quad 6] \gg [1 \quad 2 \quad 3] .$$

[13]They point in the same direction if $\lambda > 0$, and in opposite directions if $\lambda < 0$.

None of player II's pure strategies in the bimatrix game of Figure 4.2 are strongly dominated. However, pure strategy t_1 *weakly dominates* pure strategy t_2. This means that player II can *never* lose by playing t_1 instead of t_2, and may sometimes gain. The criterion is therefore that

$$\pi_2(s, t_1) \geq \pi_2(s, t_2),$$

for each value of player I's pure strategy s, with *strict* inequality for at least one value of s. In terms of the columns of player II's payoff matrix, this translates into the requirement that

$$\begin{bmatrix} 1 \\ 0 \end{bmatrix} > \begin{bmatrix} 0 \\ 0 \end{bmatrix}.$$

Similarly, it is true that

$$\begin{bmatrix} 1 \\ 0 \end{bmatrix} > \begin{bmatrix} -1 \\ 0 \end{bmatrix} \quad \text{and} \quad \begin{bmatrix} 0 \\ 0 \end{bmatrix} > \begin{bmatrix} -1 \\ 0 \end{bmatrix}.$$

Hence, pure strategy t_1 weakly dominates pure strategy t_3, and pure strategy t_2 weakly dominates pure strategy t_3.

If strategy a strongly dominates strategy b, then it is also true that a weakly dominates b. Thus, to say that one strategy weakly dominates another includes the possibility that the domination may be strong. Confusion on this point can be avoided by simply saying that *a dominates b* where necessary. This implies that a weakly dominates b without risking the misunderstanding that the possibility of strong domination is to be excluded.

4.6.1 Deleting Dominated Strategies

A rational player will never use a strongly dominated strategy. In seeking the Nash equilibria of a bimatrix game, one may therefore begin by deleting all the rows and columns corresponding to strongly dominated strategies. For example, row s_1 may be deleted in the bimatrix game of Figure 4.2. This leaves the simple 1×3 bimatrix game of Figure 4.11.

In the 1×3 bimatrix game of Figure 4.11, none of player II's pure strategies are dominated, not even in the weak sense.

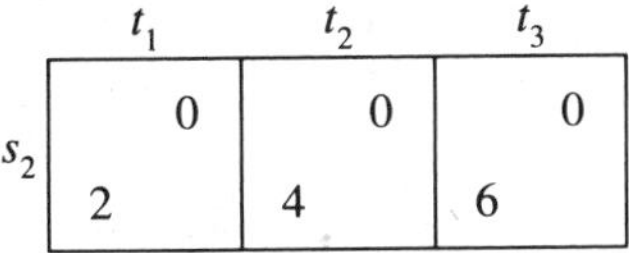

Figure 4.11 A simplified version of Figure 4.2.

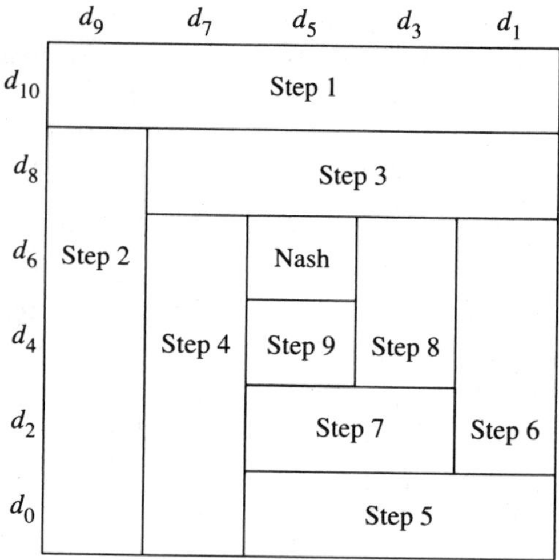

Figure 4.12 Successively deleting dominated strategies in Duel.

No further reductions can therefore be achieved using domination arguments. One can check that (s_2, t_1), (s_2, t_2) and (s_3, t_3) are all Nash equilibria of the game Figure 4.2. However, it will not always be true that only Nash equilibria are left after the process of deleting dominated strategies is complete.

Figure 4.12 demonstrates the use of the same technique with the 6×5 bimatrix game of Figure 4.1. Domination considerations are used to reduce the game to the single cell (d_6, d_5) that we already know to be the unique Nash equilibrium of this version of Duel. The steps in the reduction are listed below:

Step 1. Delete row d_{10} because it is *strongly* dominated by row d_8.

Step 2. In the 5×5 bimatrix game remaining, delete column d_9 because it is *strongly* dominated by column d_7.

Step 3. In the 5×4 bimatrix game remaining, delete row d_8 because it is *strongly* dominated by row d_6.

Step 4. In the 4×4 bimatrix game remaining, delete column d_7 because it is *strongly* dominated by column d_5.

Step 5. In the 4×3 bimatrix game remaining, delete row d_0 because it is *strongly* dominated by row d_6.

These deletions lead to a 3×3 bimatrix game in which no pure strategies are strongly dominated. If further progress is to be made, *weakly* dominated strategies must be deleted. But some caution is necessary in doing so. It cannot harm a rational player to discard his or her weakly dominated strategies, but this does not imply that it can *never* be rational to use a weakly dominated strategy. After the process of deleting dominated strategies is concluded, the simplified game that remains will always include at least one Nash equilibrium of the original game. But other Nash equilibria of the original game may have been lost if it became necessary to resort to weak domination along the way.

Step 6. In the 3×3 bimatrix game remaining after Step 5, delete column d_1 because it is *weakly* dominated by column d_3.

Step 7. In the 3×2 bimatrix game remaining, delete row d_2 because it is *strongly* dominated by row d_6.

Step 8. In the 2×2 bimatrix game remaining, delete column d_3 because it is *weakly* dominated by column d_5.

Step 9. In the 2×1 bimatrix game remaining, delete row d_4 because it is *strongly* dominated by row d_6.

This long sequence of deletions leaves the 1×1 bimatrix game consisting of the single cell of the original game that lies in row d_6 and column d_5. Thus, the pure strategy pair (d_6, d_5) must be a Nash equilibrium of the original game.

4.6.2 Rationality and Dominated Strategies

A player does not need to know anything about the opponent to decide that it can never be optimal to use a strongly dominated strategy. It is irrational to use a strongly dominated strategy regardless of whether the opponent is Von Neumann or a chimpanzee. However, to justify deleting column d_9 at Step 2 in Section 4.6.1, player II has to know that player I is sufficiently rational that he can be relied upon not to use the strongly dominated strategy d_{10}. Similarly, to justify deleting row d_8 at Step 3, player I has to know that player II will delete column d_9 at Step 2. Thus player I has to know that player II knows that player I is not so irrational as to play a strongly dominated strategy. To justify the deletion of column d_7 at Step 4, player II has to know that player I knows that player II knows that player I is not so irrational as to play a strongly dominated strategy. To justify an arbitrary number of deletions of strongly dominated strategies, it is necessary to assume that it is *common knowledge* that no player is sufficiently irrational as to play a strongly dominated strategy.

This is not the first time that common knowledge has been mentioned. At this stage, however, it is important that the terminology be understood in the technical sense in which game theorists use it. In game theory, something is common knowledge if everybody knows it; everybody knows that everybody knows it; everybody knows that everybody knows that everybody knows it; and so on. Game theorists usually assume that the rules of the game and the preferences of the players are common knowledge. In analyzing a game, they typically need also to assume that the fact that all the players subscribe to appropriate rationality principles is also common knowledge, although they are seldom explicit on this point. The weakest of all such rationality principles is that which counsels against the use of strongly dominated strategies.[14]

4.6.3 Perfection and Dominated Strategies

The game to be used in this section is given in Figure 4.13. Both its extensive form and its strategic form are shown. (Notice that player II has *four* pure strategies LL, LR, RL and RR for the reasons given in Section 1.3.) The best payoffs for player I in each column of the strategic form have been circled. Similarly, for player II's best payoffs in each row. This allows us to identify the *three* pairs of pure strategies that are Nash equilibria: namely, (r, LR), (l, RL) and (r, RR). The doubled edges in the extensive form are obtained by using Zermelo's algorithm. This reveals that only (r, RR) is a subgame-perfect equilibrium. Recall from Section 1.8.2 that some Nash equilibria are not acceptable, since they call upon players to plan to make irrational moves at nodes that would not be reached if the Nash equilibrium strategies were used. For example, the Nash equilibrium (r, LR) calls upon player II to take action L at node b. This is an irrational plan because choosing L at node b gives player II a payoff of 0 while choosing R at node b gives her a payoff of 3. Similarly, the Nash equilibrium (l, RL) calls upon player II to make the irrational choice L at node c. Only the subgame-perfect

[14] More on these issues appears in Chapter 10. Section 10.8.2 is particularly relevant.

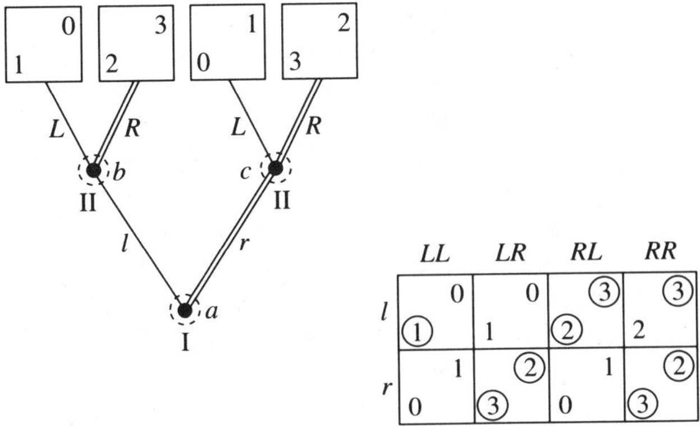

	LL	LR	RL	RR
l	①, 0	1, 0	②, ③	2, ③
r	0, 1	③, ②	0, 1	③, ②

Figure 4.13 Nash and subgame-perfect equilibria.

Nash equilibrium (r, RR) is free from such irrationalities and hence is viable as a rational solution of the game.

One might object that it does not matter that player II plans to act irrationally at node c when the Nash equilibrium (l, RL) is used, because node c will not be reached if player I chooses l at node a. But this is not correct. The reason that players continue to use their equilibrium strategies is because of what *would happen* if they *were* to deviate. Suppose, for example, that a supposedly authoritative game theory book recommended the Nash equilibrium (l, RL) for rational players in the game of Figure 4.13. After reading the book, player I would anticipate that player II would play R if node b were reached, and L if node c were reached. He would therefore want to follow the book's advice to play l because this gives him a payoff of 2 whereas playing r gives him a payoff of only 0. Thus node c would not be reached. But the book's statement of what II should plan to do if node c is reached is far from irrelevant. It is this plan that deters player I from choosing r. But player I should not be so easily deterred. Instead of trusting the game theory book, he should ask himself: will player II really follow the book's advice and choose L if I play r? Since it is incredible that a rational player II would do so, player I ought to conclude that the game theory book's advice is worthless. A game theory book that recommends (l, RL) therefore cannot sustain a reputation for being authoritative. It will only survive the type of critical examination outlined above if it recommends the subgame-perfect equilibrium (r, RR).

So far this section has been a reprise of ideas that have been presented earlier. Now the time has come to link the ideas with the deletion of dominated strategies. In the strategic form of

Figure 4.13, player II's pure strategy RR strongly dominates LL. It also weakly dominates both LR and RL. On deleting LL, LR and RL, we are left with a 2×1 game in which player I's pure strategy r strongly dominates l. Thus, the successive deletion of dominated strategies leads to the subgame-perfect equilibrium (r, RR).

This is no accident. Zermelo's algorithm and the deletion of dominated strategies are closely related in finite games of perfect information.[15] For example, the edge R at node b is doubled in the game tree of Figure 4.13 because the use of R at b gives player II a payoff of 3 while the use of L at b gives her only 0. In terms of strategies, this observation may be expressed by saying that Rx weakly dominates Lx, both when $x = L$ and when $x = R$. That is to say, Rx is at least as good as Lx, whatever player I may do. Similarly, the doubling of edge R at node c corresponds to the observation that yR weakly dominates yL, both when $y = L$ and when $y = R$. Doubling the R edges at nodes b and c therefore corresponds to deleting the dominated strategies LL, LR and RL from the strategic form. Doubling edge r at node a corresponds to deleting the dominated strategy l in the game that then remains.

4.6.4 Words of Warning

Some game theorists are very enthusiastic about the successive deletion of dominated strategies. You will therefore sometimes find the method recommended without reservation as a way of "solving" those games in which its use leads to a unique strategy profile. My own view is that, since it is not necessarily irrational to use a *weakly* dominated strategy, caution is necessary when such strategies are deleted lest something that matters is thrown away by mistake.[16]

However, there is no doubt of the value of the technique as a computational device, provided that it is used with discretion. In particular, it is important to bear in mind that equilibria may be lost when weakly dominated strategies are deleted. Section 4.6.1 makes this point for the case of Nash equilibria, but it is also true that subgame-perfect equilibria

[15]Recall that a game of perfect information is one in which a player always knows what has happened in the game so far. Information sets always enclose only one node. The simultaneous-move games of Section 4.2.1 are therefore games of imperfect information.

[16]The literature now contains a number of examples that confirm the need for such caution. Van Damme's example appears as Exercise 7.9.34.

can be eliminated—even in finite games of perfect information. Usually, the equilibria that get eliminated deserve no better fate, because nobody would ever use them in the real-world situation from which the game was abstracted. But one cannot count on this being the case.

For this reason, the method of successively deleting dominated strategies is used sparingly in this book—and never to decide which of several equilibria should be regarded as the "solution" of a game. For example, in Section 4.7, it is used as an auxiliary device to determine the subgame-perfect equilibria of a finite game of perfect information whose strategic form is known. As Section 4.6.3 explains, it can be used for this purpose provided that dominated strategies are deleted from the strategic form *in the same order* that they would be deleted when Zermelo's algorithm is used in the extensive form. One is then guaranteed that no subgame-perfect equilibria will be lost along the way.[17] If the end product is unique, it *must* therefore be a subgame-perfect equilibrium.[18]

The *order* in which dominated strategies are deleted has been emphasized in the preceding discussion because it really can sometimes make a difference. It never matters in which order *strongly* dominated strategies are deleted, but Exercise 4.8.20 illustrates that different end products may sometimes be obtained by changing the order in which *weakly* dominated strategies are eliminated. In particular, it is possible to lose subgame-perfect equilibria in a finite game of perfect information if one deletes weakly dominated strategies in the wrong order.

Math

4.7 Russian Roulette Again

The game of Russian Roulette was introduced in Section 3.3 to make it clear that one cannot analyze games in general without information about the players' attitudes to taking

[17]However, one is not guaranteed that *only* subgame-perfect equilibria will be left at the end of the process. Even in finite games of perfect information, there need be no precise correspondence between using Zermelo's algorithm and deleting dominated strategies in the appropriate order. The reason is that, when using Zermelo's algorithm, one sometimes has a choice to make about which of several equally good edges to double—as in the game of Figure 1.18. No strategies are dominated in the strategic form of this game, and hence the successive deletion of dominated strategies eliminates nothing at all.

[18]Since Zermelo's algorithm necessarily terminates after a finite number of steps, finite games of perfect information always have at least one subgame-perfect equilibrium.

risks. Von Neumann and Morgenstern utility functions take care of this problem. This section returns to Russian Roulette to see how this works out in practice.

In Russian Roulette, each player has to evaluate three outcomes, $\mathcal{L}$, $\mathcal{D}$ and $\mathcal{W}$, which we can think of as death, disgrace and triumph. Let $\Omega = \{\mathcal{L}, \mathcal{D}, \mathcal{W}\}$, and choose Von Neumann and Morgenstern utility functions $u_1 : \Omega \to \mathbb{R}$ and $u_2 : \Omega \to \mathbb{R}$ so that

$$u_1(\mathcal{L}) = 0, \qquad u_1(\mathcal{D}) = a, \qquad u_1(\mathcal{W}) = 1,$$
$$u_2(\mathcal{L}) = 0, \qquad u_2(\mathcal{D}) = b, \qquad u_2(\mathcal{W}) = 1.$$

Recall that $u_i(\mathcal{D}) = q$ means that player i will swap $\mathcal{D}$ for the lottery $\mathbf{q}$ in which he gets $\mathcal{L}$ with probability $1 - q$ and $\mathcal{W}$ with probability q. Thus, the smaller the value of $u_i(\mathcal{D})$, the readier a player will be to take a risk.[19]

Figure 4.14(a) shows an extensive form of version 2 of Russian Roulette in which each terminal node is labeled with the payoffs corresponding to the outcome it represents. Figure 4.14(b) is a simplified strategic form in which only four of each player's eight pure strategies have been included. Russian Roulette is a game of timing like Duel. All that really matters is how long a player is prepared to wait before chickening out. Thus we only really need one pure strategy for each possible waiting time.

Figure 4.15 illustrates a method for calculating the entries in the strategic form for the pure strategy pair (AAD, ADD). When this pure strategy pair is used, the possible plays of the game that might result depend on the choices made by Chance. Her choices are denoted by a for "across" and d for "down". The play $[AaAaAd]$ occurs if Chance plays a at the first and second chance move and then d at the third chance move. The probability[20] of this play is $\text{prob}(aad) = \frac{5}{6} \times \frac{4}{5} \times \frac{1}{4} = \frac{1}{6}$. The expected utility of the

---

[19]If you feel that the awfulness of being dead is being undervalued in this discussion, note first that it would make no substantive difference to the analysis if we were to take $u_i(\mathcal{L}) = -1{,}000$ instead of $u_i(\mathcal{L}) = 0$. This would just represent a recalibration of the utility scales as explained in Section 3.5. It would be totally unrealistic to take $u_i(\mathcal{L}) = -\infty$, even if this were allowed by the Von Neumann and Morgenstern theory. Such a choice would imply that a player would be unwilling to cross a busy street even if offered a million dollars to do so. The reason is that, no matter how much care he took, there would still remain some small but positive probability of his being run over. The player's expected utility from taking up the offer would therefore necessarily be $-\infty$.

[20]Rather than calculate, one may simply observe that this is the probability $\frac{1}{6}$ that the bullet is in the third chamber of the revolver.

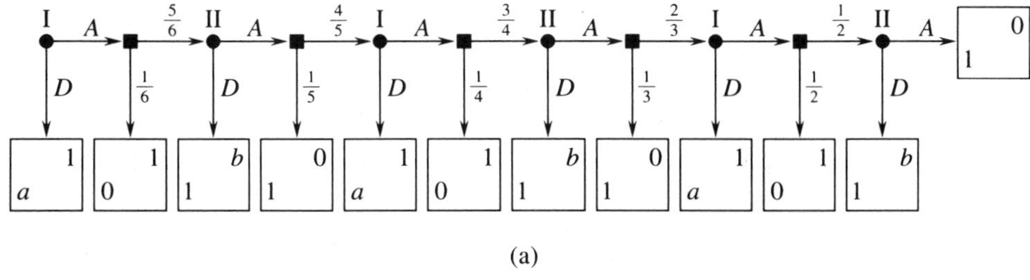

(a)

	DDD	*ADD*	*AAD*	*AAA*
DDD	a, 1	a, 1	a, 1	a, 1
ADD	$\frac{5}{6}$, $\frac{1}{6}+\frac{5}{6}b$	$\frac{1}{6}+\frac{2}{3}a$, $\frac{5}{6}$	$\frac{1}{6}+\frac{2}{3}a$, $\frac{5}{6}$	$\frac{1}{6}+\frac{2}{3}a$, $\frac{5}{6}$
AAD	$\frac{5}{6}$, $\frac{1}{6}+\frac{5}{6}b$	$\frac{2}{3}$, $\frac{1}{3}+\frac{1}{2}b$	$\frac{1}{3}+\frac{1}{3}a$, $\frac{2}{3}$	$\frac{1}{3}+\frac{1}{3}a$, $\frac{2}{3}$
AAA	$\frac{5}{6}$, $\frac{1}{6}+\frac{5}{6}b$	$\frac{2}{3}$, $\frac{1}{3}+\frac{1}{2}b$	$\frac{1}{2}$, $\frac{1}{2}+\frac{1}{6}b$	$\frac{1}{2}$, $\frac{1}{2}$

(b)

Figure 4.14 A simplified strategic form for Russian Roulette.

lottery resulting from the use of (AAD, ADD) is obtained by multiplying each of a player's payoffs by the probability with which it occurs and then summing the resulting products. Thus

$$\pi_1(AAD, ADD) = 0 \times \tfrac{1}{6} + 1 \times \tfrac{1}{6} + 0 \times \tfrac{1}{6} + 1 \times \tfrac{1}{2} = \tfrac{2}{3},$$
$$\pi_2(AAD, ADD) = 1 \times \tfrac{1}{6} + 0 \times \tfrac{1}{6} + 1 \times \tfrac{1}{6} + b \times \tfrac{1}{2} = \tfrac{1}{3} + \tfrac{1}{2}b.$$

Case 1 of Figure 4.16 has $a = 0.25$ and $b = 0.55$. Thus player I is more reckless than player II. How does this affect the way the game is played? To answer this question, we shall study the the subgame-perfect equilibria of the game.

As Exercise 4.8.25 illustrates, the chance moves in the extensive form of Russian Roulette complicate the direct use of Zermelo's algorithm. However, we can mimic the use of

Plays	[*Ad*]	[*AaAd*]	[*AaAaAd*]	[*AaAaAaD*]
Payoffs	0 / 1	1 / 0	0 / 1	1 / b
Probabilities	$\frac{1}{6}$	$\frac{5}{6} \times \frac{1}{5} = \frac{1}{6}$	$\frac{5}{6} \times \frac{4}{5} \times \frac{1}{4} = \frac{1}{6}$	$\frac{5}{6} \times \frac{4}{5} \times \frac{3}{4} = \frac{1}{2}$

Figure 4.15 The lottery that results from the use of (*AAD, ADD*).

Zermelo's algorithm in the extensive form of the game by deleting dominated strategies from the strategic form in the same order that they would be eliminated if Zermelo's algorithm were used in the extensive form. In using Zermelo's algorithm, we would begin at the last decision node, where player II has to choose between A and D. As explained in Section 4.6.3, this choice is equivalent to deciding between her pure strategies AAA and AAD. Our first step in deleting strategies from case 1 of Figure 4.16 is therefore to decide which of the columns AAA and AAD dominates the other. For the second step, it is necessary to transfer our attention to the last decision node but one. At this node, player I has to choose between A and D. This choice is equivalent to deciding between his pure strategies AAA and AAD. Thus step 2 consists of determining which of rows AAA and AAD dominates the other after the column deleted at step 1 has been removed. The full sequence of steps is as follows:

Step 1. Delete column AAA because it is dominated by column AAD.

Step 2. Delete row AAD in the game that remains because it is dominated by row AAA.

Step 3. Delete column AAD in the game that remains because it is dominated by column ADD.

Step 4. Delete row ADD in the game that remains because it is dominated by row AAA.

Step 5. Delete column ADD in the game that remains because it is dominated by column DDD.

Step 6. Delete row DDD in the game that remains because it is dominated by row AAA.

After these deletions have been made, only the pure strategy pair (AAA, DDD) remains. For the reasons given in

	DDD	ADD	AAD	AAA
DDD	(1.00) / 0.25	(1.00) / 0.25	(1.00) / 0.25	(1.00) / 0.25
ADD	0.63 / (0.83)	(0.83) / 0.33	(0.83) / 0.33	(0.83) / 0.33
AAD	0.63 / (0.83)	0.61 / (0.67)	(0.67) / 0.42	(0.67) / 0.42
AAA	(0.63) / (0.83)	0.61 / (0.67)	0.59 / (0.50)	0.50 / (0.50)

Case 1: $a = 0.25,\ b = 0.55$

	DDD	ADD	AAD	AAA
DDD	(1.00) / 0.25	(1.00) / 0.25	(1.00) / 0.25	(1.00) / 0.25
ADD	0.37 / (0.83)	(0.83) / 0.33	(0.83) / 0.33	(0.83) / 0.33
AAD	0.37 / (0.83)	0.46 / (0.67)	0.67 / 0.42	(0.67) / 0.42
AAA	0.37 / (0.83)	0.46 / (0.67)	(0.54) / (0.50)	0.50 / (0.50)

Case 2: $a = 0.25,\ b = 0.25$

	DDD	ADD	AAD	AAA
DDD	(1.00) / (0.95)	(1.00) / (0.95)	(1.00) / (0.95)	(1.00) / (0.95)
ADD	(0.96) / 0.83	0.83 / 0.80	0.83 / 0.80	0.83 / 0.80
AAD	(0.96) / 0.83	0.81 / 0.67	0.67 / 0.65	0.67 / 0.65
AAA	(0.96) / 0.83	0.81 / 0.67	0.66 / 0.50	0.50 / 0.50

Case 3: $a = 0.95,\ b = 0.95$

Figure 4.16 Three special cases.

	Parameter values		Player I	Player II
I reckless, II cautious	$a = 0.25$	$b = 0.55$	*AAA*	*DDD*
Both reckless	$a = 0.25$	$b = 0.25$	*AAA*	*AAD*
Both cautious	$a = 0.95$	$b = 0.95$	*DDD*	*DDD*

Figure 4.17 Comparing behavior in the three cases studied.

Section 4.6.4, it follows that this is the unique subgame-perfect equilibrium of the game.[21]

Case 2 of Figure 4.16 has $a = 0.25$ and $b = 0.25$, so that both player I and player II are reckless. Proceeding as in case 1 by deleting dominated strategies in the appropriate order, we find that the unique subgame-perfect equilibrium is (AAA, AAD).

Case 3 has $a = 0.95$ and $b = 0.95$, so that both player I and player II are cautious. Here the unique subgame-perfect equilibrium is (DDD, DDD). (Notice that, in case 3, there are *four* Nash equilibria, but three of these get deleted along the way and so are not subgame-perfect.)

Figure 4.17 summarizes the conclusions. The important thing to observe is that the players' attitudes to taking risks make a big difference to the way the game is played. But do not seek to draw any conclusions from the *payoffs* that each player gets in different versions of the game. Recall from Section 3.5.3 that it does not necessarily make any sense to compare different players' utils.

One should not, for example, compare case 2 and case 3, and conclude that two middle-aged, cautious gentlemen do better in playing the game against each other than two hot-blooded youngsters. It is true that both players get a payoff of about 1 in case 3, while both players get a payoff of only about $\frac{1}{2}$ in case 2. But how sweet is it to triumph for certain when you are an old man? Not nearly as sweet perhaps as half a chance of triumphing may seem to a youth, even if the down side of the coin is half a chance of getting shot.

---

[21] An alternative route to the same conclusion is to circle the best payoff for player I in each column and the best payoff for player II in each row. This will show that the only pure strategy pair that is a Nash equilibrium is (AAA, DDD). Since a subgame-perfect equilibrium exists and any subgame-perfect equilibrium is also a Nash equilibrium (Section 1.8.2), it follows that (AAA, DDD) must be subgame-perfect.

4.8 Exercises

1. Construct a simplified strategic form for Duel just as in Section 4.1.2, but taking $p_1(d) = p_2(d) = 1 - d^2$. (This case was studied in Exercise 2.6.13, but here $D = 1$.) Circle the best payoff for player I in each column and the best payoff to player II in each row. Hence locate a Nash equilibrium. How close will the players be when someone fires? Who will fire first?

2. Jerry can hide in the bedroom, the den or the kitchen. Tom can search in one and only one of these locations. If he searches where Jerry is hiding, he catches Jerry for certain. Otherwise Jerry escapes.
   (a) Assign appropriate Von Neumann and Morgenstern utilities to the possible outcomes.
   (b) Draw the game tree for the case when Tom can see where Jerry hides before searching. Find the 3×27 bimatrix game that is the corresponding strategic form. (Jerry is player I.)
   (c) Draw the game tree for the case when Jerry can see where Tom searches before hiding. Find the 27×3 bimatrix game that is the corresponding strategic form.
   (d) Draw two game trees that both correspond to the case when Tom and Jerry each make their decisions in ignorance of the other's choice. Find the 3×3 bimatrix game that is the corresponding strategic form.
   (e) In each case, find all pure strategy pairs that are Nash equilibria.[22]

Review

3. Given

$$A = \begin{bmatrix} 2 & 1 & 3 \\ -1 & 4 & 0 \end{bmatrix}, \quad B = \begin{bmatrix} 1 & 2 \\ 0 & -1 \\ 3 & 0 \end{bmatrix}, \quad C = \begin{bmatrix} 0 & 1 \\ -1 & 2 \\ 0 & 4 \end{bmatrix}$$

decide which of the following expressions are meaningful. Where they are meaningful, find the matrix they represent.

(a) $A + B$ (b) $B + C$ (c) $A^\top + B$
(d) $3A$ (e) $3B - 2C$ (f) $A - (B + C)^\top$

[22]The economics literature is often confusing when considering economic equivalents of such cat-and-mouse games. See Section 7.2.2 for a discussion of the notion of a "Stackelberg equilibrium".

Review 4. Answer the following questions for the matrices

$$A = \begin{bmatrix} 0 & 2 \\ 4 & 1 \\ 0 & 3 \end{bmatrix}, \quad B = \begin{bmatrix} 0 & 1 \\ 2 & 0 \end{bmatrix}, \quad C = \begin{bmatrix} 1 & 2 \\ 2 & 1 \end{bmatrix}.$$

(a) Why is AB meaningful? Why is BA not meaningful? Calculate AB.
(b) Why are both BC and CB meaningful? Is it true that $BC = CB$?
(c) Work out $(AB)C$ and $A(BC)$ and show that these are equal.
(d) Check that $(BC)^\top = C^\top B^\top$.

Review 5. Show that the system of "linear equations"

$$\left.\begin{aligned} 2x_1 - x_2 &= 4 \\ x_1 - 2x_2 &= 3 \end{aligned}\right\}$$

can be expressed in the form $Ax = b$, with

$$A = \begin{bmatrix} 2 & -1 \\ 1 & -2 \end{bmatrix}, \quad x = \begin{bmatrix} x_1 \\ x_2 \end{bmatrix}, \quad \text{and} \quad b = \begin{bmatrix} 4 \\ 3 \end{bmatrix}.$$

Review 6. Given the 2×1 column vectors

$$x = \begin{bmatrix} 2 \\ 1 \end{bmatrix}, \quad y = \begin{bmatrix} 4 \\ -3 \end{bmatrix}, \quad z = \begin{bmatrix} 0 \\ 2 \end{bmatrix},$$

find
(a) $x + y$
(b) $3y$
(c) $-2z$
(d) $y - z$
(e) $2x + y$
Illustrate each result geometrically.

Review 7. If x and y are $n \times 1$ column vectors, explain why $x^\top y$ and $xy^\top$ are always both defined, but $x^\top y \neq xy^\top$ unless $n = 1$. Why is it true that $x^\top y = y^\top x$ for all n?

Review 8. Given the 3×1 column vectors

$$x = \begin{bmatrix} 3 \\ 2 \\ 1 \end{bmatrix}, \quad y = \begin{bmatrix} -3 \\ 1 \\ -2 \end{bmatrix}, \quad z = \begin{bmatrix} 1 \\ -1 \\ -2 \end{bmatrix},$$

find
(a) $x^\top x$ (b) $x^\top y$ (c) $x^\top z$
(d) $y^\top z$ (e) $\|x\|$ (f) $\|x - y\|$
Verify that $x^\top(3y + 2z) = 3x^\top y + 2x^\top z$.

Review 9. Use the results of Exercise 4.8.8 to determine each of the following:

(a) The distance from 0 to x
(b) The distance from x to y
(c) Which two of the vectors x, y and z are orthogonal

Review

10. For each 1×2 vector y, the sets

$$A = \{x : x \geq y\}$$
$$B = \{x : x > y\}$$
$$C = \{x : x \gg y\}$$

represent regions in $\mathbb{R}^2$. Sketch these regions in the case $y = (1, 2)$. For each of the following 1×2 vectors z, decide whether z is a member of A, B or C:
(a) $z = (2, 3)$ (b) $z = (2, 2)$
(c) $z = (1, 2)$ (d) $z = (2, 1)$

11. Each of the following equations defines a plane in $\mathbb{R}^3$. In each case, write down a vector p that is orthogonal to the plane and has the property that $p_1 \geq 0$, $p_2 \geq 0$, $p_3 \geq 0$ and $p_1 + p_2 + p_3 = 1$.
(a) $x_1 + 2x_2 + 3x_3 = 10$
(b) $-x_1 - 3x_2 - 2x_3 = 6$
(c) $x_2 + x_3 = 0$

12. Each of the following equations defines a line in $\mathbb{R}^2$. In each case, write down a vector p that is orthogonal to the line and has the property that $p_1 \geq 0, p_2 \geq 0$ and $p_1 + p_2 = 1$.
(a) $x_1 + 2x_2 = 10$
(b) $-x_1 - 3x_2 = 6$
(c) $x_2 = 0$

How is the slope of each of these lines related to the ratio p_1/p_2?

Math

13. Find $\nabla g(1, 2)$ in the case when $g : \mathbb{R}^2 \to \mathbb{R}$ is defined by $g(x_1, x_2) = x_1^2 x_2$. Hence determine a normal vector to the curve $x_1^2 x_2 = 2$ at the point $(1, 2)^\top$. Write down the equation of the tangent line at $(1, 2)^\top$.

Econ

14. Pandora's utility function $U : \mathbb{R}^2_+ \to \mathbb{R}$ is defined by $U(x_1, x_2) = x_1^2 x_2$. The price vector p is given by $p = (2, 1)^\top$. She has \$4 to spend. What is her optimal consumption bundle subject to her budget constraint?

Econ

15. Pandora's utility function $U : \mathbb{R}^3_+ \to \mathbb{R}$ is defined by $U(x_1, x_2, x_3) = x_1^2 x_2 x_3$. The price vector p is given by $p = (1, 1, 1)^\top$. She has \$8 to spend. What is her optimal consumption bundle subject to her budget constraint?

Fun

16. Colonel Blotto can send each of his five companies to one of ten locations whose importance is valued at 1,

2, 3, ..., 10 respectively. No more than one company can be sent to any one location. His opponent, Count Baloney, must simultaneously do the same with his four companies. A commander who attacks an undefended location, captures it. If both commanders attack the same location, the result is a stand-off at that location. A commander's payoff is the sum of the values of the locations he captures minus the sum of the values of the locations captured by the enemy. What would Colonel Blotto do if he knew what a dominated strategy was?

17. Use the method of successively deleting dominated strategies in the simplified strategic form obtained in Exercise 4.8.1. Why is the result a subgame-perfect equilibrium?
18. Show that the game of Section 1.9.2 has two subgame-perfect equilibria. Write down a strategic form and apply the method of successively deleting dominated strategies insofar as this is possible. Hence, show that the method does not necessarily eliminate pure strategy pairs that are not Nash equilibria.
19. Use the bimatrix game of Figure 4.18 to show that Nash equilibria may be lost when the method of successively deleting dominated strategies is applied. Is the Nash equilibrium that is lost one that we should be sorry to lose?

<table>
<tr><td>1
1</td><td>0
100</td></tr>
<tr><td>100
0</td><td>100
100</td></tr>
</table>

Figure 4.18 The bimatrix game for Exercise 4.8.19.

20. Use the bimatrix game of Figure 4.19 to show that different end products may be obtained if weakly dominated strategies are deleted in different orders.

Phil

21. If the pure strategy pair (d_6, d_5) were to be defended as the solution of the bimatrix game of Figure 4.1 on the basis of statements like:

> Everybody knows that everybody knows that ... everybody knows that nobody ever uses a weakly dominated strategy,

<table>
<tr><td>0
0</td><td>1
0</td></tr>
<tr><td>0
1</td><td>0
0</td></tr>
</table>

Figure 4.19 The bimatrix game for Exercise 4.8.20.

how many times would the phrase "everybody knows" need to appear?

22. Construct a finite game of perfect information in which a subgame-perfect equilibrium is lost if weakly dominated strategies are deleted from the strategic form in a suitable order. (Your game tree need not be very complicated.)

23. In version 2 of Russian Roulette, explain why

$$\pi_1(ADD, AAD) = \tfrac{1}{6} + \tfrac{2}{3}a\,,$$
$$\pi_2(ADD, AAD) = \tfrac{5}{6}\,.$$

24. Show that there are two Nash equilibria in the simplified strategic form of Russian Roulette in the case when $a = 0.25$ and $b = 0.65$ (Section 4.7). Why is only one of these subgame-perfect?

25. Use Zermelo's algorithm for version 2 of Russian Roulette to find all subgame-perfect equilibria in cases 1, 2 and 3 of Section 4.7. (Use a different copy of the skeleton of the game tree given in Figure 4.20 for each case. Work backwards from the end of the tree, doubling the edges that represent optimal play. In the boxes drawn above each nonterminal node x, write down the payoffs that

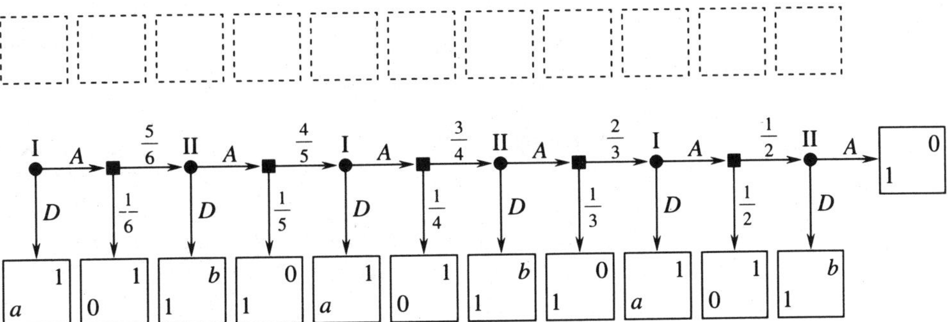

Figure 4.20 A skeleton game tree for Russian Roulette.

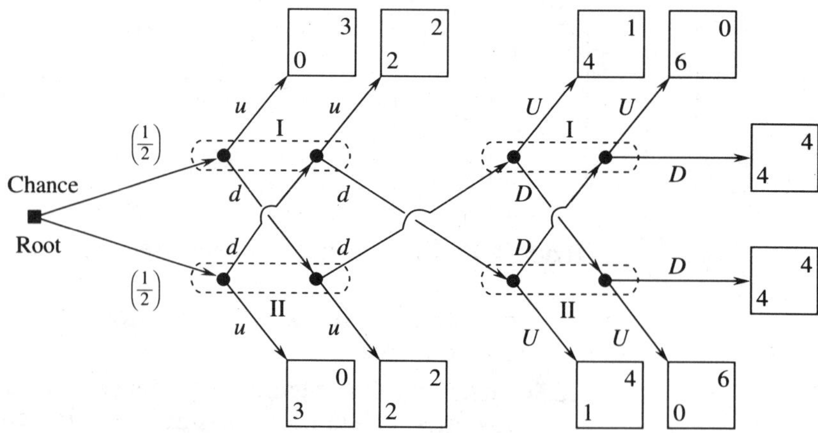

Figure 4.21 The extensive form for Exercise 4.8.27.

each player will get if node x were to be reached and the players were to play optimally in the subgame whose root is x.)

26. Explain which pure strategies you are categorizing as weakly dominated when doubling edges while using Zermelo's algorithm for case 1 in Exercise 4.8.25.

27. Obtain the 4×4 strategic form of the game whose extensive form is given in Figure 4.21. By deleting dominated strategies, show that (dU, dU) is a Nash equilibrium. Are there other Nash equilibria?

28. Write down the 3×8 strategic form of the version of Gale's Roulette given in Exercise 3.7.15 for the utility functions specified in Exercise 3.7.16. Apply the method of successive deletion of dominated strategies to this strategic form.

Econ 29. An eccentric philanthropist is prepared to endow a university with up to a billion dollars. He invites the presidents of Yalebridge and Harford to a hotel room where he has the billion dollars in a suitcase. He explains to his guests that he would like the two presidents to play a game[23] in order to decide whose university gets endowed. The game tree is illustrated in Figure 4.22. The first move consists of an offer of \$1 by the philanthropist to player I (Yalebridge) who can accept or refuse. If he refuses, the philanthropist offers \$100 to player II (Harford). If she refuses, \$1,000 is then

[23]The game is an adaptation by Reny of a game introduced by Rosenthal. It is commonly called the Centipede because the game tree has many "legs".

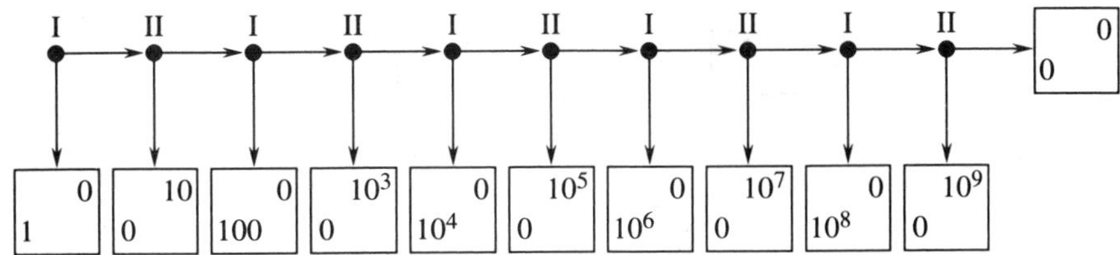

Figure 4.22 Rosenthal's Centipede.

offered to player I, and so on. After each refusal, an amount ten times larger is offered to the other player. If there are ten refusals, player II will be offered the whole billion dollars. (A billion is $10^9 = 1,000,000,000$.) If she refuses, the philanthropist takes his money back to the bank.

(a) Analyze this game using Zermelo's algorithm and hence find the unique subgame-perfect equilibrium. What would be the result of successively deleting weakly dominated strategies in the game?

(b) Is it likely that the presidents of Yalebridge and Harford are so sure of each other's rationality that one should expect to see the subgame-perfect equilibrium played in practice? (See Section 1.8.3.) What prediction would you make about what the president of Yalebridge would do when offered \$100,000 if it happened that both presidents had refused all smaller offers?

(c) How would you play this game?[24]

Econon

30. Player I first plays the Chain-store Game of Figure 1.24 with player II and then he plays the game again with player III replacing player II. The result is the three-player game illustrated in Figure 4.23.

(a) Show that either Zermelo's algorithm or the successive deletion of weakly dominated strategies leads to the conclusion that all players will choose "left" in the game of Figure 4.23.

[24]Some people see a similarity between this problem and the story of the "unexpected test". A teacher tells her pupils that she is going to give them a test on one of the days in the coming week. They ask which day it will be. She replies that the test will be on a day when they don't expect it. They deduce that the test cannot be on Friday, because they would expect the test on Friday if it had not taken place on Monday, Tuesday, Wednesday or Thursday. They then reason that the test therefore cannot take place on Thursday either. And so on. Thus, so the class argues, the test cannot take place at all, and nobody studies. But on Monday morning the teacher runs a test and everybody is surprised!

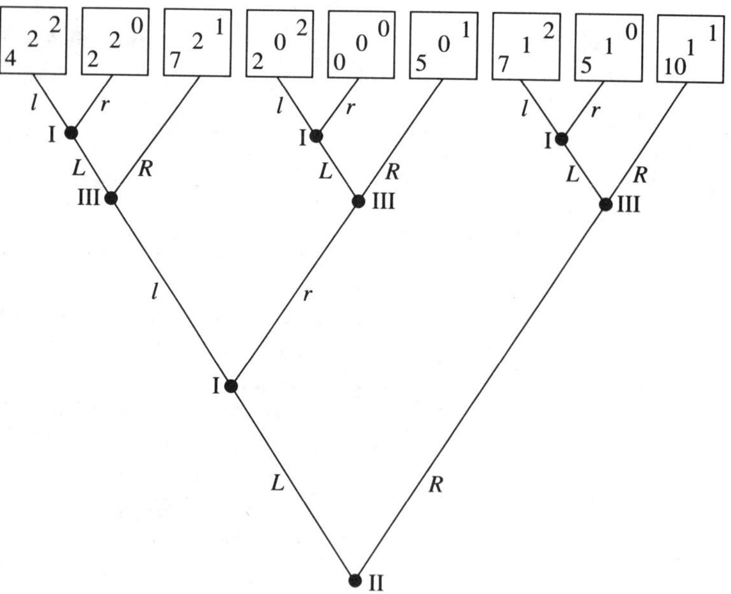

Figure 4.23 The Chain-store Game played twice.

(b) Explain why the same conclusion will result if player I plays the Chain-store Game successively against 100 different people.[25]

(c) Review Exercises 1.10.22 and 1.10.23. Interpret player I as an incumbent monopolist and the other players as independent potential entrants in 100 different towns. If it happened that the potential entrants did actually enter the market in 99 towns and the incumbent monopolist chose to respond by fighting in all 99 towns, what prediction would the potential entrant in the last town be likely to make about how the monopolist would respond to his entering the market? How would the last potential entrant behave after making the prediction you have attributed to him? How does this compare with the behavior assigned to the last potential entrant when Zermelo's algorithm or the successive deletion of weakly dominated strategies is used to analyze the game?

(d) What would you do as the incumbent monopolist? Why is this behavior not irrational?

[25]This is Selten's "Chain-store paradox". The remainder of the exercise is concerned with why the conclusion should be thought to be paradoxical.

CHAPTER

5

Making Deals

5.1 Introduction

Game theory is not only about conflict; it is also about cooperation. For example, if one person wants to sell a house and a second person wants to buy it, then the two individuals have a common interest in transferring the property from one to the other. This requires their cooperation in signing a deed of sale. However, there are many prices at which the house can be sold. The seller prefers high prices and the buyer prefers low prices. Potential therefore exists for conflict. If the buyer and seller are not to lose the joint gains available from cooperation, they have to find some way of resolving this conflict.

Social institutions have arisen that govern how such transactions are made. In particular, house sales are usually prefixed by a period of bargaining followed by the signing of a binding contract. The current chapter is concerned with attempts to model such institutions using game-theoretic ideas.

5.2 Convexity

Review 5.3 ⟶

The first part of the chapter describes an axiomatic approach to the problem of bargaining. The approach requires some preliminary discussion of the notion of a convex set. This is an idea that will be valuable in later chapters as well.

5.2.1 Convex Combinations

If α and β are scalars and x and y are vectors in $\mathbb{R}^2$, the *linear combination* $\alpha x + \beta y$ is defined by

$$\alpha x + \beta y = \alpha(x_1, x_2) + \beta(y_1, y_2) = (\alpha x_1 + \beta y_1, \alpha x_2 + \beta y_2).$$

A linear combination $w = \alpha x + \beta y$ is said to be an *affine combination* of x and y when $\alpha + \beta = 1$. Thus

$$w = \alpha x + (1 - \alpha)y = y + \alpha(x - y)$$

is an affine combination of x and y. Figure 5.1(a) illustrates that the set of all affine combinations of x and y is the straight line through the points located at x and y. (Or, equivalently, it is the straight line through y in the direction of the vector $v = x - y$.)

A *convex combination* of two vectors x and y is a linear combination $w = \alpha x + \beta y$ in which $\alpha + \beta = 1$, $\alpha \geq 0$ and $\beta \geq 0$. Figure 5.1(b) illustrates the fact that the set of all convex combinations of x and y is the straight line segment joining x and y.

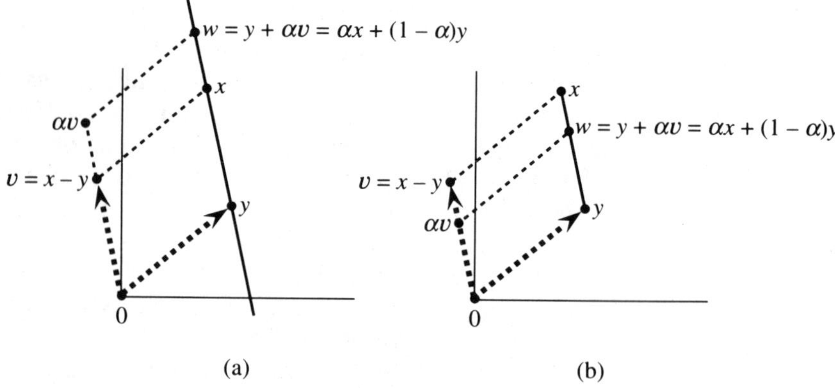

Figure 5.1 Affine and convex combinations.

Let the length of the vector $v = x - y$ in Figure 5.1(b) be d. Then the length of the vector $\frac{2}{3}v$ is $\frac{2}{3}d$. It follows that

$$w = \tfrac{2}{3}x + \tfrac{1}{3}y$$

is located at the point on the line segment joining x and y that is a distance $\frac{1}{3}d$ from x and a distance $\frac{2}{3}d$ from y. Think of the line segment as a weightless piece of rigid wire with a weight of mass $\frac{2}{3}$ at x and a weight of mass $\frac{1}{3}$ at y. Then w lies at the *center of gravity* of the system. As shown in Figure 5.2(a), the system will balance if supported at w.

The expression

$$w = \alpha_1 x_1 + \alpha_2 x_2 + \cdots + \alpha_k x_k$$

is a linear combination of the k vectors $x_1, x_2, \ldots, x_k$. This becomes an affine combination when $\alpha_1 + \alpha_2 + \cdots + \alpha_k = 1$.

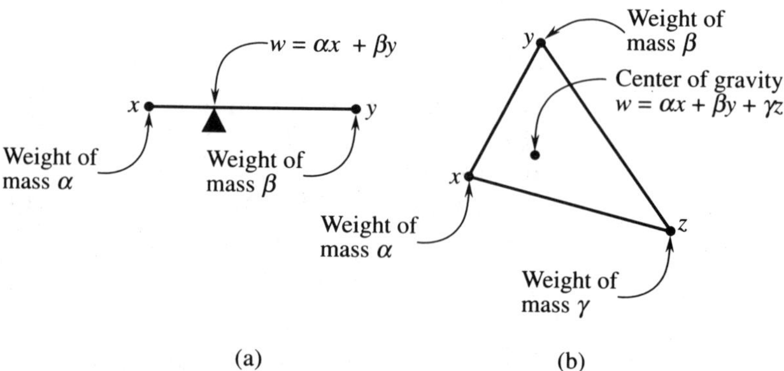

Figure 5.2 Centers of gravity.

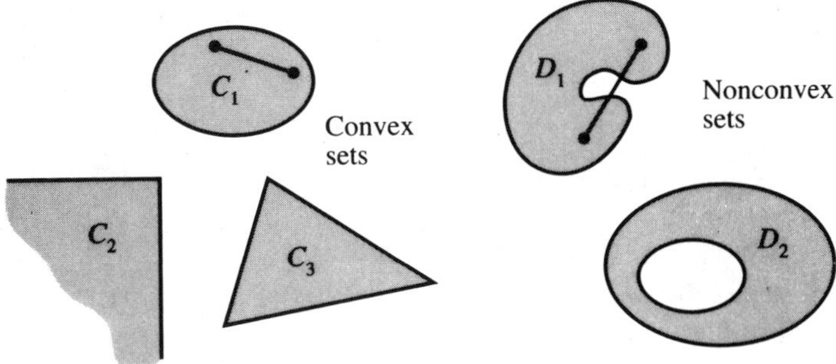

Figure 5.3 Convex and nonconvex sets.

It is a convex combination when $\alpha_1 + \alpha_2 + \cdots + \alpha_k = 1$ and $\alpha_1 \geq 0, \alpha_2 \geq 0, \ldots, \alpha_k \geq 0$. Figure 5.2(b) illustrates that the convex combination $w = \alpha_1 x_1 + \cdots + \alpha_k x_k$ lies at the center of gravity of the system with weights of mass α_i at the points x_i.

In economics, vectors are used in describing commodity bundles. For example, in Section 3.2.1, the vector $(2, 6)$ signifies the bundle in which Pandora gets 2 bottles of gin and 6 bottles of vodka. The bundle $(5, 3)$ assigns her 5 bottles of gin and 3 bottles of vodka. The convex combination

$$\tfrac{1}{3}(2, 6) + \tfrac{2}{3}(5, 3) = (4, 4)$$

then corresponds to a physical mixture of the two bundles. The amount of each commodity in the mixture is obtained by taking $\frac{1}{3}$ of that commodity in the first bundle and combining it with $\frac{2}{3}$ of the commodity in the second bundle.

5.2.2 Convex Sets

A set C is convex if, whenever it contains two points x and y, it also contains the line segment joining x and y. Figure 5.3 shows some convex sets C_1, C_2 and C_3 together with some sets D_1 and D_2 that are not convex.

In algebraic terms,[1] a set C is *convex* if, whenever $x \in C$ and $y \in C$, then

$$\alpha x + \beta y \in C,$$

for any convex combination $\alpha x + \beta y$ of x and y. It is easy to check that a convex set necessarily contains all convex combinations of any number of its members.

[1]Recall that $x \in S$ means that x is an element (or member) of the set S.

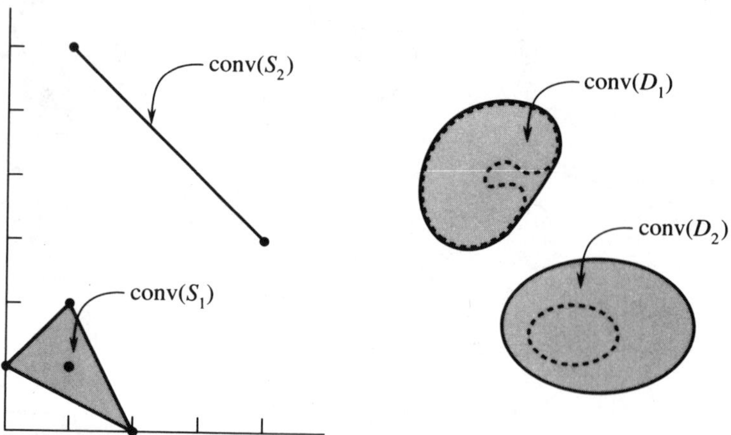

Figure 5.4 Convex hulls.

The *convex hull* of a set S is denoted by conv(S). It is the smallest convex set containing S. This is simply the set of all convex combinations of points in S. Figure 5.4 shows the convex hulls of the sets $S_1 = \{(0,1),(2,0),(1,3),(1,1)\}$ and $S_2 = \{(1,6),(4,3)\}$. It also shows the convex hulls of the sets D_1 and D_2 of Figure 5.3.

5.2.3 Supporting Lines

A line splits the plane $\mathbb{R}^2$ into two "half-spaces" as illustrated in Figure 5.5. If the interior of a convex set C lies in one of the half-spaces defined by a line l that passes through a boundary point b of C, then l is said to be a *supporting line* of C at b.

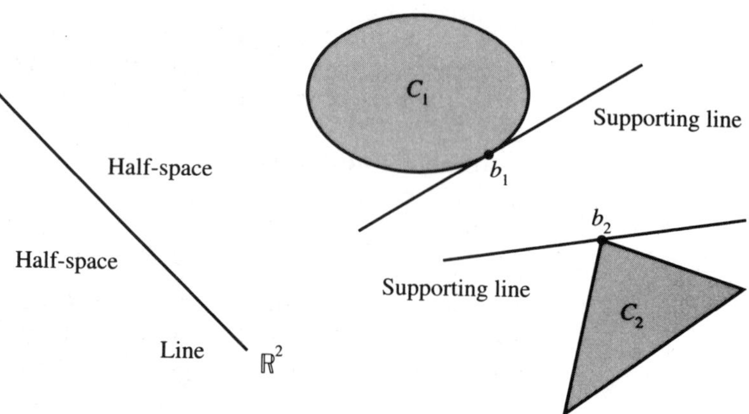

Figure 5.5 Supporting lines.

5.2.4 Concave, Convex and Affine Functions

Recall that the criterion for a concave function is that chords drawn to its graph lie on or below the graph. Thus, in Figure 3.7, the line segment joining the points $(1, u(1))$ and $(16, u(16))$ must lie on or below the graph of the function $u : \mathbb{R}_+ \to \mathbb{R}$ defined by $u(x) = 4\sqrt{x}$. Points on this line segment are convex combinations of $(1, u(1))$ and $(16, u(16))$. The point P indicated in Figure 3.7 is the convex combination

$$\tfrac{4}{5}(1, u(1)) + \tfrac{1}{5}(16, u(16)) = (4,\ \tfrac{4}{5}u(1) + \tfrac{1}{5}u(16))\ .$$

Since this point lies on or below the graph, it must be the case that

$$u(4) = u(\tfrac{4}{5} \times 1 + \tfrac{1}{5} \times 16) \geq \tfrac{4}{5}u(1) + \tfrac{1}{5}u(16)\,.$$

The general version of this argument leads to the following algebraic criterion for a concave function. Let C be a convex set. A function $f : C \to \mathbb{R}$ is concave on C if and only if, for each x and y in C,

$$f(\alpha x + \beta y) \geq \alpha f(x) + \beta f(y)$$

whenever $\alpha + \beta = 1$, $\alpha \geq 0$ and $\beta \geq 0$. Geometrically, this translates into the requirement that the set of points on or below the graph of the function is convex.

For a convex function, the requirement is that, for each x and y in C,

$$f(\alpha x + \beta y) \leq \alpha f(x) + \beta f(y)$$

whenever $\alpha + \beta = 1$, $\alpha \geq 0$ and $\beta \geq 0$. Geometrically, this translates into the requirement that the set of points on or above the graph of the function is convex.

For an affine function, the requirement is that, for each x and y in C,

$$f(\alpha x + \beta y) = \alpha f(x) + \beta f(y)$$

whenever $\alpha + \beta = 1$, $\alpha \geq 0$ and $\beta \geq 0$.[2] Affine functions are therefore characterized by the fact that they preserve convex combinations. More precisely, if z is a convex combination of x and y, then $f(z)$ is the same convex combination of $f(x)$ and $f(y)$. That is, $z = \alpha x + \beta y \Rightarrow f(z) = \alpha f(x) + \beta f(y)$. It follows that affine functions preserve convex structures. For

[2]If $C = \mathbb{R}^n$, the requirement that $\alpha \geq 0$ and $\beta \geq 0$ is redundant. Without the requirement that $\alpha + \beta = 1$, the condition $f(\alpha x + \beta y) = \alpha f(x) + \beta f(y)$ characterizes a linear function.

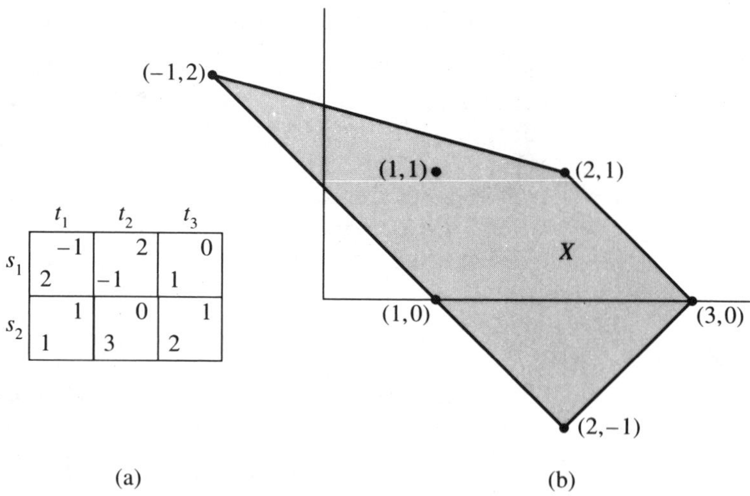

Figure 5.6 A payoff region.

example, if l is a supporting line to the convex set S at b, then $f(l)$ is a supporting line to the convex set $f(S)$ at $f(b)$.[3]

5.3 Cooperative Payoff Regions

Suppose that the players in a game can sign a *binding* agreement before the game is played about what strategies should be used. The set of payoff pairs that they can achieve in this way will be called the *cooperative payoff region* for the game.

5.3.1 Contracts That Specify Lotteries

Figure 5.6(a) shows a bimatrix game. The convex hull of all the payoff pairs that appear in this bimatrix game is shown in Figure 5.6(b).

If the players are allowed to sign a binding contract before the game is played about what pure strategies are to be used, then they can achieve any payoff pair in the set X. This is obvious, for example, in the case of the payoff pair $(1,1)$. The contract need only specify that the pure strategy pair (s_2, t_1) be used. However, no pure strategy pair leads to the payoff pair $(2,0)$.

To achieve the payoff pair $(2,0)$, the players must sign a

[3]When X is a set, the notation $f(X)$ denotes the image of the set X under the function f. That is,

$$f(X) = \{f(x) : x \in X\}.$$

contract that specifies the use of a lottery. For example, the contract may specify that a fair coin is to be tossed. If this shows heads, then the pure strategy pair (s_2, t_3) is to be used. If it shows tails, the pure strategy pair (s_1, t_1) is to be used. The Von Neumann and Morgenstern utility that player I then gets is

$$\tfrac{1}{2}\pi_1(s_2, t_3) + \tfrac{1}{2}\pi_1(s_1, t_1) = \tfrac{1}{2} \times 2 + \tfrac{1}{2} \times 2 = 2 ,$$

where π_i denotes player i's payoff function. Player II gets

$$\tfrac{1}{2}\pi_2(s_2, t_3) + \tfrac{1}{2}\pi_2(s_1, t_1) = \tfrac{1}{2} \times 1 + \tfrac{1}{2} \times (-1) = 0 .$$

Notice that the resulting payoff pair $(2, 0)$ is given by

$$(2, 0) = \tfrac{1}{2}(2, 1) + \tfrac{1}{2}(2, -1) ,$$

where $(2, 1)$ is the payoff pair that results when (s_2, t_3) is used and $(2, -1)$ is the payoff pair that results when (s_1, t_1) is used.

Similar reasoning shows that *all* the convex combinations in X are achievable by signing contracts that specify suitable lotteries.

If no other expedients are available to the players in signing contracts, then X is the cooperative payoff region for the game.

5.3.2 Free Disposal

What other expedients might be available to the players in signing contacts? One possibility is that each might contract to burn some money before the game begins. This is not likely to be an attractive prospect for either player, but it is not a possibility that can logically be excluded. When this possibility is included, economists say that *free disposal* is being admitted.

With free disposal, the set X of Figure 5.6(b) needs to be replaced by the set Y of Figure 5.7(a). For example, to achieve the payoff pair $(3, -2)$, a contract can specify that the pure strategy pair (s_2, t_2) is to be used in the game but, before the game is played, player II must burn just enough money to ensure that her resulting payoff of 0 is reduced to -2.

5.3.3 "Transferable Utility"

Sometimes it is assumed that contracts can be written that specify that some utils are to be transferred from one player to another after the play of the game. If this is possible, then the set Y of Figure 5.7(a) must be replaced by the set Z of

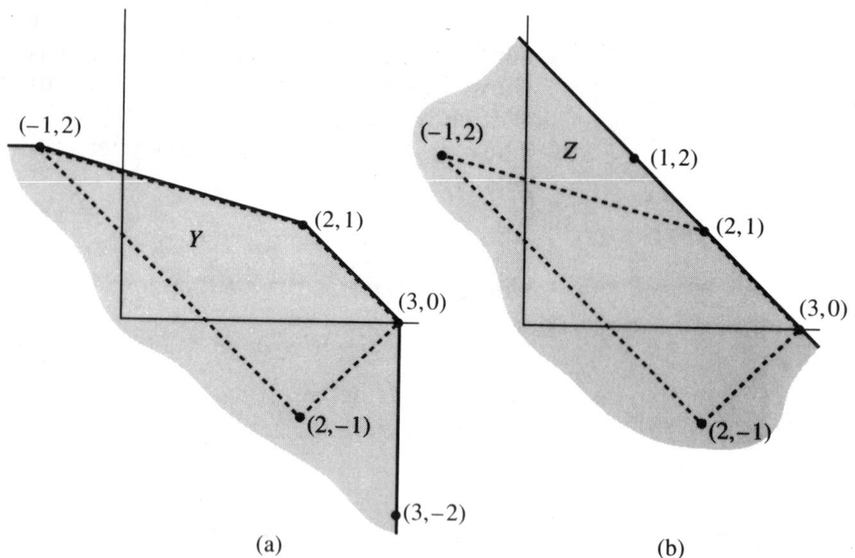

Figure 5.7 More cooperative payoff regions.

Figure 5.7(b). For example, to achieve the payoff pair $(1,2)$, the contract may specify the use of the pure strategy pair (s_2, t_3) followed by a transfer of one util from player I to player II. The use of (s_2, t_3) yields the payoff pair $(2,1)$. Transferring one util from player I to player II changes this to

$$(2-1, 1+1) = (1,2) .$$

Alert readers will be suspicious about such transfers of utils for the reasons given in Section 3.5.3. Utils are not real objects and so cannot really be transferred; only physical commodities can actually be exchanged. Transferable utility therefore only makes proper sense in special cases. The leading case is that in which both players are risk-neutral and their Von Neumann and Morgenstern utility scales have been chosen so that their utility for a sum of money x is simply $u_i(x) = x$. Transferring one util from one player to another is then just the same as transferring one dollar.

5.4 The Bargaining Set

What can be said about the contracts that rational players faced with the game of Figure 5.6(b) might sign? Von Neumann and Morgenstern argued that the most that a game theorist can say is that the result will lie in what they called the *bargaining set*.[4] This is the set of all individually rational, Pareto-efficient payoff pairs in the cooperative payoff region X. What this means is explained in the following subsections.

5.4.1 Pareto-Efficiency

Something is feasible if it is possible to select it. An outcome x in a feasible set X is *Pareto-efficient*[5] if there is no other outcome y in X that all the players like at least as much as x and some players like more than x.

If X is a set of payoff pairs, the requirement that a point x in X is Pareto-efficient translates into the condition that, for all y,

$$y > x \;\Rightarrow\; y \notin X\,. \tag{5.1}$$

Recall that the notation $y \geq x$ means that $y_i \geq x_i$ for each i. The notation[6] $y \gg x$ means that $y_i > x_i$ for each i. The notation $y > x$ means that $y \geq x$ but $y \neq x$. If $y > x$, then y is a Pareto improvement on x. The condition (5.1) therefore says that x is Pareto-efficient when no Pareto improvements on x are feasible.

Figure 5.8 shows the Pareto-efficient points[7] of the sets X, Y and Z of Figures 5.6 and 5.7. The shaded sets indicate the Pareto improvements on x. In each case, z is a feasible point for which x is a Pareto improvement.

---

[4]The idea of a bargaining set is closely related to the notion of a *contract curve* introduced by the economist Edgeworth. It is also closely related to the two-player case of the *core* as defined in cooperative game theory. It coincides with the second notion when the disagreement payoffs happen to be the same as the players' security levels.

[5]The notion is named after the Italian sociologist Pareto who introduced the idea. Sometimes a Pareto-efficient point is said to be *Pareto-optimal*, but this is an unfortunate piece of terminology since it suggests that a Pareto-efficient point cannot be improved on. But it is Pareto-efficient for a mother to give all the cookies in her cooky jar to one of her children, leaving the others with nothing. No child can then have its situation improved without making another worse off. However, nobody would wish to claim that the mother's decision is necessarily socially optimal.

[6]One may define weak Pareto-efficiency by $y \gg x \Rightarrow y \notin X$. The condition given in the text may then be referred to as strong Pareto-efficiency. The latter is stronger than the former because fewer x satisfy the latter criterion.

[7]Notice that it is not true that all boundary points of Y are Pareto-efficient. However, it is true that all boundary points of Y are *weakly* Pareto-efficient.

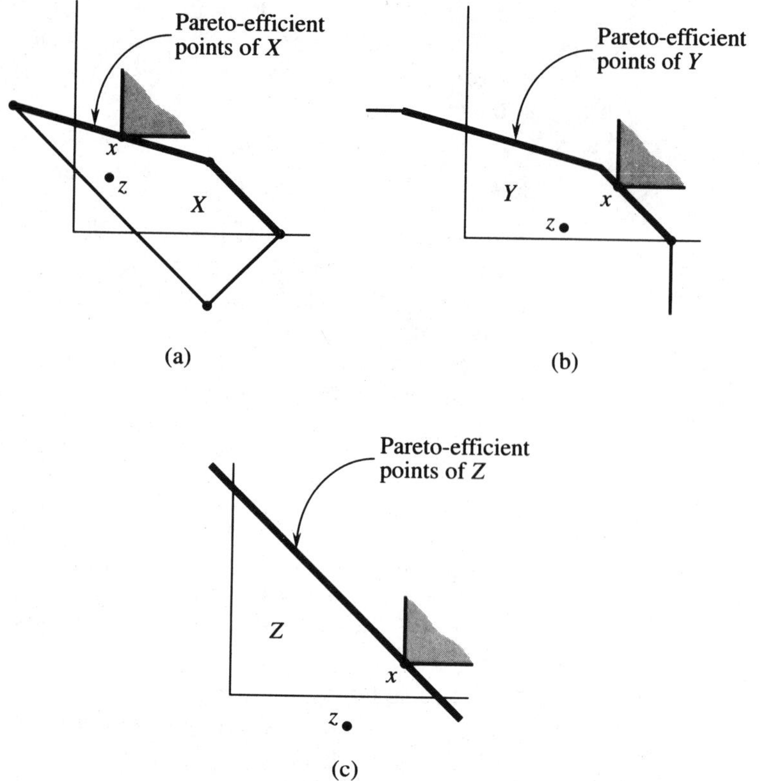

Figure 5.8 Pareto-efficient points.

5.4.2 Individual Rationality

An agreement is *individually rational* if it assigns each player a utility that is at least as large as a player can guarantee for himself in the absence of an agreement. In this chapter, it will be taken for granted that a *disagreement point* d in the set X exists.[8] The interpretation is that, if the players are unable to agree on which contract to sign, then it is common knowledge that the consequence will be that player I gets a payoff of d_1 and player II gets a payoff of d_2. A payoff pair x in the set X then corresponds to an individually rational contract if and only if $x \geq d$.

[8]What should one do if no disagreement point is given? There are no easy answers. Section 6.9 considers one possible way of determining a disagreement point, but there are many others.

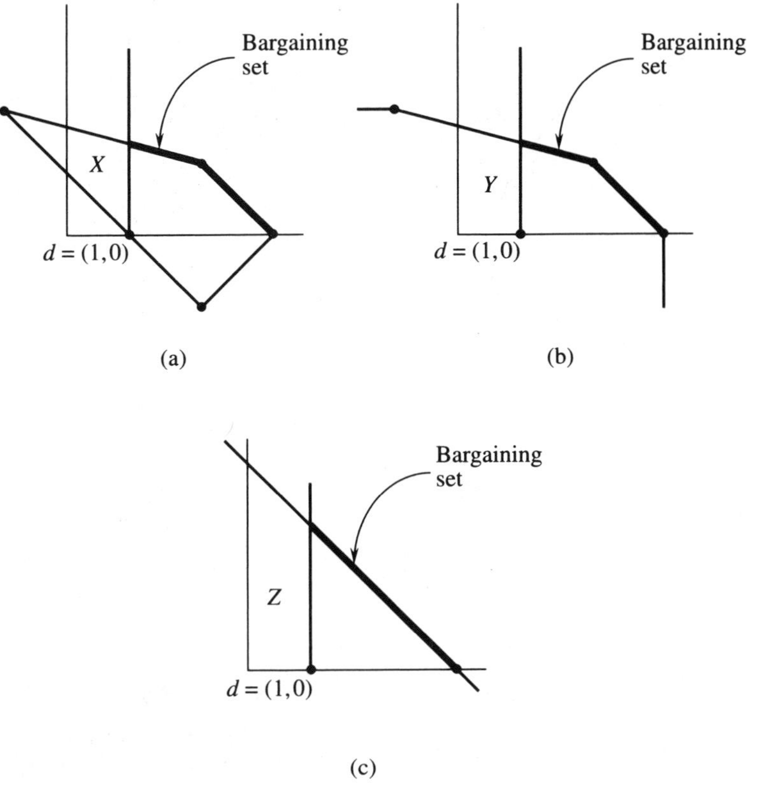

Figure 5.9 Some bargaining sets.

5.4.3 Some Bargaining Sets

Recall that the bargaining set consists of all individually rational, Pareto-efficient points in X. Figure 5.9 shows the bargaining sets for the sets X, Y and Z of Figure 5.8 in the case when the disagreement point $d = (1, 0)$.

It will be obvious why Von Neumann and Morgenstern suggested that rational players will not sign a contract that is not individually rational. Rather than sign such an agreement, at least one of the players would prefer to disagree and hence pick up the disagreement payoff. It is only slightly less obvious why they excluded contracts that are not Pareto-efficient. In the diagrams of Figure 5.8, the point z is not Pareto-efficient because x is a feasible Pareto improvement. If it were proposed that a contract be signed yielding the outcome z, at least one player would have an incentive to propose a contract yielding the outcome x

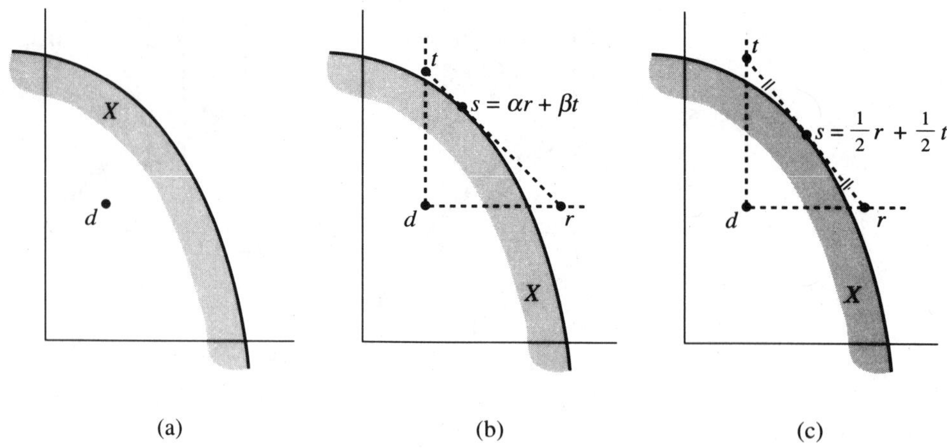

Figure 5.10 Nash bargaining problem.

instead, and the other player would have no rational objection to make.[9]

5.5 Nash Bargaining Solutions

John Nash argued that more can be said about the payoff pair on which two rational players will agree than merely that it must be in the bargaining set. He gave a list of "axioms" that such a payoff pair should satisfy for an abstract bargaining problem and then proved that only *one* payoff pair satisfies the axioms. This payoff pair is said to be the *Nash bargaining solution* of the problem.

5.5.1 Nash Bargaining Problems

Mathematically, a Nash bargaining problem is simply a pair (X, d) in which X represents the set of feasible payoff pairs and d is a point in X representing the consequences of disagreement. Figure 5.10(a) illustrates such a pair (X, d). Only certain types of feasible sets will be considered. The requirements are:

1. The set X is convex.

[9]If the second player is indifferent between x and z, the first player can propose an outcome y that is a little bit worse than x for the first player and a little bit better than z for the second player.

2. The set X is closed and bounded above.[10]
3. Free disposal is allowed.

The set of all bargaining problems (X, d) satisfying these requirements will be denoted by $\mathcal{B}$.

5.5.2 Bargaining Solutions

A *bargaining solution* is a function $F : \mathcal{B} \to \mathbb{R}^2$ with the property that $F(X, d)$ is in the set X. One interprets $F(X, d)$ as the payoff pair on which rational players will agree when confronted with the bargaining problem (X, d).

For an example of a bargaining solution, take $\alpha \geq 0$ and $\beta \geq 0$ with $\alpha + \beta = 1$. Then define $G(X, d)$ to be s in Figure 5.10(b). In this diagram, s is a boundary point of X and the line through r, s and t is a supporting line to X at s. The point s and the supporting line are chosen to ensure that

$$s = \alpha r + \beta t\ .$$

The function $G : \mathcal{B} \to \mathbb{R}^2$ defined in this way is called the *generalized Nash bargaining solution* corresponding to the "bargaining powers" α and β. The larger a player's bargaining power, the more he or she will get when the *generalized Nash bargaining solution* is used. Nash himself considered only the case when the players have equal bargaining powers. For this reason, the *regular* Nash bargaining solution $N : \mathcal{B} \to \mathbb{R}^2$ is understood to refer to the special case when $\alpha = \beta = \frac{1}{2}$. If the Nash bargaining solution is mentioned without a qualifier, it will be the regular version that the author has in mind.

Figure 5.10(c) illustrates the fact that s will be halfway between r and t when the regular Nash bargaining solution is used. Of course, neither the point s nor the supporting line to X at s will be the same as in Figure 5.10(b). A point halfway between r and t in Figure 5.10(b) would not even be in the set X.

5.5.3 Finding Nash Bargaining Solutions

It is particularly easy to compute Nash bargaining solutions in the case of a set like Z in Figure 5.7(b). A supporting line

---

[10] A set is closed if it contains all its boundary points. Thus the interval $[0,1]$ is closed because it contains both its boundary points 0 and 1. The open interval $(0,1)$ contains neither of its boundary points. A set S is bounded above if there exists b such that $x \leq b$ for each x in S.

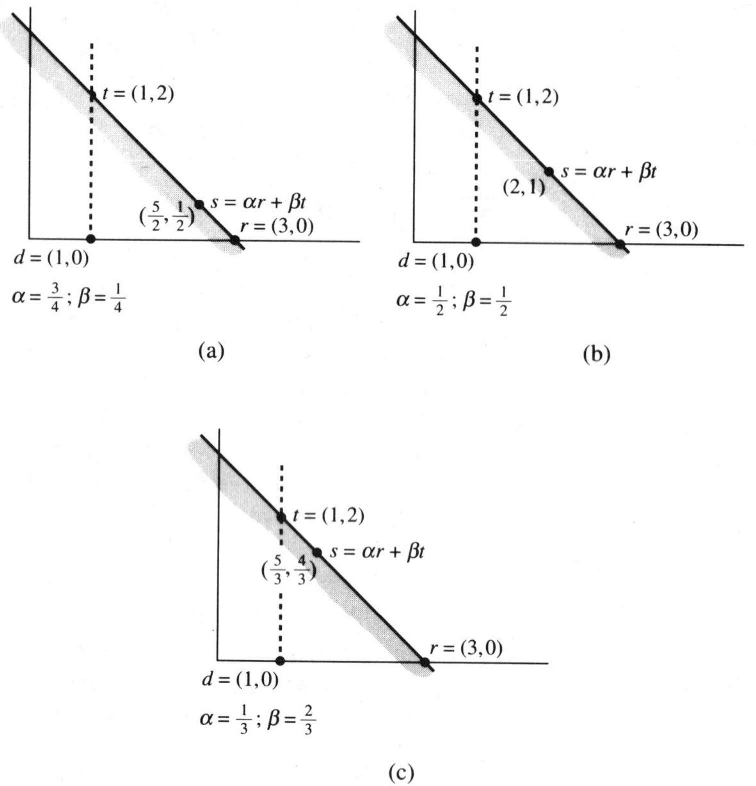

Figure 5.11 Nash bargaining solutions.

to a point s on the boundary of Z is simply the straight line that forms the boundary of Z. It follows that r and t are necessarily located where the horizontal and vertical lines through the disagreement point d cut the boundary of Z. The situation is illustrated in Figure 5.11 for the case when $d = (1, 0)$. It is then true that $r = (3, 0)$ and $t = (1, 2)$. Figure 5.11(a) shows the location of the generalized Nash bargaining solution $s = G(Z, d)$ in the case when $\alpha = \frac{3}{4}$ and $\beta = \frac{1}{4}$. Figure 5.11(c) shows the location of $s = G(Z, d)$ when $\alpha = \frac{1}{3}$ and $\beta = \frac{2}{3}$. Figure 5.11(b) shows the location of the regular Nash bargaining solution $s = N(Z, d)$.

In locating these bargaining solutions, it is worth remembering that $s = \alpha r + \beta t$ is true if and only if $s_1 = \alpha r_1 + \beta t_1$ and $s_2 = \alpha r_2 + \beta t_2$. For example, when $s = N(Z, d)$ so that $\alpha = \frac{1}{2}$ and $\beta = \frac{1}{2}$, $s_1 = \frac{1}{2} \times 3 + \frac{1}{2} \times 1 = 2$ and $s_2 = \frac{1}{2} \times 0 + \frac{1}{2} \times 2 = 1$.

It is not always so easy to work out bargaining solutions. The set Y of Figure 5.7(a) will serve to illustrate this point.

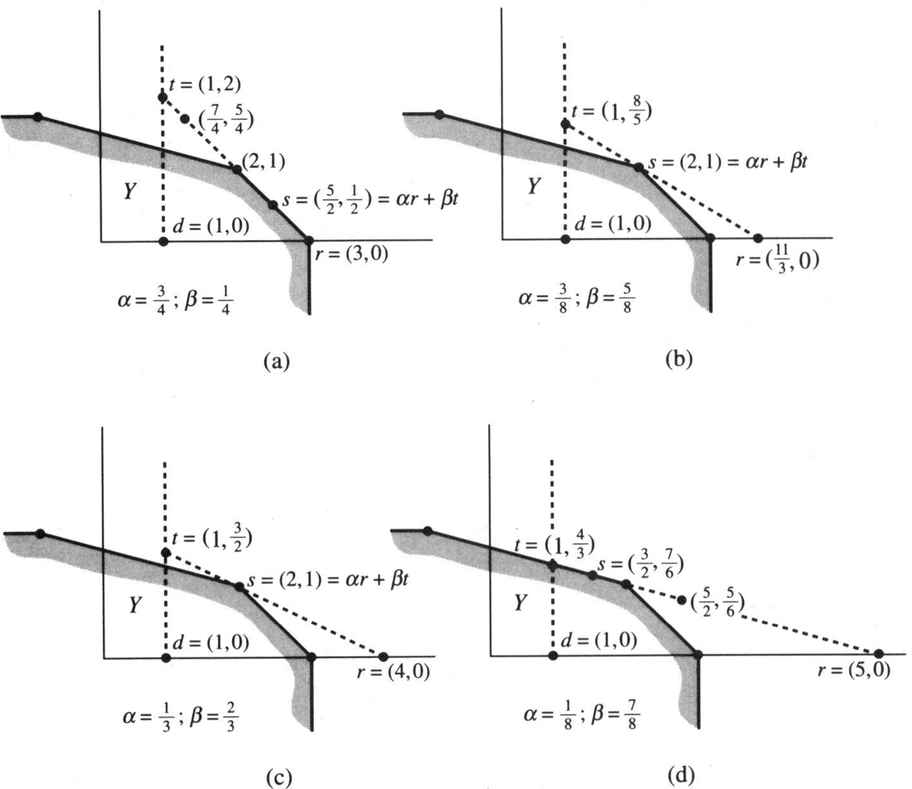

Figure 5.12 More Nash bargaining solutions.

Figure 5.12 shows the generalized Nash bargaining solution $s = G(Y, d)$ for $d = (1, 0)$ and four different pairs of bargaining powers. Notice that the supporting line at s is different in each case. In particular, both when $\alpha = \frac{3}{8}$ and $\beta = \frac{5}{8}$ and when $\alpha = \frac{1}{3}$ and $\beta = \frac{2}{3}$, the solution s is located at $(2, 1)$, but *different* supporting lines to Y at s have to be chosen in the two cases.

One may evade making this choice in a simple problem like (Y, d) by arguing like Sherlock Holmes. As he said, when all other possibilities have been eliminated, the remaining possibility *must* be correct. We know that s lies in the bargaining set, as illustrated in Figure 5.10(b). It follows that, unless s is located at one of the corners $(3, 0)$ or $(2, 1)$, a supporting line to Y at s must either be as illustrated in Figure 5.12(a) or as in Figure 5.12(d). But r and t cannot, for example, be located as in Figure 5.12(a) when $\alpha = \frac{3}{8}$ and $\beta = \frac{5}{8}$, because $(\frac{7}{4}, \frac{5}{4}) = \alpha r + \beta t$ would then not be in the set Y. Similarly, r and t cannot be located as in Figure 5.12(d), because $(\frac{5}{2}, \frac{5}{6}) = \alpha r + \beta t$ would not be in the set Y. Thus, when $\alpha = \frac{3}{8}$ and $\beta = \frac{5}{8}$, s must lie at one of the corner points $(3, 0)$ or $(2, 1)$. It cannot be that $s = (3, 0)$, since then $\alpha = 0$. Thus, $s = (2, 1)$ as shown in Figure 5.12(b). For similar reasons, it is also true that $s = (2, 1)$ when $\alpha = \frac{1}{3}$ and $\beta = \frac{2}{3}$, as shown in Figure 5.12(c).

It is worth noting that, in all these examples, the larger α is relative to β, the more the bargaining solution assigns to player I. Similarly, the larger β is relative to α, the more the bargaining solution assigns to player II. Thus, if the bargaining problem is to be solved using a generalized Nash bargaining solution, then it is good to be a player with a large bargaining power.

5.5.4 Nash's Axioms

What properties would be satisfied by a rational procedure for settling bargaining problems? The criteria proposed by Nash can be loosely expressed as follows:

- The final outcome should not depend on how the players' utility scales are calibrated.
- The agreed payoff pair should always be in the bargaining set.
- If the players sometimes agree on the payoff pair s when t is feasible, then they never agree on t when s is feasible.
- In symmetric situations, both players get the same.

The first property simply recognizes the fact that the choice of an origin and a unit for a utility scale is arbitrary. The second property was discussed in the previous section. The fourth property is not so much a rationality assumption as a decision to confine attention to bargaining procedures that treat the players symmetrically. It will not be used in proving the theorem that follows. This leaves the third property to be considered.

The third property is a version of the *Independence of Irrelevant Alternatives.* The kind of story told in defense of the assumption goes like this. Two people are choosing a dish to share in a Chinese restaurant. The menu lists three alternatives: Chow Mein, Chop Suey and Egg Foo Young. After much discussion, they choose Chop Suey. The waiter then appears and informs them that Chow Mein is actually not available. If this leads the diners to change their decision from Chop Suey to Egg Foo Young, then they will be violating the Independence of Irrelevant Alternatives. The idea is that the choice between Chop Suey and Egg Foo Young should be independent of the availability of Chow Mein. The latter is an irrelevant alternative because it would not get chosen even if it were available.

To prove a theorem, it is necessary to formulate the properties given above as mathematical assumptions about a bargaining solution $f : \mathcal{B} \to \mathbb{R}^2$. Once expressed mathematically, the properties are somewhat grandiosely referred to as axioms.

Math 5.6 ⟶ The first axiom must say that it does not matter how the utility scales are calibrated. Suppose, for example, that the bargaining solution awards 50 utils to player II. She now adopts a new utility scale so that an outcome whose old utility was u is assigned a utility of $U = \frac{9}{5}u + 32$ on the new scale. If nothing else has changed, player II should then be awarded $\frac{9}{5} \times 50 + 32 = 112$ new utils by the bargaining solution.

To express this idea more generally, two strictly increasing affine transformations $\tau_1 : \mathbb{R} \to \mathbb{R}$ and $\tau_2 : \mathbb{R} \to \mathbb{R}$ are needed. Recall that a strictly increasing affine transformation is defined by $\tau_i(u) = A_i u + B_i$ where $A_i > 0$. A function $\tau : \mathbb{R}^2 \to \mathbb{R}^2$ can be constructed from τ_1 and τ_2 by defining

$$\tau(x) = (\tau_1(x_1), \tau_2(x_2)) = (A_1 x_1 + B_1, A_2 x_2 + B_2).$$

Axiom 5.1 Given any strictly increasing affine transformations τ_1 and τ_2,

$$F(\tau(X), \tau(d)) = \tau(F(X, d)).$$

The second axiom must say that $F(X, d)$ lies in the bargaining set for the bargaining problem (X, d). It therefore has two parts. The first part says that $F(X, d)$ is individually rational. The second part says that $F(X, d)$ is Pareto-efficient.

Axiom 5.2

$$\text{(i)} \quad F(X, d) \geq d$$
$$\text{(ii)} \quad y > F(X, d) \quad \Rightarrow \quad y \notin X.$$

The third axiom is the Independence of Irrelevant Alternatives. It is illustrated in Figure 5.13. The set Y is a subset of X that contains $F(X, d)$. The members of X that are not in Y are irrelevant alternatives. If the bargaining solution selects $F(X, d)$ for the bargaining problem (X, d), then it should also select $F(X, d)$ for the bargaining problem (Y, D), because the choice should be independent of the availability or unavailability of irrelevant alternatives.

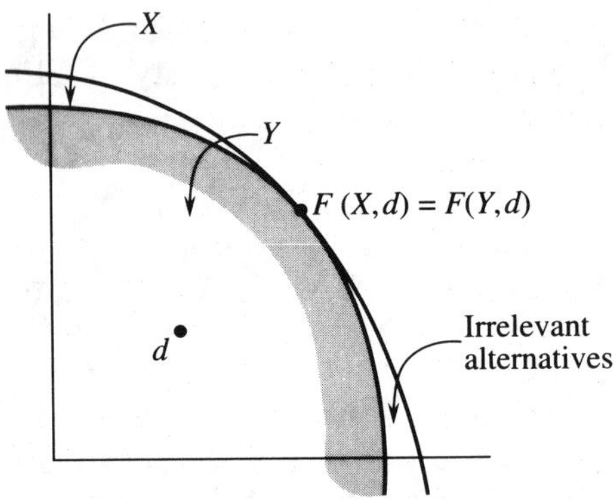

Figure 5.13 Independence of Irrelevant Alternatives.

Axiom 5.3 If $d \in Y \subseteq X$, then

$$F(X,d) \in Y \ \Rightarrow \ F(Y,d) = F(X,d).$$

Any generalized Nash bargaining solution $G : \mathcal{B} \to \mathbb{R}^2$ satisfies Axioms 5.1, 5.2 and 5.3. The interest of the next theorem is that it says that these are the *only* bargaining solutions that satisfy the axioms.

Theorem 5.5.1 (Nash) If $G : \mathcal{B} \to \mathbb{R}^2$ satisfies Axioms 5.1, 5.2 and 5.3, then F is a generalized Nash bargaining solution for some bargaining powers α and β.[11]

Proof. Begin with the simple bargaining problem $(Z, 0)$ in which the disagreement point is the zero vector $0 = (0,0)$, and the feasible set Z consists of all payoff pairs x that satisfy $x_1 + x_2 \leq 1$. The problem $(Z, 0)$ is illustrated in Figure 5.14(a).

By Axiom 5.2, the solution $s' = F(Z, 0)$ for the bargaining problem $(Z, 0)$ lies somewhere on the line segment joining $r' = (1,0)$ and $t' = (0,1)$.

Choose α and β satisfying $\alpha + \beta = 1, \alpha \geq 0, \beta \geq 0$ so that

$$s' = \alpha r' + \beta t'.$$

Next consider any bargaining problem (X, d). A typical problem is illustrated in Figure 5.14(c). Let $s = G(X, d)$, where G is the generalized Nash bargaining solution

[11]This is actually a generalization of the theorem proved by Nash. It can be generalized further by omitting Axiom 5.2(ii) provided that the conclusion is altered to admit the possibility that $F(X,d) = d$ for all (X,d).

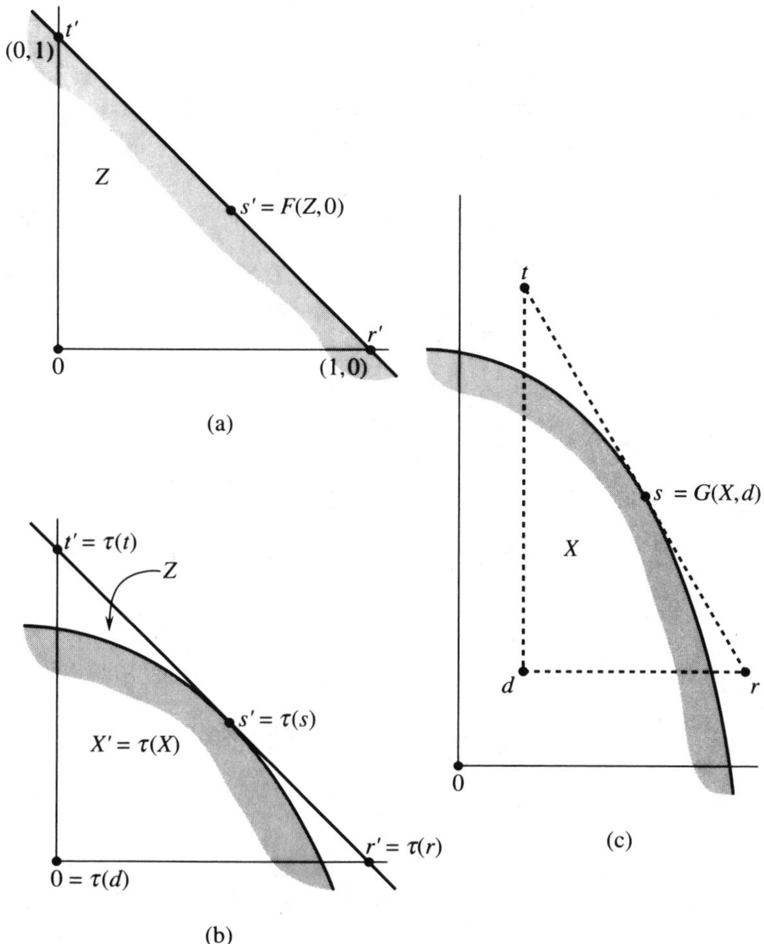

Figure 5.14 Diagrams for Nash's bargaining theorem.

corresponding to the bargaining powers α and β. Then $s = \alpha r + \beta t$ in Figure 5.14(c). The aim is to prove that $F(X,d) = G(X,d)$.

Change player I's utility scale using a strictly increasing, affine transformation $\tau_1 : \mathbb{R} \to \mathbb{R}$ chosen so that $\tau_1(d_1) = 0$ and $\tau_1(r_2) = 1$. Similarly, change player II's utility scale using a strictly increasing, affine transformation $\tau_2 : \mathbb{R} \to \mathbb{R}$ chosen so that $\tau_2(d_2) = 0$ and $\tau_2(t_2) = 1$. The affine function $\tau : \mathbb{R}^2 \to \mathbb{R}^2$ then has the property that $\tau(d) = 0$, $\tau(r) = r'$ and $\tau(t) = t'$, as illustrated in Figure 5.14(b).

Notice that, since affine functions preserve convex structures, the image of the line through r, s and t remains a supporting line to the image of the set X. That is, the line $x_1 + x_2 = 1$ through r', s' and t' is a supporting line to the convex set $X' = \tau(X)$. In particular, since τ preserves convex combinations, $s' = \tau(s)$. Thus, by Axiom 5.1,

$$F(Z, 0) = \tau(G(X, d)). \tag{5.2}$$

The next sentence is the heart of the proof. It consists of the simple observation that, since $X' \subseteq Z$, it follows from Axiom 5.3 that $F(X', 0) = F(Z, 0)$. The rest of the proof is just mathematical book-keeping.

Since $X' = \tau(X)$ and $0 = \tau(d)$, it follows from (5.2) that

$$F(\tau(X), \tau(d)) = \tau(G(X, d)).$$

Thus,

$$G(X, d) = \tau^{-1}(F(\tau(x), \tau(d))), \tag{5.3}$$

where $\tau^{-1} : \mathbb{R}^2 \to \mathbb{R}^2$ is the inverse function[12] to τ.

It remains to apply Axiom 5.1 to the right-hand side of (5.3). Axiom 5.1 is applied, not with τ, but with τ^{-1}. Thus

$$G(X, d) = F\left(\tau^{-1}(\tau(x)), \tau^{-1}(\tau(d))\right) = F(X, d).$$

This is what had to be proved. □

5.5.5 Symmetry

Recall that the regular Nash bargaining solution $N : \mathcal{B} \to \mathbb{R}$ is the special case of a generalized Nash bargaining solution that occurs when the bargaining powers α and β are equal ($\alpha = \beta = \frac{1}{2}$). Since the bargaining powers are equal, the regular Nash bargaining solution treats the players symmetrically. This fact can be expressed mathematically using the function $\rho : \mathbb{R}^2 \to \mathbb{R}^2$ defined by $\rho(x_1, x_2) = (x_2, x_1)$.

Thus ρ simply swaps the players' payoffs over. In particular, the regular Nash bargaining solution satisfies the following symmetry axiom.

---

[12]A function $f : X \to Y$ has an inverse function if the equation $y = f(x)$ has a unique solution $x \in X$ for each $y \in Y$. The inverse function $f^{-1} : Y \to X$ is then defined by $x = f^{-1}(y) \Leftrightarrow y = f(x)$. Observe that $f^{-1}(f(x)) = f^{-1}(y) = x$.

If the affine function $\tau_i : \mathbb{R} \to \mathbb{R}$ is defined by $\tau_i(u) = a_2 u + b_i$ where $a_i > 0$, then the equation $v = a_i u + b_i$ has a unique solution $u = (v - b_i)/a_i$ for each v. Thus $\tau_i^{-1}(v) = (v - b_i)/a_i$. The inverse of $\tau : \mathbb{R}^2 \to \mathbb{R}^2$ is then given by $\tau^{-1}(x) = (\tau_1^{-1}(x_1), \tau_2^{-1}(x_2))$.

Axiom 5.4 $F(\rho(X), \rho(d)) = \rho(F(X,d))$.

This axiom says that the bargaining solution does not care who is labeled player I and who is labeled player II. If the players' labels are reversed, each will still get the same payoff.

Corollary 5.5.1 (Nash) If $F : \mathcal{B} \to \mathbb{R}^2$ satisfies Axioms 5.1–5.4, then F is the regular Nash bargaining solution N.

Proof. The bargaining problem $(Z, 0)$ in the proof of Theorem 5.5.1 is symmetric. Thus Axiom 5.4 requires that the solution be symmetric. This forces $\alpha = \beta = \frac{1}{2}$. □

5.5.6 Nash Products

The generalized Nash bargaining solution $G(X, d)$ corresponding to the bargaining powers α and β may be characterized as the point s at which

$$\max_{\substack{x \in X \\ x \geq d}} (x_1 - d_1)^\alpha (x_2 - d_2)^\beta$$

is achieved. The product in this expression is called a generalized *Nash product.*

Figure 5.15 illustrates the situation. It is necessary to confirm that, if r and t are located on the tangent line to $(x_1 - d_1)^\alpha (x_2 - d_2)^\beta = c$ at s as indicated in the figure, then $s = \alpha r + \beta t$ in accordance with the definition of G.

As we saw in Section 4.5.1, if $f : \mathbb{R}^2 \to \mathbb{R}$ is differentiable, then

$$f_{x_1}(s)(x_1 - s_1) + f_{x_2}(s)(x_2 - s_1) = 0$$

is a general formula[13] for the tangent line to $f(x_1, x_2) = c$ at the point s. When $f(x_1, x_2) = (x_1 - d_1)^\alpha (x_2 - d_2)^\beta$, the tangent line is therefore

$$\alpha \left(\frac{x_1 - s_1}{s_1 - d_1} \right) + \beta \left(\frac{x_2 - s_2}{s_2 - d_2} \right) = 0.$$

This can be written as

$$\alpha \left(\frac{x_1 - s_1}{s_1 - t_1} \right) + \beta \left(\frac{x_2 - s_2}{s_2 - r_2} \right) = 0,$$

[13]The formula may be expressed more briefly as $\nabla f(s)^T (x - s) = 0$.

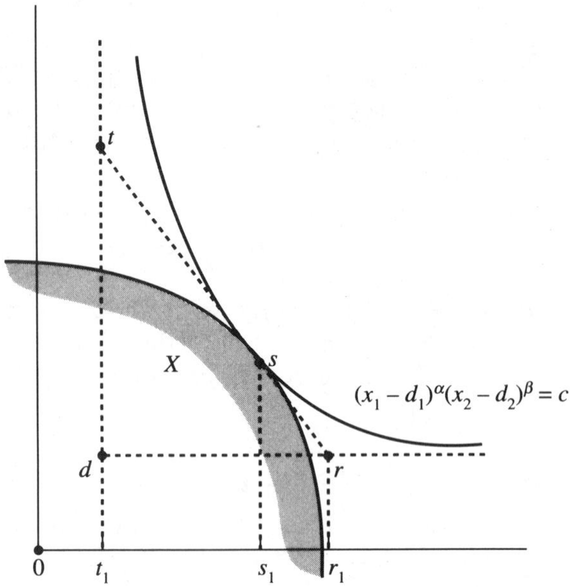

Figure 5.15 Maximizing a Nash product.

because $d = (d_1, d_2) = (t_1, r_2)$. Since r and t lie on the tangent line,

$$\alpha\left(\frac{r_1 - s_1}{s_1 - t_1}\right) - \beta = 0\,; \qquad -\alpha + \beta\left(\frac{t_2 - s_2}{s_2 - r_2}\right) = 0\,.$$

Solving these equations for s_1 and s_2, we obtain that

$$s_1 = \alpha r_1 + \beta t_1\,; \qquad s_2 = \alpha r_2 + \beta t_2\,.$$

It follows that $s = \alpha r + \beta t$, which is what had to be shown.

The definition given so far for a generalized Nash bargaining solution with bargaining powers a and b requires that $a + b = 1$. This limitation is sometimes inconvenient. If it is only given that $a \geq 0$, $b \geq 0$ and $a + b > 0$, then the generalized Nash bargaining solution with bargaining powers a and b is taken to be the same as that with powers $\alpha = a/(a + b)$ and $\beta = b/(a + b)$. This definition works out well with generalized Nash products because

$$(x_1 - d_1)^a(x_2 - d_2)^b = \left\{(x_1 - d_1)^\alpha(x_2 - d_2)^\beta\right\}^{(a+b)}\,.$$

Thus the expression $(x_1 - d_1)^a(x_2 - d_2)^b$ is maximized wherever $(x_1 - d_1)^\alpha(x_2 - d_2)^\beta$ is maximized. Notice that, since

$a/b = \alpha/\beta$, the bargaining solution continues to depend only on the *ratio* of the bargaining powers.

Recall that the regular Nash bargaining solution has $\alpha = \beta = \frac{1}{2}$. In this case, it is simplest to replace α and β by values of a and b with $a = b = 1$. The regular Nash bargaining solution $N(X, d)$ may then be characterized as the point s at which

$$\max_{\substack{x \in X \\ x \geq d}} (x_1 - d_1)(x_2 - d_2)$$

is achieved. The product in this expression is simply called a *Nash product.*

5.6 Dividing the Dollar

Econ 5.7 →

If a fancy house is worth \$2m to its owner and \$3m to a potential buyer, then a deal is possible. By getting together and arranging a sale, the buyer and the seller can create a *surplus* of \$1m. How this surplus is divided between them is a matter for bargaining. Matters are very similar when a firm and a union negotiate a wage contract. If a contract is signed, the firm and the workers will cooperate in creating a surplus. What needs to be negotiated is how this surplus should be divided.

A simple model that captures the essence of such bargaining situations is traditionally known as "dividing the dollar". The story that goes with the model envisages a philanthropist who offers John and Mary the opportunity to divide a dollar between them, provided that they can agree on how to divide it. If they can agree who should get how much of the dollar, then each gets the agreed amount. If they cannot agree, each gets nothing. In this story, the dollar represents the surplus over which two economic agents bargain. The philanthropist's provision that the dollar is available only if John and Mary can reach an agreement represents the fact that there will be no surplus unless the agents get together to create it.

This section examines how a generalized Nash bargaining solution can be used to resolve such a problem. We shall be particularly interested in how a player's attitude to taking risks affects the share of the surplus that the player gets.

In money terms, John and Mary can agree on any pair $m = (m_1, m_2)$ of dollar amounts in the set $M = \{m : m_1 + m_2 \leq 1\}$.

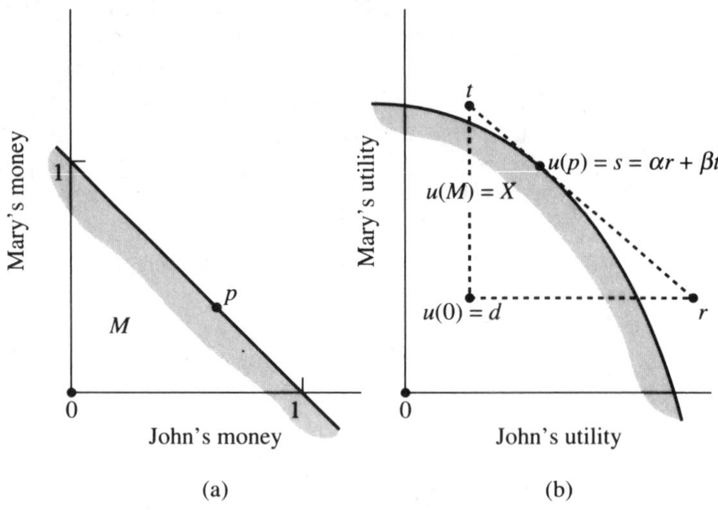

Figure 5.16 Risk-averse players dividing a dollar.

This set[14] is illustrated in Figure 5.16(a). Disagreement corresponds to the zero vector 0. To apply Nash's theory, it is necessary to translate the situation into utility terms using the players' Von Neumann and Morgenstern utility functions.

Suppose that $v_i : \mathbb{R} \to \mathbb{R}$ represents player i's utility for money.[15] It will be assumed that both players care about nothing except how much money they get from the deal. In particular, John is neither interested in helping Mary along nor in doing her any injury, unless this results in some financial benefit for himself. Mary feels exactly the same about John. With these understandings, a player's Von Neumann and Morgenstern utility function $u_i : M \to \mathbb{R}$ for deals is given by

$$u_i(m) = v_i(m_i).$$

That is, player i's utility for the deal m depends only on the amount m_i that he or she gets from the deal.

[14]For example, to achieve the point $(0.4, 0.6)$, the dollar is split so that John gets 40 cents and Mary gets 60 cents. To achieve the point $(2.4, -1.4)$, they agree to split the dollar 40 : 60 and then Mary pays John a further two dollars from her pocket. To achieve the point $(-3, -3)$, they can agree that the philanthropist's dollar should be refused and then each player should burn three dollars taken from his or her own pocket.

[15]It will be taken for granted that v_i is strictly increasing, continuous and unbounded below on $\mathbb{R}$. Together with the assumption that v_i is concave, these assumptions guarantee that the feasible set X of payoff pairs satisfies the conditions given in Section 5.4.1.

Figure 5.16(b) illustrates the bargaining problem (X, d) that corresponds to dividing the dollar in the case when John and Mary are risk-averse so that u_1 and u_2 are concave functions. In this case $u(M)$ is convex[16] and so one simply takes $X = u(M)$ and $d = u(0)$. The generalized Nash bargaining solution $s = G(X, d)$ corresponding to the bargaining powers α and β is shown in Figure 5.16(b). This corresponds to the pair p of dollar amounts that satisfies $s = u(p)$.

5.6.1 Risk-Averse Players

As an example, consider the case when $v_1 : \mathbb{R}_+ \to \mathbb{R}$ is defined by $v_1(z) = z^\gamma$ and $v_2 : \mathbb{R}_+ \to \mathbb{R}$ by $v_2(z) = z^\delta$. (Since these functions are not defined when $z < 0$, we have to proceed on the assumption that the players have no money in their pockets to burn or give away in this example.) If $0 < \gamma \leq 1$ and $0 < \delta \leq 1$, then v_1 and v_2 are strictly increasing and concave. Thus the players prefer more money to less and are risk-averse.

The Pareto-efficient utility pairs in X are of the form $(z^\gamma, (1-z)^\delta)$, where z is the share of the dollar that John gets and $1 - z$ is Mary's share. The disagreement utility pair is $d = (0, 0)$. Thus the value of the generalized Nash product $(x_1 - d_1)^\alpha (x_2 - d_2)^\beta$ when $x_1 = z^\gamma$ and $x_2 = (1 - z)^\delta$ is

$$z^{\alpha\gamma}(1 - z)^{\beta\delta}.$$

The generalized Nash bargaining solution $G(X, d)$ occurs where this product is maximized (subject to the constraint that $0 \leq z \leq 1$). The solution[17] to this optimization problem is

$$z = \frac{\gamma\alpha}{\gamma\alpha + \delta\beta}; \qquad 1 - z = \frac{\delta\beta}{\gamma\alpha + \delta\beta}.$$

The regular Nash bargaining solution is the special case

---

[16]Just as m is the pair (m_1, m_2), so $u(m)$ is the pair $(u_1(m), u_2(m))$. The set $u(M)$ is then defined by $u(M) = \{u(m) : m \in M\}$. An argument that $u(M)$ is convex goes like this. Suppose that x and y are in $u(M)$. This means that $x = u(m)$ and $y = u(n)$ for some m and n in M. To prove that $u(M)$ is convex, it must be shown that $ax + by$ is in $u(M)$ for each a and b with $a + b = 1$, $a \geq 0$ and $b \geq 0$. Since M is convex, $am + bn$ is in M. Thus $u(am + bn)$ is in $u(M)$. If $u(am + bn) \geq z$, it follows that z is in $u(M)$ because free disposal is possible in the situation under discussion. The utility function u_i is concave. Thus $u_i(am + bn) \geq au_i(m) + bu_i(n)$ $(i = 1, 2)$. Hence, $u(am + bn) \geq au(m) + bu(n) = ax + by$. It follows that $z = ax + by$ is in $u(M)$ and so $u(M)$ is convex.

[17]Differentiate $z^{\gamma\alpha}(1 - z)^{\delta\beta}$ with respect to z and set the result equal to zero.

when the bargaining powers are equal. Observe that, when $\alpha = \beta$, the dollar is split in the ratio $\gamma : \delta$. The moral of this story is that it is disadvantageous to be risk-averse in this kind of bargaining situation. The more risk-averse you are, the less money you get. For example, if $\gamma = 1$, then John is risk-neutral. If Mary were risk-neutral as well so that $\delta = 1$ also, then they would split the dollar 50 : 50. But suppose that $\delta = \frac{1}{3}$ so that Mary is strictly risk-averse. Then the split will be 75 : 25.

It is for this kind of reason that real-life bargainers seek to conceal the extent of the distress they would feel if the negotiations were to break down. However, in the simple models considered in this chapter, such attempts at deception are not possible since it is taken for granted that the players' preferences are common knowledge.

5.6.2 Risk-Loving Players

If $\gamma > 1$ and $\delta > 1$ in the previous example, both players are risk-loving. One could carry through the algebra of the preceding subsection, but the answer would be completely wrong because Figure 5.16(b) does not apply in this case. The reason is that $u(M)$ is not convex. The set X of feasible deals is therefore not $u(M)$ but the convex hull of $u(M)$. Figure 5.17(b) illustrates the situation. (As in the previous subsection, arguments that require players to dip into their pockets are excluded.)

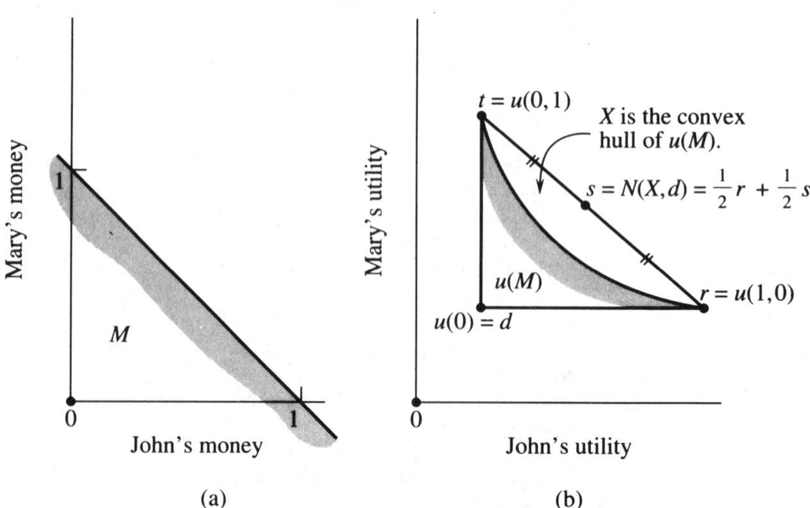

Figure 5.17 Risk-loving players dividing a dollar.

The regular Nash bargaining solution is easily found. It is the point s halfway between r and t. Since r corresponds to assigning the whole dollar to John and t corresponds to assigning the whole dollar to Mary, s corresponds to the lottery in which John and Mary agree to toss a fair coin. If it falls heads, John gets the dollar. If it falls tails, Mary gets the dollar.

We shouldn't be surprised that John and Mary should agree on a deal in which each risks getting nothing. It is true that most people would not be very enthusiastic about such a deal, but most people are risk-averse in such situations. However, John and Mary *love* to take risks.

5.7 Cooperative and Noncooperative Games

Phil 5.8 ⟶ Von Neumann and Morgenstern introduced the subject of game theory in a book called *The Theory of Games and Economic Behavior*, published in 1944. Their approach was mildly schizophrenic in that the style of analysis in the first part differs markedly from the second. This schizoid tendency is preserved in modern game theory by the distinction drawn between cooperative game theory and noncooperative game theory.

Noncooperative game theory is the more fundamental of the two. It calls for a complete description of the rules of the game to be given so that the *strategies* available to the players can be studied in detail. The aim is then to find a suitable pair of *equilibrium* strategies to label as the solution of the game. All the games in Chapters 1, 2, 3 and 4 were studied from this viewpoint.

Cooperative game theory takes a more freewheeling attitude. It is concerned with those situations in which players can negotiate before the game is played about what to do in the game. Moreover, it is assumed that these negotiations can be concluded by the signing of a *binding* agreement. Under these conditions, so it is argued, the precise strategies available in the game will not matter very much. What matters is the *preference* structure of the game, since it is this that determines what contracts are feasible. The material covered so far in the current chapter therefore counts as cooperative game theory.

5.7.1 Nash Program

Both cooperative and noncooperative theory have their pluses and their minuses. A big plus for cooperative theory is that it offers simple-minded answers to simple-minded questions. This makes it easy to use in applications. The corresponding minus is that one can never be entirely sure that one is supplying the right simple-minded answer to the right simple-minded question.

The big plus for noncooperative theory is that it cuts no corners and so, if an analysis leads to an unambiguous conclusion, one can be confident that the problem is genuinely solved. The corresponding minus is that the conclusion only applies to one specific game. If the details of the rules are changed slightly, the conclusion need no longer be valid.

Nash did not regard cooperative and noncooperative theory as rivals. He regarded them as providing complementary insights. For example, he recognized that the plausibility of his axioms for the Nash bargaining solution is open to question, and therefore proposed constructing noncooperative bargaining models to test the axioms. The idea is to model the various ploys open to the players when they are negotiating as strategies within a bargaining game whose rules are explicitly specified in detail. If the equilibrium outcomes of a sufficiently wide class of such bargaining games turn out to satisfy the Nash axioms, then the Nash bargaining theory will be vindicated. Otherwise it had best be abandoned.

This proposed line of research is referred to as the *Nash program*. In principle, it can be applied whenever a concept from cooperative game theory is in doubt. However, in what follows, attention will be restricted to generalized Nash bargaining solutions and to one particularly interesting type of noncooperative bargaining model.[18]

5.8 Bargaining Models

Econ 5.9 ⟶

Section 5.6 studied how a generalized Nash bargaining solution can be used to resolve "divide the dollar" problems. But why should we use a generalized Nash bargaining solution rather than one of the many other "bargaining solutions"

[18]Some authors misunderstand Nash's motives in formulating his bargaining solution and imagine that his axioms can sensibly be interpreted as criteria for a "fair arbitration scheme". It would take too long to explain why Nash's axioms are ill-suited for this purpose. However, other axiom systems have been introduced to characterize other so-called "bargaining solutions" that do make sense as fair arbitration schemes. It would, of course, be silly to use the Nash program to "test" axiom systems of this type. There is no reason why rational agents exploiting whatever bargaining power they may possess should arrive at a "fair" outcome.

that economists have proposed? It is true that Section 5.5.4 gives a list of characterizing axioms for the generalized Nash bargaining solution that seem very reasonable. However, people other than Nash have also given lists of axioms that seem very reasonable when stated in the abstract. For example, the Kalai-Smorodinsky bargaining solution described in Exercise 5.9.19 can also be characterized in terms of a system of axioms that look reasonable at first sight. Rather than discussing the competing claims of such rival axiom schemes, this section tries to tackle the question directly by examining the strategic realities of situations in which bargains are reached by a process of offer and counteroffer that continues until an agreement is concluded.

This is an ambitious project. It will therefore be wise for us to begin by first examining some primitive bargaining models in which only one or two offers are allowed. These are not very interesting in themselves, but they provide an opportunity to review the ideas of Nash equilibrium[19] and subgame-perfect equilibrium that were introduced in Section 1.8 and Section 4.6.3.

5.8.1 The Ultimatum Game

The bargaining problem will be that of "dividing a dollar" as studied in Section 5.6. To keep things simple, let $v_i(x) = x$. We can then identify dollars and utils. In Section 5.6, nothing was said about the *procedure* that governs the manner in which John and Mary bargain. The Ultimatum Game provides a model for the simplest of all possible bargaining procedures.

In the Ultimatum Game, player I makes a proposal to player II on how to divide the dollar. Player II may then accept or refuse. If she accepts, player I's proposal is adopted. If she refuses, the game ends with both players getting nothing. Although this procedure is very simple, it is not entirely unrealistic. It is, in fact, the bargaining procedure that is normally employed when you buy something in a store. The store writes a price on an item of merchandise. You then take it or leave it.

The game tree is illustrated in Figure 5.18. The edges at the root are labeled with the amounts that player I claims for himself. After each such claim, player II can choose Y or

[19]The temptation to confuse a Nash equilibrium with a Nash bargaining solution is hard to resist. However, the only thing they have in common is that they were both invented by John Nash.

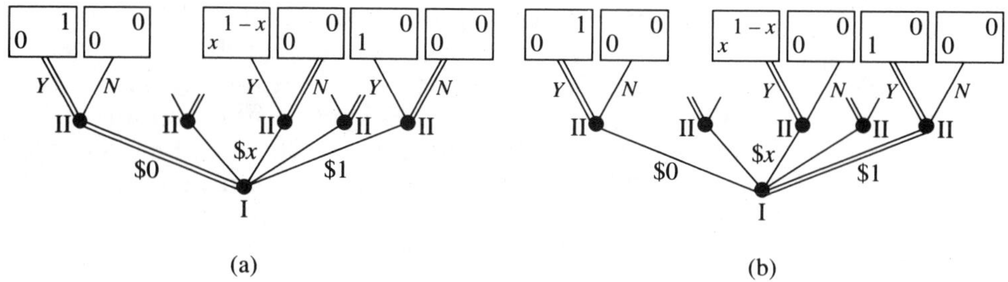

Figure 5.18 The Ultimatum Game.

N. To choose Y signifies acceptance. To choose N signifies a refusal. After a refusal, both players get nothing. Each player is assumed to prefer more money to less, and to care about nothing else.

The doubled edges in Figure 5.18(a) indicate one of the many Nash equilibria of the game. The outcome is very counterintuitive. Player I offers everything to player II who accepts. How can such an odd outcome result from Nash equilibrium play?

Denote the pure strategy for player I indicated in Figure 5.18(a) by s. Thus s calls upon player I to offer the entire dollar to player II. A pure strategy for player II is much more complicated. For each possible proposal that I might make, she must say whether she would accept it or refuse it. The pure strategy t indicated in Figure 5.18(a) calls for her to refuse every proposal except that in which she is offered the whole dollar.

The pure strategy pair (s, t) is a Nash equilibrium. To check this, it is necessary to confirm that s is a best reply to t and t is simultaneously a best reply to s. This is not hard for player II. She cannot get more than the whole dollar, and this is what she gets when she plays t in reply to s. Player I's situation is less rosy. He gets nothing by replying to t with s. But nor would he get anything if he used any other pure strategy, because any other proposal will be refused if player II uses t. Therefore s is a best reply to t since it does at least as well as any other reply.

However, the pair (s, t) is not subgame-perfect. It calls for player II to plan to play *irrationally* in subgames that are not reached when (s, t) is used. A game theory apprentice might perhaps write a book recommending that (s, t) be used, but player I will find it incredible that player II would follow the advice.[20] For example, pure strategy t calls upon player II to refuse when offered ten cents. It is true that ten cents is not very much, but it is better than nothing. A rational player II will therefore accept the ten cents if it is offered. One can argue that she might refuse out of spite, or to "teach player I a lesson", or because she wishes to establish a reputation as a tough cookie. But all of these arguments require attributing motives to player II other than a love of money. Of course, if she has the opportunity, player II might *threaten* to refuse niggardly offers, but a player I who knows that player II is rational will dismiss such threats as idle bombast and ignore them.

Figure 5.18(b) illustrates the use of Zermelo's algorithm in finding the unique subgame-perfect equilibrium. This calls for player II to plan to accept all offers, and for player II to demand the whole dollar.

The use of Zermelo's algorithm is not quite so straightforward as in previous applications because the game is infinite. Player I can choose any real number in the interval $[0, 1]$ as his demand. The procedure will therefore be described carefully. Three steps are required:

Step 1. Double all the edges corresponding to an acceptance by player II of a demand $x < 1$ by player I. To accept such a demand is optimal because $1 - x > 0$.

Step 2. Double the edge in which player I demands 1. No demand $x < 1$ can be optimal because a demand y with $x < y < 1$ would be accepted and hence yield a better payoff than the demand x.

Step 3. Double the edge corresponding to an acceptance by player II of the demand 1 by player I. It is true that refusal is also optimal. But refusal does not correspond to a subgame-perfect equilibrium. If player II plans to refuse the demand of 1 by player I, then player I would do better to make some demand $x < 1$ because this will necessarily be accepted. But we have seen that such a demand cannot be optimal.

The basic principle will be met again in more complicated models, and so it is worth stating it explicitly.

In equilibrium, a proposer always plans to offer the responder an amount that will make the responder indifferent between

[20]Provided that player I *knows* that player II is rational. But this is taken as given.

accepting and refusing. In equilibrium, the responder always plans to accept such an offer or better, and to refuse anything worse.

Even if you follow the mechanics of the argument that led to the principle just stated, you may remain uncomfortable with the idea that player II must necessarily accept what she is offered in equilibrium, even though she is indifferent between accepting and refusing. Such discomfort often arises in problems involving infinite numbers of possibilities, because we are only used to thinking about finite situations. Section 5.8.2, which looks at a *finite* version of the Ultimatum Game, may help in clarifying precisely what is going on.

5.8.2 A Finite Version of the Ultimatum Game

Phil
5.8.3 ⟶

The principle that concludes the preceding subsection will prove very useful. But it is not possible to state such a simple principle for the *finite* version of the Ultimatum Game in which player I is restricted to making demands in whole numbers of cents. On the other hand, in such a finite game, Zermelo's algorithm is easier to apply. It can be applied exactly as described in Section 1.9.2.

In analyzing the Ultimatum Game when player I can only make demands in whole numbers of cents, the first step is precisely the same as in the preceding subsection. Double all the edges corresponding to an acceptance by player II of a demand by player I that leaves something positive for player II. After this step, 100 edges will be doubled, one for each whole number of cents from 0 to 99. Player II is indifferent between accepting and refusing a demand of 100 cents since she gets nothing either way. The second step is therefore to duplicate the game tree, doubling the edge corresponding to an acceptance of a demand of 100 cents in one copy and doubling the edge corresponding to a refusal in the other. Figure 5.19 shows the two cases. The third and final step is to double the edge corresponding to an optimal demand by player I. In Figure 5.19(a), where player I's demand of 100 cents will be accepted, it is optimal for player I to demand 100 cents. In Figure 5.19(b), where player I's demand of 100 cents will be refused, it is optimal for player I to demand 99 cents. Thus, in the finite version of the Ultimatum Game, there are *two* subgame-perfect equlibria[21] as illustrated in Figure 5.19.

[21] If only pure strategies are considered.

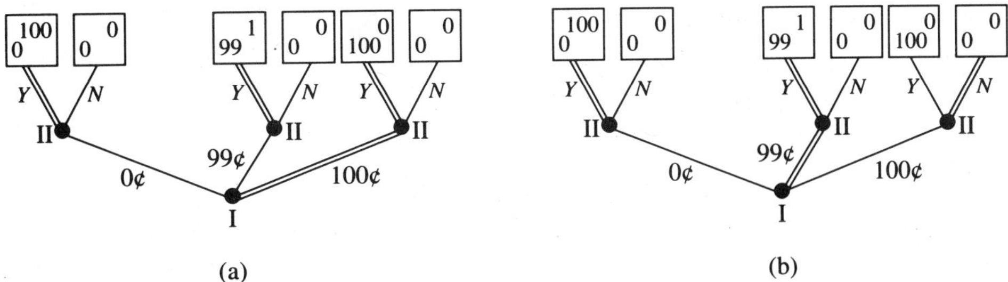

Figure 5.19 Ultimata in whole numbers of cents.

Instead of working in whole numbers of cents, one could repeat the previous discussion using smaller units of currency. If the smallest unit of currency allowed were one millionth of a dollar, then there would be two subgame-perfect equilibria: one in which player I demands the whole dollar and player II accepts, and one in which player II would refuse a demand for the whole dollar but accepts player I's demand for 0.999999 of the dollar.

This conclusion may help to dispel any doubts about the reasonableness of the principle stated at the end of Section 5.8.1. Since player II is indifferent between accepting and refusing when she is offered nothing, one feels that there should be *two* subgame-perfect equilibria; one in which she accepts when offered nothing, and one in which she refuses when offered nothing. In the finite case, we found precisely this. However, when the smallest unit of currency is allowed to become very small, *both* of these equilibria converge on the *single* subgame-perfect equilibrium of the limiting infinite game.

5.8.3 A Two-Stage Bargaining Game

The principle proposed at the end of Section 5.8.1 is now used in a model in which player II gets to make a counterproposal if she chooses to reject player I's initial proposal on how to divide the dollar. To make the problem interesting, it is necessary to suppose that the players not only prefer more money to less, but that they also prefer to get the money sooner rather than later.[22]

The basic bargaining problem remains that of "dividing the dollar" as studied in Section 5.6. We also continue to

[22]If they did not care when they got the money, player I's opening proposal would be irrelevant. Player II would ignore it and make the optimal proposal in the ensuing ultimatum game. She would then get the whole dollar.

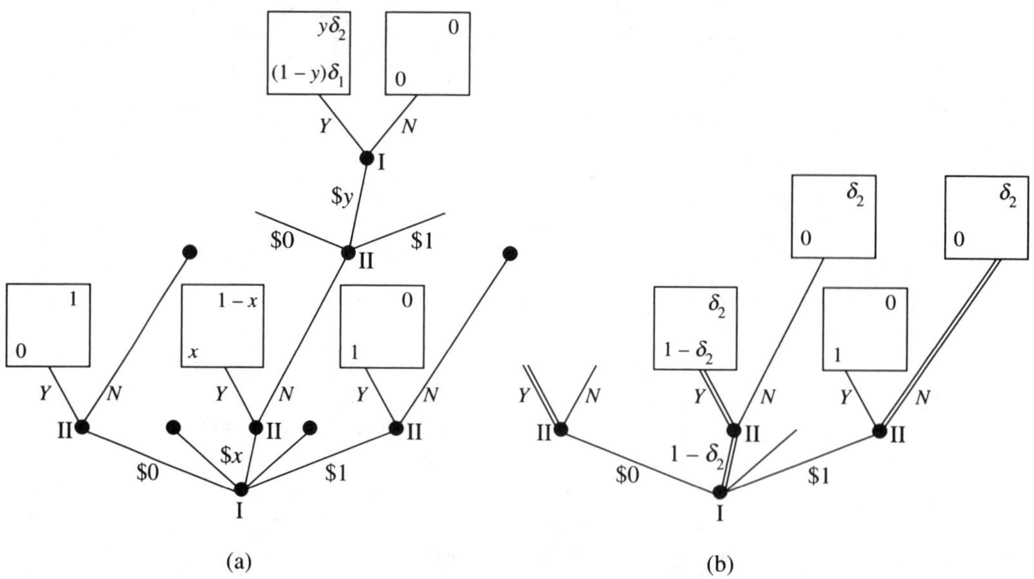

Figure 5.20 A two-stage bargaining game.

make the simplification $v_i(x) = x$. However, now it becomes necessary to introduce *discount factors* δ_1 and δ_2 satisfying $0 < \delta_i < 1$. Player i's utility for getting $\$x$ at time t is then taken to be $x\delta_i^t$.

Discount factors are a simple way of modeling how impatient players are. A player with a discount factor close to zero is very impatient. A player with $\delta_i = 1$ would not be impatient at all. For such a player, getting fifty cents now is no different from being sure of getting fifty cents in ten years time.

Figure 5.20(a) illustrates the game tree for the two-stage bargaining game. Player I makes the first proposal at time 0. If player II rejects the proposal, she makes a counterproposal at time $\tau > 0$. If this is refused by player I, then both players get nothing. No loss of generality is entailed in studying only the case $\tau = 1$. After this case has been analyzed, the corresponding results for the general case are found simply by replacing δ_i everywhere it appears by δ_i^τ.

The subgames rooted at nodes where player II makes a counterproposal are just copies of the Ultimatum Game. If such a subgame is reached and equilibrium strategies are used in the subgame, then player II will get the whole dollar. She will assign this outcome a utility of $1\delta_2 = \delta_2$ since she gets the dollar at time 1. Player I assigns the same event a utiiity of $0\delta_1 = 0$.

Zermelo's algorithm now tells us to replace each of the subgames by a terminal node labeled with the payoff pair $(0, \delta_2)$ that results from equilibrium play in the subgame. This reduces the situation to that shown in Figure 5.20(b).

In this reduced game, player I's optimal proposal is that which makes player II indifferent between accepting and refusing. He should therefore demand $1 - \delta_2$ because this leaves δ_2 for player II, and this is what she gets in equilibrium from refusing. In equilibrium, she accepts player I's demand of $1 - \delta_2$ for the reasons given in the previous section.

Notice that, if δ_2 is nearly zero so that player II is a very impatient person, then player I gets nearly all the dollar. If δ_2 is nearly 1 so that player II is a very patient person, then player II gets nearly all the dollar.

The length of the time interval that elapses between one stage of the game and the next is also significant. If this is τ instead of 1, then δ_i must be replaced everywhere by δ_i^τ. Player I will therefore demand $1 - \delta_2^\tau$ in equilibrium, which player II will accept. Since $\delta_2^\tau \to 1$ as $\tau \to 0$, it follows that player II gets nearly everything if τ is sufficiently small. Thus, if player II could choose how long to wait before making her counterproposal, she would choose to wait as short a time τ as possible.

5.8.4 The Infinite Horizon Game

The simple bargaining games of the preceding subsections were studied in preparation for the model that follows. This is perhaps the most natural of all possible bargaining models. It is therefore a striking vindication of Nash's approach to bargaining that the subgame-perfect equilibrium outcomes can be described using a generalized Nash bargaining solution.

The basic bargaining problem remains that of "dividing the dollar". In Section 5.6, player i's Von Neumann and Morgenstern utility for \$$x$ was denoted by $v_i(x)$. In Sections 5.8.1 and 5.8.3, the special case when $v_i(x) = x$ was studied. This simplification will now be abandoned. Thus we shall no longer be able to identify a util with a dollar delivered at time zero. Instead, we reintroduce the assumptions about v_i that were made in Section 5.6. In particular, the players will be risk-averse so that v_i is concave.

As in Section 5.8.3, the players' attitudes to the passage of time will also be important.[23] Player i's Von Neumann and

[23]With an infinite horizon, this point becomes transparent. If it did not matter *when* the players agreed, it would not matter *if* they agreed.

Morgenstern utility for getting $\$x$ at time t will be taken to be $v_i(x)\delta_i^t$. This makes it necessary to set $v_i(0) = 0$ so as to ensure that a player who is going to get nothing will be indifferent about when the check for zero dollars is delivered. For convenience, we also choose a utility scale with $v_i(1) = 1$.

Figure 5.16(a) shows the possible deals open to the players in money terms. They can agree on any pair $m = (m_1, m_2)$ of money payments in the set M. We must also take account of when the agreement is reached. We therefore need John and Mary's utility for a deal m reached at time t. These utilities are given by

$$u_i(m, t) = v_i(m_i)\delta_i^t \, .$$

In the bargaining game G to be studied, John makes the first proposal at time 0. If Mary rejects the proposal, she makes a counterproposal at time τ. If John rejects this proposal, he makes a counter-counterproposal at time 2τ. They continue in this way until a proposal is accepted. However, nothing prevents all proposals being refused, in which case the game will go on forever. Both players attach a utility of zero to this eventuality. As in Section 5.8.3, the case $\tau = 1$ is studied to keep the algebra simple.

A companion game H will also be needed. This is exactly the same as G except that the roles of the players are reversed. That is, Mary makes the first proposal.

The tree for the game G is shown in Figure 5.21(a). Figure 5.21(b) shows the set $X_0 = u(M, 0)$ of feasible utility pairs at time 0. The set $X_1 = u(M, 1)$ of feasible utility pairs at time 1 is smaller. The set $X_2 = u(M, 2)$ is smaller still. The economist Ariel Rubinstein, who first studied this model, likes to think of X_t as a pie that gradually shrinks over time. This shrinkage provides an incentive for the players to reach an early agreement. Each proposal that is refused means that there is less pie to be divided.

The doubled edges in the tree of Figure 5.21(a) illustrate the use of *stationary* strategies by the players. Strategies are said to be stationary when they ignore a player's history. Whatever may have happened in the past, a player using a stationary strategy always plans to play the same in the future. Thus, for example, whenever it is John's turn to make a proposal, he always proposes the deal m regardless of the history of rejected offers and counteroffers that may have gone before. Similarly, Mary always proposes the deal n.

We study the special case in which Mary always plans to

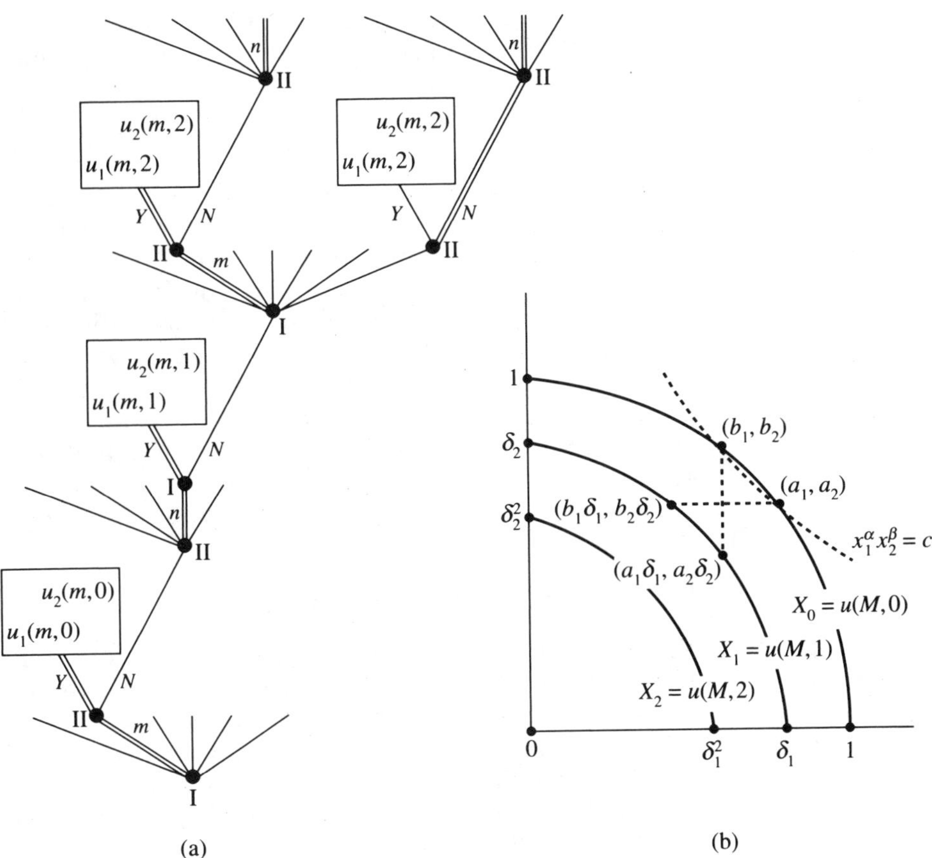

Figure 5.21 The infinite horizon game.

accept the deal m (or anything better for her) and to refuse anything worse. Similarly, John always plans to accept the deal n (or anything better for him) and to refuse anything worse. Can such pure strategies constitute a subgame-perfect equilibrium? The answer is surprisingly simple.

Let the vectors a and b be defined by $a = u(m, 0)$ and $b = u(n, 0)$. Thus, for example, $a_2 = u_2(m, 0)$ is the utility that Mary gets from accepting the deal m at time 0, and $a_1 = u_1(m, 0)$ is the utility that John gets if the deal m is accepted at time 0. From the discussion of the previous subsections, we have the principle that an equilibrium offer should make the player who responds indifferent between accepting and refusing. If John proposes m at time 0 in game G, then Mary will get a utility of a_2 from accepting. If she refuses, then she will propose n at time 1 and John will accept. She will therefore get a utility of $b_2\delta_2$ from refusing. To make her indifferent between accepting and refusing, the requirement is that

$$a_2 = b_2\delta_2 . \tag{5.4}$$

Notice that (5.4) implies that $a_2\delta_2^t = b_2\delta_2^{t+1}$ for any t. Thus Mary will be indifferent between accepting and refusing m whenever this may be proposed by John.

A similar condition is necessary for John. This is most easily formulated by repeating the preceding discussions for the companion game H in which it is Mary who makes the first proposal at time 0. If Mary proposes n at time 0 in game H, then John will get a utility of b_1 from accepting. If he refuses, then he will propose m at time 1 and Mary will accept. He will therefore get a utility of $a_1\delta_1$ from refusing. To make him indifferent between accepting and refusing, the requirement is that

$$b_1 = a_1\delta_1 . \tag{5.5}$$

Notice again that (5.5) implies that $b_1\delta_1^t = a_1\delta_1^{t+1}$ for any t. Thus John will be indifferent between accepting and refusing n whenever this may be proposed by Mary.

The conditions (5.4) and (5.5) are illustrated in Figure 5.21(b). Condition (5.4) just says that the points (a_1, a_2) and $(b_1\delta_1, b_2\delta_2)$ are on the same horizontal line. Condition (5.5) says that the points (b_1, b_2) and $(a_1\delta_1, a_2\delta_2)$ are on the same vertical line.[24]

Equations (5.4) and (5.5) characterize the equilibrium deal in the case when the time interval τ between successive proposals satisfies $\tau = 1$. However, to work out what the equilibrium deal actually is requires more calculating. Such calculation can be evaded if we turn our attention to the limiting case when $\tau \to 0$. Fortunately, this limiting case is

---

[24]Mathematicians will wish to be reassured that points a and b satisfying these requirements *exist*. Observe that $a_1 = v_1(m_1)$, $a_2 = v_2(m_2)$, $b_1 = v_1(n_1)$ and $b_2 = v_2(n_2)$. Since a and b are Pareto-efficient, $m_1 + m_2 = 1$ and $n_1 + n_2 = 1$. Thus $b_i = f(a_i)$, where $f : [0,1] \to [0,1]$ is defined by $f(x) = v_2(1 - v_1^{-1}(x))$. Equation (5.4) may therefore be written as $f(a_1) = \delta_2 f(b_1)$. Combining this with (5.5) yields that $f(a_1) = \delta_2 f(a_1\delta_1)$. A condition for existence is therefore that the function $g : [0,1] \to [0,1]$ defined by $g(x) = f(x) - \delta_2 f(x\delta_1)$ is zero somewhere in [0,1]. Note that $g(0) = 1 - \delta_2 > 0$ and $g(1) = 0 - \delta_2 f(\delta_1) < 0$. But a continuous function that is positive at 0 and negative at 1 must take the value zero somewhere between 0 and 1.

Actually, a and b are *uniquely* defined by (5.4) and (5.5) when v_1 and v_2 are concave, since the function g is then strictly decreasing on [0,1].

the case of greatest interest because, in the real world, nothing constrains a negotiator to keep to a strict timetable and, given that a player has just refused an offer, the optimal thing to do next is to make a counteroffer as soon as possible.

To deal with the case when $\tau \neq 1$, δ_1 and δ_2 in (5.4) and (5.5) must be replaced by δ_1^τ and δ_2^τ. It will make life easier if we simultaneously write $\delta_1 = e^{-\rho_1}$ and $\delta_2 = e^{-\rho_2}$. We then obtain that

$$a_2 = b_2 e^{-\rho_2 \tau}, \tag{5.6}$$

$$b_1 = a_1 e^{-\rho_1 \tau}. \tag{5.7}$$

In these formulae, ρ_1 and ρ_2 are discount *rates*.[25]

Theorem 5.8.1 Suppose that the stationary subgame-perfect equilibrium specified by (5.6) and (5.7) leads to the payoff pair $s(\tau)$. Then

$$s(\tau) \to s \quad \text{as} \quad \tau \to 0,$$

where s is the generalized Nash bargaining solution corresponding to the bargaining powers $\alpha = 1/\rho_1$ and $\beta = 1/\rho_2$ for the bargaining problem $(X_0, 0)$.

Proof. It follows from (5.6) and (5.7) that

$$\left(\frac{a_2}{b_2}\right)^\beta = \left(\frac{b_1}{a_1}\right)^\alpha = e^{-\tau} \tag{5.8}$$

because $\alpha = 1/\rho_1$ and $\beta = 1/\rho_2$. But (5.8) implies that

$$a_1^\alpha a_2^\beta = b_1^\alpha b_2^\beta .$$

Thus the points $a = (a_1, a_2)$ and $b = (b_1, b_2)$ both lie on the same curve $x_1^\alpha x_2^\beta = c$, as illustrated in Figure 5.21(b) for the case $\tau = 1$.

Since $e^{-\tau} \to 1$ as $\tau \to 0$, equation (5.8) tells us that $a_2/b_2 \to 1$ and $b_1/a_1 \to 1$ as $\tau \to 0$. Hence the points a and b converge on the same value[26] s. This tells us something interesting about Figure 5.21(b) in the case when δ_i is replaced everywhere by δ_i^τ. When $\tau \to 0$, the revised figure reduces to Figure 5.15 with $X = X_0$ and $d = 0$. Thus $s(\tau) \to s$ as $\tau \to 0$. □

[25]They correspond to what economists would call the "instantaneous rate of interest".

[26]A prior assumption that a and b converge is unnecessary. The argument shows that all limit points of a as $\tau \to 0$ are equal to s. Thus a cannot have different limit points and so converges. A similar argument applies to b.

5.8.5 The Moral of the Story

There are several lessons to be learned from the preceding analysis.

The first lesson is that the intuitions embodied in the Nash axioms of Section 5.5.4 are sound. If the interval τ between successive proposals in the Rubinstein bargaining model is sufficiently small, then a stationary subgame-perfect equilibrium outcome necessarily approximates a generalized Nash bargaining solution with bargaining powers $\alpha = 1/\rho_1$ and $\beta = 1/\rho_2$. As noted in Section 5.7.1, if no reasonably realistic bargaining model could be found with this property, then the research strategy embodied in the Nash program would call for the idea of the Nash bargaining solution to be abandoned.[27]

The second lesson concerns the interpretation of the bargaining powers $\alpha = 1/\rho_1$ and $\beta = 1/\rho_2$. Recall that ρ_2 is player i's discount rate. Since $\delta_i = e^{-\rho_i}$, a high discount rate ρ_i corresponds to a low discount factor δ_i. That is, people with high discount rates are more impatient than people with low discount rates. A patient person will therefore get a larger bargaining power than an impatient person. In consequence, his share of the dollar will be higher.

The third lesson is more a word of warning. The Rubinstein bargaining model was studied as a game of perfect information. In particular, the preferences of each player are assumed to be common knowledge. This includes how impatient they are and how averse they are to taking risks. As we have seen, both impatience and risk-aversion are undesirable properties for a successful bargainer.

However, it will seldom be realistic to assume that such characteristics of bargainers are common knowledge before the negotiations begin. In real life, people have to learn about those with whom they negotiate while the negotiations are proceeding. This may not be easy, especially if the opponent is anxious to conceal his weaknesses and is clever in doing so.

One should therefore not expect even rational bargainers to agree immediately as in the Rubinstein bargaining model

[27]When rival "bargaining solutions" to those of Nash are mentioned, it is the Kalai-Smorodinsky bargaining solution of Exercise 5.9.19 that tends to get most attention. There are noncooperative games whose unique subgame-perfect equilibrium outcome coincides with the Kalai-Smorodinsky bargaining solution. However, these noncooperative games are not at all realistic as bargaining models.

unless they are both unusually well-informed about their bargaining partner.

5.8.6 Uniqueness of Equilibrium

Math 5.9 →

The study of Rubinstein's infinite horizon model in Section 5.8.4 is incomplete. It was shown that the model has a subgame-perfect equilibrium outcome that approximates the generalized Nash bargaining solution with bargaining powers $\alpha = 1/\rho_1$ and $\beta = 1/\rho_2$. A complete analysis is much more convincing in that it shows that the game has no other subgame-perfect equilibrium outcomes. The generalized Nash bargaining solution therefore has no competitors if the players use subgame-perfect strategies.

For a proof of this result, we return to the special case in which each player's Von Neumann and Morgenstern utility for a sum of money x delivered at time 0 is simply $v_i(x) = x$. Thus an agreement that assigns x of the dollar to John and $1 - x$ of the dollar to Mary at time t will be assigned a utility of $x\delta_1^t$ by John and $(1 - x)\delta_2^t$ by Mary. As in previous sections, the algebra will be simplified by taking $\tau = 1$.

Theorem 5.8.2 (Rubinstein) The infinite horizon bargaining game G has a unique subgame-perfect equilibrium outcome.

Proof. In principle, the game G may have many subgame-perfect equilibrium outcomes from each of which John gets a different payoff. Let the largest[28] subgame-perfect equilibrium payoff to John be A_1 and let the smallest be a_1.

Recall that H denotes the companion game in which Mary makes the first proposal. Let the largest subgame-equilibrium payoff to Mary in H be B_2 and let the smallest be b_2.

The proof consists of showing that $A_1 = a_1$ and $B_2 = b_2$. Two inequalities are needed.

1. In the game G, a subgame-perfect equilibrium cannot assign Mary less than $b_2\delta_2$ because she can always refuse whatever John proposes at time 0. The game H will then be played starting at time 1. But the smallest subgame-perfect

[28]The set S of subgame-perfect equilibrium payoffs to John turns out to have a maximum and a minimum. However, it is not necessary to assume this. The proof works equally well if A_1 is taken to be the supremum of S and a_1 is the infimum.

equilibrium outcome for Mary in H is b_2, which has to be discounted by a factor δ_2 because of the delay of length 1. If Mary gets at least $b_2\delta_2$ in equilibrium, then John can get no more than $1 - b_2\delta_2$ because there is only 1 dollar to be divided. This justifies the first inequality:

$$A_1 \leq 1 - b_2\delta_2 . \tag{5.9}$$

2. Suppose that $x < 1 - B_2\delta_2$. Then it will be shown that x is not a member of the set S of subgame-perfect equilibrium payoffs for John in G.

Let $x < y < 1 - B_2\delta_2$. Since $1 - y > B_2\delta_2$, a demand by John of y at time 0 would necessarily be accepted by Mary in equilibrium. The reason is that, if she refuses, the companion game H will be played at time 1. The largest subgame-perfect equilibrium outcome for Mary in H is B_2, which has to be discounted by a factor of δ_2 because of the time delay of length 1. She therefore gets more by accepting $1 - y$ than the largest amount $B_2\delta_2$ she could get by refusing.

It follows that it cannot be optimal for John to use a strategy that results in his receiving a payoff of x because he can get y at time 0 simply by demanding y. Hence $x \notin S$. Since this is true for each $x < 1 - B_2\delta_2$, the smallest element a_1 of S must satisfy

$$a_1 \geq 1 - B_2\delta_2 . \tag{5.10}$$

Two further inequalities may be obtained by exchanging the roles of G and H in the preceding discussion. The inequalities are:

$$B_2 \leq 1 - a_1\delta_1 , \tag{5.11}$$
$$b_2 \geq 1 - A_1\delta_1 . \tag{5.12}$$

It follows from (5.12) that $-b_2 \leq -(1 - A_1\delta_1)$. This conclusion may be substituted in (5.9) and so

$$A_1 \leq 1 - b_2\delta_2 \leq 1 - \delta_2(1 - A_1\delta_1) = 1 - \delta_2 + A_1\delta_1\delta_2 .$$

It follows that

$$A_1 \leq \frac{1 - \delta_2}{1 - \delta_1\delta_2} . \tag{5.13}$$

Similarly, it follows from (5.11) that $-B_2 \geq -(1 - a_1\delta_1)$. This conclusion may be substituted in (5.10) and so

$$a_1 \geq 1 - B_2\delta_2 \geq 1 - \delta_2(1 - a_1\delta_1) = 1 - \delta_2 + a_1\delta_1\delta_2 .$$

It follows that

$$a_1 \geq \frac{1-\delta_2}{1-\delta_1\delta_2}. \tag{5.14}$$

But a_1 is the minimum of the set S and A_1 is the maximum of the set S. Hence $a_1 \leq A_1$. Thus (5.13) and (5.14) and the corresponding inequalities for B_2 and b_2 imply that

$$a_1 = A_1 = \frac{1-\delta_2}{1-\delta_1\delta_2}; \qquad b_2 = B_2 = \frac{1-\delta_1}{1-\delta_1\delta_2}.$$

This completes the proof of the theorem. □

What subgame-perfect equilibrium strategy pair yields John's unique equilibrium payoff of a_1? It turns out that the necessary pure strategies are those discussed in Section 5.8.4. In particular, John proposes the deal $a = (a_1, a_2) = (a_1, 1 - a_1)$ at time 0 and Mary accepts.[29]

Does the conclusion check with the result of Section 5.8.4 that the agreed deal a approximates the generalized Nash bargaining solution with bargaining powers $\alpha = 1/\rho_1$ and $\beta = 1/\rho_2$ when the interval τ between successive proposals is sufficiently small? To investigate this point, it is necessary to replace δ_i everywhere by δ_i^τ, and then to consider the limiting value of a_1 as $\tau \to 0$. By L'Hôpital's rule,[30]

$$\lim_{\tau \to 0} \left(\frac{1-\delta_2^\tau}{1-\delta_1^\tau \delta_2^\tau} \right) = \lim_{\tau \to 0} \left(\frac{1-e^{-\tau\rho_2}}{1-e^{-\tau(\rho_1+\rho_2)}} \right)$$

$$= \lim_{\tau \to 0} \left(\frac{\tau\rho_2}{\tau(\rho_1+\rho_2)} \right) = \frac{\rho_2}{\rho_1+\rho_2}.$$

---

[29]If it were in equilibrium for Mary to refuse John's opening proposal, then the game H would be played at time 1. The unique subgame-perfect equilibrium payoff for John in H is $b_1 = 1 - b_2$, which needs to be discounted by δ_1 because of the time delay of length 1. But it is easy to check that $b_1\delta_1 < a_1$. Hence a refusal by Mary at time 0 would make it impossible for John to get his unique equilibrium payoff.

[30]If f and g are continuous at a, then

$$\lim_{x \to a} \frac{f(x)}{g(x)} = \frac{f(a)}{g(a)}$$

provided that $g(a) \neq 0$. What happens if $g(a) = 0$? The limit may still be finite provided that $f(a) = 0$. L'Hôpital's rule says that

$$\lim_{x \to a} \frac{f(x)}{g(x)} = \lim_{x \to a} \frac{f'(x)}{g'(x)}$$

provided that f and g are differentiable close to a and the right-hand limit exists.

Thus the deal $a = (a_1, a_2)$ splits the dollar between John and Mary in the ratio $\rho_2 : \rho_1$. This is exactly what the generalized Nash bargaining solution with bargaining powers $\alpha = 1/\rho_1$ and $\beta = 1/\rho_2$ predicts.

5.9 Exercises

Review

1. Explain why the vector $w = (3 - 2\alpha, 2, 1 + 2\alpha)$ is the location of a point on the straight line through the points $x = (1, 2, 3)$ and $y = (3, 2, 1)$. For what value of α does the vector w lie halfway between x and y? For what value of α does the vector w lie at the center of gravity of a mass of $\frac{1}{3}$ at x and a mass $\frac{2}{3}$ at y?

Review

2. Draw a diagram that shows the vectors $(1, 1)$, $(4, 2)$, $(2, 4)$ and $(3, 3)$ in $\mathbb{R}^2$. Indicate the convex hull H of the set consisting of these four vectors. Why is $(3, 3)$ a convex combination of $(4, 2)$ and $(2, 4)$? Indicate in your diagram the vectors $\frac{2}{3}(1, 1) + \frac{1}{3}(4, 2)$ and $\frac{1}{3}(1, 1) + \frac{1}{3}(4, 2) + \frac{1}{3}(3, 3)$.

Review

3. Sketch the following sets in $\mathbb{R}^2$. Which are convex? What are their convex hulls?
   (a) $A = \{x : x_1^2 + x_2^2 = 4\}$
   (b) $B = \{x : x_1^2 + x_2^2 \leq 4\}$
   (c) $C = \{x : x_1 = 4\}$
   (d) $D = \{x : x_1 \leq 4\}$
   (e) $E = \{x : x_1 = 4 \text{ or } x_2 = 4\}$

Review

4. Draw supporting lines to the convex set H of Exercise 5.9.2 at the points $(1, 1)$, $(2, 4)$, $(3, 3)$ and $(2, \frac{4}{3})$. Where it is possible to draw more than one supporting line, draw several supporting lines.

Review

5. Check that the function $f : \mathbb{R}^2 \to \mathbb{R}^2$ defined by $(y_1, y_2) = f(x_1, x_2)$ if and only if

$$y_1 = x_1 + 2x_2 + 1$$
$$y_2 = 2x_1 + x_2 + 2$$

   is affine. Indicate the points $f(1, 1)$, $f(2, 4)$ and $f(4, 2)$ on a diagram. Also indicate the images $f(H)$ and $f(l)$ for the set H and one of the supporting lines l that you drew in Exercise 5.9.4.

6. Find the cooperative payoff region X for the bimatrix game of Figure 5.22 in the case when the players can make binding agreements to use a lottery, but cannot freely dispose of utils nor transfer them.

	t_1	t_2	t_3
s_1	-1 -1	3 1	0 3
s_2	0 1	1 0	3 0

Figure 5.22 The bimatrix game for Exercises 5.9.6, 5.9.7 and 5.9.8.

7. Find the cooperative payoff region Y for the bimatrix game of Figure 5.22 in the case when free disposal is permitted but utils cannot be transferred.
8. Find the cooperative payoff region Z for the bimatrix game of Figure 5.22 in the case when free disposal is permitted and utils can be transferred from one player to the other.
9. Which of the following values of y satisfy $y > x$ and hence are Pareto improvements on $x = (2, 3)$?
   (a) $y = (4, 4)$ (b) $y = (1, 2)$ (c) $y = (2, 4)$
   (d) $y = (3, 3)$ (e) $y = (2, 3)$ (f) $y = (3, 2)$
   For which of these values of y is it true that $y \geq x$? For which values of y is it true that $y \gg x$?
10. Explain why (dD, dD) is a Pareto-efficient pure strategy pair of the game of Exercise 4.8.27. Is this a Nash equilibrium of the game?
11. Find the Pareto-efficient points for the sets Y and Z of Exercises 5.9.7 and 5.9.8. What are the bargaining sets when the disagreement point is $d = (0, 1)$? What are the bargaining sets when the disagreement point is $e = (1, 0)$?
12. Find the value of the regular Nash bargaining solution for each of the problems (Y, d), (Z, d), (Y, e) and (Z, e), where Y, Z, d and e are defined as in the previous exercise.
13. Find the values of the generalized Nash bargaining solution with bargaining powers $\alpha = \frac{1}{3}$ and $\beta = \frac{2}{3}$ for each of the bargaining problems of the previous exercise.
14. Repeat the previous exercise with $\alpha = \frac{2}{3}$ and $\beta = \frac{1}{3}$.

Econon

15. A firm makes sprockets that sell at \$8 each. To make sprockets it requires various inputs, but these are all free except for labor. The firm's production function $f : \mathbb{R}_+ \to \mathbb{R}_+$ is given by $s = f(l) = \sqrt{l}$, where s is the number of sprockets produced in a day when l hours of labor are used. If the hourly wage is w, explain why the firm's daily profit is $\pi = 8\sqrt{l} - wl$. If the worker regards each hour of leisure as being worth \$1, explain why his

daily income is $I = wl + (24 - l)$. Both the worker and the firm are risk-neutral.

(a) Find the value of l that maximizes the surplus $s = \pi + I$ available to the firm and worker jointly.

(b) Suppose that the worker and the firm bargain about both the wage and the number of hours to be worked. What is their disagreement point? How will the surplus be divided if the regular Nash bargaining solution is used? What wage will be agreed upon? What will be the length of the working day?

(c) For each w, determine the length l of the working day that maximizes the firm's profit.

(d) Suppose now that the worker and the firm only bargain about the wage w. After a wage has been agreed, the firm unilaterally sets the number of hours of labor per day that it wishes to buy. Determine the value of the regular Nash product that then arises as a function of w. What wage will be agreed? What will be the length of the working day?

(e) Why will the firm say that there is overmanning (too many hours worked) in case (b)? Why can the worker respond by saying that case (d) is socially inefficient?

Phil 16. For a bargaining problem (X, d) in which X satisfies conditions (1), (2) and (3) of Section 5.5.1, explain why *every* payoff pair in the bargaining set is the generalized Nash bargaining solution for *some* bargaining powers α and β. Should we deduce that Theorem 5.5.1 is devoid of substantive content?

Math 17. For a bargaining problem (X, d) in which X satisfies conditions (1), (2) and (3) of Section 5.5.1, let m_1 be the largest value of x_1 such that $(x_1, d_2) \in X$. Let m_2 be the largest value of x_2 such that $(d_1, x_2) \in X$. Find m_1 and m_2 for each of the bargaining problems of Exercise 5.9.12. Explain why the regular Nash bargaining solution always assigns a utility of at least $\frac{1}{2}(m_i - d_i)$ to player i.

Math 18. Find two bargaining problems (X, d) and (Y, d) such that $Y \subseteq X$ but the regular Nash bargaining solution assigns more to player II in (Y, d) than in (X, d). Sometimes it is suggested that the regular Nash bargaining solution would be a good candidate for adoption by an arbitrator looking for a scheme that settles disputes fairly. Is the property of the regular Nash bargaining solution studied in this exercise likely to be one that such an arbitrator would welcome?

Econ 19. The Kalai-Smorodinsky bargaining solution $K : \mathcal{B} \to \mathbb{R}^2$ is defined by taking $K(X, d)$ to be the unique Pareto-efficient point of X that lies on the straight line joining the points d and m, where m is defined as in Exercise 5.9.17. Find $K(X, d)$ for each of the bargaining problems of Exercise 5.9.12.

Econ 20. The Kalai-Smorodinsky bargaining solution $K : \mathcal{B} \to \mathbb{R}^2$ defined in the previous exercise fails to satisfy only one of the four axioms of Section 5.5.4. Which axiom does it fail to satisfy? Give examples of specific bargaining problems for which the axiom fails when applied to $K : \mathcal{B} \to \mathbb{R}^2$.

21. John and Mary may divide a dollar between them if they can agree on how it should be divided. How will they divide the dollar if they use the generalized Nash bargaining solution with bargaining powers $\alpha = \frac{2}{5}$ and $\beta = \frac{3}{5}$ in the case when John's Von Neumann and Morgenstern utility for \$$x$ is $v_1(x) = x^\gamma$ and Mary's is $v_2(x) = x^\delta$, where $\gamma = \frac{1}{4}$ and $\delta = \frac{3}{4}$? Whose share of the dollar would increase if both γ and δ were changed to $\frac{1}{2}$?

22. Repeat the previous exercise for the case when $\gamma = 3$ and $\delta = 2$.

23. Find a Nash equilibrium for the Ultimatum Game of Section 5.8.1 that results in the dollar being split 50 : 50.

Phil 24. Take $\tau = 1$ and $\delta_1 = \delta_2 = 0.9$ in the two-stage bargaining game of Section 5.8.3. Find all subgame-perfect equilibria when proposers are confined to making proposals in whole numbers of cents.

25. Suppose that the two-stage bargaining game of Section 5.8.3 is extended so that it has three stages, with player II making the first proposal. There is a unique subgame-perfect equilibrium. How much does this assign to player II?

Econ 26. In Rubinstein's infinite horizon bargaining game of Section 5.8.4, suppose that the players are restricted to proposing either that John should get the whole dollar or that Mary should get the whole dollar.

(a) Show that there is a subgame-perfect equilibrium in which John begins by proposing that he get the whole dollar and Mary agrees.

(b) Show that there is a subgame-perfect equilibrium in which John begins by proposing that the whole dollar be given to Mary and she agrees.

(c) Show that there are other subgame-perfect equilibria in which agreement does not occur immediately.[31]

Fun

27. Suppose that John and Mary play the following bargaining game about the division of a dollar donated by a philanthropist. The philanthropist specifies that only the splits 10 : 90, 20 : 80, 50 : 50 and 60 : 40 are to be permitted. Moreover, John and Mary are to alternate in vetoing splits that they regard as unacceptable. What split will result if subgame-perfect strategies are used and John has the first opportunity to veto? What split will result if Mary begins?

---

[31] Section 5.8.2 studies a finite version of the Ultimatum Game in which the dollar can only be split into whole numbers of cents. *Two* subgame-perfect equilibria were then identified. Using the techniques required for Exercise 5.9.26, one can show that multiple equilibria may also exist in Rubinstein's infinite horizon model if proposals must be made in whole numbers of cents. In fact, if the players' discount factors are sufficiently close to 1, *any* deal is then a subgame-perfect equilibrium outcome in Rubinstein's model. This is to be contrasted with the result of Section 5.8.6 that the continuous version of the Rubinstein bargaining model has a unique subgame-perfect equilibrium. Should we conclude, as some would argue, that the latter result is nothing more than a mathematical curiosity? My own view is that it would be naive to argue that, because some aspect of the physical world is discrete, therefore a discrete model *necessarily* best models how players perceive the world. In the current case, one cannot evade asking what it is that determines the value of the smallest unit of currency. This unit changes over time, but is always so small that one unit more or less is a matter of practical indifference even to the poorest citizen. The money scale can therefore be conveniently perceived as a continuum. If one unit more or less, were *not* a matter of practical indifference, people would find their own ways of subdividing the units. For example, John might propose to Mary that she should get 47 cents if a coin falls heads, and 48 cents if it falls tails.

CHAPTER

6

Mixing Things Up

6.1 Introduction

This chapter is about mixed strategies. A player uses a mixed strategy when his or her choice of pure strategy is made at random. For example, a player with two pure strategies might decide to use one pure strategy with probability $\frac{1}{3}$ and the other with probability $\frac{2}{3}$.

It may seem odd that a rational player should choose to randomize in this way. But consider bluffing in Poker. It is obvious that rational play must involve some bluffing. Suppose, for example, that Mary never bluffs. When she bets high, everyone will therefore know that she must have a good hand. Thus her opponents will all hasten to fold, except on those rare occasions when someone thinks he has an even better hand. Mary will therefore seldom win much when dealt a good hand, and occasionally she will lose. To have a chance of winning a sizeable pot when she has a good hand, Mary must sometimes bet high when she has a bad hand. That is, she must sometimes bluff. Of course, it will do her no good at all to bluff if the other players can anticipate when she is going to bluff. She needs to make her bluffing behavior *unpredictable*. This can be guaranteed by delegating the choice of when to bluff to a carefully chosen random device. Even Mary will then not be able to predict in advance when she will be bluffing. Such a stratagem will therefore certainly keep her opponents guessing.

Those who have played Poker may see this as a clinching argument for the rational use of mixed strategies. But there remains the question of *which* mixed strategy to choose. How often should a rational player bluff, and on what hands? This question is left for a later chapter. The current chapter only considers the use of mixed strategies in much simpler games than Poker.

6.2 Minimax and Maximin

Von Neumann's minimax theorem is perhaps the most celebrated result of game theory. This section contains some preliminary material for the case when the players are restricted to using pure strategies.

6.2.1 Computing Minimax and Maximin Values

Let S be the set of rows in the matrix M of Figure 6.1, and let T be the set of columns. Denote the entry in row s and column t by $\pi(s,t)$. Then

$$\max_{s\in S} \pi(s,t) \quad \text{and} \quad \min_{t\in T} \pi(s,t)$$

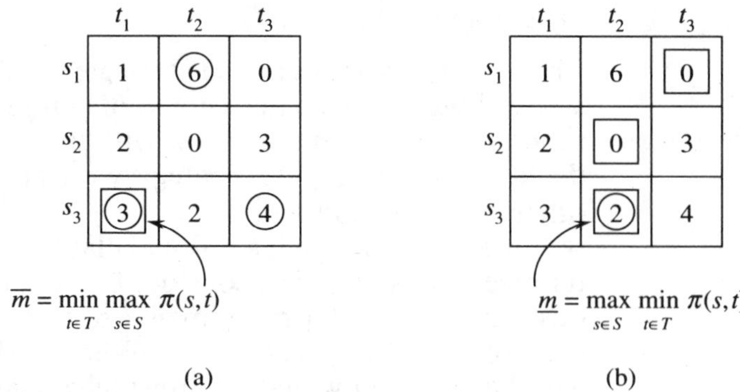

Figure 6.1 Minimax and maximin values for the matrix M.

are respectively the largest entry in column t and the smallest entry in row s. The largest entries in each column are circled in Figure 6.1(a). The smallest entries in each row are enclosed in a square in Figure 6.1(b). Notice that

$$\begin{aligned} \max_{s\in S} \pi(s,t_1) &= 3 \qquad & \min_{t\in T} \pi(s_1,t) &= 0\,, \\ \max_{s\in S} \pi(s,t_2) &= 6 \qquad & \min_{t\in T} \pi(s_2,t) &= 0\,, \\ \max_{s\in S} \pi(s,t_3) &= 4 \qquad & \min_{t\in T} \pi(s_3,t) &= 2\,. \end{aligned}$$

It follows that

$$\begin{aligned} \overline{m} &= \min_{t\in T}\{\max_{s\in S} \pi(s,t)\} = \min\{3,6,4\} = 3\,, \\ \underline{m} &= \max_{s\in S}\{\min_{t\in T} \pi(s,t)\} = \max\{0,0,2\} = 2\,. \end{aligned}$$

The quantity $\overline{m}$ is the minimax value of the matrix M. The quantity $\underline{m}$ is the maximin value of the matrix M.

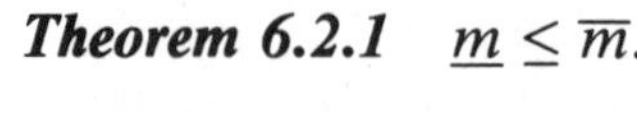

Theorem 6.2.1 $\underline{m} \leq \overline{m}$.

Proof. For any $t \in T$, $\min_{t\in T} \pi(s,t) \leq \pi(s,t)$. Hence

$$\max_{s\in S} \min_{t\in T} \pi(s,t) \leq \max_{s\in S} \pi(s,t)\,.$$

Math 6.2.2 ⟶

Now apply this inequality with the particular value of $t \in T$ that minimizes the right-hand side. □

The example that precedes Theorem 6.2.1 shows that it can happen that $\underline{m}$ is strictly smaller than $\overline{m}$ so that $\underline{m} < \overline{m}$. When is it true that $\underline{m} = \overline{m}$? This does sometimes happen, as the case of matrix N illustrated in Figure 6.2 shows. To say something more general, it is necessary to return to the idea of a saddle point previewed in Section 1.7.2.

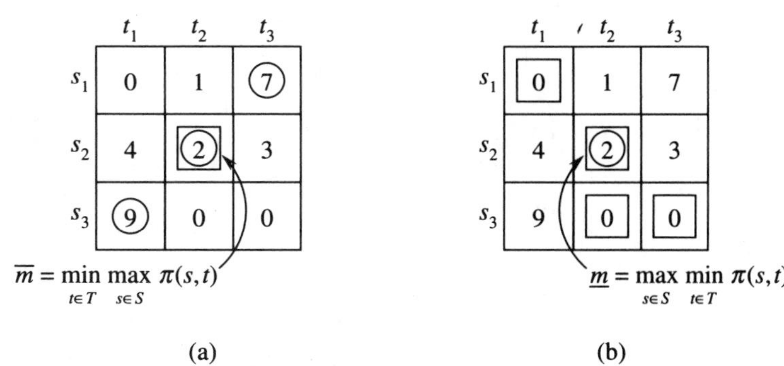

Figure 6.2 Minimax and maximin values for the matrix N.

6.2.2 Saddle Points

Let $\pi(s,t)$ be the entry in row s and column t of a matrix N. The pair (σ,τ) is a *saddle point* for the matrix N when $\pi(\sigma,\tau)$ is the largest entry in its column and the smallest entry in its row. The matrix N of Figure 6.3(a) has been copied from Figure 6.2. The largest entry in each column has been circled, and the smallest entry in each row has been enclosed in a square. The entry in row s_2 and column t_2 gets both a circle and a square. It follows that (s_2,t_2) is a saddle point of the matrix.

The heights of the obelisks in Figure 6.4(a) represent the entries in the matrix N of Figure 6.3(a). Thus the obelisk in row s_2 and column t_1 is 4 because $\pi(s_2,t_1) = 4$. If one looks closely at the picture, the reason that the pair (s_2,t_2) is called a saddle point will become apparent. However, the saddle drawn would be very uncomfortable to sit upon.

Figure 6.4(b) looks more like a saddle. It shows a saddle point (σ,τ) for a continuous function $\pi : S \times T \to \mathbf{R}$ in the

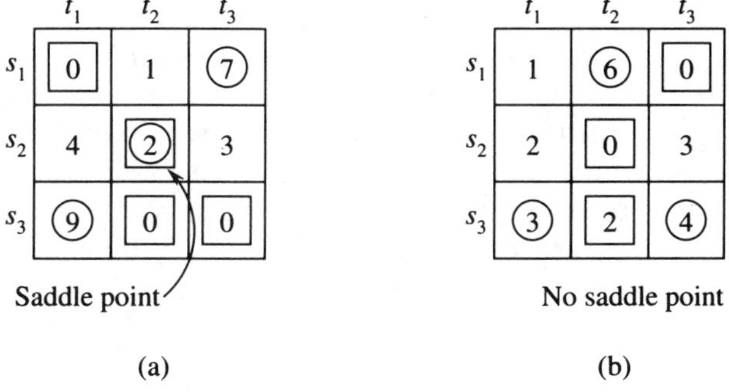

Figure 6.3 Finding saddle points.

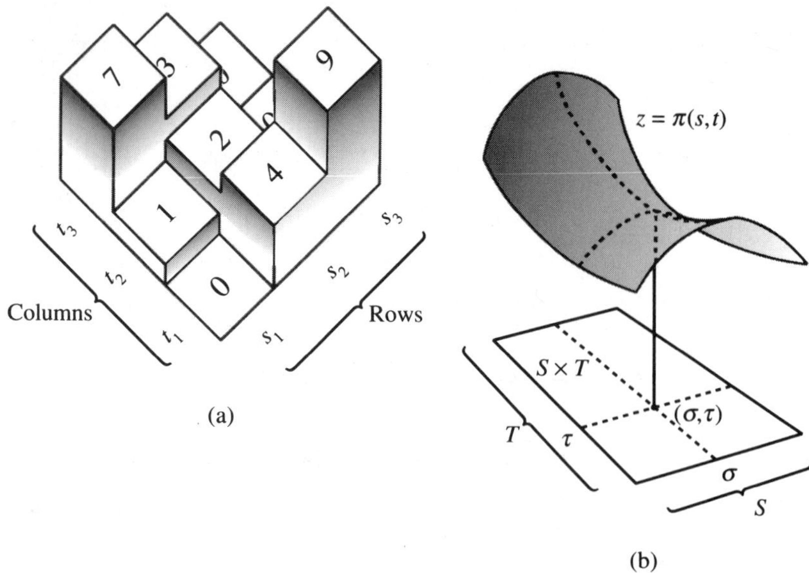

Figure 6.4 Saddle points.

case when S and T are closed intervals of real numbers. The real numbers in the set S are to be thought of as labeling the rows of a "matrix". The columns are labeled by the real numbers in the set T. The entry in the row s and column t of the "matrix" is $\pi(s,t)$. The requirement that (σ,τ) be a saddle point is that the payoff $\pi(\sigma,\tau)$ be largest in its column and smallest in its row. In mathematical terms,

$$\pi(\sigma,t) \geq \pi(\sigma,\tau) \geq \pi(s,\tau) \tag{6.1}$$

for all s in S and all t in T.

The matrix M of Figure 6.3(b) has been copied from Figure 6.1. Recall that the maximin and minimax values of M are *not* equal. The largest payoff in each column of M has been circled, and the smallest payoff in each row has been enclosed in a square. No payoff gets both a circle and a square, and so the matrix M has *no* saddle point.

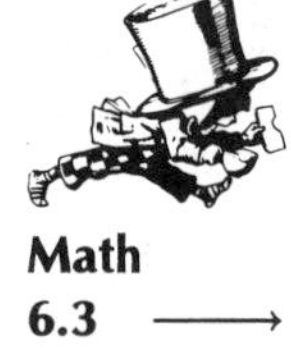

Math 6.3 ⟶

On the other hand, we have seen that the maximin and minimax values of the matrix N of Figure 6.3(a) are equal and the matrix does have a saddle point $(\sigma,\tau) = (s_2, t_2)$. An examination of Figure 6.2 shows that $\sigma = s_2$ is the row s that makes $\min_{t\in T} \pi(s,t)$ largest, and $\tau = t_2$ is the column t that makes $\max_{s\in S} \pi(s,t)$ smallest. In formal terms,

$$\min_{t\in T} \pi(\sigma,t) = \max_{s\in S} \min_{t\in T} \pi(s,t) = \underline{m} \tag{6.2}$$

$$\max_{s\in S} \pi(s,\tau) = \min_{t\in T} \max_{s\in S} \pi(s,t) = \overline{m} \tag{6.3}$$

The next theorem confirms that this connection between maximin and minimax values and saddle points holds in general.

Theorem 6.2.2 A necessary and sufficient condition that (σ, τ) be a saddle point is that σ and τ are given by (6.2) and (6.3) and $\underline{m} = \overline{m}$. When (σ, τ) is a saddle point, $\underline{m} = \pi(\sigma, \tau) = \overline{m}$.

Proof. 1. Suppose first that (σ, τ) is a saddle point. Thus, $\pi(\sigma, t) \geq \pi(\sigma, \tau) \geq \pi(s, \tau)$ for all s in S and t in T. This implies that

$$\min_{t \in T} \pi(\sigma, t) \geq \pi(\sigma, \tau) \geq \max_{s \in S} \pi(s, \tau)$$

and hence

$$\underline{m} = \max_{\sigma \in S} \min_{t \in T} \pi(\sigma, t) \geq \min_{t \in T} \pi(\sigma, t)$$
$$\geq \max_{s \in S} \pi(s, \tau) \geq \min_{\tau \in T} \max_{s \in S} \pi(s, \tau) = \overline{m}.$$

But Theorem 6.2.1 asserts that $\underline{m} \leq \overline{m}$. Thus, all the $\geq$ signs in the preceding expression may be replaced by $=$ signs.

2. Next suppose that $\underline{m} = \overline{m}$. It must then be shown that a saddle point (σ, τ) exists. Choose σ and τ to satisfy (6.2) and (6.3). Then, given any s in S and t in T,

$$\pi(\sigma, t) \geq \min_{t \in T} \pi(\sigma, t) = \underline{m} = \overline{m} = \max_{s \in S} \pi(s, \tau) \geq \pi(s, \tau).$$

Taking $s = \sigma$ and $t = \tau$ in this inequality demonstrates that $\underline{m} = \pi(\sigma, \tau) = \overline{m}$. Hence the requirement for (σ, τ) to be a saddle point is satisfied. □

6.2.3 Suprema and Infima

The discussion of the preceding subsections is technical. It would have been very much more technical if attention had not been restricted to the case when the sets S and T are finite. In the finite case, the minima and maxima under discussion always exist. However, sometimes one needs to consider infinite pure strategy sets. In this case, the existence of maxima and minima is not assured. The notion of a maximum must then be replaced by that of a supremum (abbreviated to sup) and the notion of a minimum by that of an infimum (abbreviated to inf).[1] At the same time, extra conditions must

[1]The supremum of a set is its smallest upper bound. For example, the open interval $(0, 1)$ has no maximum element. But everything in the set $(0, 1)$ is smaller than 2. Thus 2 is an upper bound for $(0, 1)$. The smallest upper bound is 1. It follows that 1 is the supremum of the set $(0, 1)$. It cannot be the maximum of the set because it is not a member of the set. By definition, the maximum of a set is its largest element. Not being in the set, 1 is therefore not even a candidate for its maximum. Note that the open interval $(0, 1)$ also has no minimum, but its infimum is 0.

be imposed on the payoff function $\pi : S \times T \to \mathbb{R}$ in order to get results. In what follows, no account is taken of the fact that such difficulties can arise beyond the fact that "sup" and "inf" will occasionally be written instead of "max" and "min".

6.3 Safety First

Security levels and security strategies were previewed in Section 1.9.1. The idea now needs to be examined more closely.

6.3.1 Security Levels

A player's *security level* in a game is the largest expected payoff he or she can *guarantee* whatever the other players may do. To compute their security levels, a player therefore has to carry out a worst-case analysis. For example, suppose that John and Mary are the protagonists in a two-player game. To compute his security level, John must ask himself what he would do under the paranoid assumption that Mary will predict his strategy choice, and then act to *minimize* his payoff. A strategy John would choose under this paranoid hypothesis is called a *security strategy*. Thus, if John uses one of his security strategies, he is guaranteed a payoff at least as large as his security level.

Suppose that John is player I and Mary is player II in the bimatrix game of Figure 6.5(a). John's payoff matrix in this game is the matrix of Figure 6.2. In working through a worst-case scenario, John may reason in the following way. If he leads off by choosing row s_1, then perhaps Mary will neglect her own welfare in favor of minimizing John's. If so, then

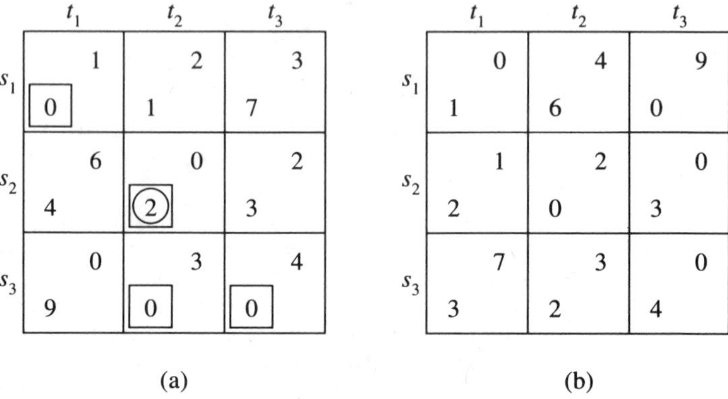

Figure 6.5 Two bimatrix games.

she will follow by choosing column t_1. John will then get a payoff of 0. If John leads with row s_2, Mary will follow with column t_2 so that his payoff is 2. If he leads with row s_3, Mary will follow with column t_2 or column t_3 so that John gets a payoff of 0. Thus a worst-case analysis places John's payoff in the set $\{0, 2, 0\}$ of payoffs enclosed in squares in the diagram of Figure 6.5(a). The best payoff in this set is the circled payoff of 2. Thus John can guarantee a payoff of at least 2 by using pure strategy s_2. Referring back to the matrix of Figure 6.2(b), we note that $2 = \underline{m}$.

The preceding argument can be employed in general to show that player I always has a pure strategy that guarantees a payoff at least as good as the maximin value $\underline{m}$ of his payoff matrix. Does this mean that $\underline{m}$ is player I's security level?

Theorem 6.3.1 If player I's payoff matrix has a saddle point (σ, τ), then his security level is $\underline{m} = \pi_1(\sigma, \tau) = \overline{m}$, and σ is one of his security strategies.

Proof. Recall from (6.1) that the requirement for a saddle point is that $\pi(\sigma, t) \geq \pi(\sigma, \tau) \geq \pi(s, \tau)$ for each s in S and each t in T. The inequality $\pi(\sigma, t) \geq \pi(\sigma, \tau)$ says that player I must get at least $\underline{m} = \pi(\sigma, \tau)$ from playing σ whatever pure strategy $t \in T$ player II may use. The inequality $\pi(\sigma, \tau) \geq \pi(s, \tau)$ says that player I cannot guarantee more than $\underline{m} = \pi(\sigma, \tau)$ by using another pure strategy s, because player II can always respond by playing τ. □

Since John's payoff matrix N in the game of Figure 6.5(a) has a saddle point, the theorem confirms that John's security level is 2 and that s_2 is a security strategy.

Next consider John's security level in the bimatrix game of Figure 6.5(b). John's payoff matrix is then the matrix M of Figure 6.1. Its maximin value is $\underline{m} = 2$. But, since the matrix M has no saddle point, Theorem 6.3.1 does *not* tell us that 2 is John's security level. In fact, John's security level is $2\frac{2}{3}$. To understand why, it is necessary to consider the use of mixed strategies in the game. This question is taken up in Section 6.4.

6.3.2 More Dueling

Math 6.4 ⟶

The game of Duel has been analyzed twice, once in Chapter 2 using Zermelo's algorithm, and once in Chapter 4 using the method of successive deletion of dominated strategies. The game will be used here to illustrate how security strategies may be calculated in complicated games.

As in Section 4.1.2, attention is confined to a simplified strategic form in which a player is restricted to those pure strategies in which he keeps his itchy finger off the trigger only until the duelists are distance d apart. Such a pure strategy is denoted by d. In Section 4.1.2, only a finite number of values of d were permitted, but here each player will be allowed to choose any d in the closed interval $[0, D]$.[2] This leaves us with an infinite "matrix" to consider rather than the 6×5 matrix of Section 4.1.2. However, we shall take it for granted that the new "matrix" also has a saddle point[3] so that player I's security level is equal to the maximin value $\underline{m}$ of the "matrix".

Recall that the probability that a player who fires first will hit his opponent if they are distance d apart is $p_i(d)$. Suppose that player I plans to wait until the players are distance d apart before firing, and player II plans to wait until they are distance e apart. Then the entry $\pi(d,e)$ in row d and column e of player I's payoff "matrix" is the probability that he will survive when these strategies are used. Thus,

$$\pi(d,e) = \begin{cases} p_1(d), & \text{if } d > e\,, \\ 1 - p_2(e), & \text{if } d < e\,. \end{cases}$$

Player I's security level is given by

$$\underline{m} = \max_d \inf_e \pi(d,e),$$

where "inf" has been written instead of "min" for the reasons given in Section 6.2.3.

From the diagrams of Figure 6.6(a)

$$m(d) = \inf_e \pi(d,e) = \begin{cases} 1 - p_2(d), & \text{if } p_1(d) \geq 1 - p_2(d)\,, \\ p_1(d), & \text{if } p_1(d) \leq 1 - p_2(d)\,. \end{cases}$$

The quantity $m(d)$ is graphed in Figure 6.6(b). Its maximum value occurs where $1 - p_2(d) = p_1(d)$. Recalling from Section 2.4 that d^* is defined by $p_1(d^*) + p_2(d^*) = 1$, it follows that

$$\underline{m} = m(d^*) = \inf_e \pi(d^*, e) = \max_d \inf_e \pi(d,e).$$

Thus player I guarantees his security level of $\underline{m} = p_1(d^*) = 1 - p_2(d^*)$ or better by firing at distance d^*. It is no accident

[2] Something needs to be added to the story of Section 2.4.1, since this does not specify what would happen if both players were planning to fire at precisely the same distance apart. It will be assumed that the result of both players planning to fire simultaneously is that Chance selects one of the players at random to get his shot in just before the other. In the lottery that results, player I survives with probability $q = \frac{1}{2}(p_1(d) + 1 - p_2(d))$.

[3] If you are unwilling to believe this, you can work out its maximin value $\overline{m}$ by the same method as that used in the text to calculate $\underline{m}$ and then check that $\overline{m} = \underline{m}$ in accordance with Theorem 6.2.2.

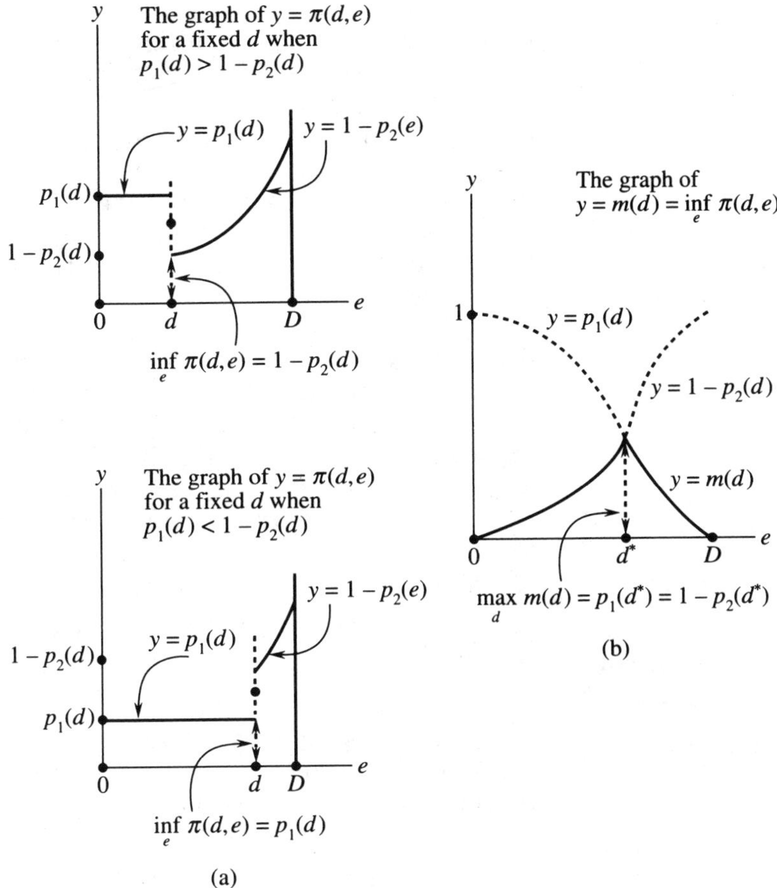

Figure 6.6 Maximin considerations for Duel.

that player I's security strategy is identical to the equilibrium strategy computed in Section 2.4.1. As we shall see, it is always true that a Nash equilibrium strategy is a security strategy in a strictly competitive game. However, this is not a result that should be cherished too dearly. Most interesting games are not strictly competitive and their Nash equilibrium outcomes usually result in the players getting more than their security levels.

6.4 Mixed Strategies

A mixed strategy for player I in an $m \times n$ bimatrix game is an $m \times 1$ column vector p with nonnegative coordinates that sum to 1. The coordinate p_j is to be understood as the probability with which player I's pure strategy s_j is to be used. Similarly, a mixed strategy for player II is an $n \times 1$ column vector q. The coordinate q_k is the probability with which player II's pure strategy t_k is to be used. The set of all player I's mixed strategies will be denoted by P and the set of all player II's mixed strategies by Q.

Consider the 3×3 bimatrix game of Figure 6.5(b). As an example of a mixed strategy for John in this game, consider the 3×1 column vector $p = (\frac{1}{4}, \frac{1}{4}, \frac{1}{2})^{\top}$. To implement this choice of mixed strategy, John might draw a card from a well-shuffled deck of cards and use his first pure strategy if he draws a heart, his second pure strategy if he draws a diamond, and his third pure strategy otherwise. An example of a mixed strategy for Mary is the 3×1 column vector $q = (\frac{1}{2}, \frac{1}{2}, 0)^{\top}$. She may implement this mixed strategy by tossing a fair coin and using her first pure strategy if heads appears and her second pure strategy if tails appears. Notice that the mixed strategy q attaches zero probability to her third pure strategy.

6.4.1 Domination and Mixed Strategies

Phil
6.4.2 ⟶

Why should rational players care about mixed strategies? One reason is that a pure strategy that is not dominated by any other pure strategy may be dominated by a mixed strategy. Consider, for example, the bimatrix game of Figure 6.5(b). John's pure strategy s_2 is strongly dominated by his pure strategy s_3. After s_2 has been deleted, the bimatrix game of Figure 6.7(a) is obtained. None of Mary's pure strategies dominates any other in this game. However, her pure strategy t_2 is strongly dominated by her *mixed* strategy $q = (\frac{1}{2}, 0, \frac{1}{2})^{\top}$ which attaches probability $\frac{1}{2}$ to t_1 and probability $\frac{1}{2}$ to t_3. To see this requires some calculation.

If Mary uses q and John uses s_1, each of the outcomes (s_1, t_1) and (s_1, t_3) will occur with probability $\frac{1}{2}$. Thus Mary's

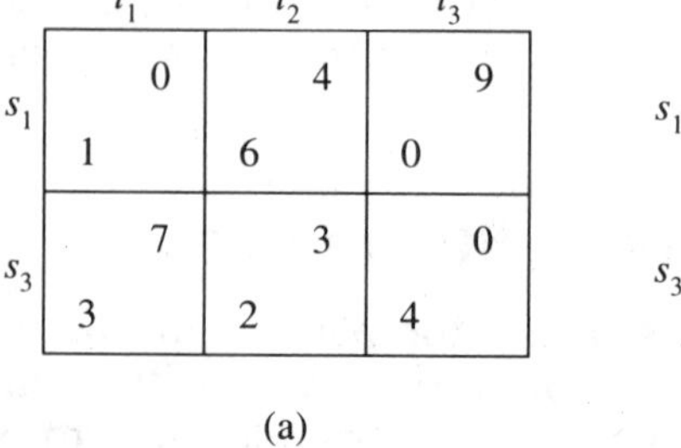

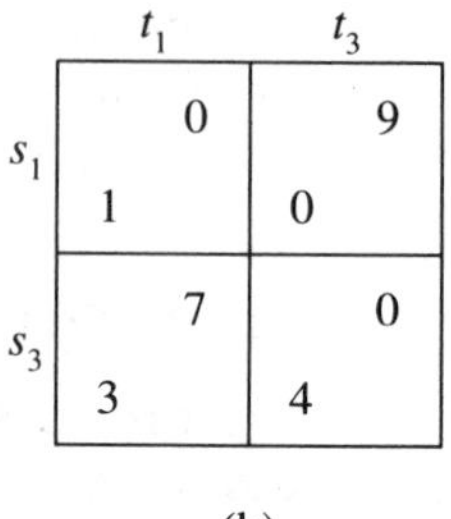

Figure 6.7 Domination by a mixed strategy.

expected payoff will be $0 \times \frac{1}{2} + 9 \times \frac{1}{2} = 4\frac{1}{2}$. Since $4\frac{1}{2} > 4$, Mary does better with q than with t_2 when John uses s_1. Mary also does better with q than with t_2 when John uses his other pure strategy s_3, because $7 \times \frac{1}{2} + 0 \times \frac{1}{2} = 3\frac{1}{2} > 3$. Thus q is better for Mary than t_2 whatever John does. This means that q strongly dominates t_2.

The game that results after column t_2 has been eliminated is shown in Figure 6.7(b). In this reduced game, s_3 strongly dominates s_1. After row s_1 has been deleted, t_1 strongly dominates t_3. The method of successive deletion of dominated strategies therefore leads to the unique pure strategy pair (s_3, t_1).

6.4.2 Securing Payoffs with Mixed Strategies

Section 6.3.1 ended with the observation that John's security level in the bimatrix game of Figure 6.5(b) is $2\frac{2}{3}$. A security strategy for John in this game is $p = (\frac{1}{6}, 0, \frac{5}{6})^\top$. Thus, to guarantee an expected payoff of $2\frac{2}{3}$, John must use a *mixed strategy*. Some calculations are necessary to see why this is true.

John's pure strategy s_2 is strongly dominated by his pure strategy s_3. Whatever scenario John contemplates, he will therefore never use pure strategy s_2. The first step is therefore to delete row s_2, leaving the bimatrix game of Figure 6.7(a). John's payoff matrix in this reduced game is shown in Figure 6.8(a).

Suppose that John uses row s_1 with probability $1 - r$ and row s_3 with probability r. That is, he uses the mixed strategy $p = (1 - r, 0, r)^\top$ in the original game. It is easy to calculate the expected payoff $x = E_k(r)$ that John will get if Mary uses column t_k. If Mary uses column t_1, then John will get a payoff of 1 with probability $1 - r$ and a payoff of 3 with probability r. His expected payoff is therefore $1(1 - r) + 3r = 1 + 2r$. Similar calculations for Mary's other columns t_2 and t_3 show that

$$E_1(r) = 1(1 - r) + 3r = 1 + 2r\,;$$
$$E_2(r) = 6(1 - r) + 2r = 6 - 4r\,;$$
$$E_3(r) = 0(1 - r) + 4r = 4r\,.$$

The three lines $x = E_1(r)$, $x = E_2(r)$ and $x = E_3(r)$ are graphed in Figure 6.8(b). (Such graphs do not usually need to be drawn with great precision, but they do need to be drawn with sufficient care to make it worthwhile having graph paper to hand.)

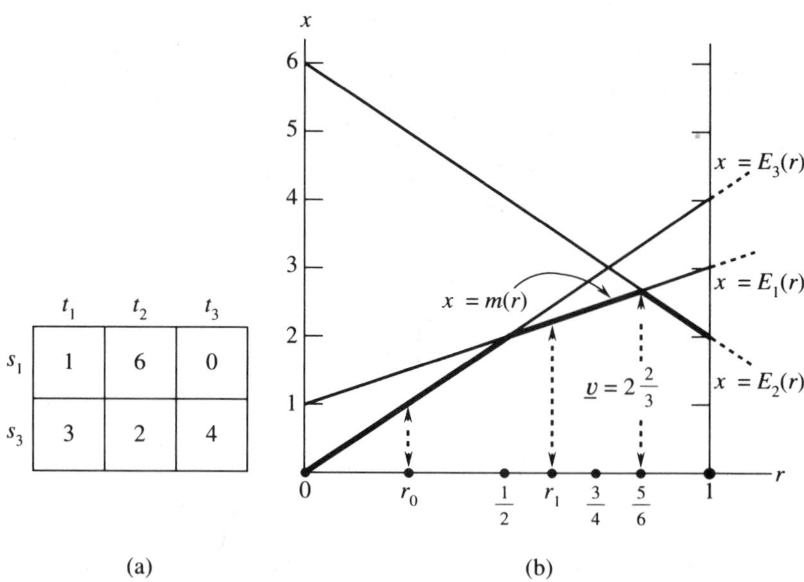

Figure 6.8 Computing a mixed security strategy for player I.

Recall that John has to contemplate a worst-case scenario in determining his security level. He therefore assumes that Mary will predict his choice of mixed strategy[4] and act to minimize his payoff.

Once John has chosen r, his paranoic assumption is that Mary will choose her strategy so as to assign John whichever of $E_1(r)$, $E_2(r)$ or $E_3(r)$ is smallest.[5] John therefore anticipates an expected payoff of

$$m(r) = \min\{E_1(r), E_2(r), E_3(r)\} .$$

The graph of $x = m(r)$ is shown with a bold line in Figure 6.8(b). For example, when $r = r_0$, $m(r) = E_3(r)$. When $r = r_1$, $m(r) = E_1(r)$.

A worst-case analysis therefore tells John that, whatever value of r he chooses, his consequent payoff will be $m(r)$. The

[4]An even worse case would be if Mary were able to predict how a tossed coin will fall, or what card will be drawn from a shuffled deck. But an analysis that attributed such superhuman powers to Mary would not be very interesting.

[5]Alert readers will want to know why Mary neglects her mixed strategies. The reason is that, for each r, the minimizing value of John's payoff is achieved using a *pure* strategy. For example, suppose that John chooses $r = r_0$ in Figure 6.8(b). Then Mary can ensure that John gets any payoff x in the interval $[E_3(r_0), E_2(r_0)]$ by using a suitable mixed strategy. But the strategy that minimizes John's payoff is the pure strategy t_3.

value of r that guarantees him the most is therefore found by maximizing $m(r)$. That is, John can ensure an expected payoff of at least

$$\underline{v} = \max_r m(r) = \max_r \min_k E_k(r)$$

by choosing r carefully.

Figure 6.8(b) shows that the value of r satisfying $0 \le r \le 1$ at which $m(r)$ is largest occurs where the lines $x = E_1(r)$ and $x = E_2(r)$ cross. Since the solution to the equation

$$1 + 2r = 6 - 4r$$

is $r = \frac{5}{6}$, John can secure an expected payoff of

$$\underline{v} = m(\tfrac{5}{6}) = E_1(\tfrac{5}{6}) = 1 + 2 \times \tfrac{5}{6} = 2\tfrac{2}{3}$$

or better by using the mixed strategy $p = (\frac{1}{6}, 0, \frac{5}{6})^\top$. In fact, $\underline{v}$ is the largest payoff that can be secured using a mixed strategy. By the end of this section, we shall know that this ensures that $\underline{v}$ is John's security level.[6]

6.4.3 Are Mixed Security Strategies Paradoxical?

The conclusion that John secures $\underline{v} = 2\frac{2}{3}$ or better by using the mixed strategy $p = (\frac{1}{6}, 0, \frac{5}{6})^\top$ strikes some people as paradoxical. How can something be secure if what you get de-

Phil

6.4.4 ⟶ pends on rolling a dice or drawing a playing card at random? It may help if a reminder of what is involved in working with Von Neumann and Morgenstern utilities is provided.

Suppose that John's Von Neumann and Morgenstern utility for a sum of money $x \ge 0$ is given by $4\sqrt{x}$ as in Section 3.4.3. Now offer him the choice of \$4 for certain or the lottery **L** in which he gets \$0 with probability $\frac{1}{4}$ and \$16 with probability $\frac{3}{4}$. He will choose the lottery **L** because this secures a Von Neumann and Morgenstern utility of $\frac{3}{4} \times 4\sqrt{16} = 12$, whereas the Von Neumann and Morgenstern utility of \$4 is only $4\sqrt{4} = 8$. One might argue that, by choosing **L**, John might end up with nothing if he is unlucky, while the \$4 on offer is a certainty. If he wants to be safe, the argument continues, he should therefore take the \$4. What this argument neglects is that Von Neumann and Morgenstern utilities *already* take into account John's feelings about taking risks in situations where the probabilities are well-defined. The Von

[6] Some authors would be willing to deduce that $\underline{v}$ is John's security level without further ado. However, it seems more satisfactory to exhibit the fact that Mary has a strategy that holds John to $\underline{v}$ or less.

Neumann and Morgenstern utility of **L** exceeds that of getting \$4 for certain because, *after* assessing the risks, John tells us that he prefers **L**.

However, when facing Mary in a game, John's uncertainties about what Mary will do are *not* given in terms of well-defined probabilities.[7] If he could reliably attach probabilities to each of her pure strategies, it would make no sense to speak of a worst-case analysis. There would only be one case to consider. John would simply choose whatever strategy maximizes his expected utility.

The moral of the story is that it is not a good idea to second-guess Von Neumann and Morgenstern. The naive interpretation of a payoff is the right one when computing security levels.

6.4.4 Payoff Functions for Mixed Strategies

Sections 6.4.1 and 6.4.2 make it clear that rational players will sometimes think it worthwhile to consider the use of mixed strategies. The current subsection develops some of the necessary apparatus.

In considering pure strategies, the payoff functions $\pi_1 : S \times T \to \mathbb{R}$ and $\pi_2 : S \times T \to \mathbb{R}$ proved useful. Recall that $\pi_i(s,t)$ is the payoff to player i when player I uses pure strategy s and player II uses pure strategy t. When mixed strategies need to be considered, more complicated payoff functions $\Pi_1 : P \times Q \to \mathbb{R}$ and $\Pi_2 : P \times Q \to \mathbb{R}$ need to be introduced. The notation $\Pi_i(p,q)$ represents player i's expected utility when player I uses mixed strategy p and player II uses mixed strategy q.

Suppose that John uses mixed strategy $p = (\frac{1}{4}, \frac{1}{4}, \frac{1}{2})^\top$ and Mary uses mixed strategy $q = (\frac{1}{2}, \frac{1}{2}, 0)^\top$ in the bimatrix game of Figure 6.5(b). What is the probability that the result will be that John's pure strategy s_2 and Mary's pure strategy t_1 will get used? To answer this question, a standard assumption

[7]Although, if he knows that Mary gets her advice on how to play from a game theory book, John will be able to predict in advance what mixed strategy she will use by looking up the appropriate page in his own copy of the book. Thus he will be able to attach probabilities to each of her pure strategies. This is one of the lines of reasoning used to justify restricting attention to Nash equilibria in games for which it is common knowledge that both players are rational. However, when in the paranoic frame of mind necessary for a security level calculation, he will not feel able to predict what strategy she will use until *after* he has made his own choice of strategy, since he proceeds as though her choice were dependent on his.

for a noncooperative analysis of a game is needed: namely, that the random devices used by the players in implementing their mixed strategies are *independent*.[8] This should always be assumed to be the case unless something is said to the contrary.

The probability of the event that both s_2 and t_1 get used is therefore obtained by multiplying their respective probabilities (Section 2.1.2). Since John uses s_2 with probability $\frac{1}{4}$ and Mary uses t_1 with probability $\frac{1}{2}$, the probability that both s_2 and t_1 are used is therefore $p_2q_1 = \frac{1}{4} \times \frac{1}{2} = \frac{1}{8}$. Thus, John will get the payoff $\pi_1(s_2, t_1) = 2$ with probability $p_2q_1 = \frac{1}{8}$.

The probability of each of John's payoffs can be calculated in the same way. Thus it is straightforward to calculate John's expected utility $\Pi_1(p, q)$. The formula to which such calculations lead is most elegantly expressed in terms of John's payoff matrix A. The formula, together with the corresponding formula for Mary's expected utility in terms of her payoff matrix B, is given by

$$\Pi_1(p, q) = p^\top A q\,; \tag{6.4}$$

$$\Pi_2(p, q) = p^\top B q\,. \tag{6.5}$$

In the case of the bimatrix game of Figure 6.5(b), the expected payoff to John when he uses mixed strategy $p = (\frac{1}{4}, \frac{1}{4}, \frac{1}{2})^\top$ and Mary uses mixed strategy $q = (\frac{1}{2}, \frac{1}{2}, 0)^\top$ is given by

$$\Pi_1(p, q) = p^\top A q = \begin{bmatrix} \frac{1}{4} & \frac{1}{4} & \frac{1}{2} \end{bmatrix} \begin{bmatrix} 1 & 6 & 0 \\ 2 & 0 & 3 \\ 3 & 2 & 4 \end{bmatrix} \begin{bmatrix} \frac{1}{2} \\ \frac{1}{2} \\ 0 \end{bmatrix} = 2\tfrac{3}{8}\,.$$

Notice that, when this expression is expanded, $\Pi_1(s_2, t_1) = 2$ gets multiplied by $p_2q_1 = \frac{1}{8}$. The expected payoff to Mary when John uses mixed strategy p and she uses mixed strategy q is given by

$$\Pi_2(p, q) = p^\top B q = \begin{bmatrix} \frac{1}{4} & \frac{1}{4} & \frac{1}{2} \end{bmatrix} \begin{bmatrix} 0 & 4 & 9 \\ 1 & 2 & 0 \\ 7 & 3 & 0 \end{bmatrix} \begin{bmatrix} \frac{1}{2} \\ \frac{1}{2} \\ 0 \end{bmatrix} = 3\tfrac{3}{8}\,.$$

---

[8] In a cooperative analysis, on the other hand, one will certainly wish to allow the players to use *correlated* random devices. For example, in Section 5.3.1, the payoff pair $(2, 0)$ is achieved by tossing a fair coin. If heads appears, player I uses pure strategy s_2 and player II uses pure strategy t_3. If tails appears, player I uses pure strategy s_1 and player II uses pure strategy t_1. This contract can be seen as requiring player I to use the mixed strategy $p = (\frac{1}{2}, \frac{1}{2})^\top$ and player II to use the mixed strategy $q = (\frac{1}{2}, \frac{1}{2}, 0)^\top$. But, since both players are to use the *same* coin, their mixed strategies will very definitely not be independent.

6.4.5 Minimax and Maximin with Mixed Strategies

This topic is easy since all that is required is some transcription of the results of Section 6.2.

Let A be an $m \times n$ matrix and define the payoff function $\Pi : P \times Q \to \mathbb{R}$ by

$$\Pi(p, q) = p^\top A q\,.$$

Thus $\Pi(p, q)$ is what a player with payoff matrix A gets if player I uses mixed strategy p and player II uses mixed strategy q.

Let the minimax value of the payoff function Π be $\overline{v}$. Let its maximin value be $\underline{v}$. Thus

$$\underline{v} = \max_{p \in P} \min_{q \in Q} \Pi(p, q) = \min_{q \in Q} \Pi(\tilde{p}, q) \tag{6.6}$$

$$\overline{v} = \min_{q \in Q} \max_{p \in P} \Pi(p, q) = \max_{p \in P} \Pi(p, \tilde{q}) \tag{6.7}$$

where $\tilde{p}$ is the mixed strategy p in P for which $\min_{q \in Q} \Pi(p, q)$ is largest, and $\tilde{q}$ is the mixed strategy q in Q for which $\max_{p \in P} \Pi(p, q)$ is smallest.

A saddle point for the payoff function Π is a pair $(\tilde{p}, \tilde{q})$ of mixed strategies such that

$$\Pi(\tilde{p}, q) \geq \Pi(\tilde{p}, \tilde{q}) \geq \Pi(p, \tilde{q})\,,$$

for all p in P and all q in Q.

If one thinks of $\Pi(p, q)$ as being the entry in row p and column q of a generalized "matrix", then the following theorems are natural. Their proofs can be copied from those of Theorems 6.2.1, 6.2.2 and 6.3.1.

Theorem 6.4.1 $\underline{v} \leq \overline{v}$.

Theorem 6.4.2 A necessary and sufficient condition that $(\tilde{p}, \tilde{q})$ be a saddle point is that $\tilde{p}$ and $\tilde{q}$ are given by (6.6) and (6.7) and $\underline{v} = \overline{v}$. When $(\tilde{p}, \tilde{q})$ is a saddle point, $\underline{v} = \Pi(\tilde{p}, \tilde{q}) = \overline{v}$.

Theorem 6.4.3 If player I's payoff function Π has a saddle point $(\tilde{p}, \tilde{q})$, then his security level is $\underline{v} = \Pi(\tilde{p}, \tilde{q}) = \overline{v}$, and $\tilde{p}$ is one of his security strategies.

These results make it important to know under what circumstances it is true that $\underline{v} = \overline{v}$. Von Neumann's minimax theorem says that, when there is only a finite number of pure strategies, the answer is: *always*. Thus, in finite games, $\underline{v}$ is always player I's security level.

6.4.6 Minimax Theorem

Math 6.5 ⟶ The following "proof" of Von Neumann's minimax theorem is loosely based on an inductive argument of Guillermo Owen. His proof has the advantage that it does not depend on any deep theorems. However it does require some smart footwork with matrix algebra that beginners would find troublesome. In the "proof" offered below, the algebra will still be troublesome for beginners, but it has been reduced to some manipulations with maxima and minima. However, simplifying the algebra in this way makes it necessary to appeal to a more complicated induction argument. The fact that this argument is intuitively appealing is taken as an excuse to gloss over its details.

Theorem 6.4.4 (Von Neumann) $\underline{v} = \overline{v}$.

Proof. We know from Theorem 6.4.1 that $\underline{v} \leq \overline{v}$. The proof of Von Neumann's minimax theorem consists of showing that, if $\underline{v} < \overline{v}$, then the strategy sets P and Q can be replaced by nonempty convex subsets P' and Q', one of which is a *strictly* smaller set, without decreasing the size of the gap $\overline{v} - \underline{v}$. That is, $\overline{v}' - \underline{v}' \geq \overline{v} - \underline{v}$. The same can then be done to P' and Q'. And so on.

But a nonempty set is smallest when it contains only one point. Thus, if the minimax theorem is false for a "matrix" with rows P and columns Q, it must also be false for some "matrix" with just *one* row and column.[9] But the maximin and minimax values of a 1×1 matrix are obviously the same. Thus the assumption that $\underline{v} < \overline{v}$ leads to a contradiction. It follows that $\underline{v} = \overline{v}$, which is what the theorem says.

If $\underline{v} < \overline{v}$, then either[10] $\underline{v} < \Pi(\tilde{p}, \tilde{q})$ or $\Pi(\tilde{p}, \tilde{q}) < \overline{v}$. The former inequality will be assumed to hold. If the latter inequality holds, a parallel argument is necessary in which it is P that shrinks in size rather than Q as in the line followed below.

---

[9]Provided that the induction process ever gets as far as the smallest possible nonempty set. To achieve this end, the induction needs to be transfinite. To justify the transfinite jumps, it is enough if the strategy spaces are compact and the payoff function is continuous. These requirements are automatically true if the original sets of pure strategies are finite. However, cognoscenti will note that the proof goes through under much weaker conditions.

[10]If $\underline{v} \geq \Pi(\tilde{p}, \tilde{q})$ and $\Pi(\tilde{p}, \tilde{q}) \geq \overline{v}$, then $\underline{v} \geq \overline{v}$.

Take Q' to be the convex set consisting of all q in Q for which

$$\Pi(\tilde{p}, q) \le \underline{v} + \varepsilon, \tag{6.8}$$

where $0 < \varepsilon < \Pi(\tilde{p}, \tilde{q}) - \underline{v}$. Then Q' is strictly smaller than Q because it does not contain $\tilde{q}$. Let $P' = P$.

With $\tilde{p}'$ and $\tilde{q}'$ defined in the obvious way, consider the convex combinations $\hat{p} = \alpha\tilde{p} + \beta\tilde{p}'$ and $\hat{q} = \alpha\tilde{q} + \beta\tilde{q}'$. Observe that[11]

$$\begin{aligned}\overline{v} = \min_{q\in Q}\max_{p\in P}\Pi(p,q) &\le \max_{p\in P}\Pi(p,\hat{q})\\ &= \max_{p\in P}\{\alpha\Pi(p,\tilde{q}) + \beta\Pi(p,\tilde{q}')\}\\ &\le \alpha\max_{p\in P}\Pi(p,\tilde{q}) + \beta\max_{p\in P'}\Pi(p,\tilde{q}')\\ &= \alpha\overline{v} + \beta\overline{v}'\,. \end{aligned}\tag{6.9}$$

An inequality for $\underline{v}$ requires more effort. Note to begin with that[12]

$$\begin{aligned}\min_{q\in Q'}\Pi(\hat{p},q) &\ge \alpha\min_{q\in Q'}\Pi(\tilde{p},q) + \beta\min_{q\in Q'}\Pi(\tilde{p}',q)\\ &\ge \alpha\min_{q\in Q}\Pi(\tilde{p},q) + \beta\min_{q\in Q'}\Pi(\tilde{p}',q)\\ &= \alpha\underline{v} + \beta\underline{v}'\,. \end{aligned}\tag{6.10}$$

Also,[13]

$$\begin{aligned}\inf_{q\notin Q'}\Pi(\hat{p},q) &\ge \alpha\inf_{q\notin Q'}\Pi(\tilde{p},q) + \beta\inf_{q\notin Q'}\Pi(\tilde{p}',q)\\ &\ge \alpha(\underline{v}+\varepsilon) + \beta c\,. \end{aligned}\tag{6.11}$$

We shall want (6.10) to be smaller than (6.11). To arrange this, $\alpha = 1 - \beta$ and β have to be carefully chosen. By taking β to be very small, (6.10) can be made as close to $\underline{v}$ as we choose. Similarly (6.11) can be made as close to $\underline{v} + \varepsilon$ as we choose. Thus, if β is chosen to be sufficiently small, then (6.10) is less than (6.11). However, it is important that β is not actually zero.

[11] In the ensuing argument, one needs to recall that $\Pi(p,q) = p^{\top}Aq$, and then to note that $p^{\top}A(\alpha\tilde{q} + \beta\tilde{q}') = \alpha p^{\top}A\tilde{q} + \beta p^{\top}A\tilde{q}'$. For the validity of the next step, consider the example: $3 = \max\{-1+2, 2+0, 0+3\} \le \max\{-1,2,0\} + \max\{2,0,3\} = 2+3$. The third step simply uses the definitions of $\tilde{q}$ and $\tilde{q}'$.

[12] At the second step, one needs to observe that the minimum of a smaller set must be larger. For example, $2 = \min\{2,3\} \ge \min\{1,2,3\} = 1$.

[13] At the second step, one must remember that, if $\Pi(\tilde{p},q) \le \underline{v} + \epsilon$, then q lies in the set Q' by (6.8). The constant c is simply an abbreviation for $\inf_{q\notin Q'}\Pi(\tilde{p}',q)$.

An inequality for $\underline{v}$ is now possible:

$$\begin{aligned}\underline{v} = \max_{p\in P}\min_{q\in Q}\Pi(p,q) &\geq \min_{q\in Q}\Pi(\hat{p},q)\\ &= \min\left\{\min_{q\in Q'}\Pi(\hat{p},q)\,,\ \inf_{q\notin Q'}\Pi(\hat{p},q)\right\}\\ &\geq \min\{\alpha\underline{v}+\beta\underline{v}'\,,\ \alpha(\underline{v}+\varepsilon)+\beta c\}\\ &= \alpha\underline{v}+\beta\underline{v}'\,. \qquad (6.12)\end{aligned}$$

Multiply inequality (6.12) by -1 and add it to inequality (6.9). Then,

$$\begin{aligned}\overline{v}-\underline{v} &\leq \alpha(\overline{v}-\underline{v})+\beta(\overline{v}'-\underline{v}')\\ \beta(\overline{v}-\underline{v}) &\leq \beta(\overline{v}'-\underline{v}')\,.\end{aligned}$$

Thus $\overline{v}-\underline{v}\leq\overline{v}'-\underline{v}'$, which is what we were trying to prove. □

6.5 Zero-Sum Games

It will usually be irrational for John to proceed on the paranoic assumption used in a security level calculation. Why should he assume that Mary is intent on doing him an injury? If she is rational she will be seeking to maximize her own payoff rather than minimizing John's. But there are games in which paranoia is entirely rational. These occur when Mary's interests are diametrically opposed to John's. Maximizing her payoff will then be the same as minimizing John's payoff. Such games were called strictly competitive in Chapter 2. Here we shall learn to call them zero-sum.

6.5.1 Diametrically Opposed Preferences

A *zero-sum* game is a game in which the payoffs always sum to zero. In the case of two players, the requirement is therefore that

$$u_1(\omega)+u_2(\omega)=0,$$

for each ω in the set Ω of final outcomes. In accordance with previous usage, $u_1:\Omega\to\mathbb{R}$ and $u_2:\Omega\to\mathbb{R}$ denote the players' Von Neumann and Morgenstern utility functions.

A two-player, zero-sum game G is necessarily strictly competitive. This is not entirely obvious when the game involves random events because the two players must then have diametrically opposed preferences, not only over the final outcomes, but also over lotteries as well. However, if $u_1 + u_2 = 0$, then $\mathcal{E}u_1 + \mathcal{E}u_2 = 0$. Thus

$$\begin{aligned} \mathbf{L} \preceq_1 \mathbf{M} &\Leftrightarrow \mathcal{E}u_1(\mathbf{L}) \leq \mathcal{E}u_1(\mathbf{M}) \\ &\Leftrightarrow -\mathcal{E}u_1(\mathbf{L}) \geq -\mathcal{E}u_1(\mathbf{M}) \\ &\Leftrightarrow \mathcal{E}u_2(\mathbf{L}) \geq \mathcal{E}u_2(\mathbf{M}) \quad \Leftrightarrow \quad \mathbf{L} \succeq_2 \mathbf{M}. \end{aligned}$$

Sometimes the attitudes that players have to taking risks are overlooked when modeling situations as zero-sum games. For example, it is often taken for granted that games like Poker and Backgammon are zero-sum because whatever sum of money is won by one player is necessarily lost by the others.[14] But it does not follow that Backgammon or two-player Poker are therefore necessarily strictly competitive. They certainly will not be if both players are strictly risk-averse. (In a zero-sum game, $u_1 = -u_2$, and hence one player's utility function is concave if and only if the other's is convex.)[15]

When games like Poker or Backgammon are analyzed as zero-sum games, the implicit understanding is that the players are *risk-neutral* so that a player's Von Neumann and Morgenstern utility function $u : \mathbb{R} \to \mathbb{R}$ can be chosen to satisfy

$$u(x) = x.$$

We know from studying the St. Petersburg paradox that risk-neutrality is unlikely to be a good assumption about people's preferences in general. But assuming risk-neutrality may not be too bad an approximation when, as in neighborhood Poker games, the sums of money that may change hands lie in a restricted range.

6.5.2 Constant-Sum Games

A *constant-sum* game is a game in which the players' payoffs always sum to a fixed constant c. For example, if player I uses pure strategy d and player II uses pure strategy e, then the probability that player I will survive in Duel was denoted by $\pi(d,e)$ in Section 6.3.2. Player I's probability of survival is therefore $1 - \pi(d,e)$. With these Von Neumann and Morgenstern utility functions, Duel is a unit-sum game, since the

[14]Except when Poker is played in casinos. Usually the house takes 10% of the pot.

[15]This was one of the reasons for restricting attention in Chapter 2 to games in which the only outcomes are $\mathcal{W}$ or $\mathcal{L}$. Only when consideration is restricted to lotteries with just two possible prizes can one deduce from the fact that players have opposing preferences over prizes that they necessarily have opposing preferences over lotteries.

(a)

	t_1	t_2	t_3
s_1	1, −1	6, −6	0, 0
s_2	2, −2	0, 0	3, −3
s_3	3, −3	2, −2	4, −4

(b)

	t_1	t_2	t_3
s_1	1	6	0
s_2	2	0	3
s_3	3	2	4

Figure 6.9 A zero-sum strategic form.

payoffs always sum to one. Any constant-sum game can be changed into a strategically equivalent zero-sum game by the simple expedient of subtracting the constant c from all of one of the player's payoffs. For example, in Duel one may replace player II's payoff of $1 - \pi(d,e)$ everywhere by $-\pi(d,e)$. This puts the game into a zero-sum format without altering player II's strategic considerations at all.

6.5.3 Matrix Games

The bimatrix game of Figure 6.9(a) is the strategic form of a zero-sum game because the payoffs in each cell sum to zero. Player I's payoff matrix A and player II's payoff matrix B therefore satisfy $A + B = 0$ and so $B = -A$. It is therefore redundant to write down player II's payoffs. Instead, the strategic form of a zero-sum game is usually represented by player I's payoff matrix alone as in Figure 6.9(b). One must remember that such a matrix only records player I's payoffs. It is easy to forget that player II seeks to *minimize* these payoffs.

6.5.4 Values of Two-Player, Zero-Sum Games

In Section 1.7.1, the value v of a strictly competitive game was defined to be an outcome with the property that player I has a strategy σ that forces a result that is at least as good for him as v, while player II simultaneously has a strategy τ that forces a result that is at least as good for her as v. The only new twist on this idea is that we will now redefine the value v of a two-player, zero-sum game to be a *payoff* to player I rather than an outcome.

It will be immediately apparent that, for a payoff v to be the value of a two-player, zero-sum game, v must be player I's security level $\underline{v}$ and σ must be one of his security strategies. Since player II gets $-v$ when player I gets v, it must simultaneously be true that $-v$ is player II's security level in the game and τ must be one of her security strategies.

Up to now, we have concentrated on calculating player I's security level in games. This is the maximin value $\underline{v}$ of $\Pi_1(p, q)$. Now it is necessary to consider player II's security level. This, of course, is the maximin value of $\Pi_2(p, q)$. In general, there is no reason why player II's security level should bear any relation to player I's. However, things are simpler in two-player, zero-sum games because, in such games, player II's security level is simply $-\overline{v}$.

To see this, it is only necessary to note that the payoffs in a zero-sum matrix game are *losses* to player II because the entries in the matrix are *gains* to player I. In considering a worst-case scenario, player II will therefore proceed on the assumption that player I will anticipate her strategy choice and then act to *maximize* her loss. She will therefore choose the strategy that *minimizes* her maximum loss. This will result in a loss of at most $\overline{v}$. This is the same as a gain of at least $-\overline{v}$.[16]

The condition for a two-player, zero-sum game to have a value v is therefore that $\underline{v} = v = \overline{v}$. But this is precisely what Von Neumann's minimax theorem says. The conclusion is worth quoting as a theorem:

Theorem 6.5.1 Any finite two-player, zero-sum game has a value $v = \underline{v} = \overline{v}$. To ensure that he gets an expected payoff of at least v or more, player I can use any of his security strategies $\tilde{p}$. To ensure that player II gets at least $-v$ or more, she can use any of her security strategies $\tilde{q}$.

6.5.5 An Example

Consider the two-player, zero-sum game of Figure 6.9. John's pure strategy s_2 is strongly dominated by his pure strategy s_3. After deleting row s_2, John is left with the payoff matrix of Figure 6.10(a). This reduced payoff matrix is identical to that given in Figure 6.8(a). Thus the calculations of Section 6.4.2

[16] A more formal derivation of player II's security level proceeds as follows:

$$\max_{q\in Q}\min_{p\in P}\{-\Pi(p,q)\} = \max_{q\in Q}\{-\max_{p\in P}\Pi(p,q)\} = -\{\min_{q\in Q}\max_{p\in P}\Pi(p,q)\} = -\overline{v}.$$

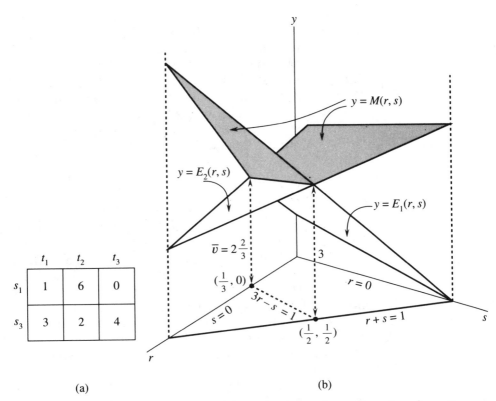

	t_1	t_2	t_3
s_1	1	6	0
s_3	3	2	4

(a)

(b)

Figure 6.10 Computing a mixed security strategy for player II.

that determined John's security level and security strategy for this payoff matrix apply here also. We therefore painlessly obtain the conclusion that the value of our zero-sum game is $v = \underline{v} = 2\frac{2}{3}$, and that John guarantees this value or better by using the mixed strategy $\tilde{p} = (\frac{1}{6}, 0, \frac{5}{6})^\top$ in the original 3×3 matrix game.

Math 6.5.6 ⟶

Von Neumann's minimax theorem assures us that Mary's security level in the game is $-\overline{v} = -2\frac{2}{3}$, but does not offer any clue as to how she secures this amount. A security strategy for Mary will be computed here using the same method as that employed in Section 6.4.2. It is not an ideal method in this case because it requires drawing the three-dimensional diagram of Figure 6.10(b). A more satisfactory method will be described later.[17]

[17]It is important also to note that neither procedure is appropriate except in two-player, zero-sum games, because only then is it guaranteed that player II's security strategy can be calculated using player I's payoff matrix. In more general games, one simply uses the method of Section 6.4.2, but with player II's payoff matrix replacing player I's.

Suppose that Mary uses column t_1 with probability $1-r-s$, column t_2 with probability r, and column t_3 with probability s. That is, she uses the mixed strategy $q = (1-r-s, r, s)^\top$. It is then easy to calculate the expected loss $y = E_k(r,s)$ that Mary will sustain if John uses row s_k. If John uses row s_1, then Mary will suffer a loss of 1 with probability $1-r-s$, a loss of 6 with probability r, and a loss of 0 with probability s. Her expected loss is therefore $1(1-r-s) + 6r + 0s = 1 + 5r - s$. A similar calculation for John's other row s_2 shows that:

$$\begin{aligned} E_1(r,s) &= 1(1-r-s) + 6r + 0s = 1 + 5r - s\,; \\ E_2(r,s) &= 3(1-r-s) + 2r + 4s = 3 - r + s\,. \end{aligned}$$

The two planes $y = E_1(r,s)$ and $y = E_2(r,s)$ are graphed in Figure 6.10(b). In Figure 6.8(b), we considered only those values of r that satisfy $0 \le r \le 1$. Here attention must be restricted to those values of r and s that satisfy $r \ge 0$, $s \ge 0$ and $r + s \le 1$. The pairs (r,s) that satisfy these restrictions lie in the triangle bounded by the lines $r = 0$, $s = 0$ and $r + s = 1$.

Recall that Mary has to contemplate a worst-case scenario in determining her security level. She therefore assumes that John will predict her choice of mixed strategy and then act to maximize her loss.

Once Mary has chosen r and s, her paranoic assumption is that John will choose his strategy so as to assign Mary whichever of $E_1(r,s)$ and $E_2(r,s)$ is larger. Mary therefore anticipates sustaining an expected loss of

$$M(r,s) = \max\{E_1(r,s), E_2(r,s)\}\,.$$

The surface $y = M(r,s)$ has been shaded in Figure 6.10(b).

A worst-case analysis therefore tells Mary that, whatever values of r and s she chooses, her consequent loss will be $M(r,s)$. The values of r and s that guarantee her the smallest loss are therefore found by minimizing $M(r,s)$. That is, Mary can ensure an expected loss of at most

$$\overline{v} = \min_{r,s} M(r,s) = \min_{r,s} \max_k E_k(r,s)$$

by choosing r and s carefully.

Figure 6.10(b) reveals that the pair (r,s) at which $M(r,s)$ is smallest occurs where the planes $y = E_1(r,s)$ and $y = E_2(r,s)$ cut. We are therefore interested in those pairs (r,s) which satisfy the equation

$$E_1(r,s) = 1 + 5r - s = 3 - r + s = E_2(r,s).$$

The pairs (r,s) that satisfy this equation therefore lie on the line $3r - s = 1$. Which of these pairs makes $M(r,s)$ smallest?

The two candidates are the points where the line $3r - s = 1$ meets $s = 0$ and where it meets $r + s = 1$. The first of these points is $(r, s) = (\frac{1}{3}, 0)$ and the second is $(r, s) = (\frac{1}{2}, \frac{1}{2})$. But $M(\frac{1}{3}, 0) = E_1(\frac{1}{3}, 0) = 1 + 5 \times \frac{1}{3} = 2\frac{2}{3}$ and $M(\frac{1}{2}, \frac{1}{2}) = E_1(\frac{1}{2}, \frac{1}{2}) = 1 + 5 \times \frac{1}{2} - \frac{1}{2} = 3$. Since $2\frac{2}{3} < 3$, the pair (r, s) that minimizes $M(r, s)$ is $(r, s) = (\frac{1}{3}, 0)$ and the minimum value is $\overline{v} = 2\frac{2}{3}$.

To summarize: Mary can guarantee that her expected loss will be no more than $\overline{v} = 2\frac{2}{3}$ by using the mixed strategy $\tilde{q} = (1 - r - s, r, s)^\top = (\frac{2}{3}, \frac{1}{3}, 0)^\top$. John can guarantee that his expected gain will be no less than $\underline{v} = 2\frac{2}{3}$ by using the mixed strategy $\tilde{p} = (\frac{5}{6}, 0, \frac{1}{6})^\top$. The value of the two-player, zero-sum game is $v = 2\frac{2}{3}$.

6.5.6 Saddle Points and Nash Equilibria

The payoff matrices of certain two-player, zero-sum games have a saddle point (σ, τ). Corollary 1.7.3, for example, says that this is true if the matrix is derived from a finite, strictly competitive game of perfect information without chance moves.[18]

Recall from (6.1) that, if $\pi(s, t)$ is the entry in row s and column t of a payoff matrix A, then the condition for (σ, τ) to be a saddle point of the matrix A is that

$$\pi(\sigma, t) \geq \pi(\sigma, \tau) \geq \pi(s, \tau),$$

for all s in S and all t in T. When a saddle point (σ, τ) exists for the payoff matrix of a two-player, zero-sum game, it follows from Theorem 6.2.2 that the value of the game is necessarily $v = \pi(\sigma, \tau)$. Player I guarantees v or better by playing σ, while player II guarantees $-v$ or better by playing τ. For example, the two-player, zero-sum game with the matrix of Figure 6.2 has value 2, because (s_2, t_2) is a saddle point of the matrix and $\pi(s_2, t_2) = 2$.

As we know, a matrix does not always have a saddle point. But the minimax theorem tells us that $\underline{v} = \overline{v}$, and so it follows from Theorem 6.4.2 that any pair $(\tilde{p}, \tilde{q})$ of security strategies for the two players is a saddle point for the mixed strategy payoff function Π. That is to say,

$$\tilde{p}^\top A q \geq \tilde{p}^\top A \tilde{q} \geq p^\top A \tilde{q}\,, \tag{6.13}$$

for all p in P and all q in Q. The value of the game is then $v = \tilde{p}^\top A \tilde{q}$.

---

[18]The restriction to games without chance moves is unnecessary. At the time the corollary was presented, chance moves had not yet been introduced.

Nash equilibria were introduced in Section 1.8.1. As noted in Section 4.1.3, the requirement that a pair $(\tilde{p}, \tilde{q})$ of strategies be a Nash equilibrium in a two-player game is that

$$\Pi_1(\tilde{p}, \tilde{q}) \geq \Pi_1(p, \tilde{q}), \tag{6.14}$$

$$\Pi_2(\tilde{p}, \tilde{q}) \geq \Pi_2(\tilde{p}, q), \tag{6.15}$$

for all p in P and all q in Q. The first inequality expresses the fact that $\tilde{p}$ is a best reply to $\tilde{q}$, and the second inequality expresses the fact that $\tilde{q}$ is a best reply to $\tilde{p}$.

In a two-player, zero-sum game, $\Pi_1(p,q) = p^\top Aq$ and $\Pi_2(p,q) = -p^\top Aq$. Thus inequality (6.15) can be rewritten as $-\tilde{p}^\top A\tilde{q} \geq -\tilde{p}^\top Aq$, which is the same as $\tilde{p}^\top Aq \geq \tilde{p}^\top A\tilde{q}$. Inequality (6.14) can be rewritten as $\tilde{p}^\top A\tilde{q} \geq p^\top A\tilde{q}$. The result of combining the rewritten inequalities is the condition (6.13) for a saddle point.

These conclusions are summarized in the theorem below:

Theorem 6.5.2 If A is player I's payoff matrix in a two-player, zero-sum game, then the following statements are equivalent:

1. Player I has $\tilde{p}$ as a security strategy, player II has $\tilde{q}$ as a security strategy, and the value of the game is $v = \tilde{p}^\top A\tilde{q}$.
2. The pair $(\tilde{p}, \tilde{q})$ is a saddle point.
3. The pair $(\tilde{p}, \tilde{q})$ is a Nash equilibrium.

6.5.7 When to Play Maximin

Some authors advocate the use of maximin strategies as a general rule for making decisions in risky situations. However, unless your relationship with the universe has reached such a low ebb that you keep your pants up with both belt and suspenders, you will probably think it right to disregard this advice. It is usually irrational to be so cautious. It is certainly *false* that, if both players use security strategies in a general bimatrix game, then each will be making a best reply to the strategy choice made by the other.

Consider, for example, the bimatrix game of Figure 6.5(b). Player I's security level of $2\frac{2}{3}$ in this game was calculated in Section 6.4.2. His security level is $\tilde{p} = (\frac{1}{6}, 0, \frac{5}{6})^\top$. Player II's security level is 2, and her security strategy is $\tilde{q} = (0, 1, 0)^\top$. (She is in the identical situation as player I in the bimatrix game of Figure 6.5(a). Her security level and strategy are therefore the same as those calculated for player I in Section 6.3.1.) However, $\tilde{p}$ is certainly *not* a best reply to $\tilde{q}$. The best reply to $\tilde{q}$ is for player I to use his first pure strategy for certain.

Phil
6.6 ⟶

The preceding example shows that a pair $(\tilde{p}, \tilde{q})$ of maximin strategies in a general bimatrix game need not be a Nash equilibrium. Theorem 6.5.2 is therefore definitely only a theorem about two-player, *zero-sum* games. However, even when playing in a two-player, zero-sum game, you would be ill-advised to use a maximin strategy when you have good reason to suppose that your opponent will play badly. Playing your security strategy will certainly guarantee you your security level however the opponent plays, but you ought to be aiming for more than your security level against a bad player. You should be probing the opponent's play for systematic weaknesses, and deviating from your security strategy in order to exploit these weaknesses. You will be taking a risk in doing so, but it is *irrational* to be unwilling to take a calculated risk when the odds are in your favor and everything is properly expressed in terms of Von Neumann and Morgenstern utilities.

The play of security strategies in a two-player, zero-sum game has only been defended for the case in which it is common knowledge that both players are rational in an appropriate sense. There is no particular reason why you should play a security strategy in a game that is not zero-sum. Nor is there any particular reason for playing a security strategy in a game that is zero-sum if you know that your opponent is irrational.

Math

6.6 Separating Hyperplanes

The theorem of the separating hyperplane has important applications. It is often used, for example, in proving the existence of clearing prices in general equilibrium models of the economy. Fortunately, in spite of its formidable name, the theorem is easy to understand. It concerns the conditions under which two convex sets can be separated by a hyperplane.

Figure 6.11(a) shows two convex sets H and K in $\mathbb{R}^2$ separated by the hyperplane $p^\top x = c$. Recall from Section 4.5 that a hyperplane in $\mathbb{R}^2$ is simply a line. The vector p is a normal to this line. (Figure 6.11(b) shows a degenerate case in which the set K consists of a single boundary point k of H. The separating line is then a supporting line as discussed in Section 5.2.3.)

In Section 5.2.3, it was noted that a line splits $\mathbb{R}^2$ into two half-spaces. Similarly, a hyperplane $p^\top x = c$ splits $\mathbb{R}^n$ into two half-spaces. The half-space "above" the hyperplane is the set

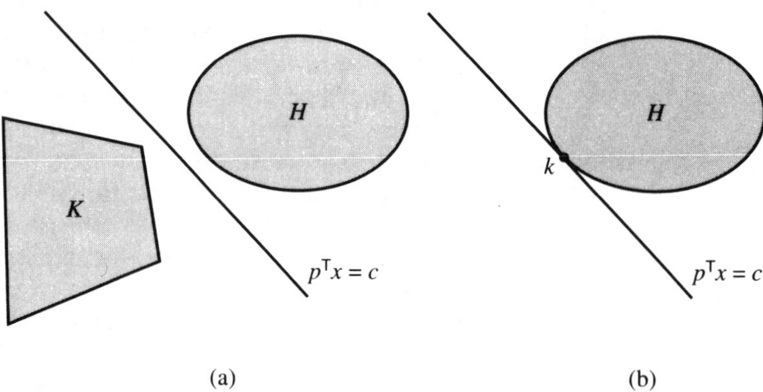

Figure 6.11 Separating hyperplanes.

of all x for which $p^\top x \geq c$. This is the half-space into which the vector p points. The half-space "below" the hyperplane is the set of all x for which $p^\top x \leq c$.

To say that H and K are separated by a hyperplane means that one of the sets lies above the hyperplane and the other lies below. The condition for H to lie above the hyperplane can be expressed algebraically as the requirement that

$$p^\top h \geq c$$

for all h in H. The condition for K to lie below the hyperplane translates into the requirement that

$$p^\top k \leq c$$

for all k in K.

Various versions of the theorem of the separating hyperplane exist. The simplest useful version is quoted below. Notice that it allows H and K to have boundary points in common.

Theorem 6.6.1 (Theorem of the Separating Hyperplane) Let H and K be convex sets in $\mathbb{R}^n$. Suppose that K has interior points, but that none of these lie in H. Then there exists a hyperplane $p^\top x = c$ that separates H and K.

6.6.1 Separation and Saddle Points

Von Neumann's minimax theorem can be seen as a special case of the theorem of the separating hyperplane. Indeed, it is often deduced from the separating hyperplane theorem.

The connection is useful to understand because it provides a geometric interpretation of the vectors $\tilde{p}$ and $\tilde{q}$ in the expression $\tilde{p}^\top Aq \geq \tilde{p}^\top A\tilde{q} \geq p^\top A\tilde{q}$ for a saddle point. Recall that $v = \tilde{p}^\top A\tilde{q}$ is the value of the zero-sum game with matrix A. Our aim in this section is therefore to investigate how the inequalities

$$\tilde{p}^\top Aq \geq v \geq p^\top A\tilde{q} \tag{6.16}$$

manifest themselves geometrically. This will then provide us with a method of finding $\tilde{p}$, $\tilde{q}$ and v that is relatively painless since it minimizes on the amount of algebra that needs to be done.[19]

The situation will be illustrated using the matrix

$$A = \begin{bmatrix} 1 & 6 & 0 \\ 3 & 2 & 4 \end{bmatrix} \tag{6.17}$$

Math 6.6.2 ⟶

of Figure 6.8(a). We then know from Section 6.4.2 that $\tilde{p} = (\frac{1}{6}, \frac{5}{6})^\top$ and $v = 2\frac{2}{3}$. From Section 6.5.5, we also know that $\tilde{q} = (\frac{2}{3}, \frac{1}{3}, 0)^\top$.

The set H is taken to be the convex hull (Section 5.2.4) of the columns of the matrix A. A point h in H is therefore a convex combination (Section 4.2.3) of the columns of A. That is, for some q in Q,

$$\begin{aligned} h &= q_1 \begin{bmatrix} 1 \\ 3 \end{bmatrix} + q_2 \begin{bmatrix} 6 \\ 2 \end{bmatrix} + q_3 \begin{bmatrix} 0 \\ 4 \end{bmatrix} \\ &= \begin{bmatrix} 1q_1 + 6q_2 + 0q_3 \\ 3q_1 + 2q_2 + 4q_3 \end{bmatrix} \\ &= \begin{bmatrix} 1 & 6 & 0 \\ 3 & 2 & 4 \end{bmatrix} \begin{bmatrix} q_1 \\ q_2 \\ q_3 \end{bmatrix} = Aq\,. \end{aligned}$$

This argument shows that the convex hull of the columns of the matrix A is the set

$$H = \{Aq : q \in Q\}$$

illustrated in Figure 6.12(a).

The set K is shown in Figure 6.12(b). It is defined by

$$K = \{k : k_1 \leq v \text{ and } k_2 \leq v\},$$

[19] If the explanation that follows is puzzling, you might try reading Section 6.6.2 first. This describes the mechanics of using the geometry to solve simple zero-sum games.

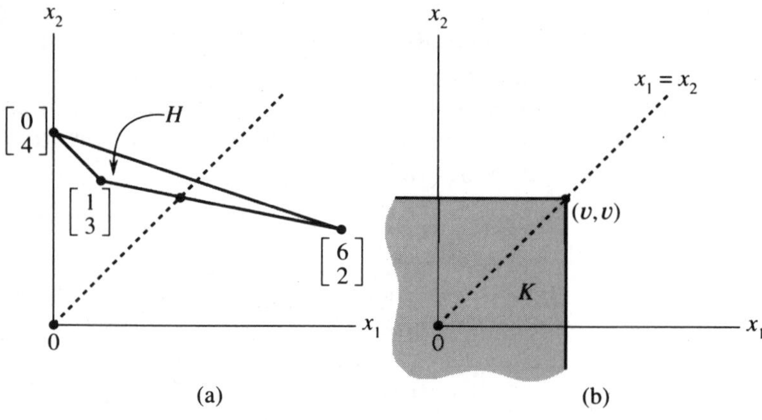

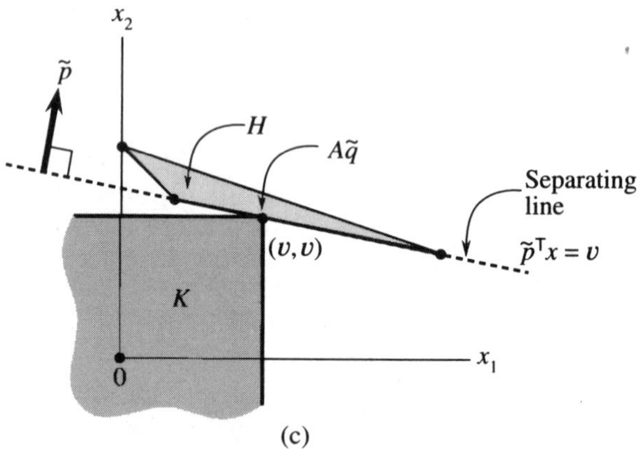

Figure 6.12 A geometric representation of security strategies.

where $v = \tilde{p}^\top A\tilde{q}$. It is helpful to note[20] that k lies in K if and only if

$$p^\top k \leq v\,, \tag{6.18}$$

for all p in P.

The hyperplane $\tilde{p}^\top x = v$ separates H and K. It is immediate that K lies below the hyperplane, because we can take $p = \tilde{p}$ in (6.18). To see that H lies above the hyperplane, we

---

[20]If $k_1 \leq v$ and $k_2 \leq v$, then

$$p^\top k = p_1 k_1 + p_2 k_2 \leq (p_1 + p_2)v = v$$

for all p in P, because $p_1 \geq 0$, $p_2 \geq 0$ and $p_1 + p_2 = 1$. Equally, if $p^\top k \leq v$ for all p in P, then $k_1 \leq v$ and $k_2 \leq v$. To see this, consider the particular values $p = (0,1)^\top$ and $p = (1,0)^\top$.

need the left half of (6.16). This says that $\tilde{p}^\top Aq \geq v$, for all q in Q. On writing $h = Aq$, it follows that

$$\tilde{p}^\top h \geq v$$

for all h in H.

The right half of (6.16) has not yet been used. This says that $p^\top A\tilde{q} \leq v$ for all p in P. Thus, $A\tilde{q}$, which we already know to lie in H, must also lie in K by (6.18). That is, the set $H \cap K$ of all points common to H and K contains $A\tilde{q}$. Although H and K are separated by the hyperplane $\tilde{p}^\top x = v$, they therefore still have the point $A\tilde{q}$ in common, as illustrated in Figure 6.12(c).

Summary. What has been shown can be briefly summarized. The inequalities (6.16) characterize $(\tilde{p}, \tilde{q})$ as a saddle point in mixed strategies with $v = \tilde{p}^\top A\tilde{q}$. An alternative geometric characterization exists. Once the sets H and K have been constructed, $\tilde{p}$ appears as a normal to the hyperplane $\tilde{p}^\top x = v$ that separates the convex sets H and K. The vector $\tilde{q}$ can be found using the fact that the point $A\tilde{q}$ lies in the set $H \cap K$.

6.6.2 Solving Games Using Separation

The preceding subsection explains how the minimax theorem can be interpreted geometrically. In this subsection, the geometry will be used to solve some two-player, zero-sum games. The method works for any payoff matrix with only two rows.

Example 1. Consider the two-player, zero-sum game with payoff matrix (6.17). This is an old friend whom we met most recently in the preceding subsection.

Step 1. Mark the location of the columns $(1, 3)^\top$, $(6, 2)^\top$ and $(0, 4)^\top$ of the matrix A on a piece of graph paper. Then draw their convex hull H as in Figure 6.12(a).

Step 2. Draw the line $x_1 = x_2$. The point $(v, v)^\top$ lies on this line. The set K is as shown in Figure 6.12(b). The number v is assigned the *smallest* value such that H and K have at least one point in common[21] as illustrated in Figure 6.12(c).

[21]The sets H and K must have a point in common because $A\tilde{q}$ belongs to both. It must contain as few other points as possible because the theorem of the separating hyperplane requires that H contain no interior point of K.

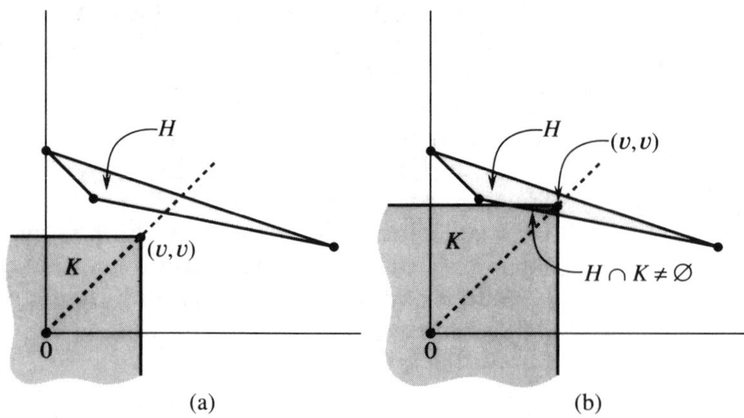

Figure 6.13 Choosing the number v.

(Figure 6.13(a) shows a case where v has been chosen too small so that H and K have no points in common. Figure 6.13(b) shows a case where v has been chosen too large. It could be made a little smaller and the sets H and K would still have points in common.)

Step 3. Draw the separating line $\tilde{p}^\top x = v$, as in Figure 6.12(c).

Step 4. Find $\tilde{p}$. This is a normal to the separating line. Often it can be found without the need to calculate, but here it is necessary to write down the equation of the separating line. Since the separating line passes through $(1, 3)^\top$ and $(6, 2)^\top$, it has equation

$$\frac{x_2 - 3}{x_1 - 1} = \frac{2 - 3}{6 - 1} = \frac{-1}{5}.$$

This can be rewritten as $x_1 + 5x_2 = 16$. From Section 4.5, we know that the coefficients 1 and 5 of this equation are the coordinates of a normal vector. Thus $(1, 5)^\top$ is a normal to the separating line. But we need to find a normal $\tilde{p}$ that satisfies $p_1 \geq 0$, $p_2 \geq 0$ and $p_1 + p_2 = 1$, and hence lies in the set P. The normal $(1, 5)^\top$ is therefore replaced[22] by the normal $\tilde{p} = (\frac{1}{6}, \frac{5}{6})^\top$.

Step 5. Find the value v of the game. Here $(v, v)^\top$ is the point where the lines $x_1 = x_2$ and $x_1 + 5x_2 = 16$ meet. Therefore $v + 5v = 16$, and so $v = 16/6 = 2\frac{2}{3}$.

---

[22]If $\lambda \neq 0$, then $\lambda(1, 5)^\top$ points in the same (or the opposite) direction to $(1, 5)^\top$, and hence is also a normal to the separating line. For a normal whose coordinates sum to 1, we take $\lambda = \frac{1}{6}$.

Step 6. Find $\tilde{q}$, using the fact that $A\tilde{q}$ lies in the set $H \cap K$. One must first identify $H \cap K$. In the current example, $H \cap K$ consists of the single point $(v, v) = (2\frac{2}{3}, 2\frac{2}{3})$. Thus,

$$\begin{bmatrix} 1 & 6 & 0 \\ 3 & 2 & 4 \end{bmatrix} \begin{bmatrix} \tilde{q}_1 \\ \tilde{q}_2 \\ \tilde{q}_3 \end{bmatrix} = \begin{bmatrix} 2\frac{2}{3} \\ 2\frac{2}{3} \end{bmatrix}.$$

One could make this into a system of three simultaneous linear equations by appending the requirement that $\tilde{q}_1 + \tilde{q}_2 + \tilde{q}_3 = 1$. However, usually there is an easier way to proceed.

Recall that H is the convex hull of the columns of A. Thus $A\tilde{q}$ is a convex combination of the columns of A. In fact, $A\tilde{q}$ lies at the center of gravity of weights $\tilde{q}_1$, $\tilde{q}_2$ and $\tilde{q}_3$ located at the points $(1, 3)^\top$, $(6, 2)^\top$ and $(0, 4)^\top$ (Section 5.2.3). In Figure 6.12(c), $(v, v)^\top = A\tilde{q}$ looks as though it is one-third of the way along the line segment joining the point $(1, 3)^\top$ to the point $(6, 2)^\top$. If so, then the appropriate weights must be $\tilde{q}_1 = \frac{2}{3}$, $\tilde{q}_2 = \frac{1}{3}$ and $\tilde{q}_3 = 0$. To check this, observe that

$$\frac{2}{3}\begin{bmatrix} 1 \\ 3 \end{bmatrix} + \frac{1}{3}\begin{bmatrix} 6 \\ 2 \end{bmatrix} + 0\begin{bmatrix} 0 \\ 4 \end{bmatrix} = \begin{bmatrix} 2\frac{2}{3} \\ 2\frac{2}{3} \end{bmatrix}.$$

Thus, with a minimum of calculation, it has been established that player II has a unique security strategy $\tilde{q} = (\frac{2}{3}, \frac{1}{3}, 0)^\top$.

To summarize: $v = 2\frac{2}{3}$, $\tilde{p} = (\frac{1}{6}, \frac{5}{6})^\top$ and $\tilde{q} = (\frac{2}{3}, \frac{1}{3}, 0)^\top$. These results agree with those obtained in Sections 6.4.2 and 6.5.5.

Example 2. Consider the two-player, zero-sum game with matrix

$$B = \begin{bmatrix} 4 & 3 & 3 \\ 5 & 2 & 0 \end{bmatrix}.$$

This yields the configuration shown in Figure 6.14(a). The separating line has equation $x_1 = 3$, and hence $\tilde{p} = (1, 0)^\top$. The value of the game is $v = 3$. The set $H \cap K$ consists of all points on the line segment ℓ joining $(3, 0)^\top$ and $(3, 2)^\top$. If $A\tilde{q}$ lies on ℓ, then $\tilde{q}$ is a security strategy for player II. If weights $\tilde{q}_1$, $\tilde{q}_2$ and $\tilde{q}_3$ are placed at $(4, 5)^\top$, $(3, 2)^\top$ and $(3, 0)^\top$, when will their center of gravity lie on ℓ? The only restriction necessary is that $\tilde{q}_1 = 0$. Thus, any $\tilde{q}$ in Q with $\tilde{q}_1 = 0$ is a security strategy for player II.

Notice that player II's first column is strongly dominated by her third column. This could therefore have been deleted

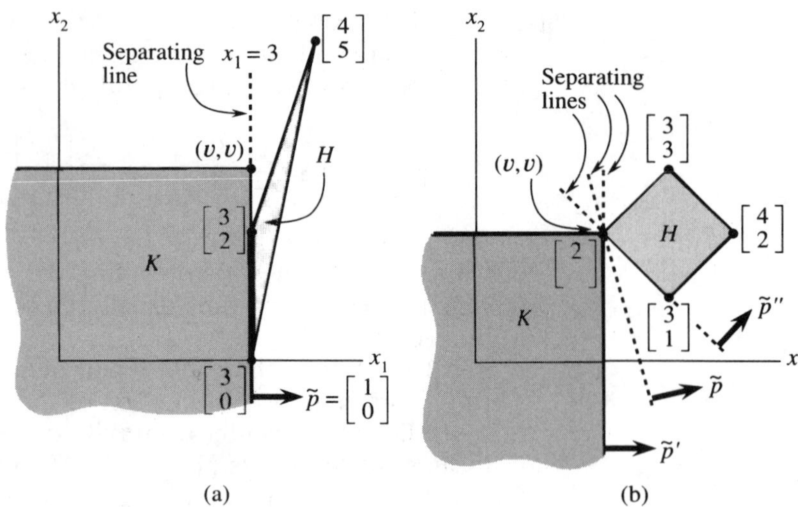

Figure 6.14 Two further examples.

to begin with. Her second column is *weakly* dominated by the third column. If this had also been deleted, all but one of her security strategies (that with $\tilde{q}_1 = \tilde{q}_2 = 0$) would have been lost.

Example 3. Consider the two-player, zero-sum game with matrix

$$C = \begin{bmatrix} 2 & 3 & 3 & 4 \\ 2 & 3 & 1 & 2 \end{bmatrix}.$$

This yields the configuration of Figure 6.14(b). There are many separating lines, of which three have been drawn: the two extremal cases with $\tilde{p}' = (\frac{1}{2}, \frac{1}{2})^\top$ and $\tilde{p}'' = (0, 1)^\top$, and an intermediate case $\tilde{p} = (1 - r, r)^\top$. Any $\tilde{p}$ with $\frac{1}{2} \leq r \leq 1$ is therefore a security strategy for player I. The value of the game is $v = 2$. The set $H \cap K$ consists of the single point $(2, 2)^\top$. For $A\tilde{q}$ to be equal to $(2, 2)^\top$, all the weight must be assigned to the single column $(2, 2)^\top$. Thus player II has a unique security strategy $\tilde{q} = (1, 0, 0, 0)^\top$.

6.6.3 Security Strategies and Domination

The method for solving two-person, zero-sum games given above works whatever the dimensions of the payoff matrix. However, it is useful as a practical tool only when the payoff matrix has only two rows or two columns.[23] In larger games,

[23]In the latter case, switch the roles of players I and II. The rows and columns of the payoff matrix A then have to be switched. This yields the

it is usually necessary to try some other tricks. If no such tricks can be found, two-player zero-sum games can always be solved using linear programming techniques. However, such techniques are beyond the scope of this book.

What tricks are available for dealing with big games? The tricks listed below are often useful if you only care about finding the value of a two-player, zero-sum game and at least one security strategy for each player. If you want to find *all* security strategies for the players, it is necessary to work harder.

- The first trick is not very clever. Simply check to see whether the payoff matrix has a saddle point. If it does, we are home and dry. There is then no need to fuss about with mixed strategies at all.
- The second trick is to look for symmetries. The example coming up in Section 6.7 shows how these can sometimes be used to simplify things.
- The third trick is even more crude. It consists of deleting dominated strategies as described in Section 4.6.1. What was said there about Nash equilibrium strategies applies directly to security strategies in two-player, zero-sum games because Theorem 6.5.2 tells us that Nash equilibrium strategies and security strategies are the same thing in two-player, zero-sum games. However, what is said below applies in any game, whether zero-sum or not.

Recall that one can always delete *strongly* dominated strategies without fear of losing anything that matters. Nash equilibrium strategies never assign positive probability to strongly dominated strategies. Nor do security strategies. Things are a little more delicate with *weakly* dominated strategies. Sometimes Nash equilibrium strategies do assign positive probability to weakly dominated strategies. So do security strategies. If you are looking for *all* Nash equilibrium strategies or *all* security strategies, you are therefore taking a risk of losing something you care about when deleting a weakly dominated strategy. However, if you are only looking for *some* Nash equilibrium strategy, or *some* security strategy, then deleting a weakly dominated strategy is harmless. There is always

---

transpose matrix $A^\top$. The signs of all the payoffs in this matrix then need to be reversed, so that they become the payoffs of the new player I (who is the old player II) rather than the payoffs of the old player I (who is the new player II). The new game therefore has payoff matrix $-A^\top$. After analyzing the new game, security stategies $\tilde{p}$, $\tilde{q}$ and a value v will be found. The *old* game then has value $-v$. A security strategy for the *old* player I is $\tilde{q}$. A security strategy for the *old* player II is $\tilde{p}$.

some Nash equilibrium strategy that assigns zero probability to a given weakly dominated strategy. This goes for security strategies also.

Fun 6.8 ⟶

6.7 Battleships

This game is popular with children. Each player has a grid on which they secretly mark a number of battleships. The players then alternate in calling out a grid reference they wish to bomb on the other player's grid. The aim is to be the first to eliminate the enemy's fleet.

A highly simplified and asymmetric version of the game will be considered here. John will have just one battleship, which he places on a 4×1 board representing a harbor. The battleship occupies two adjacent squares. The diagrams of Figure 6.15(a) show the three possible locations in the harbor where John can place his battleship. These therefore represent John's three pure strategies.

Mary does not know where John has located the battleship but seeks to destroy it by bombing. *Both* squares occupied by the battleship must be bombed for it to be destroyed. One by one, in any order she chooses, Mary bombs the squares that make up the harbor. Each time that Mary names the square she wishes to bomb, John responds by (truthfully) telling her whether or not she has scored a hit. John's aim is to place the battleship so as to maximize the expected number of bombs required to sink it. Mary's aim is to minimize the expected number of bombs.

The diagrams of Figure 6.15(b) represent Mary's pure strategies. The symbols $\circ$ or $\star$ indicate where she plans to drop the first bomb. The symbol $\circ$ is used to indicate that, if the first bomb is a miss, then the second and third bombs should be dropped on the squares marked with $\times$. The symbol $\star$ is used

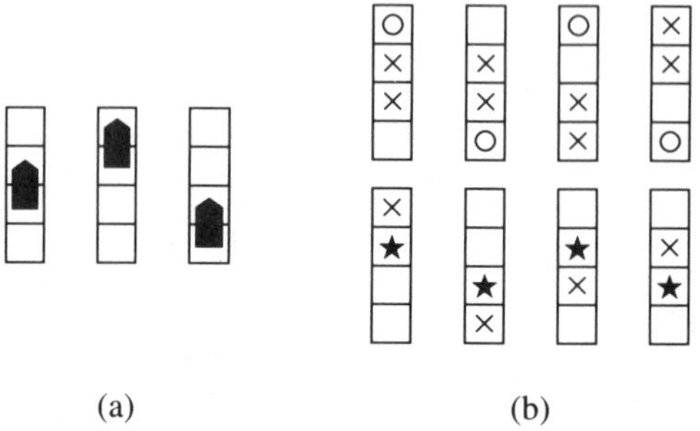

(a) (b)

Figure 6.15 Pure strategies for John and Mary in Battleships.

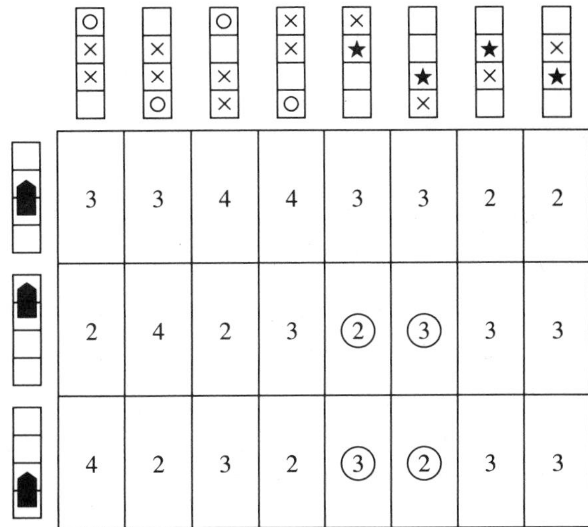

3
3
4
4
3
3
2
2
2
4
2
3
2
3
3
3
4
2
3
2
3
2
3
3

Figure 6.16 John's payoff matrix for Battleships.

to indicate that, if the first bomb is a hit, then the second bomb should be dropped on the square marked with ×. What should Mary do under other contingencies? For example, if the symbol ∘ is used and the first bomb is a hit, where should she drop the second bomb? All such questions are answered by considering only strategies that do not require Mary to continue stupidly. For example, if the symbol ⋆ is used and the first bomb is a miss, then Mary *knows* the location of the battleship precisely, and it would be stupid for her not to place her second and third bombs so as to sink it.

Figure 6.16 shows John's payoff matrix for this two-player, zero-sum game. For example, the entry 2 in row 2 and column 3 is calculated by observing that, if John uses row 2 and Mary uses column 3, then Mary's first bomb will be a hit. She then knows the location of the remainder of the battleship and hence uses her second bomb to sink it entirely. Thus only two bombs will be needed to end the game.

The 3×8 payoff matrix in Figure 6.16 takes no account of various stupid pure strategies available to Mary. Nevertheless, it is still too complicated for the method of the preceding section to be usable. A further simplification will therefore be made. If two pure strategies are the same except that north is swapped with south, then it will be assumed that each of the two pure strategies is used with equal probabilities. For example, it will be assumed that John uses row 2 and row 3 with equal probabilities. Similarly, Mary will be assumed to use columns 7 and 8 with equal probabilities. This reduces

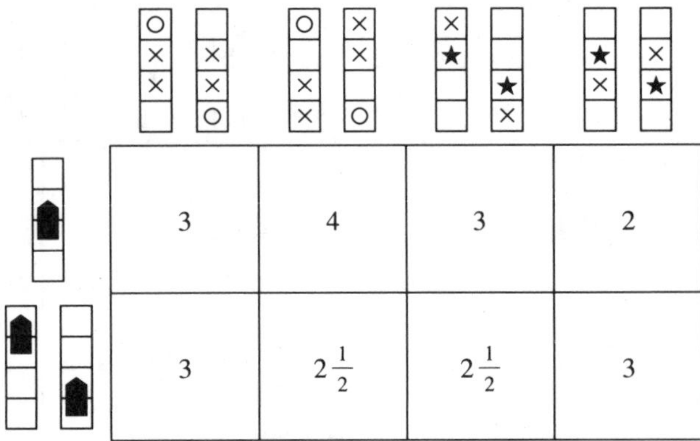

Figure 6.17 A simplified version of John's payoff matrix for Battleships.

John's payoff matrix to the manageable 2×4 matrix shown in Figure 6.17.

As an example of how the entries in this simplified matrix are calculated, consider the entry $2\frac{1}{2}$ in row 2 and column 3 of Figure 6.17. This is obtained when John uses row 2 and row 3 of Figure 6.16 each with probability $\frac{1}{2}$, and Mary independently uses column 5 and column 6 each with probability $\frac{1}{2}$. The circled payoffs in Figure 6.16 then each occur with probability $\frac{1}{2} \times \frac{1}{2} = \frac{1}{4}$. The expected payoff to John is therefore $2\frac{1}{2} = \frac{1}{4}(2 + 3 + 2 + 3)$.

Figure 6.18 shows the method of the preceding section applied with the 2×4 simplified version of the payoff matrix.[24] The separating line is $x_1 + 2x_2 = 8$. A suitable normal is $\tilde{p} = (\frac{1}{3}, \frac{2}{3})^\top$. The set $H \cap K$ consists of a single point $(2\frac{2}{3}, 2\frac{2}{3})^\top$, which can be found by solving $x_1 + 2x_2 = 8$ simultaneously with $x_1 = x_2$. The value of the game is $v = 2\frac{2}{3}$. The point $(2\frac{2}{3}, 2\frac{2}{3})$ is one third of the way along the line segment that joins $(3, 2\frac{1}{2})^\top$ and $(2, 3)^\top$. Hence $\tilde{q}$ must assign weight $\frac{2}{3}$ to column 3 of the payoff matrix of Figure 6.17 and $\frac{1}{3}$ to column 4. Columns 1 and 2 get zero weight. Thus $\tilde{q} = (0, 0, \frac{2}{3}, \frac{1}{3})^\top$.

So how should Battleships be played? In terms of the original 3×8 payoff matrix of Figure 6.16, John should[25] use the

[24]One could note that Mary's column 4 weakly dominates column 1. Also, column 3 weakly dominates column 2. Eliminating the first and second columns would simplify things slightly.

[25]You ought to check that the pair of mixed strategies advocated for John and Mary really is a saddle point for the game of Figure 6.16. No *proof* was offered that symmetric strategies should be used with equal probabilities in this game.

3	4	3	2
3	$2\frac{1}{2}$	$2\frac{1}{2}$	3

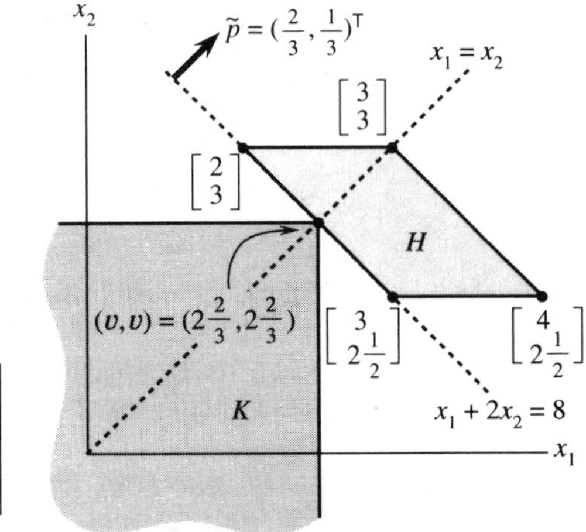

Figure 6.18 Separating convex sets for Battleships.

mixed strategy $(\frac{1}{3}, \frac{1}{3}, \frac{1}{3})^\top$ (because this assigns equal probabilities to rows 2 and 3 that sum to $\tilde{p} = \frac{2}{3}$). Mary should use the mixed strategy $(0, 0, 0, 0, \frac{1}{3}, \frac{1}{3}, \frac{1}{6}, \frac{1}{6})^\top$. If these mixed strategies are used, then the average number of bombs needed to sink the battleship will be $v = 2\frac{2}{3}$.

It is perhaps not so hard to guess that John should use each of his three possible hiding places with equal probabilities. However, Mary's bombing strategy is not so transparent.

6.8 The Inspection Game

This example combines mixed strategies in two-player, zero-sum games with the use of Zermelo's algorithm.

Econ 6.9 ⟶ An environmental protection agency knows that an unscrupulous firm is determined to discharge a pollutant into a river on one of n days. The agency will learn immediately when the river is polluted because of the telephone complaints it will receive from local residents. However, to obtain a conviction, the agency has to catch the firm red-handed. This means that it must try and guess in advance the day on which the firm will pollute the river so as to have an inspector on the spot. Unfortunately, the agency's resources are so overstretched that it can only afford to dispatch an inspector to the site on one of the n days, and the firm knows this.

This situation can be modeled as a two-player game in which player I is the agency and player II is the firm. It will be assumed that the agency wins if it chooses to inspect the firm on the day the firm pollutes the river. Otherwise the firm

	Act	Wait
Act	1	−1
Wait	−1	v_{n-1}

Figure 6.19 The Inspection Game.

wins. Both players assign a payoff of +1 to winning and −1 to losing. The game is then zero-sum. Its value will be denoted by v_n.

On each day, the players decide whether or not to act. On the first of the n days, they therefore play the matrix game of Figure 6.19. If both act, then the agency will inspect on the day the river is polluted. The agency then wins and so the entry on the top left of the payoff matrix is +1. If one player waits while the other acts, then the agency loses. Hence the entries on the top right and bottom left of the payoff matrix are both −1. What about the entry on the bottom right? If both players decide to wait on the first day, then nothing will happen until the second day. At the beginning of the second day, things will be the same as at the beginning of the first day, except that only $n-1$ days remain. The value of the inspection game played over $n-1$ days is v_{n-1}. Hence this is the appropriate payoff when both players wait on the first day.[26]

Of course, if $n = 1$, this discussion does not apply, since there will then be no second day. However, when $n = 1$, the firm has no choice about when to pollute the river and so it is sure to be caught. Thus $v_1 = 1$.

Rather than providing another illustration of the separating hyperplane method of solving zero-sum games, we take the opportunity of revising the method used in Sections 6.4.2 and 6.5.5 for finding security strategies.

If the agency (player I) uses mixed strategy $p = (1-r, r)^\top$, then its expected payoff is $E_1(r) = (1-r) - r = 1 - 2r$ when the firm acts, and $E_2(r) = -(1-r) + rv_{n-1} = -1 + r(1+v_{n-1})$ when the firm waits. To find a security strategy, the agency first needs to graph $m(r) = \min\{E_1(r), E_2(r)\}$. This graph is shown with a bold line in Figure 6.20(a). The next

[26]The use of this technique is sometimes signaled by a reference to the theory of "stochastic games". This can be confusing for the uninitiated. "Stochastic" means "random", but the technique is viable whether or not there is any randomness involved.

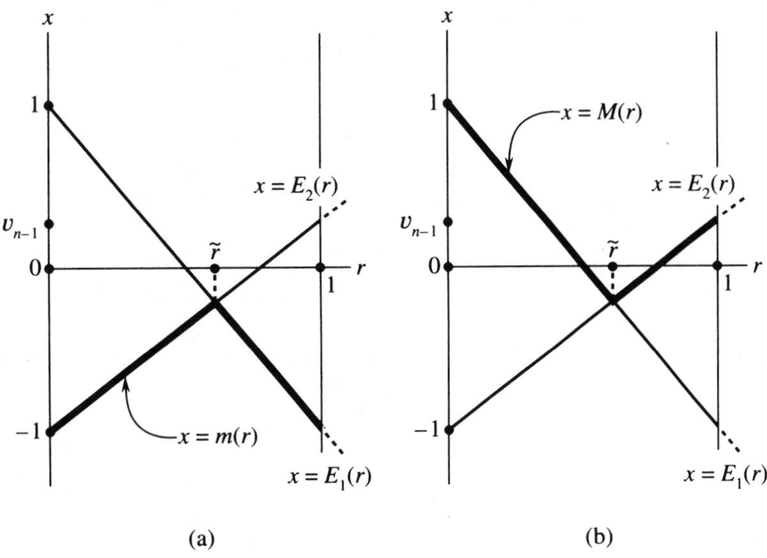

Figure 6.20 Security strategies in the Inspection Game.

step is to find the value of r at which $m(r)$ is largest. The diagram makes it clear that this occurs where the lines $x = E_1(r)$ and $x = E_2(r)$ cross. The solution to the equation $1 - 2r = -1 + r(1 + v_{n-1})$ is $\tilde{r} = 2/(3 + v_{n-1})$, and so this is the probability with which the agency should wait on the first day. The agency's security level, and hence the value v_n of the inspection game, is therefore

$$v_n = m(\tilde{r}) = 1 - 2\tilde{r} = \frac{v_{n-1} - 1}{v_{n-1} + 3}. \tag{6.19}$$

The firm (player II) can compute a security strategy in a similar way.[27] As in Section 6.5.5, it is necessary to remember that the payoffs in the matrix are *losses* to player II, and hence the roles of "max" and "min" in the discussion have to be reversed.

If the firm (player II) uses mixed strategy $q = (1 - r, r)^\top$, then its expected payoff is $E_1(r) = (1 - r) - r = 1 - 2r$ when the agency acts, and $E_2(r) = -(1 - r) + v_{n-1}r = -1 + r(1 + v_{n-1})$ when the agency waits. To find a security strategy, the firm first needs to graph $M(r) = \max\{E_1(r), E_2(r)\}$. This graph is shown with a bold line in Figure 6.20(b). The next step is to find the value of r at which $M(r)$ is smallest.

[27]Computations can be evaded by noticing that the payoff matrix is symmetric. It follows that player II's security strategy will be the same as player I's. However, it is easier to carry through the calculations than to explain why this is true. The reason is not entirely transparent.

The diagram makes it clear that this occurs where the lines $x = E_1(r)$ and $x = E_2(r)$ cross. The solution to the firm's problem is therefore the same as the solution to the agency's problem: the firm should wait on the first day with probability $\tilde{r} = 2/(3 + v_{n-1})$.

After making the substitution $v_k = w_k^{-1} - 1$ and simplifying, equation (6.19) reduces to

$$w_n - w_{n-1} = \tfrac{1}{2} \qquad (n > 1).$$

The fact that it can be reduced to this form makes it easy to understand why equations like (6.19) are called *difference equations*. Solving such equations is not always easy, but here things go very smoothly:

$$\begin{aligned} w_n - w_1 &= (w_n - w_{n-1}) + (w_{n-1} - w_{n-2}) + \cdots + (w_2 - w_1) \\ &= \tfrac{1}{2} + \tfrac{1}{2} + \cdots + \tfrac{1}{2} \\ &= \tfrac{1}{2}(n-1). \end{aligned}$$

But $w_1 = \frac{1}{2}$ because $v_1 = 1$. Hence $w_n = \frac{1}{2}n$. Thus the value v_n of the inspection game is given by

$$v_n = w_n^{-1} - 1 = -1 + \frac{2}{n}.$$

Suppose that the firm must pollute the river on one of the days in a specified week, but Sunday and Monday have passed without the river being polluted or an inspection being made. What is the probability with which the agency should inspect on Tuesday? On Tuesday morning, the players are faced with the inspection game with $n = 5$ because there are only five days left in the week. Thus the agency should inspect with probability $1 - \tilde{r}$, where $\tilde{r} = 2/(v_4 + 3) = \frac{4}{5}$. Thus, if nothing happens on Sunday and Monday, the agency should inspect with probability $\frac{1}{5}$ on Tuesday. Similarly, the firm should pollute the river with probability $\frac{1}{5}$. In general, if nothing has happened up to now and there are k days remaining, each player should act with probability $1/k$ today.

A Quick Fix. The method used to solve the Inspection Game can be used in a wide variety of circumstances. However, for the Inspection Game itself, there is a short and brutal alternative approach that exploits the fact that the strategic form of the game is particularly simple.

As with other games of timing like Duel or Russian Roulette, the only pure strategies that need to be considered are those that say when a player proposes to act. Each player has n such strategies, one for each of the days on which the river might be polluted. Player I therefore has an $n \times n$ payoff matrix. The entries are $+1$ on the main diagonal,[28] and -1 everywhere else. This reflects the fact that the agency wins if the two players choose to act on the same day, and loses otherwise.

The entries in each column of the matrix sum to $-(n-2)$. Thus, if player I uses each of his pure strategies with equal probability, then he guarantees an expected payoff of $-(n-2)/n$ whatever player II may do. The entries in each row also sum to $-(n-2)$. Playing each pure strategy with equal probability therefore also guarantees Player II an expected payoff of $(n-2)/n$ whatever player I may do. It follows that it is a security strategy for each player to use each of their pure strategies with equal probability.[29] The value of the game is player I's security level: namely,

$$v_n = -(n-2)/n = -1 + \frac{2}{n},$$

which is exactly what we found previously.

Econ 6.10 ⟶

6.9 Nash Threat Game

The Nash bargaining solution was discussed in Chapter 5. If (X, d) is a bargaining problem in which X is the set of feasible payoff pairs, and d is the disagreement point, recall that the regular Nash bargaining solution determines a payoff pair $s = N(X, d)$ in X as a candidate for the result of a rational agreement between the two players.

In this section, the payoff region X will be the set Z illustrated in Figure 6.21(a). The upper boundary of this set has equation $x_1 + x_2 = 12$. If John and Mary are both risk-neutral in respect of money, one can therefore think of their bargaining problem as that of dividing \$12 kindly contributed by a passing philanthropist. Figure 6.21(a) shows that the regular Nash bargaining solution $s = N(Z, d)$ is located where the line of slope 1 through d cuts the boundary of Z. Figure 6.21(b) shows that, if s is the solution when the disagreement point is d, and t is the solution when the disagreement point is e, then the solution is $\alpha s + \beta t$ when the disagreement point is

[28] Which stretches from the northwest corner of the matrix to the southeast corner.

[29] This is not inconsistent with what was said earlier. For example, suppose that $n = 3$. Let player I plan to act on the first day with probability $1/3$. Let him plan to act on the second day with probability $1/2$, *if* he did not act on the first day. Let him plan to act on the third day with probability 1, *if* he did not act on either of the two previous days. Before anything happens, the probability that he will act on the second day is then $\frac{2}{3} \times \frac{1}{2} = \frac{1}{3}$. The probability that he will act on the third day is $\frac{2}{3} \times \frac{1}{2} \times 1 = \frac{1}{3}$.

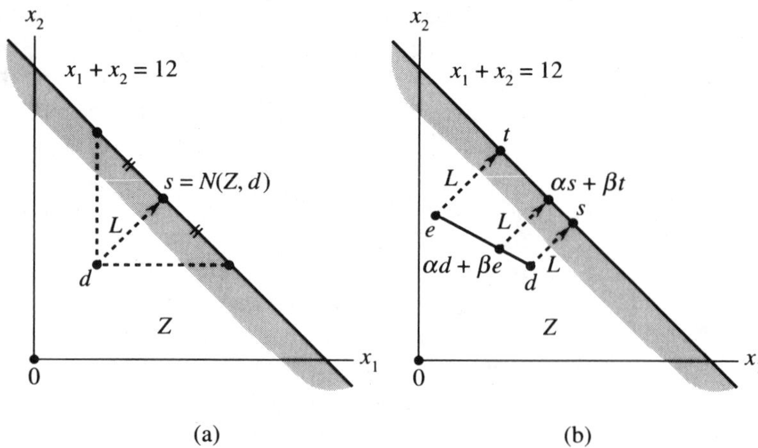

Figure 6.21 Nash bargaining solutions.

$\alpha d + \beta e$. Thus, the function defined by $L(d) = N(Z, d)$ satisfies $L(\alpha d + \beta e) = \alpha L(d) + \beta L(e)$. Mathematicians call functions with this property *linear.*

The location of the Nash bargaining solution depends heavily on where the disagreement point is. But what happens if John and Mary are not given a disagreement point in advance of their negotiation? Nash argued that, in the event of a disagreement, some game would then have to be played noncooperatively. In this example, the disagreement game is taken to have the strategic form shown in Figure 6.22(a).

Suppose that d_{ij} represents the payoff pair in the ith row and jth column of the disagreement game. Then, for example, $d_{22} = (6, 2)$. Figure 6.22(c) shows the outcomes $s_{ij} = L(d_{ij}) = N(Z, d_{ij})$ that would result if the regular Nash bargaining solution were used with d_{ij} as the disagreement point. These outcomes s_{ij} are tabulated in Figure 6.22(b).

If John and Mary are unable to commit themselves before the negotiations begin as to what they will do in the Disagreement Game should the negotiations fail, then matters are fairly simple. The Disagreement Game has a unique Nash equilibrium whose play results in the payoff pair $(4/3, 96/13)$ (Exercise 7.8.5(d)). Since both players know that this is what they will get by failing to agree, a disagreement point has been identified. Things can then proceed as in Chapter 5.

However, if John and Mary *are* able to commit themselves to a course of action in the Disagreement Game should the negotiations break down, they can use this power to exert leverage on their opponent. Nash considered the case in which the players open the negotiations by simultaneously

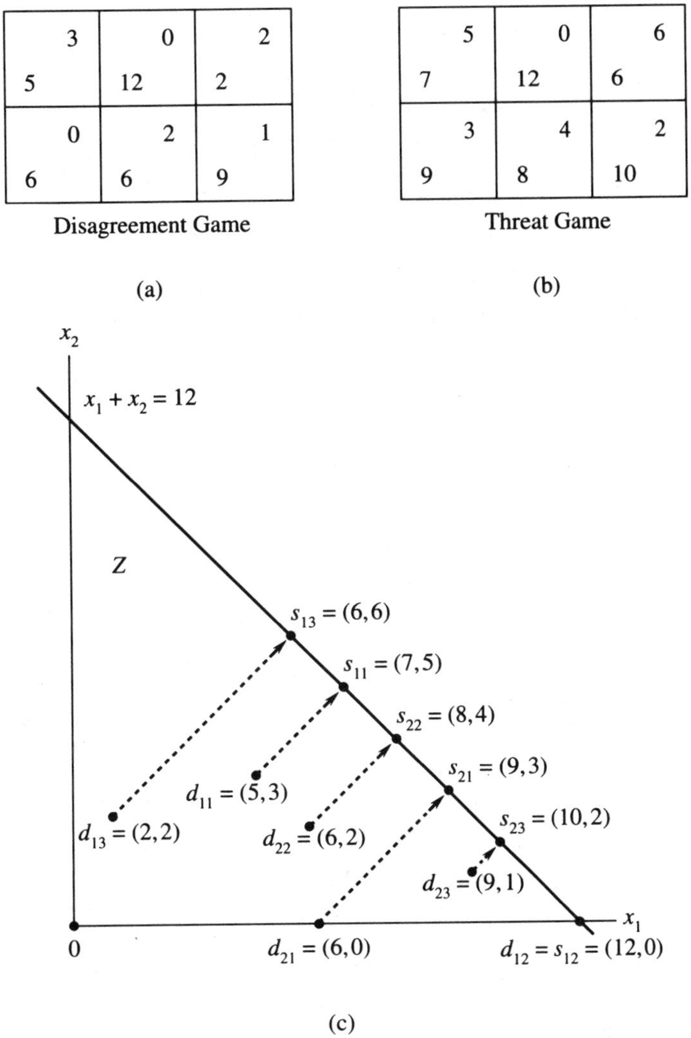

3 5	0 12	2 2
0 6	2 6	1 9

Disagreement Game

(a)

5 7	0 12	6 6
3 9	4 8	2 10

Threat Game

(b)

x_2

$x_1 + x_2 = 12$

Z

$s_{13} = (6,6)$

$s_{11} = (7,5)$

$s_{22} = (8,4)$

$s_{21} = (9,3)$

$d_{11} = (5,3)$

$s_{23} = (10,2)$

$d_{13} = (2,2)$

$d_{22} = (6,2)$

$d_{23} = (9,1)$

x_1

0

$d_{21} = (6,0)$

$d_{12} = s_{12} = (12,0)$

(c)

Figure 6.22 Nash bargaining with no disagreement point.

announcing a strategy for the Disagreement Game. These announcements are to be interpreted as *threats*. If the negotiations are unsuccessful, then the understanding is that the threat *must* be implemented. It is important that the players should not have the freedom to back down from their threats when the time comes to carry them out.

In general, John and Mary will want to threaten to use mixed strategies in the Disagreement Game. If John announces the mixed strategy p and Mary announces the mixed strategy q, then disagreement will result in John getting $d_1 = p^\top Aq$ and Mary getting $d_2 = p^\top Bq$, where A and B are their respective payoff matrices in the Disagreement Game. Thus, once their threats have been made, they know that the result of disagreement will be the payoff pair d. When the regular Nash bargaining solution is used to resolve the ensuing bargaining problem, the result is therefore $s = L(d) = N(Z, d)$.

If John and Mary are rational, they will seek to influence the outcome s in their favor by choosing p and q strategically. They will therefore see themselves as playing a game in which John chooses p, Mary chooses q, and the result is $L(p^\top Aq, p^\top Bq)$. Since L is linear, $L(p^\top Aq, p^\top Bq) = (p^\top Cq, p^\top Dq)$, where C and D are the payoff matrices in the "Threat Game" shown in Figure 6.22(b).

For example, if $p = (1,0)^\top$ and $q = (\frac{1}{2}, 0, \frac{1}{2})^\top$, then

$$\begin{aligned}(p^\top Aq, p^\top Bq) &= (\tfrac{1}{2} \times 5 + \tfrac{1}{2} \times 2, \tfrac{1}{2} \times 3 + \tfrac{1}{2} \times 2) \\ &= \tfrac{1}{2}(5,3) + \tfrac{1}{2}(2,2) \\ &= \tfrac{1}{2}d_{11} + \tfrac{1}{2}d_{13}.\end{aligned}$$

Thus,

$$\begin{aligned}L(p^\top Aq, p^\top bq) &= L(\tfrac{1}{2}d_{11} + \tfrac{1}{2}d_{13}) \\ &= \tfrac{1}{2}L(d_{11}) + \tfrac{1}{2}L(d_{13}) \\ &= \tfrac{1}{2}s_{11} + \tfrac{1}{2}s_{13} \\ &= \tfrac{1}{2}(7,5) + \tfrac{1}{2}(6,6) \\ &= (\tfrac{1}{2} \times 7 + \tfrac{1}{2} \times 6, \tfrac{1}{2} \times 5 + \tfrac{1}{2} \times 6) \\ &= (p^\top Cq, p^\top Dq).\end{aligned}$$

It follows that the solution of the game in which John and Mary negotiate after threatening to use particular mixed strategies in the Disagreement Game is the same as the solution of the Threat Game shown in Figure 6.22(b). Because Z was chosen carefully, the Threat Game is easy to solve.[30] It is constant-sum, because the payoffs in each cell always sum to 12. As noted in Section 6.5.2, such a game is strategically equivalent to a zero-sum game. In fact, subtracting 6 from each payoff yields the strategically equivalent zero-sum game of Figure 6.23(a). John's payoff matrix for this zero-sum game has been written by itself in Figure 6.23(b).

John's payoff matrix in this zero-sum game is familiar. In Sections 6.4.2 and 6.5.5, it was shown that John should play $\tilde{p} = (\frac{1}{6}, \frac{5}{6})^\top$ and Mary should play $\tilde{q} = (\frac{2}{3}, \frac{1}{3}, 0)^\top$. John will then get $2\frac{2}{3}$ and Mary will get $-2\frac{2}{3}$. Since this zero-sum game is strategically equivalent to the original Threat Game,

[30]However, the methodology would be much the same even if the Threat Game were more complicated.

1, −1	6, −6	0, 0
3, −3	2, −2	4, −4

(a)

1	6	0
3	2	4

(b)

Figure 6.23 Zero-sum form of the Threat Game.

John and Mary will play the original Threat Game in precisely the same way as they play the zero-sum game. The only difference is that their payoffs will be 6 utils larger. Thus, John will get $8\frac{2}{3}$ and Mary will get $3\frac{1}{3}$.

This concludes the analysis. John should threaten to play his first pure strategy in the Disagreement Game with probability $\frac{1}{6}$ and his second pure strategy with probability $\frac{5}{6}$. Mary should threaten to play her first pure strategy with probability $\frac{2}{3}$ and her second pure strategy with probability $\frac{1}{3}$. The result is an agreement on how to split the \$12 in which John gets $\$8\frac{2}{3}$ and Mary gets $\$3\frac{1}{3}$.

How realistic such a conclusion is depends on how reasonable it is for John and Mary to be assumed able to commit themselves irrevocably to their opening threats. In practice, making such commitments can be very difficult. John may threaten to do some dreadful thing if Mary is unwilling to make concessions, but Mary does not need to believe that he really will carry out his threat. In fact, if carrying out his threat damages John more than backing down, he will *not* carry out the threat when the time comes to do so unless he falls prey to some irrational impulse. The situation is close to that discussed in Section 4.6.3. Players who make incredible threats in bargaining situations are no more to be believed than game theory books that make incredible predictions about what players will do if there is a deviation from the equilibrium path.

6.10 Exercises

Math

1. If A and B are finite sets of real numbers, then[31]

$$A \subseteq B \quad \Rightarrow \quad \max A \leq \max B.$$

[31] Recall that $A \subseteq B$ means that each element of the set A is also an element of the set B. The notation $\max A$ means the largest element of A. If A and B are allowed to have an infinite number of elements, it would be necessary to write sup instead of max.

Math

2. Explain why

$$\max\{a_1+b_1, a_2+b_2, \dots, a_n+b_n\} \le \max\{a_1, a_2, \dots, a_n\} + \max\{b_1, b_2, \dots, b_n\}.$$

Give an example with $n = 2$ in which the inequality is strict.

Math

3. Explain why

$$\max\{-a_1, -a_2, \dots, -a_n\} = -\min\{a_1, a_2, \dots, a_n\}$$
$$\min\{-a_1, -a_2, \dots, -a_n\} = -\max\{a_1, a_2, \dots, a_n\}.$$

4. Find the maximin $\underline{m}$ and minimax $\overline{m}$ values of the following matrices:

$$A = \begin{bmatrix} 1 & 2 \\ 3 & 4 \end{bmatrix}; \qquad B = \begin{bmatrix} 1 & 3 \\ 4 & 2 \end{bmatrix};$$

$$C = \begin{bmatrix} 2 & 4 & 6 & 3 \\ 6 & 2 & 4 & 3 \\ 4 & 6 & 2 & 3 \end{bmatrix}; \qquad D = \begin{bmatrix} 3 & 2 & 2 & 1 \\ 2 & 3 & 2 & 1 \\ 2 & 2 & 3 & 1 \end{bmatrix}.$$

For which matrices is it true that $\underline{m} < \overline{m}$? For which is it true that $\underline{m} = \overline{m}$?

5. Show that, for any matrix A,

$$\text{maximin}\,(-A^\top) = -\text{minimax}\,(A).$$

6. Find all saddle points for the matrices of Exercise 6.10.4.

Math

7. For each matrix of Exercise 6.10.4, find all values of s that maximize $\min_{t \in T} \pi(s, t)$ and all values of t that minimize $\max_{s \in t} \pi(s, t)$, where $\pi(s, t)$ denotes the entry of the matrix that lies in row s and column t. What have your answers to do with Exercise 6.10.6?

Math

8. Explain why all $m \times 1$ and $n \times 1$ matrices necessarily have a saddle point.

Math

9. Explain why the open interval $(1, 2)$ consisting of all real numbers x that satisfy $1 < x < 2$ has no maximum and no minimum element. What are the supremum and infimum of this set?

10. Let M be player I's payoff matrix in a game. Show that, if M is A or D in Exercise 6.10.4, then player I has a pure security strategy. Find his security level in each case and all his pure security strategies. Decide in each case what player II should do in order to guarantee that player I gets no more than his security level.

11. Repeat Exercise 6.10.10 but with the roles of player I and player II reversed. (You may or may not find Exercise 6.10.5 helpful.)

Math

12. In Section 6.3.2, it is shown that $\underline{m} = p_1(d^*) = 1 - p_2(d^*)$. Employ a similar methodology to show also that $\overline{m} = p_1(d^*) = 1 - p_2(d^*)$, where

$$\overline{m} = \min_e \sup_d \pi(d, e).$$

Why does this confirm that firing at distance d^* is a security strategy for player I in Duel?

13. Suppose that player I has a 4×3 payoff matrix. What vector represents the mixed strategy in which he never uses his second pure strategy and uses each of his other pure strategies with equal probabilities? What random device could player I use to implement this mixed strategy?

14. If one of the matrices in Exercise 6.10.4 is taken to be player II's payoff matrix in a game, then player II has a pure strategy that is strongly dominated by a mixed strategy but not by any pure strategy. Which of A, B, C and D is the matrix with this property? What is the dominated pure strategy? What is the dominating mixed strategy?

15. Player I's payoff matrix in a game is

$$\begin{bmatrix} 1 & 2 & 3 & 4 & 5 \\ 9 & 7 & 5 & 3 & 1 \end{bmatrix}.$$

The matrix has no saddle point and hence player I's security strategies are mixed. Find player I's security level in the game and a mixed security strategy for player I.

16. Any mixed strategy is a security strategy for player I if his payoff matrix is D in Exercise 6.10.4. Why is this true? What is player I's security level?

17. Explain why the use of the mixed strategy $p = (\frac{1}{3}, \frac{1}{3}, \frac{1}{3})^\top$ by player I guarantees him an expected utility of at least 3 if his payoff matrix is C in Exercise 6.10.4. Show that the use of player II's fourth pure strategy guarantees that player I gets at most 3. What is player I's security level? What is a security strategy for player I?

18. Find player I's security strategies when his payoff matrix is B in Exercise 6.10.4.

Math

19. Let $p = (1 - x, x)^\top$ and $q = (1 - y, y)^\top$, where $0 \leq x \leq 1$ and $0 \leq y \leq 1$. If player I's payoff matrix is B in Exercise

6.10.4, show that his expected utility if he uses mixed strategy p and player II uses mixed strategy q is given by

$$\Pi_1(p,q) = f(x,y) = 1 + 3x + 2y - 4yx\,.$$

Find the values of (x,y) for which $\partial f/\partial x = \partial f/\partial y = 0$. Explain why these are saddle points of the function $f : [0,1]\times[0,1] \to \mathbb{R}$. Relate this conclusion to your answer for Exercise 6.10.18.

Math 20. Player I has payoff matrix A in a finite, two-player game. Explain why his mixed strategy $\tilde{p}$ is a best reply to some mixed strategy for player II if and only if

$$\exists q \in Q \; \forall p \in P \; (\tilde{p}^\top A\, q \geq p^\top A\, q)\,,$$

where P is player I's set of mixed strategies and Q is player II's set of mixed strategies.[32] Why is the above statement equivalent to

$$\min_{q\in Q}\max_{p\in P_0} p^\top A\, q \leq 0\,,$$

where $P_0 = \{p - \tilde{p} : p \in P\}$?

Math 21. With the notation of Exercise 6.10.20, explain why player I's mixed strategy $\tilde{p}$ is strongly dominated (possibly by a mixed strategy) if and only if

$$\exists p \in P \; \forall q \in Q \; (p^\top Aq > \tilde{p}^\top Aq)\,.$$

Deduce that $\tilde{p}$ is *not* strongly dominated if and only if[33]

$$\forall p \in P \; \exists q \in Q \; (p^\top Aq \leq \tilde{p}^\top Aq)\,.$$

Why is the second statement equivalent to

$$\max_{p\in P_0}\min_{q\in Q} p^\top Aq \leq 0\,?$$

Math 22. Use Exercises 6.10.20 and 6.10.21 to show that a mixed strategy in a finite, two-player game is a best reply to some mixed strategy choice by the opponent if and only if it is not strongly dominated. You will need to appeal to Von Neumann's minimax theorem.[34]

23. John and Mary simultaneously announce whether or not they will bet on the outcome of an election in which

---

[32] The notation "$\exists\, q \in Q$" means, "there exists a q in the set Q such that". The notation "$\forall p \in P$" means, "for any p in the set P". If this notation is unfamiliar, it may be best to skip Exercises 6.10.20 thru 6.10.22.

[33] Why is it true that "not $(\exists p \forall q \ldots)$" is equivalent to "$\forall p \exists q$ (not ...)"?

[34] With P replaced by P_0. Cognoscenti will recognize the relevance of the problem to the notion of "rationalizability".

only a Republican and a Democrat are running. If they both bet, John pays Mary \$10 if the Republican wins and Mary pays John \$10 if the Democrat wins. Otherwise neither pays anyone anything.

(a) If both are risk-neutral and attach the same probability to the event that the Republican will win, explain why the game is zero-sum.

(b) If both are risk-neutral, but John thinks the Democrat will win with probability $\frac{5}{8}$ and Mary believes the Republican will win with probability $\frac{3}{4}$, explain why the game is not zero-sum. (See Exercise 2.6.5.)

(c) If both attach the same probability to the event that the Republican will win and both are strictly risk-averse, explain why the game is not zero-sum.

24. In the version of Gale's Roulette of Exercise 3.7.15, assume that player I has the risk-loving preferences over money specified by the Von Neumann and Morgenstern utility function $\phi_1 : \mathbb{R} \to \mathbb{R}$ of Exercise 3.7.16. What must player II's utility function be if the game is to be zero-sum? What are the players' security strategies in this game? (See Exercise 4.8.28.)

Is it possible that both player I and player II can be risk-loving if the game is zero-sum? Is it possible that both can be risk-averse?

25. The game of Duel from Section 2.4 is sometimes called Noisy Duel to distinguish it from Silent Duel. This is the same except that the pistols make no noise when fired and so neither duelist knows at any time whether or not his opponent has already fired his pistol (unless, of course, he is shot). In Section 6.5.2, it was explained that Noisy Duel is a unit-sum game. Assuming that players continue to seek to maximize their probability of surviving, is the same true of Silent Duel?

Math

26. Player I's payoff matrix in a zero-sum game is A. Why would he be equally happy to be player II in a zero-sum game with payoff matrix $-A^\top$? A matrix A is skew-symmetric if $A = -A^\top$. Why is a matrix game with a skew-symmetric payoff matrix said to be "symmetric"? Show that the value of such a game is necessarily zero.

27. Find the values of the zero-sum games that have the following payoff matrices using the method of Section 6.4.2. Check that the method of Section 6.6.2 yields the same answers.

(a) $\begin{bmatrix} 9 & -5 & 7 & 1 & -3 \\ -10 & 4 & -8 & -6 & 2 \end{bmatrix}$

(b) $\begin{bmatrix} 1 & 2 & 3 & 4 & 5 \\ 5 & 4 & 3 & 2 & 1 \end{bmatrix}$

Find all security strategies for both players. What are the Nash equilibria for these games?

28. Find the values and all security strategies of the following matrix games using the method of Section 6.6.2.

(a) $\begin{bmatrix} 1 & 0 & 2 \\ 3 & 1 & 1 \end{bmatrix}$ (b) $\begin{bmatrix} 0 & 1 & 3 \\ 3 & 1 & 0 \end{bmatrix}$ (c) $\begin{bmatrix} -2 & 0 \\ -2 & 1 \\ -4 & -3 \end{bmatrix}$

29. Find the value and at least one security strategy for each player in each of the following matrix games.

(a) $\begin{bmatrix} 7 & 2 & 1 & 2 & 7 \\ 2 & 6 & 2 & 6 & 2 \\ 5 & 4 & 3 & 4 & 5 \\ 2 & 6 & 2 & 6 & 2 \\ 7 & 2 & 1 & 2 & 7 \end{bmatrix}$ (b) $\begin{bmatrix} 1 & 3 & 2 & 5 \\ 0 & -1 & 6 & 7 \\ 3 & 4 & 2 & 3 \\ -7 & 2 & 2 & 1 \end{bmatrix}$

Math 30. A 2×2 matrix A has no saddle point. If A is player I's payoff matrix in a zero-sum game, show that:
(a) A player who uses a security strategy will get the same payoff whatever the opponent does.
(b) A player will get the same payoff whatever he or she does, provided the opponent uses a security strategy.

Math 31. A 2×2 matrix A has no saddle point. If A is player I's payoff matrix in a zero-sum game, show that the value of the game is given by $v = \{e^{\top}A^{-1}e\}^{-1}$, where $e = (1, 1)^{\top}$.

32. Find the values of the following matrix games by exploiting any symmetries you can find.

(a) $\begin{bmatrix} 1 & 2 & 3 \\ 3 & 1 & 2 \\ 2 & 3 & 1 \end{bmatrix}$

(b) $\begin{bmatrix} 1 & 2 & 3 & 0 \\ 3 & 1 & 2 & 0 \\ 2 & 3 & 1 & 0 \\ 0 & 0 & 0 & 1 \end{bmatrix}$

(c) $\begin{bmatrix} 1 & 2 & 4 & 1 \\ 2 & 1 & 1 & 4 \\ 3 & 1 & 1 & 0 \\ 1 & 3 & 0 & 1 \end{bmatrix}$

Math 33. Let $(\tilde{p}, \tilde{q})$ and $(\tilde{P}, \tilde{Q})$ be two Nash equilibria for a two-player, zero-sum game with matrix A. Prove that the two Nash equilibria are equivalent and interchangeable (Section 1.9.2). (It is enough to show that $(\tilde{p}, \tilde{Q})$ is a Nash equilibrium and that $\tilde{p}^{\top}A\tilde{q} = \tilde{P}^{\top}A\tilde{Q}$.)

Fun 34. Colonel Blotto[35] has four companies that he can distribute among two locations in three different ways: $(3, 1)$, $(2, 2)$ or $(1, 3)$. His opponent, Count Baloney, has three companies that he can distribute among the same two locations in two different ways: $(2, 1)$ or $(1, 2)$. Suppose that Blotto sends m_1 companies to location 1 and Baloney sends n_1 companies to location 1. If $m_1 = n_1$, the result is a stand-off and each commander gets a payoff of zero for location 1. If $m_1 \neq n_1$, the larger force overwhelms the smaller force without loss to itself. If $m_1 > n_1$, Blotto gets a payoff n_1 and Baloney gets a payoff of $-n_1$ for location 1. If $m_1 < n_1$, Blotto gets a payoff $-m_1$ and Baloney gets a payoff of m_1 for location 1. Each player's total payoff is the sum of his payoffs at both locations.

Find the strategic form of this simultaneous-move game. Show that it has no saddle point. Determine a mixed-strategy Nash equilibrium.

Fun 35. Repeat the previous exercise for the case when Blotto has five companies and Baloney has four companies. (You may want to use the trick from Section 6.7 by means of which Figure 6.16 was reduced to Figure 6.17.)

Fun 36. Analyze the game of Battleships from Section 6.7 on the assumption that Mary has only three bombs. Her aim is to win by sinking the battleship before her bombs are exhausted. John's aim is to avoid being sunk.

Math 37. The Inspection Game of Section 6.8 is modified so that the agency may inspect on *two* days freely chosen from the n days on which the river might be polluted. The firm still chooses just *one* of the n days on which to pollute the river. If the value of this game is u_n, show that, for $n \geq 3$,

$$u_n = \frac{u_{n-1} + v_{n-1}}{u_{n-1} - v_{n-1} + 2},$$

[35]This is not the Colonel Blotto we met in Exercise 4.8.16. There are many variants of the Colonel Blotto game. That described in the current exercise is not very similar in structure to that of Exercise 4.8.16.

where $v_k = -1 + 2/k$, as in Section 6.8. Work out the value of u_4 and determine the probability with which the agency should inspect on the first day when $n = 4$.

Fun

38. Colonel Blotto has to match wits with Count Baloney in yet another new military situation. This time Blotto commands two companies, and Baloney commands only one. Each tries to succeed in capturing the enemy camp without losing his own. Every day, each commander sends however many companies he chooses to attack the enemy camp. If the defenders of a camp are outnumbered by the attackers, then the camp is captured. Otherwise the result is a stand-off. This continues for a period of n days, unless someone is victorious in the interim. Anything short of total victory counts for nothing. Each army then abandons any gain it may have made and retreats to its own camp until the next day.

    Counting a defeat as -1, a victory as $+1$, and a stand-off as 0, determine optimal strategies for the two players, and compute Blotto's expected payoff if the optimal strategies are used.

Econ

39. Sketch the cooperative payoff regions (Section 5.3) for each of the games of Figure 6.24. Assume "free disposal" and "transferable utility".

	3, 3	0, 6
	6, 0	2, 1

	1, 1	0, 2
	2, 0	−2, −1

Figure 6.24 Games for Exercise 6.10.39.

In each case, John and Mary can get any payoff pair in the cooperative region on which they are able to agree. Once a disagreement point is located, they will use the regular Nash bargaining solution. However, no *a priori* disagreement point is given. If they fail to agree, the given game will have to be played without an agreement. As in Section 6.9, the negotiations open with each player simultaneously making an irrevocable commitment to a mixed strategy that is to be used without fail if no agreement is reached. For each of the two given games, determine what the final outcome will be and what threats the players will make.

40. Odd Man Out is a three-player, zero-sum game. Each of three risk-neutral players simultaneously chooses heads or tails. If all make the same choice, no money changes hands. If one player chooses differently from the others, he must pay the others one dollar each. What is a security strategy for a player in this game? Find a Nash equilibrium in which no player uses his security strategy. Why does the existence of such a Nash equilibrium contrast with the situation in the two-player case?

41. In O'Neill's Card Game, each of two players has the A, K, Q and J from one of the suits in a deck of playing cards. They each simultaneously show a card. Player I wins if both show an A or if there is a mismatch of picture cards. Player II wins if both show the same picture card or if one shows an A and the other doesn't.
    (a) Why can this game be analyzed without further information being supplied about the players' attitudes to taking risks?
    (b) Find the 4×4 strategic form of the game.
    (c) Reduce the strategic form to a 2×2 matrix using the trick from Section 6.7 by means of which Figure 6.16 was reduced to Figure 6.17.
    (d) Find the unique, mixed-strategy Nash equilibrium of the game.

CHAPTER

7

Keeping Your Balance

Libra is a sign of the Zodiac. It represents the scales used in ancient times for weighing things. The term *equilibrium* therefore means something like "equally balanced". In game theory, the most important type of equilibrium is a Nash equilibrium. Recall from Section 1.8.2 that (s, t) is a Nash equilibrium if and only if s is an optimal response to t, and t is simultaneously an optimal response to s. Thus, if player I predicts that player II will use strategy t, and player II predicts that player I will use strategy s, neither will have reason to behave other than as their opponent predicted. In this sense, their predictions are "in balance".

This chapter explores the idea of a Nash equilibrium in more depth than was possible in previous chapters. It begins by observing that Nash equilibria occur where the players' optimal response curves cross. This raises two problems. The first concerns what we should do when the curves cross more than once. Each crossing point corresponds to a Nash equilibrium. Which of these Nash equilibria should be selected? The second difficulty arises if the curves do not cross at all. What is one to do in a game without Nash equilibria? Nash showed that the second problem cannot arise in a finite game. The proof he gave depends on Brouwer's important fixed point theorem. It is fun to be able to round off the chapter by outlining how Brouwer's theorem can be deduced from the fact that Hex cannot end in a draw.

7.1 Reaction Curves

Economists use the word *reaction* as a synonym for what has so far been called a best reply or an optimal response.

7.1.1 Reaction Curves with Pure Strategies

Consider the payoff matrix for a two-person, zero-sum game of Figure 6.3(a). This is repeated in Figure 7.1(a). If both players are restricted to pure strategies in this game, player I has the best reply correspondence $R_1 : T \to S$ and player II has the best reply correspondence $R_2 : S \to T$ defined by

$$\begin{aligned} R_1(t_1) &= \{s_3\}, & R_2(s_1) &= \{t_1\}, \\ R_1(t_2) &= \{s_2\}, & R_2(s_2) &= \{t_2\}, \\ R_1(t_3) &= \{s_1\}, & R_2(s_3) &= \{t_2, t_3\}. \end{aligned}$$

This means, for example, that $R_1(t_1) = \{s_3\}$ is the set of best replies by player I to the choice of t_1 by player II. Similarly,

	t_1	t_2	t_3
s_1	0	1	7
s_2	4	2	3
s_3	9	0	0

(a)

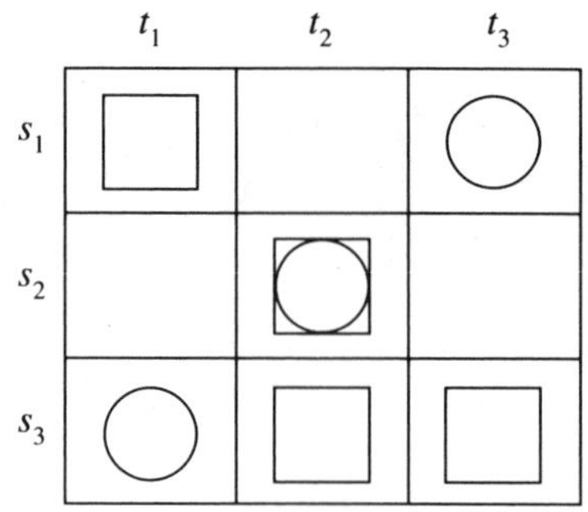

(b)

Figure 7.1 Reaction curves.

$R_2(s_3) = \{t_2, t_3\}$ is the set of best replies by player II to the choice of s_3 by player I.

Notice that R_1 and R_2 are what economists call *correspondences*. They are *not* functions. The requirement that $R_2 : S \to T$ be a function is that, for each s in S, $R_2(s)$ is uniquely defined as an *element* of T. For a correspondence, $R_2(s)$ is not an element[1] of T, but a *subset* of T. For example, $R_2(s_3)$ is the subset $\{t_2, t_3\}$. Either of t_2 and t_3 is a best reply to s_3.

Figure 7.1(b) shows the reaction curves for players I and II. Player I's reaction curve is indicated by circles, and player II's by squares. The requirement that a pair (s, t) of strategies lie on player I's reaction curve is that

$$s \in R_1(t).$$

This says that s is a best reply for player I to the choice of t by player II. The requirement that a pair (s, t) of strategies lie on player II's reaction curve is that

$$t \in R_2(s).$$

This says that t is a best reply for player II to the choice of s by player I.

A pair (s, t) of strategies is a Nash equilibrium if and only if

$$s \in R_1(t) \text{ and } t \in R_2(s),$$

[1]It is for this reason that $R_2(s_1)$ is written as $\{t_1\}$ rather than as t_1. The notation $\{t_1\}$ means the *set* whose only element is t_1. Although this distinction may seem pedantic, it is important in some contexts. However, in this book, it will be ignored if there seems no risk of confusion resulting.

so that s and t are best replies to each other. The Nash equilibria therefore occur where the reaction curves cross. Thus, for the game of Figure 7.1(a), there is a unique Nash equilibrium at (s_2, t_2).

This observation is nothing new. An identical pattern of circles and squares to that of Figure 7.1(b) appears in Figure 6.3(a). Section 6.2.2 explained why the pair (s_2, t_2) of strategies is a Nash equilibrium by pointing out that the cell (s_2, t_2) contains both a circle and a square. But this is exactly what is required for the reaction curves to cross at (s_2, t_2).

7.1.2 Reaction Curves with Mixed Strategies

We have been discussing the game of Figure 6.3(a). The circles and squares in Figure 6.3(b) show two reaction curves for another two-person, zero-sum game. These reaction curves do not cross. It follows that this game has *no* Nash equilibrium if the players are confined to using pure strategies. Such difficulties led to the introduction of mixed strategies in Chapter 6.

Reaction curves when mixed strategies are involved are easy to draw only in the 2×2 case. Consider, for example, the payoff matrix for a two-person, zero-sum game shown in Figure 7.2(a). This game has no Nash equilibrium in pure strategies, and so mixed strategies must be considered.

A mixed strategy for player I is a vector $(1-p, p)^\top$, where $1-p$ is the probability with which s_1 is to be played, and p is the probability with which s_2 is to be played. Each mixed strategy for player I therefore corresponds to a real number p in the interval $[0, 1]$. Similarly, each mixed strategy $(1-q, q)^\top$ for player II corresponds to a real number q in the interval $[0, 1]$. Each pair of mixed strategies for the two players therefore corresponds to a point (p, q) in the square of Figure 7.2(b).

If player II chooses the mixed strategy corresponding to q, then player I's expected payoff when he uses his first pure strategy is

$$E_1(q) = (1-q) + 4q = 1 + 3q\,.$$

If he uses his second pure strategy, his expected payoff is

$$E_2(q) = 3(1-q) + 2q = 3 - q\,.$$

It is therefore best for him to reply with his first pure strategy if $q > \frac{1}{2}$, because this inequality holds if and only if

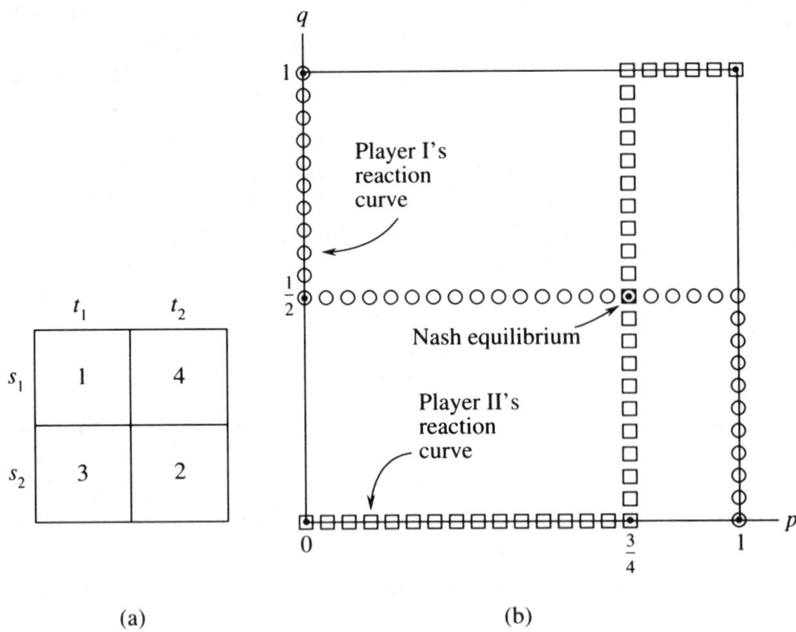

Figure 7.2 Reaction curves with mixed strategies.

$1 + 3q > 3 - q$. Similarly, it is best for him to reply with his second pure strategy if $q < \frac{1}{2}$.

What if $q = \frac{1}{2}$? In this case, player I is indifferent between his first and second pure strategies. Thus, either is a best reply to $q = \frac{1}{2}$. Not only this, any mixture of his first and second pure strategies is also a best reply to $q = \frac{1}{2}$. This illustrates a principle that is often useful:

> A mixed strategy is a best reply to something if and only if each of the pure strategies to which it assigns positive probability is also a best reply to the same thing. A player who optimizes by using a mixed strategy will therefore necessarily be *indifferent* between all the pure strategies to which the mixed strategy assigns positive probability.

The reason is simple. Nobody would ever want to make a reply that used some pure strategy s with positive probability if there were another strategy t that was definitely a better reply than s. Whenever you were supposed to use s, you could use t instead.

To summarize: player I's best reply when $q < \frac{1}{2}$ is to use his second pure strategy. This corresponds to taking $p = 1$. His best reply when $q > \frac{1}{2}$ is to use his first pure strategy. This corresponds to taking $p = 0$. Any mixed strategy is a best reply when $q = \frac{1}{2}$. His best reply correspondence $R_1 : [0,1] \to [0,1]$ is therefore given by

$$R_1(q) = \begin{cases} \{1\}, & \text{if } 0 \le q < \frac{1}{2}, \\ [0,1], & \text{if } q = \frac{1}{2}, \\ \{0\}, & \text{if } \frac{1}{2} < q \le 1. \end{cases}$$

The reaction curve that represents this correspondence is shown with small circles in Figure 7.2(b). For example, the set of best replies for player I to $q = \frac{1}{3}$ is found by locating the values of p at which the horizontal line $q = \frac{1}{3}$ cuts player I's reaction curve. In this case, only $p = 1$ has this property. Thus, $p = 1$ is the only best reply to $q = \frac{1}{3}$.

Player II's reaction curve can be found in a similar way. If player I uses the mixed strategy corresponding to p, then player II gets

$$E_1(p) = -(1-p) + -3p = -1 - 2p,$$

if she uses her first pure strategy, and

$$E_2(p) = -4(1-p) + -2p = -4 + 2p,$$

if she uses her second pure strategy. Her first pure strategy is therefore her only best reply if $p < \frac{3}{4}$, because this inequality holds if and only if $-1 - 2p > -4 + 2p$. Her second pure strategy is her only best reply if $p > \frac{3}{4}$. If $p = \frac{3}{4}$, any of her mixed strategies is a best reply. Her best reply correspondence $R_2 : [0,1] \to [0,1]$ is therefore given by

$$R_1(p) = \begin{cases} \{0\}, & \text{if } 0 \le p < \frac{3}{4}, \\ [0,1], & \text{if } p = \frac{3}{4}, \\ \{1\}, & \text{if } \frac{3}{4} < p \le 1. \end{cases}$$

The reaction curve that represents this correspondence is shown with small squares in Figure 7.2(b). For example, the set of best replies for player II to $p = \frac{1}{4}$ is found by locating the values of q at which the vertical line $p = \frac{1}{4}$ cuts player II's reaction curve. In this case, only $q = 0$ has this property. Thus, $q = 0$ is the only best reply to $p = \frac{1}{4}$.

Nash equilibria occur where the reaction curves cross. From Figure 7.2(b), it is clear that only $(\tilde{p}, \tilde{q}) = (\frac{3}{4}, \frac{1}{2})$ corresponds to a Nash equilibrium. Since we are dealing with a two-person, zero-sum game, it follows from Chapter 6 that $\tilde{p} = \frac{3}{4}$ is a security strategy for player I, and $\tilde{q} = \frac{1}{2}$ is a security strategy for player II.

7.1.3 Games for the Birds

The games studied in the preceding subsections are zero-sum, but the same methodology works equally well for any two-person game.[2] As an example, consider the Hawk-Dove Game of Figure 7.3(a). This is the standard bimatrix game used to introduce evolutionary ideas in a game theory context.

Two birds of the same species compete for a territory whose value in terms of evolutionary fitness is V. Each bird can adopt a hawkish or a dovelike strategy in a simultaneous-move game. If both behave like doves, they split the territory. If one behaves like a dove and the other like a hawk, the hawk gets the territory. If both behave like hawks, there is a fight. The evolutionary fitness of a bird that has to fight is W. Usually it is understood that each bird is equally likely to win the fight and hence gain the territory. However, the fight is costly because of the risk of injury. Thus, $W = \frac{1}{2}V - C$, where C represents the cost of fighting.

More will be said about this game in Chapter 9. At the moment, just note that the choice of parameters $V = 6$ and $C = 2$ produces a version of what is undoubtedly the most famous of all the "toy games" that game theorists love to cite. This is the Prisoners' Dilemma to which we will return repeatedly in the remainder of this book. However, at this stage, more will be said about a second "toy game" called Chicken. This is obtained from the Hawk-Dove Game by choosing the parameters to be $V = 2$ and $C = 2$.

Both the Prisoners' Dilemma and Chicken come with little stories quite separate from that used to motivate the general Hawk-Dove Game. Such stories are not to be taken too seriously. Chiefly they exist to help everyone remember what the payoffs in the games are. The usual story that goes with Chicken concerns teenage virility rites. However, its strategic structure would seem equally well to represent the game

---

[2]Indeed, it works equally well with any number of players. If the set of player i's mixed strategies is P^i, then P^{-i} is often used to denote the set of strategy vectors jointly available to all the players except player i. Thus, for example, in a three-player game, $P^{-2} = P^1 \times P^3$, and hence denotes the set of all vectors of the form (p_1, p_3), where p_1 is a mixed strategy for player I and p_3 is a mixed strategy for player III. If $R_2 : P^{-2} \to P^2$ is player II's best reply correspondence, then $R_2(p_1, p_3)$ represents the set of player II's best replies to the use of p_1 by player I and p_3 by player III. For a Nash equilibrium, one looks for a triple at which the three reaction "surfaces" representing R_1, R_2 and R_3 cross. Nothing of what is discussed in this chapter fails in the n-person case. Attention is confined to the two-person case only to keep the algebra manageable.

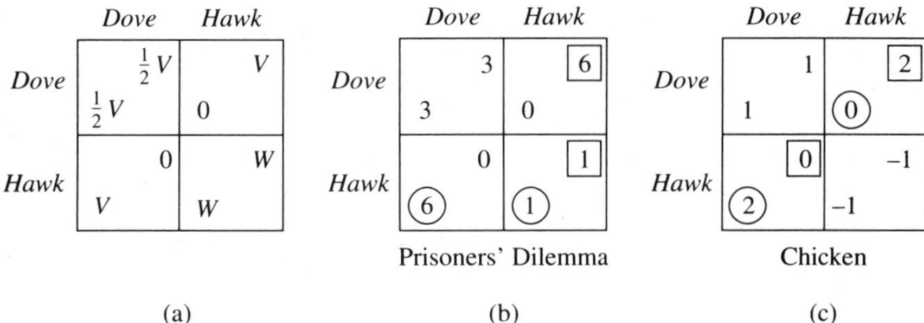

Figure 7.3 Hawk-Dove Games.

played in grim earnest by middle-aged businessmen whose cars approach one another at speed along city streets that are too narrow for the cars to pass safely unless at least one driver slows down. If one player chickens out by slowing while the other continues to speed, the player who slows loses self-esteem and the other gains. If both slow, their initial levels of self-esteem remain unchanged. If neither slows, the consequences are unpleasant for both.[3]

Reaction curves for the Prisoners' Dilemma and Chicken when both players are restricted to the use of pure strategies are indicated by circles and squares in Figure 7.3. Notice that (*hawk, hawk*) is a Nash equilibrium for the Prisoners' Dilemma. Chicken has two Nash equilibria in pure strategies: (*hawk, dove*) and (*dove, hawk*). But we should not be content with these Nash equilibria. It may be that further Nash equilibria will emerge when mixed strategies are considered. In fact, since games typically have an *odd* number of Nash equilibria, we ought to look especially closely at the mixed strategies for Chicken. On the other hand, no further Nash equilibria will be found for the Prisoners' Dilemma, because *dove* is strongly dominated by *hawk*, and hence no rational player will ever choose to play *dove* with positive probability.

Figure 7.4 shows reaction curves for the Prisoners' Dilemma and for Chicken when mixed strategies are allowed. These reaction curves are calculated as in Section 7.1.2. The only difference is that player II's payoff matrix B is no longer equal to $-A$, as in a two-person, zero-sum game.

In the Prisoners' Dilemma, the reaction curves cross only

[3]It is a pity that this version of the story requires confusing a chicken with a dove. But most readers of this book will perhaps be city folk for whom one domestic fowl is much the same as another.

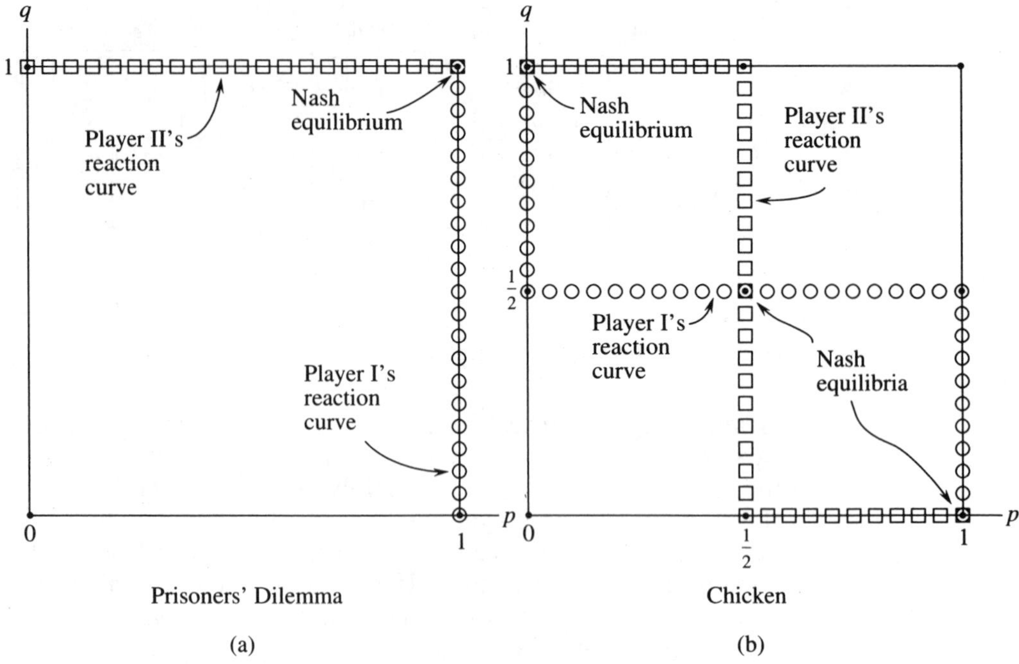

Figure 7.4 Reaction curves for the Prisoners' Dilemma and Chicken.

where $(\tilde{p}, \tilde{q}) = (1, 1)$. This confirms that the only Nash equilibrium is for both players to play *hawk*.

In Chicken, the reaction curves cross in three places: where $(\tilde{p}, \tilde{q}) = (0, 1)$, where $(\tilde{p}, \tilde{q}) = (1, 0)$ and where $(\tilde{p}, \tilde{q}) = (\frac{1}{2}, \frac{1}{2})$. The first and second of these alternatives are the pure strategy Nash equilibria already located. The third alternative is a mixed strategy Nash equilibrium in which both players use each of *hawk* and *dove* with probability $\frac{1}{2}$.

Notice that player I's reaction curve for Chicken is vertical when player II uses $\tilde{q} = \frac{1}{2}$. Similarly, player II's reaction curve is horizontal when player I uses $\tilde{p} = \frac{1}{2}$. These observations illustrate the fact that a player will necessarily be *indifferent* between all the pure strategies that he or she should play with positive probability when a mixed strategy equilibrium is in use. This fact can often be useful in finding a mixed equilibrium without first constructing best reply correspondences.

For example, to find the mixed Nash equilibrium in Chicken, one need only look for the $\tilde{p}$ that makes player I indifferent between *dove* and *hawk*, and the $\tilde{q}$ that makes player II indifferent between *dove* and *hawk*. These requirements generate the equations:

$$1(1-\tilde{p})+0\tilde{p}=2(1-\tilde{p})+(-1)\tilde{p},$$
$$1(1-\tilde{q})+0\tilde{q}=2(1-\tilde{q})+(-1)\tilde{q}.$$

The equations have the unique solution $\tilde{p}=\tilde{q}=\frac{1}{2}$.

7.1.4 Mixing in Chicken

Phil 7.2 ⟶ Unless some outside factor is available to break the symmetry, a game theorist cannot recommend either of the pure Nash equilibria in Chicken because any argument in favor of one is equally good as an argument in favor of the other. On the other hand, Section 1.8.1 explains why it would be self-defeating to recommend anything other than a Nash equilibrium. If our game theorist is to make any recommendation at all, there therefore seems little choice but to recommend the mixed strategy Nash equilibrium. But this reasoning is entirely negative. Is there anything positive that can be said in favor of the mixed equilibrium?

The defense offered in Chapter 6 for the use of mixed strategy Nash equilibria in two-person, zero-sum games will no longer suffice. An equilibrium strategy is necessarily a security strategy in such games. Its use therefore guarantees a player's security level or more. Since a player cannot reasonably anticipate getting more than this in a two-person, zero-sum game, one has a good positive argument to put to a doubtful player about the wisdom of following the game theorist's recommendation. But this argument is not valid for a general bimatrix game.[4]

It is tempting for the game theorist to argue that a game theory book need contain no defense of the Nash equilibrium it recommends beyond the fact that it is the Nash equilibrium that the game theorist chooses to nominate. But such a patrician attitude will cut no ice with a player I who reads the book and then notices that all his strategies in Chicken are equally good if his opponent follows the book's advice and uses the mixed equilibrium strategy recommended for her.

[4]Exercise 6.10.40 provides an example of a three-person, zero-sum game, Odd-Man-Out, for which equilibrium strategies are not necessarily security strategies. Chicken is a bimatrix game that is not zero-sum. The players' security levels are both 0 which they guarantee by playing *dove*. But (*dove*, *dove*) is not a Nash equilibrium. Moreover, each player gets a payoff of $\frac{1}{2}$ when they use the mixed Nash equilibrium.

If player I is confident that player II will follow the book's recommendation, he might as well deviate and play any strategy that takes his fancy.[5] But then he must ask himself how reasonable it is to be confident that player II will follow the book's advice if he sees no particular reason to do so himself.

Such considerations expose the weakness of introducing Nash equilibria only with a story about the recommendations that game theorists should write in books about the play of a one-shot game (played once and once only). In Chapter 9, situations will be discussed in which mixed Nash equilibria emerge as a consequence of the players' learning to play better as time goes by during a long sequence of *repetitions* of the same game.[6] For the moment, it will perhaps be enough to observe that a Nash equilibrium need not be naively interpreted as a straightforward prescription on how to play a game. Instead it can be seen as describing the probabilities that rational players can reasonably assign to the actions open to their opponents.[7] Thus $(\tilde{p}, \tilde{q})$ becomes a pair of *predictions* rather than a pair of *prescriptions*. The game theory book then no longer tells players what they should *do*: only what they should *believe*. This may sometimes not be very helpful, as when players in Chicken are told to regard the choice of *dove* and *hawk* by the opponent as being equally likely. But such anodyne advice might be the best that can be offered in the absence of extra information about the circumstances in which the game is played.

7.2 Oligopoly and Perfect Competition

Econ 7.3 ⟶ Economists are enthusiastic about the merits of perfect competition as opposed to imperfect competition. A proper ac-

[5]In Exercises 7.9.29 and 7.9.30, this problem is even more severe than in Chicken.

[6]Section 6.1 already anticipates such a scenario by motivating mixed strategies using the example of bluffing during a long sequence of Poker games.

[7]A player need then not be seen as deliberately randomizing. His or her choice may be entirely determinate from the player's own standpoint. But it need not seem so to an opponent. For example, decisions about when to devalue a currency are typically made by "experts" who certainly do not toss any coins during their deliberations. Nevertheless, their decisions are difficult for speculators to predict because the speculators do not know on what data the "experts" will condition their decision. Such "purification" stories are more convincing when accompanied by a detailed account of *how* the actual choice gets made and *why* this process is not fully known by the opponent. The best known model that satisfies these criteria is due to Harsanyi. This is discussed in Section 11.6.

count of the reasons for their enthusiasm is beyond the scope of this book. However, something of the flavor of the arguments they offer can be garnered from this section, which is devoted to the game-theoretic analysis of some very simple models of imperfect competition. This is one of the major areas in which game-theoretic reasoning has revolutionized the way that people think about certain types of economic problem.

7.2.1 Cournot Models

Widgets are a small novelty item produced at a cost of $\$c$ each. A lot of people will buy a few widgets each if the price is not too high. The market behavior of such potential consumers is described in this example by a demand equation[8]

$$p + q = M,$$

in which M is a much larger number than c. If the price of a widget is $\$p$, the demand equation tells us that the number of widgets that will be sold is $q = M - p$.

Very simple assumptions have been made about the behavior of consumers so that attention can be concentrated on the producers. Economists speak of perfect competition when there is a very large number of firms, each of whose production has a negligible effect on the market. Such a firm does not need to consider what impact its own production will have on the price at which widgets sell. However, in an oligopoly, matters are not so simple.

An oligopoly is an industry with n producers, each of which is of appreciable size. No firm can therefore neglect the effect that its own production decisions will have on the market price. A monopoly occurs when $n = 1$. This case is not very interesting from a game theory point of view, but it will be useful to analyze it first so as to have a benchmark for later comparison.

Monopoly. How many widgets will a monopolist manufacture if his aim is to maximize profit? It would be stupid for him to make more widgets than he can sell at the price he proposes to set. If he produces q widgets, he will therefore

[8]Only prices and quantities in the range $[0, M]$ are considered. But be warned that economists will often speak of "linear" demand even when prices $p > M$ are permitted, although the quantity q then demanded will always be zero, so that the demand curve will necessarily have a kink where $(q, p) = (0, M)$.

sell them at price $p = M - q$ because this is the largest price at which they will all be sold.[9]

Profit is always the difference between the revenue obtained by selling what is produced and the cost of making it. The monopolist's profit is therefore

$$\pi(q) = pq - cq = (p - c)q = (M - q - c)q.$$

To find the output $\tilde{q}$ that maximizes profit, $\pi(q)$ is differentiated, and the derivative set equal to zero. Since

$$\frac{d\pi}{dq} = M - c - 2q,$$

profit is maximized when $\tilde{q} = \frac{1}{2}(M - c)$. Price is then $\tilde{p} = \frac{1}{2}(M + c)$ and the maximum profit is $\pi = \{\frac{1}{2}(M - c)\}^2$.

Duopoly. Now consider the case when there are two producers. The widget industry is then said to be a *duopoly*. For this special situation, the French economist Cournot anticipated the idea of a Nash equilibrium by more than a century. Economists therefore sometimes refer to a Cournot-Nash equilibrium when speaking about what is called a Nash equilibrium in this book.

Cournot's model has both producers choosing their output in ignorance of the choice of the other. The price at which widgets are sold is then determined by the demand for widgets. That is, the price adjusts until supply equals demand. Supply is simply the total number $q = q_1 + q_2$ of widgets produced. The demand for widgets when the price is p is $M - p$. Thus the price at which widgets are sold satisfies

$$p = M - q_1 - q_2\,.$$

In modeling the situation as a game, the two firms become player I and player II. They play a simultaneous-move game in which each player chooses a number q_i from the interval $[0, M]$. The players' payoffs in the game are identified with their profits. The payoff functions are therefore

$$\pi_1(q_1, q_2) = (p - c)q_1 = (M - c - q_1 - q_2)q_1\,,$$
$$\pi_2(q_1, q_2) = (p - c)q_2 = (M - c - q_1 - q_2)q_2\,.$$

[9]Sometimes a monopolist is able to *price discriminate* by selling the same thing to different people at different prices. Airlines, for example, sell tickets cheaper to students than to professors. However, in this example, a firm must sell all the widgets it makes at the same price.

The game is infinite because each player's strategy set is infinite. Such games are not necessarily harder to analyze than finite games because one can often get quick answers using calculus. Here, for example, it is easy to find the unique Nash equilibrium $(\tilde{q}_1, \tilde{q}_2)$.

To find his best replies to player II's choice of q_2, player I need only differentiate his profit function and set the derivative equal to zero. Since

$$\frac{\partial \pi}{\partial q_1} = M - c - 2q_1 - q_2,$$

player I has a unique best reply to q_2, namely,

$$q_1 = R_1(q_2) = \tfrac{1}{2}(M - c - q_2).$$

Notice that it is necessary to differentiate *partially* with respect to q_1 keeping q_2 fixed, because player II's choice of q_1 is *independent* of player II's choice of q_2. Player I's reaction curve[10] is illustrated in Figure 7.5(a).

Player II's reaction curve is illustrated in Figure 7.5(b). Because things are symmetric, its equation is obtained simply by swapping q_1 and q_2 in the formula for $R_1(q_2)$. Thus player II's unique best reply to the choice of q_1 by player I is

$$q_2 = R_2(q_1) = \tfrac{1}{2}(M - c - q_1).$$

A Nash equilibrium $(\tilde{q}_1, \tilde{q}_2)$ occurs where the reaction curves cross. To find $\tilde{q}_1$ and $\tilde{q}_2$, the equations $q_1 = R_1(q_2)$ and $q_2 = R_2(q_1)$ must be solved simultaneously. The two equations are:

$$2\tilde{q}_1 + \tilde{q}_2 = M - c,$$
$$\tilde{q}_1 + 2\tilde{q}_2 = M - c,$$

and so $\tilde{q}_1 = \tilde{q}_2 = \frac{1}{3}(M - c)$. (Exercise 10.9.36 indicates how this same conclusion can be obtained using the method of successively deleting strongly dominated strategies.)

---

[10]The curves drawn with broken lines are player I's *isoprofit curves*. Along such a curve, player I's profit is constant. For example, $\pi_1(q_1, q_2) = 3$ is the isoprofit curve along which player I's profit is equal to 3. This curve has equation $(M - c - q_1 - q_2)q_2 = 3$ and hence is a *hyperbola* with asymptotes $q_1 + q_2 = M - c$ and $q_2 = 0$. (It may help to note that all hyperbolas of the form $(ax + by + c)(Ax + By + C) = d$ have the same asymptotes, which can be found by looking at the degenerate member of the family obtained by setting $d = 0$. This degenerate hyperbola consists of the pair of lines $ax + by + c = 0$ and $Ax + By + C = 0$. These two lines are the asymptotes for the family.) Notice that each horizontal line $q_2 = Q$ is tangent to an isoprofit curve where $q_1 = R_1(Q)$. This is because, in computing a best reply to $q_2 = Q$, player I must find the point on $q_2 = Q$ at which his profit is largest.

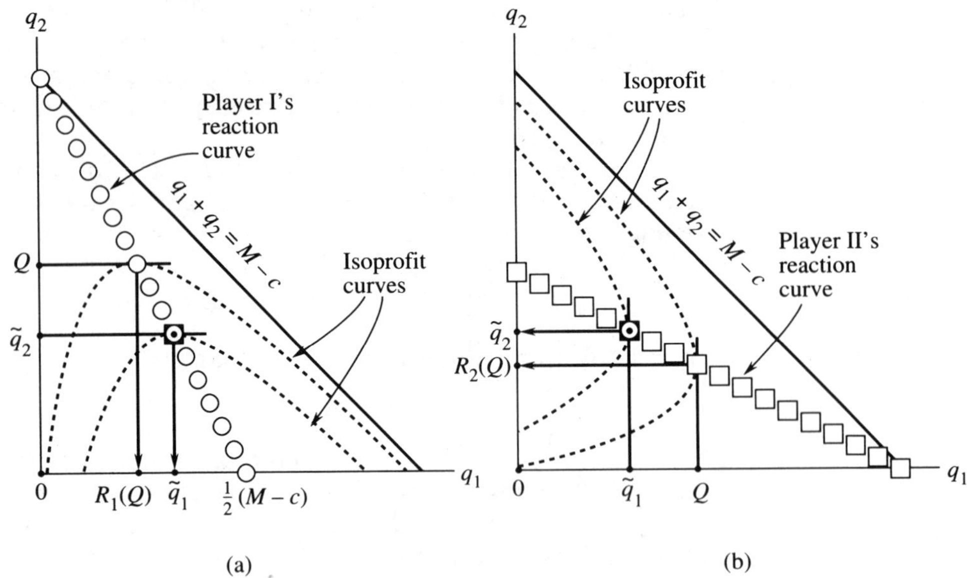

Figure 7.5 Cournot duopoly.

Thus, in the Cournot model of duopoly, there is a unique Nash equilibrium in which each player produces $\frac{1}{3}(M-c)$ widgets. The total number of widgets produced is therefore $\frac{2}{3}(M-c)$, and so the price at which they are sold is $\tilde{p} = M - \frac{2}{3}(M-c) = \frac{1}{3}M + \frac{2}{3}c$. Each player's profit is $\{\frac{1}{3}(M-c)\}^2$.

Oligopoly. The duopoly story can be told again, but with n players instead of only two. Player I's profit function is then

$$\pi_1(q_1, q_2, \ldots, q_n) = (M - c - q_1 - q_2 - \cdots - q_n)q_1 .$$

A Nash equilibrium is found by solving the equations

$$\begin{aligned}
2\tilde{q}_1 + \tilde{q}_2 + \cdots + \tilde{q}_n &= M - c\,, \\
\tilde{q}_1 + 2\tilde{q}_2 + \cdots + \tilde{q}_n &= M - c\,, \\
&\vdots \\
\tilde{q}_1 + \tilde{q}_2 + \cdots + 2\tilde{q}_n &= M - c\,.
\end{aligned}$$

These have the unique solution

$$\tilde{q}_1 = \tilde{q}_2 = \cdots = \tilde{q}_n = \frac{1}{n+1}(M-c)\,.$$

Suppose, for example, that $n = 9$. Then each firm produces $\frac{1}{10}(M-c)$ widgets. The total number of widgets produced is therefore $\frac{9}{10}(M-c)$, and so the price at which they are sold is $\tilde{p} = M - \frac{9}{10}(M - c) = \frac{1}{10}M + \frac{9}{10}c$. Each player's profit is $\{\frac{1}{10}(M - c)\}^2$.

Perfect Competition. Firms are "price-takers" in a perfectly competitive industry. They do not believe that anything they do can affect the price at which widgets sell. The reason is that $p = M - q$, where q is the *total* number of widgets produced, and each individual firm is assumed not to be able to produce enough by itself to alter q appreciably. In seeking to maximize its profit

$$\pi(q) = (p - c)q\,,$$

a firm therefore treats p as a constant $\tilde{p}$. If $\tilde{p} < c$, profit is maximized by producing nothing. Hence no firms would be in business. If $\tilde{p} > c$, profit cannot be maximized because, however much a firm produces, it would increase its profit by producing more. But a firm that produced a huge amount would not have a negligible impact on the market price. Thus, the only value of $\tilde{p}$ consistent with a perfectly competitive story is $\tilde{p} = c$. In a perfectly competitive market, the price at which widgets sell is therefore the unit cost of manufacturing them, and each firm makes zero profit.

To check the validity of this rather abstract argument, consider what happens when the number of firms in an oligopoly is allowed to become very large. If $n \to \infty$ in the preceding oligopoly model, then the number of widgets produced converges to $M - c$, and the price at which they are sold converges to $\tilde{p} = c$. Each firm then gets zero profit. These are exactly the conclusions obtained by considering the idealized case of perfect competition.

The table of Figure 7.6 compares the equilibrium outcomes for each of the market structures considered in this subsection.[11] Notice the improvement in the lot of the consumers as the industry becomes more competitive. The price of widgets goes down and the number of widgets produced goes up. This goes a long way towards explaining why economists enthuse about the virtues of perfectly competitive industries.

[11]The entries in the *consumer surplus* column show how much the consumers as a whole save in dollars compared with what they would have to pay a monopolist who did not have to charge each consumer the same price, but was able to extract from everybody the maximum they would be willing to pay to get another widget (Exercise 7.9.20). Economists regard this quantity as a measure of how well off the consumers are under differing regimes.

	Total output	Price	Total profit	Consumer surplus
Monopoly	$\frac{1}{2}(M-c)$	$\frac{1}{2}M+\frac{1}{2}c$	$\frac{1}{4}(M-c)^2$	$\frac{1}{8}(M-c)^2$
Duopoly	$\frac{2}{3}(M-c)$	$\frac{1}{3}M+\frac{2}{3}c$	$\frac{2}{9}(M-c)^2$	$\frac{2}{9}(M-c)^2$
Oligopoly	$\frac{n}{n+1}(M-c)$	$\frac{1}{n+1}M+\frac{n}{n+1}c$	$\frac{n}{(n+1)^2}(M-c)^2$	$\frac{n^2}{2(n+1)^2}(M-c)^2$
Competition	$M-c$	c	0	$\frac{1}{2}(M-c)^2$

Figure 7.6 Comparing different market structures.

7.2.2 Following the Leader

The chief subject for this subsection is the Stackelberg duopoly model. The way economists discuss this topic can be very confusing for those who know some game theory. It may therefore help to begin by describing how a standard economics text would present a Stackelberg analysis of the simple bimatrix game of Figure 7.7(a).

One of the players is designated as the *leader*, and the other as the *follower*. Who is the leader and who the follower usually makes a big difference (as in the cat-and-mouse games of Exercise 4.8.2). Here player I will be the leader and player II the follower. This means that player I chooses between s_1 and s_2 *first*. *After* player II has learned his choice, she chooses

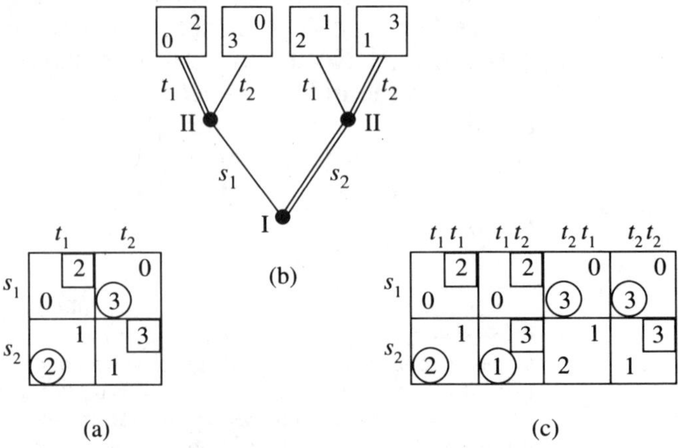

Figure 7.7 Following the leader.

between t_1 and t_2. She can therefore be *sure* of making a best reply to whatever player I chooses. He will anticipate that she will make such a best reply. Thus he operates on the assumption that, whatever row he selects, the final outcome will be the cell in the row he chooses in which player II's payoff is enclosed in a square. Of the two cells (s_1, t_1) and (s_2, t_2) with this property, player I prefers the latter, because $1 > 0$. He will therefore select s_2, to which player II will respond with t_2. Economists call the pair (s_2, t_2) a "Stackelberg equilibrium" after the German economist Von Stackelberg.

It is easy to be misled by such language because it tempts one to think of the bimatrix game of Figure 7.7(a) as being the strategic form of the game under study. But it is *not*. It is the strategic form of the *simultaneous-move* game in which both player I and player II make their choices in ignorance of the choice of the other. The strategy pair (s_2, t_2) is certainly not a Nash equilibrium of this simultaneous-move game. The simultaneous-move game has no pure strategy Nash equilibria at all (Exercise 7.9.1).

To find the strategic form of the leader-follower game whose "Stackelberg equilibrium" is (s_2, t_2), it is a good idea to begin by looking at its extensive form[12] as illustrated in Figure 7.7(b). Player II has two decision nodes at each of which she can make one of two choices. She therefore has $2 \times 2 = 4$ pure strategies. In the terminology of Section 1.3, these are labeled t_1t_1, t_1t_2, t_2t_1 and t_2t_2. For example, t_2t_1 means that t_2 is to be played if player I uses s_1, and t_1 is to be played if player I uses s_2. In the leader-follower game, player I's choice of action is therefore a *function* that makes her choice contingent on the choice made by player I. In the simultaneous-move game, the players make their choices independently.

The 2×4 strategic form of the leader-follower game is illustrated in Figure 7.7(c). The use of Zermelo's algorithm in the extensive form[13] shows that the game has a unique subgame-perfect equilibrium (s_2, t_1t_2). In the notation of Section 1.3, the play that results from the use of this subgame-perfect equilibrium is $[s_2t_2]$. It is this *play* of the leader-follower game that economists call a "Stackelberg equilibrium".[14]

[12]This differs from the extensive form of the simultaneous-move game in that player II's two decision nodes are not enclosed in an information set (as in Figure 4.3(a)).

[13]Or the observation that (s_1, t_1t_2) is a unique Nash equilibrium for the strategic form.

[14]It would be less confusing if they spoke of a "Stackelberg play". Better still, they could identify Stackelberg with the follow-the-leader scenario and speak of a subgame-perfect equilibrium in a Stackelberg *game*.

Stackelberg Duopoly. Stackelberg's model differs from Cournot's only in that player I decides first on how many widgets to produce. He is therefore the leader. Player II observes player I's production decision, and then decides how many widgets she will produce. She is therefore the follower.[15]

In analyzing the model, the important consideration to keep in mind is that a pure strategy for player II is a *function* $f : [0, M] \to [0, M]$. When player I chooses q_1, player II then replies by producing $q_2 = f(q_1)$. She has a unique best reply $R_2(q_1)$ to each q_1. Her optimal pure strategy is therefore the *function* $R_2 : [0, M] \to [0, M]$. Player I knows that player II will select R_2, and hence anticipates a profit of

$$\pi_1(q_1, R_2(q_1))$$

from choosing q_1. Since he is a profit maximizer, he will therefore choose the output $\tilde{q}_1$ that maximizes this quantity. The "Stackelberg equilibrium" will therefore be $(\tilde{q}_1, \tilde{q}_2)$, where $\tilde{q}_2 = R_2(\tilde{q}_1)$.

All the necessary calculations have already been made while analyzing the Cournot model. Since $R_2(q_1) = \frac{1}{2}(M - c - q_1)$

---

[15]Such stories are often complicated in the economics literature by a reluctance on the part of authors to commit themselves to a particular set of rules that govern the actions of the agents. Instead, the agents are seen as being constrained by the type of "conjecture" they find themselves entertaining about their opponent. For example, in the simultaneous-move game used earlier to model a Cournot duopoly, the two firms make once-and-for-all production decisions. They are offered no later opportunity to revise this decision once they have observed the output of the other firm. Often, however, the Cournot outcome will be defended with a story in which the firms can revise their output level if they so choose. The story is that, in making their initial production choice, they conjecture that, if they were to revise their output at a later stage, the opposing firm would not respond at all, but stick with its initial production decision. If firms have such *Cournot conjectures* , they will choose their initial outputs precisely as the Cournot model in the text specifies.

The equivalent story for the Stackelberg model attributes Cournot conjectures to player II, but *Stackelberg conjectures* to player I. He is supposed to believe that player II is so flexible that she will respond to any revision of his initial output decision with an immediate switch to an optimal response.

Game theorists are traditionally suspicious of such stories on the grounds that one can defend almost any outcome by being sufficiently ingenious in the type of "conjectural variations" to which the agents are assumed to confine their attention. They feel that proponents of "conjectural variation" theories have a duty to explain why the type of irrationality they attribute to their agents is more plausible than all of the many other kinds of irrationality to which the human species is prey.

	Total output	Price	Total profit	Consumer surplus
Stackelberg	$\frac{3}{4}(M-c)$	$\frac{1}{4}M+\frac{3}{4}c$	$\frac{3}{16}(M-c)^2$	$\frac{9}{32}(M-c)^2$

Figure 7.8 The Stackelberg duopoly model.

and $\pi_1(q_1, q_2) = (M - c - q_1 - q_2)q_1$, player I has to maximize

$$(M - c - q_1 - R_2(q_1))q_1 = \tfrac{1}{2}(M - c - q_1)q_1 \,.$$

This expression for a Stackelberg leader's profit is always exactly half what a monopolist who produced q_1 would get. Player I will therefore make the same output decision $\tilde{q}_1 = \frac{1}{2}(M - c)$ as a monopolist. Player II's output is then $\tilde{q}_2 = R_2(\tilde{q}_1) = \frac{1}{4}(M - c)$. Total production is therefore $\frac{3}{4}(M - c)$, and so widgets are sold at price $\tilde{p} = \frac{1}{4}M + \frac{3}{4}c$. Figure 7.8, which is to be compared with Figure 7.6, indicates why consumers prefer a Stackelberg duopoly to a Cournot duopoly.

7.3 Equilibrium Selection

It often happens that the players' reaction curves cross several times. The game will then have more than one Nash equilibrium. Which of these should be selected?

Sometimes the appropriate response is that the question is misconceived. For example, the Ultimatum Game studied in Section 5.8.1 has many Nash equilibria, but the issue is not really which of these should be selected. Only subgame-perfect equilibria make sense for rational players in such a game, and the Ultimatum Game has only one subgame-perfect equilibrium.

However, this section is concerned with what is to be done when the equilibrium selection problem cannot be evaded in this kind of way.[16]

[16]Some game theorists would maintain that the equilibrium selection problem can nearly always be solved by replacing the idea of a Nash equilibrium by some more refined equilibrium notion. However, no consensus exists on what the appropriate refinement should be, except in simple cases. This is one of the reasons that little is said about refinements other than subgame-perfect equilibrium in this book. There is more than enough material to cover without getting into controversial areas.

7.3.1 Interchangeability and Equivalence

Occasionally, it does not matter which equilibrium is selected. This happens if all the Nash equilibria are interchangeable and equivalent. Recall from Section 1.9.2 that two Nash equilibria (s, t) and (s', t') are *equivalent* if $\pi_1(s, t) = \pi_1(s', t')$ and $\pi_2(s, t) = \pi_2(s', t')$. Since both players then get the same payoff at each equilibrium, neither will then care which gets selected. Two Nash equilibria (s, t) and (s', t') are *interchangeable* if (s, t') and (s', t) are also Nash equilibria.

If the Nash equilibria of a game have the property that any pair are equivalent and interchangeable, then the selection problem disappears. Even if Von Neumann had written a book recommending the equilibrium (s, t), and Morgenstern had written a rival book recommending (s', t'), their failure to agree would not trouble the players at all. If player I follows Von Neumann, then he will play s. If player II follows Morgenstern, she will play t'. The result will be the Nash equilibrium pair (s, t') which assigns each player exactly the payoff they were anticipating.

Theorem 6.5.2 shows that the Nash equilibria of a two-person, zero-sum game are necessarily interchangeable and equivalent, but this is seldom the case otherwise.

7.3.2 Conventions

Two saboteurs are parachuted into enemy territory. During the jump, they unexpectedly get separated, but it is essential to their mission that they meet up again. If you were such a saboteur, seeking to rendezvous with your colleague, where would you go on the map shown in Figure 7.9(a)? Nearly everyone answers that they would go to the bridge. It is what Schelling[17] calls a *focal point*.

In the jargon of Section 1.9.1, the saboteurs are playing a team game. Each chooses a location on the map. Both can then be seen as receiving a winning payoff of 1 if they choose the same location, and a losing payoff of 0 otherwise. Their objectives are therefore identical. Since their goals do not conflict in the slightest, their problem is one of *pure coordination*.

Figure 7.9(b) shows a simpler game of pure coordination. As in the saboteurs' game, the pure strategy Nash equilibria are equivalent but not interchangeable. However, here no focal point is apparent. Nor is there any point in looking at the

[17]One of the essays in his evergreen *Strategy of Conflict* contains many ingenious and instructive examples of this type.

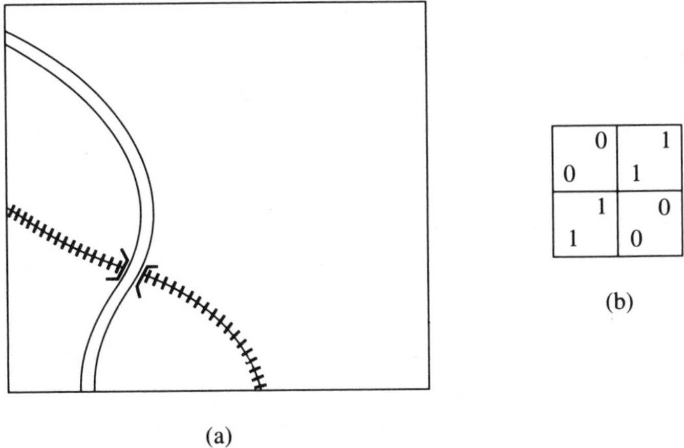

Figure 7.9 Looking for focal points.

structure of the game itself in seeking a reason to select one equilibrium rather than the other. To locate a focal point, it is necessary to look for clues, not in the game itself, but in the real-world situation from which the game has been abstracted.[18]

Fortunately, human societies abound with *conventions* that exist precisely for such purposes. In their purest form, such conventions are entirely arbitrary. People do not imagine that making contact at the "meeting point" in an airport terminal will enhance the joys of reunion. They meet at the "meeting point" because it is conventional to do so. The same is true of other conventions like "driving on the right"[19] or "doing things in alphabetical order".

It is easy to underestimate the importance of such coordinating conventions. But notice that the words in this book have meaning only by convention. Money is only valuable because it is conventional to regard it as valuable. Indeed, such considerations have led some authors to claim that society is "nothing but" the system of conventional understandings that bind it together.

[18]Recall that, in Section 1.9.2, an analogy was drawn between selecting an equilibrium in a game and deciding which root of a quadratic equation to choose.

[19]Although one can argue that "driving on the right" is not so much arbitrary, as perverse. The British, for example, claim that it is sensible to drive on the left on the grounds that right-handed people can then keep their more adept hand on the wheel when changing gear. However, driving on the right is certainly preferable to the convention of selecting the mixed equilibrium in which the side of the road on which to drive is chosen at random.

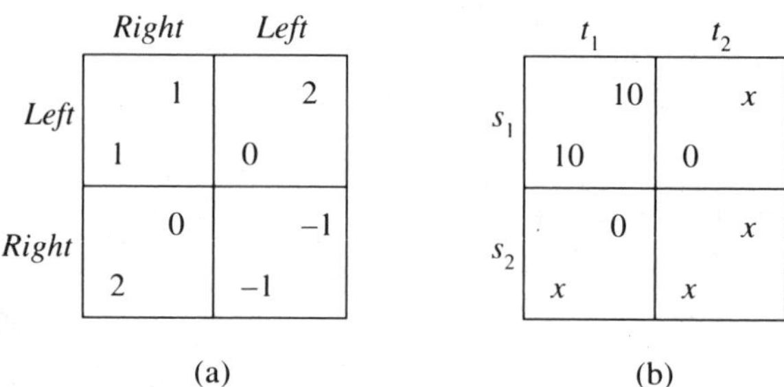

Figure 7.10 More focal points.

However, the conventions to which one may appeal in selecting equilibria in simple games are of a more humble character. Often, the necessary contextual clues for locating a focal point are retained in the labeling of the strategies. For example, if one were modeling the real-life game in which two cars approach each other along a street, one might use the pure coordination game of Figure 7.9(b) with player I's first and player II's second pure strategies labeled *left*, and the remaining pure strategies labeled *right*. In the United States, nobody would then hesitate in selecting (*right*, *right*) as the focal equilibrium.

This also goes for Chicken if it is introduced, as in Section 7.1.3, in a driving context and labeled as in Figure 7.10(a). Player II will wish that British conventions were in force, but will usually readily agree that any convention is better than none at all.[20]

7.3.3 Pareto-Dominance

Sometimes one Nash equilibrium (s, t) is a Pareto improvement (Section 5.4.1) on all the other Nash equilibria in a game. Usually (s, t) is then said to *Pareto-dominate* the other Nash equilibria.[21] It is often argued that this is enough to guarantee focal point status for (s, t), and even that the selection of any other equilibrium is somehow irrational.

To help evaluate such claims, consider the game of Figure 7.10(b). If $0 \leq x \leq 10$, the game has two pure strategy Nash equilibria, (s_1, t_1) and (s_2, t_2). If $x < 10$, (s_1, t_1) is a Pareto improvement on (s_2, t_2). Should it therefore always be selected?

[20]Some of the difficulties that arise when Chicken must be studied in the absence of a convention were discussed in Section 7.1.4. But matters can be even more troublesome in other games. See Exercises 7.9.29 and 7.9.30.

[21]In spite of the risk of this use of the word "dominate" being confused with the notion of strategic dominance introduced in Section 4.6.

Nobody would deny (s_1, t_1) focal point status when $x = 1$. But what if $x = 9$? What if $x = 9.9$? What if $x = 9.99$?[22]

7.3.4 Stability

A convention for selecting an equilibrium will not survive for long if it is not stable.[23] What this means in precise terms will depend on the context. Roughly speaking, the idea is that small mistakes in using the convention should not lead to disastrous coordination failures.

Only one example in which this idea is important will be worked through. However, this example is the Nash Demand Game, which is sufficiently important to deserve a section of its own.

Econ 7.5 ⟶

7.4 Nash Demand Game

The Nash Demand Game is a simultaneous-move game based on a Nash bargaining problem (X, d) of the type described in Section 5.5.1. Its study will not only illustrate how "stability" considerations can sometimes assist in equilibrium selection problems, it will also provide some further insight into the circumstances under which the Nash bargaining solution of Section 5.5.2 can usefully be employed.

John and Mary each simultaneously announce a demand. Their demands x_1 and x_2 are either compatible or incompatible. They are compatible if the pair $x = (x_1, x_2)$ lies in the set X of feasible payoff pairs. Otherwise they are incompatible. If the demands are compatible, both players get their demands. If the demands are incompatible, both players

---

[22]Harsanyi and Selten distinguish between "Pareto-dominance" and "risk-dominance". The latter notion is intended to embody the idea that some equilibria are riskier than others. For example, (s_1, t_1) is riskier than (s_2, t_2) because a player aiming for the latter is sure to get x, while a player aiming for the former will get nothing if there is a coordination failure. The manner in which Harsanyi and Selten quantify the risk involved makes (s_2, t_2) risk-dominate (s_1, t_1) when $x > 5$. But does risk-dominance ever outweigh Pareto-dominance? For Harsanyi and Selten's answers to such questions, you will have to read their book, *A General Theory of Equilibrium Selection in Games.*

[23]Cognoscenti should note that reference is not being made to stability in the technical sense of Kohlberg and Mertens, or others. Nor is an opportunity being taken to sneak refinement ideas in through a back door. In refinement theory, the "trembles" implicitly or explicitly considered are derived from the structure of the game itself. Here the intention is that the "trembles" actually exist in the real-life situation from which the game was abstracted.

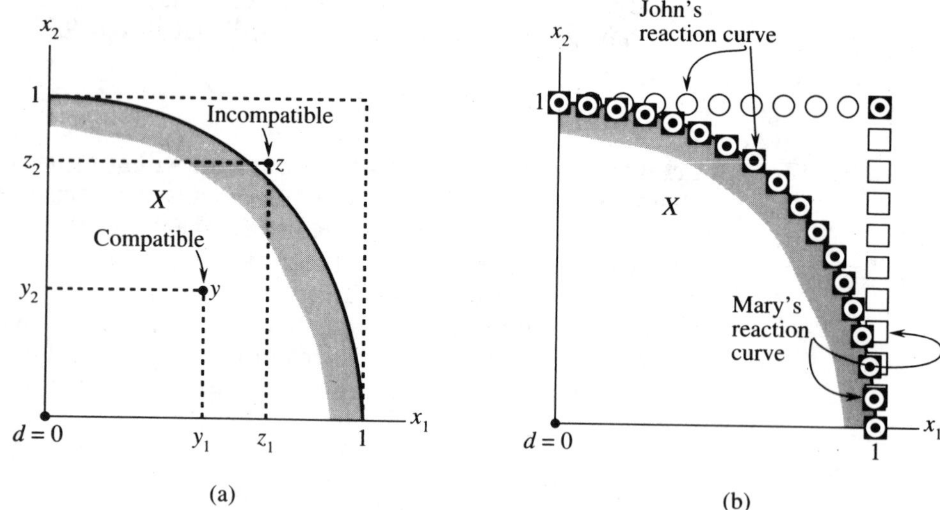

Figure 7.11 The Nash Demand Game.

receive their disagreement payoffs. The players' payoff functions $\pi_i : \mathbb{R}^2 \to \mathbb{R}$ are therefore defined by

$$\pi_i(x) = \begin{cases} x_i, & \text{if } x \in X\,, \\ d_i, & \text{if } x \notin X\,. \end{cases}$$

Figure 7.11(a) illustrates a bargaining problem (X, d). Recall that the zero and the unit on a player's Von Neumann and Morgenstern utility scale can be chosen in any way that it is convenient. In this problem it simplifies the mathematics slightly if the utility scales are chosen so that $d = 0$. Nothing much is simplified by making a specific choice for the units in which the utility scales are measured, but these have been chosen so that the frontier of X passes through the points $(0, 1)$ and $(1, 0)$. As a further simplification, John and Mary will be restricted to making demands from the interval $[0, 1]$.

The players' reaction curves for this specialized version of the game are shown in Figure 7.11(b). Notice that if Mary makes a demand satisfying $0 \leq x_2 < 1$, then John's best reply is to choose the demand x_1 that makes (x_1, x_2) Pareto-efficient in X. It would be stupid for John to claim less because he would then get less. It would be equally stupid to claim more, since the demands would then be incompatible, and so John would get only $d_1 = 0$. If Mary makes her maximum demand of $x_2 = 1$, then John will get nothing whatever he does. Thus any demand is a best reply for him in this case.

Figure 7.11(b) shows that any point in the bargaining set

(Section 5.4) for the bargaining problem (X, d) corresponds to a Nash equilibrium for the Nash Demand Game. There is also a "non-cooperative" Nash equilibrium that results if both players are greedy enough to make their maximum possible demand. They both then get nothing.

An infinite number of Nash equilibria therefore exist for the Nash Demand Game. This creates a major equilibrium selection problem. However, only one convention for selecting an equilibrium from the many available is "stable".

7.4.1 The "Smoothed" Nash Demand Game

To explain the sense in which the word "stable" is intended, it is necessary to consider a "smoothed" version of the Nash Demand Game in which the players are not quite sure what

Math 7.5 ⟶ the feasible set X is. They therefore do not know in advance whether a pair (x_1, x_2) will prove to be compatible or not. The best they can do is to attach a probability $p(x_1, x_2)$ to the event that a pair of demands (x_1, x_2) will be compatible.

Figure 7.12(a) indicates some contours for the function $p : [0,1]^2 \to [0,1]$. For example, if a demand pair $x = (x_1, x_2)$ lies on or below the contour $p(x) = \frac{2}{3}$, then the probability that the demand pair x will prove to be compatible is at least $\frac{2}{3}$. In such a situation the players know that the frontier of the set X is somewhere in the strip sandwiched between the regions labeled $p(x) = 0$ and $p(x) = 1$. If the

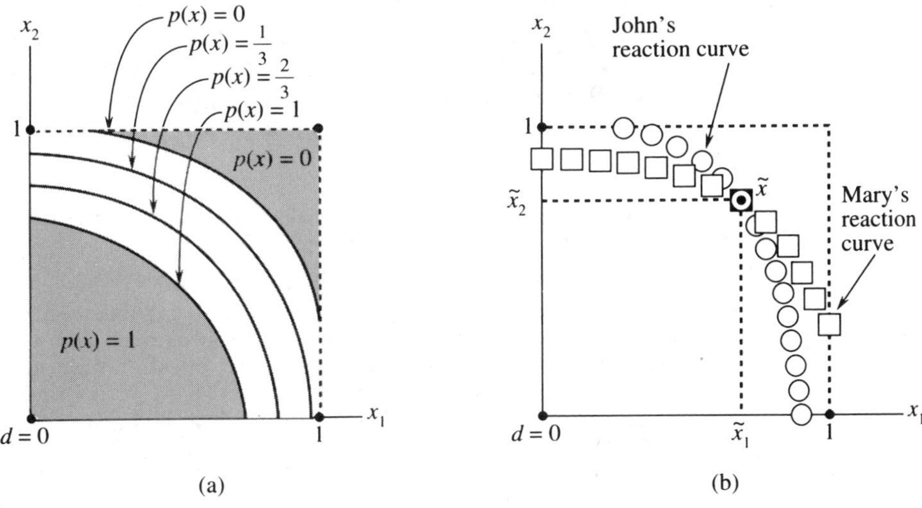

Figure 7.12 The "smoothed" Nash Demand Game.

amount of uncertainty to which they are subject is small, then the strip will be narrow. The focus of the study will be on what happens as its width becomes vanishingly small.

Player i's payoff function in the smoothed demand game is

$$\pi_i(x_1, x_2) = x_i p(x_1, x_2)$$

because, if the pair of demands (x_1, x_2) is chosen, the result is a lottery in which player i gets x_i with probability $p(x_1, x_2)$ and nothing with probability $1 - p(x_1, x_2)$.

It will be assumed that the function $p : [0,1]^2 \to [0,1]$ is sufficiently well-behaved that a naive approach to calculating the players' reaction functions for the smoothed demand game will be successful.[24] In finding his best replies to Mary's demand of x_2, John can then simply differentiate his payoff function partially with respect to x_1, keeping x_2 fixed. The resulting partial derivative $\partial \pi_1 / \partial x_1$ is then set equal to zero. This yields the equation[25]

$$x_1 p_{x_1}(x_1, x_2) + p(x_1, x_2) = 0 \qquad (7.1)$$

for John's reaction curve. Similarly, Mary's reaction curve has the equation

$$x_2 p_{x_2}(x_1, x_2) + p(x_1, x_2) = 0\,. \qquad (7.2)$$

Figure 7.12(b) shows the typical shape of the reaction curves.[26]

A Nash equilibrium $\tilde{x} = (\tilde{x}_1, \tilde{x}_2)$ occurs where these two reaction curves cross. Figure 7.12(b) shows the two reaction curves crossing once. But it may happen that the reaction curves cross several times, so that multiple Nash equilibria exist. But, however many Nash equilibria there may be, the following analysis shows that they all approximate the regular

[24]Amongst the assumptions normally made are that p is differentiable, quasi-concave and strictly decreasing.

[25]Recall that the notation p_{x_1} simply means $\partial p / \partial x_1$.

[26]If John and Mary were less naive in calculating their reaction curves, they might pay special attention to what happens when $x_1 = 1$ or $x_2 = 1$. Depending on what is assumed about p, they might or might not discover that their reaction curves bend back, as in Figure 7.11(b), and cross at a "non-cooperative" Nash equilibrium in which both players get nothing because each greedily demands everything. This possibility is ignored in the text because, if it did occur, one would simply reject the "non-cooperative" Nash equilibrium as a candidate for selection anyway.

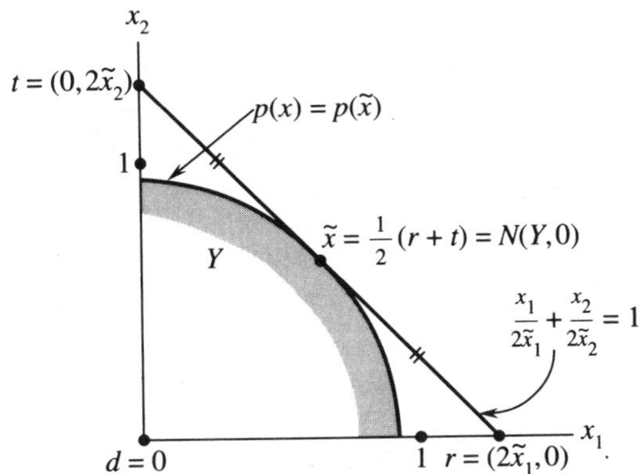

Figure 7.13 Characterizing Nash equilibria in the "smoothed" game.

Nash bargaining solution when the players are fairly certain about what X is.[27]

As explained in Section 4.5.1, the tangent to the curve $p(x) = p(\tilde{x})$ at the point $\tilde{x}$ has equation $\nabla p(\tilde{x})^\top(x - \tilde{x}) = 0$. When written in full, the equation for the tangent becomes

$$p_{x_1}(\tilde{x}_1, \tilde{x}_2)(x_1 - \tilde{x}_1) + p_{x_2}(\tilde{x}_1, \tilde{x}_2)(x_2 - \tilde{x}_2) = 0\,. \tag{7.3}$$

If $\tilde{x} = (\tilde{x}_1, \tilde{x}_2)$ is a Nash equilibrium, it must lie on both John's and Mary's reaction curves. Thus (7.1) and (7.2) are both true with $x = \tilde{x}$. This observation allows the partial derivatives in (7.3) to be eliminated, yielding the simpler equation

$$\frac{p(\tilde{x}_1, \tilde{x}_2)}{\tilde{x}_1}(x_1 - \tilde{x}_1) + \frac{p(\tilde{x}_1, \tilde{x}_2)}{\tilde{x}_2}(x_2 - \tilde{x}_2) = 0\,.$$

A little algebra reduces this to

$$\frac{x_1}{2\tilde{x}_1} + \frac{x_2}{2\tilde{x}_2} = 1\,.$$

Figure 7.13 serves as a reminder that this is the equation of the tangent line to $p(x) = p(\tilde{x})$ at the point $\tilde{x}$.

In Figure 7.12, the tangent line cuts the x_1 axis at the point $r = (2\tilde{x}_1, 0)$. It cuts the x_2 axis at the point $t = (0, 2\tilde{x}_2)$. Thus, the Nash equilibrium $\tilde{x} = (\tilde{x}_1, \tilde{x}_2)$ lies at the midpoint of the line segment joining r and t. If Y is the shaded region

[27] Figure 5.10(b) shows how the regular Nash bargaining solution is defined. If your recollection of this material is hazy, it would be wise to review Section 5.5.

in Figure 7.13, it then follows that $\tilde{x}$ is the regular Nash bargaining solution for the bargaining problem $(Y, 0)$. In the notation of Section 5.5, $\tilde{x} = s = N(Y, 0)$.

The frontier of the set Y is a probability contour. All such contours converge on the frontier of the set X as the width[28] of the strip shown in Figure 7.11(a) approaches zero. It follows that $N(Y, 0)$ converges on $N(X, 0)$. That is to say, when the amount of uncertainty about the location of X is sufficiently small, all Nash equilibria of the smoothed game approximate the regular Nash bargaining solution of the bargaining problem $(X, 0)$.

This conclusion was offered by Nash as a reason for using the Nash bargaining solution as a convention for selecting a Nash equilibrium in the (unsmoothed) Nash Demand Game. His argument was that any other convention is necessarily unstable because, although such an alternative convention may serve perfectly well as a device for selecting a Nash equilibrium when everyone is certain about the feasible set X, the slightest hint of doubt will generate a game for which the convention does not even come near selecting a Nash equilibrium at all. If such doubts are endemic, then only the Nash bargaining solution can be expected to survive as an equilibrium selection convention because it is the only convention that is stable when such doubts are present.

7.5 Pre-play Negotiation

The preceding sections on equilibrium selection assume that the players have no opportunity for pre-play negotiation. Any common understandings between the players are *tacit*. In this section, players will be *vocal*. They will be able to talk to each other before the play of the game. Often, such pre-play negotiation is referred to as a "bull session" taking place "in the bar" the night before the game is to be played. In such "bull sessions", the players may rewrite their game theory books, or invent new conventions. Even the fact that they may jointly observe the fall of a coin will turn out to be significant.

Phil 7.5.1 ⟶ Of course, pre-play negotiation properly falls under the heading of bargaining. The Nash program, described briefly

[28]Mathematicians should note that the "width" of the strip may be taken to be the Hausdorff distance between the set where $p = 0$ and the set where $p = 1$. They will need to reassure themselves that the Nash bargaining solution is continuous with respect to the Hausdorff metric.

in Section 5.7.1, calls for all negotiation ploys in a bargaining situation to be modeled explicitly as moves in a formal bargaining game. If this ambitious program were carried through, each player would be faced with the problem of choosing a grand strategy for an enlarged game. This would incorporate a bargaining strategy for conducting the negotiations and then a strategy for playing the original game that would be contingent on the course the negotiations took. Since the enlarged game would need to be analyzed *tacitly*, it follows that tacit games should be regarded as being more fundamental than vocal games.[29] That is to say, if game theory were properly worked out, the theory of vocal games would appear as a consequence of the theory of tacit games. However, such deep questions will be irrelevant for the elementary considerations to which this section is confined.

7.5.1 Commitment and Cooperation

It is easy to get confused about what is or is not allowed during pre-play negotiations. Recall from Section 5.7 that, in *cooperative* game theory, any agreement reached during pre-play negotiations is taken to be *binding* on the players. It has the status of a legal contract. A player cannot agree to play strategy s before the game, and then sneakily switch to something more advantageous later. A player's agreement to play s imposes a *commitment* on the player. In game theory, this term is not used loosely. When a player has made a commitment, the door is closed to second thoughts. For better or worse, a committed player is one who has *no choice* but to carry out the commitment.

However, the study of Nash equilibria, with which this chapter is mainly concerned, belongs very definitely to *non-cooperative* game theory. In non-cooperative game theory, nothing that happens during any pre-play negotiations binds anyone to anything. If players honor agreements, it is not because they *must* honor them, but because they believe it advantageous to do so.

This section seeks to make it clear why these distinctions matter. Examples illustrating the ideas appear in Sections 7.5.4 and 7.5.5. However, first a brief review of what Chapter 5 had to say about cooperative game theory is required.

[29] I like to use the word *contest* to refer to games that have to be analyzed without any common understandings at all between the players, whether vocalized or not. Such games are even more fundamental than what are called tacit games in the text.

Cooperative Payoff Regions. The power to make commitments, or to conclude binding agreements, can be very useful indeed. For example, if the players have the ability to write binding agreements during the pre-play negotiations, they need not confine their attention to Nash equilibria of the game to be played the next morning. They can agree to implement any payoff pair in the *cooperative payoff region* of the game. Section 5.3 explains why this is simply the convex hull of the payoff pairs in the game's strategic form.[30]

As an example, the cooperative payoff region for the Prisoners' Dilemma is shown in Figure 7.14(b). It is the convex hull of the payoff pairs (3, 3), (0, 6), (6, 0) and (3, 3) that appear in the strategic form for the Prisoners' Dilemma of Figure 7.14(a).

Recall that *hawk* strongly dominates *dove* in the Prisoners' Dilemma. Thus the only Nash equilibrium for the game is (*hawk*, *hawk*). This yields the outcome (1, 1). Players who are able to make binding agreements can therefore do a whole lot better than those confined to choosing Nash equilibria. For example, they can achieve the outcome (3, 3) simply by signing an agreement to play (*dove*, *dove*). (Alternatively, they might agree to toss a fair coin together and to play (*hawk*, *dove*) if the coin falls heads, and (*dove*, *hawk*) if it falls tails.) When the time comes to play according to the agreement, neither player will *want* to play *dove* because this is strongly dominated by *hawk*. But, in cooperative game theory, agreements *must* be honored.

Econ 7.5.2 ⟶

Nash's Threat Theory. One may ask: On which of all the possible outcomes in the cooperative payoff region will the players agree? Such a question takes us into the realm of bargaining theory considered in Chapter 5. One might, for example, seek to answer the question by using some version of the Nash bargaining solution. Among the problems that then have to be faced is the location of the disagreement point d.

For an environment in which the players have the power to make unlimited commitments, as usually envisaged in cooperative game theory, Nash offers a convincing answer. In such an environment, player I would be in deep trouble if he delayed making a commitment. Player II would then get in first, and commit herself to play the game in a very damaging way for player I *unless* he agrees to sign a contract

[30]To keep things simple, the possibility of free disposal or "transferable utility" is neglected for the moment.

on *her* terms. He would then be stuck in a take-it-or-leave-it situation with no room for maneuver.[31]

Since neither player can afford to delay, pre-play negotiation between rational players in such an environment would be telescoped into the opening instant of the negotiation period. In the spirit of the Nash program, Nash sought to model the situation by having the players simultaneously commit themselves once-and-for-all to a threat of the form: unless you sign an agreement that grants me my demand of D, I will carry out threat T in the game.

This sketch of the Nash threat theory is incidental to the main thrust of the section, and so it will only be noted that the relevance of the *regular* Nash bargaining solution in an unlimited commitment environment can be justified by an appeal to the preceding section on the Nash Demand Game, where the players were envisaged as simultaneously exchanging nonnegotiable demands. Threats become significant when no disagreement point is given. The mechanics of how to work out what the final outcome will be were described in Section 6.9.

In the case of the Prisoners' Dilemma, things turn out to be particularly simple. Each player demands a payoff of 3 and threatens to play *hawk* if this demand is not met. In consequence, the players agree to play (*dove*, *dove*) or some other strategy combination that leads to the outcome $(3, 3)$.

7.5.2 Incredible Threats and Promises

Agreements between two parties that are legally binding are nothing remarkable. But, one must bear in mind that the range of circumstances for which such contracts can be written is restricted, and that they are not binding in the strict sense. They bind only to the extent that each party prefers not to incur the penalties that may arise from breaching the contract. However, in many cases, it will not pay the other party to sue even if you do fail to live up to your legal obligations. Nevertheless, cooperative game theory has a wide range of application.

On the other hand, the assumptions built into Nash's threat theory about the power that players have to make *unilateral* commitments are almost never satisfied. The following

[31] Read Section 5.8.1 on the Ultimatum Game again if you are tempted to respond that player I should not submit to such blackmail even if it does damage him to be defiant. This behavior is not rational unless there is some payoff to establishing a reputation for being hard to blackmail.

kidnapping story[32] is often told to illustrate how difficult it is in practice to convince another person that what you *say* is a commitment is *in fact* a commitment.

John has kidnapped Mary. The ransom has been paid, and John is now considering Mary's release. He does not wish to kill her. Indeed, he would be delighted to release her if he could count on her not revealing his identity once she is free. Mary does not wish to be killed, and fervently promises that she will remain silent if released. But what is her promise worth? She needs to convince John that she is *committed* to remaining silent. If she had some incriminating documents proving her guilty of some major crime of her own, she could perhaps post these with John as a bond for her good behavior. But Mary almost certainly has no such expedient to fall back on. Her promises, no matter how earnestly they are expressed, will strike John as *incredible.* He will simply not believe her.

The same goes for incredible threats. Consider, for example, the discussion of subgame-perfect equilibrium in Section 4.6.3. Player II may *threaten* that she will follow player I's choice of r by playing L. Her aim in making such a threat during pre-play negotiations would be to blackmail player I into an agreement on the Nash equilibrium (l, RL). But, unless she has some way of convincing player I that her threat has the status of a commitment, he will dismiss it as idle bombast. He knows that, if she is rational, she will not carry out her threat if he actually does play r because she will then get a payoff of 1 instead of the payoff of 2 that she would get from playing R. It is for this reason that the rationale behind the notion of a subgame-perfect equilibrium is often expressed by saying that the players only recognize threats that are *credible.* These are threats that it would actually be in the interests of a rational player to carry out if called upon to do so.

Phil 7.5.3 ⟶

None of this means that it is *never* possible to make commitments. However, game theorists usually prefer to build any opportunities that the players have for making commitments into the formal structure of the game. The enlarged game is then analyzed using an equilibrium concept like subgame-perfection that does not take commitment possibilities for granted. Nor does the fact that Nash's own defense of the Nash bargaining solution is flawed by modern standards imply that it has no value. It has other more powerful justifications. One of these was studied in Section 5.8.4.

[32]For this story, and other cautionary tales of a similar nature, see again Schelling's *Strategy of Conflict.*

7.5.3 Cheap Talk

In non-cooperative game theory, players cannot make commitments in any pre-play negotiation. Nor can they make binding agreements. Pre-play interchanges between the players are therefore confined to "cheap talk". Nothing anyone says constrains their future behavior. Thus, if a player chooses to honor an agreement that has been made, it will be because it is optimal to do so. The only agreements that will be honored are therefore those that are *self-policing* in the sense that nobody deviates because nobody has anything to gain from deviating. The only worthwhile deals that can result from cheap talk are therefore agreements to coordinate on an *equilibrium*. An agreement on anything else is doomed because there will then necessarily be at least one player with an incentive to cheat who cannot be prevented from doing so. It is for this reason that modern economists have learned to restrict their attention to what they call *incentive-compatible* agreements. However, the essence of what matters was already clear to the philosopher Thomas Hobbes way back in 1661, when he dramatized the point by writing, "Covenants without the sword are but words".

Phil 7.5.5 ⟶

Game theorists are often accused of being naive about human nature for saying such things. It is argued that people are guided by more than narrow self-interest: they also pay heed to moral promptings. It may perhaps be in an individual's narrow self-interest to cheat, but the story is that we can often count on people to keep their word because they feel a moral obligation to do so.

But such accusations miss a major point. Game theory is *neutral* on moral issues. It is *not* wedded to the notion that the "end justifies the means"[33] or any other Machiavellian principles. Those who maintain otherwise are simply confused.

When game theorists describe players as "rational", they mean no more than that they make choices *consistently*. With the morally neutral assumptions on consistent behavior made in Chapter 3, it turns out that a consistent person can be characterized as one who acts *as though* maximizing the expected value of a Von Neumann and Morgenstern utility function. In Chapter 4, such expected values were called *payoffs*. But nothing in the theory says that consistent players must pursue selfish goals. Nor is there any reason why unselfish people

[33] Indeed, a game-theoretic formulation makes "ends" inseparable from the "means" by which they are achieved. Each terminal node in an extensive form is determined uniquely by the play that leads to it.

who follow moral imperatives should be inconsistent. Both types of people will behave as though seeking a maximum payoff, but outcomes that yield a high payoff for one will not be the same as those that yield a high payoff for the other. Game theory does not say that one sort of behavior is somehow preferable to the other. It takes a player's aspirations as *given*, and confines itself to offering advice on how the player can best achieve whatever his or her aspirations may be.

The usual arena for debate on such issues is the Prisoners' Dilemma. Further discussion is therefore postponed until the next subsection. Howard Tucker could have had no notion of the enormous literature his invention of this simple "toy game" would spawn. However, for those who understand game theory, there is little that needs to be said.

7.5.4 The Prisoners' Dilemma

A version of the Prisoners' Dilemma was introduced in Section 7.1.3. The bimatrix game is reproduced in Figure 7.14(a). Its cooperative payoff region is shown in Figure 7.14(b).

Suppose that cheap talk leads to both players promising to play *dove* in the Prisoners' Dilemma. Game theory says that it is irrational for either player to keep their promise because *hawk* strongly dominates *dove*. But, if both follow the game-theoretic recommendation and break their promises, the result is that both do worse than they would have done if both had kept their promises. Indeed, the outcome $(1, 1)$ that results from the play of (*hawk*, *hawk*) is arguably the very worst outcome possible in the game. Many authors have therefore claimed that it is not only immoral, but foolish, to be rational in the Prisoners' Dilemma.

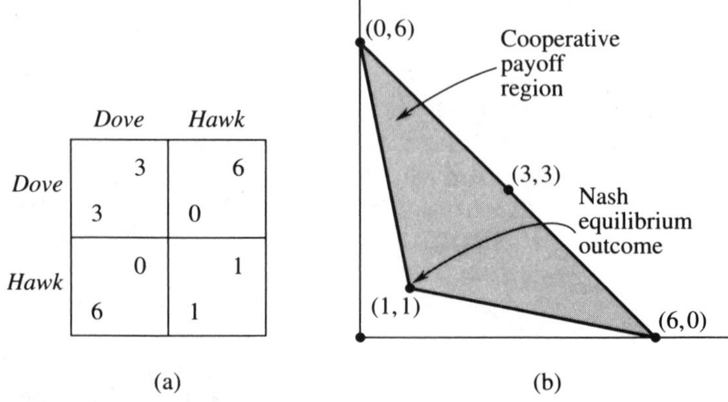

Figure 7.14 The Prisoners' Dilemma.

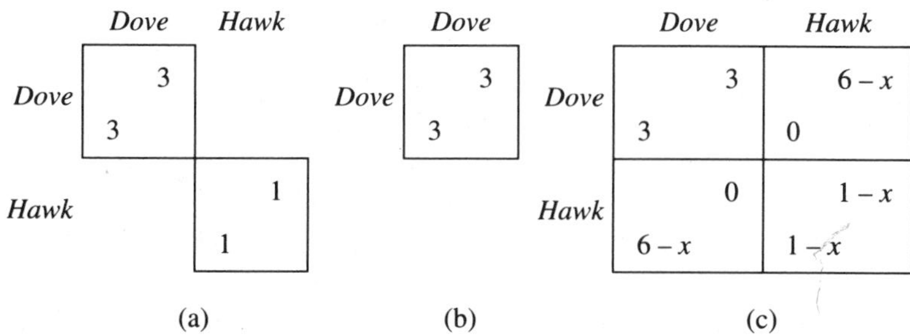

Figure 7.15 Games that are not the Prisoners' Dilemma.

Fallacy of the Twins. Those who claim that breaking your promise in the Prisoners' Dilemma is an act of folly are often victims of some version of the "fallacy of the twins". The fallacy is particularly inviting in the Prisoners' Dilemma because the game is symmetric. Assuming that the players do not use mixed strategies and nothing external intervenes to break the symmetry, it is not unreasonable to argue that rational players will make the same choice of pure strategy. The final outcome will therefore be either (*hawk*, *hawk*) or (*dove*, *dove*). Both players prefer the latter to the former. Thus, so this particular fallacy goes, rationality demands the choice of the latter.

The fallacy is commonplace in contexts much grander than the Prisoners' Dilemma. Its appearance is usually signaled by the question, "What if everyone were to behave like that?"[34]

This question misdirects attention only to what happens when everybody does the same thing. Since it is nearly always worse for everyone if everyone behaves "selfishly" than if everyone behaves "unselfishly", the mistaken conclusion is drawn that "selfish" behavior makes no sense.

In brief, it is false that rational players can restrict their attention in the Prisoners' Dilemma to the main diagonal of the payoff table as indicated in Figure 7.15(a). This would only make sense if the two players did not reason *independently*. If player I could count on player II reasoning *precisely* as he reasons, then it would be as though he could *force* her

---

[34]The philosopher Spinoza introduces his version of the fallacy by writing, "What if a man could save himself from the present danger of death by treachery? ... If reason should recommend that, it would recommend it to all men". He then implicitly concludes that only his equivalent of the outcomes (*hawk*, *hawk*) or (*dove*, *dove*) need to be considered. Kant's celebrated "categorical imperative" is that one should *act only on the maxim which you can at the same time will to become a universal law*. What does this mean for the Prisoners' Dilemma? Nobody seems to know for sure. What do you think?

to choose whichever strategy he found expedient simply by choosing it himself. Perhaps this conclusion could be justified in the case when the players are an idealized pair of twins who are so indistinguishable that they might as well be the same person. Such an hypothesis would reduce the Prisoners' Dilemma to a one-player game for which any game theorist would be happy to recommend the play of *dove.* But two rational players are not such a pair of twins. If they reason in the same way in identical circumstances, it is not because they have no alternative but to think identically: it is because the rational thing to think is the same in both cases.[35]

It is rational in the Prisoners' Dilemma to play *hawk* because this strongly dominates *dove.* A rational player I who knows that his opponent is rational therefore knows that she will play *hawk.* He knows that he will play *hawk* as well because he is rational too. In a passing moment of whimsy, he might perhaps contemplate the play of *dove.* If he were feeling especially whimsical, he might even contemplate the possibility that his opponent is simultaneously experiencing an identical bout of whimsy. But this would only reinforce his conviction that *hawk* is a good idea since the use of *dove* by player II makes *hawk* even more attractive for him than her use of *hawk.*

Morality. What of the claim that game theory is immoral to advocate breaking cheap-talk promises? Such criticism seems very unreasonable to a game theorist. If a moral theorist wishes to maintain that there are "natural laws" of behavior that should be honored regardless of the consequences, then a game theorist will be very happy to put the tools of the game theory trade at his disposal. Such "natural laws" can be incorporated into the rules of the game under study. However, if one of the rules is that promises should never be broken, then players will *not be able* to play the Prisoners' Dilemma after a cheap-talk promise to use *dove.* The game they will be playing is shown in Figure 7.15(b). The possibility of *hawk* being played has been eliminated because its use is incompatible with the "natural law" being postulated. To proceed in this way is to deny that the Prisoners' Dilemma can be preceded by talk that is "cheap"

[35]A player cannot argue: I am rational. Therefore, my acceptance of argument A makes it a rational argument. Hence a rational opponent will necessarily accept argument A. Therefore my opponent will do whatever I do. This puts the horse before the cart. An argument is not rational because it is accepted by a rational person. On the contrary, a person is rational because he or she accepts only rational arguments.

in any meaningful sense. Cheap talk is simply impossible in such a setting.

Similar considerations apply to those who are anxious to deny that people seek only their own narrowly conceived selfish ends. They argue that the players may care about the welfare of their opponents, or that they may actively want to keep their promises out of feelings of group solidarity or because they would otherwise suffer the pangs of a bad conscience. Such players will *not* be playing the Prisoners' Dilemma. They will be playing some other game with different payoffs. Figure 7.15(c) shows one possibility. It is derived from the Prisoners' Dilemma by supposing that the players have made cheap-talk promises to play *dove* that they prefer not to break because they do not like breaking promises. This disposition to keep promises is reflected in the payoffs written into the table. Playing *hawk* is not impossible for these players, but it results in their losing x utils. If $x > 3$, *hawk* does not dominate *dove* in the new game. On the contrary, *dove* now dominates *hawk*. Thus rational play will result in the outcome (*dove, dove*). As many commentators have observed, this is a situation where everybody will end up better off if it is common knowledge that everyone likes to keep their promises. (Similarly, both John and Mary would be better off in the kidnapping story of Section 7.5.2 if it were common knowledge that Mary suffers unbearable mental distress if she breaks a promise.) But notice that, in this story, it is *not* the Prisoners' Dilemma that gets played after promises have been made. Again, a story has been invented that makes cheap talk impossible. Far from being cheap, breaking a promise in the story costs at least three utils.

In summary, the reaction of game theorists to their critics in this context goes something like this. Perhaps you know the right way to think about some social problem. If so, it may be helpful in persuading others if you are able to deduce what you believe to be right from a game-theoretic analysis of a suitable game. But make sure you analyze the right game. However right your conclusion, nothing whatever is to be gained by deducing it from a wrong analysis of the wrong game.[36] The critic may respond that the game theorist's victory in the debate is at best Pyrrhic, since it is bought at the cost of

[36] My own view is that the Prisoners' Dilemma is almost never a suitable paradigm for the cooperation problems it is said to epitomize. The repeated Prisoners' Dilemma, as studied in Chapter 8, makes a lot more sense in such a role. But, if one insists on restricting the search for a suitable paradigm to one-shot games, there is much to be said for something like the Nash Demand Game.

reducing the propositions of game theory to the status of "mere" tautologies. But such an accusation disturbs a game theorist not in the least. There is nothing a game theorist would like better than for his propositions to be entitled to the status of tautologies, just like proper mathematical theorems.

7.5.5 Collusion in Cournot Duopoly

Econ 7.6 ⟶

Profit-maximizing firms do not like competition, whether perfect or imperfect. They prefer to get together in cosy cartels whose members do not make their economic decisions independently, but *collude* to avoid the inroads into their profits that competition brings. Such collusion can take many forms. At its crudest, it may consist of a straight price-fixing deal, or an arrangement that assigns each cartel member a negotiated market share. At its most subtle, there may be no explicit deal at all. Instead, over the years, the firms may establish an unspoken understanding that neither will press the other too hard. At this stage, only crude collusive deals will be considered. To study more subtle arrangements, the theory of repeated games introduced in the next chapter is required.

One advantage of studying pre-play negotiation in the context of an oligopoly is that most people are only too ready to take for granted that moral scruples will be of small importance in determining the behavior of commercial enterprises. This prejudice is incorporated into the discussion of the Cournot Duopoly Game that follows by assuming, as we have in the past, that each firm cares only about maximizing its own profit. Defending such an assumption is particularly easy when collusion is under study. After all, even when collusive deals are not illegal, it is hardly compatible with an upright nature to enter into a conspiracy whose aim is to screw the consumer. Indeed, in real life, colluding executives seem to take relish in their shady dealing by choosing to meet in smoke-filled hotel rooms late at night—just like gangsters in the movies.

We begin by finding the cooperative payoff region Z for the Cournot Duopoly Game. This is easy to determine because the most money that can be squeezed from the consumers is the amount $\tilde{\pi}$ that a profit-maximizing monopolist would achieve. As Figure 7.6 records, this profit level is achieved when a monopolist's output is $\tilde{q} = \frac{1}{2}(M - c)$. A colluding pair of duopolists will therefore maximize the cake they have to share between them by ensuring that their outputs satisfy $q_1 + q_2 = \tilde{q}$. The total profit they earn between

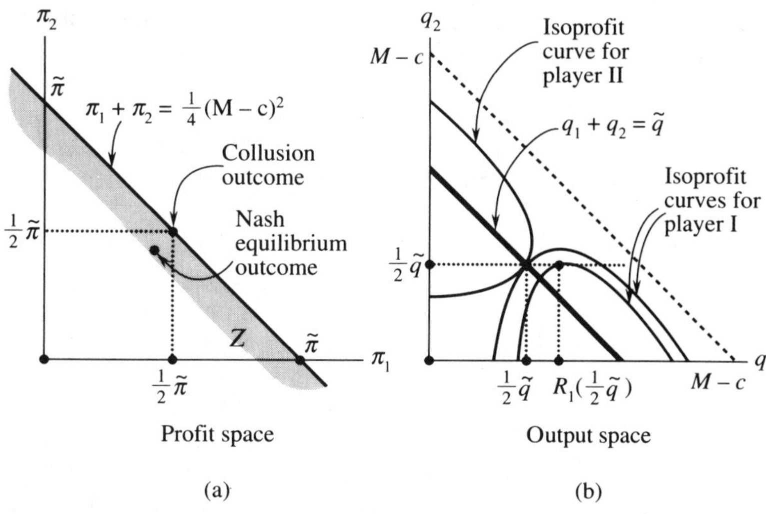

Figure 7.16 Collusion in a Cournot duopoly.

them will then satisfy $\pi_1 + \pi_2 = \tilde{\pi}$. In this context, it makes most sense to assume that both "transferable utility" and free disposal are possible. The cooperative payoff region Z is then as illustrated in Figure 7.16(a). Figure 7.16(b), which should be compared with Figure 7.5, does not show profit pairs (π_1, π_2), but output pairs (q_1, q_2). The line $q_1 + q_2 = \tilde{q}$ of Pareto-efficient output deals is marked.[37]

What profit pair in Z will result if the duopolists negotiate under the assumption that their agreement will be binding? This will depend on the circumstances under which they bargain. Since the whole setup is symmetric, the most likely outcome is that they will split fifty-fifty[38] so that each produces $\frac{1}{2}\tilde{q}$ and receives a profit of $\frac{1}{2}\tilde{\pi}$.

However, the point of this example is that any such collusive deal is inherently unstable. Talk is cheap when

[37]Notice that the isoprofit curves touch along this line. Economists who know about Pareto-efficiency in the Edgeworth box will be familiar with this phenomenon. Others should ask themselves why an output pair at which the isoprofit curves cross cannot be Pareto-efficient.

[38]This would be the result, for example, if the regular Nash bargaining solution were used with the disagreement point d located at the pair of profits each would receive if they were to use the unique Nash equilibrium that results when the Cournot Duopoly Game is analyzed without collusion. The same result would also follow if the Nash threat theory were applied. For an asymmetric result, some asymmetry would need to be introduced into the bargaining procedure. Perhaps, for example, it might be appropriate to place the disagreement point d at the pair of profits each receives in a Stackelberg model.

executives meet in smoke-filled hotel rooms. The deals reached will *not* be binding. Often the deals will be downright illegal. One must then anticipate that any agreement will be broken if one of the firms has an incentive to do so. Figure 7.16(b) indicates that neither firm has an incentive to honor an agreement on the output pair $(\frac{1}{2}\tilde{q}, \frac{1}{2}\tilde{q})$. Player I has an incentive to deviate to $R_1(\frac{1}{2}\tilde{q})$, which is his best reply to player II's choice of $\frac{1}{2}\tilde{q}$. Player II has a similar incentive to deviate. The only deal on which neither has an incentive to rat is the output pair $(\frac{2}{3}\tilde{q}, \frac{2}{3}\tilde{q})$. But this is just the Nash equilibrium of the noncollusive Cournot Duopoly Game, for which no collusion is required at all.

Of course, the fact that collusive deals are inherently unstable in the one-shot Cournot Duopoly Game does not imply that the same is true when the game is played *repeatedly*. However, this is a story that will have to wait until Section 8.3.3.

7.6 Pre-play Randomization

The previous section concentrated on what *cannot* be achieved through pre-play cheap talk. This section offers some simple examples of what such cheap talk *can* achieve if the circumstances are favorable.

7.6.1 Tossing Coins

Tossing a coin is a traditional way of settling coordination problems. For example, this is how the question of who goes first in sporting events is usually decided. Even the Bible has favorable things to say about the "casting of lots".

To see how the use of jointly observed random events can assist in equilibrium selection, consider the variant of Chicken shown in Figure 7.17(a). Its cooperative payoff

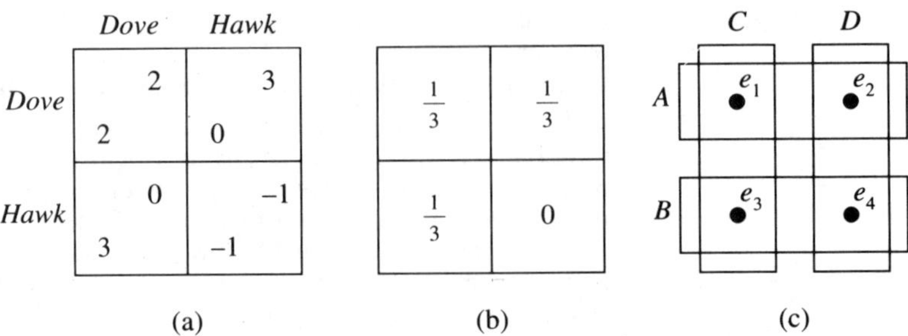

Figure 7.17 A second version of Chicken.

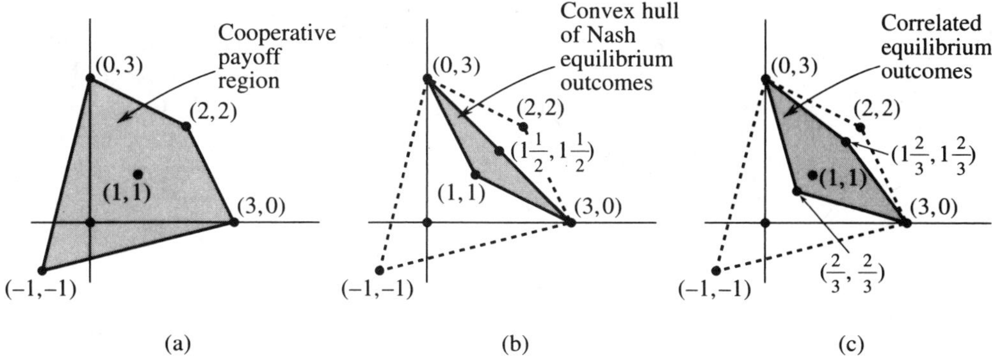

Figure 7.18 Payoff regions for Chicken.

region is shown in Figure 7.18(a). The game has three Nash equilibria: (*dove, hawk*), (*hawk, dove*), and a mixed equilibrium in which each player uses *dove* and *hawk* with equal probability.

If binding agreements are possible, the players can agree on the outcome $(2, 2)$. Without the possibility of making a binding agreement, the players are confronted with an equilibrium selection problem. As we have seen in studying Chicken previously, such selection problems may not be easy to resolve when no obvious convention is at hand to break the symmetry. But, if cheap talk is permitted, the players may be able to invent a convention of their own.

For example, they can break the symmetry by jointly watching the toss of a fair coin. Before the toss, they agree to play (*dove, hawk*) if it falls heads, and (*hawk, dove*) if it falls tails. Each will evaluate the agreed lottery to be worth $1\frac{1}{2}$ utils. The outcome $(1\frac{1}{2}, 1\frac{1}{2})$ is not as good as $(2, 2)$, but it is better than the outcome $(1, 1)$ that results from the use of the mixed Nash equilibrium.

The set of all outcomes they can achieve in this way is indicated in Figure 7.18(b). This set is the convex hull (Section 5.2.2) of the three Nash equilibrium outcomes: $(0, 3)$, $(3, 0)$ and $(1, 1)$. For example, to achieve the outcome

$$(1, 1\tfrac{3}{4}) = \tfrac{1}{4}(0, 3) + \tfrac{1}{4}(1, 1) + \tfrac{1}{2}(3, 0)\,,$$

the players can jointly watch the fall of two independent fair coins. They play (*dove, hawk*) if the result is *HH*, and the mixed Nash equilibrium if the result is *HT*. Otherwise they play (*hawk, dove*).

Notice that such an agreement is *self-policing* provided there is no opportunity for the players to try and renegotiate the arrangement *after* the fall of the coin has been observed.[39] The observation of HH, for example, establishes (*dove, hawk*) as a focal point. Player I will wish that what had been observed was TH or TT, but will have little choice but to live with his disappointment. Given that HH has been observed, he will anticipate that player II will honor the deal by playing *hawk*. If she does, it is optimal for player I to play *dove*.

7.6.2 Correlated Equilibrium

Even when cheap talk is allowed, it may not always be easy to find a jointly observable random event that takes place after the players' opportunity for discussion is over. It will be even harder to organize things so that Aumann's notion of a *correlated equilibrium* can be employed. However, if the circumstances are favorable, all the outcomes in the set shown in Figure 7.18(c) become available. This set includes the outcome $(1\frac{2}{3}, 1\frac{2}{3})$, which is a definite improvement on the outcome $(1\frac{1}{2}, 1\frac{1}{2})$ obtained by using each of the Nash equilibria (*dove, hawk,*) and (*hawk, dove*) with equal probabilities.

Suppose that, during their cheap-talk discussion, the players are able to hire a referee at negligible cost. Their instructions to the referee are that he is to use a random device to select one of the cells in the payoff table for Chicken according to the probabilities shown in Figure 7.17(b). The referee is *not* to inform either player of the cell that is selected. Instead, he secretly tells player I to use the row in which the cell occurs, and player II to use the column in which the cell occurs. The players' agreement is that they will do whatever the referee tells them to do. If they honor the agreement, the result will be that (*dove, dove*), (*dove, hawk*) and (*hawk, dove*) each get played with probability $\frac{1}{3}$. Thus the agreement corresponds to the outcome

$$(1\tfrac{2}{3}, 1\tfrac{2}{3}) = \tfrac{1}{3}(2,2) + \tfrac{1}{3}(0,3) + \tfrac{1}{3}(3,0)\,.$$

What is important is that this agreement is *self-policing*. It is optimal for each player to honor the agreement.[40] The

[39]This does not mean that attempts at renegotiation by a disappointed player will necessarily succeed in displacing the focal point established by the fall of the coin, but matters then become much less clear-cut.

[40]Provided that renegotiation is not an option, and that there are no opportunities for a player to find out more about the random event organized by the referee than the player is supposed to learn.

notion of a conditional probability introduced in Section 2.1.4 is required to explain why this is true.

For example, in the sample space $\Omega = \{e_1, e_2, e_3, e_4\}$ of Figure 7.17(c), the probability that the event A will occur, conditional on the knowledge that the event C has already occurred, is given by

$$\text{prob}(A|C) = \frac{\text{prob}(A \cap C)}{\text{prob}(C)} = \frac{\text{prob}(e_1)}{\text{prob}(e_1) + \text{prob}(e_2)}.$$

Now suppose that the referee tells player II to use *dove.* She can then calculate

$$\text{prob}(\text{I hears } \textit{dove} \,|\, \text{II hears } \textit{dove}) = \frac{\frac{1}{3}}{\frac{1}{3} + \frac{1}{3}} = \tfrac{1}{2},$$

$$\text{prob}(\text{I hears } \textit{hawk} \,|\, \text{II hears } \textit{dove}) = \frac{\frac{1}{3}}{\frac{1}{3} + \frac{1}{3}} = \tfrac{1}{2}.$$

Her expected payoff from honoring her agreement to play *dove* when told to do so is therefore $\frac{1}{2} \times 2 + \frac{1}{2} \times 0 = 1$. Her expected payoff from cheating on the agreement and playing *hawk* when told to play *dove* is $\frac{1}{2} \times 3 + \frac{1}{2} \times (-1) = 1$. She therefore loses nothing by honoring the deal when told to play *dove.*

What if the referee tells her to play *hawk*? She then calculates

$$\text{prob}(\text{I hears } \textit{dove} \,|\, \text{II hears } \textit{hawk}) = \frac{\frac{1}{3}}{\frac{1}{3} + 0} = 1,$$

$$\text{prob}(\text{I hears } \textit{hawk} \,|\, \text{II hears } \textit{hawk}) = \frac{0}{\frac{1}{3} + 0} = 0.$$

Hence it is again optimal for her to honor the deal by playing *hawk*, because $1 \times 3 + 0 \times (-1) = 3 > 2 = 1 \times 2 + 0 \times 0$.

Because the situation is symmetric, exactly the same considerations show that player II also has nothing to gain by deviating from the agreement. The result is an example of what Aumann calls a correlated equilibrium.

7.7 When Do Nash Equilibria Exist?

Nash equilibria occur where the players' reaction curves cross. So far we have been mostly concerned with what to do if the reaction curves cross several times. But suppose the reaction curves do not cross at all? It is tempting to respond by echoing the author of the little piece of doggerel verse that goes:

Yesterday upon the stair,
I met a man that wasn't there.
He wasn't there again today.
How I wish he'd go away!

However, the fact that Nash equilibria may not exist is a problem that has to be taken seriously. Infinite games often do have no Nash equilibria, even when mixed strategies are admitted. Fortunately, Nash accompanied his definition of Nash equilibrium with a proof that such a problem can never arise in a *finite* game.

Math 7.9 ⟶

Strategies and Payoffs. The proof to be outlined shortly does not only work for finite games. It works for any game in which player I chooses his strategies from a set P and player II chooses her strategies from a set Q, provided that these sets and the payoff functions $\Pi_1 : P \times Q \to \mathbb{R}$ and $\Pi_2 : P \times Q \to \mathbb{R}$ satisfy some simple properties. The proof also works equally well for the case when there are many players. But, as elsewhere in this book, the multi-player case is neglected so as not to complicate the algebra.

The notation introduced above has been encountered previously for finite games in Section 6.4.4. But it will help to review their significance by seeing what these various mathematical objects turn out to be in the case of a 2×2 bimatrix game like those considered in Section 7.1.3.

A mixed strategy $(1-p, p)^\top$ in a 2×2 bimatrix game is determined by naming a real number p in the interval $I = [0, 1]$. In 2×2 bimatrix games, it is therefore possible to take $I = P = Q$. As explained in Section 6.4.4, the payoff functions may be expressed in terms of the players' 2×2 payoff matrices, A and B, as described in Section 6.4.4. If player I chooses p and player II chooses q, then player I's expected payoff is

$$\Pi_1(p, q) = [\,1-p \quad p\,] \begin{bmatrix} a_{11} & a_{12} \\ a_{21} & a_{22} \end{bmatrix} \begin{bmatrix} 1-q \\ q \end{bmatrix} .$$

Thus, for example, in the version of Chicken given in Section 7.1.3,

$$\Pi_1(p, q) = (1-q) + p(1-2q) .$$

This conclusion illustrates the fact that, for each fixed value of q, $\Pi_1(p,q)$ is an affine[41] function of p. Affine functions are not only always continuous, they are also simultaneously convex and concave.

In what follows, the things that will matter about the strategy sets and payoff functions are the following:

- Each player's strategy set must be convex and compact.[42] This is automatically true for the strategy sets P and Q in a finite game.
- Each player's payoff function must be continuous. It must also be concave when the other players' strategies are held constant. The reasons why these conditions are automatically satisfied for a finite game were indicated above.

These properties are required to ensure that the players' best reply correspondences $R_2 : P \to Q$ and $R_1 : Q \to P$ are nicely behaved. Recall that these objects were introduced in Section 7.1.1.

Fixed Points. For a correspondence $R : X \to Y$ to be nicely behaved in the sense that will be needed, it must satisfy the following properties when X and Y are convex, compact sets:

- For each $x \in X$, the set $R(x)$ is nonempty and convex.
- The graph G of $R : X \to Y$ is a closed subset of $X \times Y$.

Figure 7.19(a) illustrates the case when both X and Y are compact intervals. It shows the graph G of a nicely behaved correspondence $R : X \to Y$.

Figure 7.19(b) illustrates a nicely behaved correspondence $F : X \to X$ that maps X back into *itself*. Kakutani's fixed point theorem says that such correspondences necessarily have at least one *fixed point*. This is a point $\tilde{x}$ with the property

$$\tilde{x} \in F(\tilde{x}).$$

[41]As explained in Section 3.4.3, an affine function $f : \mathbb{R} \to \mathbb{R}$ has a straight line graph. Such functions are often said to be "linear" although such a usage is not stricly kosher. The text invites some small confusion on this point. The reason is that the notation in use differs from that of Section 6.4.4. In Section 6.4.4, p does not denote a real number, but the *vector* that appears above as $(1-p,p)^\top$. With the old notation, $\Pi_1(p,q) = p^\top Aq$, and so $\Pi_1(p,q)$ is indeed a linear function of p when q is held fixed.

[42]To be compact, a set in $\mathbb{R}^n$ must be both closed and bounded. To be closed, it must contain all its boundary points. Thus, the compact interval $[0, 1]$ is closed because it contains both its boundary points 0 and 1.

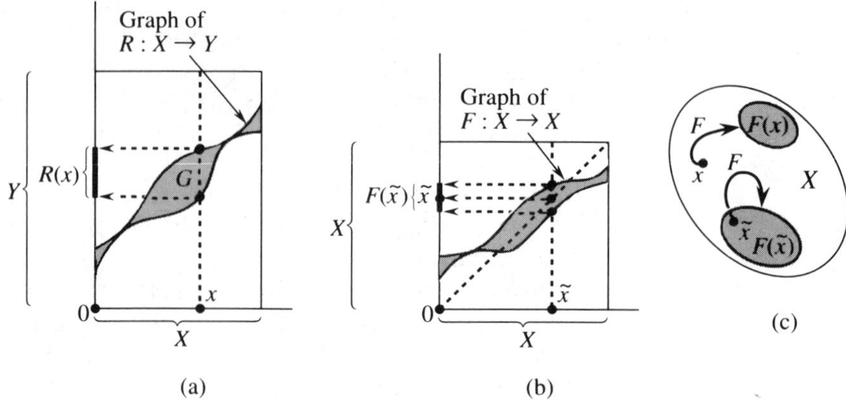

Figure 7.19 Nicely behaved correspondences and fixed points.

As Figure 7.19(b) shows, it is evident that $F : X \to X$ must have a fixed point $\tilde{x}$ when X is a compact interval. However, it is far from evident that this is always true when X is any nonempty, convex, compact set in $\mathbb{R}^n$. But this is what Kakutani's fixed point theorem says. More will appear on this subject in the next section. For the moment, the theorem will be taken for granted. Figure 7.19(c) illustrates the conclusion of Kakutani's theorem in the case when X is a convex, compact set in $\mathbb{R}^2$.

Theorem 7.7.1 (Nash) Every finite game has at least one Nash equilibrium if mixed stategies are allowed.

Proof. The proof is sketched only for the two-player case. The first step is to check that, in a finite game, the players' best reply correspondences $R_2 : P \to Q$ and $R_1 : Q \to P$ are nicely behaved. Properties of strategy sets and payoff functions that guarantee this conclusion are listed above, but the linking algebra is omitted even though it is not very difficult.

The second step in the proof is to construct a correspondence $F : P \times Q \to P \times Q$ to which Kakutani's fixed point theorem can be applied. For each (p, q) in $P \times Q$, $F(p, q)$ is defined as a *set* in $P \times Q$. To be precise,

$$F(p, q) = R_1(q) \times R_2(p)\,.$$

This definition is illustrated in Figure 7.20(a) for the 2×2 bimatrix game case when $P = Q = I$.

The third step is to deduce that F is nicely behaved using the fact that the same is true of R_1 and R_2. Again, the not very difficult algebra is omitted.

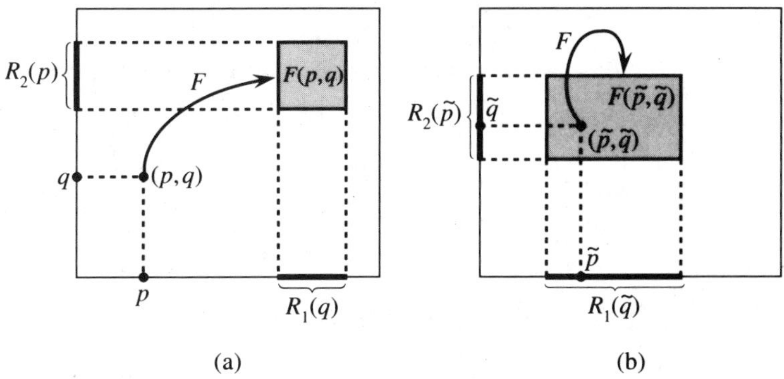

Figure 7.20 The correspondence F in Nash's theorem.

The fourth step is to apply Kakutani's fixed point theorem. This demonstrates the existence of a fixed point $(\tilde{p}, \tilde{q})$ satisfying

$$(\tilde{p}, \tilde{q}) \in F(\tilde{p}, \tilde{q}) = R_1(\tilde{q}) \times R_2(\tilde{p}) \,.$$

The situation is illustrated in Figure 7.20(b).

The final step is to notice that $(\tilde{p}, \tilde{q})$ is a Nash equilibrium. The mixed strategy $\tilde{p}$ is a best reply to $\tilde{q}$ because $\tilde{p} \in R_1(\tilde{q})$. The mixed strategy $\tilde{q}$ is a best reply to $\tilde{p}$ because $\tilde{q} \in R_2(\tilde{p})$. □

7.8 Hexing Brouwer

Fun 7.9 ⟶

Fixed point theorems are widely used in many disciplines. They are particularly important for economists because of their preoccupation with equilibria in economic systems. The proof of Nash's theorem given in the previous section exhibits the archetypal method by means of which the existence of such equilibria may be demonstrated.

Brouwer's fixed point theorem is quoted below. This is the big daddy of the family of such theorems. It is even simpler than Kakutani's theorem.

Theorem 7.8.1 (Brouwer) Suppose that X is a nonempty, compact, convex set in $\mathbb{R}^n$. If the function $f : X \to X$ is continuous, then a fixed point $\tilde{x}$ exists satisfying

$$\tilde{x} = f(\tilde{x}) \,.$$

Usually, Brouwer's theorem is proved by appealing to a combinatorial result called Sperner's lemma. However, David Gale has shown that Sperner's lemma can be replaced by an appeal to the fact that the game of Hex cannot end in a draw, as established in Section 1.6.1. His argument is something of a curiosity from the mathematical point of view, but it is far too much fun to be passed over in a book on game theory, especially since the version of Hex to be used was invented by Nash. Proving Brouwer's theorem will, in any case, allow an opportunity for some brief discussion of compactness and continuity.

Math 7.8.2 ⟶

7.8.1 Continuity and Compactness

Continuity and compactness are profound mathematical ideas, but one does not need to know much about them to avoid being intimidated by the use that is made of them in most economics texts.

Continuity. It first needs to be emphasized that the discussion has now turned to *functions* rather than *correspondences* as in the previous section. In what follows, X and Y will be subsets of $\mathbb{R}^n$ and $\mathbb{R}^m$ respectively. A function $f : X \to Y$ assigns a unique *element* y of the set Y to each element x in the set X. The element y in Y assigned by f to x is denoted by $f(x)$.

Like most really important mathematical concepts, the notion of a function is accompanied by a bewildering array of alternative terminologies and notations. The language an author chooses to use in discussing a function will depend on the use to which the idea is to be put. Here it is perhaps most useful to think of a function as some sort of process that acts on x and changes it into $f(x)$. This way of thinking is often signaled by calling a function an *operator*, a *transformation* or a *mapping*.

For example, in discussing Brouwer's theorem, one may think of X as a tank full of water. A continuous function $f : X \to X$ can then be envisaged as a stirring of the water. After the water has been stirred, a droplet that was located at point x will have been shifted to a new location $f(x)$ in the tank. Brouwer's theorem can then be seen as the far from obvious proposition that, however the water is stirred, there will always be at least one droplet that is returned to its initial location.[43]

---

[43]The metaphor incidentally helps to explain why the statement of Brouwer's theorem is confined to *convex* sets. Imagine a car's inner tube filled with water. The water is now rotated a few degrees about the car's axle. Such a rotation defines a continuous function that clearly has no fixed point. But the space inside an inner tube is not convex because of the hole at its center.

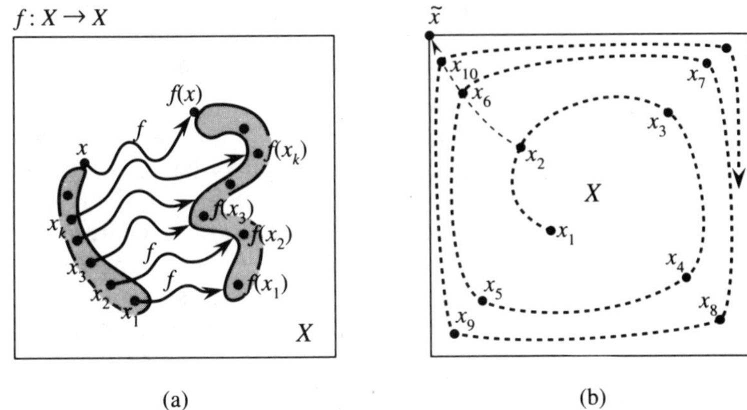

(a) (b)

Figure 7.21 Continuity and compactness.

A function $f : X \to Y$ is *continuous* if it is always true that $x_k \to x$ as $k \to \infty$ implies that $f(x_k) \to f(x)$ as $k \to \infty$.[44] Such a definition forbids discontinuities like that created by Moses when he parted the waters of the Red Sea. If water is shifted around according to a continuous process, sets of droplets that are neighbors at the beginning will still be neighbors at the end. Our definition of continuity focuses on a point x that is assumed to be a neighbor[45] of the set $S = \{x_1, x_2, \ldots\}$. After the water has been stirred, the requirement for continuity can then be interpreted as saying that the droplet of water that started at x should still be a neighbor of the set of droplets of water that were initially located in S. Figure 7.21(a) provides a schematic representation of the idea.

When X and Y are intervals of real numbers, it is easy to tell whether a function $f : X \to Y$ is continuous just by looking at its graph. If the graph can be drawn without having to lift the pencil off the paper, then the function is continuous. Things are less straightforward in the multidimensional case. Fortunately, only the very easy proposition that affine functions are always continuous was needed for Nash's theorem.

[44]To say that $y_k \to y$ as $k \to \infty$ means that the distance $\|y_k - y\|$ between y_k and y can be made as small as one chooses by taking k to be sufficiently large. This may seem simple enough if you have not met the idea before. Be warned, however, that it is an idea that has broken the heart of many aspiring mathematics majors!

[45]It is, in fact a boundary point of the set S. The French call x a *point d'adhérence* of S. This captures nicely the idea that x is somehow "glued" to the set S.

Compactness. It has been explained several times that a compact set in $\mathbb{R}^n$ is one that is closed and bounded. This makes it easy to know when a set is compact and when it is not. But it does not help to explain why compact sets are so useful. The reason is that any sequence of points chosen from a compact set necessarily has a *convergent* subsequence. The importance of this proposition[46] is not easy to appreciate until one has seen it being used repeatedly in the proofs of important theorems. Its use in the next paragraph to prove a stepping stone to Brouwer's theorem is typical.

In proving Brouwer's theorem, it will be shown that, for each natural number k, a vector x_k in the compact set X can be found that satisfies

$$\|x_k - f(x_k)\| < \frac{1}{k}. \tag{7.4}$$

From this, the existence of a fixed point $\tilde{x}$ satisfying $\tilde{x} = f(\tilde{x})$ can be deduced, provided that the function $f : X \to X$ is continuous. How is this done?

The first step is to check that the function $g : X \to \mathbb{R}$ defined by $g(x) = \|x - f(x)\|$ is continuous. If $x_k \to \tilde{x}$ as $k \to \infty$, it then follows that $g(x_k) \to g(\tilde{x})$ as $k \to \infty$. But it is given that $g(x_k) \to 0$ as $k \to \infty$. Thus, it would seem that $g(\tilde{x}) = 0$ and the required result has been obtained.

Unfortunately, there is no guarantee that the sequence $x_1, x_2, x_3, \ldots$ converges. If X were not compact, this would be an obstacle that might well be insuperable. But if X is compact, the possible failure of the sequence to converge, as illustrated in Figure 7.21(b), is something to be taken in one's stride. One simply discards the original sequence and replaces it by a convergent subsequence. In Figure 7.21(b), the convergent subsequence marked begins with the terms $x_2, x_6, x_{10}, \ldots$.

Only two of the many other consequences of the availability of this technique will be mentioned here. The first is the fact that continuous functions necessarily attain a maximum and a minimum value on a compact set. Economists are particularly fond of this conclusion since they are always maximizing or minimizing something or other.

The second fact is that a function is continuous on a compact set if and only if it has a closed graph. This fact is mentioned to provide some intuition about why Kakutani's theorem can be seen as a consequence of Brouwer's. Given

---

[46]Which is a version of a nontrivial theorem attributed jointly to the mathematicians Bolzano and Weierstrass.

a nicely behaved correspondence $F : X \to X$, one can imagine using it to construct a function $f : X \to X$ that satisfies $f(x) \in F(x)$, for each $x \in X$. (The easiest thing to do would be to make $f(x)$ the center of gravity, or centroid, of the nonempty, convex set $F(X)$.) If the function $f : X \to X$ so constructed is continuous, an application of Brouwer's theorem to $f : X \to X$ then demonstrates the existence of an $\tilde{x}$ satisfying $\tilde{x} = f(\tilde{x})$. Since $f(\tilde{x}) \in F(\tilde{x})$, the conclusion of Kakutani's theorem follows immediately. Of course, if the original correspondence $F : X \to X$ were not continuous in some generalized manner that makes sense for correspondences, then there would be no hope that $f : X \to X$ could be continuous. However, nicely behaved correspondences do satisfy such a generalized criterion. In particular, they have closed graphs.

7.8.2 Proof of Brouwer's Theorem

This outline of a proof will be confined to the two-dimensional case. Moreover, the set X will be taken to be the unit square $I^2 = [0, 1] \times [0, 1]$. The second restriction is easily relaxed.[47] Relaxing the first restriction requires extending the argument of Section 1.6.1 to show that n-dimensional Hex cannot end in a draw. This is not difficult but the details are tedious.

The version of Hex invented by Nash is explained in Exercise 1.10.13. The board is reproduced in Figure 7.22(a). The hexagon superimposed on the board is intended to help clarify why Nash's Hex is really the same as the more conventional version studied in Section 1.6. The board of Figure 7.22(b) shows a winning situation for player I in Nash's Hex. His circles label all the nodes on a route linking N and S. Player II's aim is to label all the nodes on a route linking W and E with crosses. Since the game is equivalent to regular Hex, it cannot end in a draw. More than this, if all the nodes on the board are labeled with either a circle or a cross, then either player I must have won or player II must have won.[48]

Pick some $d > 0$. Let O_N be the set of all x in I^2 that f shifts a distance of more than d towards the north. Let X_E

[47]If $g : X \to I^2$ is a homeomorphism, one gets Brouwer's theorem for X by considering the continuous function $F : I^2 \to I^2$ defined by $F = g \circ f \circ g^{-1}$. A homeomorphism is something that preserves the topological properties of a set. Here the relevant topological property of I^2 is that it has no holes. Mathematically, a homeomorphism is a continuous function that has a continuous inverse.

[48]The fact that *both* players cannot have won may be used to prove the Jordan curve theorem, but that is another story!

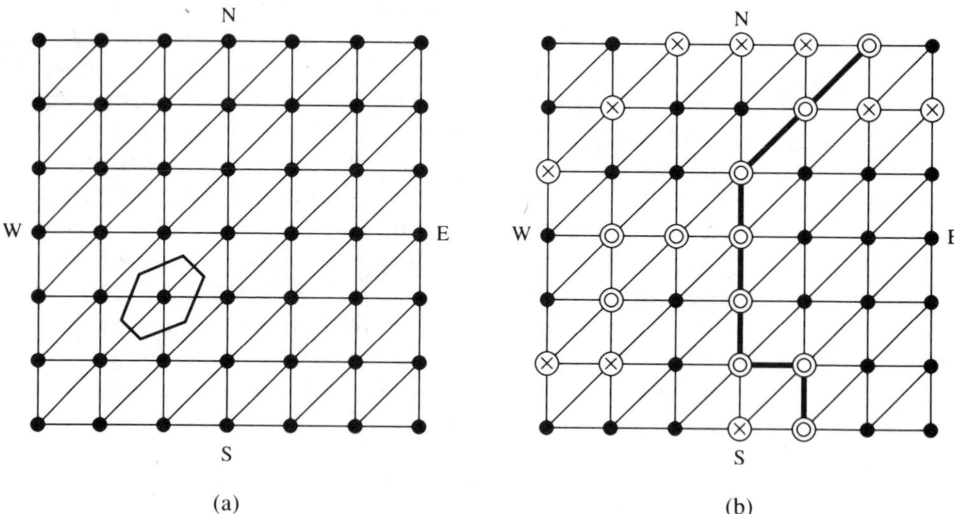

Figure 7.22 Nash's Hex.

be the set of all x in I^2 that f shifts a distance of more than d towards the east. Similarly for the sets O_S and X_W. Figure 7.23(a) shows what these sets might look like. The unshaded set S in the diagram is the set of all x in I^2 that belong to *none* of the four sets O_N, O_S, X_E or X_W.

If S is not an empty set, then there must be at least one x in I^2 that f does not shift very far in any direction. In fact, $f(x)$ must lie within a square of side $2d$ centered at x. The point x is therefore "nearly" fixed. If such an approximate fixed point can be found no matter how small the positive

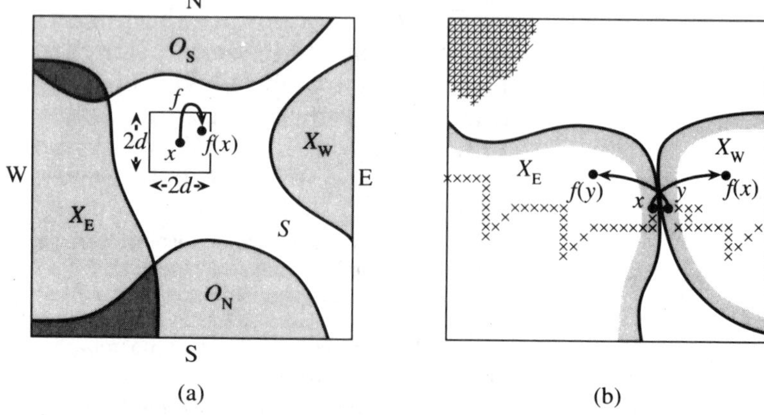

Figure 7.23 Proving Brouwer's theorem.

number d may be, then (7.4) of the previous subsection must always be valid. But we have seen that the compactness of X and the continuity of f then imply the existence of an *exact* fixed point $\tilde{x}$. The problem has therefore been reduced to showing that S is never empty. This will be proved using an argument by contradiction.

Suppose that S were empty for some $d > 0$. Then each x in I^2 would be in one of the two sets $O = O_N \cup O_S$ or $X = X_E \cup X_W$. Cover I^2 with a Hex grid of tiny mesh, as shown in Figure 7.23(b). Each node on this grid is now labeled with a circle or a cross depending on whether it lies in the set O or the set X. (If it lies in both sets, label it at random.) One of the players must have won the Hex position created in this way. Suppose that the winner is player II.

A westernmost node on player II's winning route must be in X_E. An easternmost node on her winning route must be in X_W. Somewhere in between, there must therefore be a pair of adjacent nodes, x and y, one of which lies in X_W and the other in X_E.

This implies that f shifts a point x at least d to the west, and simultaneously shifts the adjacent point y to the east. Since the distance between x and y can be made as small as we please by taking the mesh of the Hex grid sufficiently tiny, this conclusion contradicts the assumption that f is without discontinuities.[49]

7.9 Exercises

1. Find the best reply correspondences for the bimatrix game of Figure 7.7(a). Draw reaction curves in the manner of Figure 7.2. Explain why the game has a unique Nash equilibrium, and determine what it is. Check that it can be located by using the fact that each player's Nash equilibrium strategy must make the other player indifferent between each of the pure strategies that he or she is supposed to use with positive probability.

---

[49] A formal expression of the argument must go to the compactness well again. The text establishes that, for each sufficiently large natural number k, x_k and y_k can be found so that $\|x_k - y_k\| < 1/k$ but $\|f(x_k) - f(y_k)\| \geq d$. If $x_k \to \xi$ as $k \to \infty$, then it follows that $y_k \to \xi$ as $k \to \infty$. Also, since f is continuous, $f(x_k) \to f(\xi)$ as $k \to \infty$, and $f(y_k) \to f(\xi)$ as $k \to \infty$. But this implies that $0 \geq \|f(\xi) - f(\xi)\| \geq d$. The derivation of this contradiction assumes that the sequence $x_1, x_2, x_3, \ldots$ converges; but it may not. However, the compactness of X comes to the rescue. There will always be at least one *subsequence* that does converge.

2. Find the best reply correspondences for the bimatrix games[50] of Figure 7.24. Draw reaction curves in the manner of Figure 7.2. Determine *all* Nash equilibria for both games.

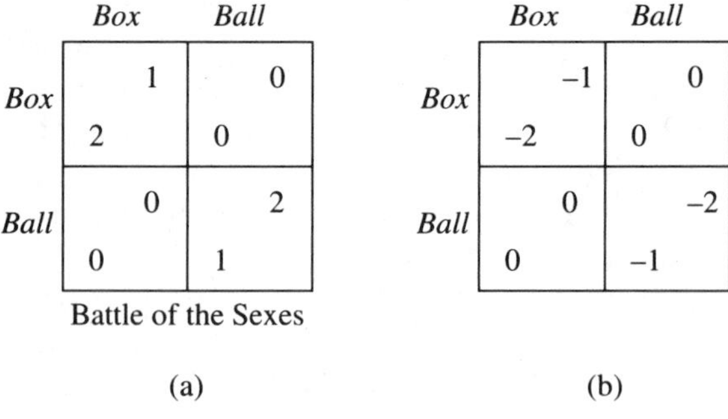

Figure 7.24 Games for Exercise 7.9.2.

3. Show that the best reply correspondence for a bimatrix game remains unchanged if a constant is added to each of player I's payoffs in some column. Show that the same is true if a constant is added to each of player II's payoffs in some row. Use this fact to show that the two versions of Chicken that appear in this chapter necessarily have the same Nash equilibria.[51]

4. Explain why a mixed strategy is a best reply to something if and only if every pure strategy to which it assigns positive probability is a best reply to the same thing.

Math

5. Consider the bimatrix game of Figure 6.22(a). Each mixed strategy $(1-p, p)^\top$ for player I is determined by

---

[50]The first of these is another well-known "toy game" that passes under the name of the Battle of the Sexes. Although it dates from before women's liberation, it does at least treat both players symmetrically. A young married couple on their honeymoon get separated in a large city with which they are unfamiliar. Each has to decide independently of the other where to go in the evening in the hope of getting together again. At breakfast, they ruled out all possible evening entertainments except for a boxing match and a ballet performance. Preferences between these are assumed to fit the traditional stereotypes.

[51]Sometimes it is argued that, once the best reply correspondences for a game have been determined, all the remaining structure of the game can be abandoned as irrelevant. If so, then the fact that one Nash equilibrium may Pareto-dominate the others cannot be a significant fact in selecting an equilibrium. For example, in the Battle of the Sexes of Figure 7.24(a), one may make (box, box) Pareto-dominate $(ball, ball)$ by adding 2 to each of player I's payoffs in column 1 and to each of player II's payoffs in row 1. This does not change the best reply correspondences.

	A	B
A	−4 2 2	0 0 0
B	0 0 0	−8 4 4

Player III chooses A.

	A	B
A	−6 3 3	0 0 0
B	0 0 0	−2 1 1

Player III chooses B.

Figure 7.25 The three-player game for Exercise 7.9.6.

a real number p satisfying $0 \leq p \leq 1$. Each mixed strategy for player II is determined by a pair (q, r) of real numbers q and r satisfying $0 \leq q$, $0 \leq r$ and $q + r \leq 1$.

(a) For each (q, r), find the set $R_1(q, r)$ of all player I's best replies. Sketch the three-dimensional graph $p = R_1(q, r)$. (The plane $7q - 6r = 1$ will be relevant.)

(b) For each p, find the set $R_2(p)$ of all player II's best replies to p. Sketch the three-dimensional graph $(q, r) = R_2(p)$. (The values $p = \frac{1}{2}$ and $p = \frac{2}{3}$ will be relevant.)

(c) Where do the best reply graphs cross? What is the unique Nash equilibrium? Who gets how much when this is played?

(d) The game studied here is the disagreement game of Section 6.9. Who gets how much if the regular Nash bargaining solution is used on the assumption that, if agreement cannot be reached, the Nash equilibrium will be played in the disagreement game?[52]

6. Consider the three-person, zero-sum, simultaneous-move game of Figure 7.25 in which each player chooses between A or B.

(a) Find the two Nash equilibria in pure strategies.

(b) Find the Nash equilibrium in mixed strategies.

(c) Suppose that, before the game, it is common knowledge that players I and II can make a binding agreement on what to play. What agreement do you predict they would make? Would it be in player II's interests to honor the agreement if she were released from her obligation to do so without the other players

[52] As opposed to the assumption of Section 6.9, which is that the players are forced to carry out the threats to which they have earlier made commitments. The assumption of Exercise 7.9.5 makes sense when such commitments are not possible.

becoming aware of this? What if both player I and player II were released from their obligations without player III becoming aware of this?

7. Explain why a Nash equilibrium strategy never calls for a strongly dominated strategy to be used with positive probability. Give an example of a game in which a Nash equilibrium strategy is weakly dominated. Explain why every finite game has at least one Nash equilibrium in which no weakly dominated strategy is used with positive probability.[53]

Math

8. Why is a bimatrix game "symmetric" if the payoff matrices satisfy $A = B^\top$. Prove that a symmetric bimatrix game necessarily has a symmetric Nash equilibrium.

Math

9. A *completely mixed* strategy assigns positive probability to each of a player's pure strategies. If each player's payoff matrix in a bimatrix game is nonsingular, show that the game can have at most one Nash equilibrium in which both players use completely mixed strategies.

Math

10. Let $\Pi_i : P \times Q \to \mathbb{R}$ be player i's payoff function in a bimatrix game in which player I's set of mixed strategies is P and player II's set of mixed strategies is Q. Show that, for any Nash equilibrium $(\tilde{p}, \tilde{q})$,

$$\max_{p\in P}\min_{q\in Q}\Pi_1(p,q) \le \min_{q\in Q}\max_{p\in P}\Pi_1(p,q) \le \Pi_1(\tilde{p},\tilde{q}).$$

What is the corresponding inequality for player II's payoff function? Why do the two inequalities imply that neither player can get less than their security level at a Nash equilibrium? Can you think of a way of seeing why this must be true without calculating at all?

11. Recall from Exercise 7.9.1 that the bimatrix game of Figure 7.7(a) has a unique Nash equilibrium. Show that the play of this Nash equilibrium results in the players getting only their security levels. Show, however, that player I's security strategy is not the same as his Nash equilibrium strategy.

Econ

12. Sketch the cooperative payoff regions for the Prisoners' Dilemma[54] and Chicken given in Figure 7.3. If the players negotiate a binding agreement using the Nash threat

[53]For the last sentence, begin by applying Nash's theorem on the existence of Nash equilibria in finite games to the game obtained by deleting all weakly dominated strategies.

[54]You can cheat by copying this payoff region from Figure 7.14, but do not copy the other cooperative payoff region from Figure 7.18 because this is derived from a different version of Chicken.

theory of Section 6.9, decide in each game which of the outcomes in its cooperative payoff region will be selected. Find the threats that the players will make about the mixed strategy they will use in the game if negotiations break down.

Econon

13. In Section 7.2.1, all firms manufacture the same product at a unit cost of c. Consider instead the case when the goods are *differentiated.* Perhaps player I continues to produce widgets at unit cost c_1, but player II now produces wowsers at unit cost c_2. If q_1 widgets and q_2 wowsers are produced, the respective prices for the two goods are determined by the demand equations $p_1 = M - 2q_1 - q_2$ and $p_2 = M - q_1 - 2q_2$. Adapt Cournot's duopoly model to this new situation, and find:
    (a) The players' reaction curves
    (b) The quantities produced in equilibrium and the prices at which the goods are sold
    (c) The equilibrium profits

Econ

14. Repeat Exercise 7.9.13 with the demand equations $p_1 = M - 2q_1 + q_2$ and $p_2 = M + q_1 - 2q_2$. Comment on how the consumers' view of the products must have changed to yield these new demand equations.

Econ

15. In the Cournot duopoly model of Section 7.2.1, it is common knowledge that both players have unit cost c. Suppose this continues to be true of player II's unit cost, but that player I's unit cost is now known only by himself, so that player II is forced to guess at it when she makes her production decision. Take it to be common knowledge that player II is sure that player I's unit cost is in the set $C = \{c_1, c_2, \ldots, c_k\}$, and that she attaches probability r_i to each alternative c_i. Both players should be assumed to aim at maximizing *expected* profit.

    Model this situation as a game by introducing an initial chance move that selects player I's unit cost. Player I learns the outcome of this chance move, but player II does not. Then the Cournot simultaneous-move game is played.
    (a) Draw a schematic game tree for this situation. Pay particular attention to where the information sets go.
    (b) Explain why a pure strategy q_2 for player II is just a number in the interval $[0, M]$, but a pure strategy for player I is a function $q_1 : C \to [0, M]$.[55]
    (c) If player I will produce $q_1(c_i)$ widgets after learning that his unit cost is c_i, what will player II's expected

[55]Section 7.2.2 is a place in the text where a pure strategy is also a function.

profit be if she produces q_2 widgets? What is her best reply to player I's use of the pure strategy q_1?

(d) If player II produces q_2 widgets, how much would it be optimal for player I to produce *after* learning that his unit cost is c_i. But player I has to choose a pure strategy q_1 *before* learning his unit cost. What is his best reply to player II's use of the pure strategy q_2?

(e) What is a Nash equilibrium in this game? How much does player II produce in equilibrium? How much does player I produce if his unit cost is c_i?

Econon

16. Now consider the n-player Cournot oligopoly game of Section 7.2.1.

(a) Suppose that the game is modified so that each firm has to pay a fixed cost of F regardless of the quantity it produces in order to enter the widget industry. Show that nodody's behavior is modified, provided that the fixed cost F is less than each player's equilibrium profit.

(b) If the fixed cost exceeds the equilibrium profit with n players, then at least one firm would have been better off if it had not entered the widget industry. Assuming there are no barriers to entry other than payment of the fixed entry cost of F, determine the number of firms that will end up producing widgets. What happens as $F \to 0$?

Econ

17. In the Cournot duopoly model of Section 7.2.1, the firms independently decide how many widgets to produce, and then the price at which widgets are sold is determined by the demand equation. The Bertrand model of imperfect competition is quite different. In the Bertrand model, the firms independently select the *price* at which they will sell widgets.[56] The firm that sets the lower price then supplies the entire demand at that price. The firm with the higher price sells no widgets at all.[57] If everything else is as in Section 7.2.1, prove that the only Nash equilibrium requires both firms to sell widgets at the unit cost c of production. What will their profits then be? How is this

[56]A firm is *not* allowed to lower its price if it finds it is getting no customers. This is seldom a realistic assumption. Nor does it become more realistic if the model is explained in terms of the players having "Bertrand conjectures". With this story, the players could change prices if they wished, but each firm conjectures that a change in its own price will not lead the other firm to change its price.

[57]Assume that the demand is divided equally among the firms if they set the same price.

conclusion related to perfect competition? How do things change if the firms do not have the same unit cost?

Econon

Econ

18. Exercises 7.9.13 and 7.9.14 are about the Cournot duopoly model with differentiated products. Repeat these exercises for the case of a Bertrand duopoly.

Econ

19. Widget consumers are located with uniform density[58] ρ along a single street of length l. Each consumer has a need for at most one widget. A consumer will buy the widget he needs from whatever source costs him the least.[59] In counting costs he considers not only the price at which a widget is sold at an outlet, but his transportation expenses. It costs a consumer $\$tx^2$ to travel a distance x and back again.

Two widget firms are to open outlets in the street. Each firm independently decides on where to locate its outlet. After their outlets have been opened, they engage in Bertrand competition. They simultaneously announce the prices at which they will trade and then meet whatever demand is forthcoming at that price. The unit cost to a firm is always $\$c$. There are no fixed costs.

(a) Suppose that player I locates his outlet a distance x from the west end of the street and the second player locates her outlet a distance X from the east end of the street. If player II now sets price P, determine the number of customers player I will get if he sets price p. What will his profit be?

(b) After x and X have been chosen, the subgame that ensues is a simultaneous-move game in which the pure strategies for players I and II are their prices p and P. Find the unique Nash equilibrium of this subgame for all values of x and X. What profits will the players get if this Nash equilibrium is played?

(c) Now consider the simultaneous-move game in which the locations x and X are chosen. Take for granted that a Nash equilibrium will be played in the price-fixing game that follows. What is the unique Nash equilibrium?

(d) Comment on the relevance of the idea of a subgame-perfect equilibrium to the preceding analysis.

(e) Where do the firms locate in equilibrium? What prices do they set? What are their profits?

---

[58]This means that there are ρx consumers in any segment of the street of length x.

[59]His reservation price for a widget is so high that it need not be considered.

Econ

20. In the story of Section 7.2.1, all consumers pay the same price for widgets. However, sometimes a firm is able to discriminate among customers and to charge some a higher price than others. A perfectly discriminating[60] monopolist is one who is able to sell each widget at the maximum price its purchaser would be willing to pay to get it.

    Suppose that $\$A$ is spent on buying widgets when all widgets are sold at price $\$P$. The *consumer surplus* is then $\$(B - A)$, where $\$B$ is the amount that would be spent on buying widgets if a perfectly discriminating monopolist were to sell the same widgets to the same consumers. If the demand equation is $p = M - q$, explain why the consumer surplus is the area trapped between the lines $q = 0$, $p = P$ and $p + q = M$. Check that the values given for consumer surpluses in Sections 7.2.1 and 7.2.2 are correct.

21. Analyze the leader-follower game of Figure 7.7(a) as in Section 7.2.2, except with player II as the leader and player I as the follower. What is the "Stackelberg equilibrium"?

Econ

22. The Nash Demand Game of Section 7.4 is a simultaneous-move game. What would the outcome be if player I were to act as a leader by moving first, and player II were to act as a follower by moving second. How is this situation related to the Ultimatum Game of Section 5.8.1?

Econ

23. Analyze the n-player oligopoly model of Section 7.2.1 again, but without the assumption that the players move simultaneously. Assume instead that they play follow-the-leader. Player I chooses the quantity q_1 that he will produce first. Player II chooses her quantity q_2 second, after having observed player I's choice. Then player III chooses q_3, after having observed q_1 and q_2. And so on.

    What is a "Stackelberg equilibrium" for this game. Show that the equilibrium outcome approaches perfect competition as $n \to \infty$.

Econ

24. Analyze the n-player oligopoly model of Section 7.2.1 again, but without the assumption that the players all move simultaneously. Assume instead that player I chooses the quantity q_1 first. After observing his choice, all the remaining players then choose how much to produce simultaneously. What happens as $n \to \infty$?

[60] This is "first degree" price discrimination. Economists also distinguish second and third degrees.

Econ

25. In the location game of Exercise 7.9.19, show that the conclusion is unchanged if one firm acts as a leader by locating first, provided that everything else remains the same.

Econ

26. Each of n farmers can costlessly produce as much wheat as he chooses. Suppose that the kth farmer produces W_k, so that the total amount of wheat produced is $W = W_1 + W_2 + \cdots + W_n$. The price p at which wheat sells is then determined by the demand equation $p = e^{-W}$.
   (a) Show that the strategy of producing one unit of wheat strongly dominates all of a profit-maximizing farmer's other strategies. Check that the use of this strategy yields a profit of e^{-n} for a farmer.
   (b) Explain why the best of all agreements that treat each farmer equally requires each to produce only $1/n$ units of wheat. Check that a farmer's profit would then be $1/en$. Why would such an agreement need to be binding for it to be honored by profit-maximizing farmers?
   (c) Confirm that xe^{-x} is largest when $x = 1$. Deduce that all the farmers would make a larger profit if they all honored the agreement rather than each producing one unit and so flooding the market.
   (d) Political scientists refer to such situations as "tragedies of the commons".[61] Why is such an n-player game a generalization of the Prisoners' Dilemma?

27. A problem that political scientists see as being related to the "tragedy of the commons" discussed in Exercise 7.9.26 concerns the reasons why people vote. Suppose that 100 people live in a village of whom 51 support the conservative candidate and 49 support the liberal candidate. Villagers get a payoff of $+10$ if their candidate gets elected, and a payoff of -10 if the opposition candidate gets elected. But voting is a nuisance that costs voters one util. Those who stay at home and do not vote evade this cost, but are rewarded or punished just the same as those who shoulder the cost of voting.
   (a) Why is it not a Nash equilibrium for everybody to vote?
   (b) Why is it not a Nash equilibrium for nobody to vote?

[61] The usual story concerns peasants who can each put as many animals as they choose to graze on a piece of land they hold in common. The result is that the common is ruined through overgrazing. Of course, in Exercise 7.9.26, it is no tragedy for the consumer that the market is flooded with wheat.

(c) Find a Nash equilibrium in which all conservatives use the same strategy and all liberals use the same strategy.[62] What is the expected number of villagers who will vote when this Nash equilibrium is used?

28. In Victorian England, a lady and a gentleman approach a newfangled revolving door. In the variant of Chicken with which they are confronted, there are two pure strategy Nash equilibria: the lady can wait for the gentleman to go first, or the gentleman can wait for the lady. Which of these equilibria is focal?

29. The Battle of the Sexes is given in Figure 7.24(a).
   (a) Sketch a diagram that shows the cooperative payoff region for the Battle of the Sexes on the assumption that neither free disposal nor transferable utility is admitted. Verify that the outcome $(\frac{3}{2}, \frac{3}{2})$ is feasible when binding pre-play agreements are possible.
   (b) Sketch a diagram that shows the convex hull of the Nash equilibria for the Battle of the Sexes. What non-binding agreement made during pre-play cheap talk could lead to the outcome $(\frac{3}{2}, \frac{3}{2})$?
   (c) Sketch a diagram that shows the non-cooperative payoff region for the Battle of the Sexes. This is the set of outcomes that can result when the players make their choices of strategy completely independently. Pre-play coordination is therefore disbarred.[63] Confirm that the non-cooperative payoff region is not convex. If both players independently use the mixed strategy that assigns probability $\frac{1}{2}$ to each pure strategy, the resulting outcome is $(\frac{3}{4}, \frac{3}{4})$. Show that this outcome is a Pareto-efficient point of the non-cooperative payoff region. In particular, the point $(\frac{3}{2}, \frac{3}{2})$ is not available as an outcome when the players are forced to choose independently.
   (d) Suppose that the players have no opportunity for pre-play negotiation in the Battle of the Sexes, but that

[62]If an equal number of liberals and conservative turn out to vote, the election is decided by tossing a fair coin.

[63]This is harder than it looks at first sight. One way of proceeding is to consider first the outcomes that are possible if player I uses the mixed strategy $(1-p,p)^\top$. When $p=0$, this is the line segment joining $(2,1)$ and $(0,0)$. When $p=1$, it is the line segment joining $(0,0)$ and $(1,2)$. When $p=\frac{1}{2}$, it is the line segment joining $a=\frac{1}{2}(2,1)+\frac{1}{2}(0,0)$ and $b=\frac{1}{2}(0,0)+\frac{1}{2}(1,2)$. The point a is located halfway between $(2,1)$ and $(0,0)$. The point b is located halfway between $(0,0)$ and $(1,2)$. After such line segments have been drawn for $p=0, \frac{1}{10}, \frac{2}{10}, \ldots, 1$, the shape of the non-cooperative payoff region will be apparent. The use of graph paper is recommended!

the same convention for selecting an equilibrium as considered in Exercise 7.9.28 is in force. What will be the outcome?

(e) Suppose that the players not only have no opportunity for pre-play negotiation in the Battle of the Sexes, but that no convention is available to break the symmetry. Why does this leave only the mixed Nash equilibrium as a possible recommendation for a game theory book to make? The mixed Nash equilibrium calls for player I to use his first pure strategy with probability $\frac{2}{3}$ and for player II to use her second pure strategy with the same probability. Confirm that the resulting outcome is $(\frac{2}{3}, \frac{2}{3})$.

(f) Show that each player's security level in the Battle of the Sexes is $\frac{2}{3}$, but that the players' security strategies are not the same as their mixed equilibrium strategies. Player I's security strategy calls for him to use his first pure strategy with probability $\frac{1}{3}$ and player II's security strategy calls for her to play her second pure strategy with probability $\frac{1}{3}$.

30. One might call the game of Figure 7.24(b) Australian Battle of the Sexes because its cooperative and noncooperative payoff regions are "upside-down" versions of those for the Battle of the Sexes. For each of the questions posed for the Battle of the Sexes in Exercise 7.9.29, answer an analogous question for its Australian cousin.

31. Suppose that, before the Battle of the Sexes is played, player I has the opportunity to make a commitment to one of his pure strategies. If he makes such a commitment, he *must* honor the commitment when the Battle of the Sexes is played later. If he chooses not to make a commitment, the Battle of the Sexes is played in the regular way. Draw the extensive form of a game in which this commitment opportunity is modeled as an opening move by player I. Assume that player II knows what choice player I made at the opening move when the Battle of the Sexes is played later. Analyze the game you have constructed.

How would your extensive form differ if player II did not know what player I chose at his opening move? Would this affect your analysis?

32. Suppose that the payoffs in the Battle of the Sexes of Figure 7.24(a) are dollar amounts, and that both players are risk neutral in money. Before the Battle of the Sexes is played, player I first gets the opportunity to

threaten player II. He may commit himself to the play of any mixed strategy when the Battle of the Sexes is played, unless player II pays him a specified amount of money. Player II may then pay up or refuse. If she refuses, player I *must* carry out his threat. If she pays up, he has no further opportunity for blackmail, but may commit himself to one of his pure strategies in the Battle of the Sexes, as in Exercise 7.9.31. What will player I threaten[64] and how much will he demand? Why will player II pay up?

Phil 33. When the Battle of the Sexes is played tacitly without a symmetry-breaking convention, a game theory book that recommends anything has no choice but to recommend the mixed equilibrium. In Exercise 7.9.29, it was noted that both players get only their security levels when this mixed equilibrium is used. But they can *guarantee* their security levels by deviating from the book's advice and playing their security strategies. One might counter this objection by observing that a player gets more with the mixed equilibrium strategy than with the security strategy if the opponent switches to the security strategy. Check that this is true for the Battle of the Sexes, but false for the Australian version of Exercise 7.9.30.

Comment on the soundness of a recommendation in favor of the mixed equilibrium in such circumstances. Review Exercise 7.9.11 and then comment on the proposition that, when a bimatrix game has only one Nash equilibrium, this *must* be what a game theory book should recommend that the players use.[65]

Phil 34. Player I and player II are risk neutral in money. They are to play a version of the Battle of the Sexes given in Figure 7.24(a) in which the payoffs are dollar amounts, and each 2 is replaced by a 4. The only pre-play interaction allowed is for player I to produce two dollars from his pocket, which he may then burn or not burn as he chooses. Player II passively watches this display. Figure 7.26(a) is a schematic for the enlarged game in which this pre-play action is incorporated as a formal move.

(a) Write down the 4×4 strategic form of the enlarged game.

[64]If player II is defiant, the worst possible consequence is that she gets her security level. Why is Von Neumann's minimax theorem relevant to this conclusion?

[65]As observed in Section 7.1.4, one cannot always offer advice that a player will find very useful.

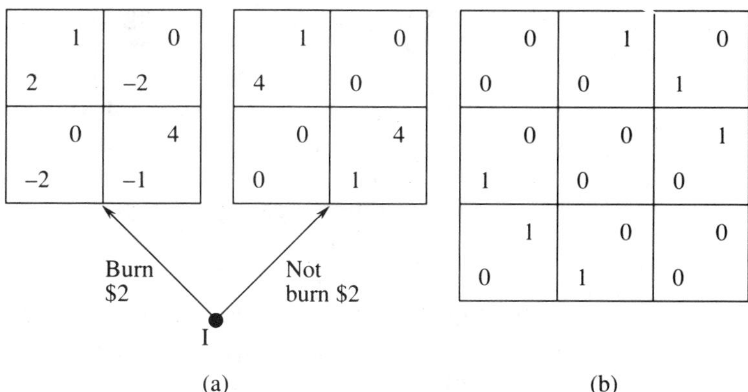

Figure 7.26 The games for Exercises 7.9.34 and 7.9.40.

(b) Find all Nash equilibia in pure stategies. Which of these are subgame-perfect equilibria?

(c) Using the method of successive deletion of weakly and strongly dominated strategies, reduce the equilibria to just one.[66]

(d) The remaining equilibrium should call on player I *not* to burn the money, and for the equilibrium most favorable to him to be played in the Battle of the Sexes subgame that ensues. It is often argued that equilibria that do not survive the successive deletion of dominated strategies should never be selected. Is your confidence in such a principle shaken by this example?[67]

Econ

35. Section 7.5.5 discusses collusive behavior in the Cournot Duopoly Game.

---

[66] Do not be disturbed if you delete a subgame-perfect equilibrium. This is a game of imperfect information because the players move simultaneously in the Battle of the Sexes subgames.

[67] The example exhibits the controversial idea of "forwards induction" proposed by Kohlberg and Mertens, in which a player's actions in the early stages of the game are seen as "signaling" the equilibrium the player is aiming at. In evaluating the equilibrium selection argument offered in the example, ask yourself what you would believe about an opponent who ostentatiously burnt two dollars before sitting down to play the Battle of the Sexes with you. There are situations in which it might pay him to advertise his contempt for money, but here such behavior cannot be rational unless the equilibrium selection argument is invalid. However, during the iterated deletion of dominated strategies used to defend the equilibrium selected, we have to proceed as though this display of irrationality were irrelevant. As we know from Exercise 4.8.21, justifying such deletions requires quite strong assumptions about what the players know about each other's rationality.

(a) Suppose that binding agreements can be made, and the alternative to an agreement is that the noncollusive Cournot Duopoly Game is played. What is the bargaining set (Section 5.4.3) for the bargaining problem that then arises?
(b) Suppose that player I can be relied upon to keep any agreement reached, but that player II will fink on any deal if she has an incentive to do so. What Pareto-efficient deal is then incentive-compatible?

Econon

36. Suppose that the firms in the version of the Cournot Duopoly Game given in Exercise 7.9.13 attempt to collude.
(a) What is the cooperative payoff region? (Assume "transferable utility" and free disposal.)
(b) If binding agreements are possible, determine the profit pair that will result if the Nash bargaining solution with bargaining powers $\alpha = \frac{1}{3}$ and $\beta = \frac{2}{3}$ is used, and the disagreement point d is placed at the profit pair that results when the unique Nash equilibrium of the noncollusive game is played. What will each firm's output be under this collusive arrangement?
(c) If the agreement were not binding on player I, what would he do?

Econ

37. Suppose that binding threats and agreements are possible in the collusive version of a Cournot duopoly studied in Section 7.5.5. It is then obvious that, if the players use the Nash threat theory described in Section 6.9, then their collusive arrangement will be that each produces half a monopolist's output. Why is this? It is not so obvious what threats the firms will make when the negotiations begin.
(a) If the regular Nash bargaining solution is used in Figure 7.16(a) with the disagreement point $d = (\pi_1, \pi_2)$, what agreement will be reached?
(b) Deduce that the choice of threats in Nash's threat theory reduces to a zero-sum game in which player I seeks to maximize $\pi_1 - \pi_2$.
(c) Express $\pi_1 - \pi_2$ in terms of the outputs q_1 and q_2. Hence compute player I's security level in the zero-sum game.
(d) Explain why each player will open the negotiations by threatening to produce the monopoly output if the negotiations should fail.

38. Section 7.6.2 discusses the idea of a correlated equilibrium for the variant of Chicken given in Figure 7.17(a).

Suppose that the matrix of Figure 7.17(b) is replaced by a matrix whose entries are the probabilities p_{ij}. If the story of Section 7.6.2 is repeated with this new matrix of probabilities, show that the result is a correlated equilibrium if and only if each probability on the main diagonal of the new matrix exceeds neither of the probabilities off the main diagonal.

Math

39. Exercise 7.9.38 characterizes all correlated equilibria for the variant of Chicken given in Figure 7.17(a). Express the four inequalities obtained in Exercise 7.9.38 in terms of p_{11}, p_{12} and p_{21} using the fact that probabilities must sum to one. Write down the further inequalities that these three quantities must satisfy simply because, together with p_{22}, they form a system of probabilities. The system of inequalities you have constructed defines a convex set in $\mathbb{R}^3$. Find the extreme points of this set.

40. Show that the bimatrix game of Figure 7.26(b) has a unique Nash equilibrium in which both players use each pure strategy with probability $\frac{1}{3}$. Show that the players get more if they are able to use a correlated equilibrium in which each cell off the main diagonal is assigned a probability of $\frac{1}{6}$. Draw the cooperative payoff region (Section 5.3) for the game. Explain why the correlated equilibrium outcome you have found is a Pareto-efficient point of this region.

Math

41. A firm's output consists of a commodity bundle chosen from a compact and strictly convex production set Y in $\mathbb{R}^n$. The output bundle is chosen to maximize profit $p^\top y$, where p is the price vector.[68] Because Y is *strictly* convex, there is always a unique profit-maximizing ouput $y = s(p)$ for each price vector p. The function $s : \mathbb{R}^n_+ \to Y$ is then the firm's *supply function*. Answer the parenthetical questions in the following "proof" that the supply function is continuous, and point to a flaw in the argument. What can be done to patch up the proof?[69]

    Let $p_k \to p$ as $k \to \infty$. Write $y_k = s(p_k)$. Then, for any z in Y, $p_k{}^\top z \leq p_k{}^\top y_k$. (Why?) If $y_k \to y$ as $k \to \infty$, it follows that, for any z in Y, $p^\top z \leq p^\top y$. (Why?) Hence $y = s(p)$. (Why?) Thus, $s(p_k) \to s(p)$ as $k \to \infty$, and so s is continuous.

[68] Some of the coordinates of y may be negative, and so represent *inputs.* It is not therefore being assumed that production is costless.

[69] A sequence $y_1, y_2, y_3, \ldots$ of points in a compact set Y converges to y if and only if all its convergent subsequences converge to y. (*Proof?*)

Math

42. The equilibria of economic theory are not always the equilibria of some game. It may be, for example, that the ith player's strategy set is S_i, but that some constraint prevents a free choice from all the strategies in S_i. Often the subset T_i to which the player is confined depends on the vector s of *all* the players' choices.[70] That is, $T_i = G_i(s)$, where $G_i : S_1 \times S_2 \times \cdots \times S_n \to S_i$.
   (a) Use Kakutani's fixed point theorem to outline a proof that there is at least one $\tilde{s}$ for which $\tilde{s}_i \in G_i(\tilde{s})$ $(i = 1, 2, \ldots, n)$. List the mathematical assumptions that your proof takes for granted.
   (b) Soup up your argument to obtain a version of Debreu's "social equilibrium theorem". This asserts that $\tilde{s}$ can be found for which it is not only true that (a) holds, but $\tilde{s}_i$ is player i's *optimal* choice from the set $G_i(\tilde{s})$.

[70] Such a situation arises, for example, in a simple exchange economy. Economic activity in such an economy is restricted to trading of the players' initial endowments of goods. Each player can be envisaged as selling his or her endowment at the going prices. The sum realized then imposes a *budget constraint* on what the player can then buy with the money. However, the going prices are determined by supply and demand in the market as a whole. That is, they depend on how *everybody* chooses to spend their money. What each player *can* choose is therefore a function of what everybody actually *does* choose.

CHAPTER

8

Repeating Yourself

8.1 Reciprocity

Game theorists speak of *one-shot* games when they wish to emphasize that the recommendation they are offering applies only when the game is to be played once and once only. But people seldom play a game just once in real life. Games usually get played over and over again. Repeated games are therefore of much practical importance.

Only one of many the issues that arise in the study of repeated games will receive any emphasis in this chapter.[1] As we learned in Chapter 7, rational players have to forgo the full fruits of cooperation in one-shot games like the Prisoners' Dilemma, unless some external means of *enforcing* their pre-play agreements is available. One might say that rational players need a policeman to help them cooperate in one-shot games. However, this difficulty often disappears when the game is repeated many times. Cooperative agreements may then become available as *equilibrium* outcomes in the enlarged situation.

The reason is simple. Without a policeman, pre-play promises may be broken with impunity in a one-shot game. But, if player I breaks his word in a *repeated* game, then player II has the opportunity to punish him later for his bad behavior. Sometimes, it is enough if player II simply plans to withdraw from their previous understanding. In such circumstances, player I will choose not to fink on their deal, because the prospective future benefits from continuing his relationship with player II outweigh the momentary advantage to be obtained from finking. If player II also sees it as being in her interest to stay honest for the same reason, then the two players will not need any help in getting along together. No policeman is necessary, because each player polices the behavior of the other.

Everybody understands that such *self-policing* or *incentive-compatible* arrangements are important in ordinary life. The essence of what is involved is summarized in the phrase, "I'll scratch your back if you'll scratch mine". People provide a service to others expecting to get something in return. If the service a person provides is *not* reciprocated to his or her satisfaction, then the service will be withdrawn. Sometimes, some disservice will be offered instead. Many authors believe that this type of *reciprocity* is the glue that holds human

[1]Reputation is one of the important issues that is neglected. It may be stupid to act tough in a one-shot game, but very sensible to act tough if the situation is to be repeated. The reason is that a reputation for toughness may be a very valuable asset in future play.

societies together. It is certainly true that many more ongoing relationships between human beings are buttressed by a reciprocity understanding than is generally acknowledged. We like to tell ourselves that it is from the goodness of our hearts that we help our neighbors. It is no accident, however, that what our hearts commend often turns out to coincide with what our heads would command if given the chance.

We all maintain a complex network of reciprocal arrangements with those around us, but, as with riding bicycles, the fact that we do it does not imply that we understand *how* we do it. What game theory has to offer is some insight into the nuts-and-bolts of self-policing agreements. How do they work? Why do they survive? What outcomes can be supported in such a way?

8.2 Repeating a Zero-Sum Game

When investigating any new problem, it is nearly always best to look at very simple cases first. We therefore begin the study of repeated games by seeing what happens when a two-player, zero-sum game is played twice. This means that the search for insight into the nature of self-policing agreements in repeated games will have to wait for a short while. There is no scope at all for agreements of any type between two players in a zero-sum situation because the players' interests are diametrically opposed. However, this fact leaves us free to concentrate on the technical problems raised by the study of repeated games. It is particularly important not to get confused about what pure strategies look like in repeated games.

Consider the simple two-player, zero-sum game Z of Figure 8.1(a). Recall that the matrix shows only player I's payoffs. The players' security strategies in the game are $(1-p,p)^\top = (\frac{1}{2},\frac{1}{2})^\top$ and $(1-q,q)^\top = (\frac{1}{2},\frac{1}{2})^\top$. The value of the game is $v = \frac{1}{2}$.

Suppose that the game Z is played *twice* by the same players. Then Z is said to be the *stage-game* of a repeated[2] game Z^2. In this section, it will be assumed that the payoffs in the repeated game Z^2 are obtained simply by summing the payoffs in each stage-game. For example, if the strategy pair (s_1,t_2) is used at the first stage and the strategy pair (s_2,t_2) is used at the second stage, then player I is assumed to get $0+1=1$ in the repeated game Z^2.

[2]If the stage-games are not all the same, one says *supergame* instead.

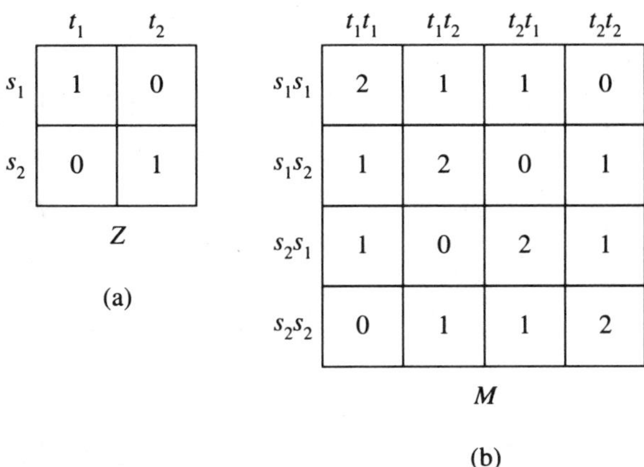

Figure 8.1 Two zero-sum games.

It is tempting, but badly mistaken, to think that the strategic form of Z^2 can be identified with the matrix game M of Figure 8.1(b). If $0 \leq p \leq \frac{1}{2}$, it is easy to check that the mixed strategy $(\frac{1}{2} - p, p, p, \frac{1}{2} - p)^\top$ guarantees an expected payoff of $+1$ to player I in the game with matrix M. Similarly, $(\frac{1}{2} - q, q, q, \frac{1}{2} - q)^\top$ guarantees -1 to player II, provided $0 \leq q \leq \frac{1}{2}$. Thus, for example, $(0, \frac{1}{2}, \frac{1}{2}, 0)^\top$ is a security strategy for player I in M.

Suppose, however, that player I were to toss a fair coin to decide which of s_1s_2 and s_2s_1 to play. Assume that player II knows or guesses that this is what player I is doing. Then, if player I uses s_i at stage one, player II should use t_i at stage two. She will then get 0 at the second stage. Her expected payoff will then be $-\frac{1}{2} + 0 = -\frac{1}{2}$. Thus, player I gets only $+\frac{1}{2}$, which is less than the supposedly secure $+1$.

The reason for this anomaly is that the pure strategies for M ignore the fact that players will wish to make their behavior at the second stage *contingent* on what happened at the first stage. A pure strategy for Z^2 is therefore more complicated than for M.

Let $S = \{s_1, s_2\}$ be the set of pure strategies for player I in the stage-game Z. These pure strategies will be called *actions* so as not to confuse them with pure strategies in Z^2. The set of actions for player II in the stage-game Z is $T = \{t_1, t_2\}$. At the second stage, the players will remember what happened at the first stage. Four possible *histories* of the game must therefore be considered. These are the four elements of the set $H = S \times T$. For example, the history $h_{12} = (s_1, t_2)$ means that player I used action s_1 and player II used action t_2 at the first stage.

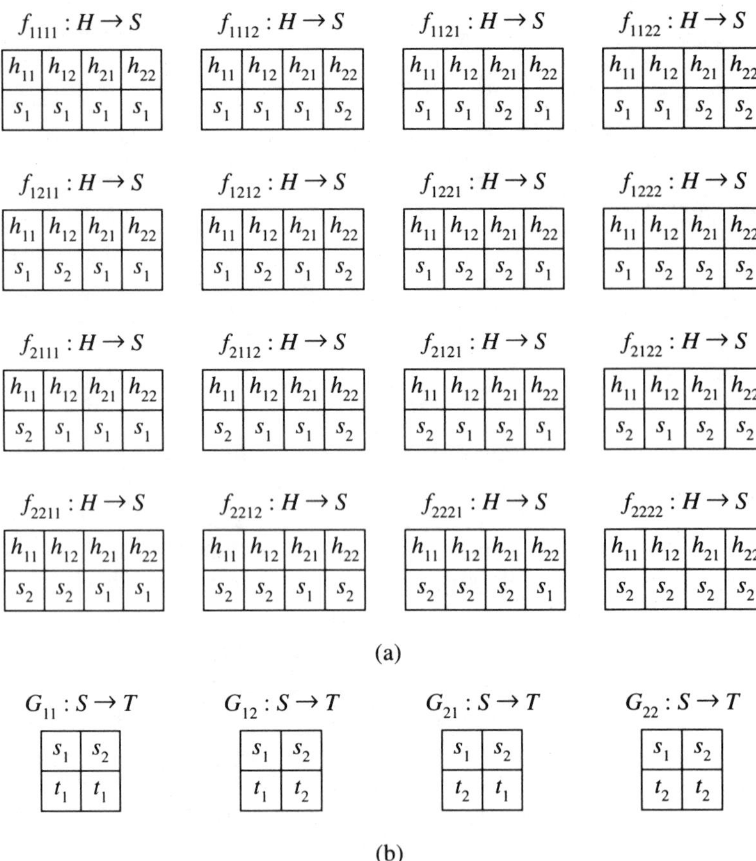

Figure 8.2 Some functions.

A pure strategy for player I in Z^2 is a pair (s, f) in which s is an action in S to be used at the first stage, and $f : H \to S$ is a *function*. If player II uses action t at the first stage, then the history of the game at the second stage will be $h = (s, t)$, and so player I will take action $f(h) = f(s, t)$ at the second stage.

There are 16 possible functions $f : H \to S$. These are shown as tables in Figure 8.2(a). For example, $f_{1212}(h_{21}) = s_1$ and $f_{2221}(h_{11}) = s_2$. Since player I has two choices for s and 16 choices for f, he has 2×16 choices in Z^2. The situation for player II is the same, and so the strategic form of Z^2 is represented by a 32×32 matrix. It is therefore much more complicated than the 4×4 matrix of the game M.

The 32×32 strategic form of the repeated game Z^2 is shown in Figure 8.3(a). This is not so horrendous as it appears at first, because each row and column is repeated four

<table>
<tr><th></th><th>(t_1, g_{1111})</th><th>(t_1, g_{1112})</th><th>(t_1, g_{1121})</th><th>(t_1, g_{1122})</th><th>(t_1, g_{1211})</th><th>(t_1, g_{1212})</th><th>(t_1, g_{1221})</th><th>(t_1, g_{1222})</th><th>(t_1, g_{2111})</th><th>(t_1, g_{2112})</th><th>(t_1, g_{2121})</th><th>(t_1, g_{2122})</th><th>(t_1, g_{2211})</th><th>(t_1, g_{2212})</th><th>(t_1, g_{2221})</th><th>(t_1, g_{2222})</th><th>(t_2, g_{1111})</th><th>(t_2, g_{1112})</th><th>(t_2, g_{1121})</th><th>(t_2, g_{1122})</th><th>(t_2, g_{1211})</th><th>(t_2, g_{1212})</th><th>(t_2, g_{1221})</th><th>(t_2, g_{1222})</th><th>(t_2, g_{2111})</th><th>(t_2, g_{2112})</th><th>(t_2, g_{2121})</th><th>(t_2, g_{2122})</th><th>(t_2, g_{2211})</th><th>(t_2, g_{2212})</th><th>(t_2, g_{2221})</th><th>(t_2, g_{2222})</th></tr>
<tr><td>(s_1, f_{1111})</td><td colspan="8" rowspan="8">2</td><td colspan="8" rowspan="8">1</td><td colspan="4" rowspan="4">1</td><td colspan="4" rowspan="4">0</td><td colspan="4" rowspan="4">1</td><td colspan="4" rowspan="4">0</td></tr>
<tr><td>(s_1, f_{1112})</td></tr>
<tr><td>(s_1, f_{1121})</td></tr>
<tr><td>(s_1, f_{1122})</td></tr>
<tr><td>(s_1, f_{1211})</td><td colspan="4" rowspan="4">0</td><td colspan="4" rowspan="4">1</td><td colspan="4" rowspan="4">0</td><td colspan="4" rowspan="4">1</td></tr>
<tr><td>(s_1, f_{1212})</td></tr>
<tr><td>(s_1, f_{1221})</td></tr>
<tr><td>(s_1, f_{1222})</td></tr>
<tr><td>(s_1, f_{2111})</td><td colspan="8" rowspan="8">1</td><td colspan="8" rowspan="8">2</td><td colspan="4" rowspan="4">1</td><td colspan="4" rowspan="4">0</td><td colspan="4" rowspan="4">1</td><td colspan="4" rowspan="4">0</td></tr>
<tr><td>(s_1, f_{2112})</td></tr>
<tr><td>(s_1, f_{2121})</td></tr>
<tr><td>(s_1, f_{2122})</td></tr>
<tr><td>(s_1, f_{2211})</td><td colspan="4" rowspan="4">0</td><td colspan="4" rowspan="4">1</td><td colspan="4" rowspan="4">0</td><td colspan="4" rowspan="4">1</td></tr>
<tr><td>(s_1, f_{2212})</td></tr>
<tr><td>(s_1, f_{2221})</td></tr>
<tr><td>(s_1, f_{2222})</td></tr>
<tr><td>(s_2, f_{1111})</td><td colspan="2" rowspan="2">1</td><td colspan="2" rowspan="2">0</td><td colspan="2" rowspan="2">1</td><td colspan="2" rowspan="2">0</td><td colspan="2" rowspan="2">1</td><td colspan="2" rowspan="2">0</td><td colspan="2" rowspan="2">1</td><td colspan="2" rowspan="2">0</td><td>2</td><td>1</td><td>2</td><td>1</td><td>2</td><td>1</td><td>2</td><td>1</td><td>2</td><td>1</td><td>2</td><td>1</td><td>2</td><td>1</td><td>2</td><td>1</td></tr>
<tr><td>(s_2, f_{1112})</td><td>1</td><td>2</td><td>1</td><td>2</td><td>1</td><td>2</td><td>1</td><td>2</td><td>1</td><td>2</td><td>1</td><td>2</td><td>1</td><td>2</td><td>1</td><td>2</td></tr>
<tr><td>(s_2, f_{1121})</td><td colspan="2" rowspan="2">0</td><td colspan="2" rowspan="2">1</td><td colspan="2" rowspan="2">0</td><td colspan="2" rowspan="2">1</td><td colspan="2" rowspan="2">0</td><td colspan="2" rowspan="2">1</td><td colspan="2" rowspan="2">0</td><td colspan="2" rowspan="2">1</td><td>2</td><td>1</td><td>2</td><td>1</td><td>2</td><td>1</td><td>2</td><td>1</td><td>2</td><td>1</td><td>2</td><td>1</td><td>2</td><td>1</td><td>2</td><td>1</td></tr>
<tr><td>(s_2, f_{1122})</td><td>1</td><td>2</td><td>1</td><td>2</td><td>1</td><td>2</td><td>1</td><td>2</td><td>1</td><td>2</td><td>1</td><td>2</td><td>1</td><td>2</td><td>1</td><td>2</td></tr>
<tr><td>(s_2, f_{1211})</td><td colspan="2" rowspan="2">1</td><td colspan="2" rowspan="2">0</td><td colspan="2" rowspan="2">1</td><td colspan="2" rowspan="2">0</td><td colspan="2" rowspan="2">1</td><td colspan="2" rowspan="2">0</td><td colspan="2" rowspan="2">1</td><td colspan="2" rowspan="2">0</td><td>2</td><td>1</td><td>2</td><td>1</td><td>2</td><td>1</td><td>2</td><td>1</td><td>2</td><td>1</td><td>2</td><td>1</td><td>2</td><td>1</td><td>2</td><td>1</td></tr>
<tr><td>(s_2, f_{1212})</td><td>1</td><td>2</td><td>1</td><td>2</td><td>1</td><td>2</td><td>1</td><td>2</td><td>1</td><td>2</td><td>1</td><td>2</td><td>1</td><td>2</td><td>1</td><td>2</td></tr>
<tr><td>(s_2, f_{1221})</td><td colspan="2" rowspan="2">0</td><td colspan="2" rowspan="2">1</td><td colspan="2" rowspan="2">0</td><td colspan="2" rowspan="2">1</td><td colspan="2" rowspan="2">0</td><td colspan="2" rowspan="2">1</td><td colspan="2" rowspan="2">0</td><td colspan="2" rowspan="2">1</td><td>2</td><td>1</td><td>2</td><td>1</td><td>2</td><td>1</td><td>2</td><td>1</td><td>2</td><td>1</td><td>2</td><td>1</td><td>2</td><td>1</td><td>2</td><td>1</td></tr>
<tr><td>(s_2, f_{1222})</td><td>1</td><td>2</td><td>1</td><td>2</td><td>1</td><td>2</td><td>1</td><td>2</td><td>1</td><td>2</td><td>1</td><td>2</td><td>1</td><td>2</td><td>1</td><td>2</td></tr>
<tr><td>(s_2, f_{2111})</td><td colspan="2" rowspan="2">1</td><td colspan="2" rowspan="2">0</td><td colspan="2" rowspan="2">1</td><td colspan="2" rowspan="2">0</td><td colspan="2" rowspan="2">1</td><td colspan="2" rowspan="2">0</td><td colspan="2" rowspan="2">1</td><td colspan="2" rowspan="2">0</td><td>2</td><td>1</td><td>2</td><td>1</td><td>2</td><td>1</td><td>2</td><td>1</td><td>2</td><td>1</td><td>2</td><td>1</td><td>2</td><td>1</td><td>2</td><td>1</td></tr>
<tr><td>(s_2, f_{2112})</td><td>1</td><td>2</td><td>1</td><td>2</td><td>1</td><td>2</td><td>1</td><td>2</td><td>1</td><td>2</td><td>1</td><td>2</td><td>1</td><td>2</td><td>1</td><td>2</td></tr>
<tr><td>(s_2, f_{2121})</td><td colspan="2" rowspan="2">0</td><td colspan="2" rowspan="2">1</td><td colspan="2" rowspan="2">0</td><td colspan="2" rowspan="2">1</td><td colspan="2" rowspan="2">0</td><td colspan="2" rowspan="2">1</td><td colspan="2" rowspan="2">0</td><td colspan="2" rowspan="2">1</td><td>2</td><td>1</td><td>2</td><td>1</td><td>2</td><td>1</td><td>2</td><td>1</td><td>2</td><td>1</td><td>2</td><td>1</td><td>2</td><td>1</td><td>2</td><td>1</td></tr>
<tr><td>(s_2, f_{2122})</td><td>1</td><td>2</td><td>1</td><td>2</td><td>1</td><td>2</td><td>1</td><td>2</td><td>1</td><td>2</td><td>1</td><td>2</td><td>1</td><td>2</td><td>1</td><td>2</td></tr>
<tr><td>(s_2, f_{2211})</td><td colspan="2" rowspan="2">1</td><td colspan="2" rowspan="2">0</td><td colspan="2" rowspan="2">1</td><td colspan="2" rowspan="2">0</td><td colspan="2" rowspan="2">1</td><td colspan="2" rowspan="2">0</td><td colspan="2" rowspan="2">1</td><td colspan="2" rowspan="2">0</td><td>2</td><td>1</td><td>2</td><td>1</td><td>2</td><td>1</td><td>2</td><td>1</td><td>2</td><td>1</td><td>2</td><td>1</td><td>2</td><td>1</td><td>2</td><td>1</td></tr>
<tr><td>(s_2, f_{2212})</td><td>1</td><td>2</td><td>1</td><td>2</td><td>1</td><td>2</td><td>1</td><td>2</td><td>1</td><td>2</td><td>1</td><td>2</td><td>1</td><td>2</td><td>1</td><td>2</td></tr>
<tr><td>(s_2, f_{2221})</td><td colspan="2" rowspan="2">0</td><td colspan="2" rowspan="2">1</td><td colspan="2" rowspan="2">0</td><td colspan="2" rowspan="2">1</td><td colspan="2" rowspan="2">0</td><td colspan="2" rowspan="2">1</td><td colspan="2" rowspan="2">0</td><td colspan="2" rowspan="2">1</td><td>2</td><td>1</td><td>2</td><td>1</td><td>2</td><td>1</td><td>2</td><td>1</td><td>2</td><td>1</td><td>2</td><td>1</td><td>2</td><td>1</td><td>2</td><td>1</td></tr>
<tr><td>(s_2, f_{2222})</td><td>1</td><td>2</td><td>1</td><td>2</td><td>1</td><td>2</td><td>1</td><td>2</td><td>1</td><td>2</td><td>1</td><td>2</td><td>1</td><td>2</td><td>1</td><td>2</td></tr>
</table>

(a)

	(t_1, G_{11})	(t_1, G_{12})	(t_1, G_{21})	(t_1, G_{22})	(t_2, G_{11})	(t_2, G_{12})	(t_2, G_{21})	(t_2, G_{22})
(s_1, F_{11})	2	2	1	1	1	1	0	0
(s_1, F_{12})	2	2	1	1	0	0	1	1
(s_1, F_{21})	1	1	2	2	1	1	0	0
(s_1, F_{22})	1	1	2	2	0	0	1	1
(s_2, F_{11})	1	0	1	0	2	1	2	1
(s_2, F_{12})	1	0	1	0	1	2	1	2
(s_2, F_{21})	0	1	0	1	2	1	2	1
(s_2, F_{22})	0	1	0	1	1	2	1	2

(b)

Figure 8.3 Some big matrices.

times. If each distinct row and column is written down only once, the 8×8 matrix of Figure 8.3(b) is obtained. This 8×8 matrix is a *reduced* strategic form for Z^2 in which the only pure strategies included are those in which a player conditions his or her behavior at the second stage only on what the *opponent* did at the first stage.[3] A pure strategy for a player II who ignores what she did herself at the first stage, is a pair (t, G) in which t is an action in T and $G : S \to T$ is a function. If player I uses action s at the first stage, then player II will use action t at the first stage and action $G(s)$ at the second stage. The four possible functions $G : S \to T$ are shown as tables in Figure 8.2(b).[4]

The symmetries in the zero-sum game of Figure 8.3(b) make it easy to solve. For example, it is a security strategy for player I to use each of his pure strategies with probability $\frac{1}{8}$. He then gets an expected payoff of 1, whatever player II does. She similarly guarantees an expected payoff of -1 by playing each of her pure strategies with probability $\frac{1}{8}$.

These are not the only security strategies. The choice of (s_1, F_{12}), (s_1, F_{21}), (s_2, F_{12}) and (s_2, F_{21}), each with probability $\frac{1}{4}$, is also secure. So is the choice of (s_1, F_{11}), (s_1, F_{22}), (s_2, F_{11}) and (s_2, F_{22}), each with probability $\frac{1}{4}$.

It is this last security strategy that comes naturally to mind. Notice that, since player I uses only F_{11} and F_{22}, he ignores what player II does. In fact, the security strategy can be realized by player I choosing each action s_1 and s_2 at the first stage with probability $\frac{1}{2}$, and then *independently* doing the same thing at the second stage. This ensures that player II is unable to deduce anything about what player I will do at the second stage from what he did at the first stage.

This conclusion should come as no surprise. It is obvious that rational players with a sequence of two-player, zero-sum games to play will act so as to ensure that their past play

---

[3]If player II plans to use action t_2 at stage one, it will not help her much to say what she would do at stage two if she found she had actually used action t_1 at stage one.

[4]Consider, for example, $G_{21} : S \to T$. If player II is using this function and player I uses s_1 at stage one, then player II will use $t_2 = G_{21}(s_1)$ at stage two regardless of what she did at stage one. Thus, for both histories $h_{11} = (s_1, t_1)$ and $h_{12} = (s_1, t_2)$, she plans to play t_2 at stage two. If player I uses s_2 at stage one, player II will use $t_1 = G_{21}(s_2)$ at stage two, regardless of what she did at stage one. Thus, for both histories $h_{21} = (s_2, t_1)$ and $h_{22} = (s_2, t_2)$, she plans to play t_1 at stage two. The function $G_{21} : S \to T$ therefore corresponds to $g_{2211} : H \to T$. Following this through, one can check that the matrix of Figure 8.3(b) is obtained from that at the top by taking the 1st, 6th, 11th, 16th, 17th, 22nd, 27th and 32nd rows, and the 1st, 4th, 13th, 16th, 17th, 20th, 29th and 32nd columns.

will not help the opponent predict their future play. This is because, whatever is good for one player in a two-player, zero-sum game is necessarily bad for the other. What then have we learned in this section?

One useful feature of the discussion has been that it contains a full account of how a strategic form may be reduced to something simpler by eliminating duplicated rows or columns. The details of the procedure were skimped when it was used previously in discussing Duel (Section 4.1.2) and Russian Roulette (Section 4.7).

However, what matters most is that the notion of a pure strategy in a repeated game has been clarified. In general, a pure strategy for a repeated game does not simply name an action for each stage of the game. It names an action for the first stage of the game and then, for each later stage, it names a *function* that makes the choice of action at that stage contingent on the *history* of the game so far. A repeated game with many stages therefore has a very complicated set of pure strategies.

8.3 Repeating the Prisoners' Dilemma

The Prisoners' Dilemma (Sections 7.1.3 and 7.5.4) is reproduced in Figure 8.4(a). In this section, the game obtained by repeating it n times will be studied. If $n = 10$, each player then has $2^{349,525}$ pure strategies (Exercise 8.6.3). This is an unimaginably large number. The repeated game therefore has an enormously large strategic form even when n is comparatively small. Nevertheless, the game is easy to analyze. There is a unique subgame-perfect equilibrium in which each player always chooses *hawk*.

The reason is straightforward. Before the last stage of the repeated game, it is possible that a player might be deterred from choosing *hawk* because of the fear of retaliation by the opponent later in the game. But, at the *final* stage, no later retaliation is possible. Since *hawk* dominates *dove* in the Prisoners' Dilemma, both players will therefore choose *hawk* at the nth and last stage, whatever the previous history of play may have been.

Now consider the penultimate stage. Both players know that, regardless of their current choice, (*hawk*, *hawk*) will be played at the final stage. Nobody can therefore be punished for playing *hawk* at the penultimate stage because the worst punishment the opponent could inflict at the final stage is to use *hawk*. But the opponent is planning to use *hawk* at the final stage anyway, no matter what happens previously. Both

	Dove	Hawk
Dove	3 3	6 0
Hawk	0 6	1 1

(a)

$3 + y(h)$ $3 + x(h)$	$6 + y(h)$ $0 + x(h)$
$0 + y(h)$ $6 + x(h)$	$1 + y(h)$ $1 + x(h)$

(b)

Figure 8.4 Prisoners' Dilemma.

players will therefore use *hawk* at the last stage but one. The same argument can then be applied at the last stage but two. And so on.

A more formal version of the argument is given as the proof of the following mini-theorem.

Theorem 8.3.1 The finitely repeated Prisoners' Dilemma has a unique subgame-perfect equilibrium in which both players plan always to use *hawk.*

Math 8.3.1 ⟶

Proof. Let $P(n)$ be the proposition that the theorem is true for the n-times repeated Prisoners' Dilemma. Then $P(1)$ is correct for the reasons given in Section 7.1.3. To deduce the theorem from the Principle of Induction, it is necessary to show, in addition, that $P(n) \Rightarrow P(n+1)$ for each $n = 1, 2, \ldots$.

To this end, assume that $P(n)$ holds for some particular value of n, and consider the $(n+1)$-times repeated Prisoners' Dilemma. Suppose that the last stage has been reached after a history h of play. If the play at the kth stage during this history resulted in a payoff of x_k to player I, then he will have accumulated a total payoff of $x(h) = x_1 + x_2 + \cdots + x_n$ by the time the $(n+1)$st and final stage comes to be played. Player II will similarly have accumulated a payoff of $y(h)$.

The game to be played at the $(n+1)$st stage is therefore as illustrated in Figure 8.4(b). Since *hawk* strongly dominates *dove* in this game, it has the unique Nash equilibrium $(hawk, hawk)$. In fact, the game of Figure 8.4(b) is *strategically identical* to the Prisoners' Dilemma of Figure 8.4(a). The new Von Neumann and Morgenstern utility function obtained by adding $x(h)$ to each of player I's payoffs describes precisely the *same* preferences as the old Von Neumann and Morgenstern utility function (Section 3.5).

Subgame-perfect equilibria are found using Zermelo's algorithm (Section 1.8.2). The game of Figure 8.4(b) is a smallest subgame of the $(n+1)$-times repeated Prisoners' Dilemma. Zermelo's algorithm calls for each such smallest subgame to be replaced by a terminal node labeled with the payoff pair that results from using a Nash equilibrium in the subgame. Since (*hawk*, *hawk*) is the only Nash equilibrium in Figure 8.4(b), the required payoff pair is $(1 + x(h), 1 + y(h))$.

The new game obtained by this reduction is precisely the same as the n-times repeated Prisoners' Dilemma, except that 1 is added to each payoff.[5] It is therefore strategically equivalent to the n-times repeated Prisoners' Dilemma. Since $P(n)$ is being assumed, *hawk* will therefore always be used by both players in the new game. We already know that they will play *hawk* at the final stage of the $(n+1)$-times repeated Prisoners' Dilemma. It follows that they *always* play *hawk* in the $(n+1)$-times repeated Prisoners' Dilemma. Thus $P(n+1)$ has been established.

The argument shows that $P(1)$ holds, and that $P(n) \Rightarrow P(n+1)$, for all $n = 1, 2, \ldots$. The fact that $P(n)$ is always true then follows from the Principle of Induction (Section 1.7). □

8.3.1 Rational Fools?

Phil 8.3.2 →

We saw in Section 7.5.4 that there are people who argue that it is foolish to be rational in the one-shot Prisoners' Dilemma. Usually, they labor under the mistaken impression that the assumptions about rationality that game theorists make in recommending the play of *hawk* are the same in the finitely repeated case as they are in the one-shot case. This misapprehension leads them to concentrate their fire on the *finitely repeated* Prisoners' Dilemma, where the failure of two rational players in an ongoing relationship to succeed in cooperating certainly is disturbing to the intuition.

Since *hawk* strongly dominates *dove*, it is best for a rational player in the one-shot Prisoners' Dilemma to choose *hawk*, whatever may or may not be known about the rationality of the opponent. This is far from being the case in the finitely repeated Prisoners' Dilemma. The question of what rational players need to know or believe to justify backwards induction arguments was discussed in Section 1.8.3, and again in Section 4.6.3. In brief, it is not enough that the players are rational. It is

[5]Not to the stage-game payoffs, but to the payoffs in the n-times repeated Prisoners' Dilemma as a whole.

not even enough that it is common knowledge that the players are rational, although this is much more to ask. It also needs to be assumed that the players' beliefs about these matters are so firmly rooted that nothing that happens in the game can lead to their being abandoned. No matter how often a player behaves irrationally, the opponent continues to attribute the behavior to some transient influence that cannot be expected to persist into the future. If a player's rationality was common knowledge before the game, it remains common knowledge during the game *no matter what may happen.*[6]

Of course, in real life, such idealizing assumptions will seldom be realistic. In particular, *towards the end of a long repeated game*, one has to work hard in suspending disbelief to maintain that a player with an unbroken history of irrationality will still be likely to behave rationally in the future. But this does *not* imply that the analysis of the finitely repeated Prisoners' Dilemma given in this section is wrong: only that the assumptions on which the analysis is based are overly simple. When the *same* method of analysis is applied with more realistic assumptions, different conclusion are obtained. In particular, equilibria exist that call for the play of *dove.*

Game theorists have considered various ways of making the underlying model more realistic. The most popular involves looking at repetitions of the Prisoners' Dilemma that may go on forever. In such a game, *any* history of play will necessarily be *short* compared with the potential length of the game. Deviations from rationality during such a short history will therefore not cost the deviant much compared with what he or she stands to gain in the future. The assumption that a player will behave rationally in the future, in spite of having behaved irrationally in the past, therefore ceases to be quite so implausible.

One might object that one implausibility has been eradicated only by introducing another. Surely it is impossible that a real-life game could go on forever? However, games with a potentially infinite horizon are often more realistic than those with a finite horizon.

When people interact in real life, they seldom know in advance how long their relationship will last. They know it will come to an end eventually because neither expects to live forever. But they will almost never be sure of the *precise* date of their final meeting.

[6] In fact, only sentences of the form "[Everybody knows that]^N everybody is rational" need to hold for large enough values of N. How large N needs to be is discussed in Exercise 4.8.21.

The simplest way of modeling such uncertainty in the case of the repeated Prisoners' Dilemma is by introducing a chance move after each repetition that decides whether or not the game will continue. Consider, in particular, the case in which the probability is $\frac{1}{3}$ that any stage reached is the last. One might, for example, roll a fair dice after each stage and continue if and only if neither 5 nor 6 appears.

Such a model does not have a finite horizon. Whatever N may be, the game is not certain to end at the Nth stage or sooner. The probability that it will persist until at least the Nth stage is $(\frac{2}{3})^{N-1}$. This is the probability that no 5 nor 6 will ever appear in $N - 1$ rolls of a fair dice. It is true that $(\frac{2}{3})^N \to 0$ as $N \to \infty$, and hence the probability that the game will literally go on forever is zero. But it is still a game with an infinite horizon. Its study is taken up in the next subsection.

8.3.2 An Infinite Horizon Example

Cooperation is *not* necessarily irrational when the Prisoners' Dilemma is repeated an *indefinite* number of times. In this example, we study the case when the probability that the game will continue from whatever stage it has reached to the next is always $\frac{2}{3}$. At the beginning of the game, the probability that the Nth stage will be reached is therefore $(\frac{2}{3})^{N-1}$.

Consider the strategy s that calls for *dove* to be played as long as the opponent reciprocates by playing *dove* also.[7] If the opponent ever fails to do so, the strategy calls for *hawk* always to be played thereafter. Any deviation will therefore be well and truly punished. However, if both players use the strategy s, no occasion for punishment will arise. The players will cooperate forever. Each player's expected payoff will then be

$$C = 3 + 3(\tfrac{2}{3}) + \cdots + 3(\tfrac{2}{3})^{N-1} + 3(\tfrac{2}{3})^N + 3(\tfrac{2}{3})^{N+1} + 3(\tfrac{2}{3})^{N+2} + \cdots .$$

Can a player gain by deviating? If a player deviates by playing *hawk* for the first time at the $(N + 1)$st stage, then the deviant will get at most

$$D = 3 + 3(\tfrac{2}{3}) + \cdots + 3(\tfrac{2}{3})^{N-1} + 6(\tfrac{2}{3})^N + 1(\tfrac{2}{3})^{N+1} + 1(\tfrac{2}{3})^{N+2} + \cdots .$$

[7]This is called the GRIM strategy in the next section.

If $C \geq D$, then it is unprofitable to deviate. We therefore consider,

$$\begin{aligned} C - D &= (3-6)(\tfrac{2}{3})^N + (3-1)(\tfrac{2}{3})^{N+1} + (3-1)(\tfrac{2}{3})^{N+2} + \cdots \\ &= (\tfrac{2}{3})^N \left\{-3 + 2(\tfrac{2}{3} + (\tfrac{2}{3})^2 + \cdots)\right\} \\ &= (\tfrac{2}{3})^N \left\{-3 + 2\left(\frac{\frac{2}{3}}{1-\frac{2}{3}}\right)\right\} \\ &= (\tfrac{2}{3})^N(-3+4) = (\tfrac{2}{3})^N \geq 0 . \end{aligned}$$

Since $C \geq D$, it follows that it is unprofitable to deviate, provided that the opponent sticks to the strategy s. Thus, (s, s) is a Nash equilibrium that requires players to cooperate all the time in the infinite horizon game.

This story explains why rational cooperation may be viable in a repeated Prisoners' Dilemma with an infinite horizon. It is such a good story that it deserves to be told over and over again—and it will be, since this chapter has every intention of living up to its title. The story is first retold for the case of the colluding duopolists considered in Section 7.5.5. This retelling of the story will serve to make it clear that one should expect a close connection between the outcomes that would be available to players in the one-shot case if binding agreements were possible, and the outcomes that can be achieved by the use of equilibrium strategies when the game is repeated with an infinite horizon. The chapter then continues by exploring this issue in detail for a class of particularly simple infinite horizon, repeated games.

8.3.3 Collusion in a Repeated Cournot Duopoly

Econ 8.4 ⟶

Section 7.5.5 explained that collusion is difficult to sustain in a one-shot Cournot Duopoly Game because the players have an incentive to cheat on any deal that is worth the trouble of negotiating. A natural response is that the one-shot game is not very realistic. In the real world, oligopolists have to make repeated production decisions over long time periods of indefinite duration. As we shall see, such a climate is very much more favorable for sustaining collusive deals than a harsh one-shot environment. To demonstrate this, it is only necessary to copy the argument of Section 8.3.2 that shows cooperation to be feasible in the indefinitely repeated version of the Prisoners' Dilemma.

In the collusive deal studied in Section 7.5.5, the two firms agree that their total production should be chosen to be

$\tilde{q}$, which is the output of a profit-maximizing monopolist. In the repeated version to be studied now, let us suppose that they agree that player I will produce q_1 in each period and that player II will produce q_2, where $q_1 + q_2 = \tilde{q}$. Suppose that the implementation of this agreement leads to player I earning a profit of a per period and player II earning a profit of b. However, unlike in the one-shot case, the firms can now build a provision into their agreement about what action should be taken if someone cheats. The simplest provision is that, if someone cheats, then the partnership is dissolved and both then play their one-shot Nash equilibrium strategies in all succeeding periods. The question we care about is whether such a deal is incentive-compatible. Does either player have an incentive to cheat?

Consider what player I gets if he does not cheat. If his discount factor (Section 5.8.3) is δ, where $0 < \delta < 1$, he will evaluate the income stream he gets when neither deviates from the agreement as being worth

$$C = a + a\delta + a\delta^2 + \cdots + a\delta^N + \cdots .$$

If player II sticks to the agreement but player I deviates, how much will player I get? Suppose that player I deviates for the first time at the $(N+1)$st stage. He will then get

$$D = a + a\delta + \cdots + a\delta^{N-1} + B\delta^N + c\delta^{N+1} + c\delta^{N+2} + \cdots ,$$

where B is the bonanza that player I enjoys from cheating on player II at the $(N+1)$st stage, and c is the profit per period that each firm receives when each plays the one-shot Nash equilibrium strategy. The precise values[8] of a, B and c do not matter much, since all that is necessary for the argument that follows is that $c < a < B$.

The requirement for it to be unprofitable for player I to cheat is that $C \geq D$. We therefore consider

$$\begin{aligned} C - D &= \delta^N\{(a - B) + (a - c)\delta + (a - c)^2\delta^2 + \cdots\} \\ &= \delta^N\{(a - B) + (a - c)\frac{\delta}{1 - \delta}\} . \end{aligned}$$

The agreement is therefore incentive-compatible for player I when

$$\delta \geq \frac{B - a}{B - c} .$$

---

[8]In fact, if $q_1 = q_2$, then $a = b = \frac{1}{8}(M - c)^2$ and $c = \frac{1}{9}(M - c)^2$. The optimal deviation for player I at the Nth stage is $Q_1 = R_1(q_2) = \frac{3}{8}(M - c)$, for which the corresponding profit is $B = \{\frac{3}{8}(M - c)\}^2$.

This condition is satisfied when the discount factor δ is sufficiently large because the right hand side is less than 1 when $c < a < B$. Since a similar condition holds for player II under similar circumstances, it follows that collusion is indeed viable in the repeated Cournot Duopoly Game, provided that the players do not discount the future too heavily.

We have seen that a range of collusive deals can be sustained as Nash equilibrium outcomes when a Cournot duopoly is modeled as a repeated game with an infinite horizon, provided that the players care sufficiently about their future income streams. Does this mean that we should expect collusion to be endemic in oligopolistic situations? It is certainly true that many cases of blatant collusion have come to light, and the documented cases are doubtless only the tip of a very large iceberg. However, one must remember that the model we have been studying neglects many important issues. In particular, the notion of a repeated game introduced in Section 8.2 takes for granted that both players know for certain what action the other took at all previous stages of the game. This makes it easy for each player to monitor whether the other is sticking to the deal. But in the real world, things are seldom so clear-cut. Random events outside both players' control may intervene to confuse the issue. If player's II's profit falls below what she expects, this may be because player I has cheated, but it also may be because of some external glitch over which he has no control. Designing incentive-compatible collusive deals when such informational difficulties intrude is not necessarily easy, as we shall see when the subject of mechanism design is touched upon briefly in Section 11.7. Hasty conclusions about what is or is not possible in the real world are therefore inappropriate.

8.4 Infinite Repetitions

The preceding examples make it clear that the study of infinitely repeated games is worth pursuing. However, the study of such games is technically demanding, and so attention will

Phil 8.4.1 ⟶

be restricted here to some highly simplified situations. At least three problems will be finessed:

- As Section 8.2 shows, strategy sets in repeated games are huge and complicated. This difficulty is handled by restricting attention to strategies that can be represented by finite automata (Section 8.4.1).
- Realistic models require that payoffs received late in the game are discounted more than payoffs received early in

the game, as in the models of Sections 8.3.2 and 8.3.3. If the discount factor is sufficiently small, it can then happen that what players do early in the game makes a significant difference to their final earnings. The mathematical difficulties created by such considerations are evaded here by not discounting at all. Thus it is only what the players do in the *long run* that matters to what they finally get.

- As noted at the end of Section 8.3.3, monitoring the opponent's play can often be a problem. In particular, problems arise if mixed strategies are allowed. Perhaps player II is supposed to use one of two actions with equal probability each time she moves, but player I observes that she has always used her first action in the past. Should he now conclude that she has cheated and therefore deserves punishment? Or should he give her the benefit of the doubt on the grounds that it is not actually impossible that her coin fell heads every time? Rather than face the statistical problems raised by such questions, the monitoring issue will be avoided altogether by restricting players to the use of pure strategies.

8.4.1 Finite Automata

A *finite automaton* is an idealized computing machine.[9] When strategies can be represented by finite automata, one can therefore think of a player's choice of strategy as being a decision to delegate the play of the game to a suitably programmed computer.

Mathematicians distinguish various types of finite automata. Those suitable for playing repeated games are called *Moore machines.* When stimulated by an appropriate input, a Moore machine responds by generating an output. The Moore machine chosen by player I will have player II's stage-game actions as its possible inputs. Its outputs will be player I's stage-game actions. The machine then responds to what player II does at the nth stage by choosing an action for player I at the $(n+1)$st stage. Information other than player II's last action has to be held in the machine's memory.[10] As we shall

---

[9]Or, if you prefer, it is the program that runs such a machine.

[10]One could reduce the demands on a machine's memory by increasing the set of signals it can accept as inputs. One might, for example, allow the machine to input, not only the opponent's last action, but its own last action as well. Or one might let the machine have access to a clock, so that it can know what stage the game has reached without having to keep track of this internally. Or one might let the machine have access to random inputs so that it can play mixed strategies. However, all these possibilities and others are suppressed so as to keep things simple.

see, a finite automaton can only remember a finite number of things. For this reason, a finite automaton cannot keep track of all possible histories in a repeated game. Confining attention to strategies that can be represented by a finite automaton is therefore a definite restriction on what the players can choose.

Each conceivable configuration of memories that a finite automaton can sustain is a possible *state* of the machine. A careful description of a finite automaton would begin by listing the set of all its possible states. This set must be finite. One of these states is its *initial state*: the state in which the machine finds itself at the beginning of the game. To complete the description, an *output function* and a *transition function* are required. The output function specifies what action the machine will take in each state. The transition function tells the machine how to move from one state to another after it receives as input the action taken by the opponent.

However, for the purposes of this chapter, it will be adequate to describe finite automata pictorially as in Figure 8.5. This shows various finite automata capable of playing the repeated Prisoners' Dilemma. Each circle represents a possible state of the machine. The letter written within the circle is the output the machine offers in that state.[11] The arrows indicate transitions.

Consider, for example, the machine of Figure 8.5(d), which is called TIT-FOR-TAT because it always does next time what its opponent did last time. In particular, if it is in the state in which it outputs H, it will stay in the same state if it receives the input H (indicating the play of *hawk* by the opponent). On the other hand, if it receives the input D, it switches to the state in which it outputs D. Each machine has one arrow that comes from nowhere. This indicates the machine's initial state. For example, TIT-FOR-TAT is a nice machine in that it begins by playing *dove*.

Figure 8.6(a) shows what happens when TIT-FOR-TAT plays TWEEDLEDUM. Figure 8.6(b) shows what happens when TWEEDLEDUM plays his brother TWEEDLEDEE. Notice that, in both cases, the two machines end up by cycling through the same sequence of states forever. In Figure 8.6(a), the cycle is four stages long and begins immediately. In Figure 8.6(b), the cycle is only one stage long and it begins only after some preliminary jostling in stages one, two and three.

Any two finite automata playing each other in a repeated game will eventually end up cycling through the same

[11] The letter D means that *dove* is to be played. The letter H means that *hawk* is to be played.

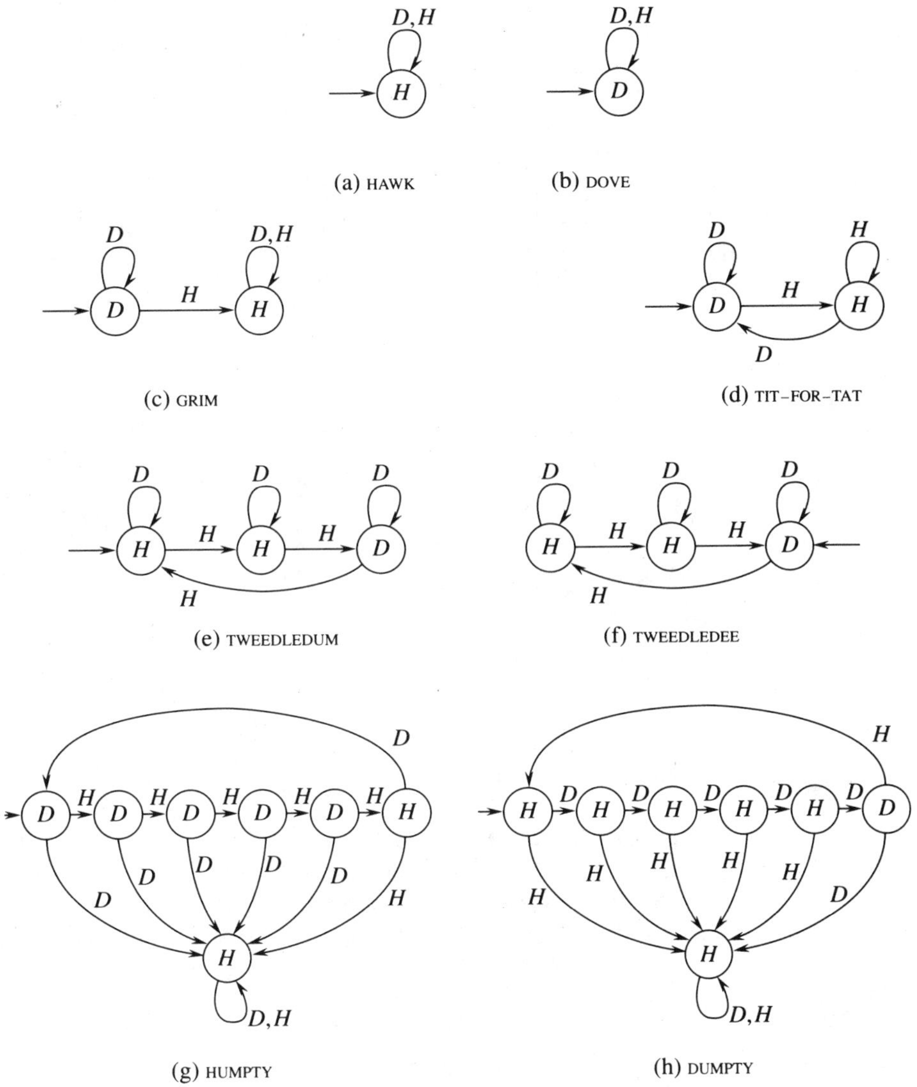

(a) HAWK

(b) DOVE

(c) GRIM

(d) TIT-FOR-TAT

(e) TWEEDLEDUM

(f) TWEEDLEDEE

(g) HUMPTY

(h) DUMPTY

Figure 8.5 Some finite automata.

sequence of states over and over again. As we shall see in Section 8.4.2, this makes it easy to work out their total payoffs in the repeated game.

8.4.2 Evaluating Income Streams

Math 8.4.3 ⟶

Suppose that the result of player I's choosing strategy a and player II's choosing strategy b in a repeated game is that player I uses action s_n at the nth stage of the game and player II uses

		Cycle				Cycle				Cycle					
I	Payoff	0	1	1	6	0	1	1	6	0	1	1	6	0	1
I	TIT-FOR-TAT	D	H	H	H	D	H	H	H	D	H	H	H	D	H
	Stage	1	2	3	4	5	6	7	8	9	10	11	12	13	14
II	TWEEDLEDUM	H	H	H	D	H	H	H	D	H	H	H	D	H	H
II	Payoff	6	1	1	0	6	1	1	0	6	1	1	0	6	1

(a)

					Cycle	Cycle	Cycle	Cycle						Cycle	
I	Payoff	6	1	1	3	3	3	3	3	3	3	3	3	3	3
I	TWEEDLEDUM	H	H	H	D	D	D	D	D	D	D	D	D	D	D
	Stage	1	2	3	4	5	6	7	8	9	10	11	12	13	14
II	TWEEDLEDEE	D	H	H	D	D	D	D	D	D	D	D	D	D	D
II	Payoff	0	1	1	3	3	3	3	3	3	3	3	3	3	3

(b)

Figure 8.6 Computer wars.

action t_n at the nth stage. Player I will then get a payoff of $\pi_1(s_n, t_n)$ at the nth stage of the game. To determine his total payoff in the repeated game as a whole when he uses strategy a and player II uses strategy b, he must therefore evaluate the *income stream*

$$\pi_1(s_1, t_1),\ \pi_1(s_2, t_2),\ \pi_1(s_3, t_3),\ \ldots .$$

In economics, there are often good reasons for supposing that an agent will maximize the discounted sum of such an income stream. Player I's payoff function $\pi_1 : S \times T \to \mathbf{R}$ in the repeated game would then take the form

$$\pi_1(a, b) = \pi_1(s_1, t_1) + \delta\pi_1(s_2, t_2) + \delta^2\pi_1(s_3, t_3) + \cdots ,$$

where δ is player I's *discount factor*.[12] For example, player I's income stream in Figure 8.6(a) is $0, 1, 1, 6, 0, 1, 1, 6, 0, \ldots$.

[12]Suppose for example, that an economic agent wishes to compare two income streams of money payments. This is done by computing their present values. For example, if the yearly interest rate is fixed at r%, then the *present value* of an IOU promising to pay $\$X$ three years from now is $\$Y = \$X/(1 + r)^3$. This is because $\$Y$ is the amount you would have to

This income stream can be evaluated as a discounted sum with a discount factor δ satisfying $0 < \delta < 1$. If a is TIT-FOR-TAT and b is TWEEDLEDUM, a player I who evaluates income streams this way would then get a payoff in the repeated game equal to

$$\begin{aligned} U_1(a,b) &= 0 + \delta + \delta^2 + 6\delta^3 + 0 + \delta^5 + \delta^6 + 6\delta^7 + \cdots \\ &= (0 + \delta + \delta^2 + 6\delta^3) + (0 + \delta + \delta^2 + 6\delta^3)\delta^4 \\ &\qquad + (0 + \delta + \delta^2 + 6\delta^3)\delta^8 + \cdots \\ &= (0 + \delta + \delta^2 + 6\delta^3)(1 + \delta^4 + \delta^8 + \cdots) \\ &= (0 + \delta + \delta^2 + 6\delta^3)\left(\frac{1}{1-\delta^4}\right). \end{aligned} \tag{8.1}$$

Earlier in the chapter, when considering *finitely* repeated games, income streams were evaluated using a discount factor $\delta = 1$.[13] One cannot simplify so gracefully in the infinite horizon case because the series obtained when $\delta = 1$ will usually *diverge*. For example, $0 + 1 + 1 + 6 + 0 + 1 + 1 + 6 + \cdots$ diverges to $+\infty$. A little fancy footwork is therefore required.

First, recall from Section 3.5.1 that the utility functions U_1 and $AU_1 + B$ represent the same preferences. Thus U_1 can be replaced by $(1-\delta)U_1$ without changing the strategic situation. One can then consider the limit as $\delta \to 1$. For example, in Equation (8.1),

$$\begin{aligned} \lim_{\delta\to 1}(1-\delta)U_1(a,b) &= \lim_{\delta\to 1}(0 + \delta + \delta^2 + 6\delta^3)\left(\frac{1-\delta}{1-\delta^4}\right) \\ &= \tfrac{1}{4}(0 + 1 + 1 + 6) = 2, \end{aligned}$$

which is simply what player I gets on average as his stage-game payoffs cycle through the values 0, 1, 1 and 6, as indicated in Figure 8.6(a).[14]

---

invest in a bank now to get \$$X$ three years hence. Equivalently, \$$Y$ is the largest amount at which you could hope to sell the IOU right now. Nobody would pay \$$Z >$ \$$Y$, because \$$Z$ invested in a bank would yield \$$Z(1+r)^3$ three years from now, which is more than \$$X$.

The present value of an *income stream* $X_0, X_1, X_2, \ldots$, in which \$$X_t$ is to be received t years from now, is simply $X_0 + \delta X_1 + \delta^2 X_2 + \cdots$, where $\delta = (1+r)^{-1}$ is the discount factor associated with the fixed interest rate r.

[13] However, Section 8.3.3 used a discount factor $\delta < 1$, and in Section 8.3.2, the discount factor was $\delta = \frac{2}{3}$.

[14] There are various ways of calculating the limit of $(1-\delta)/(1-\delta^4)$ as $\delta \to 1$. One can use L'Hôpital's rule as in Section 5.8.6. Alternatively, one can remember the formula for a geometric progression: namely $1 + \delta + \delta^2 + \delta^3 = (1-\delta^4)/(1-\delta)$. The limit of $1 + \delta + \delta^2 + \delta^3$ as $\delta \to 1$ is obviously 4.

One of the advantages of working with finite automata is that this trick always works. When two finite automata play each other in a repeated game, they will eventually end up cycling through a fixed sequence of states. Each will then be assumed to evaluate the income stream they obtain by taking the average of the payoffs they receive *during this cycle.*[15] This corresponds to the case $\delta = 1$ in finite-horizon games.

Figure 8.6(b) provides a second example. Each player evaluates their income stream as being worth 3 utils. Notice that the initial jostling for position at the beginning of the game is ignored in this evaluation. The players are assumed to care only about what happens *in the long run.*

8.4.3 Nash Equilibria

What equilibria can be found for the infinitely repeated Prisoners' Dilemma? It would be pleasant to give some neat answers in which the equilibria considered were subgame-perfect. However, except for the sketchy remarks of Section 8.4.5, attention will be confined to the case of Nash equilibria, so as to keep things reasonably simple.

Throughout the rest of this chapter, it will be taken for granted that the players evaluate income streams in terms of their long-run average payoff as discussed in Section 8.4.2. In the case when the stage-game is the Prisoners' Dilemma of Figure 8.4(a), Figure 8.7 then shows the strategic form of the game that would result if the players were restricted to choosing one of the finite automata of Figure 8.5.

A careful count will reveal that this strategic form admits 18 Nash equilibria in pure strategies. *All* of these remain Nash equilibria when the players are allowed to select any finite automaton to play the infinitely repeated Prisoners' Dilemma. As we shall see, these 18 Nash equilibria are just representatives of a huge class of other Nash equilibria in the game when any finite automaton may be chosen. However, for the

---

[15]Since evaluating in this way is equivalent to using a utility function defined by

$$V_1(a,b) = \lim_{N\to\infty} \frac{1}{N}\sum_{n=1}^{N} \pi_1(s_n, t_n),$$

it is often referred to as the limit-of-the-means criterion. Nothing guarantees that the limit-of-the-means exists in the general case. This is one reason for confining attention to strategies representable by finite automata. The expedient of writing "lim inf" for "lim" when the latter does not exist is not very satisfying.

	HAWK	DOVE	GRIM	TIT-FOR-TAT	TWEEDLEDUM	TWEEDLEDEE	HUMPTY	DUMPTY
HAWK	①, ①	⑥, 0	1, ①	1, ①	$2\frac{2}{3}$, $\frac{2}{3}$	$2\frac{2}{3}$, $\frac{2}{3}$	1, ①	①, ①
DOVE	0, ⑥	3, 3	③, 3	③, 3	0, ⑥	③, 3	1, 1	①, 1
GRIM	①, 1	3, ③	③, ③	③, ③	$2\frac{2}{3}$, $\frac{2}{3}$	③, ③	1, 1	①, 1
TIT-FOR-TAT	①, 1	3, ③	③, ③	③, ③	2, 2	③, ③	1, 1	①, 1
TWEEDLEDUM	$\frac{2}{3}$, $2\frac{2}{3}$	⑥, 0	$2\frac{2}{3}$, $\frac{2}{3}$	2, 2	③, ③	③, ③	1, 1	①, 1
TWEEDLEDEE	$\frac{2}{3}$, $2\frac{2}{3}$	3, ③	③, ③	③, ③	③, ③	③, ③	1, 1	①, 1
HUMPTY	①, 1	1, 1	1, 1	1, 1	1, 1	1, 1	1, 1	①, ⑤
DUMPTY	①, ①	1, ①	1, ①	1, ①	1, ①	1, ①	⑤, ①	①, ①

Figure 8.7 A restricted strategic form.

moment, only four of the equilibria will be examined more closely.

Hawk v. Hawk. If one player always uses *hawk*, then the other player can do no better than always to use *hawk* as well. Thus (HAWK, HAWK) is a Nash equilibrium in the repeated game.

This illustrates a general fact. Whenever (s, t) is a Nash equilibrium of the one-shot game, it is invariably a Nash equilibrium of the repeated game for player I always to plan to use s and for player II always to plan to use t. However, such equilibria in the repeated game are seldom those on which it is interesting to focus.

Grim v. Grim. Notice that, when the GRIM automaton plays itself, the result is cooperation. Both machines always use the action *dove*. To check that (GRIM, GRIM) is a Nash equilibrium for the repeated game, it is necessary to confirm that GRIM is a best reply to itself.

If this were false, then there would be some other machine DEVIANT that got a bigger payoff than 3 when playing GRIM. Thus DEVIANT could not always use *dove* when playing GRIM. Eventually, it would have to use *hawk*. But, as soon as DEVIANT plays *hawk*, GRIM retaliates by switching to a state in which it plays *hawk* itself. Thus, when DEVIANT plays GRIM, the latter will be using *hawk* and only *hawk* in the long run. The best that DEVIANT can then do is to play *hawk* as well in the long run. Thus DEVIANT will get a payoff of 1, which is certainly not better than 3. This contradiction shows that there is *no* DEVIANT machine that does better than GRIM when playing GRIM. It follows that (GRIM, GRIM) is a Nash equilibrium.

Tit-for-Tat v. Tit-for-Tat. The GRIM strategy gets its name because it punishes any deviant behavior relentlessly. An offender is offered no opportunity for repentance. Once a transgression has been observed, the opponent is damned forever.

The TIT-FOR-TAT strategy is more forgiving. It punishes any transgression enough to make the transgression unprofitable. But, after the punishment has been administered, the offender is welcomed back to the fold once more until he or she offends again.

Notice that, when TIT-FOR-TAT plays itself, the result is cooperation and both machines get a payoff of 3. To check that (TIT-FOR-TAT, TIT-FOR-TAT) is a Nash equilibrium, consider a machine DEVIANT that gets a payoff of more than 3 when playing TIT-FOR-TAT. The DEVIANT machine would have to play *hawk* eventually. But then TIT-FOR-TAT retaliates by playing *hawk* until DEVIANT plays *dove* again. Thus, as Figure 8.8 makes clear, DEVIANT gains nothing. For each stage at which

					Deviation				Penance	
I	Payoff	3	3	3	6	1	1	1	0	3
I	DEVIANT	*D*	*D*	*D*	*H*	*H*	*H*	*H*	*D*	*D*
	Stage	1	2	3	4	5	6	7	8	9
II	TIT-FOR-TAT	*D*	*D*	*D*	*D*	*H*	*H*	*H*	*H*	*D*
II	Payoff	3	3	3	0	1	1	1	6	3
						Punishment				

Figure 8.8 Punishment and redemption.

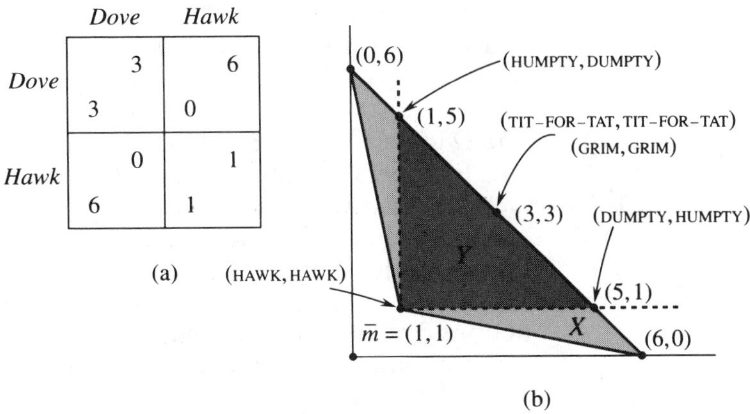

Figure 8.9 Nash equilibrium outcomes.

it gets a stage-game payoff of 6 by playing *hawk* when TIT-FOR-TAT plays *dove*, DEVIANT has to suffer a counter-balancing stage-game payoff of 0 when it plays *dove* to get TIT-FOR-TAT out of its punishment phase.

Humpty v. Dumpty. When HUMPTY plays DUMPTY, they cycle through the sequence of action pairs (D, H), (D, H), (D, H), (D, H), (D, H), (H, D) over and over again. If either were to deviate, eternal punishment would follow as in the GRIM strategy. Thus (HUMPTY, DUMPTY) is a Nash equilibrium.

8.4.4 Folk Theorem

Figure 8.9(a) shows the one-shot Prisoners' Dilemma yet again. Figure 8.9(b) illustrates its cooperative payoff region X. All the Nash equilibrium outcomes for the infinitely repeated version of the Prisoners' Dilemma studied in Section 8.4.3 are shown in Figure 8.9(b). There are also many more Nash equilibrium outcomes. If they were all marked in Figure 8.9(b), they would fill up the deeply shaded part of X completely.[16]

This fact is a consequence of a general result that game theorists call the *folk theorem*.[17] Its proof is easy, but some time will be spent getting ready for the proof. Most of what

[16]To be precise, any x in X satisfying $x \geq (1, 1)$ is a Nash equilibrium provided that x_1 and x_2 are rational numbers. The latter restriction is necessary because only strategies representable by finite automata are being considered.

[17]Folk as in folklore. In the early days of game theory it seems that everybody knew the theorem but nobody knew to whom it should be attributed.

needs to be done consists simply of restating ideas already introduced for the infinitely repeated Prisoners' Dilemma in a more general way.

Math 8.5 ⟶

The Game $G^{\#}$. In what follows, the role previously played by the Prisoners' Dilemma will be taken over by a general finite game G. This will be the stage-game for an infinitely repeated game G^{∞}. Player I's pure strategy set S for the one-shot game G will be the set of actions available to him at each stage of G^{∞}. Player II's pure strategy set T for G will be the set of actions available to her at each stage of G^{∞}.

As we know, the pure strategies for the players in G^{∞} are very complicated. Attention will therefore be restricted to pure strategies in G^{∞} that can be represented by finite automata. The set of Moore machines with input set T and output set S will be denoted by A. The set of Moore machines with input S and output set T will be denoted by B. The sets A and B will be the pure strategy sets for a game $G^{\#}$ that is to be the final object of study. One may regard player I's choice of an automaton a in A as being the decision to delegate responsibility for playing G^{∞} to the machine a. Similarly, player II's choice of b in B can be seen as the decision to delegate responsibility to b.

To analyze $G^{\#}$, payoff functions $V_i : A \times B \to \mathbb{R}$ need to be introduced. The definitions make use of the payoff functions $\pi_i : S \times T \to \mathbb{R}$ of the original one-shot game G.

If player I chooses a in A, and player II chooses b in B, then the two automata will eventually cycle through the same sequence of states forever.[18] Figure 8.6 gives some examples. Suppose the cycle is N stages long, and that the pairs of actions through which the machines cycle are $(s_1, t_1), (s_2, t_2), \ldots, (s_n, t_n)$. Then player i's payoff in $G^{\#}$ is defined as

$$V_i(a, b) = \frac{1}{N} \sum_{n=1}^{N} \pi_i(s_n, t_n) . \tag{8.2}$$

Thus, a player's payoff in $G^{\#}$ is what the player gets on average during the cycle into which play finally settles. As explained in Section 8.4.2, evaluating the players' income streams in this way is an attempt to evade the difficulties that would arise with a discount factor $\delta = 1$.

[18]If a has m states and b has n states, then there are only mn pairs of states. Thus, after mn stages, the two machines *must* return to a situation identical to one they have jointly experienced previously. They are then doomed to reiterate their past behavior from that point on.

Consider, as an example, the case illustrated in Figure 8.6(a). The one-shot game G is the Prisoners' Dilemma. The automaton a is TIT-FOR-TAT and the automaton b is TWEEDLEDUM. The length of a cycle is $N = 4$, and $(s_1, s_2) = (D, H)$, $(s_2, t_2) = (s_3, t_3) = (H, H)$, $(s_4, t_4) = (H, D)$. Thus

$$\begin{aligned}(V_1(a,b), V_2(a,b)) &= \tfrac{1}{4}\{(0,6) + (1,1) + (1,1) + (6,0)\} \\ &= \tfrac{1}{4}(0,6) + \tfrac{1}{2}(1,1) + \tfrac{1}{4}(6,0) = (2,2)\,.\end{aligned}$$

Lemma 8.4.1 Any outcome of $G^\#$ is necessarily a point of the cooperative payoff region of the one-shot game G.

Proof. Suppose that (s, t) is a pure strategy pair for G. Then $(\pi_1(s,t), \pi_2(s,t))$ is the pair of payoffs that goes in the sth row and tth column of the strategic form of G. The cooperative payoff region of G is the convex hull of all such payoff pairs (Section 5.3). From (8.2),

$$(V_1(a,b), V_2(a,b)) = \frac{1}{N}\sum_{n=1}^{N}(\pi_1(s_n, t_n), \pi_2(s_n, t_n))\,,$$

and hence the outcome $(V_1(a,b), V_2(a,b))$ of the game $G^\#$ is a convex combination (Section 5.2.1) of payoff pairs in the strategic form of G. It therefore lies in the cooperative payoff region of G. □

Minimax Point. Player i's *maximin value* $\underline{m}_i$ for the one-shot game G is defined in terms of his or her payoff matrix M_i as discussed in Section 6.2. This is player i's security level in G if the players are confined to using pure strategies (Section 6.3.1). It is important to emphasize that it is not player i's maximin value that will matter here, but his or her *minimax value* $\overline{m}_i$. It is always true that $\underline{m}_i \leq \overline{m}_i$ (Theorem 6.2.1), but $\underline{m}_i = \overline{m}_i$ if and only if it happens that the payoff matrix M_i has a saddle point (Theorem 6.2.2).[19]

The minimax point $\overline{m} = (\overline{m}_1, \overline{m}_2)$ for the Prisoners' Dilemma is $(1, 1)$. In this special case $(1, 1)$ is also the maximin point $\underline{m}$. The minimax point $\overline{m}$ for the bimatrix game[20] of

[19] Von Neumann's minimax theorem (Theorem 6.4.4) says that $\underline{v}_i = \overline{v}_i$. But $\underline{v}_i$ and $\overline{v}_i$ are player i's maximin and minimax values *when mixed strategies are allowed.* In this section, mixed strategies are excluded in an attempt to keep things reasonably simple, although the results would be more elegant if mixed strategies were admitted. (Exercise 8.6.26.)

[20] Its payoff matrices will be familiar from Section 6.2. Player I's payoff matrix is M of Figure 6.1. Player II's payoff matrix is the transpose of the matrix N of Figure 6.2 (Why the *transpose* of N?)

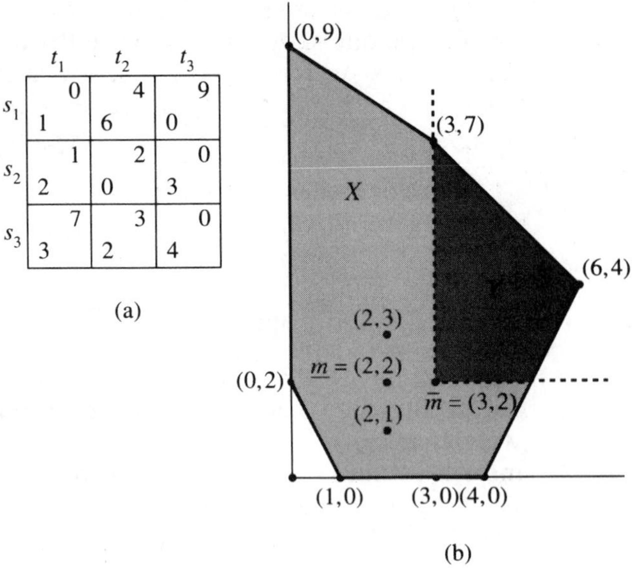

Figure 8.10 A minimax point.

Figure 8.10(a) is (3, 2). Its maximin point $\underline{m}$ is (2, 2). As always, $\underline{m} \leq \overline{m}$. Figure 8.10(b) shows the cooperative payoff region of the game together with the location of $\underline{m}$ and $\overline{m}$.

Some rephrasing of the definition of the minimax value $\overline{m}_1$ will help with the next lemma. For each pure strategy t in T available to player II, let $r_1(t)$ be one of player I's best replies in S (Section 7.1.1). Then

$$\pi_1(r_1(t), t) = \max_{s \in S} \pi_1(s, t) .$$

It follows that

$$\overline{m}_1 = \min_{t \in T} \max_{s \in S} \pi_1(s, t) = \min_{t \in T} \pi_1(r_1(t), t) . \qquad (8.3)$$

One trivial consequence of this rephrasing of the definition is that any Nash equilibrium (σ, τ) in pure strategies of the one-shot game G necessarily assigns each player at least his or her minimax value. The reason is simple. Since σ is a best reply to τ,

$$\pi_1(\sigma, \tau) = \pi_1(r_1(\tau), \tau) \geq \min_{t \in T} \pi_1(r_1(t), t) = \overline{m}_1 .$$

Similarly, the fact that τ is a best reply to σ implies that $\pi_2(\sigma, \tau) \geq \overline{m}_2$.

The following lemma says something that is superficially very similar. But remember that $G^{\#}$ is a very different game from G. The pure strategies in $G^\#$ are automata that play the *repeated* game G^∞.

Lemma 8.4.2 Any Nash equilibrium of $G^\#$ assigns each player at least his or her minimax value in the one-shot game G.

Proof. It will be shown that, if player I's payoff $V_1(a,b)$ is less than $\overline{m}_1$, then player I has a better reply to b than a, and hence (a,b) cannot be a Nash equilibrium for $G^\#$. The better reply is easy to find. Simply take an automaton c in A that makes a best one-shot reply to b at every stage of the repeated game.[21] If $\pi_1(s_n,t_n)$ is the very worst stage-game payoff that c ever gets in playing b, then

$$\begin{aligned} V_1(c,b) &\geq \pi_1(s_n,t_n) \\ &= \pi_1(r_1(t_n),t_n) \\ &\geq \min_{t\in T} \pi_1(r_1(t),t) = \overline{m}_1 . \end{aligned}$$

Nobody says that c is a *best* reply to b, but it is a better reply than a when $V_1(a,b) < \overline{m}_1$. It follows that, if (a,b) is a Nash equilibrium for $G^\#$, then $V_1(a,b) \geq \overline{m}_1$. Similarly, $V_2(a,b) \geq \overline{m}_2$. □

The conclusions of Lemmas 8.4.1 and 8.4.2 are illustrated in two special cases by Figures 8.9(b) and 8.10(b). All pure strategy, Nash equilibrium outcomes for the game $G^\#$ lie in the set $Y = \{x : x \in X \text{ and } x \geq \overline{m}\}$.

In the case of the Prisoners' Dilemma of Figure 8.10(b), various particular Nash equilibrium outcomes for $G^\#$ are indicated. When G is the game of Figure 8.10(a), no Nash equilibrium outcomes for $G^\#$ have been studied so far. One equilibrium is easy to identify. Since (s_3,t_1) is a Nash equilibrium for the *one-shot* game G, it must be a Nash equilibrium in $G^\#$ for player I to choose an automaton that always plays s_3, and for player II to choose an automaton that always plays t_1. Thus $(3,7)$ is a Nash equilibrium outcome for $G^\#$. However, the next theorem shows that this Nash equilibrium outcome for $G^\#$ is only one of many more.

Theorem 8.4.1 (Folk Theorem) Let X be the cooperative payoff region of a finite one-shot game G, and let $\overline{m}$ be its

---

[21] If b plays t_1 at stage one, then c should play $r_1(t_1)$ at stage one. After observing c's play, b will switch states and play t_2 at stage two. Thus c should play $r_1(t_2)$ at stage two. And so on. Eventually, b will return to a state it has occupied previously. The two automata will then begin to cycle. Note that c needs no more states than b.

minimax point. Then the outcomes corresponding to Nash equilibria in pure strategies of the game $G^\#$ are dense[22] in the set

$$Y = \{x : x \in X \text{ and } x \geq \overline{m}\}.$$

Math 8.4.5 ⟶

Proof. Suppose that $x_1, x_2, \ldots, x_K$ are payoff pairs that appear in the strategic form of G. Let $q_1, q_2, \ldots, q_K$ be nonnegative rational numbers satisfying $q_1 + q_2 + \cdots + q_K = 1$. Then

$$y = q_1 x_1 + q_2 x_2 + \cdots + q_K x_K$$

is a convex combination of $x_1, x_2, \ldots, x_K$ and hence lies in X. The set of all such y is dense in X. The idea of the proof is to show that, if $y \geq \overline{m}$, then y is a Nash equilibrium outcome of $G^\#$.

Let the pure strategy pairs that generate the outcomes $x_1, x_2, \ldots, x_K$ of G be (s_1, t_1), (s_2, t_2), ..., (s_K, t_K). This means that $x_k = (\pi_1(s_k, t_k), \pi_2(s_k, t_k))$, for $k = 1, 2, \ldots, K$.

Next look at the fractions q_1, q_2, ..., q_K. These can be written with a common denominator N so that $q_k = n_k/N$ $(k = 1, 2, \ldots K)$, where n_k is a nonnegative integer. It is then true that

$$n_1 + n_2 + \cdots + n_K = N.$$

To achieve the outcome y of $G^\#$, two automata a and b will be constructed that perpetually cycle through a sequence of N action pairs. First they play (s_1, t_1) for n_1 stages, then they play (s_2, t_2) for n_2 stages, then they play (s_3, t_3) for n_3 stages, and so on. Finally, they complete the cycle by playing (s_K, t_K) for n_K stages, after which the cycle begins again. Player i's payoff in $G^\#$ is then

$$\frac{1}{N}\sum_{k=1}^{K} n_k \pi_i(s_k, t_k) = \sum_{k=1}^{K} q_k \pi_i(s_k, t_k),$$

which is the ith coordinate of y. Thus, when automaton a plays automaton b, the outcome of $G^\#$ that results is the payoff pair y.

[22]For example, the rational numbers are dense in the set $\mathbb{R}$ of all real numbers. Each real number can be approximated arbitrarily closely by a rational number. Consider, for example, the real number $\pi = 3.14159\ldots$. A rational number that approximates π to within an accuracy of 0.0005 is 3.142. A rational number that approximates π within an accuracy of 0.00005 is 3.1416.

Recall that a rational number is a fraction m/n in which m and $n \neq 0$ are integers. The integers are $0, \pm 1, \pm 2, \pm 3, \ldots$.

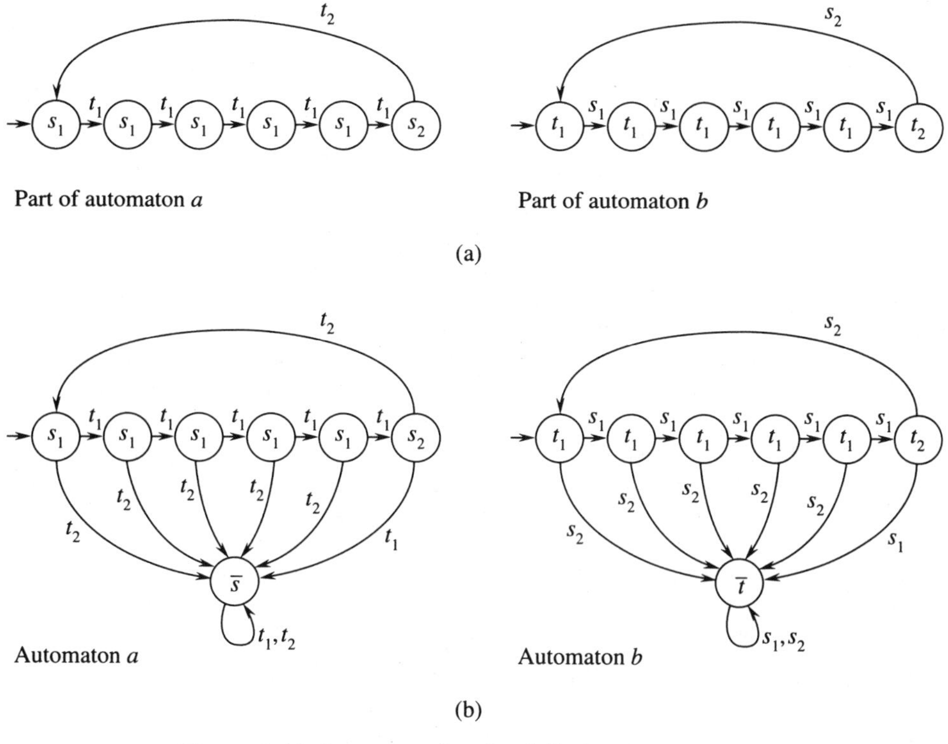

Figure 8.11 Automata for the folk theorem.

As an example, consider the case when $K = 2$ and $q_1 = \frac{5}{6}$, $q_2 = \frac{1}{6}$. Then the common denominator of the fractions q_1 and q_2 is $N = 6$, with $n_1 = 5$ and $n_2 = 1$. Figure 8.11(a) shows the structure of the automata a and b so far specified in this special case.

The automata HUMPTY and DUMPTY of Figure 8.5 provide a fully specified version of the example just considered. In their case, the one-shot game G is the Prisoners' Dilemma, for which X and $\overline{m}$ are as in Figure 8.9(b). The payoff vectors x_1 and x_2 are (0,6) and (6,0) respectively. (These are generated by the pure strategy pairs $(s_1, t_1) = (D, H)$ and $(s_2, t_2) = (H, D)$.) The payoff pair y that results when HUMPTY plays DUMPTY in $G^\#$ is given by

$$y = q_1 x_1 + q_2 x_2 = \tfrac{5}{6}(0,6) + \tfrac{1}{6}(6,0) = (1,5)\,.$$

Notice that y lies in the set Y of Figure 8.9(b).

HUMPTY and DUMPTY have more structure than the uncompleted automata drawn in Figure 8.11(a). Their extra structure guarantees that each is a best reply to the other, so that (HUMPTY, DUMPTY) is a Nash equilibrium for $G^\#$. The extra structure specifies how the opponent is to be *punished* if it ever deviates from the specified cycle of behavior in which one (H, D) stage is always followed and preceded by five (D, H) stages. In the case of HUMPTY and DUMPTY, the punishment consists of the grim expedient of always playing *hawk* after a deviation by the opponent. Neither player can therefore gain by replacing HUMPTY or DUMPTY or by a DEVIANT machine for the reasons given in Section 8.4.3.

To finish the proof of the folk theorem, it remains to complete the construction of a and b. As in HUMPTY and DUMPTY, punishments must be found that will deter either player from replacing a or b by a deviant machine that departs from the cycle of behavior leading to the outcome y in $G^\#$.

The significant feature about *hawk* as a punishment in the infinitely repeated Prisoners' Dilemma is that it *minimaxes* the opponent. In general, the action $\bar{s}$ by player I that *minimaxes* player II in G satisfies

$$\pi_2(\bar{s}, r_2(\bar{s})) = \min_{s \in S} \pi_2(s, r_2(s)) = \overline{m}_2 .$$

Thus, even if player II makes a best reply $r_2(\bar{s})$ to $\bar{s}$, she still gets no more than her minimax value $\overline{m}_2$.

The idea of minimaxing actions $\bar{s}$ and $\bar{t}$ for players I and II in the one-shot game G allows the construction of the automata a and b to be completed as illustrated in Figure 8.11(b). If there is a departure from the sequence that sustains y, the deviant is minimaxed by the opponent at all later stages.

Player I, for example, will now have nothing to gain by replacing a by some deviant automaton c provided that $y \geq \overline{m}_1$. If c plays like a, it will get only y_1. If it deviates from the way a plays, it will trigger b's punishment phase and get only $\overline{m}_1$. Similarly, player II can do no better than b provided that $y_2 \geq \overline{m}_2$.

This proves the folk theorem. Provided $y \geq \overline{m}$, each of a and b is a best reply to the other. Since the outcome when a plays b in $G^\#$ is y, it follows that y is a Nash equilibrium outcome of $G^\#$. □

The preceding proof leaves some loose ends that need to be tied up. The first question that arises is why only Nash equilibria have been discussed, although previous chapters have stressed the importance of subgame-perfect equilibria. This question is taken up in Section 8.4.5. For the moment, attention will be focused on a second question. What happens if the minimax point $\overline{m}$ does not lie below the Pareto frontier of X, as in Exercise 8.6.23? Lemmas 8.4.1 and 8.4.2 then tell us that $G^{\#}$ has no Nash equilibria at all in pure strategies. In such cases, the lesson of Chapter 6 is that one should look for equilibria in mixed strategies. The folk theorem then continues to hold, but $\overline{m}$ is replaced by $\overline{v}$ (the minimax point of G when mixed strategies are allowed).[23]

8.4.5 Who Guards the Guardians?

In previous chapters, much fuss was made about the inadequacy of the Nash equilibrium concept. However, in discussing the folk theorem, only Nash equilibria were considered. **Phil 8.5** → Why have subgame-perfect equilibria been neglected?

It is *not* that the issues that led to our introducing subgame-perfect equilibria are irrelevant here. On the contrary, the problems raised in Sections 1.8.2, 4.6.3 and 7.5.2 are at least as pressing for repeated games as anywhere else. For example, in the preceding section, Nash equilibria were studied that sustained cooperative outcomes. In these equilibria, players are deterred from departing from cooperative play by the prospect of being punished. They believe that, if they were to deviate, the opponent would retaliate by minimaxing them. Hence they never *actually* deviate and so the punishment is never *actually* inflicted. In such situations, one should always ask whether the beliefs attributed to the players make sense. Is it really credible that, if player I were to deviate, player II would minimax him relentlessly thereafter, regardless of how damaging this may be to her own payoff in the game?[24] Clearly the answer is *no*. The question then arises: can equilibrium strategies be found in which the planned punishments *are* always credible, and hence *will* deter rational players from deviating? The answer to this question is *yes*. That is to say, a version of the folk theorem holds with Nash equilibria replaced by subgame-perfect equilibria.

A precise proof for such a souped-up version of the folk theorem is not offered because it is full of fussy details. However, it is not hard to explain what a subgame-perfect strategy

---

[23]By Von Neumann's minimax theorem (Theorem 6.4.4), $\overline{v} = \underline{v}$. By Nash's theorem (Theorem 7.7.1), the one-shot game G always has a Nash equilibrium if mixed strategies are allowed. If this Nash equilibrium generates the outcome y, then we know from Exercise 7.9.10 that $\overline{v} \leq y \in X$. It follows that the set Y of the folk theorem with mixed strategies is never empty.

[24]For example, in the game of Figure 8.10(a), if player I always minimaxes player II, he gets less than his own minimax value, assuming that she responds by making the optimal reply.

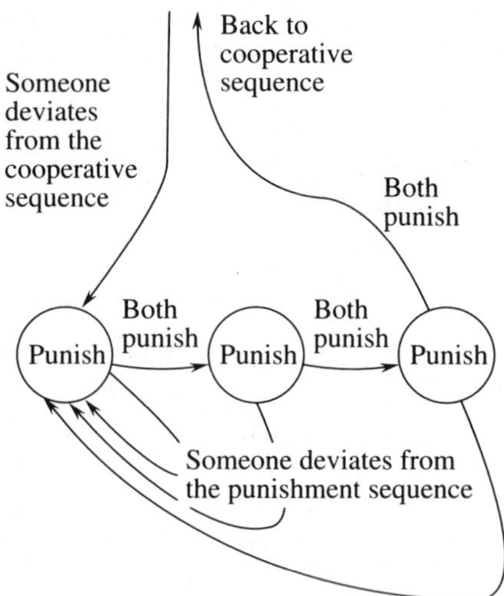

Figure 8.12 Guarding the guardians.

looks like in general terms. Figure 8.12 shows a suitable punishment scheme. If someone departs from the cooperative sequence,[25] they are then punished for however many stages are necessary to render the deviation unprofitable.[26] If the punishment is successfully administered, both players then return to their cooperative phase. But what if someone fails to punish when punishment is called for? Then *this* behavior is punished. And if someone fails to punish someone who has failed to punish when punishment is called for, then *this* behavior is punished also. And so on.

Such constructions provide a formal answer to an age-old question that is usually posed by quoting in Latin from the Roman satirist Juvenal:

> Pone seram; cohibe:
> *Sed quis custodiet ipsos custodes*?
> Cauta est, et ab illis incipit uxor.[27]

The italicized phrase translates as: who guards the guardians?[28] The game-theoretic answer is that, if things are properly

[25] In the story told here, *both* players then switch into the punishment schedule. This means that the Moore machines would need to input, not only what the opponent did, but also what they did themselves last time.

[26] In Figure 8.12, three stages of punishment are taken to be adequate.

[27] Who says this isn't a classy text?

[28] Who they are guarding and why the guards might prove untrustworthy is best left unsaid. Someone with Juvenal's views about the status of women would not last long on a modern university campus.

organized, they can successfully be left to *guard each other.* Of course, this answer comes as no surprise to those who run secret police forces in totalitarian states.

Phil
8.6 ⟶

8.5 Social Contract

What is the cement that holds society together? Since ancient times, philosophers have tried to frame explanations in terms of a "social contract". This is to be envisaged as an implicit agreement to which we are all party and which we use to regulate our dealings with each other.

The word "contract" is unfortunate. It suggests both that we are fully conscious of the terms of the agreement, and that something enforces our adherence to its terms. But neither of these properties of a contract as normally understood necessarily applies in the case of a *social* contract. In particular, if it does make sense to envisage a social contract as providing the organizing principle of a society, then it has to be explained why people honor the terms of the contract. One cannot postulate any policemen for this purpose. Before the social contract was in place, there were no policemen. Indeed, part of what a social contract is about is the provision of a police force.

By this stage, it will be clear what answer a game theorist will make. If the social contract embodies an agreement to coordinate on a suitable *equilibrium*, then people will honor the terms of the social contract because it is in their interests to do so. The social contract will be *self-policing*. The guardians will guard each other. *No* cement will be necessary to hold society together. It will have the character of a dry-stone wall in which each stone is held in place by its neighbors and reciprocates, in its turn, by helping to hold its neighbors in their places.

Such a viewpoint identifies the idea of a social contract with the notion of a *convention* as discussed in Section 7.3.2. In discussing conventions, the philosopher David Hume emphasized the fact that society is not a one-shot game. In a famous passage from his *Treatise on Human Nature* he says:

> I learn to do service to another, without bearing him any real kindness: because I foresee that he will return my service, in expectation of another of the same kind, and in order to maintain the same correspondence of good offices with me or others. And accordingly, after I have serv'd him and he is in possession of the advantage arising from my action, he is induc'd to perform his part, as foreseeing the consequences of his refusal.

This was written more than 200 years before the theory of repeated games was conceived, but it already captures everything that matters about equilibria that sustain cooperative outcomes. The secret is *reciprocity*. Usually, this word is used to describe I'll-scratch-your-back-if-you'll-scratch-mine principles.[29] However, Hume mentions not only the importance to someone I help of his maintaining good offices *with me*, but also the importance of his maintaining good offices *with others*. How might such an I-won't-scratch-your-back-if-you-won't-scratch-*their*-backs principle work?

8.5.1 An Overlapping Generations Model

This simple model is intended to answer the question that concluded the preceding discussion of the social contract. It will also serve as a further example of the ideas behind the folk theorem.

Imagine a world in which there are only two people alive at any stage: a mother and a daughter.[30] Each individual lives for precisely two periods. The first of these is a player's *youth* and the second is her *old age*. Some details of a player's life history are fixed. In her youth, she works, and earns two units of a perishable good. This is wholesome if and only if it is consumed in the *same* period that it is earned. At the end of her youthful stage, each player gives birth to a daughter. The mother then enters her elderly stage during which she is too feeble to work, and so earns nothing.[31]

Everyone would prefer not to consume all their earnings in their youth. All players would prefer to consume one unit in their youth and one unit in their old age. Unfortunately, the consumption good cannot be stored, and so the second possibility cannot be achieved unless there are transfers of the good from one player to another.

One equilibrium is for each player to consume everything she earns in her youth. Everyone will then have to endure a miserable old age, but everyone will be optimizing given the choices of the others.

---

[29]These would be better phrased as I-*won't*-scratch-your-back-if-you-*won't*-scratch-mine.

[30]As the world in which the game is played contains no males, one must imagine that reproduction is parthenogenetic.

[31]To avoid chicken and egg problems, assume that the past has an infinite horizon just like the future. The resulting model will not strictly be a game, because it has no first move. However, this does not affect anything important here.

A more socially desirable outcome would be for each daughter to give her mother one of the two units of the daughter's consumption good. Everyone would then be able to enjoy one unit of consumption in each period of her life. But is such behavior sustainable as an equilibrium?

Suppose first that each daughter adopts the strategy of giving one unit of her earnings to her mother if and only if her mother behaved similarly in the previous period. This is a *Nash* equilibrium. No deviant would gain anything if everybody else stuck to their equilibrium strategies. The best a deviant could do is to consume all her own income in her youth, but then her daughter's equilibrium strategy calls for the daughter to punish such selfish behavior. The punishment consists of the daughter's withholding the gift of one unit of the consumption good that she would otherwise make. The deviant will then be left with nothing in her old age.

Notice, however, that a daughter would not *want* to punish her deviant mother. If she did, she too would be punished by *her* daughter. The Nash equilibrium we have discovered is therefore not a subgame-perfect equilibrium because it calls for behavior off the equilibrium path that is not credible for rational players. A *subgame-perfect* equilibrium that sustains the cooperative outcome is easy to find. Each daughter gives one unit of the consumption good to her mother if and only if *nobody* has *ever* done anything different in the past. The punishments in this subgame-perfect equilibrium are grim indeed. Punishment extends, not only to the third and fourth generation as in the Bible, but to *all* descendants of the transgressor. Can we not find a subgame-perfect equilibrium in which only the guilty are punished?

To this end, call a player a *conformist* if she gives her mother one unit of the consumption good, provided that her mother acts as a *conformist* should. Otherwise, a *conformist* daughter gives her mother nothing. In this set-up, *conformists* reward other *conformists* and punish *nonconformists*. Thus, it is a subgame-perfect equilibrium for everybody to be a *conformist*.[32]

Some people are outraged by such stories about how societies might, in principle, be held together. The stories are said to "denigrate the human spirit", or to "devalue the human capacity for love". To react this way is to miss the point of such stories. Game theorists are just as fond of apple pie and

---

[32]The circularity built into the definition of a *conformist* is only apparent. Once a daughter at time t who gives her mother a unit of the consumption good at time t has been judged to have conformed, this determines whether any player at a later time is *conformist* or *nonconformist*.

their mothers as anyone else. They know perfectly well that daughters often look after their elderly mothers because they love them. The overlapping generations model is a *parable*. It is not meant to be a realistic statement about the human condition. It is meant to focus attention very sharply on just one aspect of human existence, and it does so very successfully. It teaches us that, even if all daughters were stonyhearted and selfish, it would not necessarily follow that their mothers would be neglected. In a society that has coordinated on a suitable social contract, mothers would be cared for because it would be in the daughters' best interests to do so. If what their heads tell them to do happens to be what their hearts yearn for, so much the better for the daughters—and for the stability of the society in which they live.

8.6 Exercises

1. Section 8.2 studies the twice-repeated, zero-sum game Z of Figure 8.1(a) under the assumption that a player's payoff in the repeated game Z^2 is $x + y$, where x is the player's payoff at the first stage and y is his or her payoff at the second stage. What matrix would replace Figure 8.3(b) if the payoffs in Z^2 were taken to be
   (a) $x + \frac{1}{2}y$ (b) xy ?
2. The set H in Section 8.2 is the set of possible histories of play just before Z is played for the second time. How many elements does Z have? How many elements would H have if Z were a 3×4 matrix game? How many elements would H have if it were the set of histories of play just before Z was played for the fifth time?

Math

3. Show that the n-times repeated Prisoners' Dilemma has

$$2^{4^0} \times 2^{4^1} \times 2^{4^2} \times \cdots \times 2^{4^{n-1}} = 2^{(4^n-1)/3}$$

   pure strategies. Give an estimate of how many decimal digits it takes to write down the number of pure strategies in the ten-times repeated Prisoners' Dilemma.
4. A repeated game G^n results when G is played precisely n times in succession. The payoffs in G^n are obtained by summing the payoffs in each stage-game. If G has a unique Nash equilibrium, show that G^n has a unique subgame-perfect equilibrium and that this requires each player to plan always to use his or her Nash equilibrium strategy at every stage.

5. Recall that the game Chicken of Figure 7.3(c) has three Nash equilibria. Why does it follow that the game obtained by repeating Chicken twice and summing the stage-game payoffs has at least nine subgame-perfect equilibria?

Math 6. Theorem 8.3.1 shows that, when the Prisoners' Dilemma is repeated a finite number of times, there is a unique *subgame-perfect* equilibrium in which each player always plans to play *hawk*. Prove that all *Nash* equilibria also lead to *hawk* always *actually* being played, but that Nash equilibria exist in which players plan to use *dove* under certain contingencies that never arise when the equilibrium is used.

Econ 7. Theorem 8.3.1 shows that, when the Prisoners' Dilemma is repeated a finite number of times, there is a unique subgame-perfect equilibrium in which each player always plans to play *hawk*. Use a similar formal argument to prove the conclusion of Exercise 4.8.30(b) for the finitely repeated Chain-store Game.

8. Section 8.3.2 studies a version of the repeated Prisoners' Dilemma in which the probability p that any particular repetition will be the last is given by $p = \frac{1}{3}$. What is the largest value of p for which the pair of GRIM strategies described in Section 8.3.2 constitutes a Nash equilibrium? What is the largest value of p for which the same is true when the underlying Prisoners' Dilemma game has the payoffs shown in Figure 8.13(a)?

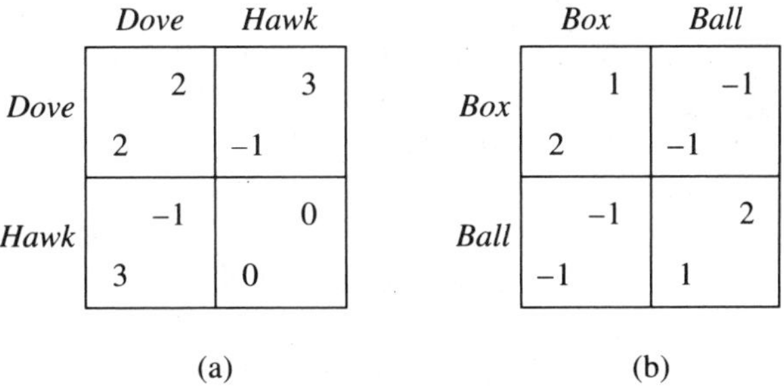

Figure 8.13 The games for Exercises 8.6.8 and 8.6.29.

Phil 9. Section 8.3.1 concerns *perfectly* rational players whose behavior may look foolish to a kibitzer. *Imperfectly* rational players may find it easier to cooperate in the finitely repeated Prisoners' Dilemma. Consider, for example, players who are "satisficers" in the sense proposed by Herbert Simon. Such players are satisfied with a strategy that yields *nearly* the optimum payoff.[33] For satisficers, the idea of a Nash equilibrium should perhaps be replaced by that of an ε-equilibrium. This is a pair (σ, τ) of strategies for which requirement (4.3) for a Nash equilibrium is replaced by the requirement that

$$\left.\begin{array}{l}\pi_1(\sigma,\tau) \geq \pi_1(s,\tau) - \varepsilon \\ \pi_2(\sigma,\tau) \geq \pi_2(\sigma,t) - \varepsilon\end{array}\right\}$$

for all s in S and all t in T. Here ε is some small positive number that represents how close the players need to be to the optimum in order to be satisfied.

Consider the n-times repeated Prisoners' Dilemma of Figure 8.4(a) in which the payoffs are taken to be the *average* of the payoffs in the stage-games. If n is sufficiently large, show that Nash equilibria exist for this repeated game in which the players cooperate at every stage. (Consider a pair of GRIM strategies, as described in Section 8.3.2.) How large does n need to be as a function of ε? How large does n need to be when the stage-game is the version of the Prisoners' Dilemma given in Figure 8.13(a)?

Econon

10. **Econ** Figure 7.16(a) shows the cooperative payoff region Z when the firms can make binding collusive agreements in the Cournot duopoly problem of Section 7.2.1. Indicate the bargaining set obtained in Exercise 7.9.35(a) on a copy of this diagram. On the same diagram, show the set of all pairs (a, b) of profits per period that can be sustained as equilibrium outcomes in the manner described in Section 8.3.3, provided that the discount factor δ is sufficiently large.

11. **Econ** In Exercise 4.8.30 and in Exercise 8.6.7, we learned that an incumbent monopolist in the finitely repeated Chain-store Game cannot establish a reputation for being tough by fighting early entrants into his markets. This exercise concerns the infinitely repeated case. Assume that the monopolist evaluates his income stream using a discount factor δ satisfying $0 < \delta < 1$.

[33] They may, for example, care about the costs involved in calculating the precise optimum. If so, one should then properly model the costs of calculation, and how the players go about estimating these. However, as is frequently the case, doing things properly is not very easy.

Consider a strategy s for the monopolist that calls for him to fight an entrant if and only if he has never acquiesced to an entry in the past. Consider a strategy t_i for the ith potential entrant that calls for entering the market if and only if the monopolist has acquiesced to an entry in the past. Is this strategy profile a Nash equilibrium if δ is sufficiently large? Is it subgame-perfect?

12. Figure 8.5 gives pictorial representations of some finite automata suitable for playing the repeated Prisoners' Dilemma. Draw pictures of the 26 such machines that have at most two states.

Phil 13. Exercise 8.6.9 considers one way in which imperfect rationality can lead to cooperation in the finitely repeated Prisoners' Dilemma. In the current exercise, the players are perfectly rational, but they are forced to express their strategies as computer programs drawn from a restricted set. The computer programs are modeled as Moore machines of the type considered in Section 8.4.1, with the proviso that only machines with at most 100 states are available for selection.[34] Why can such a machine not count up to 101? Why does it follow that the pair (GRIM, GRIM) is a Nash equilibrium in the automaton-selection game when the Prisoners' Dilemma is to be repeated 101 times?[35]

Math 14. Given an input set T and an output set S, a Moore machine is formally a quadruple $\langle Q, q_0, \lambda, \mu \rangle$ in which Q is a set of states, q_0 is the initial state, $\lambda : Q \to S$ is the output function, and $\mu : Q \times T \to Q$ is the transition function.

Which of the machines of Figure 8.5 is determined by the following specifications?

- $S = T = \{D, H\}$
- $q_0 = D$
- $\lambda(D) = D$; $\lambda(H) = H$
- $\mu(D, D) = D$; $\mu(D, H) = H$; $\mu(H, D) = D$; $\mu(H, H) = H$

[34]A kibitzer who didn't know that the players had been forced to delegate the play of the repeated game to simple computer programs might therefore think that the players are boundedly rational. It would seem to him that the players are incapable of solving computational problems whose resolution requires a finite automaton with more than 100 states.

[35]Neyman has shown that cooperation remains possible as a Nash equilibrium outcome even when the number of states allowed is very large compared with the number of times the Prisoners' Dilemma is to be repeated.

15. When cooperation in the infinitely repeated Prisoners' Dilemma is discussed, attention is often concentrated on strategies that are "nice" in that they are never the first to play *hawk*. Thus, for example, GRIM and TIT-FOR-TAT of Figure 8.5(c) and Figure 8.5(d) are both "nice".
    (a) Explain why the finite automaton TAT-FOR-TIT of Figure 8.14 is "nasty".
    (b) Draw diagrams like those of Figure 8.6 showing what happens when TAT-FOR-TIT plays itself, and what happens when it plays TIT-FOR-TAT in the repeated Prisoners' Dilemma based on Figure 8.13(a).

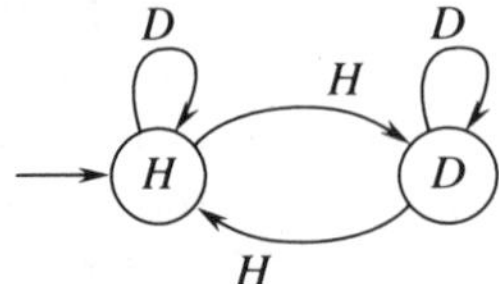

Figure 8.14 The machine TAT-FOR-TIT.

Math

16. Exercise 8.6.14 discusses the formal specification of a Moore machine as a quadruple $\langle Q, q_0, \lambda, \mu \rangle$. Give such a specification for the machine TAT-FOR-TIT of Figure 8.14.

Econ

17. The interest rate is fixed at 10%. You are offered an asset that pays \$1,000 from now until eternity at yearly intervals. You find its present value by calculating the sum of the discounted annual payments in the income stream secured by the asset. What discount factor will you use? Assuming there are no uncertainties, at what price will the asset be traded?

Econ

18. You borrow \$1,000 and agree to pay back 12 monthly installments of \$100.
    (a) It cost you \$200 to borrow \$1,000 for a year. Why is your yearly interest rate not equal to $200/1{,}000 = 20\%$?
    (b) What is the present value of the income stream 1,000, $-100, -100, \ldots, -100$ if the *monthly* interest rate is m? Find the approximate monthly interest rate μ you are paying by determining the value of m that makes this present value equal to zero.
    (c) What *yearly* interest rate is equivalent to the monthly interest rate μ?

Math

19. Suppose that TWEEDLEDUM evaluates his income stream in Figure 8.6(a) by computing its discounted sum using the discount factor δ, where $0 < \delta < 1$. Find the result

$U_2(a, b)$ of this calculation, and show that $(1-\delta)U_2(a, b) \to \frac{1}{4}(6+1+1+0) = 2$ as $\delta \to 1$. What is the corresponding result for TWEEDLEDUM in the case of the income stream of Figure 8.6(b)?

20. Find a restricted strategic form like that of Figure 8.7 for the infinitely repeated Prisoners' Dilemma based on Figure 8.13(a). Include only the strategies HAWK, DOVE, GRIM, TIT-FOR-TAT, together with the strategy TAT-FOR-TIT of Figure 8.14. Find all pure strategy Nash equilibria for this restricted strategic form.

Math

21. Show that a pair of TAT-FOR-TIT strategies, as specified in Figure 8.14, is a Nash equilibrium for the infinitely repeated Prisoners' Dilemma game based on Figure 8.13(a). (Assume that only strategies representable by finite automata are possible, and that players evaluate income streams by calculating their long-run average payoff.)

22. Consider the strategic form of Figure 7.10(a) for a value of x satisfying $0 < x < 10$.
    (a) Sketch the cooperative payoff region X on the assumption that neither free disposal nor transferable utility is possible. (Section 5.3.)
    (b) Find the maximin and minimax points, assuming that only pure strategies are permitted. Mark these on your diagram. (Sections 6.2.1 and 8.4.4.)
    (c) What does the folk theorem tell us about pure strategy Nash equilibria in the infinitely repeated version of the game? (Assume that only strategies representable by finite automata are possible, and that players evaluate an income stream by calculating its long-run average payoff.)
    (d) What happens if $x > 10$? What happens if $x < 0$?

23. Consider the strategic form of Figure 7.7(a).
    (a) Sketch the cooperative payoff region X on the assumption that neither free disposal nor transferable utility is possible. (Section 5.3.)
    (b) Why do all Nash equilibrium payoff pairs lie in X?
    (c) Find the maximin and minimax points, assuming that only pure strategies are permitted. Mark these on your diagram. (Sections 6.2.1 and 8.4.4.)
    (d) It follows from your diagram and Lemma 8.4.2 that the strategic form has no Nash equilibria in pure strategies. Why is this?
    (e) Check the preceding conclusion directly by circling payoffs in the strategic form that correspond to best replies. (Section 7.1.1.)

(f) What does the folk theorem tell us about pure strategy Nash equilibria in the infinitely repeated version of the game? (Assume that only strategies representable by finite automata are possible, and that players evaluate an income stream by calculating its long-run average payoff.)
(g) Find the unique Nash equilibrium in *mixed* strategies for the one-shot game. (Exercise 7.9.1.)
(h) Find a Nash equilibrium for the twice-repeated game. Find a Nash equilibrium for the infinitely repeated game.

24. Suppose that the two-player, zero-sum game of Figure 6.3(a) is repeated infinitely often. (Assume that only strategies representable by finite automata are possible, and that players evaluate an income stream by calculating its long-run average payoff.) What does the folk theorem tell us about pure strategy Nash equilibria in the repeated game? Answer the same question for the infinitely repeated version of the two-player, zero-sum game of Figure 6.3(b).

25. Find the maximin amd minimax points in the Cournot Duopoly Game of Section 7.2.1. What is the cooperative payoff region X if neither "transferable utility" nor free disposal are allowed? What does the folk theorem tell us about pure strategy Nash equilibria in the infinitely repeated version? (Assume that only strategies representable by finite automata are possible, and that players evaluate an income stream by calculating its long-run average payoff.)

Math

26. Obtain a version of the folk theorem that concerns mixed strategy equilibria. Assume that each player can directly observe the randomizing devices employed by the opponent in the past, and not just the actions that the opponent actually used. Why does this assumption matter?

Phil

27. Suppose that it is common knowledge that the players in a repeated game always jointly observe the fall of a coin before each stage is played. Give an example to show why this might be relevant.

28. The version of Chicken given in Figure 7.17(a) is repeated 100 times. The repeated game payoffs are just the sum of the stage-game payoffs. Consider a strategy s that tells you always to choose *dove* up until the 100th stage and to use *dove* and *hawk* with equal probabilities at the 100th stage—*unless* the two players have failed to use

the same actions at every preceding stage. If such a coordination failure has occurred in the past, s tells a player to look for the first stage at which differing actions were used and then always to use whatever action he or she did *not* play at that stage.

(a) Why is (s, s) a Nash equilibrium?
(b) Prove that (s, s) is a subgame-perfect equilibrium.
(c) Give some examples of income streams other than $2, 2, 2, \ldots, 2, 1$ that can be supported as equilibrium outcomes in a similar way.
(d) What is it about Chicken that allows such "folk theorem" results to be possible in the finitely repeated case?

29. Consider the version of the Battle of the Sexes given in Figure 8.13(b). Find the three Nash equilibria and explain why there is an equilibrium selection problem in the one-shot case. Now suppose that this version of the Battle of the Sexes is repeated n times. The repeated game payoffs are just the sum of the stage-game payoffs.

    Consider a strategy s that tells you always to choose *box* and *ball* with equal probabilities up until the last stage of the game, unless your choice coincides with that of the opponent at some stage. If the latter eventuality occurs, s requires you to continue by alternating between *box* and *ball* to the end of the game. If the last stage is reached without the players' choices ever being the same at any previous stage, s tells you to use your one-shot mixed equilibrium strategy at the final stage. Explain why (s, s) is a Nash equilibrium. Is it a subgame-perfect equilibrium?

Math

30. If both players use the strategy s in Exercise 8.6.29, let the expected payoff to one of the players be x_n, where n is the number of stages in the repeated game. Show that, for $n \geq 2$,

$$40x_n - 20x_{n-1} = 30n - 33 + (-1)^n 13\,.$$

    Solve this difference equation with the boundary condition $x_1 = \frac{1}{5}$, and hence compute a player's expected utility in the case when $n = 100$.

CHAPTER

9

Adjusting to Circumstances

9.1 Spontaneous Order

The buzz words for this chapter are *spontaneous order* and *bounded rationality*. Spontaneous combustion will perhaps be a familiar term. It is usually applied to hay stacks that catch fire by themselves without anybody setting them alight. Spontaneous order is said to arise when order emerges from confusion without anybody doing any organizing.

The favorite example of spontaneous order among economists is the perfectly competitive market. Buyers and sellers in a market do not care whether the scarce commodities in which they trade are produced and distributed in an efficient manner. They just want to make money. Nevertheless, their interaction in the market pushes the prices at which commodities are traded to the equilibrium levels at which supply is equal to demand.[1] Not only this, when trading at the equilibrium prices is complete, the outcome is Pareto-efficient. That is, nobody can be made better off without someone else being hurt. No socialist economy has ever come anywhere near such an achievement, in spite of the armies of planners and organizers that they traditionally use in seeking to make things better.

Biologists have even better examples. If the theory of evolution is to be believed, then all living organisms are examples of spontaneous order. Anthropologists can point to the organization of primitive societies. Nobody planned these. They evolved along with man himself. Sociologists and political scientists can similarly observe that much of what matters about modern societies is also unplanned. Even when attempts are made to reorganize society in a more humane or efficient manner, things seldom turn out to be much like the planners intended.

9.1.1 Chance and Necessity

Schelling's *Micromotives and Macrobehavior* contains a version of Solitaire that very effectively demonstrates how orderly arrangements can arise spontaneously, although nobody plans it that way. In his example, the order that arises is socially undesirable. However, there is a real sense in which nobody can be blamed. It was nobody's intention that the

[1] Subjects in laboratory simulations of market mechanisms often complain of a feeling of helplessness as they watch the prices quoted zeroing in on the market-clearing values, in spite of all their attempts to buck the trend.

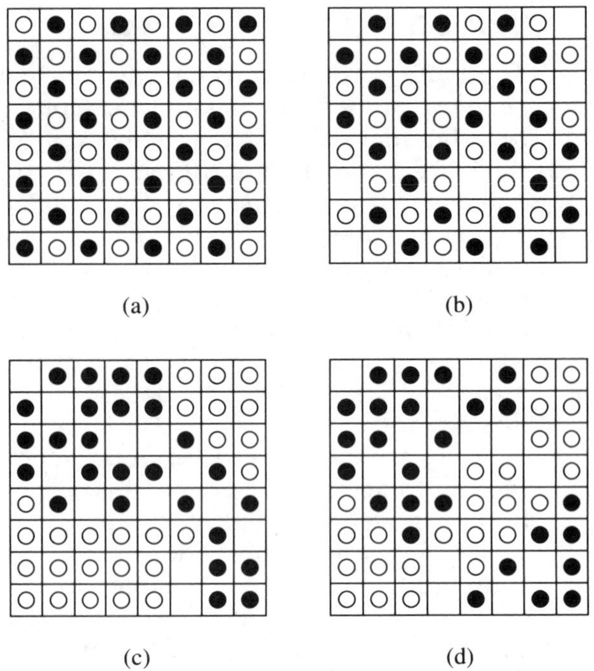

Figure 9.1 Schelling's Solitaire.

simulated neighborhoods in his example should turn out to be segregated.

Schelling's Solitaire is played on a Chessboard with black and white counters as illustrated in Figure 9.1. Each counter represents a householder. The square the counter occupies represents his or her house. The surrounding squares (up to eight) represent the householder's neighborhood. A counter occupying one of these squares is therefore a neighbor.

Each counter is sensitive to the colors of its neighbors. Whites wish one half or more of their neighbors to be white. Blacks wish one third or more of their neighbors to be black. Discontented counters are moved to squares on which they are content until everybody is satisfied, or else no squares remain where discontented counters would be content. The order in which discontented counters are chosen for removal and the new location to which they are moved are not of great significance for the point being made. One can make these choices at random.

Schelling recommends that the process be started from a housing scheme like that shown in Figure 9.1(b). This is obtained by making some random removals from the scheme of Figure 9.1(a) in which black and white counters are evenly distributed. Only a few counters in Figure 9.1(b) are discontented, but as they move elsewhere, others are made discontent in a chain reaction that typically culminates in a segregated pattern like those of Figure 9.1(c) or 9.1(d). This is one of those statements that it is better not to take on trust. It is not until you have played Schelling's Solitaire a number of times that you get any feeling for how inexorable the separation process can be.

Phil 9.2 ⟶

Biologists like to emphasize the roles of chance and necessity in such a process. If the process converges, it is *necessary* that the end-product be orderly. However, the particular end-product that emerges is a matter of *chance*. For example, before the discovery of Australia, it would perhaps have been possible to predict that something would occupy the ecological niche of the duck-billed platypus. But who could have guessed that the occupant of this niche would be an egg-laying mammal with the beak of a duck? The conventions of Section 7.3.2 provide another example. It is *necessary* for the survival of a convention that it select an equilibrium. But it may well be only by *chance* that a society comes to adopt one particular convention rather than another. Driving on the right rather than the left is a particularly clear-cut case.

Such interplay between chance and necessity will be manifest in several of the models of this chapter. When the processes studied converge, they always converge to an equilibrium of the underlying game. But, when the game has several equilibria, the particular equilibrium to which the process converges will depend on the historical accident of where the process started from.

9.1.2 Teleological Language

Human languages are not good at expressing the spontaneous order idea. Teleological imagery[2] is almost impossible to avoid in discussing the subject. Adam Smith's reference to an *invisible hand* that somehow equates supply and demand is a particularly well-known example. Even in writing a book specifically to deny the "argument by design", Richard Dawkins finds *The Blind Watchmaker* an irresistible title.[3] Game theory goes even further down this primrose path. It does not just tolerate teleological metaphors; it uses them

[2]That is, imagery which attributes a *purpose* to what is being described.

[3]To recognize the phenomenon of spontaneous order is not to deny the existence of God. Who is to say that what sceptics attribute to Chance is not actually the workings of Divine Providence?

as a positive tool in describing aspects of the phenomenon of spontaneous order with which it would otherwise be very hard to come to grips. But one must not allow oneself to become a victim of the imagery. Often nobody is optimizing at all. Sometimes there aren't even any players. Nevertheless, things work out *as though* fully rational players were choosing equilibrium strategies. How and why is the subject of this chapter.

9.2 Bounded Rationality

Real people are not very good at figuring things out from first principles. They learn by trial-and-error. Sometimes they learn by imitating the behavior of other people who seem to be getting by reasonably well. Sometimes they learn by reading books, or through attending classes. Often they do not understand *why* what they have learned works out in practice. Indeed, many people become impatient when asked how the method they are using works. It is not a question they see as relevant to anything practical.[4]

Riding bicycles is an example. Nobody can easily explain *how* they keep their balance. Nevertheless they do. A robot designed for riding bicycles might have a complicated program that monitors such factors as the wind speed and the camber of the road, and then solves a complicated system of differential equations to decide what action to take. But people manage to achieve the same effect without being aware of doing any of this. They only behave *as though* they were consciously gathering all the necessary data and then calculating an optimal response.

When *bounded rationality* is mentioned, it signals that players are no longer assumed to be mathematical prodigies with access to encyclopedic manuals written by omniscient game theorists. The question then is: how can it come about that people behave *as though* they were the idealized decision-makers with which traditional game theory is concerned?

The answer usually offered is that people can sometimes find their way to optimal solutions by trial-and-error adaptation if the situation is encountered sufficiently frequently. In a game-theoretic context, this means that players need not necessarily be supplied with an authoritative game theory book in order to get to equilibrium. If they play the game *repeatedly*, they may gradually adjust their behavior over time

[4]It if ain't broke, don't fix it.

until there is no further room for improvement. At this stage, they will have achieved equilibrium. Their behavior will be *as though* they had consulted the game theory book. But nobody organized this result. It just happened by itself. A kibitzer[5] would therefore be able to congratulate himself on having observed a case of spontaneous order.

The reference to repeated games in the previous paragraph is important. A player cannot adapt to situations that are encountered only once. However, one must not confuse the method of analysis used in this chapter with that of the preceding chapter on repeated games. Both chapters study games that are played repeatedly, but the players are *fully rational* in Chapter 8. They use all the information available to them in an optimal manner. In this chapter, the players are *boundedly rational*. Economists call such players *myopic* or *short-sighted* to indicate that they see only what is under their noses, and perhaps not even that. In biological applications, the players often cannot be said to think at all. Their rationality is so bounded that even a chocolate dispensing machine might score higher on an IQ test. Nevertheless, game theory may still be useful in describing what happens in the long run.

Adaptation, adjustment, *tâtonnement*, learning-by-doing, evolution—these are just some of the words used in describing the processes that may lead players who have no clear idea about what is going on to behavior that may look very rational indeed to a kibitzer. We shall use the word *libration* as a generic term for any such equilibriating process. However, it is important to understand that there is very little that can be said about librations *in general*. Asking how such processes work is like opening Pandora's box.[6] The equilibriating processes that one might study are innumerable. Entirely different processes operate in different environments. Sometimes they may work fast; sometimes they may work slow. Different librations may converge to different equilibria of the same game. One cannot even rely on a given libration converging at all. Often perfectly respectable looking processes will generate wildly erratic behavior.

No attempt will be made to try and classify all the possibilities. Instead, attention will be confined to a few examples. The first examples will be of what might be called *economic*

---

[5]A kibitzer is someone who watches a game but does not play himself. It seems to be a law of nature that kibitzers are always more expert than those actually playing.

[6]Recall that she opened the box containing mankind's gifts from the gods, and all but one flew away and were lost. The only exception was the gift of hope.

libration, in which people learn on the job. The next example will be a case of *social* libration, in which learning is passed on to the next generation through the educational system. Finally, but most importantly, there is *biological* libration.

Everybody knows that Darwin's theory of evolution is based on the principle of the "survival of the fittest". For example, the dodo illustrated in the frontispiece to this chapter is extinct because it was unable to adapt to the invasion of its habitat by nineteenth century sailors hungry for fresh meat. Section 9.5 attempts to sketch how such natural selection may serve to guide animal populations to an equilibrium of an underlying game. However, a warning is necessary. All of the librations studied in this chapter are highly stylized. In particular, the successes that biologists have had in modeling evolutionary processes should not be judged by stripped-down models examined here. Nor would it be wise to repeat what is said in this chapter about the natural history of the dodo in the hearing of any zoologists.

9.3 Economic Libration

9.3.1 Cournot Duopoly

The Cournot model of duopoly was discussed in Section 7.2.1. Figure 9.2(a) shows the reaction curves for the two players. These are copied from Figure 7.5. Recall that a Nash equilibrium occurs where the reaction curves cross. In Section 7.2.1,
Econ 9.3.2 ⟶
it is shown that the unique Nash equilibrium $(\tilde{q}_1, \tilde{q}_2)$ for the Cournot duopoly game has $\tilde{q}_1 = \tilde{q}_2 = \frac{1}{3}(M - c)$.

Suppose now that the duopolists are not fully rational. In fact, they are so unable to think clearly that, when they play the Cournot duopoly game repeatedly with the same opponent, they always proceed on the assumption that the other guy will always produce this period exactly what he or she produced last period. Their predictions will always be wrong, but the players are too stubborn or stupid to switch to a more sophisticated method of predicting what their opponent will do.

Suppose that, in period t, player I produces q_1^t and player II produces q_2^t. If player II assumes that player I will also produce q_1^t in period $t + 1$, then player II's best reply is $q_2^{t+1} = R_2(q_1^t) = \frac{1}{2}(M - c - q_1^t)$. The algebra merits less attention than the geometry illustrated in Figure 9.2(a). Observe that q^{t+1} is located at the opposite corner of the shaded rectangle from q^t.

Figures 9.2(b) and 9.2(c) show what happens as time passes. The amounts produced converge to the Nash equilibrium levels. This is true whatever the initial q^0 may be. (See Exercise

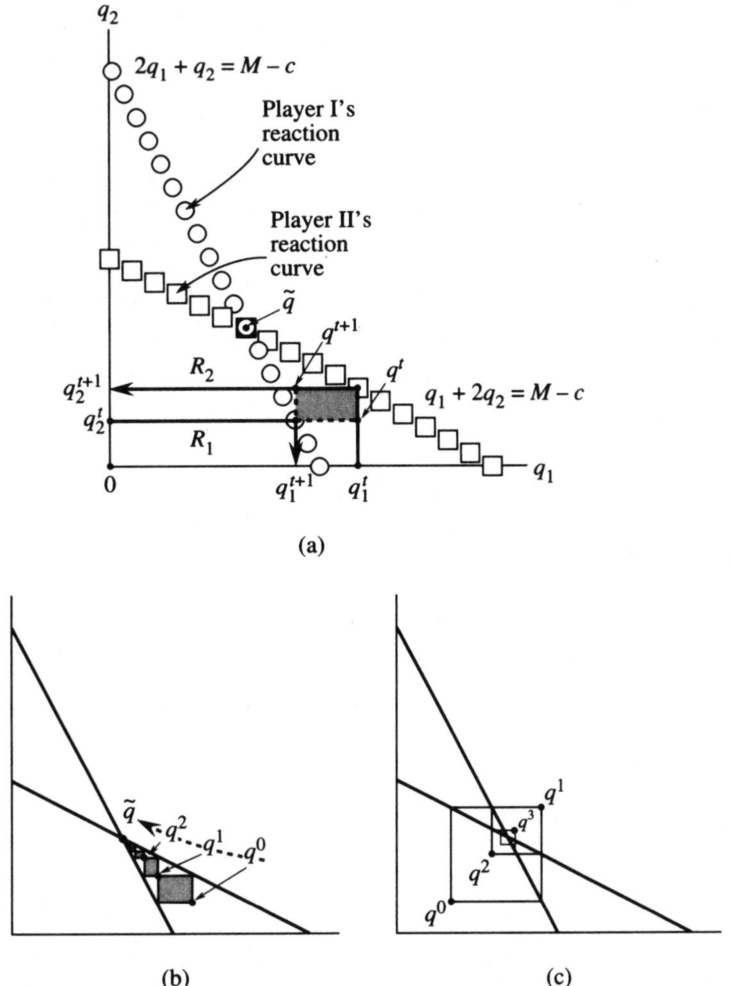

Figure 9.2 Myopic responses in a Cournot duopoly.

10.9.36.) Thus the players get to the Nash equilibrium even though neither has thought things out properly.

Unfortunately, matters do not always work out so well. Figure 9.3(a) is derived from Figure 9.2(a) by swapping the players' reaction curves over.[7] In the new situation, it is

[7]This is easily achieved by adapting the Cournot duopoly model of Section 7.2.1 so that the demand equation is $p = \frac{1}{2}M - q_1 - q_2$, and the cost to a firm of producing q_i is $\frac{1}{2}cq_i - \frac{3}{4}q_i^2$. A firm with such a cost function enjoys *increasing returns to scale*. The more it produces, the less each extra unit costs to manufacture. However, it would not make much sense for the cost of an extra unit to become negative, and so attention should be restricted to the case when $q_i < \frac{1}{3}c$.

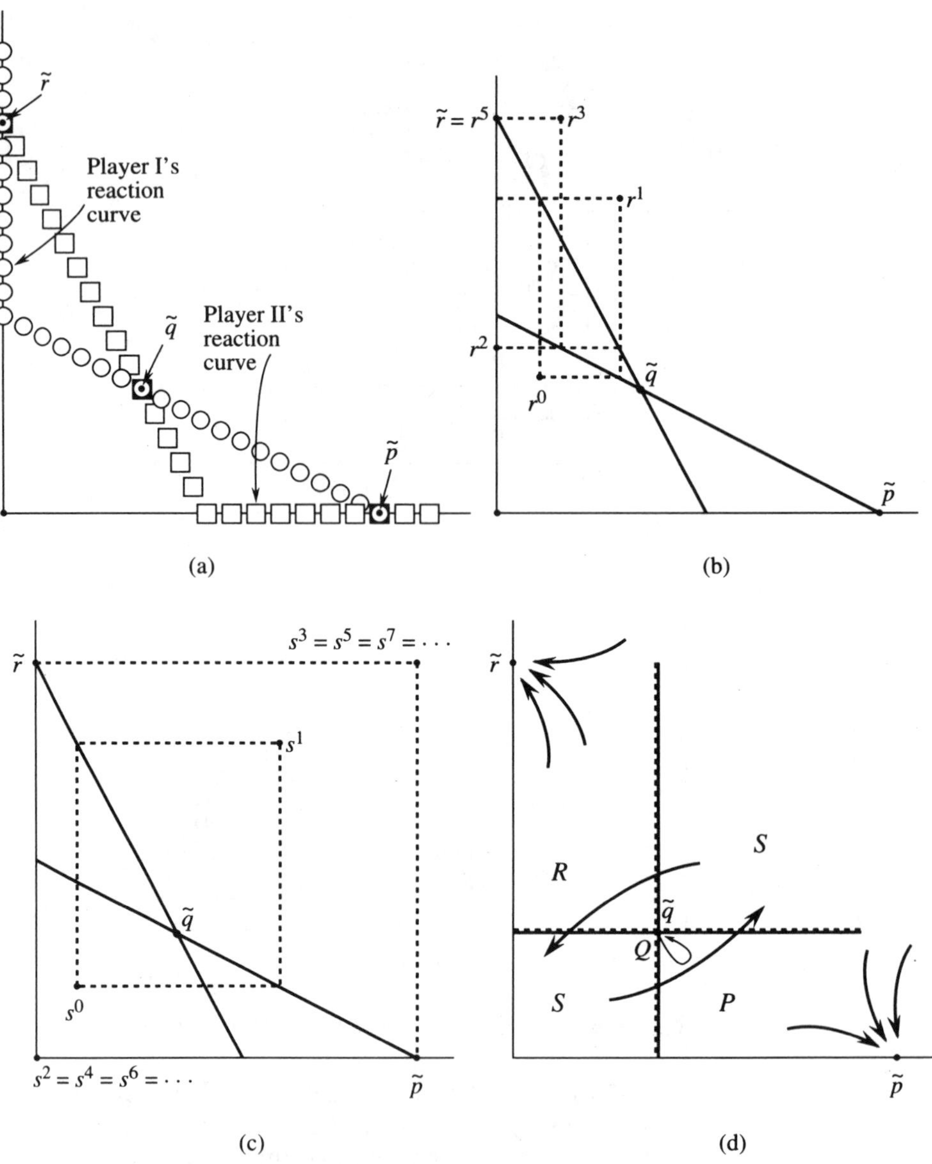

Figure 9.3 Basins of attraction.

necessary to take account of when a player's best reply is to produce nothing at all. This will always be the correct response if the opponent produces an excessively large amount, but the segments of the reaction curves corresponding to this possibility have been irrelevant until now. However, if they were neglected here, two of the *three* Nash equilibria, $\tilde{p}$, $\tilde{q}$ and $\tilde{r}$, indicated in Figure 9.3(a) would be overlooked.

Figures 9.3(b) and 9.3(c) show that what happens as time passes depends on the historical accident of where the process begins. If the initial point p^0 is in the set P of Figure 9.3(d), the process converges to the Nash equilibrium $\tilde{p}$. If the initial point r^0 is in the set R, the process converges to the Nash equilibrium $\tilde{r}$ as shown in Figure 9.3(b). If the initial point s^0 is in the set S, the process *oscillates* as shown in Figure 9.3(c). An oscillating process never converges at all. Finally, there is the possibility that the initial point q^0 lies in the set Q consisting just of the single point $\tilde{q}$. Only in this case is there convergence to the Nash equilibrium $\tilde{q}$.

An important moral can be drawn from this second example. It concerns the problem of equilibrium selection discussed at much length in Chapter 7. When equilibrium is achieved as the result of a trial-and-error adjustment process, the question of *which* equilibrium is reached may be answerable only if something is known about the history of interaction between the players. No quantity of armchair philosophizing, however erudite, will substitute for real-world data in such situations.

9.3.2 Dynamic Processes

The preceding discussion is about the convergence of a discrete dynamic process. The dynamic processes studied in the remainder of the chapter are all continuous. However, the same terminology will do for both.

An *initial point* of a dynamic process is the point from which it begins at time 0. In the Cournot duopoly model just examined, the initial point was q^0. Starting from the designated initial point, the process describes a *trajectory* (or a *flow* or *orbit*). In Figure 9.2(b), the trajectory described is the sequence $q^0, q^1, q^2, \ldots$.

A trajectory may do various things. In particular, it may converge or diverge. In Figure 9.2(b), the trajectory illustrated converges to $\tilde{q}$. Except in pathological cases, a convergent trajectory will converge to a *rest point* (or a *fixed point*) of the process. The rest points are found by locating those initial points from which the dynamic process never moves. If it begins at a rest point, it remains there forever. For example, in Figure 9.3(d) there are three rest points, $\tilde{p}$, $\tilde{q}$ and $\tilde{r}$.

A rest point is often said to be an "equilibrium" of the dynamic process. This is a very reasonable piece of terminology, but it invites confusion in a game theory context. In the Cournot duopoly model, for example, the rest points of the dynamic process all turn out to be Nash equilibria of the underlying Cournot duopoly game. However, we would be in danger of deceiving ourselves into thinking that this did not need to be proved if we were in the habit of referring to rest points as "equilibria" of the dynamic system.

The *basin of attraction* of a rest point r is the set of initial points from which the dynamic process converges to r. The basin of attraction of $\tilde{r}$ in Figure 9.3(d) is the set R. If the basin of attraction consists of every possible initial point, then the rest point is a *global attractor*.[8] For example, $\tilde{q}$ is a global attractor in Figure 9.2(b). *Local* attractors are also important.[9] The local attractors that will be of most interest in this chapter are asymptotic attractors. An *asymptotic attractor* is a rest point that lies in the interior of its basin of attraction.[10] For example, $\tilde{p}$ and $\tilde{r}$ are local attractors in Figure 9.3(d). The rest point $\tilde{q}$ in Figure 9.3(d) is not an attractor of any kind.

Figure 9.4(a) shows a global attractor for a continuous dynamic process together with a number of trajectories. Figure 9.4(b) shows two local attractors and a rest point that is not an attractor at all. No economist would ever want to be found predicting that the long-run outcome of a dynamic process will be a rest point that is not an attractor. Even if the process started at such a rest point, any small disturbance could push it onto a trajectory that heads off somewhere else entirely. His prediction would then not only be wrong, it would be wildly wrong.

Dynamic processes that do not converge are said to diverge. We only consider bounded processes that cannot wander off to infinity. If they diverge, they must therefore oscillate in some way. The oscillation shown in Figure 9.3(c) is *periodic*. After some preliminary jostling, the trajectory $s^0, s^1, s^2, \ldots$ settles into a cycle of period 2. That is to say, $s^{t+2} = s^t$, once t is sufficiently large. Figure 9.4(c) shows some periodic trajectories of a continuous dynamic process. Take note of the rest point that is labeled as a local attractor in

[8]Sometimes a less stringent definition is used.

[9]Global or local attractors are often said to be globally or locally "stable equilibria" of the dynamic process.

[10]This means that the rest point is not a boundary point of its basin of attraction, and so all trajectories that start near enough the rest point finish there. In deciding whether something is a boundary point, do not consider possibilities that cannot be initial points. For example, points with a negative coordinate are not admissible in the Cournot duopoly model. In the language of topology, the rest point must be in the *relative* interior of its basin of attraction.

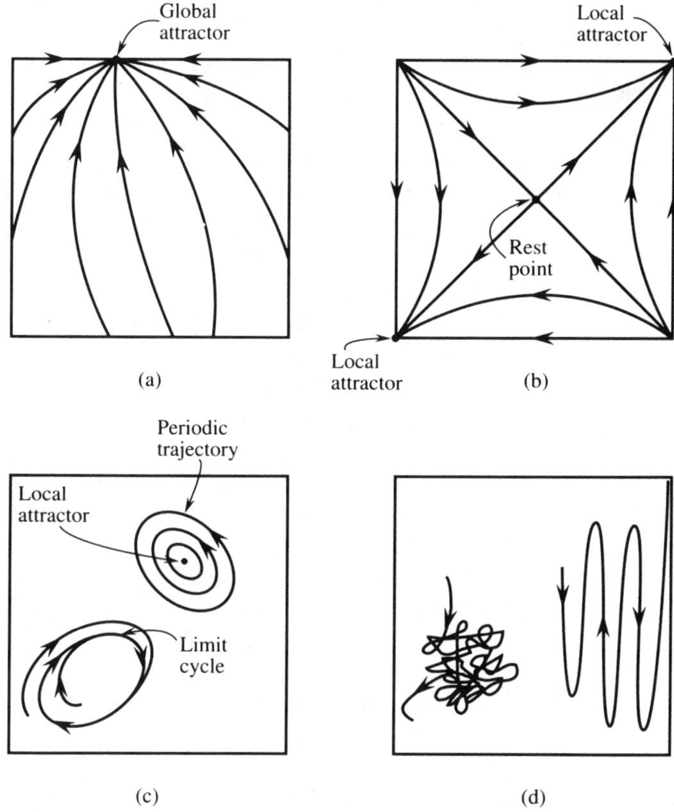

Figure 9.4 Continuous trajectories.

this diagram. The general requirement for a *local attractor* is simply that trajectories that begin near it remain near it. However, in Figure 9.4(c) the trajectories that begin near the local attractor do not converge to it, and so the local attractor is not an asymptotic attractor.

Figure 9.4(d) shows some less pleasant things that trajectories can do. One has to live with the fact that there is nothing outlandish about such behavior. Even chaotic behavior, in which a trajectory comes arbitrarily near every point in some region arbitrarily often, is not uncommon. There are no good reasons at all for assuming that the trajectories of a dynamic process will behave nicely.[11] It is something that needs to be checked out.

[11]However, a trajectory that crosses itself many times as illustrated in Figure 9.4(d) will not be possible with the dynamic processes considered in this chapter.

Math
9.4 →

9.3.3 Mixed Strategies

Dynamic processes can behave very wildly, but people do not need to use wild dynamic processes. The process studied in Section 9.3.1, for example, assumes that the Cournot duopolists are very myopic indeed. If they start in the oscillating region S of Figure 9.3(d), they are so short-sighted that they never notice that their predictions are always absurdly wrong. They just keep on predicting that the opponent will behave exactly as in the previous period. But real people are not so stupid, especially if substantial sums of money are involved.[12] They will notice if their predictions are always wrong and try out different ways of making predictions.

Simply guessing that the opponent will always do tomorrow what he or she did yesterday is very naive. A more sophisticated prediction rule will therefore be examined here. Its study will lead us to an interpretation of a mixed strategy that is not vulnerable to the difficulties discussed in Section 7.1.4. However, because the adjustment process is more sophisticated, the game to which it is applied needs to be simpler than the Cournot duopoly game, unless the analysis is to get harder.

We met the game to be studied previously in Figure 7.7(a) and Exercise 7.9.1. Its payoff table is repeated here as Figure 9.5(a). Figure 9.5(b) shows mixed-strategy reaction curves like those drawn for the Prisoners' Dilemma and Chicken in Figure 7.4. The reaction curves cross at $(\frac{1}{2}, \frac{1}{2})$. This confirms that the game has a unique Nash equilibrium in which both players use each pure strategy with equal probability.

The game will be played repeatedly by myopic players. At every stage, each player estimates the probability with which the opponent will use each of his or her pure strategies. After estimating these probabilities, the players choose their own pure strategy for the next stage so as to maximize their estimated expected payoff. The calculation is the same as finding a best reply to a mixed strategy.

How does player I estimate the probability q with which player II will use her second pure strategy? Suppose that n stages have elapsed, and that she used her second pure strategy on m of these occasions. The *frequency* with which she used her second pure strategy is therefore m/n. The frequency with

[12]Behavioral psychology notwithstanding. My own laboratory experiments, and those of other economists, show that people do not behave stupidly, provided that: the task is comprehensible; the subjects have time to learn and to experiment with possible solutions; and the incentives for success are adequately large.

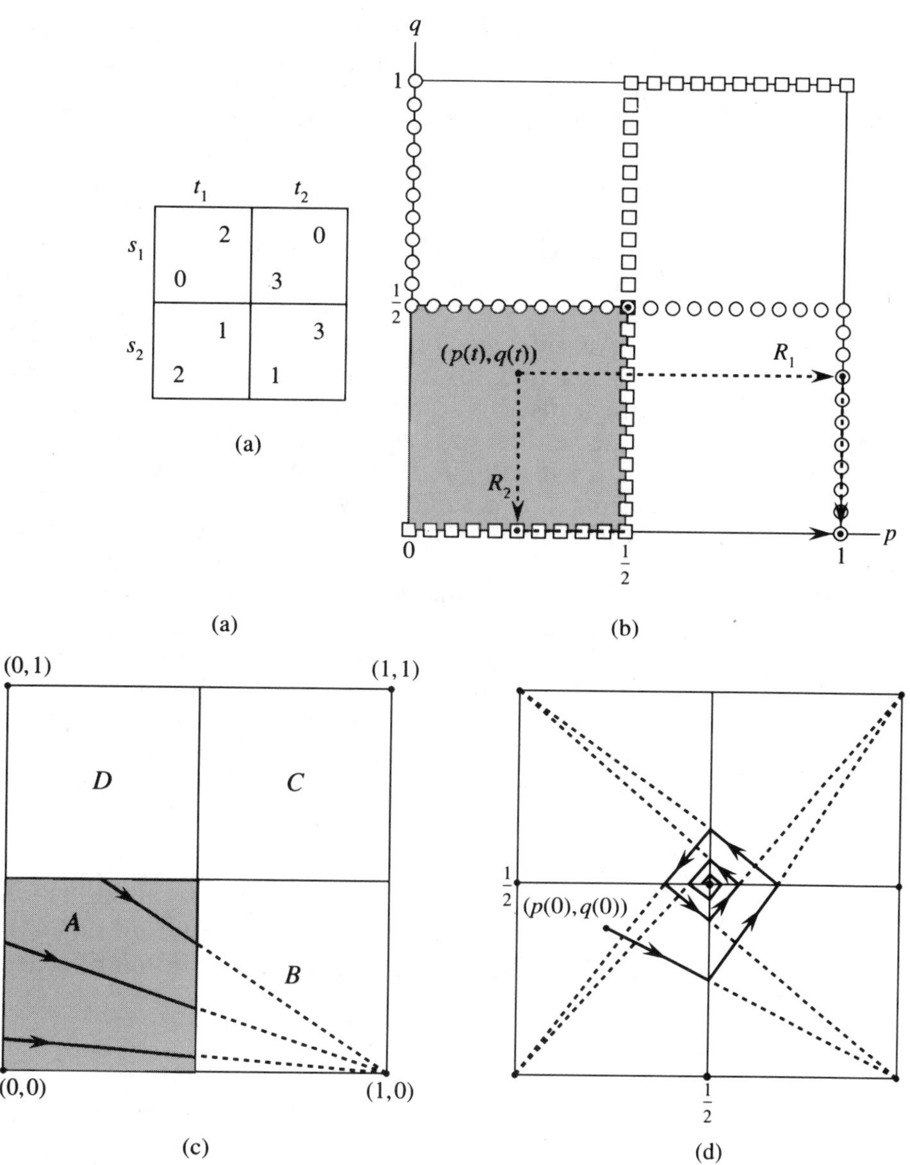

Figure 9.5 Convergence to a mixed equilibrium.

which she used her first pure strategy is $(n - m)/n$. These frequencies will be player I's estimates of the probabilities $1 - q$ and q with which player II will use her first and second strategies at the $(n + 1)$st stage. Player II will make her estimates of player I's behavior in a similar way.

This way of guessing what the opponent will do is not naive, but neither is it fully rational. For example, if player

II were trained in game theory, she might easily guess player I's guessing rule. She would then be able to predict his next action *precisely*, instead of needing to estimate probabilities.

The model described so far is not complicated but its analysis requires some attention to detail. This will be evaded here by adopting the mathematician's trick of moving from discrete time to *continuous* time. Let $p(t)$ denote the frequency with which player I has used his second pure strategy up to time t, and let $q(t)$ denote the frequency with which player II has used her second pure strategy up to time t. As long as $(p(t), q(t))$ remains in the shaded region A of Figure 9.5(c), a study of the reaction curves shows that player I will want to use his second pure strategy and player II will want to use her first pure strategy. If $(p(t), q(t))$ is inside the region A, then it will continue to lie inside A until time $t+\tau$, provided $\tau > 0$ is sufficiently small. Thus player I will be using his first pure strategy and player II will be using her second pure strategy between time t and time $t+\tau$.

How many times will player I have played his second pure strategy at time $t+\tau$? If λT represents the number[13] of games played during a period of length T, he will have played his second pure strategy $\lambda t p(t)$ times up to time t. Between t and $t+\tau$, he plays $\lambda\tau$ games, using his second pure strategy on each occasion. The second pure strategy is therefore played $\lambda t p(t) + \lambda\tau$ times between 0 and $t+\tau$. Its frequency of play is therefore

$$p(t+\tau) = \frac{\lambda t p(t) + \lambda\tau}{\lambda(t+\tau)} = \frac{tp(t)+\tau}{t+\tau}.$$

This information will be used to find a *differential equation*[14] for the function p. By the definition of a derivative,

$$\begin{aligned} p'(t) &= \lim_{\tau\to 0} \frac{p(t+\tau)-p(t)}{\tau} \\ &= \lim_{\tau\to 0} \frac{1}{\tau}\left\{\frac{tp(t)+\tau}{t+\tau} - p(t)\right\} \\ &= \lim_{\tau\to 0} \left\{\frac{tp(t)+\tau - p(t)t - \tau p(t)}{\tau(t+\tau)}\right\} \\ &= \lim_{\tau\to 0} \frac{1-p(t)}{t+\tau} = \frac{1-p(t)}{t}. \end{aligned} \tag{9.1}$$

[13]When T is a small number, one can think of λT as being the probability that a game will be played during the period.

[14]If c is a constant, the equation $f(x) = x + c$ defines a function $f : \mathbb{R} \to \mathbb{R}$. If the equation is differentiated, the result is the *differential equation* $f'(x) = 1$. Usually one needs to reverse this process. A differential

It is now necessary to derive a similar differential equation for the function q. Since player II uses only her *first* pure strategy between t and $t+\tau$,

$$q(t+\tau) = \frac{\lambda t q(t) + \lambda\tau 0}{\lambda(t+\tau)} = \frac{tq(t)}{t+\tau}.$$

Thus

$$\begin{aligned} q'(t) &= \lim_{\tau\to 0} \frac{q(t+\tau)-q(t)}{\tau} \\ &= \lim_{\tau\to 0} \frac{1}{\tau}\left\{\frac{tq(t)}{t+\tau} - q(t)\right\} \\ &= \lim_{\tau\to 0} \left\{\frac{tq(t) - tq(t) - \tau q(t)}{\tau(t+\tau)}\right\} = \frac{-q(t)}{t}. \qquad (9.2) \end{aligned}$$

Solving differential equations can be very difficult. Fortunately, our differential equations can be solved without knowing anything whatever about the theory. From (9.1), we have the differential equation $tp' + p = 1$. Notice that the left-hand side is what is obtained by differentiating the product tp. The differential equation can therefore be written as

$$\frac{d}{dt}(tp) = 1\,.$$

Integrating[15] both sides, we obtain that

$$\begin{aligned} tp &= t - a \\ 1 - p &= \frac{a}{t}, \qquad (9.3) \end{aligned}$$

where a is a constant of integration.[16]

---

equation is given, and the problem is to integrate it. This can be very difficult indeed, even when the differential equation looks quite simple. But the techniques for solving differential equations will not be needed in this book. This footnote is only intended to make the point that a differential equation does not have a unique solution. For example, each value of the constant c determines a different solution $f(x) = x + c$ of the differential equation $f'(x) = 1$. To tie down the solution to a differential equation uniquely, something extra is required. Physicists call the extra information a *boundary condition*, although it has nothing to do with the boundaries of the regions we shall consider. Our boundary condition will always simply be a specification of the *initial point* of the dynamic process that the differential equation describes. For example, a boundary condition for the differential equation $f'(x) = 1$ is the requirement that $f(0) = 2$. The only solution that satisfies this boundary condition is $f(x) = x + 2$.

[15] Remember Newton's great discovery that integrating is the opposite of differentiating.

[16] If you don't believe that $tp = t - a$ is a solution of $tp' + p = 1$ for each constant a, differentiate both sides of the equation with respect to t.

The same method solves the differential equation of (9.2). Rewrite the equation $tq' = -q$ as

$$\frac{d}{dt}(tq) = 0.$$

Integrating both sides, we obtain that

$$tq = b$$

$$q = \frac{b}{t}, \tag{9.4}$$

where b is a constant of integration.

Dividing equations (9.3) and (9.4), we obtain the formula

$$\frac{1-p}{q} = \frac{a}{b}.$$

The points (p, q) that satisfy this equation lie on a straight line that passes through the point $(1, 0)$ in Figure 9.5(c). It follows that, *in the shaded region A* of Figure 9.5(c), $(p(t), q(t))$ moves along a straight line trajectory towards the *target point* $(1, 0)$. Several such trajectories are drawn. When such a trajectory reaches the edge of the shaded region, our analysis needs to be sent back to the workshop for a retread.

What changes when the trajectory reaches the edge of one of the regions of Figure 9.5(c) is the target point. In region B, the target point becomes $(1, 1)$. In region C, it is $(0, 1)$. In region D, it is $(0, 0)$. Figure 9.5(d) shows the complete trajectory when the initial point is $(p(0), q(0))$. The important observation is that the process converges. It converges to $(\frac{1}{2}, \frac{1}{2})$ whatever the initial point may be. Thus $(\frac{1}{2}, \frac{1}{2})$ is a global attractor. Game theorists are interested in this conclusion because $(\frac{1}{2}, \frac{1}{2})$ is also the unique Nash equilibrium of the game under study.

An important lesson to be learned from this analysis relates to the interpretation of mixed strategy equilibria. As we saw in Section 7.1.4, problems arise when attention is restricted to the one-shot case with fully rational players. But with a myopic adjustment story, these difficulties evaporate. No player need ever be asked to toss coins or roll dice in deciding what to do. Players always choose a pure strategy that maximizes expected payoff given their beliefs. But their beliefs change as they observe their opponent's play. In the long run, their beliefs converge on the Nash equilibrium of the game. The Nash equilibrium is therefore an equilibrium *in beliefs* rather than an equilibrium *in actions*.

To a kibitzer, of course, it may not be obvious that the players are not randomizing. He will see the players sometimes doing one thing and sometimes another. If he observes the long-run frequency with which each pure strategy is used, it will match the Nash equilibrium probability for that pure strategy. To the kibitzer, it will therefore be *as though* the players were randomizing their choices, even though the players are behaving entirely deterministically.

9.3.4 Shapley's Shimmy

Math 9.4 ⟶

Early game theorists, having formulated the idea of an equilibrium, were much concerned with the problem of how equilibria in complicated games should be calculated. One method they explored is called *fictitious play*. It consists of nothing more than seeing what happens in the long run when the game is played by robots programmed to use the trial-and-error adjustment process we considered in Section 9.3.3. Thus, each robot computes the frequency with which an opponent has used a pure strategy in the past, and optimizes on the assumption that the pure strategy will be used with that probability at the next stage.

For the game of Section 9.3.3, fictitious play led to the unique Nash equilibrium. However, Shapley produced an example that shows that the process need not converge at all. It need not even get into a cycle that repeats itself over and over again.

For us, there are two lessons. The first is that nothing should be taken for granted about the convergence of trial-and-error adjustment processes. The second is that, even when the process does not converge, equilibrium ideas are not irrelevant to the situation.

For reasons that will soon be apparent, the analog of Shapley's game to be studied here will be called Shapley's Shimmy. Its payoff table is given in Figure 7.26(b). The payoff table is repeated again with various embellishments in Figure 9.6(a). Player I's pure strategies have been labeled T, M and B. Player II's pure strategies have been labeled L, C and R. Exercise 7.9.40 was concerned with equilibria of Shapley's Shimmy. There is a unique Nash equilibrium in which both players use each of their pure strategies with probability $\frac{1}{3}$. Each then expects a payoff of $\frac{1}{3}$. Correlated equilibria were introduced in Section 7.6.2. The correlated equilibrium for Shapley's Shimmy examined in Exercise 7.9.40 was based on the probability distribution that assigns $\frac{1}{6}$ to each off-diagonal cell of the payoff table (and 0 to the diagonal cells). When this correlated equilibrium is used, each player expects a payoff of $\frac{1}{2}$.

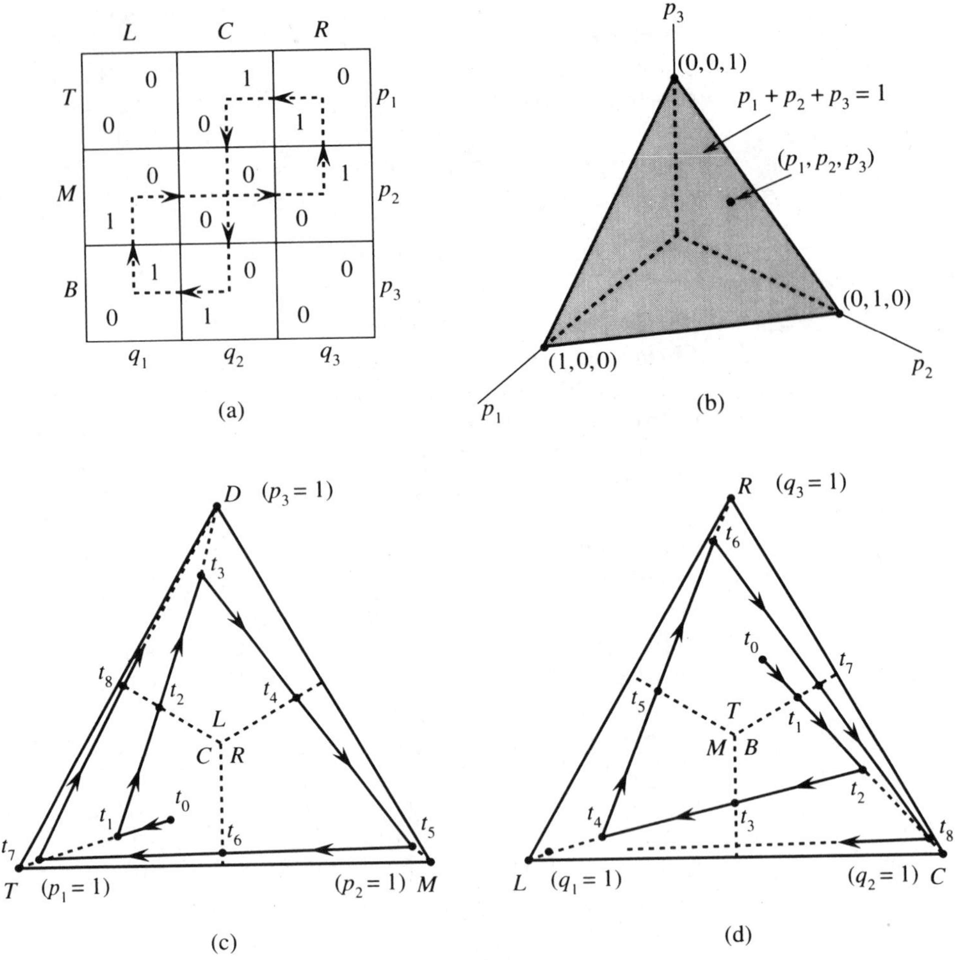

Figure 9.6 Shapley's Shimmy.

To analyze "fictitious play" in Shapley's game, it is not necessary to solve any new differential equations, because the considerations are all pretty much the same as in the previous example. We shall have to split our space up into regions. Within each region the trajectories will be straight lines aimed at a target point. This will all be taken for granted here so that attention can be concentrated on the problem of coping with the fact that we no longer have a two-dimensional situation. We have *six* variables. First, there are the frequencies p_1, p_2 and p_3 with which player I has used T, M and B in the past. Then there are the frequencies q_1, q_2 and q_3 with which player II has used L, C and R in the past. Fortunately, things are simplified somewhat because it must be true that $p_1 + p_2 + p_3 = 1$ and $q_1 + q_2 + q_3 = 1$.

Figure 9.6(b) shows a geometrical method of keeping track of the location of $p = (p_1, p_2, p_3)$ as a point in an equilateral triangle. This triangle is shown again in Figure 9.6(c). The triangle of Figure 9.6(d) keeps track of the location of $q = (q_1, q_2, q_3)$. Note that we need to trace the movement of *two* points simultaneously. As time passes, p and q will move around their triangles. Which way p moves will depend on where q is. Which way q moves will depend on where p is.

The triangle showing player II's frequencies is divided into three regions labeled T, M and B. In the region labeled T, q_3 is the largest of q_1, q_2 and q_3. When this is the case, player I's best reply to the mixed strategy (q_1, q_2, q_3) is to use pure strategy T. The regions M and B are labeled for similar reasons. So are the regions C, T and L in the triangle showing player I's frequencies. For example, p_2 is the largest of p_1, p_2 and p_3 in the region labeled R. Under these circumstances, player II's best reply to the mixed strategy (p_1, p_2, p_3) is to use pure strategy R.

This labeling of regions makes identifying target points easy. For example, when q is in region T of Figure 9.6(d), the target point for p is the vertex T of the triangle in Figure 9.6(c). When p is in region R of Figure 9.6(c), the target point for q is the vertex R of the triangle in Figure 9.6(d).

The trajectories drawn in Figures 9.6(c) and 9.6(d) give an indication of how the system develops. The state of the system at various times is shown by labeling pairs of points t_0, t_1, t_2, ... Neither trajectory converges on $(\frac{1}{3}, \frac{1}{3}, \frac{1}{3})$. A kibitzer will *not* therefore think that the players are using the unique Nash equilibrium of the game in the long run. The Nash equilibrium is not an attractor of any kind. Unless the initial point is at the Nash equilibrium, a trajectory will not converge at all. Indeed, either Figure 9.6(c) or 9.6(d) would serve well as a substitute for Figure 7.21(b), which was used to illustrate the idea of a *divergent* process.

How will things look to a kibitzer? Until time t_1, he sees the pure strategy pair (T, C) being played. At time t_1, the players switch to (D, C), where they remain until time t_2 when they switch to (D, L). If he follows their play for a long time, he will observe the players' shimmying[17] through the cells of the payoff table as shown in Figure 9.6(a).

[17]As in the immortal lines:

I wish I could shimmy like my sister Kate,
Lord how she shimmies, like a jelly on a plate.

Notice that the cells on the main diagonal are not visited at all. The long-run behavior generated by the process shares this property with the *correlated equilibrium* discussed in Exercise 7.9.40. To a kibitzer, it will therefore seem *as though* the players are employing a rough-and-ready counterpart of the idea of a correlated equilibrium.[18]

Math 9.5 ⟶

9.4 Social Libration

As we have seen, people can learn to play equilibria by trial-and-error without ever doing anything clever. But they can learn faster if they are taught by someone who is an expert already, or if they imitate the play of someone whom they see is winning.

A simple model will be used to illustrate this point. The game to be studied will be that of Figure 9.5(a). We shall find that much of the mathematics used in discussing this game in Section 9.3.3 can be redeployed here. In consequence, what needs to be said can be made very brief.

The same two players will not play each other over and over again in this model. Instead, every time the game is repeated, the players are chosen anew from the population at large. A boy is chosen at random to be player I, and a girl is chosen at random to be player II. Before entering the game-playing population, everybody attends a gaming school where they are taught the "correct" strategy, which they never think to question in later life. The players are therefore myopic in that they do not exploit their knowledge to the full.

The schooling players receive is enlightened to the extent that the strategy it designates as "correct" *is* always correct *at the time the instruction is given*. That is to say, if a fraction $p(t)$ of boys in the current population have been taught to use their pure second strategy, the girls who graduate from school at time t will be taught to optimize against the mixed strategy $(1 - p(t), p(t))$. Similarly, if a fraction $q(t)$ of girls in the current population have been taught to use their second pure strategy, then the boys who graduate from school at time t will be taught to optimize against the mixed strategy $(1 - q(t), q(t))$.

---

[18]Cognoscenti will recognize *how* rough-and-ready, especially if they have met Shapley's Shimmy elsewhere in studying "hypercycles". The text neglects the question of *how long* the process remains in each cell while shimmying through the payoff table. In fact, the time it spends in each cell before moving on to the next increases exponentially. In consequence, average payoffs to the players oscillate between $1/3$ and $2/3$. Recall, however, that players get only $1/3$ at the mixed Nash equilibrium. At the correlated equilibrium of Exercise 7.9.40, they get $1/2$.

It will be assumed that there are always exactly N boys and N girls, where N is very large. In any period of length T, the probability that any boy or girl will retire from the game-playing population is λT. Such retirements are exactly balanced by new recruits just leaving school.

If $(p(t), q(t))$ lies in the shaded region of Figure 9.5(c), then all boys who leave school between times t and $t + \tau$ will be trained to use their second pure strategy, provided that τ is sufficiently small. There will be $N\lambda\tau$ such boys, because this is the number of retirees in the period. The population of boys at time $t + \tau$ will therefore consist of $N - N\lambda\tau$ veterans and $N\lambda\tau$ recruits. How many of these use their second pure strategy? All of the recruits and a fraction $p(t)$ of the veterans play this way. The total number is therefore $N(1 - \lambda\tau)p(t) + N\lambda\tau$. But, if N is sufficiently large, this number is approximately the same as $Np(t + \tau)$. It follows that

$$\begin{aligned} p'(t) &= \lim_{\tau \to 0} \frac{p(t+\tau) - p(t)}{\tau} \\ &= \lim_{\tau \to 0} \frac{(1 - \lambda\tau)p(t) + \lambda\tau - p(t)}{\tau} = -\lambda p(t) + \lambda\,. \end{aligned}$$

Similarly

$$q'(t) = \lim_{\tau \to 0} \frac{(1 - \lambda\tau)q(t) - q(t)}{\tau} = -\lambda q(t)\,.$$

The linear differential equation[19] $p' + \lambda p = \lambda$ has solution $1 - p(t) = ae^{-\lambda t}$, where a is a constant of integration. Similarly, the linear differential equation $q' + \lambda q = 0$ has solution $q = be^{-\lambda t}$, where b is a constant of integration. It follows that, as in Section 9.3.3,

$$\frac{1 - p(t)}{q(t)} = \frac{a}{b},$$

when $(p(t), q(t))$ is in the shaded region of Figure 9.5(c).

No further discussion is necessary. The trajectories for this social adjustment model are precisely the same[20] as those

[19]The word "linear" in this orthodox usage is intended to refer to the role of p' and p in the equation. To solve the equation, multiply throughout by $e^{\lambda t}$. Then notice that

$$p'(t)e^{\lambda t} + \lambda p(t)e^{\lambda t} = (p(t)e^{\lambda t})'\,.$$

Now integrate both sides of $(p(t)e^{\lambda t})' = \lambda e^{\lambda t}$ with respect to t. This yields $p(t)e^{\lambda t} = e^{-\lambda t}a$. Hence $p(t) = 1 - ae^{-\lambda t}$.

[20]The only difference is that the trajectories are traversed *faster* because $e^{-\lambda t}$ decreases much more quickly than t^{-1}. However, one must remember that social time units will be months or years, whereas economic time units may be only seconds.

shown in Figure 9.5(d). In particular, they converge on the mixed Nash equilibrium.

9.5 Biological Libration

Maynard Smith's *Evolution and the Theory of Games* spotlights many interesting applications of game theory to biology. This section can do no more than indicate the flavor of the ideas. Even then, much of the savor will be lost, since only sexless reproduction will be considered.

9.5.1 Replicators

At first sight, it seems unlikely that game theory could be successfully applied in evolutionary biology. How could an insect, for example, be a player in a game? Insects cannot reason. Their behavior is instinctive. They just do what they are programmed to do.

Nevertheless, some of the most promising applications of game theory have been biological. Paradoxically, the *less* developed an organism's thinking abilities, the *better* the theory tends to work. It is sometimes even usable when the protagonists are trees or flowers. How can this be so?

The secret is that the players in the game are *not* taken to be the organisms under study. If the behavior being investigated is instinctive, then it is coded in the organism's genes. One may think of the genes as part of the hardware of a natural computer: the part where the computer's programs are stored. Some of the programs control the organism's behavior. The programs we shall be interested in are those that select a strategy for the organism in a particular game. It is these *programs* that must be seen as substitutes for players when game theory is applied.

An important property of computer programs is that they can be copied from one computer to another. "Computer viruses" copy *themselves* from one computer to another. They are *self-replicating* programs.[21] The programs imprinted on an animal's genes are also self-replicating. But their replication is immensely complicated compared with the replication of a computer virus. Nature not only has to copy programs from one natural computer to another, she has to create a

[21] A virus is a type of self-replicating molecule. Computer viruses usually do more than replicate themselves. Those widely publicized are akin to the biological virus for the common cold in that they create mayhem inside their host.

new natural computer to which the programs may be copied. Crick and Watson's discovery of how Nature works this trick using the device of the "double helix" is one of the great scientific adventure stories. But its thrills will have to be enjoyed elsewhere. All that is important here is that we understand that *something* exists that does two things:

- It replicates itself.
- It determines strategic behavior in a game.

Such an entity will be called a *replicator*.[22]

Replicators do not only arise in a biological context. Rules-of-thumb, codes-of-conduct, fashions, life-styles, creeds and scientific ideas are all replicators of a kind.[23] Their mode of replication is not biological. They spread from one human mind to another through imitation or education (as in Section 9.4). However, given our current state of knowledge, one can only speculate about the detailed mechanics of such socio-economic replication. It therefore seems wiser to stick with the biological paradigm in what follows.

All this insistence on the importance of replicators is a preliminary to a discussion of Charles Darwin's notion of *natural selection*, which the philosopher Spencer encapsulated in the phrase "survival of the fittest".

To survive, replicators need hosts in whose genes they are imprinted. If we define the fitness of a host to be some measure of how frequently it gets to reproduce its genes, then it becomes almost a tautology that replicators that confer high fitness on their hosts will come to control a larger share of hosts than those that confer low fitness. If the environment will only support a restricted number of hosts, the replicator conferring low fitness on its hosts may die out altogether. The fittest replicator will then have survived.

A kibitzer watching the situation evolve might try to make sense of what he sees by attributing a goal or purpose to a replicator: that of maximizing the fitness of its hosts. If natural selection operates for long enough in a stable

[22]This follows Dawkin's usage in his magnificent book, *The Selfish Gene*. The term is not intended to denote anything physical here. A computer program should not be confused with the hardware that stores it, nor a story with the book in which it is written. Similarly, when a double helix unravels, two different molecules result whose atoms are arranged in the same pattern. Neither of these molecules is the replicator. It is their common *pattern* that is the replicator.

[23]In the *Selfish Gene*, Dawkin's calls such socio-economic replicators "memes".

environment, only those replicators that are good at maximizing the fitness of their hosts will remain in existence. To the kibitzer, it would therefore seem *as though* the surviving replicators were consciously seeking to attain the goal he had assigned to them. In brief, it would seem as though a replicator were acting like a *player in a game.*

Game theory is relevant because the behavior that confers high fitness on a host will often depend on what other hosts in the population are doing. Evolution should therefore be expected to generate an *equilibrium* of some kind among the surviving replicators. In this equilibrium, each replicator will be maximizing the fitness of its hosts, given the behavior induced in other organisms in the population by the replicators they are hosting.

9.5.2 Fitness

Maynard Smith's *Evolution and the Theory of Games* uses the Hawk-Dove Game of Figure 7.3(a) to illustrate the ideas of Section 9.5.1. To make things even simpler, the special form of the Hawk-Dove Game called Chicken in Figure 7.3(c) will be used here. This is shown again in Figure 9.7(a). Recall from Section 7.1.2 that Chicken has three Nash equilibria. It has two Nash equilibria in pure strategies, (*hawk, dove*) and (*dove, hawk*). It also has a mixed Nash equilibrium in which both players use each pure strategy with probability $\frac{1}{2}$. The latter is a *symmetric* equilibrium because both players do the same thing.

Although the pure strategies are labeled *hawk* and *dove*, Chicken is *not* to be interpreted as an inter-species game between hawks and doves. Think of it in terms of conflict between different members of the *same* species. To emphasize that the example is only an illustrative parable, we shall call the animal being studied the dodo. Dodos are extinct in real life, and so we are free to follow the example of historians in inventing any facts about them that suit our convenience. In particular, our dodos are all female and so reproduce asexually.[24]

A dodo's day is not 24 hours long, but some fraction of τ of a year. During the daylight hours, dodos search for food. All dodos are equally good at foraging, but some may be unlucky because there is only enough food to support N dodos. Those

[24]The assumption of an all-female species is not so crazy as it may seem. Certain beetles dispense with a male sex and reproduce parthogenetically.

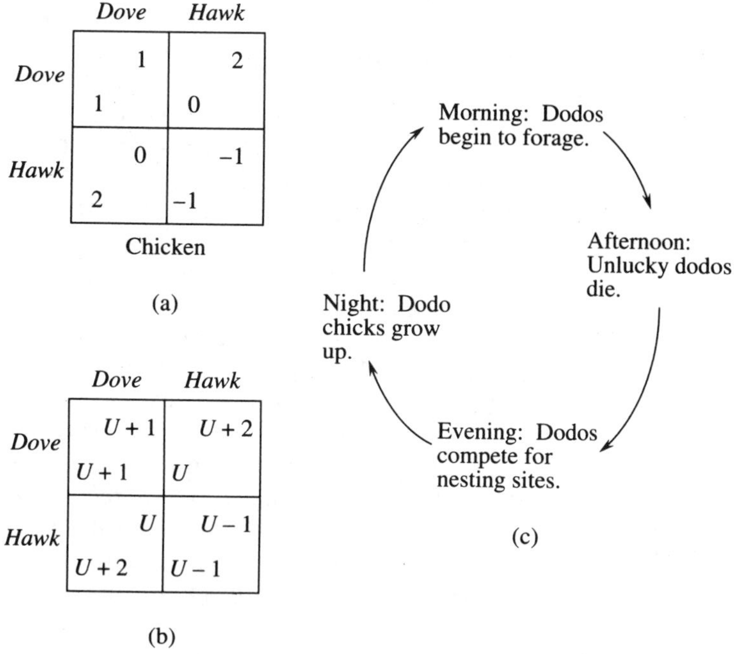

Figure 9.7 The facts of dodo life.

who fail to find food die. This is particularly tragic since a dodo that found food every day would be immortal.

In the evening, the N surviving dodos compete for favored nesting sites in the following way. Pairs of dodos chosen at random from the population are matched against each other to play Chicken. Remember that the *real* players are not the dodos, but the replicators that they are hosting. Only two types of replicator are considered at this stage: a replicator D that induces its host to play *dove*, and a replicator H that induces its host to play *hawk*.

A dodo that plays *hawk* against an opponent who plays *dove* gets exclusive possession of a favored nesting site. The opponent is excluded altogether. If both play *dove*, the site is shared. If both play *hawk*, there is a fight.

These different outcomes each affect the chances of a dodo laying an egg that evening differently. The dodo chicks that hatch out grow to maturity overnight, and are indistinguishable next morning from other dodos. Since older dodos have forgotten everything they knew the day before, they all start the new day on an equal basis. Figure 9.7(c) illustrates a dodo's daily round.

The precise fitnesses for the various possible strategy combinations for Chicken are shown in Figure 9.7(b). These are given as the expected number of chicks a dodo will mother in a year. This means, for example, that a mother excluded altogether from a favored nesting site will expect $U\tau$ chicks on any particular evening. A mother who is sharing a site will expect $(U + 1)\tau$ chicks. A mother who has exclusive possession of a site will expect $(U + 2)\tau$ chicks. A mother who had to fight will expect $(U - 1)\tau$ chicks.

Notice that everything is stated in terms of *expected* number of chicks. We do not care about the number of chicks born to any particular dodo on any particular evening. We only care about the *total* number of dodos who will be hosting a particular replicator tomorrow.

Since reproduction is asexual, a chick's genes will be a copy of its mother's.[25] A chick therefore hosts the same replicator as her mother. To find the number of chicks hosting the D replicator tonight, we therefore have to add up all the chicks born to mothers hosting the D replicator. If the number of such mothers is sufficiently large, adding up the *expected* numbers of chicks and the *actual* numbers will nearly be the same thing.

This is why it is *expected* fitness that matters in biological discussions, just as it is *expected* Von Neumann and Morgenstern utility that matters in conventional game theory. In fact, nothing goes wrong if fitnesses are treated *exactly* like Von Neumann and Morgenstern payoffs. In particular, subtracting U from each entry in the fitness table of Figure 9.7(b) makes no difference to anything, as we shall see in Section 9.5.3. One therefore might as well confine attention to the regular Chicken game of Figure 9.7(a) in which the payoffs are *incremental* fitnesses.[26]

9.5.3 The Replicator Equation

The time has now come to follow the evolution of the dodo population in detail. To this end, let $1 - p(t)$ denote the fraction of dodos hosting the D replicator who survive the daylight hours on some particular day. Let $p(t)$ denote the fraction hosting the H replicator. We shall abbreviate $p(t)$ to p in what follows, but the fact that p depends on time must not be forgotten.

---

[25]Unless a mutation occurs. But this possibility is neglected for the moment.

[26]That is, fitnesses in excess of the background level of U. In general, Nature cares nothing about absolutes. She cares only about how well one replicator does *relative* to another.

How many chicks does a mother hosting the D replicator expect *before* Chicken is played to apportion nesting sites? The answer is

$$\tau f_D(p) = \tau U + \tau(1-p), \tag{9.5}$$

which is what the play of *dove* in Figure 9.7(b) would yield if the opponent used the mixed strategy $(1-p, p)^T$. It is true that the opponent will not use a mixed strategy, but the effect is the same because the opponent is chosen at random from a population in which a fraction $1-p$ play *dove* and a fraction p play *hawk*.

Since only N dodos survive until the evening, there will be $N(1-p)$ mothers hosting the D replicator. Thus $N(1-p)\tau f_D(p)$ chicks hosting the D replicator will be born. Since the mothers will be around in the morning too, the total number of dodos hosting the D replicator next morning is

$$N(1-p)(1+\tau f_D(p)).$$

The corresponding expression for the total number of dodos next morning hosting the H replicator is

$$Np(1+\tau f_H(p)),$$

where

$$\tau f_H(p) = \tau U + 2\tau(1-p) - \tau p. \tag{9.6}$$

Because all dodos have an equal chance of surviving the next day, the fraction $p(t+\tau)$ of dodos hosting the H replicator who make it to the next evening is necessarily the same as the fraction of dodos hosting the H replicator next morning. Thus

$$p(t+\tau) = \frac{Np(t)(1+\tau f_H(p))}{N(1+\tau\overline{f}(p))} = p(t)\left(\frac{1+\tau f_H(p)}{1+\tau\overline{f}(p)}\right)$$

where $\tau\overline{f}(p) = (1-p)\tau f_D(p) + p\tau f_H(p)$, so that $N(1+\tau\overline{f}(p))$ is the total number of dodos next morning.

It remains to rewrite the expression for $p(t+\tau)$ as

$$\frac{p(t+\tau)-p(t)}{\tau} = p\left\{\frac{f_H(p)-\overline{f}(p)}{1+\tau\overline{f}(p)}\right\}.$$

After Section 9.3.3, it will come as no surprise that the limit will now be taken as $\tau \to 0$. The result is the *replicator equation*

$$p' = p(f_H(p) - \overline{f}(p)). \tag{9.7}$$

In this differential equation, recall that $p(t)$ is the fraction of dodos hosting the H replicator. The quantity $f_H(p)$ is the fitness[27] conferred on a host by the H replicator, given the current population mix. The quantity $\overline{f}(p) = (1-p)f_D(p) + pf_H(p)$ is the average fitness of the population as a whole.

The story that led us to the replicator equation is more than a little far-fetched. But it is only one of many stories that lead to the same conclusion. Other stories require less fanciful assumptions about the natural history of the organism under study, but they take longer to tell.

9.5.4 Who Survives?

Substitute (9.5) and (9.6) in the replicator equation (9.7). Notice that the background fitness U cancels out, confirming that only the *incremental* fitnesses of Figure 9.7(a) are relevant. The result is the differential equation

$$\frac{dp}{dt} = p(1-p)(1-2p)\,. \tag{9.8}$$

This differential equation governs the evolution of the dodo population. If we could solve it, we would know the fraction of hawkish dodos at every time t. But solving complicated differential equations is a headache even for experts. Fortunately, we can evade this difficult task because we care only about what happens in the long run.

As we know from our previous study of dynamic processes, the rest points of the process are likely to be significant. The rest points for (9.8) are $\tilde{p} = 0$, $\tilde{p} = 1$ and $\tilde{p} = \frac{1}{2}$. If the process is started at one of these points, it will never move anywhere else, because the replicator equation tells us that the rate at which it starts moving is $p'(0) = \tilde{p}(1-\tilde{p})(1-2\tilde{p}) = 0$.

Our study of Shapley's Shimmy warns us not to leap to any conclusions about the convergence properties of the dynamic process when it does not start at a rest point. However, here things are easy. If $p > \frac{1}{2}$, then

$$p'(t) = p(1-p)(1-2p) < 0$$

and so the function p is *strictly decreasing*. If $p < \frac{1}{2}$, then $p'(t) > 0$ and so the function p is *strictly increasing*. This tells us what the shape of the graph of p must look like. The possibilities are illustrated in Figure 9.8(a). Only $\tilde{p} = \frac{1}{2}$ is a local attractor.

Neither of the rest points $\tilde{p} = 0$ or $\tilde{p} = 1$ is stable. The first corresponds to a population in which only the H replicator is present. If no D replicator ever appears, the population just

[27] Expressed in expected number of chicks per year.

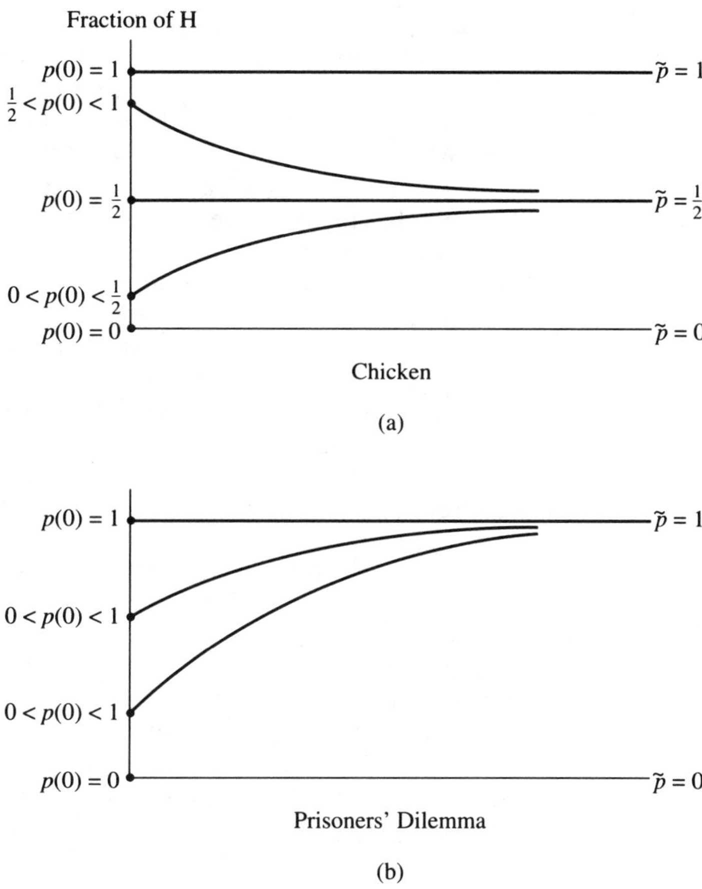

Figure 9.8 The evolution of dodos.

stays the way it is. But, if there should be a *mutation* that generates even a tiny fraction of dodos hosting the D replicator, then that fraction will grow over time until the numbers of dodos hosting the H and D replicators are equalized. The same goes for the rest point $\tilde{p} = 1$. A population in which only the D replicator is present is vulnerable to an invasion by a tiny fraction of H mutants. Such a tiny fraction will grow until the numbers of H and D replicators are equalized.

The only population invulnerable to such invasions is one in which half the population is hosting the H replicator and half is hosting the D replicator. This corresponds to the rest point $\tilde{p} = \frac{1}{2}$ for the replicator equation.

Recall that Chicken has three Nash equilibria. The local attractor $\tilde{p} = \frac{1}{2}$ corresponds to the *mixed* Nash equilibrium in which both players use each pure strategy with probability $\frac{1}{2}$. However, no dodo tosses any coins. We have yet another interpretation of a mixed-strategy equilibrium in which no player actually randomizes. The randomization is done by Nature when she pairs off the dodos to play Chicken. To a kibitzer, it will seem *as though* a dodo is choosing *hawk* and *dove* with probability $\frac{1}{2}$. But this is only because the kibitzer is ignorant of the replicator the dodo is hosting. In fact, a dodo's behavior is entirely deterministic.

Biologists refer to populations in which distinct behaviors coexist together as polymorphous.[28] However, it will be evident that it is not only in biology that polymorphy matters. In particular, when mixed Nash equilibria are important, it will often be because the players have been randomly selected from a polymorphous population even when the context is economic or sociological.

Of the three Nash equilibria for Chicken, only the mixed equilibrium corresponds to a local attractor. What is wrong with (*hawk, dove*) and (*dove, hawk*)? In brief, they are not symmetric. Nothing asymmetric can emerge from the story told about the evolution of dodos, because both player I and player II are chosen at random from the *same* population. Hence, the probability that any pure strategy is used must be the *same* for each player.

It remains to say something about Figure 9.8(b). Exercise 9.8.10 asks for the replicator equation to be obtained for the case in which Chicken is replaced by the Prisoners' Dilemma of Figure 7.3(b). Since the only Nash equilibrium of the Prisoners' Dilemma is (*hawk, hawk*), it is no surprise that the only local attractor is then $\tilde{p} = 1$, which corresponds to the case when all dodos are hosting the H replicator. It is true that $\tilde{p} = 0$ is also a rest point, but a population consisting of dodos hosting the D replicator can be invaded by a mutant H replicator that takes over a tiny fraction of the dodo population. The fraction of the population hosting the H replicator will expand over time until the D replicator is displaced altogether.

9.6 Evolutionary Stability

Local attractors for the replicator dynamics in Chicken and the Prisoners' Dilemma correspond to symmetric Nash equilibria. This is no accident. It is another example in which a trial-and-error adjustment process leads to the use of optimal strategies, even though nobody did any conscious optimizing. Mutations

---

[28] This means "many forms".

provide the source of new strategies to be tried,[29] and natural selection is the mechanism for the correction of errors.

It is tempting to seek to short-circuit the painful study of the mathematics of replication, and to leap directly to the conclusion that evolution is bound to lead to optimizing behavior in the long run. The idea of evolutionary stability is an attempt to put such intuitions into concrete form.

9.6.1 Mutant Invasions

Imagine that only one replicator is present in a population of dodos. This replicator will be denoted by N to indicate that it is the "normal" replicator. A new *mutant* replicator M now appears. At first, the fraction of the population hosting M is some tiny number $\epsilon > 0$. Will this mutant invasion be repelled, or will the mutant replicator establish itself permanently? The condition for *evolutionary stability* is that the mutant replicator will necessarily be driven to extinction, provided that ϵ is sufficiently small.

Figure 9.9(a) is a fitness table. For example, $f(N, M)$ is the fitness of a dodo hosting the N replicator when it is matched against a dodo hosting the M replicator. Any dodo has probability $1 - \epsilon$ of being matched against a dodo carrying the N replicator and probability ϵ of being matched against a dodo carrying the M replicator. The overall fitness of a dodo carrying the N replicator is therefore

$$(1 - \epsilon)f(N, N) + \epsilon f(N, M).$$

The overall fitness of a dodo carrying the M replicator is

$$(1 - \epsilon)f(M, N) + \epsilon f(M, M).$$

The condition that the mutant invasion be repelled is that mutant dodos be less fit than normal dodos. Evolutionary stability therefore requires that

$$(1 - \epsilon)f(N, N) + \epsilon f(N, M) > (1 - \epsilon)f(M, N) + \epsilon f(M, M), \tag{9.9}$$

for sufficiently small $\epsilon > 0$.

[29] Here biologists have an advantage over economists. Their discipline provides them with hard information about what mutations it is sensible to include in the model. For example, the phrase "dead as a dodo" would perhaps not be in common usage if a mutant strain of evil-smelling, skunk-like dodos had appeared at the appropriate time. However, science-fiction movies to the contrary, biologists know enough about how genes work to be able to dismiss such an eventuality as absurdly unlikely. However, very little is known about how humans come up with new "mutant" ideas for making money. Economists can therefore only guess at what strategies they should include in deciding what game to study.

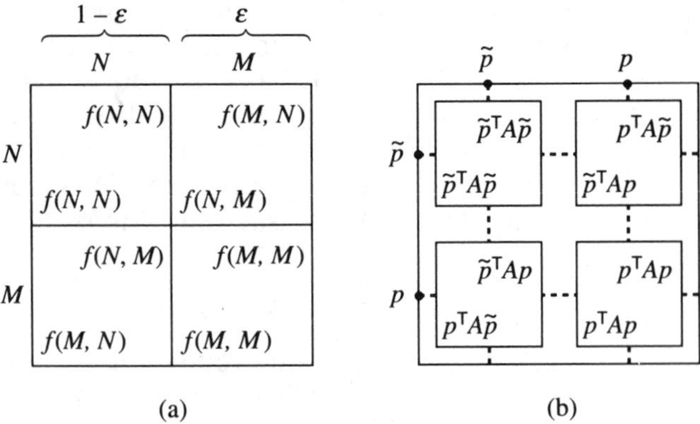

Figure 9.9 Evolutionary stability.

Evolutionary fitness in our dodo story depends on how a game is played. In Section 9.5.2, the game was Chicken. Here it will be any symmetric bimatrix game. An entry in the $n \times n$ payoff matrix A is to be interpreted as player I's incremental fitness. The game is symmetric because we are modeling a situation that looks precisely the same to both players. In algebraic terms, the requirement for symmetry is that player II's payoff matrix B be given by $B = A^{\top}$. Figure 9.9(b) shows what the fitnesses will be if the N replicator induces its hosts to use the mixed strategy $\tilde{p}$, and M induces its hosts to use the mixed strategy p.

9.6.2 Symmetric Nash Equilibria

A mixed strategy in a symmetric $n \times n$ bimatrix game is an $n \times 1$ column vector. Recall from Section 6.4.4 that player I's payoff from using mixed strategy p when player II uses mixed strategy q is $\Pi_1(p,q) = p^{\top}Aq$. Player II's payoff[30] is $\Pi_2(p,q) = p^{\top}Bq = q^{\top}Ap = \Pi_1(q,p)$. Section 6.5.6 gives the requirement that $(\tilde{p},\tilde{q})$ be a Nash equilibrium in the form

$$\Pi_1(\tilde{p},\tilde{q}) \geq \Pi_1(p,\tilde{q})$$
$$\Pi_2(\tilde{p},\tilde{q}) \geq \Pi_2(\tilde{p},q)\,.$$

The first inequality says that $\tilde{p}$ is a best reply to $\tilde{q}$ since it is at least as good as any other reply p. The second inequality says that $\tilde{q}$ is a best reply to $\tilde{p}$ since it is at least as good as any other reply q.

[30] Since $p^{\top}Bq$ is a scalar, it is equal to its transpose. For the reasons given in Section 4.3.1, $(p^{\top}Bq)^{\top} = q^{\top}B^{\top}p = q^{\top}Ap$. The last step uses the symmetry of the game. Since $B = A^{\top}$, $B^{\top} = (A^{\top})^{\top} = A$.

Only *symmetric* Nash equilibria in our symmetric game are of interest here. For a symmetric equilibrium, $\tilde{p} = \tilde{q}$. The second of the two inequalities characterizing a Nash equilibrium then becomes $\Pi_2(\tilde{p}, \tilde{p}) \geq \Pi_2(\tilde{p}, q)$, which is the same as $\Pi_1(\tilde{p}, \tilde{p}) \geq \Pi_1(q, \tilde{p})$. If q is replaced by p, this is exactly the same as the first inequality:

$$\Pi_1(\tilde{p}, \tilde{p}) \geq \Pi_1(p, \tilde{p}) . \tag{9.10}$$

In brief, the condition that $(\tilde{p}, \tilde{p})$ be a Nash equilibrium for our symmetric game is that the inequality (9.10) holds for all mixed strategies p. This guarantees that $\tilde{p}$ is a best reply to $\tilde{p}$ for *both* players.

9.6.3 Evolutionarily Stable Strategies

Suppose that the normal replicator N induces its host to use the mixed strategy $\tilde{p}$, and the mutant replicator M induces its host to use the mixed strategy p.[31] Then (9.9) translates into the requirement that, for all sufficiently small $\epsilon > 0$,

$$(1-\epsilon)\Pi_1(\tilde{p}, \tilde{p}) + \epsilon\Pi_1(\tilde{p}, p) > (1-\epsilon)\Pi_1(p, \tilde{p}) + \epsilon\Pi_1(p, p) . \tag{9.11}$$

If this requirement holds for all mixed strategies p, then the mixed strategy $\tilde{p}$ is said to be an *evolutionarily stable strategy*.[32]

Lemma 9.6.1 A necessary and sufficient condition that $\tilde{p}$ be an evolutionarily stable strategy is that

$$\text{(i)}\ \Pi_1(\tilde{p}, \tilde{p}) \geq \Pi_1(p, \tilde{p}) \qquad \text{(for all } p\text{)}$$

$$\text{and (ii)}\ \Pi_1(\tilde{p}, \tilde{p}) = \Pi_1(p, \tilde{p}) \Rightarrow \Pi_1(\tilde{p}, p) > \Pi_1(p, p) \qquad \text{(for all } p \neq \tilde{p}\text{)}$$

Proof. To obtain necessary conditions, we begin with (9.11) and see what follows. The first step is to consider the limit as $\epsilon \to 0$. This yields (i) immediately.[33] Item (ii) is even easier

[31] For a biologist, N and M are *genotypes*. These express themselves in the *phenotype* of an animal. An animal's phenotype is the set of its observable attributes. In our case, what matters about the phenotype of a dodo is the mixed strategy it uses in the game.

[32] To be precise, the requirement is that, for any p there exists $\delta > 0$ such that the inequality holds for each ϵ satisfying $0 < \epsilon < \delta$. Notice that several different replicators may induce $\tilde{p}$. Thus the evolutionary stability of $\tilde{p}$ does not guarantee evolutionary stability for any particular replicator.

[33] It does *not* yield the conclusion $\Pi_1(\tilde{p}, \tilde{p}) > \Pi_1(p, \tilde{p})$. For example, if $\epsilon > 0$, then $2\epsilon > \epsilon$. But we cannot take the limit as $\epsilon \to 0$ in this inequality and deduce that $0 > 0$. We can only deduce that $0 \geq 0$. If you suspect that even this is wrong (on the grounds that what is true is $0 = 0$), then consider carefully what $0 \geq 0$ *means*.

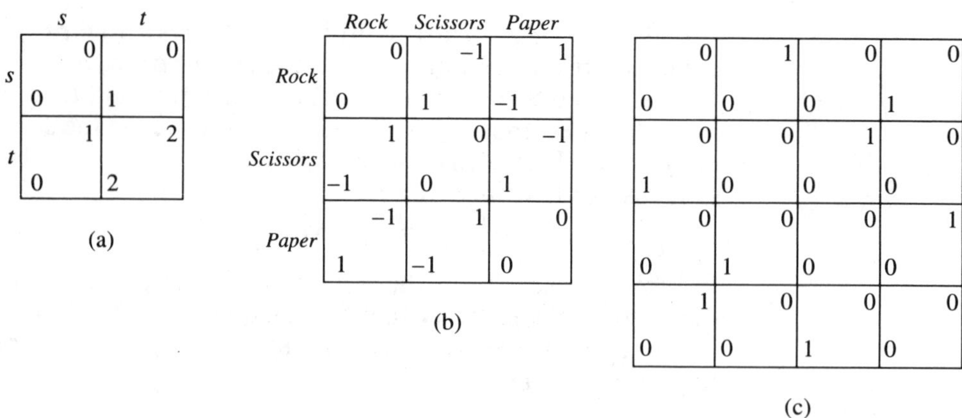

Figure 9.10 Evolutionarily stable strategies.

to deduce. Just put $\Pi_1(\tilde{p},\tilde{p}) = \Pi_1(p,\tilde{p})$ in (9.11) and see what happens.

For (i) and (ii) to be sufficient conditions, we must be able to use them to derive (9.11). If (i) holds, then either $\Pi_1(\tilde{p},\tilde{p}) > \Pi_1(p,\tilde{p})$ or $\Pi_1(\tilde{p},\tilde{p}) = \Pi_1(p,\tilde{p})$. In the second case, (9.11) follows immediately from (ii). For the first case, simply note that the left side of (9.11) can be made as close to $\Pi_1(p,\tilde{p})$ as we choose by taking $\epsilon > 0$ sufficiently small. Similarly, the right side can be made as close to $\Pi_1(p,\tilde{p})$ as we choose. Thus, when $\Pi_1(\tilde{p},\tilde{p}) > \Pi_1(p,\tilde{p})$, the inequality (9.11) must hold provided $\epsilon > 0$ is chosen to be small enough.[34] □

The criteria for an evolutionarily stable strategy $\tilde{p}$ given in Lemma 9.6.1 have a straightforward game-theoretic interpretation. Criterion (i) is identical to (9.10) and hence says that $(\tilde{p},\tilde{p})$ is a Nash equilibrium. Thus $\tilde{p}$ is a best reply to itself. But $\tilde{p}$ need not be the only best reply to itself. Criterion (ii) asks us to consider an *alternative best reply* p to $\tilde{p}$. It then insists that, for $\tilde{p}$ to be evolutionary stable, $\tilde{p}$ must be a better reply to p than p is to itself.

Figure 9.10(a) shows a 2×2 symmetric game in which the symmetric Nash equilibria in pure strategies are (s,s) and (t,t). Although t is evolutionarily stable, s is not. The reason is that t is an alternative best reply to s, but s is not a better reply to t than t is to itself.

[34]Let $a = \Pi_1(\tilde{p},\tilde{p}) - \Pi_1(p,\tilde{p})$ and $b = \Pi_1(p,p) - \Pi_1(\tilde{p},p)$. If $b \leq 0$, any $\epsilon > 0$ will suffice. Otherwise $a > 0$ and $b > 0$, and ϵ must be chosen to satisfy $0 < \epsilon < a/(a+b)$.

9.6.4 Replicator Dynamics

Evolutionarily stable strategies were introduced in an attempt to short-circuit the difficulties involved in modeling the details of biological adaptation processes. How successful are they in this role? Our crazy model of the evolution of dodos can be used to examine this question. Its lack of realism is no handicap for this purpose because, if the ideas that led us to the concept of evolutionary stability are valid, then they would still be valid in crazy *counterfactual* worlds like that inhabited by our dodos. The use of such unrealistic, oversimplified formal models for the purpose of testing the *internal consistency* of theories that do claim to be realistic is very important indeed, although widely misunderstood.[35]

Before discussing how evolutionarily stable strategies are related to attractors of the replicator dynamics, it is necessary to say something about mixed strategies. Animals *do* sometimes use mixed strategies, but it seems that they seldom do so in one-on-one contests. If a mixed strategy is used, it will usually be when an animal is "playing the field". That is, when it is competing simultaneously with a large number of its fellows. So why take the trouble to define an evolutionarily stable mixed strategy? Why not stick to pure strategies? As regards the replicator dynamics, we shall do precisely that. Only replicators that induce their hosts to use pure strategies will be considered. However, in studying Chicken, we discovered that *polymorphic* populations may turn out to be stable. These are populations in which different animals may be hosting different replicators. Although we shall not study the case when any particular animal makes random choices, we shall find the idea of an evolutionarily stable mixed strategy useful in describing stable polymorphic populations.

It is not necessary to repeat the derivation of the replicator equation (9.7) from Section 9.5.3. When Chicken is replaced by a symmetric game in which player I's payoff matrix is A, it is true that things get a little more complicated. Instead of two replicators, one needs n replicators, one for each pure strategy. At any time, the *state* of the population will then be determined by a vector $p = (p_1, p_2, \ldots, p_n)^\top$ that gives the

[35]Some social scientists are touchy about the "scientific" status of their subject, and insist that a model is worthwhile if and only if it predicts actual behavior. One might characterize this attitude as "naive positivism". Physicists, of course, know better. In particular, they understand mathematics well enough to appreciate the importance of searching for logical *counterexamples* when confronted with a conjecture.

fractions of the population hosting each replicator. If the ith replicator induces its host to play the ith pure strategy, its fitness $f_i(p)$ can be calculated from the matrix A.[36] The argument of 9.5.3 then yields the replicator equation in the form

$$p_i' = p_i(f_i(p) - \overline{f}(p)). \tag{9.12}$$

Let A be any symmetric 2×2 matrix whose rows are not both the same.[37] The replicator dynamics for such a matrix are not difficult to study. The argument of Section 9.5.4 suffices to prove part (ii) of the simple proposition stated below (Exercise 9.8.12). Part (i) is equally easy (Exercise 9.8.16).

Proposition 9.6.1 When $n = 2$,

(i) The payoff matrix A always admits at least one evolutionarily stable strategy $\tilde{p}$.

(ii) A population state $\tilde{p}$ is an asymptotic attractor of the replicator dynamics if and only if $\tilde{p}$ is an evolutionarily stable strategy.

When $n > 2$, the world becomes more complicated. Neither (i) nor (ii) is then true. The Rock-Scissors-Paper game of Figure 9.10(b) is a counterexample to (i). It has no evolutionarily stable strategy.[38] (Exercise 9.8.17). The 4×4 analog of Shapley's Shimmy given in Figure 9.10(c) is a counterexample to (ii). The population state $\tilde{p} = (\frac{1}{4}, \frac{1}{4}, \frac{1}{4}, \frac{1}{4})^\top$ is an asymptotic attractor of the replicator dynamics, but $\tilde{p}$ is not an evolutionarily stable strategy.[39] However, some useful things are true in the general case. The following proposition summarizes some of these.

Proposition 9.6.2 Let $\tilde{p}$ be an $n \times 1$ vector whose coordinates are nonnegative and sum to one. Then, for any symmetric $n \times n$ game, the following implications hold:

---

[36]The fitnesses $f_i(p)$ are incremental fitnesses per unit of time. The $n \times 1$ column vector $f(p)$ is given by $f(p) = Ap$. The average fitness $\overline{f}(p)$ of a member of the population is given by $\overline{f}(p) = p^\top f(p) = p^\top Ap$.

[37]If both rows are the same, then both pure strategies are equally good no matter what the other player does. This trivial case therefore has to be excluded (Exercise 9.8.12(c)).

[38]The only Nash equilibrium is for each player to use the mixed strategy $\tilde{p} = (\frac{1}{3}, \frac{1}{3}, \frac{1}{3})^\top$. Both players then get zero. Anything is a best reply to $\tilde{p}$. In particular, *rock* is an alternative to $\tilde{p}$ as a best reply to $\tilde{p}$. But $\tilde{p}$ is not a strictly better reply to *rock* than *rock* is to itself.

[39]This is a little troublesome to prove. Exercise 9.8.26 provides a less elegant example that is easier to analyze.

(i) $\tilde{p}$ is an evolutionarily stable strategy

$\Rightarrow$ (ii) $\tilde{p}$ is an asymptotic attractor of the replicator dynamics

$\Rightarrow$ (iii) $\tilde{p}$ is a Nash equilibrium

$\Rightarrow$ (iv) $\tilde{p}$ is a rest point of the replicator dynamics.

The failure of Proposition 9.6.1 to generalize means that the idea of an evolutionarily stable strategy does not allow us to escape the painful task of studying the replicator dynamics in detail. However, it remains a useful tool. The fact that evolutionarily stable strategies sometimes fail to exist at all should not lead us to change our minds on this point.[40] Indeed, the nonexistence of an evolutionarily stable strategy may well be a useful indication in itself that the replicator dynamics need particularly careful study.

9.7 The Evolution of Cooperation

Axelrod's *Evolution of Cooperation* has been so influential a book that it is often taken for granted that the repeated Prisoners' Dilemma is the right and proper vehicle for the study of this question. However, it is complicated to study repetitions of a repeated game. Moreover, the question of how cooperative behavior may evolve becomes entangled with a second even more important question: namely, how do *learning rules* evolve? This second question is unavoidable when boundedly rational players confront each other in a *repeated* game. A replicator that did not program its host to respond to the way the opponent is playing would usually not stand much chance of surviving.

Since little seems to be known about the evolution of learning rules, it seems wiser to continue to use Chicken to illustrate how cooperation may evolve. However, it will be necessary to examine a souped-up version of Chicken with *four* pure strategies instead of two.

9.7.1 Chicken Soup

If two hawkish dodos are matched to play the original version of Chicken, they fight and thereby risk injury. However, in real life, contests between animals of the same species are often settled by a *ritualized* battle. Both animals begin by

[40]Some game theorists make existence for all games a *sine qua non* for an equilibrium concept.

	D	H	B	R
D	1 1	2 0	2 0	$1+\varepsilon$ $1-\varepsilon$
H	0 2	-1 -1	0 2	$-1-\varepsilon$ $-1+\varepsilon$
B	0 2	2 0	1 1	2 0
R	$1-\varepsilon$ $1+\varepsilon$	$-1+\varepsilon$ $-1-\varepsilon$	0 2	1 1

Figure 9.11 Displaying in Chicken.

displaying their prowess. One animal will then often concede what is in dispute to the other, and neither gets hurt.

Figure 9.11 is a souped-up version of Chicken that attempts to capture the idea of a preliminary round in which animals have the opportunity to signal to each other. The *hawk* and *dove* strategy are as before, except that one must imagine that those dodos using *hawk* signal their hawkishness before Chicken gets played, and those dodos using *dove* signal that they are dove-like.

In addition to these truthful strategies, there is the *bully* strategy and the *retaliator* strategy. A dodo using the *bully* strategy never fights, but she displays as though she intends to. This strategy deceives only dodos playing *dove*.

If a bullying dodo resembles Benito Mussolini, then a retaliator is like the character portrayed by Clint Eastwood in a spaghetti Western. A dodo using the *retaliator* strategy begins by acting like a dove, but switches to a hawkish stance at the first hint of hawkishness from the opponent. The value of $\epsilon > 0$ in Figure 9.11 is very small. It is included to give *hawk* a slight advantage over *retaliator*, since a hawkish dodo will have the initiative in a fight. Similarly, *retaliator* gets a slight advantage over *dove*.[41]

Figure 9.6(c) shows how to represent a population state $p = (p_1, p_2, p_3)^\top$ as a point in a triangle. Here we have to cope with a four-dimensional population state $p = (p_1, p_2, p_3, p_4)^\top$. This can be represented as a point in a tetrahedron as

---

[41]Without these added touches of realism, the replicator dynamics need not converge.

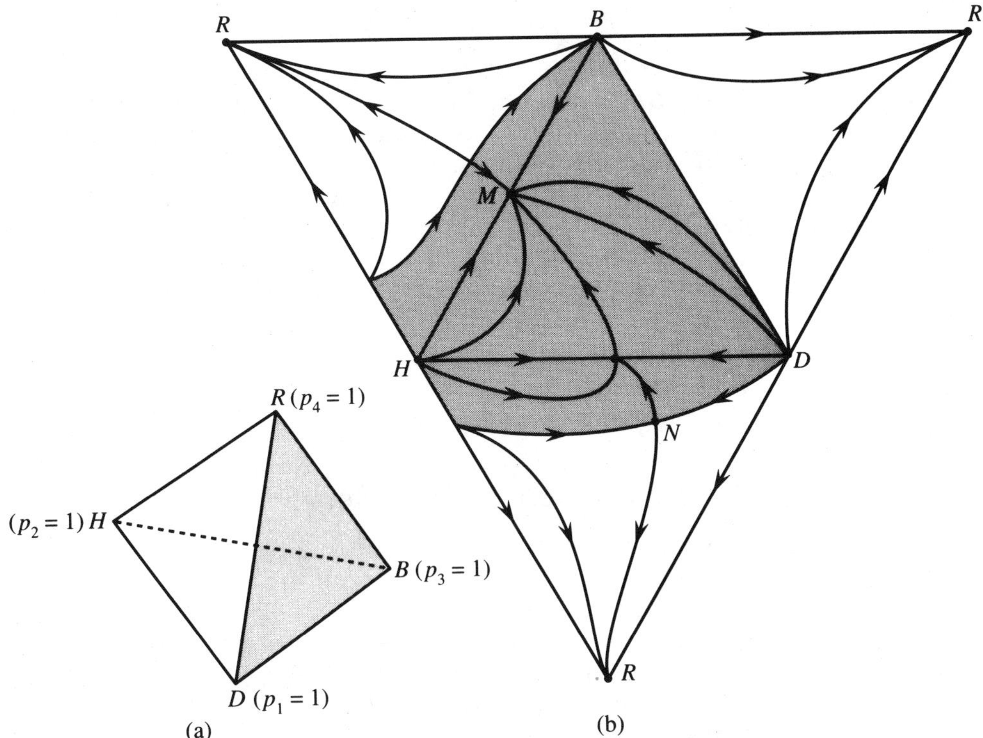

Figure 9.12 Replicator dynamics for Souped-Up Chicken.

illustrated in Figure 9.12(a). Figure 9.12(b) shows the faces of the tetrahedron unfolded with the trajectories of the replicator dynamics indicated.[42]

Figure 9.12(b) shows three rest points, M, N and R. The first corresponds to a polymorphic population of half hawks and half bullies. The second to a polymorphic mixture of hawks, doves and retaliators. The third to a population of all retaliators. In accordance with Proposition 9.6.2, each of these rest points corresponds to a Nash equilibrium of Souped-Up Chicken. The rest point N is not a local attractor. Proposition 9.6.2 therefore tells us that it does not correspond to an evolutionarily stable strategy. Both M and R are asymptotic attractors. This need not imply that they correspond to evolutionarily stable strategies, but in this case they do. (Exercise 9.8.27)

[42]This diagram follows the mathematician Zeeman, who elaborated on Maynard Smith's original model.

9.7.2 Cheap-Talking Dodos

The first thing to notice is that cooperation need not triumph. The hawk-bully equilibrium M is equivalent to the hawk-dove equilibrium discovered for regular Chicken in Section 9.5.4. The only difference is that bullies replace doves.

This observation prompts some comment about cheap talk (Section 7.5.3) in the animal kingdom. Sometimes the displays observed are very elaborate indeed, but if the display conveys no hard information about the displayer's physical characteristics,[43] then the opponent often appears unimpressed by this animal equivalent of cheap talk. Presumably, those replicators that were deceived no longer survive, just as the D replicator no longer survives at the hawk-bully equilibrium.

9.7.3 Strong-but-Silent Takeover

In studying the evolution of cooperation, it is the equilibrium in which all dodos host the R replicator that is of interest. At the R attractor in Figure 9.12, a kibitzer will never see any fighting. All games will be settled with both dodos behaving like doves and dividing the disputed resource between them. But how could the strong-but-silent R replicator get established in the first place? If the population at time 0 contains positive fractions only of the D, H and B replicators, then the initial population state will lie inside the triangle DHB of Figure 9.12 and hence in the basin of attraction of the attractor M. If a mutant R replicator were to appear and to take over a tiny fraction of the population, this would not be enough to break out from the basin. Thus, eventually the R replicator would be squeezed to extinction.

Here are various ways in which enough R replicators might appear on the scene to force the population state out of M's basin of attraction. The simplest supposes that mutations appear at a specific locality in the first instance. As hosts carrying the mutant replicator wander, the mutant replicator will later diffuse throughout the whole habitat if it is successful. But to begin with, mutants will only be encountered in a restricted area. Within that area, the mutant need not be hosted by a negligible fraction of the *local* population. For example, although the members of your family form a negligible fraction of the world's population, they very definitely do not

[43]That is, information that cannot be simulated by an animal without these characteristics. Certain spiders, for example, apparently convey information about their body weight to their rivals by strumming the spider web over whose possession they are in dispute.

form a negligible fraction of the people you encounter in the family home. The *local* population state may therefore lie outside *M*'s basin of attraction. If so, all the replicators except *R* will be squeezed out *locally*. But then the area within which the above analysis applies will expand. Eventually it will expand until the whole habitat is included. All but the *R* replicator will then be eliminated, and evolution will have created a cooperative world for dodos to live in.

9.7.4 Axelrod's Olympiad

In his *Evolution of Cooperation*, Robert Axelrod describes two computer tournaments for which he invited various people to submit computer programs that would then compete against each other in the repeated Prisoners' Dilemma. The strategy TIT-FOR-TAT of Figure 8.5(d) won both times. His next step was to simulate the effect of running further tournaments. He began with an initial population in which each of the 63 strategies used in his second tournament was equally numerous. He then used a version of the replicator dynamics to make a guess at the profile of strategies that would have been submitted in later tournaments. The idea is that strategies that have been unsuccessful in the past are unlikely to be popular candidates for submission in the future. In the long run, the process settled on a polymorphic profile in which TIT-FOR-TAT had the largest share.[44]

In consequence of Axelrod's study, some authors use the phrase TIT-FOR-TAT as though it were a synonym for a self-enforcing, cooperative agreement. It is certainly true that TIT-FOR-TAT is an elegant embodiment of a number of ideas studied in this and the previous chapter. If both players use TIT-FOR-TAT, cooperation is sustained because neither player has anything to gain by deviating. Any such deviation will be punished. At the same time, TIT-FOR-TAT is a close enough cousin to the *retaliator* strategy studied in Section 9.7.1 for

[44]Axelrod's methodology has been criticized. In particular, although his second tournament was advertised as an infinite-horizon Prisoners' Dilemma, his evolutionary simulation used a *finite*-horizon version. If *all* pure strategies for this finite-horizon Prisoners' Dilemma had been in the initial population, then the replicator dynamics would necessarily converge on a population state in which everyone always plays *hawk*. However, replications of his simulation that use the advertised *infinite*-horizon Prisoners' Dilemma yield much the same conclusion as that reported in the text. On the other hand, such simulations do not show TIT-FOR-TAT coming out on top most of the time when different initial mixtures of the original 63 strategies are used. In fact, TIT-FOR-TAT wins out only about 26 percent of the time in simulations for which the initial mixture is chosen at random.

it to be clear how a story would go that sought to make it plausible that evolutionary forces could lead to a population who all play TIT-FOR-TAT.

However, there is nothing inevitable about TIT-FOR-TAT, even when attention is restricted to the infinite-horizon Prisoners' Dilemma. What evolution produces will largely be a matter of historical accident. In particular, one ought not to be at all confident that evolution will necessarily eliminate "nasty" strategies that, unlike TIT-FOR-TAT, begin by playing *hawk*.[45] Such strategies need not be stupid. For example, the strategy TAT-FOR-TIT of Figure 8.14 is "nasty", but the pair (TAT-FOR-TIT, TAT-FOR-TIT) is a Nash equilibrium that yields the cooperative outcome in the long run. (Exercises 8.6.15 and 8.6.21)

9.8 Exercises

1. The initial position for Schelling's Solitaire in Figure 9.1(b) has 26 black counters and 26 white counters. Is it possible to find a stable configuration with the same number of black and white counters in which all the black counters are on the black squares of a chessboard and all the white counters on the white squares?

Econ

2. Exercises 7.9.13 and 7.9.14 ask for the reaction curves and the Nash equilibria for two Cournot models with differentiated products. Draw the reaction curves in each case. Show some trajectories for the libration described in Section 9.3.1. What are the basins of attraction for the Nash equilibria?

Econ

3. Exercise 7.9.18 asks for a Bertrand analysis of the two models of the previous exercise. In a Bertrand model, each firm selects the *price* at which it sells its product (Exercise 7.9.17). Draw the Bertrand reaction curves for

---

[45]Maynard Smith's *Evolution and the Theory of Games* quotes Axelrod as having proved that TIT-FOR-TAT is an evolutionarily stable strategy for the infinitely repeated Prisoners' Dilemma, provided that this is played with a sufficiently high discount factor. This result is false, since a mutant invasion by any other "nice" machine will obviously not be driven out. What Axelrod proves is that TIT-FOR-TAT is what he calls "collectively stable". This just means that it is a Nash equilibrium against itself as proved in Section 8.4.3 for limit-of-the-means payoffs. Axelrod observes that, with one exception, the propositions in his book *Evolution of Cooperation* remain valid if collective stability is replaced by evolutionary stability, provided that attention is restricted to "nice" machines. However, this does not imply that collective stability is an adequate substitute for evolutionary stability, even if it were appropriate to exclude "nasty" machines from consideration.

each model. Show some trajectories for a libration that is the same as that of Section 9.3.1 except that each firm chooses its *price* in the current period on the assumption that the other firm will choose the same *price* as it chose in the previous period.

Econ

4. Consider the following libration. Both players nearly always just do the same in the current period as they did in the previous period. However, in each period there is a small probability that a bell will ring in a player's mind. If the bell rings, the player takes note of the other player's action in the previous period, and switches to a best reply to this.

   Show that this new libration always converges in both the Cournot duopoly models of Section 9.3.1. Describe the nature of the historical accidents that determine what the libration converges to in the second model.

Econ

5. Investigate a less naive libration for the second Cournot model of Section 9.3.1. The players are now slightly more sophisticated and do not simply predict that the opponent will do the same as in the last period. Instead, each firm predicts that the opponent will produce the average of what it produced in the previous two periods. Each firm then makes a best reply to their prediction of the opponent's output. Find the trajectory that results when the output pair in period 0 is $\tilde{p}$ in Figure 9.3(a) and the output pair in period 1 is $\tilde{r}$. Does this trajectory converge?

Econ

6. Repeat Exercise 9.8.5 with even more sophisticated players. They predict that the opposing firm's output will be $\frac{2}{3}a + \frac{1}{3}b$, where a is the opposing firm's output last period, and b is its output in the period before that.

7. Draw a diagram showing basins of attraction and typical trajectories for the "fictitious play" libration of Section 9.3.3 in the case of each of the following games:
   (a) Prisoners' Dilemma (Figure 7.3(b))
   (b) Chicken (Figure 7.3(c))
   (c) Battle of the Sexes (Figure 7.24(a))
   (d) Australian Battle of the Sexes (Figure 7.24(b))
   How will these diagrams differ if the libration of Section 9.4 is used instead?

Math

8. Show that the considerations of Section 9.3.3 remain unchanged if Shapley's Shimmy is replaced by the Rock-Scissors-Paper game of Figure 9.10(b).

Math

9. In the libration story of Section 9.4, veteran players retire from the game-playing population at the same rate as they

are replaced by rookies. The population size N therefore remains unchanged. Consider a different model in which veterans never fade away or die, but rookies continue to join the population at the same rate as before.

(a) If the population at time t is $N(t)$, why will the population at time $t + \tau$ be approximately $N(t)(1 + \lambda\tau)$?

(b) Derive differential equations for the new libration.

(c) Why do these new differential equations lead to the same trajectories as the old differential equations?

10. To what does the replicator equation (9.7) reduce when the underlying game is not Chicken, but the Prisoners' Dilemma of Figure 7.3(b)? Explain why solutions to the equation have graphs like those of Figure 9.8.

11. Show that the replicator equation (9.7) is unchanged if each payoff x in the Chicken matrix of Figure 9.7(a) is replaced by $ax + b$, where $a > 0$ and b are constants.

12. A general symmetric 2×2 bimatrix game is given in Figure 9.13(a). With this game, show that the replicator equations (9.7) for the fractions p_1 and p_2 of the population using strategies s_1 and s_2 respectively are:

$$p_1' = p_1(1 - p_1)\{p_1(a - c) + (1 - p_1)(b - d)\}$$
$$p_2' = p_2(1 - p_2)\{p_2(d - b) + (1 - p_2)(c - a)\}$$

	s_1	s_2
s_1	a, a	b, c
s_2	c, b	d, d

(a)

	s_1	s_2	s_3
s_1	0, 0	6, −3	−4, −1
s_2	−3, 6	0, 0	5, 3
s_3	−1, −4	3, 5	0, 0

(b)

Figure 9.13 Evolutionary stability problems.

(a) Explain why $(\tilde{p}_1, \tilde{p}_2) = (1, 0)$ is always a rest point of the replicator dynamics. Show that it is an asymptotic attractor if and only if (i) $a > c$ or (ii) $a = c$ and $b > d$.

(b) Explain why $(\tilde{p}_1, \tilde{p}_2) = (0, 1)$ is always a rest point of the replicator dynamics. Show that it is an asymptotic attractor if and only if (i) $d > b$ or (ii) $d = b$ and $c > a$.

(c) Explain why any pair $(\tilde{p}_1, \tilde{p}_2)$ is a rest point of the replicator dynamics if $a = c$ and $d = b$. Explain why none of these rest points is an asymptotic attractor (although they are local attractors).

(d) Suppose that $(a, d) \neq (c, b)$. Let $\tilde{p}_1 = (d - b)/(a - c + d - b)$ and $\tilde{p}_2 = 1 - \tilde{p}_1$. Explain why $(\tilde{p}_1, \tilde{p}_2)$ is a rest point of the replicator dynamics if and only if either $a \geq c$ and $d \geq b$ or else $a \leq c$ and $d \leq b$.

(e) Show that a rest point $(\tilde{p}_1, \tilde{p}_2)$ of the type considered in part (d) is an asymptotic attractor if and only if $a < c$ or $d < b$.

(f) If a rest point $(\tilde{p}_1, \tilde{p}_2)$ is completely mixed, explain why it is an asymptotic attractor if and only if $a < c$ and $d < b$. (Recall that a completely mixed strategy uses each pure strategy with positive probability.)

13. Show that any Nash equilibrium of the general symmetric 2×2 bimatrix game of Figure 9.13(a) is a rest point of its replicator dynamics. Give a counterexample to the proposition that a rest point of the replicator dynamics is always a Nash equilibrium of the game.

14. Prove the following assertions for the general symmetric 2×2 bimatrix game of Figure 9.13(a):
    (a) The pure strategy s_1 is evolutionarily stable if and only if (i) $a > c$ or (ii) $a = c$ and $b > d$.
    (b) The pure strategy s_2 is evolutionarily stable if and only if (i) $d > b$ or (ii) $d = b$ and $c > a$.
    (c) A completely mixed strategy is evolutionarily stable if and only if $a < c$ and $d < b$.

15. Use Exercises 9.8.12 and 9.8.14 to show that a population state is an asymptotic attractor of the replicator dynamics for the general symmetric 2×2 bimatrix game of Figure 9.13(a) if and only if the corresponding strategy is evolutionarily stable.

16. Show that an evolutionarily stable strategy for the general symmetric 2×2 bimatrix game of Figure 9.13(a) fails to exist only in the case $a = c$ and $d = b$.

17. Show that the Rock-Scissors-Paper game of Figure 9.10(b) has no evolutionarily stable strategy.

18. Why can a strongly dominated strategy not be evolutionarily stable? Is it possible for a weakly dominated strategy to be evolutionarily stable?

19. Evolutionary stability is studied throughout the chapter for the case when both players are drawn from the *same* population to fill the roles of player I and player II. Another possibility is that player I is drawn from one population and player II is drawn from an entirely separate population. Mutations will appear in only *one* of these two populations at a time. Explain why the condition for evolutionary stability of Section 9.6.1 then becomes
$$f(n,n) > f(m,n),$$
instead of the more complicated formula (9.9). What is the corresponding version of Lemma 9.6.1? Relate your answer to the notion of a strong Nash equilibrium.[46]
20. Section 9.6 discusses the replicator dynamics for a population state $p = (p_1, p_2, \ldots, p_n)^\top$ when player I's $n \times n$ payoff matrix in the underlying symmetric game G is A. Prove that the replicator equation (9.7) reduces to
$$p_i' = p_i\{(Ap)_i - p^\top Ap\},$$
where $(Ap)_i$ denotes the ith coordinate of the $n \times 1$ column vector Ap.
21. Explain why $A^\top = -A$ in a symmetric, zero-sum, bimatrix game. Deduce that $p^\top Ap = 0$ for all p. Hence show that the replicator equation in the previous exercise reduces to $p_i' = p_i(Ap)_i$ in the zero-sum case.

Math

22. Let $\tilde{p}$ be a completely mixed, evolutionarily stable strategy for a symmetric bimatrix game in which player I's $n \times n$ payoff matrix is A.
    (a) Explain why there is a constant w such that $(A\tilde{p})_i = w$ for all values of i. Deduce that $\tilde{p}^\top A\tilde{p} = p^\top A\tilde{p}$ for all p.
    (b) Explain why any p is an alternative best reply to $\tilde{p}$.
    (c) Deduce that $\tilde{p}^\top Ap > p^\top Ap$ for all $p \neq \tilde{p}$.
    (d) If the game is zero-sum, $A^\top = -A$. Deduce that $\tilde{p}^\top A\tilde{p} < p^\top Ap$ for all p. Use this fact and the previous exercise to show that a symmetric zero-sum game cannot have a completely mixed, evolutionarily stable strategy.
23. Show that the replicator equations for the Rock-Scissors-Paper game of Figure 9.10 are
$$p_1'/p_1 = p_2 - p_3,$$
$$p_2'/p_2 = p_3 - p_1,$$
$$p_3'/p_3 = p_1 - p_2.$$
Prove that the only rest point for these equations is

[46]This is a pair of strategies, each of which is a strong best reply to the other. That is, each strategy is *strictly* better than any alternative.

$\tilde{p} = (\frac{1}{3}, \frac{1}{3}, \frac{1}{3})$. Confirm that $(\tilde{p}, \tilde{p})$ is a symmetric Nash equilibrium for the game.

Math

24. Add the three equations of the previous exercise. Hence show that the trajectories have equations of the form $p_1 p_2 p_3 = c$, where c is a constant whose value depends on the initial point. (Do not forget that only states with $p = (p_1, p_2, p_3)$ satisfying $p_1 \geq 0$, $p_2 \geq 0$, $p_3 \geq 0$ and $p_1 + p_2 + p_3 = 1$ are admissible.)
    (a) Prove that $p_1 p_2 p_3$ achieves a strict maximum of $\frac{1}{27}$ subject to the constraint $p_1 + p_2 + p_3 = 1$ when $p_1 = p_2 = p_3 = \frac{1}{3}$. Deduce that no trajectory $p_1 p_2 p_3 = c$ with $c < \frac{1}{27}$ approaches $\tilde{p} = (\frac{1}{3}, \frac{1}{3}, \frac{1}{3})$. Why does this imply that there are no asymptotic attractors in this model?
    (b) If $0 \leq c \leq \frac{1}{27}$, let $p_1(c)$ denote the smallest value of p_1 that satisfies $p_1 p_2 p_3 = c$ and $p_1 + p_2 + p_3 = 1$. Show that $p_1(c)(1 - p_1(c))^2 = 4c$, and deduce that $p_1(c) \to \frac{1}{3}$ as $c \to \frac{1}{27}$. Why does this imply that a trajectory that starts near $\tilde{p} = (\frac{1}{3}, \frac{1}{3}, \frac{1}{3})$ remains near $\tilde{p}$? Why is $\tilde{p}$ a local attractor but not an asymptotic attractor?
    (c) Using a triangular diagram like those of Figure 9.6, sketch the trajectories for the replicator dynamics in the Rock-Scissors-Paper game.

25. Show that s_1 is an evolutionarily stable strategy for the game of Figure 9.13(b). If $\tilde{p} = (\frac{1}{3}, \frac{1}{3}, \frac{1}{3})$, show that $(\tilde{p}, \tilde{p})$ is a Nash equilibrium for the game, but that $\tilde{p}$ is not an evolutionarily stable strategy.

Math

26. Use Exercise 9.8.20 to help write down the replicator equations for the game of Figure 9.13(b).
    (a) Why is $\tilde{p}$ of the previous exercise a rest point for these dynamics?
    (b) Change the variable in the replicator equations from p to $q = p - \tilde{p}$. Use the fact that $q_1 + q_2 + q_3 = 0$ to eliminate q_3 from the first two equations. Hence reduce the system to the form

$$q_1' = \frac{17}{9} q_1 + \frac{27}{9} q_2 + \varepsilon_1(q_1, q_2),$$

$$q_2' = -\frac{19}{9} q_1 - \frac{23}{9} q_2 + \varepsilon_2(q_1, q_2),$$

where the error terms $\varepsilon_1(q_1, q_2)$ and $\varepsilon_2(q_1, q_2)$ are quadratic and hence small when q is close to 0.[47]

[47] You have "linearized" the system of differential equations. Provided that q stays near 0, its trajectory will be approximately the same as the trajectory obtained from the linear system that results from suppressing the error terms ε_1 and ε_2.

(c) Check that the eigenvalues of the matrix of coefficients in the system of differential equations of part (b) are $\frac{1}{3}(-1 \pm i\sqrt{2})$.

(d) The eigenvalues obtained in part (c) have negative real part. Why does this imply that $\tilde{p}$ is an asymptotic attractor even though it is not an evolutionarily stable strategy?

27. In the Souped-Up Chicken game of Figure 9.11,

(a) Show that R is an evolutionarily stable strategy.

(b) Show that the mixed strategy in which H and B are each used with probability $\frac{1}{2}$ is an evolutionarily stable strategy.

Math

28. In the game of Figure 9.14(a), show that s_3 is stable against invasion by s_1 or s_2 alone, but not against an invasion by both s_1 and s_2 simultaneously.

	s_1	s_2	s_3
s_1	0 / 0	10 / 10	1 / 1
s_2	10 / 10	0 / 0	1 / 1
s_3	1 / 1	1 / 1	1 / 1

(a)

	Dove	*Mix*	*Hawk*
Dove	1 / 1	$\frac{3}{2}$ / $\frac{1}{2}$	2 / 0
Mix	$\frac{1}{2}$ / $\frac{3}{2}$	$\frac{1}{2}$ / $\frac{1}{2}$	$\frac{1}{2}$ / $-\frac{1}{2}$
Hawk	0 / 2	$-\frac{1}{2}$ / $\frac{1}{2}$	−1 / −1

(b)

Figure 9.14 More evolutionary stability problems.

Math

29. The mixed strategy $\tilde{p}$ in which *dove* and *hawk* are each used with probability $\frac{1}{2}$ is an evolutionarily stable strategy for the game of Chicken given in Figure 9.7(a). The game of Figure 9.14(b) is constructed from Chicken by introducing a new pure strategy *mix*. The payoffs assigned to the pure strategy *mix* in the new game are the same as those that would be obtained from the use of the mixed strategy $\tilde{p}$ in Chicken.

(a) Show that *mix* is not evolutionarily stable in the new game.

(b) Show that the mixed strategy in which *dove* and *hawk* are each used with probability $\frac{1}{2}$ is not evolutionarily stable in the new game.

Math

30. The game of Chicken of Figure 7.3(c) comes with a story about cars that approach each other at speed along a narrow city street, with neither driver wishing to lose face by taking evasive action. It is true that Chicken captures the essentials of this strategic situation, but the following variant of a game called the War of Attrition does so better. It is a game of timing like Duel or Russian Roulette.

As in the game of Russian Roulette studied in Section 4.7, think of the outcomes for each player as death, disgrace or triumph. Both players attach payoffs of 0, a and 1 to these outcomes, where $0 < a < 1$. Decisions are made at times $t_0, t_1, t_2, \ldots$, where $0 = t_0 < t_1 < t_2 < \cdots < T$ and $t_k \to T$ as $k \to \infty$. At these times, both players simultaneously decide whether to hold on or to chicken out. A player who chickens out is disgraced. A player who holds on when the opponent has chickened out is triumphant. A collision leads to certain death. If both players hold out until time t_k without a collision occurring, the probability of a collision between time t_k and time t_{k+1} is $\pi(t_k)$. The function $\pi : [0, T] \to [0, 1]$ is continuous and strictly increasing with $\pi(0) = 0$ and $\pi(T) = 1$.

(a) Why are times after T being neglected?

(b) Show that it is a Nash equilibrium for player I always to plan to chicken out and for player II always to plan to hold on.

(c) Suppose that both players have held on until time t_k. If player I believes that player II will now chicken out with probability $p(t_k)$, why will he be indifferent between chickening out now and chickening out at time t_{k+1} if

$$a = p(t_k) + (1 - \pi(t_k))a\,?$$

(d) Why is it a symmetric Nash equilibrium for both players to plan to chicken out at each time t_k with probability $p(t_k) = a\pi(t_k)$ unless someone chickened out previously?[48]

(e) What is the probability that there will be a collision if the symmetric Nash equilibrium strategies are used? If there is no collision, what is the probability that

[48]The mixed strategies that the players use in this symmetric equlibrium are not described directly in terms of the probabilities to be assigned to each pure strategy. Instead they are specified indirectly in terms of the conditional probabilities with which each available action is taken at a decision node, should that decision node ever be reached. In Section 10.4.3, we shall learn to call such a specification a *behavioral strategy*.

someone will chicken out before time t? You may find it more convenient to give the answers for a continuous time version of the model.

Phil

31. A souped-up version of Chicken was introduced in Section 9.7.1. A dynamic version of Chicken was introduced in Exercise 9.8.30. What would correspond to the *dove*, *hawk* and *bully* strategies of Section 9.7.1 in the game of Exercise 9.8.30?

Symmetric Nash equilibria in the version of Chicken studied in the previous exercise require the players to use mixed strategies (Exercise 9.8.30(d)). Modify the game of Exercise 9.8.30 so that each player observes not only what the opponent did in the time period just finished, but also the *probability* that the opponent assigned to holding on or chickening out in that period. A *retaliator* strategy can then be seen as one that assigns a high probability p to holding on in any particular period,[49] provided that the opponent has been holding on with probability p in the past. If the opponent fails to behave this way, the *retaliator* strategy calls for switching to the strategy of a hawk at all future times.

(a) Does the hypothesis that players can observe the probability with which each uses a particular action make any sense in the context of a contest between animals?

(b) Show that, if the time interval between successive stages is sufficiently small and the value of p is sufficiently high, then two players who both use the *retaliator* strategy will do nearly as well as two players who both use *dove*.

(c) Use the model proposed in this exercise to evaluate the plausibility of the payoffs in the Souped-Up Chicken matrix of Figure 9.11.

[49]Notice that this does not imply that there will be a high probability that two retaliators will meet with a disaster. Even if the probability of holding on at the kth stage, should this be reached, is 0.99, the probability that a player will chicken out at some time in the first hundred stages is $1 - (.99)^{100}$, which is approximately 0.6.

CHAPTER

10

Knowing Your Place

10.1 Bob's Your Uncle

The frontispiece to this chapter shows three travelers in a Victorian railway carriage. They are Bob, his niece Alice, and an old family retainer affectionately known as Nanny. Each has a dirty face. However, nobody is blushing with shame, even though any Victorian traveler who was conscious of appearing in public with a dirty face would surely do so. We can therefore deduce that none of the travelers knows that his or her own face is dirty, although each can clearly see the dirty faces of their companions.

A railway guard now looks in through the window and announces that someone in the carriage has a dirty face. He is the sort of person who can be relied upon to make such an announcement if and only if it is true. One of the travelers now blushes. Why should this be? Did not the guard simply tell the travelers something they *already knew*?

To understand what is going on, it is necessary to examine the nuts and bolts of the chain of reasoning that leads to the conclusion that one of the travelers must blush. If neither Bob nor Nanny blushes, Alice would reason as follows:

> *Alice:* Suppose that my face were clean. Then Bob would reason as follows:
>
> > *Bob:* I see that Alice's face is clean. Suppose that my face were also clean. Then Nanny would reason as follows:
> >
> > > *Nanny:* I see that Alice and Bob's faces are clean. If my face were clean, nobody's face would be dirty, which I know to be false. Thus my face is dirty and I must blush.
> >
> > *Bob:* Since Nanny has not blushed, my face is dirty. Thus I must blush.
>
> *Alice:* Since Bob has not blushed, my face is dirty. Thus I must blush.

What the guard added to what the travelers already knew is information about what the travelers would know under various hypothetical circumstances. Thus Alice needs to know what Bob would know if she had a clean face. Moreover, she needs to know what Bob would know about what Nanny would know if Alice and Bob had clean faces. It is *this* information that the guard's announcement supplied. [1]

---

[1]Notice that no claim is made that *all* the travelers will necessarily blush. In fact, the information supplied is insufficient to allow this conclusion to be drawn. (See Section 10.3.4.)

In brief, the guard's announcement ensures that it will be *common knowledge* that a dirty-faced traveler is present whenever this is actually true. The idea of common knowledge has been touched upon several times in previous chapters. The current chapter begins by using the story of Alice, Bob and Nanny as a hook on which to hang a general discussion of how game theory tackles problems of knowledge and information within a game.[2] More details are given for this topic than for corresponding topics elsewhere in the book because the theory is not yet part of the folklore of the subject. The chapter concludes with a thorough airing of the notion of common knowledge.

10.2 Knowledge

Phil 10.4 ⟶ The hallmark of philosophical accounts of knowledge is grandiose terminology. The subject itself is called *epistemology*. And, in this context, the humble sample space Ω of Section 2.1.1 becomes a set of possible *states of the world*. The set Ω itself is sometimes called the *universe of discourse*. However, as previously, a subset E of Ω is simply called an *event*.

If the subject under discussion is the roll of a dice, the universe of discourse will be $\Omega = \{1, 2, 3, 4, 5, 6\}$. If the result of rolling the dice is 6, then $\omega = 6$ is the state of the world. When the true state of the world is ω, an event E is said to have occurred if and only if $\omega \in E$. For example, the event $E = \{2, 4, 6\}$ that an even number is rolled occurs when the true state of the world is $\omega = 6$.

10.2.1 Knowledge Operators

What Alice knows can be specified with the aid of a *knowledge operator* $\mathcal{K}$. For each event E, the set $\mathcal{K}E$ is the set of states of the world in which Alice knows that E has occurred. More briefly, $\mathcal{K}E$ is the event that Alice knows E.

For the story of the dirty-faced travelers, a set Ω with eight states is required. These will be numbered as in Figure 10.1. The event that Alice's face is dirty is then $D_A = \{2, 5, 6, 8\}$. If blushing were not part of the story, she would know that her face was dirty after the guard's announcement only when the true state of the world is $\omega = 2$, because this is the only state in which the other two travelers have clean faces. Thus, under these circumstances, $\mathcal{K}D_A = \{2\}$. But the true state of the

[2]This part of the chapter is based on an article written jointly with Adam Brandenburger.

	1	2	3	4	5	6	7	8
Alice	Clean	Dirty	Clean	Clean	Dirty	Dirty	Clean	Dirty
Bob	Clean	Clean	Dirty	Clean	Dirty	Clean	Dirty	Dirty
Nanny	Clean	Clean	Clean	Dirty	Clean	Dirty	Dirty	Dirty

Figure 10.1 Victorian states of the world.

world is given to be $\omega = 8$. Without a blushing component to the story, Alice would therefore not know she had a dirty face because it would then be true that $8 \notin \mathcal{K}D_A$.

The properties that game theorists assume about knowledge are listed in Figure 10.2.1. Properties (K0) and (K1) are book-keeping assumptions.[3] It follows from property (K1) that $E \subseteq F \Rightarrow \mathcal{K}E \subseteq \mathcal{K}F$ (because $E \subseteq F \Leftrightarrow E \cap F = E$). Property (K2) says that Alice cannot know something unless it actually happens. In property (K3), $\mathcal{K}^2E$ means $\mathcal{K}(\mathcal{K}E)$. Thus $\mathcal{K}^2E$ is the event that Alice knows that she knows E has occurred. Property (K3) therefore says that Alice cannot know something without knowing that she knows it.

To interpret (K4), it is necessary to discuss the *possibility operator* $\mathcal{P}$. Not knowing that something didn't happen is the same as thinking it possible that it did happen. The possibility operator is therefore defined by $\mathcal{P}E = {\sim}\mathcal{K}{\sim}E$, where ${\sim}F$ means the complement of the set F as explained in Section 1.7. Property (K4) therefore says that, if Alice thinks something is possible, then she knows that she thinks it possible. The list (P0)–(P4) of properties for the possibility operator $\mathcal{P}$ in Figure 10.2.1 are straightforward deductions from (K0)–(K4).

Assumptions (K0)–(K4) are too strong to be generally applicable to all situations in which knowledge needs to be

(K0) $\mathcal{K}\Omega = \Omega$	(P0) $\mathcal{P}\emptyset = \emptyset$
(K1) $\mathcal{K}(E \cap F) = \mathcal{K}E \cap \mathcal{K}F$	(P1) $\mathcal{P}(E \cup F) = \mathcal{P}E \cup \mathcal{P}F$
(K2) $\mathcal{K}E \subseteq E$	(P2) $\mathcal{P}E \supseteq E$
(K3) $\mathcal{K}E \subseteq \mathcal{K}^2E$	(P3) $\mathcal{P}E \supseteq \mathcal{P}^2E$
(K4) $\mathcal{P}E \subseteq \mathcal{K}\mathcal{P}E$	(P4) $\mathcal{K}E \supseteq \mathcal{P}\mathcal{K}E$

Figure 10.2 Knowledge and possibility.

[3]The text takes it for granted that Ω is a finite set. If infinite sets Ω are to be considered, (K1) must be replaced by the requirement that, for any index set I, $\mathcal{K}\bigcap_{i \in I} E_i = \bigcap_{i \in I} \mathcal{K}E_i$.

discussed. The assumptions only make good sense when the universe of discourse is sufficiently small that all the possibilities can be enumerated in advance of any action being taken, and all the implications of all possibilities explored in detail so that they can be neatly labeled and placed in their proper pigeonholes. The statistician Savage (Section 3.6.2) called this proviso on the type of universe of discourse to be considered, the *small world* assumption.

The English language dimly recognizes that some distinction should be made between discussions of knowledge in small and large worlds. For example, (K4) seems plausible enough when expressed in terms of what Alice thinks is *possible.* But suppose we choose to interpret it as saying that, if something is *conceivable* for Alice, then she knows that it is conceivable. We are then claiming that Alice has *already* conceived of everything of which she is capable of conceiving. Only in a small world is such a claim defensible.

Fortunately, the possible things that can happen within a game are firmly tied down by its rules. The rules therefore create precisely the type of microcosm to which the small world assumption applies.[4]

10.2.2 Truisms

A *truism* for Alice is something that cannot be true without her knowing it. More precisely, T is a truism if and only if $T \subseteq \mathcal{K}T$.

For example, if the guard can be relied upon to announce that someone has a dirty face if and only if this is true, then it is a truism for Alice that someone has a dirty face. If one thinks of a truism as embodying the essence of what is involved in making a direct observation, then there is a sense in which all knowledge is derived from truisms. The following theorem expresses this formally. It is not a result of any substance, but its proof will provide some practice in using the knowledge properties (K0)–(K4).

Theorem 10.2.1 Alice knows that E has occurred if and only if a truism T that implies E has occurred.

Proof. To say that E has occurred means that the true state ω of the world satisfies $\omega \in E$. To say that Alice knows that E has occurred means that $\omega \in \mathcal{K}E$. Take $T = \mathcal{K}E$. Then

[4]As observed in Section 10.8.2, this does *not* apply to a world large enough to encompass the thinking processes of the players.

$T \subseteq E$, by (K2). Moreover, T is a truism because $\mathcal{K}T = \mathcal{K}^2E \supseteq \mathcal{K}E = T$, by (K3). If $\omega \in \mathcal{K}E$, we can therefore find a truism T such that $\omega \in T \subseteq E$. Thus a truism that implies E has occurred. This deals with the *only if* part of the theorem. For the *if* part, one begins with a truism T for which $\omega \in T \subseteq E$. Since $T \subseteq E$, $\mathcal{K}T \subseteq \mathcal{K}E$ by (K1). Since T is a truism, $T \subseteq \mathcal{K}T$. Thus $\omega \in T \subseteq \mathcal{K}T \subseteq \mathcal{K}E$, and so Alice knows that E has occurred. □

10.3 Possibility

Recall that $\mathcal{P}E$ is the set of states of the world in which Alice thinks that event E is possible. Thus $\mathcal{P}\{\omega\}$ is the event that Alice thinks it possible that ω has occurred.

Theorem 10.3.1 The smallest truism containing ω is $\mathcal{P}\{\omega\}$.

Proof. The fact that $\omega \in \mathcal{P}\{\omega\}$ follows immediately from (P2) of Figure 10.2.1. That $\mathcal{P}\{\omega\}$ is a truism follows immediately from (K4). It remains to show that $\mathcal{P}\{\omega\}$ is the smallest truism containing ω.

Suppose that T is another truism containing ω. We need to show that $\mathcal{P}\{\omega\} \subseteq T$. Rewrite $\omega \in T \subseteq \mathcal{K}T$ in the form $\{\omega\} \subseteq T \subseteq \mathcal{K}T$. Then it follows that

$$\mathcal{P}\{\omega\} \subseteq \mathcal{P}T \subseteq \mathcal{P}\mathcal{K}T \quad \text{(by (P1))}$$
$$\mathcal{P}\mathcal{K}T \subseteq \mathcal{K}T \subseteq T \quad \text{(by (P4) and (K2))}$$

Thus $\mathcal{P}\{\omega\} \subseteq T$ and so $\mathcal{P}\{\omega\}$ is smaller than any other truism T. □

10.3.1 Possibility Sets

Let $P(\omega)$ be the set of states that Alice thinks are possible when ω occurs. As we shall see, this idea is closely related to the notion of an *information set* which we encountered in Section 3.3.1. However, $P(\omega)$ will be called a *possibility set*. If ω occurs, Alice will not necessarily know that ω has occurred. She will only be able to say that something in $P(\omega)$ has occurred.

It turns out that $P(\omega) = \mathcal{P}\{\omega\}$. Recall that $\mathcal{P}\{\omega\}$ is the set of states in which Alice thinks ω is possible. It is now claimed that $\mathcal{P}\{\omega\}$ is also the set of states that Alice thinks is possible when ω occurs.

To see this, imagine that ω has occurred. If $\omega \in T$ and T is a truism, then Alice knows that anything outside T is impossible. Hence $P(\omega)$ must be a subset of all truisms containing

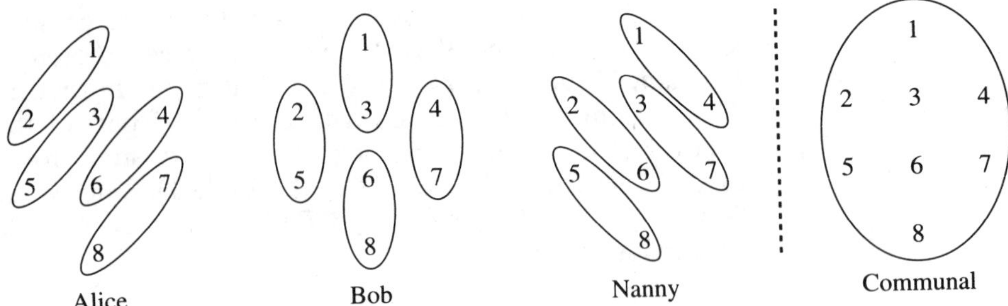

Figure 10.3 Possibility sets *before* the guard speaks.

ω. But $P(\omega)$ must itself be a truism, because Alice cannot fail to know what it is that she regards as possible. Thus $P(\omega)$ is the smallest truism containing ω, namely $\mathcal{P}\{\omega\}$.

The story of the dirty-faced travelers provides some examples of possibility sets. Recall from Section 10.2 that the universe of discourse is $\Omega = \{1, 2, 3, 4, 5, 6, 7, 8\}$. Figure 10.3 shows possibility sets for each of the travelers *before* the guard makes his announcement. (Ignore the fourth column for the moment.) For example, whatever Alice sees when she looks at the faces of her companions, it remains possible for Alice that her own face is clean or dirty. Thus, writing P_A to indicate that we are discussing what Alice thinks is possible, $P_A(1) = P_A(2) = \{1, 2\}$.[5]

Figure 10.4 shows possibility sets for the travelers *after* the guard's announcement, but *before* any blushing takes place. (Ignore the fourth column again.) When Alice sees two clean faces, she can now deduce the state of her own face from whether or not the guard says anything. Thus $P_A(1) = \{1\}$ and $P_A(2) = \{2\}$.

Knowledge and Possibility. Describing a person's knowledge with possibility sets simplifies things a great deal because of the following theorem.

Theorem 10.3.2 Alice knows that E has occurred in state ω if and only if $P(\omega) \subseteq E$.

[5]Since we know that the *actual* state of the world is $\omega = 8$, why does Figure 10.3 list possibility sets other than $P_A(8)$, $P_B(8)$ and $P_N(8)$? The reason for not neglecting what people *would* believe if the actual state *were* something other than $\omega = 8$ is so that we will to be able to follow the arguments of someone who does not share our omniscient viewpoint, and hence does not know the true state of the world. The argument that Alice used in Section 10.1 is a good example. She was forced to consider several hypotheses about the nature of the true state that other players might be entertaining before reaching the conclusion that her face was dirty.

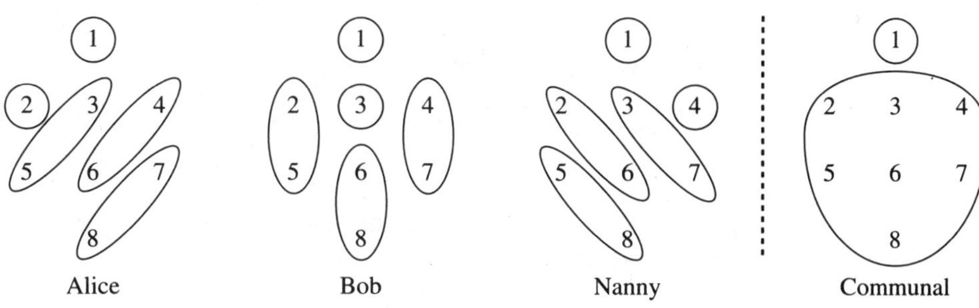

Figure 10.4 Possibility sets *after* the guard speaks, *before* blushing begins.

Proof. If $P(\omega) \subseteq E$, then Theorem 10.2.1 tells us that Alice knows E in state ω because $P(\omega)$ is a truism that contains ω. On the other hand, if Alice knows that E has occurred, there must be a truism T such that $\omega \in T \subseteq E$. But $P(\omega)$ is the smallest truism containing ω. Thus $\omega \in P(\omega) \subseteq T \subseteq E$. □

Math 10.3.3 ⟶

10.3.2 Partitions

An important feature of the possibility sets in Figures 10.3 and 10.4 is that they partition the set Ω. In general, a collection $\mathcal{C}$ of sets with union Ω is a *partition* of Ω if distinct members of $\mathcal{C}$ have no elements in common.

The next theorem says that the collection of all possibility sets $P(\omega)$ partitions the set Ω.

Theorem 10.3.3

$$\mathcal{P}\{\omega_1\} \neq \mathcal{P}\{\omega_2\} \Rightarrow \mathcal{P}\{\omega_1\} \cap \mathcal{P}\{\omega_2\} = \emptyset$$

Proof. The theorem is proved[6] by showing that, if $\mathcal{P}\{\omega_1\}$ and $\mathcal{P}\{\omega_2\}$ have an element ζ in common, then $\mathcal{P}\{\omega_1\} = \mathcal{P}\{\omega_2\}$.

The statement $\zeta \in \mathcal{P}\{\omega_1\}$ means that Alice thinks ω_1 is possible when ζ occurs. The statement $\omega_1 \in P(\zeta)$ also means that Alice thinks that ω_1 is possible when ζ occurs. Since $P(\zeta) = \mathcal{P}\{\zeta\}$, it follows that $\zeta \in \mathcal{P}\{\omega_1\}$ if and only if $\omega_1 \in \mathcal{P}\{\zeta\}$.

The next step is to note that, if $\zeta \in \mathcal{P}\{\omega_1\}$, then $\mathcal{P}\{\zeta\} \subseteq \mathcal{P}\{\omega_1\}$ (by (P1) and (P3)). But $\omega_1 \in \mathcal{P}\{\zeta\}$, and so it is also true that $\mathcal{P}\{\omega_1\} \subseteq \mathcal{P}\{\zeta\}$. Hence, if $\zeta \in \mathcal{P}\{\omega_1\}$, $\mathcal{P}\{\zeta\} = \mathcal{P}\{\omega_1\}$.

Thus, if $\zeta \in \mathcal{P}\{\omega_1\}$ and $\zeta \in \mathcal{P}\{\omega_2\}$, then $\mathcal{P}\{\omega_1\} = \mathcal{P}\{\zeta\} = \mathcal{P}\{\omega_2\}$. □

[6]The statement $A \Rightarrow B$ is equivalent to its "contrapositive" (not B) $\Rightarrow$ (not A).

Some possibility partitions can be compared. A partition $\mathcal{C}$ is a *refinement* of a partition $\mathcal{D}$ if each set in $\mathcal{C}$ is a subset of a set in $\mathcal{D}$. Under the same circumstances, $\mathcal{D}$ is said to be a *coarsening* of $\mathcal{C}$. For example, Alice's partition in Figure 10.4 is a refinement of her partition in Figure 10.3. Equivalently, her partition in Figure 10.3 is a coarsening of her partition in Figure 10.4. This reflects the fact that she is better informed in the latter case.

10.3.3 Refining Your Knowledge

In general, as people get more information, their possibility partitions get more refined. Figure 10.5(a) illustrates this point. It is constructed on the assumption that the opportunity to blush rotates among the three travelers, starting with Alice. This leads to the following sequence of events.

Step 1. Before the guard has the opportunity to speak the knowledge situation is as illustrated in Figure 10.3.

Step 2. After the guard has had the opportunity to speak, the knowledge situation is as illustrated in Figure 10.4. This is repeated as the first row of Figure 10.5(a) but with the states in which a traveler has a dirty face indicated by the addition of some shading. (Ignore the fourth column of the figure until Section 10.6.4.)

Step 3. Alice now has the opportunity to blush (but not Bob or Nanny). She will blush only in state 2 because this is the only state in which she knows her face to be dirty. Alice's own information is unchanged whether she blushes or not. However, Bob and Nanny learn something from her behavior. If Alice blushes, the true state must be $\omega = 2$. This allows Bob to split his possibility set $\{2, 5\}$ into two subsets $\{2\}$ and $\{5\}$. Notice that, like the dog that *didn't* bark in the Sherlock Holmes story, observing that Alice does *not* blush is as useful information for Bob when his possibility set is $\{2, 5\}$ as observing that she *does*. Her not blushing then excludes the possibility that the true state is $\omega = 2$. It must therefore be that $\omega = 5$. Nanny also makes similar inferences and so is able to split her possibility set $\{2, 6\}$ into $\{2\}$ and $\{6\}$. The result is shown in the second row of Figure 10.5(a).

Step 4. Bob now has the opportunity to blush (but not Nanny or Alice). He blushes only in states 3 and 5. This is very informative for Nanny whose new possibility partition

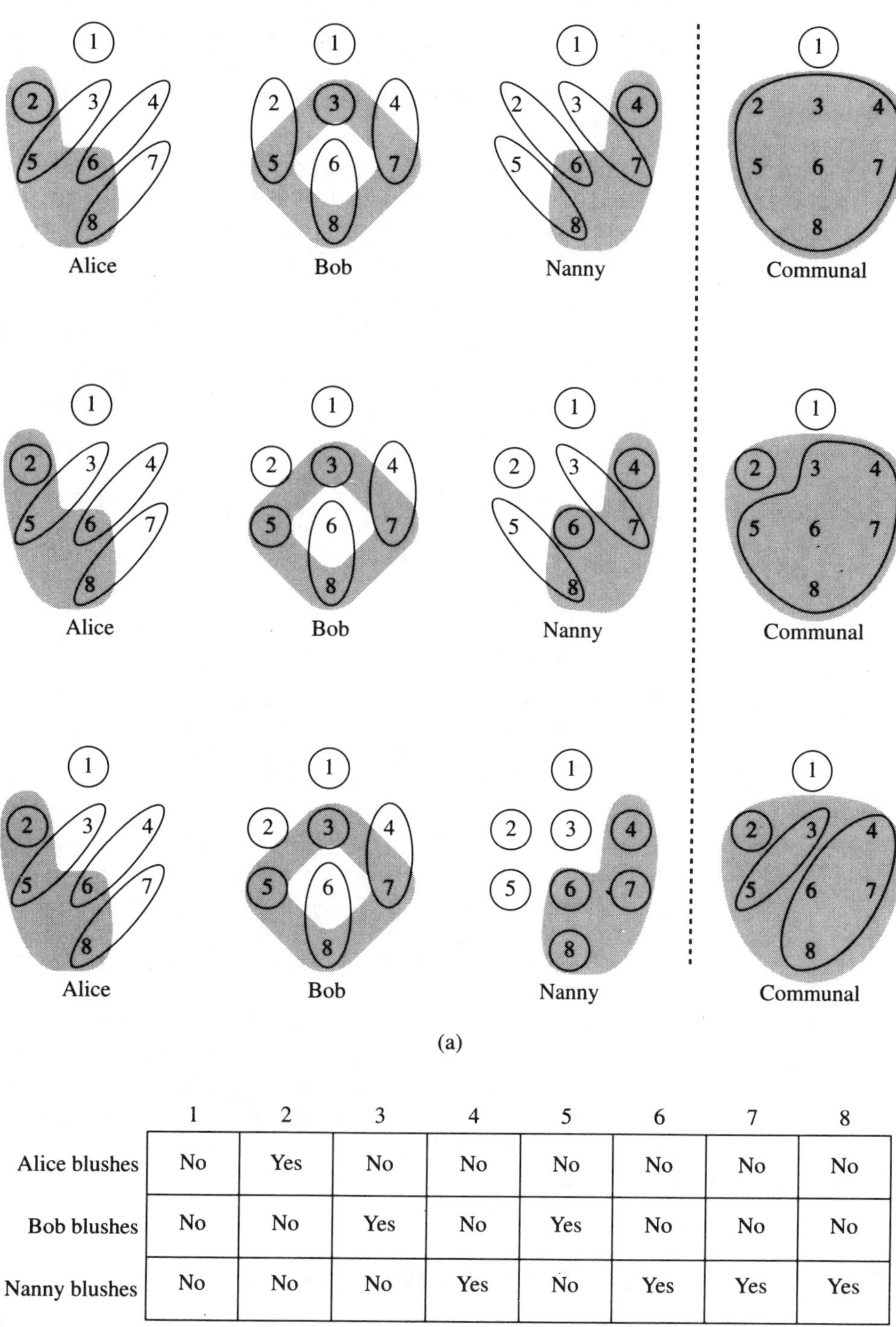

(a)

	1	2	3	4	5	6	7	8
Alice blushes	No	Yes	No	No	No	No	No	No
Bob blushes	No	No	Yes	No	Yes	No	No	No
Nanny blushes	No	No	No	Yes	No	Yes	Yes	Yes

(b)

Figure 10.5 Blushing in rotation.

becomes as refined as it can possibly get. Alice, however, learns nothing. In particular, her possibility set $\{3, 5\}$ cannot be refined because Bob will blush both in state 3 and in state 5. The result is shown in the third row of Figure 10.5(a).

Step 5. Nanny now has the opportunity to blush (but not Alice or Bob). She blushes in states 4, 6, 7 and 8. However, neither Alice nor Bob can refine their possibility partitions on the basis of this information.

Step 6. Alice now has the opportunity to blush again. She blushes only in state 2. This helps neither Bob nor Nanny.

Step 7. Bob now has the opportunity to blush again. He blushes only in states 3 and 5. This helps neither Alice nor Nanny.

No further steps need be examined since steps 5, 6 and 7 will just repeat over and over again. The final informational situation is therefore as recorded in the third row of Figure 10.5(a).

10.3.4 Who Blushes?

The preceding discussion allows something to be said about *who* blushes in the story of the dirty-faced travelers. Recall that persons who know they have a dirty face necessarily blush. The blushing table of Figure 10.5(b) can therefore be constructed using the third row of Figure 10.5(a). For example, Bob's possibility set when $\omega = 8$ is $P_B(8) = \{6, 8\}$. The event that he has a dirty face is $D_B = \{3, 5, 7, 8\}$. It is therefore false that $P_B(8) \subseteq D_B$. Hence, by Theorem 10.3.2, Bob does not blush when the true state is $\omega = 8$. However, $P_N(8) = \{8\}$ and $D_N = \{4, 6, 7, 8\}$. Thus $P_N(8) \subseteq D_N$, and therefore Nanny blushes when the true state is $\omega = 8$.

However, the story of blushing in rotation is only one of several stories that could have been told that are consistent with the informational specifications given in the tale of the dirty-faced travelers. Other possibilities are explored in Exercises 10.9.13 and 10.9.14. Someone always blushes, but who it is depends on how the blushing mechanism works.

10.4 Information Sets

The time has now come to begin to relate what has been learned so far about the theory of knowledge to game theory.

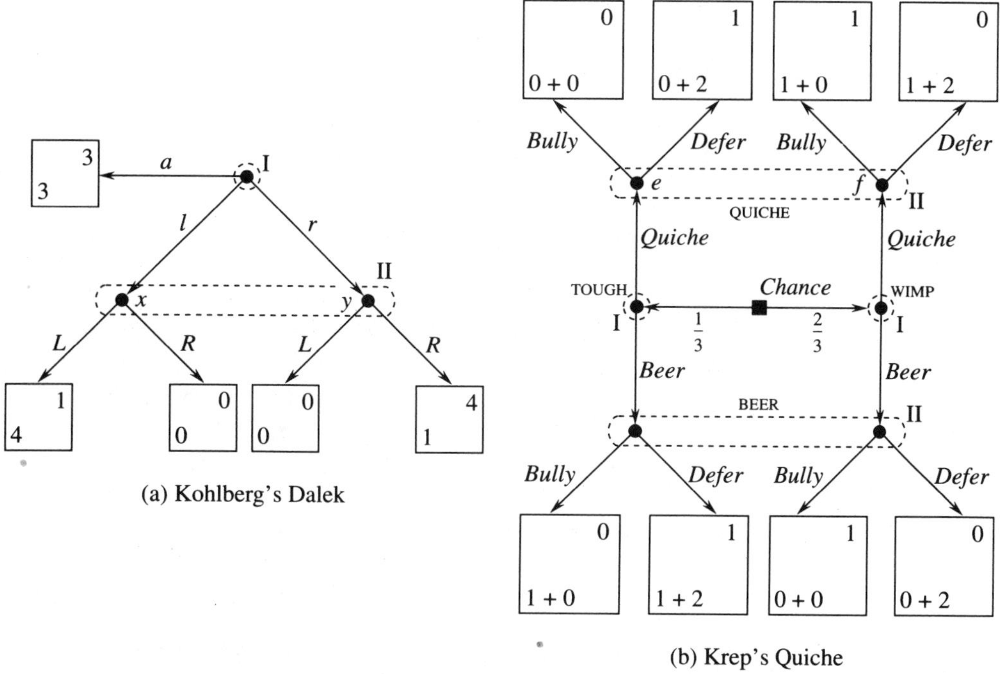

(a) Kohlberg's Dalek

(b) Krep's Quiche

Figure 10.6 Games of imperfect information.

The immediate topic for study is the notion of an *information set.* Information sets were introduced in Section 3.3.1, and have been used since then without any critical discussion of their properties. However, now that possibility sets are part of our lexicon, it is feasible to discuss the implications of modeling the players' knowledge during a game with information sets.

The most important property of information sets is that they must not overlap. More precisely, a player's information sets must partition the player's set of decision nodes. After Theorem 10.3.3, we know that this simply reflects the fact that the assumptions to be made about the knowledge a player has about where he or she is in the game are the standard assumptions listed in Figure 10.2.1.

Figure 10.6 shows information sets in use in two well-known games. In a game of *perfect information,* each information set contains exactly one decision node. Thus, when a player makes a decision in a game of perfect information, he or she knows everything that has happened so far in the game. Kohlberg's Dalek game of Figure 10.6(a) is an example of a game of *imperfect information.* When player II decides between L and R, she knows only that player I did not

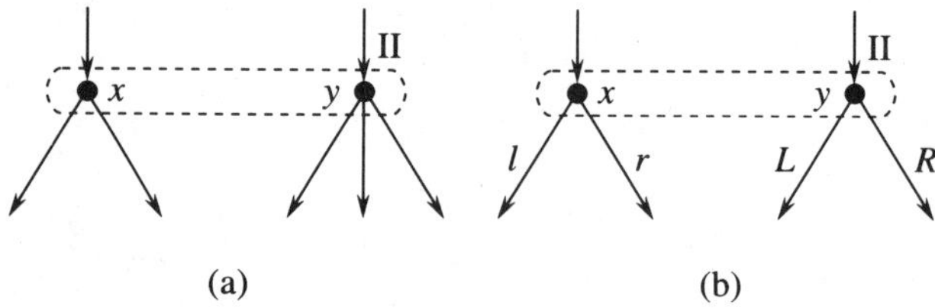

Figure 10.7 Illegal information sets.

begin by choosing a. If he had done so, she would not have been called upon for a decision. However, she does not know which of l or r were chosen by player I. If he chose l, then she is deciding at node x. If he chose r, then she is deciding at node y. Her possibility set is therefore $\{x, y\}$. She may have reason to believe that one of the two possibilities x and y is more likely than the other, but what she *knows* is simply that she is deciding at one of these two nodes.

One cannot partition a player's set of decision nodes just anyhow and expect to obtain a game in which the information sets make sense. In particular, neither of the situations of Figure 10.7 is admissible if $\{x, y\}$ is to be interpreted as an information set. In Figure 10.7(a), Player II could tell which decision node he was at by counting the choices available to him. In Figure 10.7(b), he could deduce where he was from the labels used to describe his choices.

10.4.1 Perfect Recall

The word "perfect" is over-used in game theory. In particular, it is easy to confuse a game of perfect recall with a game of perfect information. However, both the games of Figure 10.6 are games of perfect recall, but neither are games of perfect information.

In a game of perfect recall , nobody ever forgets something they once knew. Figure 10.8 shows two one-player games that do *not* exhibit perfect recall. The single player in each case will be called Terence, in honor of an Oxford economist who is well-known for being absent-minded. In Figure 10.8(a) Terence is assumed to forget that he has already made a decision in the game when he gets to node y. If he remembered that he had already visited the information set $\{x, y\}$, he would necessarily know that he must now be at its second node.

In Figure 10.8(b), which shows a game beginning with a Chance move, Terence must have forgotten at node X that he just chose action r. Otherwise he would know that he was at node X.

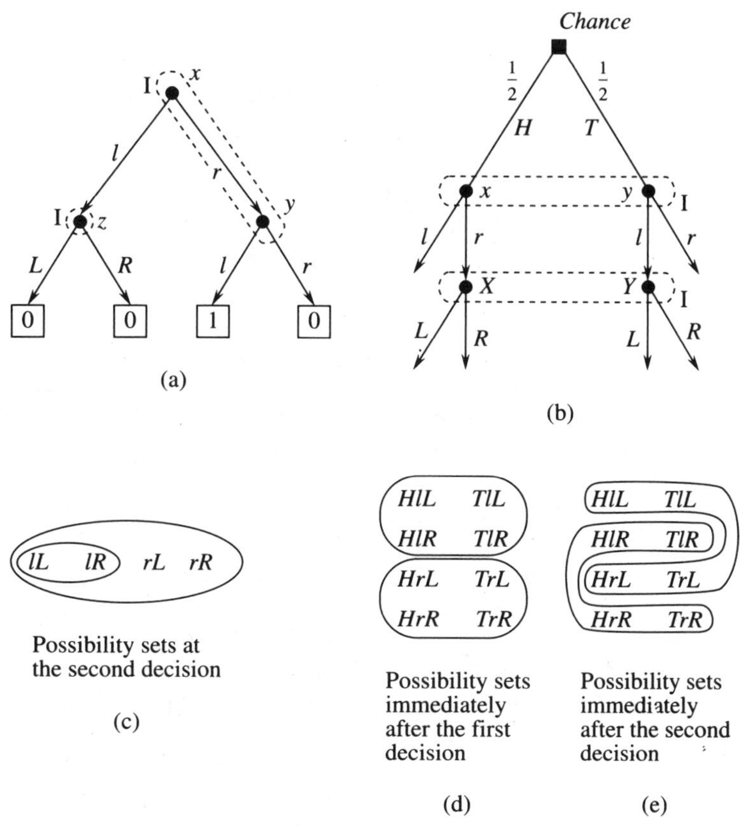

Figure 10.8 Forgetful players.

Phil 10.4.3 ⟶ It may help to relate the notion of perfect recall to the knowledge considerations explored in earlier sections. For this purpose, take the state space Ω to be the set of Terence's pure strategies in the game of Figure 10.8(a). Recall that a pure strategy for a player assigns an action to each of his information sets. In this case, there are two information sets, and the set of pure strategies is $\Omega = \{lL, lR, rL, rR\}$. Imagine that Terence has consulted a game theorist who, knowing him to be absent-minded, has written advice on what pure strategy to use on a piece of paper pinned to Terence's shirt.

The first time Terence has to make a decision, he consults his paper and acts accordingly. However, he forgets not only what the paper says, but even the fact that he has already made a decision in the game. Now he is called upon for a second decision. But, although Terence is forgetful, he has an enquiring mind. He therefore asks himself what he can deduce about what is written on the paper from the nature of the decision he is now asked to make.

He will be at node z if and only if lL or lR is written on the paper. He can deduce that he is at node z from the fact that his current choice is between L and R. Thus two of his possibility sets are $P(lL) = P(lR) = \{lL, lR\}$. He will be at node y if and only if rL or rR is written on the paper. He cannot deduce that he is at node y from the fact that he is asked to choose between l and r. This would also be true at node x. Thus $P(rL) = P(rR) = \{lL, lR, rL, rR\}$ as indicated in Figure 10.8(c). The point here is that Terence's possibility sets at this stage of the game do not partition Ω. Terence therefore violates one of our knowledge requirements.

One can proceed similarly with the game of Figure 10.8(b). But here Terence has to take account, not only of the fact that he does not know what the game theorist wrote on the paper pinned to his shirt, but also of his ignorance of whether Chance has selected H or T. Thus Ω contains the eight elements listed in Figure 10.8(d). There is no violation of the knowledge requirements here, but notice that the partition of Figure 10.8(e) is not a refinement of the partition of Figure 10.8(d). This is a straightforward case of forgetfulness. For someone who never forgets, later partitions are always refinements of earlier partitions.

Few people would claim to be perfectly rational. But, if we were perfectly rational, we would not need to go around with reminders pinned to our shirts. Hence, in the idealized world inhabited by game theorists, perfect recall should always be taken for granted unless something is said to the contrary. In a game of perfect recall, players are always able to deduce from their current circumstances everything that they once knew. Thus, even if players were to forget things, it would never do them any harm provided they always take into account all the implications of having arrived at a particular information set.

10.4.2 Agents

Games like that of Figure 10.8(a) are unlikely ever to be useful as models because they generate incoherent knowledge structures.[7] However, models in which there is some forgetfulness can sometimes be useful. Bridge is an example.

[7]Not all game theorists would agree with this. My wife does not even agree that fully rational folk can dispense with reminders pinned to their shirts.

One may study Bridge as a four-player game. It will then be a game of imperfect information and perfect recall. North and South will be two separate players who happen to have identical preferences. Sometimes such a set of players is called a *team*. East and West will also be a team, but with diametrically opposed preferences to the North-South partnership.

Alternatively, one may study Bridge as a two-player, zero-sum game. Player I is then a manager for the North-South partnership. North and South act as puppets who simply follow his instructions given in detail before the game begins. One says that North and South are player I's *agents*. Similarly East and West are agents for player II. This may seem a simpler formulation because two-player games are easier than four-player games. But notice that, if Bridge is formulated according to the second model, it is a game of imperfect recall. It would make nonsense of the game if, when player I puts himself into South's shoes, he were able to remember what cards North had when player I was in his shoes a moment before.

10.4.3 Behavioral Strategies

The reason it is worth distinguishing games of perfect recall from their more forgetful cousins, is because one can work with behavioral strategies in such games. If you can remember what a behavioral strategy is, and that such strategies can be used as substitutes for mixed strategies in games of perfect recall, then you have a grip on what really matters in this part of the chapter. Perfect recall of all the details is not necessary for most purposes.

A *pure strategy* assigns a specific action to each of a player's information sets. For example, when $n = 10$, player I has five information sets in the game Duel of Figure 2.6. At each information set, he has two choices. It follows that he has $2^5 = 32$ pure strategies in all.

A *mixed strategy* p is a vector whose coordinates correspond to the pure strategies of a game. A player's use of the mixed strategy p results in his or her ith pure strategy being played with probability p_i. Since Duel has 32 pure strategies, its mixed strategies are cumbersome objects requiring the specification of 32 probabilities $p_1, p_2, \ldots, p_{32}$.

A *behavioral strategy* is like a pure strategy in that it says what to do at each of a player's information sets. But instead of selecting a specific action at each information set, it assigns a *probability* to each of the available actions. One may imagine that a player using a behavioral strategy is delegating his decisions to an army of agents, one for each of the player's information sets. Each agent is given a piece of paper saying with what probability the agent should select each of the available actions at the information set the agent is responsible for. Each agent then acts *independently* of all the others.[8]

Using behavioral strategies often simplifies things immensely. For example, in Duel, a behavioral strategy is determined by only five probabilities $q_1, q_2, \ldots, q_5$, where q_i is the probability with which player I is to fire his pistol if his ith information set is reached.

A player who uses a behavioral strategy delays his randomizing activity until the last possible moment. Only when an information set is reached does the player rattle a dice-box or spin a roulette wheel. This contrasts sharply with the case of a player using a mixed strategy. Such a player does all his or her randomizing *before* the game begins. This determines a pure strategy to which the player sticks throughout the rest of the game.

Since mixed and behavioral strategies are so different, it is something of a surprise that they should turn out to be effectively equivalent in games of perfect recall. The next result states this fact in precise terms. To understand the result, it is necessary to recall that, once all the players have chosen their strategies (whether pure, mixed or behavioral), what is determined is a *lottery* over the outcomes of the game.

Proposition 10.4.1 (Kuhn) Whatever mixed or behavioral strategy s that player i may choose in a game of perfect recall, he or she has a strategy t of the other type with the property that, however the opponents play, the resulting lottery over the outcomes of the game is the same for both s and t.

Kuhn's theorem is one of those propositions that has very little substantive content, but which requires marshalling much mathematical notation if a formal proof is to be given. For this reason, all that will be offered in its defense is an illustration of how it works for the simple game of Figure 10.9. However, simple though the game is, it exhibits all the considerations that matter for Kuhn's theorem.

Figure 10.9(a) shows player II's pure strátegy LLR. Figure 10.9(b) shows her pure strategy RRL. Our aim will be to

[8] An economist might say that the player thereby *decentralizes* his or her decision process.

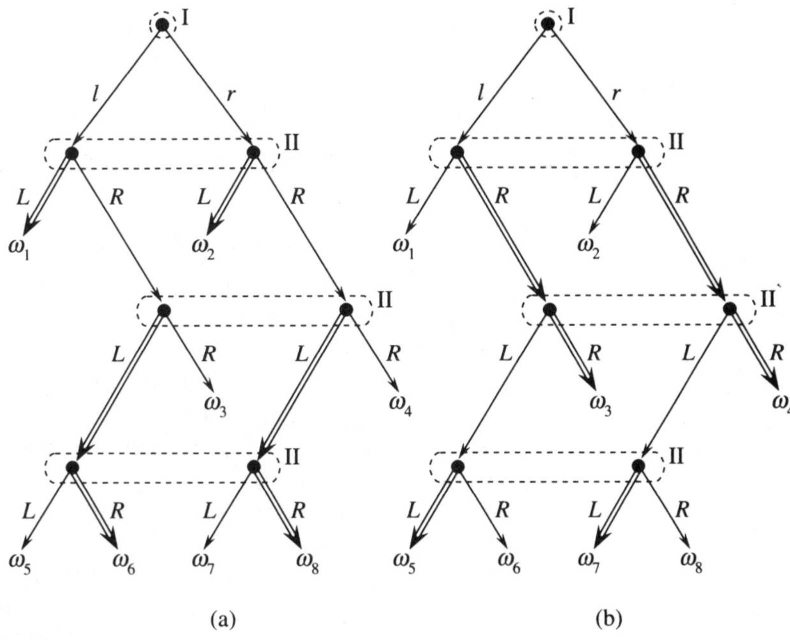

Figure 10.9 Kuhn's theorem.

find a behavioral strategy b that is equivalent to the mixed strategy m that assigns probability $\frac{1}{3}$ to LLR and $\frac{2}{3}$ to RRL. The behavioral strategy will be specified by three probabilities q_1, q_2 and q_3, representing the probabilities with which player II is to use R at each of her three information sets.

Suppose that player II's first information set is reached. If the randomizing specified by m leads the use of LLR, then L will get played at this information set. If the randomizing leads to the use of RRL, then R will be played at the information set. Hence L will be played at the information set with probability $\frac{1}{3}$ and R with probability $\frac{2}{3}$. To mimic this behavior with the behavioral strategy b, it is only necessary to take $q_1 = \frac{2}{3}$. Player II's second information set will never be reached if the randomizing specified by m leads to the use of LLR. Hence, if the second information set is reached, the randomizing called for by m must have led to the use of RRL. Thus R will be played for certain at the second information set. To mimic this behavior with b, take $q_2 = 1$. The third information set cannot be reached at all when m is used. Hence q_3 can be chosen to be anything. Figure 10.10 shows the lottery over outcomes that results if player II uses b or m, and player I chooses l with probability $1 - p$ and r with probability p.

ω_1	ω_2	ω_3	ω_4	ω_5	ω_6	ω_7	ω_8
$\frac{1}{3}(1-p)$	$\frac{1}{3}p$	$\frac{2}{3}(1-p)$	$\frac{2}{3}p$	0	0	0	0

Figure 10.10 A lottery over outcomes.

10.5 Bayesian Updating

In game theory, it is necessary to keep track not only of what players *know*, but also of what they *believe*. As explained in Section 3.6.2, decision-makers who honor certain rationality postulates behave *as though* maximizing expected Von Neumann and Morgenstern utility relative to a probability measure $\text{prob}: \Omega \to [0,1]$. The number $\text{prob}(E)$ is then said to be the player's *prior* subjective probability for the event E. It describes the player's belief about the event E *before* any information is available.

For example, in the story of the dirty-faced travelers, Alice will not be able to exclude any of the possible states listed in Figure 10.1 until after she enters the railway carriage. Before she enters the railway carriage, she *knows* nothing whatever about what is the true state. But this does not prevent her having *beliefs*. These are summarized by a prior probability measure defined on the set Ω of all possible states. For example, it may be that:

$$\text{prob}\{1\} = 0.2; \quad \text{prob}\{2\} = \text{prob}\{3\} = \text{prob}\{4\} = 0.15;$$
$$\text{prob}\{5\} = \text{prob}\{6\} = \text{prob}\{7\} = 0.1; \quad \text{prob}\{8\} = 0.05.$$

The event $D_A = \{2,5,6,8\}$ that her own face is dirty therefore has a prior probability of $\text{prob}(D_A) = 0.15 + 0.1 + 0.1 + 0.05 = 0.4$. This is a *prior* probability because it represents her belief about D_A *before* she gets any information.

When she gets into the railway carriage, she sees the faces of her fellow travelers. This will lead her to update her probability for D_A. The new probability will be her *posterior* probability for D_A, because it represents her belief about D_A *after* she gets some information. If the true state is $\omega = 8$, she will know that only states in the set $E = \{7,8\}$ are possible after she sees the faces of her companions. (The event E is the possibility set $P_A(8)$ illustrated in Figure 10.3.) Her posterior probability for D_A is therefore the conditional probability $\text{prob}(D_A|E)$. Conditional probabilities are calculated as explained in Section 2.1.4. In this case,

$$\text{prob}(D_A|E) = \frac{\text{prob}(D_A \cap E)}{\text{prob}(E)} = \frac{\text{prob}\{8\}}{\text{prob}\{7,8\}} = \frac{0.05}{0.1+0.05} = \tfrac{1}{3}.$$

Alice's prior probability of $\frac{2}{5}$ for the event D_A is therefore revised downwards to a posterior probability of $\frac{1}{3}$.

Although Bayes' rule is only sometimes used in the process, the activity of deducing posterior probabilities from prior probabilities after receiving some information is called *Bayesian updating*. Often, Alice's prior probability measure is referred to simply as her *prior*. Similarly, her *posterior* is not what she sits upon, but her posterior probability measure.

10.5.1 Real Men Don't Eat Quiche

Kreps' Quiche of Figure 10.6(b) is an example of a signaling game. However, the version studied in this chapter is not very interesting for making points about signaling because, as we shall see, it has only one Nash equilibrium. It is introduced here for two purposes. The first is to provide a serious example of how Bayesian updating is used in computing equilibria in a game of imperfect information. The second is to clear the way for the next chapter, where this and other versions of Quiche will be used in illustrating how game theory copes with problems of *incomplete* information.[9]

In Quiche, Chance begins by deciding whether player I will be tough or wimpish. In either case, player I then has to face player II who may choose to *bully* player I or *defer* to him. She would defer to him if she knew he were tough, and she would bully him if she knew he were a wimp. But only player I knows for sure the temperament with which he has been endowed by Nature. However, he can send signals to player II by acting tough or behaving like a wimp. Here the signals are stylized as drinking *beer* or eating *quiche*. Tough guys prefer beer and wimps prefer quiche. But they will not necessarily consume what they prefer. For example, a wimp may conceal his distaste for beer in the hope of being mistaken for a tough guy.

Figure 10.6(b) shows that Nature chooses tough guys with probability $\frac{1}{3}$, and wimps with probability $\frac{2}{3}$. The information sets labeled TOUGH and WIMP show that player I knows his own temperament. The information sets labeled QUICHE and BEER show that player II knows only the signal sent by player I but not whether he is tough or wimpish. The payoffs are chosen so that player I gets a bonus of 2 if player II defers to him, plus a bonus of 1 if he avoids consuming something he dislikes. Player II gets a bonus of 1 for guessing right.

[9]Incomplete information is not the same as imperfect information. The former arises, for example, if the players do not know each other's preferences.

	bb	*bd*	*db*	*dd*
qq	$\frac{2}{3}$, $\frac{2}{3}$	$\frac{2}{3}$, $\frac{2}{3}$	$\frac{8}{3}$, $\frac{1}{3}$	$\frac{8}{3}$, $\frac{1}{3}$
qb	0, $\frac{2}{3}$	$\frac{4}{3}$, 0	$\frac{2}{3}$, 1	2, $\frac{1}{3}$
bq	1, $\frac{2}{3}$	$\frac{5}{3}$, 1	$\frac{7}{3}$, 0	3, $\frac{1}{3}$
bb	$\frac{1}{3}$, $\frac{2}{3}$	$\frac{7}{3}$, $\frac{1}{3}$	$\frac{1}{3}$, $\frac{2}{3}$	$\frac{7}{3}$, $\frac{1}{3}$

Figure 10.11 The strategic form for Quiche.

Player I has four pure strategies.[10] These are:

(*quiche, quiche*); (*quiche, beer*); (*beer, quiche*); (*beer, beer*).

Player II also has four pure strategies:

(*bully, bully*); (*bully, defer*); (*defer, bully*); (*defer, defer*).

Quiche therefore has a 4×4 strategic form. For the sake of completeness, this is given in Figure 10.11. However, painful experience has taught us that such strategic forms are often laborious to compute, and not always very illuminating once computed. How can we get by without using it?

Nash Equilibria in Pure Strategies? It seems sensible to begin by looking for Nash equilibria in pure strategies. If player II uses (*bully, bully*), player I's best reply is (*beer, quiche*), because if he is going to get bullied anyway, there is no point in his consuming something distasteful. But, player II's best reply to (*beer, quiche*) is not (*bully, bully*). It is (*bully, defer*). If player I simply consumes what he likes, he gives his identity away and player II can then exploit this information. The conclusion is that there are no Nash equilibria in which player II uses (*bully, bully*).

Suppose that player II uses (*bully, defer*). Then player I's best reply is (*beer, beer*). It pays him to drink beer even when he is a wimp because he thereby avoids getting bullied. But player II's best reply to (*beer, beer*) is not (*bully, defer*). It is (*???, bully*). That is, what she should do if player I eats quiche

[10]The decision at his left information set TOUGH is written as the first component of each pair. For player II's pure strategies, the decision at her top information set QUICHE is written first.

is undetermined. However, she should bully if he drinks beer. To see why, it is necessary to consider what her beliefs will be after seeing her opponent quaff a glass of ale. If it is correct[11] for player I to use (*beer, beer*), then the fact that he drinks beer gives her no information at all. Her prior probabilities therefore remain unchanged. She believes that he is tough with probability $\frac{1}{3}$ and wimpish with probability $\frac{2}{3}$. But her payoffs are such that she always bullies when it is more likely that he is a wimp. Thus (*???, bully*) is a best reply to (*beer, beer*). The conclusion is that there are no Nash equilibria in which player II uses (*bully, defer*).

In fact there are no Nash equilibria in pure strategies at all. This can easily be confirmed by following through similar chains of reasoning to those just given for the cases when player II uses (*defer, bully*) or (*defer, defer*). We therefore have to look for an equilibrium in mixed strategies. Nash's theorem (Theorem 7.7.1) assures us that such a search is sure to be successful. However, mixed strategies are complicated things. In a game of perfect recall like Quiche, they can be replaced by behavioral strategies.

Behavioral Strategies. A behavioral strategy for player I must state the probability B with which he will drink beer at the information set TOUGH, and the probability b with which he will drink beer at the information set WIMP. The corresponding probabilities for eating quiche are $Q = 1 - B$ and $q = 1 - b$. A behavioral strategy for player II must state the probability d with which she will defer at the information set QUICHE, and the probability D with which she will defer at the information set BEER.

If player I's equilibrium behavioral strategy (B, b) is written in a game theory book, player II will know what it is. She can use this knowledge to *update* her beliefs about player I's temperament. If player I uses (B, b), the probability that node e will be reached in Figure 10.6(b) is $\frac{1}{3}Q$. The probability that node f will be reached is $\frac{2}{3}q$. Hence, at the information set QUICHE, player II's posterior probabilities are

$$\text{prob}(\text{I is tough}\,|\,\text{I eats quiche}) = \frac{\text{prob}(e)}{\text{prob}(e) + \text{prob}(f)} = \frac{\frac{1}{3}Q}{\frac{1}{3}Q + \frac{2}{3}q},$$

[11]That is, written in a game theory book for all to see.

$$\text{prob}(\text{I is a wimp}\,|\,\text{I eats quiche}) = \frac{\text{prob}(f)}{\text{prob}(e) + \text{prob}(f)} = \frac{\frac{2}{3}q}{\frac{1}{3}Q + \frac{2}{3}q}\,.$$

Recall that she defers if she thinks it more likely that I is tough. She therefore defers at QUICHE when $Q > 2q$. She bullies at QUICHE when $Q < 2q$. She is indifferent between deferring and bullying when $Q = 2q$.

The same analysis applies at player II's information set BEER. She defers at BEER when $B > 2b$. She bullies at BEER when $B < 2b$. She is indifferent between deferring and bullying when $B = 2b$.

From our discussion of pure strategies, we know that player II must randomize in equilibrium. It can only be optimal to randomize among a set of possible choices if the player is indifferent about which choice is made. Thus, either $Q = 2q$ or $B = 2b$ (or both).

Consider first the case $Q = 2q$. Then $1 - B = 2(1 - b)$, and so $2b = 1 + B$. Thus $2b > B$. It follows that player II will bully at BEER. But then player I has nothing to gain by drinking beer at WIMP, and so he will eat quiche for certain. Thus $q = 1$. But then $Q = 2q = 2$, which is impossible. It follows that there cannot be a Nash equilibrium with $Q = 2q$.

The only remaining possibility is $B = 2b$. Then $(1 - Q) = 2(1 - q)$, and so $2q = 1 + Q$. Thus $2q > Q$. It follows that player II will bully at QUICHE. But then player I has nothing to gain from eating quiche at TOUGH, and so he will drink beer for certain. Thus $B = 1$, and so $b = \frac{1}{2}B = \frac{1}{2}$. Since $b = \frac{1}{2}$, player I is randomizing between *quiche* and *beer* at WIMP. Because he gets a payoff of 1 from eating quiche at WIMP, he must also get a payoff of 1 from drinking beer. Thus player II must be randomizing at BEER. In fact, it must be true that $1 = 0(1 - D) + 2D$. Therefore, $D = \frac{1}{2}$, and so player II bullies with probability $\frac{1}{2}$ and defers with probability $\frac{1}{2}$ at BEER.

Conclusion. This method of systematically eliminating possible Nash equilibria is a very powerful technique. One considers the possibilities one by one and investigates what would follow if the possibility *were* a Nash equilibrium. If a contradiction is obtained, the possibility is *not* a Nash equilibrium. Here the method leads to a unique Nash equilibrium.

In this equilibrium, player I drinks beer for certain at TOUGH. Player II bullies for certain at QUICHE. Player I vacillates at WIMP. With probability $\frac{1}{2}$ he eats quiche in accordance with his wimpish nature. But with probability $\frac{1}{2}$, he drinks beer and hopes to be mistaken for a tough guy. This keeps player II guessing at BEER. In equilibrium, she bullies with probability $\frac{1}{2}$ and defers with probability $\frac{1}{2}$.

In terms of mixed strategies, player I uses $(0, 0, \frac{1}{2}, \frac{1}{2})^T$ and player II uses $(\frac{1}{2}, \frac{1}{2}, 0, 0)^T$. It is easy to check that it is indeed a Nash equilibrium by using the strategic form of Figure 10.11.[12] It is even easier to check that there are no Nash equilibria in pure strategies.

10.6 Common Knowledge

Phil 10.9 ⟶

This chapter began with a discussion of the theory of knowledge. It continued by exploring the implications for game theory of some of the basic ideas. This took us quite far afield. But now the time has come to return to the theory of knowledge, since further progress in game theory requires us to square up to the idea of *common* knowledge.

As always, the story of the dirty-faced travelers will be used to illustrate the necessary concepts. Section 10.1 emphasized the importance of the fact that the guard's announcement made it common knowledge that someone has a dirty face. Earlier chapters also occasionally mentioned in passing that this or that was assumed to be common knowledge. What is common knowledge and why does it matter?

The philosopher David Lewis defined something to be common knowledge if everybody knows it, everybody knows that everybody knows it, everybody knows that everybody knows that everybody knows it; and so on. This section describes how the game theorist Robert Aumann[13] put this idea into operational form.

10.6.1 Mutual Knowledge

Different people often know different things. For the story of the dirty-faced travelers we therefore need three knowledge operators, $\mathcal{K}_A$, $\mathcal{K}_B$ and $\mathcal{K}_N$.

Something is *mutual knowledge* if everybody knows it. More precisely, if the relevant individuals are Alice, Bob and Nanny, then the "everybody knows" operator is defined by

$$(\text{everybody knows})E = \mathcal{K}_A E \cap \mathcal{K}_B E \cap \mathcal{K}_N E\,.$$

[12] After the labor of constructing the strategic form is over, one can delete dominated strategies until only a 2×2 bimatrix game remains. The mixed-strategy Nash equilibrium of this is easy to compute.

[13] In spite of the paper hat, Uncle Bob of Section 10.1 is not meant as a caricature of this distinguished scholar.

Thus E is mutual knowledge when the true state of the world is ω if and only if $\omega \in$ (everybody knows)E.

For example, before the guard made his announcement, it was mutual knowledge that someone in the railway carriage has a dirty face. To see this, recall that $D_A = \{2, 5, 6, 8\}$ is the event that Alice's face is dirty. Similarly, $D_B = \{3, 5, 7, 8\}$ and $D_N = \{4, 6, 7, 8\}$ are the events that Bob and Nanny have dirty faces. The event that someone has a dirty face is therefore $D = D_A \cup D_B \cup D_N = \{2, 3, 4, 5, 6, 7, 8\}$. Notice that $\mathcal{K}_A D = \{3, 4, 5, 6, 7, 8\}$, $\mathcal{K}_B D = \{2, 4, 5, 6, 7, 8\}$ and $\mathcal{K}_N D = \{2, 3, 5, 6, 7, 8\}$. Hence

$$\text{(everybody knows)}D = \mathcal{K}_A D \cap \mathcal{K}_B D \cap \mathcal{K}_N D = \{5, 6, 7, 8\}.$$

The true state of the world is actually $\omega = 8$. Thus, D is mutual knowledge because $8 \in$ (everybody knows)D.

The operator $\mathcal{K} =$ (everybody knows) satisfies properties (K0), (K1) and (K2) of Figure 10.2.1. It does not satisfy (K3). For example, in state 5 of Figure 10.3, everybody knows that someone has a dirty face, but Bob thinks state 2 is possible. In state 2, Alice thinks state 1 is possible. Since everybody has a clean face in state 1, it is therefore false that everybody knows that everybody knows someone has a dirty face in state 5. To find an operator that satisfies (K3), a little more work is necessary.

10.6.2 Common Knowledge Operator

Because the (everybody knows) operator satisfies (K2) of Figure 10.2.1, it follows that

$$\begin{aligned} E &\supseteq \text{(everybody knows)}E \\ &\supseteq \text{(everybody knows)}^2 E \\ &\supseteq \text{(everybody knows)}^3 E \\ &\;\vdots \\ &\supseteq \text{(everybody knows)}^N E \\ &= \text{(everybody knows)}^{N+1} E \\ &= \text{(everybody knows)}^{N+2} E \\ &\;\vdots \end{aligned}$$

Why do the inclusions start becoming identities at the Nth step? The reason is simple. If the finite set Ω contains only N elements, we will run out of things that can be discarded to make (everybody knows)$^n E$ a strictly smaller set on or before the Nth step.

The *common knowledge* operator[14] is defined by

$$\text{(everybody knows)}^{\infty} E = \text{(everybody knows)}^{N} E\,.$$

Lewis' criterion for something to be common knowledge can now be expressed fairly easily. An event E is common knowledge when the true state is ω if and only if

$$\omega \in \text{(everybody knows)}^{\infty} E\,.$$

There is no dificulty in checking that the common knowledge operator $\mathcal{K} = \text{(everybody knows)}^{\infty}$ satisfies (K3) of Figure 10.2.1 along with (K0)–(K2). It is more painful to show that it also satisfies (K4), but this is true as well. Thus the common knowledge operator has the same properties as the knowledge operator of an individual.

10.6.3 Common Truisms

We saw in Section 10.2.2 that it was a truism for Alice that someone has a dirty face provided that the guard can be relied upon to announce this if and only if it is true. However, the event that someone has a dirty face is not only a truism for Alice, it is a truism for everybody. This makes it a *common truism.*[15] More precisely, the requirement for an event E to be a common truism is that

$$T \subseteq \text{(everybody knows)}T\,. \tag{10.1}$$

Lemma 10.6.1 An event is a common truism if and only if

$$T \subseteq \text{(everybody knows)}^{\infty} T\,. \tag{10.2}$$

Proof. If (10.1) holds, then (10.2) follows because the (everybody knows) operator satisfies (K2). If (10.2) holds then

$$T \supseteq \text{(everybody knows)}T \supseteq \text{(everybody knows)}^{\infty} T \supseteq T\,,$$

and hence $T = \text{(everybody knows)}T$. □

The common knowledge operator $\text{(everybody knows)}^{\infty}$ shares all the properties (K0)–(K4) with a regular knowledge operator. Lemma 10.6.1 shows that a common truism is just

[14] If Ω is an infinite set, $\text{(everybody knows)}^{\infty} E$ may be defined as the intersection of all the sets $\text{(everybody knows)}^{n} E$.

[15] The idea was introduced by Milgrom, who aptly described it as a *public event.* Unfortunately there seems no way to adapt his terminology so that the analogy between truisms and common truisms is preserved.

like a regular truism but with the common knowledge operator replacing a regular knowledge operator. We can therefore return to Section 10.2 and 10.3 and restate its results about the knowledge of individuals as results about the common knowledge of sets of individuals.

Proposition 10.6.1 It is common knowledge that E has occurred if and only if a common truism that implies E has occurred.

Proof. Copy the proof of Theorem 10.2.1. □

Justifying Alice's Argument. It is now at last possible to finalize the argument of Section 10.1. Alice's reasoning depends on three things. She needs to know that a dirty-faced traveler is present. She needs to know that Bob knows it. And she needs to know that Nanny knows that Bob knows it. In fact, much more than this is true. We have already seen that the presence of a dirty-faced traveler is a common triusm because of the gabby railway guard. It therefore follows from Proposition 10.6.1 that the presence of a dirty-faced traveler is *common knowledge* in state $\omega = 8$.

10.6.4 Communal Possibility Sets

Recall that the possibility operator $\mathcal{P}$ for individuals is defined by $\mathcal{P}E = \sim\mathcal{K}\sim E$. This says that something is possible if it is not known not to have occurred. The possibility operator $\mathcal{M}$ for communities is defined by

$$\mathcal{M}E = \sim(\text{everybody knows})^{\infty}\sim E$$

Proposition 10.6.2 The smallest common truism containing ω is $\mathcal{M}\{\omega\}$.

Proof. Copy the proof of Theorem 10.3.1. □

The notation $M(\omega)$ will be used for "the set of states that the community as a whole cannot reject as being irrelevant to their concerns". The set $M(\omega)$ will be called a communal possibility set. As in Section 10.3.1, $M(\omega)$ can be identified with the smallest common truism containing ω, and so $M(\omega) = \mathcal{M}\{\omega\}$.

The notion of communal possibility is a wide one. Just as it is hard for something to be common knowledge, so it is easy for something to be communally possible. For example,

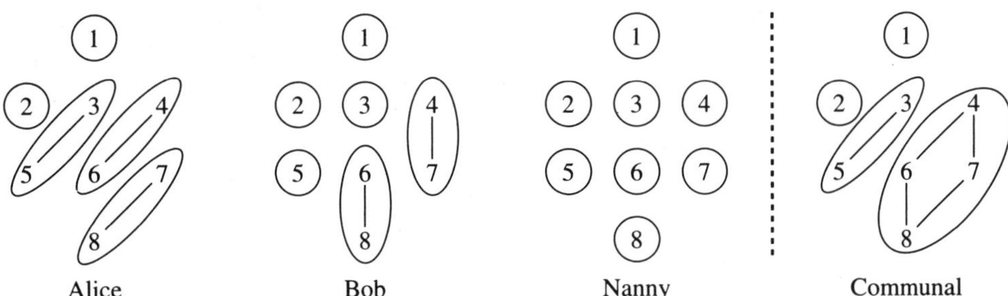

Figure 10.12 Communal possibility sets.

it is enough for something to be communally possible if Alice thinks it possible. But it is also enough if Bob thinks it possible that Alice thinks it possible; or if Nanny thinks it possible that Bob thinks it possible that Alice thinks it possible. And so on.

It is easiest to keep track of these possibility chains in a diagram. Figure 10.12 shows how this is done. The possibility partitions for Alice, Bob and Nanny are those of the third row of Figure 10.5(a). The communal possibility sets are shown in the fourth column. To find these sets, join up two states with a line if they belong to the same possibility set for at least one individual. For example, 4 and 7 get linked because they are both included in one of Bob's possibility sets. When all such links have been drawn, two states belong to the same communal possibility set if and only if they are connected by a chain of linkages. For example, 4 and 8 belong to the same communal possibility set because 4 gets linked to 7, and 7 gets linked to 8.

The advantage of thinking about communal possibility sets is that they make it easy to tell what is or is not common knowledge. All that one needs to know for this purpose appears in the following proposition.

Proposition 10.6.3 It is common knowledge that E has occurred in state ω if and only if $M(\omega) \subseteq E$.

Proof. Copy the proof of Theorem 10.3.2. □

With Proposition 10.6.3 in hand, it is possible to go back to the story of the dirty-faced travelers so as to trace the evolution of what is common knowledge as time passes. The fourth columns of Figures 10.3, 10.4 and 10.5(a) show how the communal possibility sets change as information percolates through the community. The event that someone has a dirty face is $D = \{2,3,4,5,6,7,8\}$. This becomes common knowledge in Figure 10.4 because $M(8) \subseteq D$. The event that Nanny has a dirty face is $D_N = \{4,6,7,8\}$. This becomes common knowledge in the third row of Figure 10.5(a). Only then does it become true that $M(8) \subseteq D_N$.

Math 10.7 ⟶

10.6.5 Meet

The partition of $\Omega = \{1,2,3,4,5,6,7,8\}$ shown in the fourth column of Figure 10.12 is the *meet*[16] of Alice, Bob and Nanny's possibility partitions. In general, the meet of a collection of partitions is their finest common coarsening. Thus, the meet is the most refined partition that is simultaneously a coarsening of each partition in the collection.

10.7 Agreeing to Disagree?

In Exercise 2.6.5, John believes that the Democrat will win a presidential election with probability $\frac{5}{8}$. Mary believes that the Democrat will win with probability $\frac{1}{4}$. Their beliefs are no secret because each is willing to take bets based on what they believe. But they do not believe the same thing. They "agree to disagree" about the prospects of the Democratic candidate.

There is something paradoxical about such a situation. Exercise 2.6.5 focuses on the fact that a third party can guarantee making money out of John and Mary by placing suitable bets with them. But this is not very remarkable. Bookies make a living in precisely this way.

Consider, however, the problem of splitting a dollar with which John and Mary were faced in Section 5.6. Why do they not agree that John should get the whole dollar if the Democrat wins, and Mary should get the whole dollar otherwise? Such a deal has a dollar expectation of $\$\frac{5}{8}$ for John and $\$\frac{3}{4}$ for Mary. Since the sum of their expectations exceeds the dollar to be divided, their deal has the character of a perpetual motion machine. Something is somehow created out of nothing. Their agreement to disagree violates the fundamental economic precept that there is no such thing as a free lunch.

Can rational people genuinely agree to disagree? The following story will help us to formulate an answer.

[16]Sometimes, the word "join" is substituted for "meet". But this implies a rather perverse ordering of the lattice of partitions.

10.7.1 Crime Busters

One of Alice, Bob and Nanny is guilty of a crime. The only available clues are the state of their faces in the railway carriage. John and Mary are engaged to solve the mystery. The size of their fees limits the time each is able to devote to the case. They therefore agree that John will pursue one of two possible lines of inquiry, and Mary will follow up another. At the end of the inquiry, each investigator will have reduced the state space $\Omega = \{1, 2, 3, 4, 5, 6, 7, 8\}$ to one of a number of possibility sets. However, John's possibility partition will not be the same as Mary's because they will have received different information during their separate investigations. It may be, for example, that John and Mary's possibility partitions will be as in Figure 10.13(a) after their inquiries are concluded.

Notice that each possibility set $P(\omega)$ in Figure 10.13 is labeled with one of the suspects. This is the person that the investigator will accuse if the true state is ω. Thus, if the true state is $\omega = 8$, John will accuse Nanny because $P_J(\omega) = \{6, 8\}$.

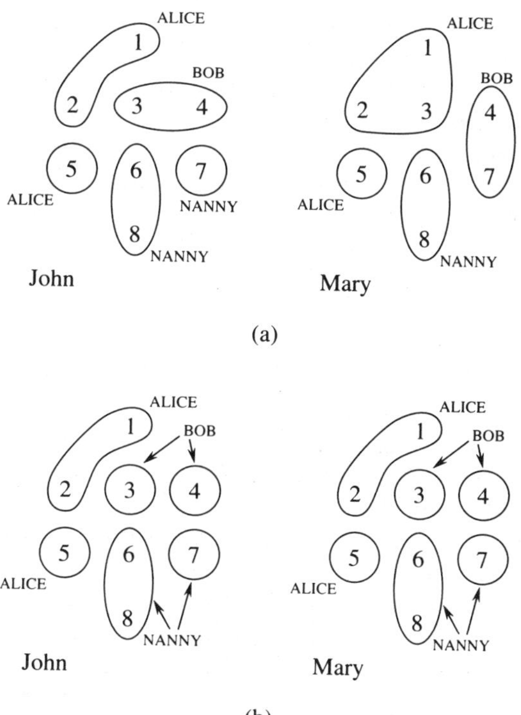

Figure 10.13 Who done it?

It is important for the story that John and Mary *reason* in the same way. Perhaps they both went to the same detective school (or read the same game theory book). Thus it is given that, if John and Mary arrive at the same possibility set, they will both accuse the same person. For example, $P_J(\omega) = P_M(\omega) = \{6, 8\}$ when $\omega = 8$. Thus John and Mary will both accuse Nanny if $\omega = 8$.

Now suppose that John and Mary discuss the case *after* both have completed their inquiries, but *before* reporting their findings. Each simply tells the other whom they plan to accuse on the basis of their current evidence. Can they agree to disagree? For example, if the true state is $\omega = 3$, will John persist in accusing Bob while Mary points the finger at Alice?

In the circumstances of Figure 10.13(a), the answer is *no*. Suppose that the true state is $\omega = 3$, and John and Mary simultaneously name the suspect they would accuse if they got no further information. Thus John names Bob, and Mary names Alice. Such a naming of suspects is very informative for both John and Mary. They use this new information to refine their possibility partitions. The new partitions are shown in Figure 10.13(b). These partitions are the *same* for both John and Mary. Thus, the investigators will now accuse the *same* person. In Figure 10.13(b), the person accused is taken to be Bob.

The point here is that John, for example, would be stupid not to react to Mary's conclusion. She reasons exactly as he would reason if he had her information. Thus, when she reports her conclusion, this conclusion is just as much a piece of hard evidence for John as the evidence he collected himself.

10.7.2 Reaching a Consensus

The preceding story makes it clear why John and Mary might reach a consensus on whom to accuse. Robert Aumann explained the circumstances under which such a result will arise in the general case. The version of his idea given here is due to Michael Bacharach. What turns out to be important is that John and Mary's conclusions be *common knowledge*. Other requirements are mentioned along the way.

Suppose that John and Mary have completed their investigations. Not only this, they have met and it is now common knowledge between them whom each plans to accuse. Can each now point a finger at a different person?

Imagine that John's final possibility partition of Ω is ALICE, BOB_1, BOB_2, BOB_3, NANNY. Here, for example, BOB_2 represents a possibility set in which John will accuse Bob. Suppose that, when the true state is ω, John actually will accuse Bob. Then, by Proposition 10.6.3,

$$M(\omega) \subseteq \text{BOB}_1 \cup \text{BOB}_2 \cup \text{BOB}_3 .$$

But the partition M is a coarsening of John's possibility partition. Thus, for example, either $\text{BOB}_2 \subseteq M(\omega)$ or $\text{BOB}_2 \subseteq {\sim}M(\omega)$. Similar inclusion relations hold for John's other possibility sets. It follows that $M(\omega)$ must be the *union* of some of the possibility sets in which John accuses Bob. It may be, for example, that

$$M(\omega) = \text{BOB}_2 \cup \text{BOB}_3 . \quad (10.3)$$

To proceed further, an assumption about John's rationality is required.[17] In his detective school, he was trained how to decide who should be accused under all possible contingencies. If his investigations lead him to the conclusion that the set of possible states of the world is E, his training will therefore tell him the right person to accuse. Denote this person by $d(E)$. For example, when $E = \text{ALICE}$, the person John will accuse is $d(E) =$ Alice.

Let E and F be disjoint events. This means that they cannot both occur simultaneously. Then John's decision rule will be required to have the following property. If $d(E) = d(F)$, then $d(E \cup F) = d(E) = d(F)$. If John's decision rule violates this requirement, he would sometimes find himself in court replying to the defense attorney as follows:

> Did you accuse my client Bob?—*Yes.*
> When you accused him, what did you know about the state of Alice's face?—*Nothing.*
> Whom would you have accused if you had known Alice's face was dirty?—*Nanny.*
> Whom would you have accused if you had known Alice's face was clean?—*Nanny.*
> Are you not using an irrational decision rule?—*I guess so.*

Returning to (10.3), we can use the rationality requirement just discussed to conclude that

$$d(M(\omega)) = \text{ Bob}, \quad (10.4)$$

when it is common knowledge that John will accuse Bob.

A second assumption is necessary. This is that John and Mary reason in the same way. To be precise, the requirement

[17]This assumption is closely related to Savage's sure-thing principle, which was mentioned in Section 3.6.2. It is therefore not surprising that Bayesian-rational people necessarily make decisions in accordance with it.

is that they use the *same* decision rule. Thus, if it were common knowledge that Mary will accuse Alice, then the same argument that led to (10.4) will yield

$$d(M(\omega)) = \text{Alice}. \tag{10.5}$$

But (10.4) and (10.5) cannot both be true, because Alice is not the same person as Bob. Thus, the argument shows that, if it is common knowledge whom John and Mary plan to accuse, they must be planning to accuse the same person. They cannot agree to disagree.

10.7.3 No Free Lunches

The Harsanyi doctrine[18] is that rational people must necessarily have common prior beliefs. That is to say, each person's prior probability measure on the set Ω is the same. The argument offered in defense of this claim is that rational human beings, like John and Mary in the preceding section, will necessarily process data in the same way. If they have different beliefs, it must therefore be because they have different data. However, *before* anything happens, two people cannot have different data. Thus, so the argument goes, their *prior* beliefs must be the same. It does not, of course, follow that their *posterior* beliefs, *after* one or both has received some private information, will necessarily be the same. For example, John and Mary's prior probabilities for the election of the Democrat might both be $\frac{1}{2}$. However, if Mary is secretly told that the Democratic candidate is involved in a scandal that will break in tomorrow's headlines, then her posterior probability may go down to $\frac{1}{4}$. John may hear something scandalous about the Republican and revise his probability up to $\frac{5}{8}$.

If this defense of the Harsanyi doctrine is thought plausible, then one should also think it plausible that it should be common knowledge that everybody has a common prior. After all, since the Harsanyi doctrine is defended on rational grounds, it cannot be correct without all rational people knowing it to be correct. It must therefore be a common truism.

Bayesian-rational people obtain their posterior probabilities by updating their priors as explained in Section 10.5. If it is common knowledge that everybody is Bayesian-rational and that the Harsanyi doctrine holds, then it follows that it is common knowledge that everybody uses the *same* decision rule for assigning probabilities to events. For the reasons

[18] Although Robert Aumann hung this label on him, John Harsanyi is not in the least doctrinaire.

given in Section 10.7.2, players cannot then agree to disagree about these probabilities (Exercise 10.9.29). Thus, it cannot become *common knowledge* that John's posterior probability for the Democrat being elected is $\frac{5}{8}$ while Mary's is $\frac{1}{4}$ without one or both changing their beliefs.

No free lunch is therefore available for John and Mary. The mere fact that John is willing to bet on terms that would be unfavorable for him if Mary's beliefs are accurate, would lead Mary to revise her beliefs. And similarly for John when he learns the terms on which Mary is willing to bet.[19]

Should we believe the Harsanyi doctrine? Alert readers will have noticed that the argument offered in its defense abandons Savage's small world hypothesis. The set Ω on which players' priors are defined is not even specified in precise terms. To my mind, this is a fatal flaw. I prefer to defend the Harsanyi doctrine as a working hypothesis rather than as a philosophical principle. Just as people with intransitive preferences can be exploited using the "money pump" described in Section 3.1.1, so groups of people who believe in communal free lunches can be exploited.

As noted at the beginning of Section 10.7, Exercise 2.6.5 provides an example of how an outsider can make a Dutch book (Section 3.6.2) against a group who agree to disagree, and hence guarantee taking money from the group no matter what happens. What the outsider has to do is very simple. In the example, John and Mary are risk-neutral. John believes that the Democrat will be elected with probability $\frac{5}{8}$. Mary believes that the Democrat will be elected with probability $\frac{1}{4}$. The outsider proposes a bet to John in which John gets \$3 if the Democrat wins, but pays the outsider \$5 if the Republican wins. John evaluates such a bet as having zero expectation and so should be willing to accept it if paid a penny. Simultaneously, the outsider proposes a bet to Mary in which she gets \$2 if the Republican wins, but pays the outsider \$6 if the Democrat wins. As with John, she should accept this bet if offered a penny to do so. The outsider is now guaranteed an income of \$3 no matter who wins the election.

[19]Economists will prefer the version of this result formulated by Paul Milgrom and Nancy Stokey . It is common knowledge that two risk-averse economic agents have a common prior. Before receiving any information, they negotiate a Pareto-efficient trading contract. The trades specified will include securities whose values are contingent on the outcome of events about which the agents are currently uninformed. Each then gets some private information. Is it possible that they will now renegotiate their contract? The answer is *no.* As with John and Mary, the mere fact that the other guy is willing to deal is evidence that the deal is not a good idea.

Such reasoning does not show that any particular individual in a group that repeatedly agrees to disagree will necessarily suffer when the group is exploited by an outsider. It shows only that the group as a whole cannot survive as an economic entity if its members have inconsistent models of the world that repeatedly lead them to estimate probabilities differently. In assuming the Harsanyi doctrine, game theorists exclude such exploitable groups. A theory that did not do so would be more widely applicable, but things are hard enough even when the Harsanyi doctrine *is* assumed.

10.8 Common Knowledge in Game Theory

The philosopher Hobbes said that a man is characterized by his strength of body, his passions, his experience, and his reason. This list of properties provides a convenient hook on which to hang a discussion of what needs to be common knowledge in a game.

Strength of body. This determines what someone can or cannot do. An athlete may plan to run a mile in four minutes, but such a plan would be impossible for most of us to execute. Game theory incorporates such considerations into the *rules of the game.* These determine what is feasible for a player. More precisely, a player is confined to choosing from his or her set of strategies in the game. This section is mostly concerned with why it is important that the rules of the game be *common knowledge* among the players.

Passion and experience. These correspond to the preferences and beliefs of a player. Both must be common knowledge for a game-theoretic analysis to be possible in most cases. However, this is an issue taken up in the next chapter.

Reason. In one-person decision problems, economists simply assume that players maximize their expected payoff given their beliefs. In a game, matters are more complicated because the idea of an equilibrium takes for granted that players know something about how everybody reasons. Only a little will be said on this topic, because exactly who needs to know how much about what remains controversial at this time.

10.8.1 Common Knowledge of the Rules

Why do the rules of a game need to be common knowledge among the players? The finitely repeated Prisoners' Dilemma of Section 8.3 will be used to clarify this point. In Exercise 8.6.6, we saw that all Nash equilibria in the n-times repeated Prisoners' Dilemma result in *hawk* being played all the time.[20] Like many results in game theory, the dependence of this conclusion on the fact that the value of n must be *common knowledge* is not immediately evident. However, as the following example shows, if the value of n is not common knowledge, Nash equilibria exist in which players use *dove*, except possibly at the very last stage of the game.

Ignorance Is Bliss. Sometimes it is claimed that rational people cannot fail to profit from being better informed. This is true in one-person decision problems. However, groups of people can certainly be made worse off through certain information becoming common knowledge. As an example, consider the ten-times repeated Prisoners' Dilemma of Figure 7.3(b). Since the rules of a game are assumed to be common knowledge, then the fact that the tenth stage is the last stage will be common knowledge. As a consequence, in a Nash equilibrium, both players will use *hawk*, and each will get a low payoff of only 10.

But suppose it were not common knowledge that the tenth stage were the last. In order to bring game-theoretic tools to bear, it is necessary to say what would be common knowledge instead. Consider, therefore, the following story. All the details of the story are common knowledge between the players.

Player I knows that he is playing a version of the repeated Prisoners' Dilemma with either $2m - 1$ or $2m$ stages. Player II knows that she is playing a version of the repeated Prisoners' Dilemma with either $2n$ or $2n + 1$ stages.[21] Actually, the game has 10 stages. Thus, player I's possibility set is $\{9, 10\}$ and player II's is $\{10, 11\}$. But player I thinks it possible that player II's possibility set is $\{8, 9\}$, and player II thinks it possible that player I's possibility set is $\{11, 12\}$. Moreover, player I thinks it possible that player II thinks it possible that player I's possibility set is $\{7, 8\}$. And so on. Figure 10.14 shows some of the possibility sets that need to be taken into account.

---

[20] On the equilibrium path. Theorem 8.3.1 says that, when a subgame-perfect equilibrium is used, players always plan to use *hawk* both on and off the equilibrium path.

[21] Unless $n = 1$. In this case, player II's possibility set is just $\{1\}$.

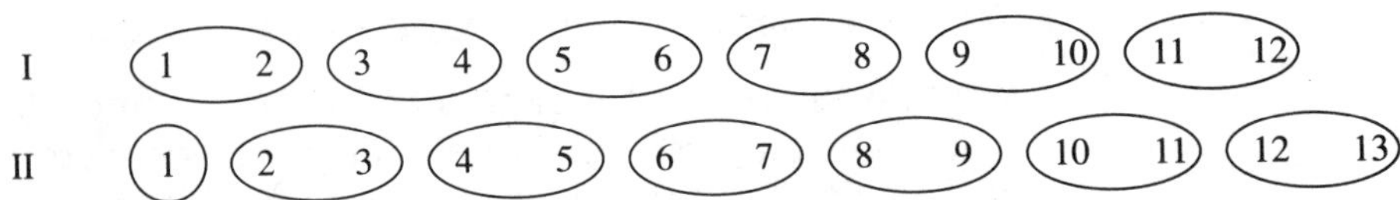

Figure 10.14 How long does this go on for?

It is not enough for us to consider what the players will do given their actual information. For example, in seeking to predict what player II will do, player I must not only consider the case in which player II's possibility set is $\{10, 11\}$. He must also consider what player II *would do* if her possibility set were $\{8, 9\}$. This partly depends on what she believes he would do if his possibility set were $\{7, 8\}$. And so on. We therefore have to say what the players *would do* for *each* of their possibility sets. Since the players are rational, the decisions that they would make at each possibility set will, of course, be optimal, given the beliefs they would then hold.

This brings us to the question of what is to be assumed about the players' beliefs. To keep things as simple as possible, suppose that a player always believes that, of the two pieces of information the opponent might have, each is equally likely.[22] Thus, for example, when player I's possibility set is $\{9, 10\}$, he thinks that player II's possibility set is $\{8, 9\}$ with probability $\frac{1}{2}$, and $\{10, 11\}$ with probability $\frac{1}{2}$.

The time has now come to say what strategies the players are to use. We will study the case in which each player uses a "grim-trigger" strategy. With such a strategy, a player uses *dove* until one of two things happen. The first possibility is that the opponent plays *hawk* on some occasion. Such an opponent is punished with the grim response of always playing *hawk* thereafter no matter what. The second possibility is that a "trigger" stage of the game is reached. *Hawk* is then played from that stage on, no matter how cooperative the opponent may have been. In this example, the trigger stage is the stage that the player knows to be the very last stage of the game when it is reached. For example, when player I's possibility set is $\{10, 11\}$, his trigger stage will be 11. Reaching this stage triggers the *hawk* strategy no matter what might have happened previously.

[22] Except again in the case when player II's possibility set is $\{1\}$. She is then certain that player I's possibility set is $\{1, 2\}$. A second problem will occur to those who recall Exercise 3.7.18(e). Some discussion of this point appears in Section 11.9.1.

If players can be relied upon always to use such a grim-trigger strategy whatever their information, then the result is an equilibrium.[23] No player would ever have an incentive to deviate.

Consider, for example, a player I whose possibility set is $\{6, 7\}$. If his opponent has the possibility set $\{5, 6\}$, then the actual length of the game must be 6. If both use the grim-trigger strategy, then player I's income stream is 3, 3, 3, 3, 3, 0. If the opponent has the possibility set $\{7, 8\}$, then the actual length of the game is 7 and player I's income stream is 3, 3, 3, 3, 3, 3, 6. Thus player I gets $\frac{1}{2}(15 + 24) = 39/2$ by sticking to his grim-trigger strategy.

What can he get by deviating? He does best by beating an opponent whose possibility set is $\{5, 6\}$ to the punch. That is, if he is going to deviate, he should plan to play *hawk* at stage 5 and thereafter. This generates the two income streams 3, 3, 3, 3, 6, 1 and 3, 3, 3, 3, 6, 1, 1. Thus the most that player I can get from deviating is $\frac{1}{2}(19 + 20) = 39/2$.

The same argument shows that no player ever has an incentive to deviate from grim-trigger. But, if grim-trigger is played when the Prisoners' Dilemma is actually repeated ten times, then the players will cooperate until the ninth stage. Only at the tenth stage will player II disturb the harmony by playing *hawk*. Player I will then get a total payoff of 27 and player II will get a total payoff of 33. This is a great improvement on the payoff of 10 that each gets when the length of the game is common knowledge.

Rational Fools? Of course, since we have to envisage an *infinite* number of possibility sets, we are really only gilding the lily of Section 8.3.2 as far as rational cooperation in the Prisoners' Dilemma is concerned. Notice, however, that the game considered here does *not* have an infinite horizon. It is common knowledge that the game has a *finite* horizon. When the game actually has length 10, everybody knows that the length is at most 11. Moreover, everybody knows that everybody knows that the length is at most 12. In fact, one can write "everybody knows that" as many times as one chooses in front of the assertion that the game has a finite horizon, and the result will be a true statement. It is therefore *false* that rational cooperation is impossible when it is common knowledge that the Prisoners' Dilemma is to be repeated a finite number of times.

[23]More on this issue will appear in Section 11.9.

Phil
10.9 ⟶

10.8.2 Common Knowledge of How Players Reason

The notion of an equilibrium is fundamental to game theory. But *why* should players be anticipated to use equilibrium strategies?

Two kinds of answers have been offered so far. First there is the *eductive* type of answer. This assumes that the players find their way to equilibrium as a result of careful reasoning. They are not frightened of sentences that begin "If I think that he thinks that I think ...". On the contrary, they pursue all such reasoning chains to the bitter end.

However, the eductive answer is not the only possible answer. There are also *evolutive* answers. These see equilibrium being achieved, not through the players thinking everything out in advance, but as a consequence of myopic players adjusting their behavior by trial-and-error as they play a game repeated over possibly long periods of time. Such evolutive libration processes were studied in Chapter 9. We found no neat and tidy theory. Economic, social and biological librations all have their own idiosyncrasies about which it is difficult to say anything very general. Nevertheless, the examples offered make it clear that the notion of an equilibrium is essential to an understanding of what is going on.

My own opinion is that *eductive* answers are less important than *evolutive* answers. This is not to deny that game theorists sometimes have to answer questions that need to be answered eductively.[24] However, the chief reason that eductive answers are interesting is because of the hope that they will provide insight into the end-product of relevant evolutionary processes. Perhaps the future will show that such optimism is ill-founded, but in the meantime enough encouraging examples exist to make the enterprise seem worthwhile.

Such an attitude lessens the importance of a single-minded investigation of the eductive foundations of equilibrium ideas. Indeed, if an eductive analysis becomes too sophisticated, there is a danger of generating concepts that are not relevant at all in an evolutionary context. However, it remains of interest to follow where eductive reasoning leads. In this section, two approaches are described. The first was proposed independently by two economists, Bernheim and Pearce. The second is the brainchild of Robert Aumann. The exposition is very much more brisk than elsewhere in

[24]For example, what is the optimal way to play Blackjack given the casino's house strategy? Or, what is the optimal way of programming an antiballistic missile?

the book because the material is controversial, and so there is not much point in attempting to do more than give the general flavor of the ideas.

Rationalizability. Recall from Section 3.6.2 how a Bayesian-rational decision-maker behaves in situations where the outcome of the decision to be made depends on events about which the decision-maker is uncertain. He or she acts *as though* equipped with a probability measure that assigns subjective probabilities to the events that are uncertain.

In a finite, two-player game, each player is uncertain about which pure strategy[25] the opponent will finally use. A Bayesian-rational player therefore assigns a subjective probability to each of the possible alternatives. The player then chooses a strategy to play that maximizes his or her expected payoff with respect to these subjective probabilities. He or she therefore behaves as though choosing a best reply to one of the opponent's mixed strategies.[26]

How does a Bayesian-rational player know what to optimize against? Where do his or her subjective beliefs come from? Game theory takes for granted that a player's beliefs about what an opponent will do depend on what the player knows about the opponent. However, it is far from clear precisely what should be assumed about what players know about their opponents. The idea of *rationalizability* is built on the assumption that it should at least be common knowledge that both players are Bayesian-rational.

Suppose that player II's set of mixed strategies is M. Then a Bayesian-rational player I will necessarily choose a strategy from the set $\mathcal{B}M$ of best replies to strategies in M. A Bayesian-rational player II who knows that player I is Bayesian-rational will therefore choose a strategy from the set $\mathcal{B}^2 M = \mathcal{B}(\mathcal{B}M)$ of best replies to strategies in $\mathcal{B}M$. A Bayesian-rational player I who knows that player II is a Bayesian-rational player who knows that player I is Bayesian-rational will therefore choose a strategy from $\mathcal{B}^3 M$. And so on, in a style that will by now be familiar.

[25]Even if the opponent mixes, the final result will be that some pure strategy gets played.

[26]If the mixed strategy to which a best reply is chosen is $q = (\frac{1}{3}, \frac{1}{3}, \frac{1}{3})^T$, it does not necessarily follow that the Bayesian-rational player believes that the opponent will use the mixed strategy q. It may equally well mean that the Bayesian-rational player is sure that the opponent will use a pure strategy but cannot think of a reason for favoring one pure strategy rather than another.

Exercise 6.10.22 can now be used to relate this line of reasoning to something we have met before. The exercise says that a mixed strategy is a best reply to some mixed strategy choice of the opponent if and only if it is not strongly dominated. It follows that the only strategies that can be played when it is common knowledge that the players are Bayesian-rational are simply those that survive the successive deletion of strongly dominated strategies as described in Section 4.6.

Some games have no strongly dominated strategies at all. In such games, *all* strategies are rationalizable. Does this mean that we can forget about the equilibria of such games and simply tell the players that anything goes?

One would have to answer *yes* to this question if it really were the case that the only piece of common knowledge available about the players was the fact that they are Bayesian-rational. However, a theory that assumed only this would be very barren. Real people, even total strangers from different countries, have a great deal more in common than rationalizability assumes. The mere fact that we are all human ensures that we share a common culture to some extent.

Orthodox game theory seeks to capture this, albeit crudely, by discussing what should be written in game theory books. The implicit assumption is that what is written in the game theory book will be common knowledge among the players. More generally, the implicit assumption behind much game-theoretic reasoning is that the way to behave in a game—the conventional thing to do—is somehow common knowledge among the players. Attention can then be concentrated on those commonly understood *conventions* that are not self-destabilizing. These are the conventions that select *equilibria*. Of course, like all idealizations, the assumption that the convention in use is common knowledge will sometimes be wildly inappropriate. But there will be few situations, especially in economics, when we can truthfully say that we know nothing at all about what the opponent will do beyond the fact that it will be something Bayesian-rational.

Correlated Equilibrium. How can one express the fact that the players in a game share a common culture? Aumann suggests that it should be assumed that it is "common knowledge" that the players share the *same* universe of discourse. He further suggests that the states ω in this universe Ω should be taken to be *all-embracing*. This means that, if you should ever get to know that state ω has occurred for sure, then you would know absolutely everything that might conceivably be relevant to you as a decision-maker. The description of a state

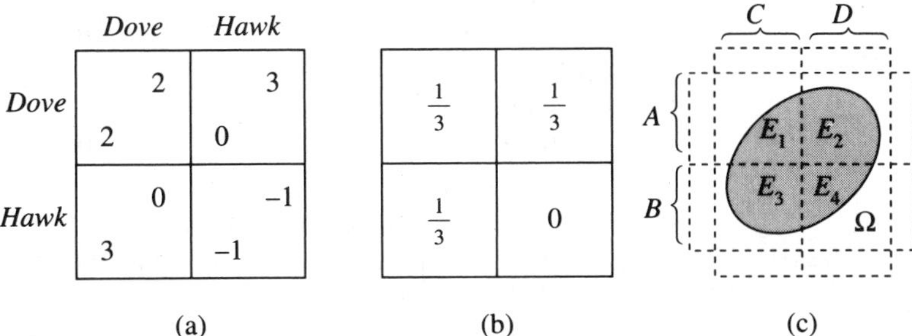

Figure 10.15 Correlated equilibrium again.

must therefore specify every detail of the "possible world" it represents. This includes not only how the players behave, but also what their states of mind are. Since the players are Bayesian-rational, their states of mind can be summarized by two things: what they know and what they believe.

One should not be surprised if such heroic assumptions lead to heroic conclusions. Consider, in particular, what the players know and believe. What Alice knows in state ω is determined by her possibility set $P(\omega)$. All this is part of the specification of the state ω. Thus it is "common knowledge" what Alice would know and believe in every state ω. It follows that Alice's possibility *partition* P and her *prior* probability measure prob : $\Omega \to [0, 1]$ are always "common knowledge".

Now consider the game of Chicken given in Figure 7.17(a). This is repeated as Figure 10.15(a). Recall that this was the version of Chicken used to illustrate the idea of a correlated equilibrium in Section 7.6.2.

Since a state ω specifies everything that there is to specify, it specifies the strategy that Alice and Bob will use if they play Chicken in state ω. For simplicity, consider only the possibility that *pure* strategies are used. Suppose that Alice uses pure strategy $a(\omega)$ when she is player II and Bob uses pure strategy $b(\omega)$ when he is player I. It is assumed that both players are Bayesian-rational in every state.[27] This implies that the strategy $t = a(\omega)$ must maximize the expected value of Alice's payoff $\pi_2(b(\omega), t)$, given her knowledge that the true state of the world lies in her possibility set $P(\omega)$.

[27]Since their behavior is determined by the state that occurs, the players cannot be said to *think* their way to an equilibrium—or, rather, their reasoning processes are not explicitly modeled. As Aumann puts it, the players "just do what they do". However, whatever the unmodeled reasoning processes may be, they result in Bayesian rational behavior.

Figure 10.15(c) shows a schematic picture of the universe Ω. The set C is the set of states in which Alice uses *dove.* That is, $C = \{\omega : a(\omega) = dove\}$. The set D is the set in which she uses *hawk.* If Alice always knows what she is doing, then C and D will be truisms for her. For reasons like those of Section 10.7.2, it follows that C and D are both unions of some of Alice's possibility sets. As in Section 10.7.2 again, this implies that Alice would choose *dove* even if she knew only that C had occurred. Similarly, she would choose *hawk* if she knew only that D had occurred. Bob's situation is analogous.

Figure 10.15 should be compared with Figure 7.17. The resemblance becomes even stronger if e_1, e_2, e_3 and e_4 of Figure 7.17(c) are identified with the events E_1, E_2, E_3 and E_4 of Figure 10.15(c). If Alice and Bob share the same prior[28] with $\text{prob}(E_1) = \text{prob}(E_2) = \text{prob}(E_3) = \frac{1}{3}$, and $\text{prob}(E_4) = 0$, then Figure 10.15 and Figure 7.17 become essentially the same. A kibitzer will therefore be unable to distinguish Alice and Bob's behavior from that of two players using the correlated equilibrium discussed in Section 7.6.2.

Aumann's approach would make it almost tautological that Bayesian-rational players will use a correlated equilibrium in a game. Where does this leave other equilibrium ideas? In particular:

What about Nash equilibrium? The idea of a Nash equilibrium fits comfortably inside Aumann's system because it can be seen as a special kind of correlated equilibrium. It is a correlated equilibrium in which the events A and B are independent of the events C and D. What this means is that Alice and Bob make their choices independently. Or to say the same thing another way, neither can learn anything about the choice of the other by examining the choice they plan to make themselves. Obviously, this is an assumption that one will wish to make very frequently.

What about rationalizability? This idea can also be fitted into Aumann's system. In describing how Aumann sees correlated equilibria arising in his very general setting, the players' priors were taken to be the same, as prescribed by the Harsanyi doctrine. If the Harsanyi doctrine is not invoked,

[28]Our assumptions do not imply that they *must* share the same prior. Unless the Harsanyi doctrine is imposed, nothing prevents players having different *priors* even when these priors are "common knowledge". The "agreeing to disagree" result of Section 10.7.3 shows that it cannot be common knowledge that people have different *posteriors* if it is given to be common knowledge that their priors are the same.

then the players' priors may be different. One is then led to a generalization of the idea of a correlated equilibrium that Aumann calls a "subjective correlated equilibrium". The fact that this is very closely connected with the notion of a rationalizable strategy was noted by the economists Brandenburger and Dekel. It turns out that the set of a player's rationalizable strategies is identical to the set of all the strategies that a player might be called upon to play in some subjective correlated equilibrium. Exercise 10.9.37 draws attention to some of the consequences.

Bayesianism. It will be apparent from the preceding discussion that Bayesianism does not call for much mental prowess on the part of the players. They mechanically update their subjective probabilities as new information becomes available, and then decide what to do by the equally mechanical procedure of maximizing their expected payoff given their current beliefs.

Naive Bayesians do not think it necessary to ask where players get their priors from, or how they know what their possibility partitions are.[29] Aumann offers this attitude some of the trappings of respectability by making the universe responsible for what players know and believe, rather than the players themselves. However, if Bayesians wish to achieve respectability by following this route, they have a heavy price to pay. They must abandon Savage's "small world" proviso. Whatever the virtues of Aumann's universe of discourse may be, smallness is not one of them!

Personally, I have little patience with Bayesianism as a creed. Bayesian decision theory seems to me no more than a useful tool to be used wherever it is appropriate. It is not a glass slipper into which any foot will fit. There is a good reason, for example, why the method used by scientists in making discoveries about the physical world is not Bayesian. It is because scientists are not sufficiently silly to imagine that they can predict in advance every idea that might occur to some scientist in the future. That is to say, they understand that concepts will be formulated in the future that are inconceivable in the present. What is true for outer space is even more sharply true for inner space. A

[29]In particular, they believe that Bayesian rationality endows those who embrace it with the capacity to pluck their subjective beliefs from the air. This attitude leads *very* naive Bayesians to argue that game theory is a waste of time. It is certainly true that, if we did not need to concern ourselves with *why* people believe what they believe, then equilibrium considerations would become irrelevant.

mind literally cannot itemize and docket every detail of its own operation, let alone the operation of other equally complex minds.

Bayesianism is therefore not an appropriate framework within which to study how people reason. Bayesians will protest that they are running the only viable game in town. I agree that alternative methodologies are simply too *ad hoc* to be worthy of serious attention. However, like Prince Charming, I would rather remain a bachelor than force the glass slipper onto the foot of one of the Ugly Sisters. Or to say the same thing in plain words, I do not agree that a Bayesian account of the foundations of equilibrium theory is better than no account at all.

10.9 Exercises

1. What subsets of the universe Ω of Figure 10.1 correspond to the following events?
   (a) Bob has a dirty face.
   (b) Nanny has a clean face.
   (c) Precisely two travelers have dirty faces.
   Which of these events occur when the true state of the world is $\omega = 3$?

Math

2. Use the knowledge properties (K0)–(K4) of Section 10.2.1 to prove the following:
   (a) $E \subseteq F \Rightarrow \mathcal{K}E \subseteq \mathcal{K}F$
   (b) $\mathcal{K}E = \mathcal{K}^2E$
   (c) $(\sim\mathcal{K})^2E \subseteq \mathcal{K}E$
   Offer an interpretation of each of these statements.

Math

3. Show that (K0)–(K4) of Section 10.2.1 are equivalent to (P0)–(P4).

Math

4. Write down properties of the possibility operator $\mathcal{P}$ that are analogous to those given in Exercise 10.9.2. Interpret these properties.
5. In the story of the dirty-faced travelers of Section 10.1, it is true that everybody has a dirty face. Why is this not a truism for Alice before the guard speaks?
6. Show that an event T is a truism if and only if $T = \mathcal{K}T$.

Math

7. Show that, for any event E, all of the following are truisms:
   (a) $\mathcal{K}E$ (b) $\sim\mathcal{K}E$ (c) $\mathcal{P}E$ (d) $\sim\mathcal{P}E$

Math

8. If S and T are truisms, show that the same is true of $\sim S$, $S \cap T$, and $S \cup T$.

Math 9. Explain why

$$\bigcap_{\omega \in \mathcal{K}E} \mathcal{K}E \subseteq \bigcap_{\omega \in \mathcal{K}E} E \subseteq \bigcap_{\omega \in \mathcal{K}(\mathcal{K}E)} \mathcal{K}E = \bigcap_{\omega \in \mathcal{K}E} \mathcal{K}E .$$

Use Theorem 10.3.1 and Exercise 10.9.6 to deduce that

$$\mathcal{P}\{\omega\} = \bigcap_{\omega \in \mathcal{K}E} E .$$

Math 10. Use Theorem 10.3.1 to prove that

$$\mathcal{K}E = \{\omega : \mathcal{P}\{\omega\} \subseteq E\} .$$

11. Suppose that the guard in the story of the dirty-faced travelers of Section 10.1 no longer announces that somebody has a dirty face whenever this is true. Instead, he announces that there are at least two dirty-faced travelers if and only if this is true. Assuming that the travelers know the guard's disposition, draw a diagram showing the travelers' possibility sets after the guard has had the opportunity to make an announcement.
12. Continue the preceding exercise by drawing diagrams like those of Figure 10.5(a) to show how the travelers refine their possibility partitions if the opportunity to blush rotates among them as in Section 10.3.1.
13. Suppose that the dirty-faced travelers no longer take turns in having the opportunity to blush as in Section 10.3.3. Instead, all three travelers have the opportunity to blush precisely one second after the guard's announcement, and then again precisely two seconds after the announcement, and so on. Draw diagrams to show how the travelers' possibility partitions get refined as time passes. Who will blush in this story? How many seconds after the announcement will the first blush occur?
14. Find a blushing story that leads to a different final configuration of possibility sets than those obtained in Section 10.3.3 and Exercise 10.9.13.
15. For the game of Figure 10.9:
    (a) Find a mixed strategy for player II that always leads to the same lottery over outcomes as the behavioral strategy in which she assigns equal probabilities to each action at each information set.
    (b) Find a behavioral strategy for player II that always leads to the same lottery over outcomes as the mixed strategy in which RLR is used with probability $\frac{2}{3}$ and LRL with probability $\frac{1}{3}$.

16. For the game of Figure 4.21:
   (a) Explain why the game has imperfect information but perfect recall.
   (b) Find a behavioral strategy for player II that always leads to the same lottery over outcomes as the mixed strategy in which she uses dD with probability $\frac{2}{3}$ and uU with probability $\frac{1}{3}$.
17. In the one-player game of Figure 10.8(a):
   (a) State the payoff that the player gets for each of his four pure strategies Ll, Lr, Rl, Rr.
   (b) Explain why all mixed strategies yield a payoff of zero.
   (c) Find a behavioral strategy that yields a payoff of $\frac{1}{4}$.
   (d) Why does Kuhn's theorem not apply?
18. In the one-player game of Figure 10.8(b):
   (a) Find a mixed strategy that leads to the same lottery over outcomes as the behavioral strategy in which r is chosen with probability p and R is chosen with probability P.
   (b) Show that no behavioral strategy results in the same lottery over outcomes as the mixed strategy that assigns probability $\frac{1}{2}$ to lL and probability $\frac{1}{2}$ to rR.
   (c) Why does Kuhn's theorem not apply?
19. Suppose that player II uses the behavioral strategy of Exercise 10.9.16(b) in the game of Figure 4.21. If player I knows this, what probabilities will he assign to the two nodes in his first information set should this be reached? What probabilities will he assign to the two decision nodes in his second information set should this be reached?
20. Nanny's prior probability measure on Ω is specified by $\text{prob}(1) = \text{prob}(2) = \cdots = \text{prob}(4) = \frac{1}{12}$, and $\text{prob}(5) = \text{prob}(6) = \cdots = \text{prob}(8) = \frac{1}{6}$. If the true state of the world is $\omega = 8$, how will these probabilities be updated as she progresses through steps 1–7 of Section 10.3.3?
21. Explain how the entries in the strategic form of Quiche given in Figure 10.11 are calculated. Write down the calculations for the entries in the cell in row (*quiche*, *beer*) and column (*defer*, *bully*). Use the method of successively deleting weakly and strongly dominated strategies to reduce the strategic form to a 2×2 bimatrix game. Find the mixed-strategy Nash equilibrium of this reduced game.
22. Use the strategic form of Figure 10.11 to check that Quiche has no Nash equilibria in pure strategies. Verify that when player I uses his mixed strategy $(0, 0, \frac{1}{2}, \frac{1}{2})^T$,

player II is indifferent between her first and second pure strategies. Verify that when player II uses her mixed strategy $(\frac{1}{2}, \frac{1}{2}, 0, 0)^T$, player I is indifferent between his third and fourth pure strategies. Check that this pair of mixed strategies is a Nash equilibrium.

23. Find all Nash equilibria in the game Quiche of Figure 10.6(b) when the Chance move is replaced by a new Chance move that selects a wimp with probability $\frac{3}{4}$ and a tough guy with probability $\frac{1}{4}$.

Phil

24. Write down the 3×2 strategic form of the Dalek game of Figure 10.6(a). Find all the Nash equilibria in pure strategies. Which of these are subgame-perfect? One of player I's pure strategies is strongly dominated. If player II assumes that it is certain that player I will never use a strongly dominated strategy, what probabilities will she assign to nodes x and y if called upon to play? What behavior will these beliefs induce? What will player I do if he predicts these beliefs? What does this say about the Nash equilibrium that will actually get played?[30]

Math

25. Prove that the $\mathcal{K}$ = (everybody knows) operator of Section 10.6.1 satisfies properties (K0), (K1) and (K2) of Figure 10.2. An example is given in Section 10.6.1 to show that everybody can know something without everybody knowing that everybody knows it. Give an alternative example.

Math

26. How should the operator $\mathcal{K}$ = (somebody knows) be defined in formal terms? Why does this operator not satisfy (K1) of Figure 10.2?

Math

27. Why does the common knowledge operator $\mathcal{K}$ = (everybody knows)$^\infty$ satisfy (K3) of Figure 10.2 as claimed in Section 10.6.2?

28. Return to Exercises 10.9.12 and 10.9.13. In each case, find the communal possibility partitions at each stage of

[30]This is a "forwards induction" argument of the same general type as that considered in Exercise 7.9.34. An objection is that, if a game theory book specifies (a, r) as "correct", then player I must have made a mistake if player II is called upon to play. However, if player I is making mistakes, why not the mistake of using a strongly dominated strategy? The objection is more difficult to sustain when the players get the opportunity for some "cheap talk" before the game is played. Player I can then adamantly deny that he regards the game theory book as authoritative. He can, moreover, explain very carefully that he understands that R is strongly dominated and so has no intention of playing it. In fact, player I will continue, he is entirely resolved to play L. Such a speech will surely convince all but the most stubborn player II.

the blushing process. Eventually, it is common knowledge that Bob and Nanny both have dirty faces when this is true. Explain why. In the case of Exercise 10.9.12, why does it never become common knowledge that Bob and Nanny both have clean faces when this is true?

Math

29. Bayesian-rational players make whatever decision maximizes their expected payoff given their current beliefs. Prove that such a decision rule satisfies the rationality principle of Section 10.7.2. That is, if E and F cannot occur simultaneously and $d(E) = d(F)$, then $d(E \cup F) = d(E) = d(F)$.

30. It is common knowledge that Gino and Polly always tell the truth. The state space is $\Omega = \{1, 2, 3, 4, 5, 6, 7, 8, 9\}$. The players' initial possibility partitions are shown in Figure 10.16(a). The players alternate in announcing how many elements their current possibility set contains.
    (a) Why does Gino begin by announcing 3 in all states of the world?
    (b) How does Gino's announcement change Polly's possibility partition?
    (c) Polly now makes an announcement. Explain why the possibility partitions afterwards are as in Figure 10.16(b).

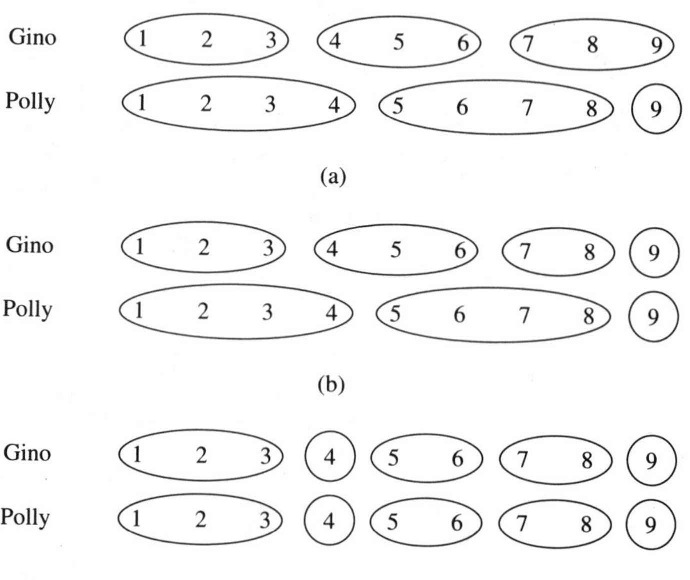

Figure 10.16 Reaching consensus.

(d) Continue updating the players' possibility partitions as announcements are made. Eventually, Figure 10.16(c) will be reached. Why will there be no further changes?

(e) In Figure 10.16(c), the event E that Gino's possibility set contains 2 elements is $\{5, 6, 7, 8\}$. Why is this common knowledge when the true state is $\omega = 5$? Is E a common truism?

31. In the previous exercise, it is common knowledge that Gino and Polly each attach a prior probability of $\frac{1}{9}$ to each element of Ω. Instead of announcing how many elements their current possibility set contains, they announce their current subjective probability for the event $F = \{3, 4\}$.

(a) In Figure 10.16(a), explain why the event that Gino announces $\frac{1}{3}$ is $\{1, 2, 3, 4, 5, 6\}$, and the event that he announces 0 is $\{7, 8, 9\}$.

(b) What is Polly's possibility partition after Gino's initial announcement? Explain why the event that Polly now announces $\frac{1}{2}$ is $\{1, 2, 3, 4\}$, and the event that she announces 0 is $\{5, 6, 7, 8, 9\}$.

(c) What is Gino's new possibility partition after Polly's announcement? Explain why the event that Gino now announces $\frac{1}{3}$ is $\{1, 2, 3\}$, the event that he announces 1 is $\{4\}$, and the event that he announces 0 is $\{5, 6, 7, 8, 9\}$.

(d) What is Polly's new possibility partition? Explain why the events that Polly will now announce $\frac{1}{3}$, 1 or 0 are the same as in (c).

(e) Explain why each player's posterior probability for the event F is now common knowledge, whatever the true state of the world.

(f) In Figure 10.16(a), why is it true that no player's posterior probability for F is common knowledge in any state?

(g) What will the sequence of announcements be when the true state of the world is $\omega = 2$?

32. Alice, Bob and Nanny's initial possibility partitions are as shown in Figure 10.17. It is common knowledge that their common prior attaches equal probability to each state. The table on the right of Figure 10.17 shows Alice, Bob and Nanny's initial posterior probabilities for F for each state, and also the average of these probabilities. Each player now *privately* informs a kibitzer of his

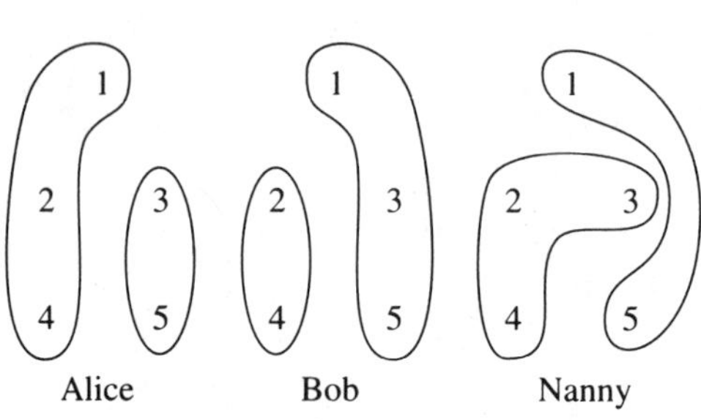

State	Alice	Bob	Nanny	Average
1	$\frac{2}{3}$	$\frac{2}{3}$	$\frac{1}{2}$	$\frac{11}{18}$
2	$\frac{2}{3}$	$\frac{1}{2}$	$\frac{2}{3}$	$\frac{11}{18}$
3	$\frac{1}{2}$	$\frac{2}{3}$	$\frac{2}{3}$	$\frac{11}{18}$
4	$\frac{2}{3}$	$\frac{1}{2}$	$\frac{2}{3}$	$\frac{11}{18}$
5	$\frac{1}{2}$	$\frac{2}{3}$	$\frac{1}{2}$	$\frac{5}{9}$

Figure 10.17 Reaching consensus again.

or her posterior probability for the event $F = \{1, 2, 3\}$. The kibitzer computes the average of these three probabilities, and announces the result of his computation *publicly*. Bob and Nanny update their probabilities for F in the light of this new information. They then privately report their current posterior probabilities to the kibitzer who again publicly announces their average. And so on.

(a) Draw Figure 10.17 again, but modified to show the situation *after* the kibitzer's first announcement.

(b) Repeat (a) for the kibitzer's second announcement.

(c) Repeat (a) for the kibitzer's third announcement.

(d) How many announcements are necessary before consensus is reached on the probability of F?

(e) What will the sequence of events be when the true state of the world is $\omega = 1$?

(f) If the true state of the world is $\omega = 1$, does this ever become common knowledge?

(g) If $\omega = 5$ is not the true state, at which stage will this fact become common knowledge?

(h) If ω is even, at what stage does this become common knowledge?

(i) Consensus is reached when everybody reports the same probability for F to the kibitzer. Why is it common knowledge that consensus has been reached as soon as it happens?

Phil 33. Explain why a Nash equilibrium will necessarily be played in a game if the strategy choice of each player is mutual knowledge, and each player is Bayesian-rational.

34. Give an example of a 2×2 bimatrix game in which *every* pair of pure strategies is rationalizable.
35. If the criterion of rationalizability from Section 10.8.2 is applied to the bimatrix game of Figure 10.18, a unique pair of pure strategies is obtained. Determine what the pair of strategies is. (Don't forget that mixed strategies may be relevant.)

<table>
<tr><td>2
5</td><td>6
2</td><td>4
1</td><td>3
0</td></tr>
<tr><td>1
4</td><td>4
3</td><td>1
2</td><td>2
1</td></tr>
<tr><td>0
1</td><td>1
1</td><td>5
1</td><td>1
5</td></tr>
<tr><td>3
2</td><td>1
0</td><td>2
0</td><td>4
4</td></tr>
</table>

Figure 10.18 A game to rationalize.

Econ

36. In the Cournot Duopoly Game of Section 7.2.1:
    (a) Confirm that each player's profit is strictly concave as a function of the player's output. Deduce that mixed strategies are never best replies in the game, and hence can be ignored in the rest of this exercise.
    (b) Use Figure 7.5 to assist in drawing a large diagram showing both player I's reaction curve $q_1 = R(q_2)$ and player II's reaction curve $q_2 = R(q_1)$, where $R(x) = \frac{1}{2}(M - c - x)$ for $0 \leq x \leq M - c$.
    (c) Let $x_0 = 0$, and define $x_{n+1} = R(x_n)$ for $n = 0, 1, \ldots$. If $x_n \to \tilde{x}$ as $n \to \infty$, explain why $\tilde{x} = R(\tilde{x})$.[31] Deduce that $\tilde{x} = \frac{1}{3}(M - c)$. Thus $(\tilde{x}, \tilde{x})$ turns out to be the same as the unique Nash equilibrium for the Cournot Duopoly Game computed in Section 7.2.1.
    (d) Mark x_1 on both players' axes in the diagram drawn for part (b). Explain why it is never a best reply for

[31] Mathematicians should confirm that the sequence $\langle x_{2n} \rangle$ is increasing and bounded above by $M - c$. It therefore converges to a limit a. The sequence $\langle x_{2n-1} \rangle$ decreases and is bounded below by 0. It therefore converges to a limit b. Explain why $b = R(a)$ and $a = R(b)$. Deduce that $a = b = \tilde{x}$.

player i to choose any $q_i > x_1$. Then erase the part of your diagram with $q_1 > x_1$ or $q_2 > x_1$.

(e) Mark x_2 on both players' axes in your diagram. Explain why it is never a best reply for player i to choose any $q_i < x_2$ if it is known that the strategy choices erased in part (d) will never be used. Then erase the part of your diagram with $q_1 < x_2$ or $q_2 < x_2$.

(f) Mark x_3 on both players' axes in your diagram, and then decide which part of your diagram should now be erased.

(g) Explain why a strategy choice q_i that never gets erased in the process whose initial three steps are described above, must satisfy $x_{2n} \leq q_i \leq x_{2n+1}$ for $n = 0, 1, \ldots$.

(h) Deduce that the only *rationalizable* strategy pair for the Cournot Duopoly Game is the game's unique Nash equilibrium $(\tilde{x}, \tilde{x})$.

(i) Show *directly* that each strategy erased in the procedure is strongly dominated in the game from which previously erased strategies have been eliminated.

(j) Use the methodology of this exercise to prove that one always obtains convergence to the unique Nash equilibrium, whatever the initial point used in the libration studied in Section 9.3.1.

Phil 37. Figure 10.19 shows some prior probabilities for the sets E_1, E_2, E_3 and E_4 of Figure 10.15(c). These priors form

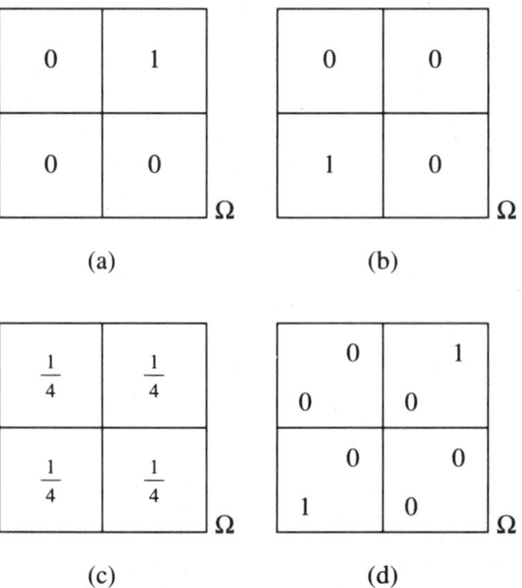

Figure 10.19 Priors for correlated equilibria in Chicken.

the basis for different correlated equilibria (Section 7.6.2) of the version of Chicken of Figure 7.17(a).

(a) Why do the prior probabilities of Figures 10.19(a), 10.19(b) and 10.19(c) correspond to Nash equilibria of Chicken? What are the Nash equilibria to which they correspond?

(b) Figure 10.19(d) shows a case where the players agree to disagree about their priors. What payoff does the "subjective correlated equilibrium" (Section 10.8.2) based on these different priors assign each player? Is this a free lunch?

CHAPTER

11

Knowing Who to Believe

11.1 Complete and Incomplete Information

The distinction between complete and incomplete information is not at all the same as that between perfect and imperfect information. To say that a game is of perfect or imperfect information is to say something about its rules.[1] To say that a game is of complete or incomplete information is to say something about what is known about the circumstances under which the game is played.

All the games studied in this book, whether they have perfect or imperfect information, are games of complete information. Roughly speaking, this means that enough information has been supplied to allow the game to be analyzed. For this to be true in general, various things are taken to be common knowledge.[2] The requirements were dramatized in Section 10.8 by quoting the philosopher Hobbes' characterization of man in terms of his strength of body, his passions, his experience and his reason.

In game theory, a player's strength of body is determined by the *rules of the game*. A player's reason is assumed to lead him to make decisions in accordance with the principles of *Bayesian rationality*.[3] This chapter focuses on the remaining properties of a man: his passions and his experience. These correspond to a player's *preferences* over the possible outcomes of the game, and the player's *beliefs* about the moves made by Chance in the game.

11.1.1 Knowing Your Enemy

Consider preferences in the first instance. It is not overly restrictive to assume that the players' preferences are common knowledge in many of the games that are used to illustrate game-theoretic ideas. In Chess, for example, it seems quite harmless to assume that it is common knowledge that both players prefer winning to losing. But what of a game like Russian Roulette? In Section 4.7, we saw that the way this game

---

[1]To be precise, a game is of perfect information if and only if the rules specify that each information set contains just one node.

[2]Although this does not mean that some games cannot be analyzed successfully under weaker assumptions. For example, to analyze the Prisoners' Dilemma, no more is needed than that each player know that *hawk* strongly dominates *dove*.

[3]The doubts of Section 10.8.2 can be put aside in this chapter. Harsanyi's theory of incomplete information is definitely a "small world" theory.

gets played by rational players depends on how risk-averse they are. However, it is not very realistic to assume that each player will have reliable information about how ready the other is to take risks, especially since both players have an incentive to pretend to be more reckless than they actually are. The same applies to bargaining games like those studied in Chapter 5. Players then have an incentive not only to misrepresent how risk-averse they are, but also to misrepresent how patient they are. In the Cournot Duopoly Game of Section 7.2.1, it seems a relatively innocent assumption that it is common knowledge that both firms seek to maximize profit. But a firm's profit depends partly on what its costs are. How reliably can one firm estimate the costs of another? The answer depends on the circumstances, but it will be clear that there will be many cases in which hard evidence about an opponent's costs may be very hard to acquire, particularly if the opponent understands the strategic importance of misleading rival firms about such matters.

Harsanyi's theory of incomplete information offers a means of getting a handle on such problems. Usually, it is said to be a theory of "games of incomplete information". However, strictly speaking, there is no such thing as a *game* of incomplete information. Harsanyi's theory is a technique for *completing* a structure in which information is incomplete. The theory leaves a great deal to the judgment of those who use it. It points a finger at what is missing in an informational structure, but does not say where the missing information is to be found. What it has to offer are the right questions. Coming up with the right answers is something that Harsanyi leaves to you and me.

If we can answer the questions adequately, the result will be a game of *imperfect* information. It is superfluous to say that the game that emerges *after* Harsanyi's theory has been applied is a game of *complete* information. If it wasn't, it wouldn't be a game.[4]

Harsanyi's theory is not very difficult. Otherwise it would not have been possible to sneak some examples of its use into

---

[4]However, it is necessary to live with the fact that many authors signal the fact that they have just used Harsanyi's theory by describing the end-product as a "game of incomplete information". Sometimes it is said that Harsanyi's theory makes "incomplete information a special case of imperfect information". However, this is a view that needs to be taken with a pinch of salt. Nothing guarantees that the questions posed by Harsanyi's theory have the sort of answers that his theory requires. If they do not, then it will simply be impossible to remodel the given problem of incomplete information as a game of imperfect information.

earlier chapters. It will be useful to return to one of these examples while the theory is being outlined in the next section.

11.2 Typecasting

The language of the theater lends itself very aptly to an exposition of Harsanyi's theory of incomplete information.[5] We can think of the rules of a two-player game as a *script*[6] with *roles* for two *actors*. The *casting director* is Chance.

There will be a set $\mathcal{M}$ of out-of-work male actors who turn up to be auditioned for the role of player I. Similarly, $\mathcal{F}$ is the set of out-of-work female actors who audition for the role of player II. Chance selects one of the actors from the set $\mathcal{M}$ to fill the role of player I. She also selects one of the actors from the set $\mathcal{F}$ to fill the role of player II. This move by Chance will be called the *casting move.*

An actor who has been cast in one of the roles will know this fact. But he or she will not know who has been cast in the opposing role. Actors must therefore decide what strategy to use in ignorance of the identity of their opponent.

The strategy an actor chooses will depend on his or her *type.* All actors are assumed to be Bayesian-rational (Section 3.6.2). It follows that an actor's type is entirely determined by his or her:

1. **Preferences.** These are specified by a Von Neumann and Morgenstern utility function defined over the set of outcomes allowed for in the script. It is important that these preferences may depend on the type of the actor who fills the opposing role.
2. **Beliefs.** These are specified by the subjective probabilities the actor assigns to the choices available to Chance at the casting move.[7]

---

[5]The standard version in which only players' preferences and beliefs are in doubt is described. However, one can use the theory equally well to deal with doubts about the rules of the game. Indeed, we did precisely this in Section 10.8.1. Aumann argues that one can also proceed in the same way when the players' rationality is in doubt, but this is a much more controversial application.

[6]Sometimes this is called a *game-form.*

[7]This casting move will be the root of the game of imperfect information that Harsanyi's theory requires be constructed. Of course, the actors' beliefs about later Chance moves will also matter, but it is assumed that these are given in terms of objective probabilities by the rules of the game. For example, if cards have to be dealt, the rules should specify a thorough and public shuffling.

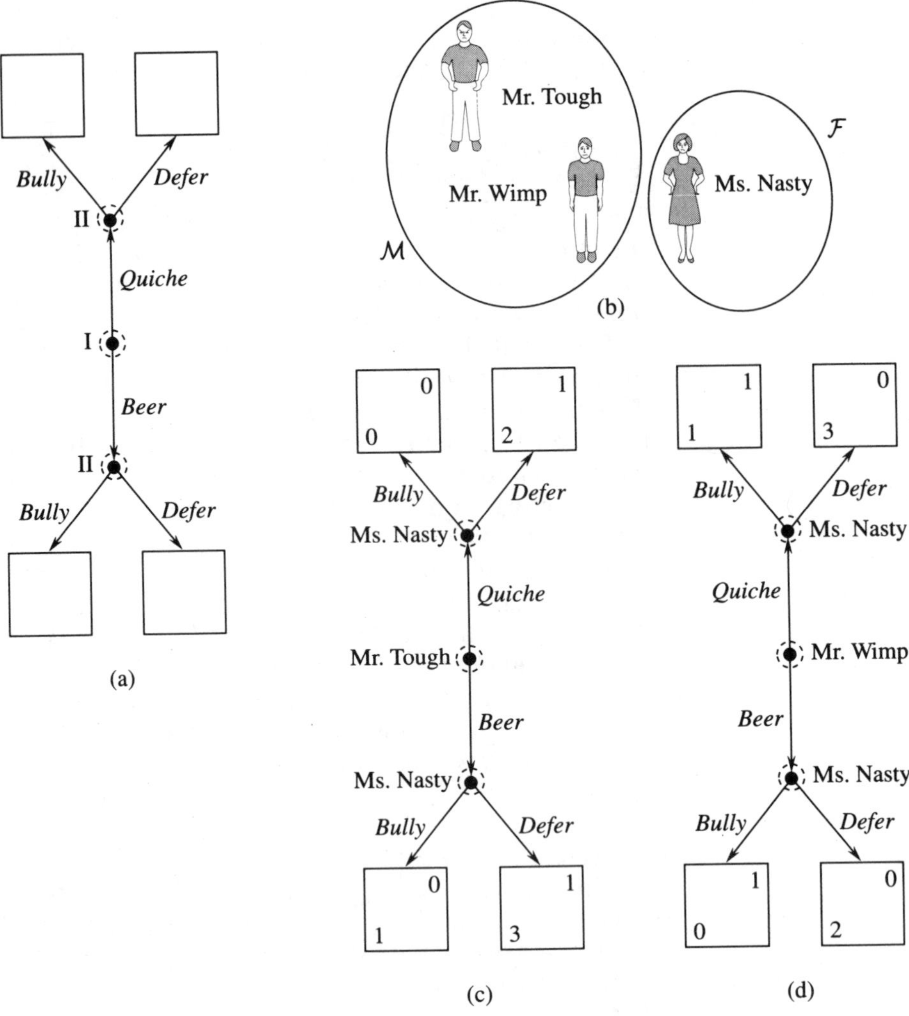

Figure 11.1 Completing an incomplete structure.

Such a description of an actor's type is too abstract to be easily appreciated without at least one concrete example. The game of Quiche studied in Section 10.5.1 will be used for this purpose.

11.2.1 Real Men Drink Beer

Quiche is an example of a game of imperfect information that emerges after Harsanyi's theory has been used to complete an incomplete information structure. What needs to be discussed is the process that leads to its emergence.

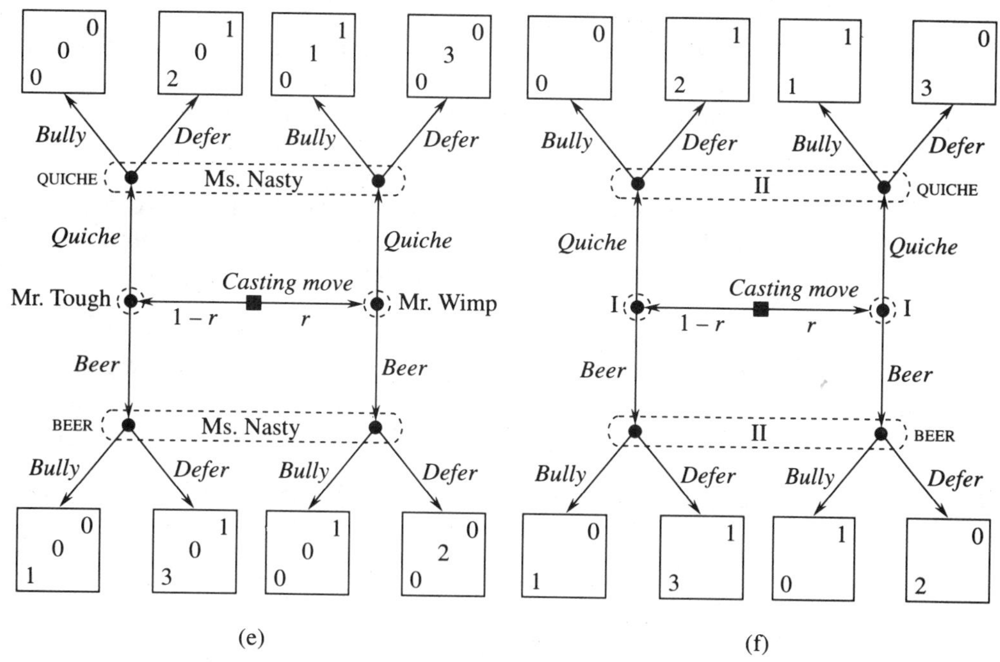

Figure 11.1 (continued)

Script. The script with which the story begins is illustrated in Figure 11.1(a). Notice that the payoff boxes are empty. Information that is necessary for a game-theoretic analysis is therefore missing. What should be written in the payoff boxes depends on the characteristics of the players. In our theatrical terminology, this means that we need to know the set of actors auditioning for each of the two roles.

Actors. The sets $\mathcal{M}$ and $\mathcal{F}$ are illustrated in Figure 11.1(b). Two actors are available for the role of player I: Mr. Tough and Mr. Wimp. Only Ms. Nasty is available for the role of player II.

Preferences. Figures 11.1(c) and 11.1(d) show how the payoff boxes would be filled if it were common knowledge who had been cast in each role. In brief, Ms. Nasty prefers deferring to Mr. Tough to bullying him. She prefers bullying Mr. Wimp to deferring to him. Both Mr. Tough and Mr. Wimp think that being deferred to is what they care about most, but, other things being equal, Mr. Tough prefers beer to quiche, and Mr. Wimp prefers quiche to beer.

Beliefs. Figures 11.1(c) and 11.1(d) summarize the *preferences* of the three types of actor. Next their *beliefs* must be considered. These beliefs concern the actors who will be selected at the casting move. All that is at issue here is whether Mr. Tough or Mr. Wimp gets selected for the role of player I. It is Ms. Nasty who will be ignorant about this question. It will be assumed that she attaches a subjective probability of $1 - r$ to Mr. Tough's being chosen and a subjective probability of r to Mr. Wimp's being chosen. (In Section 10.5.1, $r = \frac{2}{3}$).

Casting Move. Figure 11.1(e) includes the casting move. At the casting move, Chance selects Mr. Tough with probability $1 - r$, and Mr. Wimp with probability r.

Payoffs. Notice that each payoff box in Figure 11.1(e) contains *three* entries. The southwest corner has a payoff for Mr. Tough, the center has a payoff for Mr. Wimp, and the northeast corner has a payoff for Ms. Nasty. Figures 11.1(c) and 11.1(d) tell us what payoffs to write in the boxes in the case of an actor who is chosen to fill a role. An actor who is not chosen for a role is assigned a payoff of zero.[8] For example, if Mr. Tough eats quiche after being chosen for the role of player I and Ms. Nasty follows by deferring, then the appropriate triple of payoffs is $(2, 0, 1)$. The payoffs of 2 for Mr. Tough and 1 for Ms. Nasty come from Figure 11.1(c). Mr. Wimp gets 0 because he was not chosen to play.

Information Completed. Figure 11.1(a) has the form of a two-player game of perfect information. However, its information is incomplete. After the information is completed, the result is the three-player game of imperfect information given in Figure 11.1(e). It is important that all the details of this game of imperfect information are *common knowledge.* This is by no means an assumption that can be taken for granted. Sometimes it makes sense and sometimes it does not. In Quiche, for example, it is not very realistic that Ms. Nasty's beliefs should be common knowledge unless they are based on publicly available survey data about the distribution of different temperaments in the population at large.

[8]It does not matter what payoff is assigned to an actor who is not cast in a role since he or she does not get to influence anything. The choice of zero is just for convenience.

11.2.2 On with the Show

After completing an incomplete information structure, the result is a game of imperfect information. How should this be analyzed? There are two superficially different approaches depending on who is seen as being a player in the game.

Approach 1—Actors Are Players. This is the more natural approach for Quiche. Section 11.2.1 is therefore organized from this viewpoint.

In this approach, the actors are seen as separate and distinct individuals. They know that they may be cast in one of the roles in the game and so have decided in advance what strategy to use should this happen. Chance then decides who will actually play by randomly choosing a male actor for the role of player I, and a female actor for the role of player II. If the characteristics of the populations of male and female actors from which Chance makes her selection are matters of public record, then the probability with which any given actor is chosen can be assumed to be common knowledge. If there are m male actors and f female actors, the result will be an $(m + f)$-player game of imperfect information. Nothing special needs to be said about its analysis. It is just a game like any other. In particular, it is a good idea to begin by identifying its Nash equilibria.

Approach 2—Actors Are Agents. The second approach retains the *two*-player structure of the original script.

Imagine that the male actor cast in the role of player I consults Von Neumann about what strategy he should use. Similarly, the female actor cast in the role of player II consults Morgenstern. In order to induce Von Neumann and Morgenstern to give optimal advice, their commissions must be arranged so that each has identical preferences to the actor they are advising. Von Neumann will then give advice to the actor that is *contingent* on his type. For example, in Quiche, Von Neumann will recommend a different strategy to an actor cast in the role of player I who reports that he is Mr. Tough than he would to an actor who reports that he is Mr. Wimp. Similarly, Morgenstern will give type-contingent advice to the female actor cast in the role of player II.

This approach reduces the actors to puppets. The actual players in this version of the story are the guys who pull their strings: namely, Von Neumann and Morgenstern. Before Chance makes her casting decisions, Von Neumann and

Morgenstern have a complicated game to consider. Each must have instructions in readiness for every actor who might call upon them for advice. In the language of Section 10.4.2, each such actor is an *agent* for Von Neumann or Morgenstern.

At first sight, this second approach seems to lead to a simpler framework than the first approach. One can say that player I *is* Von Neumann and player II *is* Morgenstern. Only a *two*-player game need then be considered. But this two-player game is no simpler than the $(m + f)$-player game of the first approach. Although the latter game has many players, each player has a relatively simple strategy set. However, in the two-player game played by Von Neumann and Morgenstern, both players have complicated strategy sets. In fact, a pure strategy for Von Neumann consists of a *function* $F : \mathcal{M} \to S$, where S is the set of pure strategies assigned to role I in the original script. Once he has chosen F, he has decided on what instructions to give each of his agents. If the casting director casts actor a in role I, the strategy that Von Neumann recommends will be $F(a)$. As we learned in Section 8.2, the set of all functions $F : \mathcal{M} \to S$ is not something that is necessarily easy to handle even when $\mathcal{M}$ and S are not large sets.

It is therefore an illusion that the second approach is simpler than the first. The two are equivalent provided that each potential actor gets cast with positive probability. The situation is entirely analogous to that considered in Section 10.4.3. The first approach is simply a decentralized version of the second approach.

Phil 11.2.3 ⟶

Which Approach Should Be Used? From the mathematical point of view, the answer does not matter. One can pass back and forward between the two approaches, just as one can pass back and forward between mixed and behavioral strategies. Usually, the choice of approach depends on where the game came from. If there really are populations $\mathcal{M}$ and $\mathcal{F}$ from which Chance really does make an objective choice of who is to play, then the first approach is natural. But this is not always the case.

For example, in Section 10.8.1, there isn't really an infinite population of male actors auditioning for the role of player I, all with different information about how many times the Prisoners' Dilemma is to be repeated. The infinite population exists only in the *minds* of those playing. Actors other than those actually playing are mental constructs invented by the real actors in order to make sense of the information with which they are provided. The technique involved is very powerful, but one must bear in mind that, in such a story, the probabilities with which the mythical actors get chosen are entirely *subjective* constructs that exist only inside the heads of the actual players. One is assuming a great deal, when one assumes that these subjective constructs are common knowledge.

11.2.3 More Beer and Quiche

In the game of Quiche, the first approach of Section 11.2.2 reduces the original incomplete information structure to the three-player game of Figure 11.1(e), as described in Section 11.2.1. The second approach reduces it to the two-player game of Figure 11.1(f). Here Von Neumann is identified with player I and his payoffs are taken to be identical to those of Mr. Tough when he is advising Mr. Tough, and identical to those of Mr. Wimp when he is advising Mr. Wimp.[9] Morgenstern is identified with player II and hence just gets Ms. Nasty's payoff.

The strategic form of Figure 11.1(e) is a $2 \times 2 \times 4$ object. The strategic form of Figure 11.1(f) is a 4×4 object.[10] It is seldom a good idea to compute either strategic form in the first instance. An analysis that considers behavioral strategies in the extensive form is usually less troublesome. Section 10.4 does this for Quiche, using the second approach in the case when $r = \frac{2}{3}$. If the first approach had been used, the analysis would have been identical except that the wording would have occasionally been less cumbersome.

11.2.4 An Evolutionary Application

Phil 11.3 ⟶

Section 9.5.1 explains how evolutionary questions can sometimes usefully be discussed in game-theoretic terms. When doing so, we can often leave any agonizing over who the players are to the philosophy profession. But such a freewheeling attitude will not always suffice. It is then useful to think about things using the language of Harsanyi's theory.

Section 9.5 told a tale about an all-female society of dodos who compete for nesting sites by playing Chicken. To fit this into Harsanyi's framework, one must first begin by

---

[9]An alert reader might suspect that the strictures of Section 3.5.3 about comparing different players' utils is being violated here. However, if Von Neumann were awarded $3t + 5$ utils when advising a Mr. Tough whose payoff is t, and $17w - 23$ utils when advising a Mr. Wimp whose payoff is w, then the new game would be strategically equivalent to that of the text.

[10]It is given, for the case $r = \frac{2}{3}$, in Figure 10.11.

replacing the two sets $\mathcal{M}$ and $\mathcal{F}$ from which the actors are drawn by a single set $\mathcal{R}$. This will often contain only two agents: Ms. Normal and Ms. Mutant. Nature is the casting director. She selects two actors at random with replacement from $\mathcal{R}$ to fill the roles of player I and player II. The probabilities with which actors are chosen will reflect the frequencies with which the normal and mutant replicators exist in the population.

With the first approach of Section 11.2.2, we now have a game to study in which the real players are seen as Ms. Normal and Ms. Mutant with a simple strategy choice between *hawk* and *dove*. If one prefers the second approach of Section 11.2.2, the players can be identified instead with the roles I and II that the actors occupy. Neither Von Neumann nor Morgenstern must then be told the role of the actor to whom they are giving advice.[11] They will then necessarily give advice that is type-contingent but role-independent. The first approach is closer to the biological realities, but the second facilitates comparisons with the conventional equilibrium ideas of game theory.

11.3 Bayesian Equilibrium

Phil 11.4 ⟶

No special terminology is really needed to analyze the game that emerges after Harsanyi's methodology has been used to complete an incomplete information structure. Otherwise, it would not have been possible to analyze the Quiche game of Section 10.5.1 before any of the apparatus of Harsanyi's theory had been introduced. Much of the standard terminology is, in fact, more than a little confusing for beginners, and I have therefore been sparing in its use. In particular, nothing whatever has been said about the idea of a *Bayesian equilibrium*.

The economics literature is full of references to "Bayesian equilibria in games of incomplete information". What this means in precise terms usually has to be deduced from the context. The context always involves an underlying problem in which information is incomplete. The reference to a Bayesian equilibrium signals that this problem is to be dealt with using Harsanyi's methodology. It is important to understand that the manner in which the incomplete information

[11]If they were to be told, the model would need to be changed so that dodos are able to condition their behavior on whether they are player I or player II. Sometimes this is appropriate, as when one of the protagonists has a pre-established "claim" to a territory. But this possibility was excluded in Section 9.5.

structure is to be completed is not somehow built into the definition of a Bayesian equilibrium. In particular, the author still has to tell us who the potential actors are, and how Chance chooses amongst them. After this has been done, a game of imperfect information emerges. What one is to understand by a "Bayesian equilibrium in a game of incomplete information" is nothing other than a Nash equilibrium in the game of imperfect information that emerges after the incomplete information structure has been completed. Nearly always, the terminology adopted uses the second approach of Section 11.2.2, and the players' choices are expressed in terms of behavioral strategies.

Some authors like to recognize the fact that they are making use of nothing more than the idea of a Nash equilibrium by speaking of a *Bayesian-Nash* equilibrium rather than a Bayesian equilibrium. This seems like a respectable compromise to me. The "Bayesian" at the front reminds you to ask yourself who the actors are and what the casting move is, while the "Nash" at the rear tells you what calculations need to be made. However, it still makes life difficult for the novice who very reasonably thinks that the mention of Bayes must surely mean that Bayes' Rule is necessarily going to be invoked somewhere along the way.

11.4 Continuous Random Variables

Review 11.5 ⟶

It will be clear by now that Harsanyi's theory of incomplete information involves no new concepts at all. Insofar as it is difficult to use in practice, it is because one has to keep many things in mind simultaneously. Paradoxically, the technical difficulties are often eased by looking at models with *infinite* populations of actors.

Section 2.2.1 explains that a random variable is a function $X : \Omega \to \mathbb{R}$. So far, only *discrete* random variables have been considered, since attention has been restricted to finite sample spaces Ω. But, if we are to exploit the simplifications of Harsanyi's theory that become possible when infinite populations are considered, it will be necessary to allow *infinite* sample spaces.

11.4.1 Probability Density Functions

A fair pointer is spun. When it stops spinning, the clockwise angle ω between where it starts and finishes is measured in degrees. You then win $\$\sqrt{\omega/10}$. Since $0 \leq \omega < 360$, your winnings will be something between \$0 and \$6. What is the

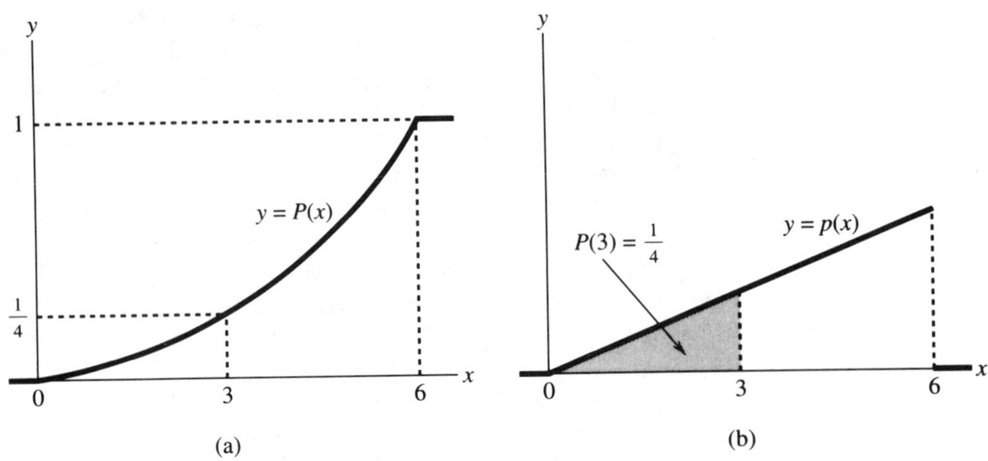

Figure 11.2 Probability distribution and density functions.

probability that you will win no more than \$3 if each angle is equally likely?

The sample space is $\Omega = [0, 360)$. The random variable $X : \Omega \to \mathbb{R}$ of interest is defined by $X(\omega) = \sqrt{\omega/10}$. The *probability distribution* of the random variable X is a function $P : \mathbb{R} \to [0, 1]$ defined by

$$P(x) = \text{prob}\{\omega : X(\omega) \leq x\}.$$

We care about the value of $P(3)$, but $P(x)$ will be calculated for all values of x.

Notice first that $P(x) = 0$ when $x < 0$, because it is impossible that you will win less than \$0. Similarly, $P(x) = 1$ when $x > 6$. When $0 \leq x \leq 6$, $P(x)$ can be calculated using the fact that $X(\omega) \leq x$ if and only if $\omega \leq 10x^2$. The value of $P(x)$ is therefore the probability that ω lies in the interval $[0, 10x^2]$. Since each angle is equally likely, this probability must be proportional to the length of the interval. Hence

$$P(x) = 10x^2/360 = \left(\frac{x}{6}\right)^2 \qquad (0 \leq x \leq 6).$$

In particular, the probability $P(3)$ that you win \$3 or less is $(3/6)^2 = \frac{1}{4}$.

Figure 11.2(a) shows the graph of the probability distribution function $P : \mathbb{R} \to [0, 1]$. Sometimes a random variable has a probability *density* function as well as a probability *distribution* function.[12] When this is true, the probability density

[12] But nothing guarantees that a random variable has a probability density function. Indeed, random variables in earlier chapters could take only

function is just the derivative of the probability distribution function, wherever the derivative is defined. For example, the probability density function $p : \mathbb{R} \to \mathbb{R}_+$ for the random variable X we have been considering is defined by

$$p(x) = P'(x) = \frac{2x}{36} = \frac{x}{18}\,.$$

when $0 < x < 6$. When $x < 0$ or $x > 6$, $p(x) = P'(x) = 0$. When $x = 0$ or $x = 6$, it does not matter how $p(x)$ is defined.

The reason that probability density functions are useful is that they allow probabilities to be expressed as integrals. For example, $\text{prob}(0 < X \leq 3)$ is equal to the shaded area in Figure 11.2(b). In general, the probability that X lies between a and b is equal to the area under the graph of the probability density function between a and b. To see this, note that $\text{prob}(a < X \leq b) = P(b) - P(a)$. But, since integrating a derivative takes you back to where you started,

$$\int_a^b p(x)\,dx = \int_a^b P'(x)\,dx = \big[\,P(x)\,\big]_a^b = P(b) - P(a)\,.$$

In particular,

$$\text{prob}(0 < X \leq 3) = \int_0^3 \tfrac{1}{18}x\,dx = \tfrac{1}{4}\,.$$

11.4.2 Fundamental Theorem of Calculus

The fundamental result of calculus is that integration is the opposite of differentiation. This fact was just used in demonstrating how to use probability density functions. However, the fundamental theorem gets used whenever someone carries through an integration. If p is continuous on $[a, b]$ and

one of a set of discrete values. Such a *discrete random variable* does not have a probability density function. A graph of its probability distribution function looks like a flight of steps. Such a step function can be differentiated except where it jumps. It therefore has a zero derivative "almost everywhere". But this zero derivative is useless as a candidate for a probability density function p because we certainly shall not recover the probability distribution function P by integrating the zero function. Even probability distribution functions that increase continuously can have zero derivatives "almost everywhere". Cognoscenti will know that *almost everywhere* means "on a set of Lebesgue measure zero". They will also know that the condition for a probability distribution function to admit a probability density function is that it be *absolutely continuous*. Others should simply note that there will sometimes be unstated restrictions on the range of validity of what is said in the text. In particular, various equations would be qualified with the phrase "almost everywhere" in a formal discussion.

$Q'(x) = p(x)$ for each x in (a, b), then the fundamental theorem tells us that

$$\int_a^b p(x)\,dx = \int_a^b Q'(x)\,dx = \Big[\,Q(x)\Big]_a^b = Q(b) - Q(a)\,.$$

The function Q can be anything whose derivative is p. Such a Q is called a *primitive* or *indefinite integral* for p. Primitives are never unique. If Q is a primitive, then so is $Q + c$, where c is any constant.

The simplest example of a primitive for p is the function P defined by

$$P(x) = \int_a^x p(y)\,dy\,.$$

To check that P is a primitive, one need only remember that the fundamental theorem tells us that differentiation is the opposite of integration, and so[13]

$$P'(x) = \frac{d}{dx}\int_a^x p(y)\,dy = p(x)\,. \tag{11.1}$$

It may seem superfluous to state something so obvious as (11.1), but the appalling notation commonly used for primitives often leads to confusion on this issue. The appalling notation consists of writing $Q(x) = \int p(x)\,dx$ in specifying a primitive Q. This notation invites beginners to imagine that, when they use the fact that $Q'(x) = p(x)$, they have somehow contrived to carry out the absurd operation of differentiating with respect to a variable of integration.[14] However, once this misunderstanding is put aside, nothing could be simpler than differentiating an indefinite integral as in (11.1). One simply evaluates the integrand at the upper limit of integration. This will be a useful fact to remember in the next chapter.

11.4.3 Integrating by Parts

Let u and v be functions that are continuous on $[a, b]$ and differentiable on (a, b). Let U and V be primitives for the two functions. The formula for differentiating a product says that $(UV)' = U'V + UV' = uV + UV'$. From the fundamental theorem, it follows that

$$\int_a^b (uV + UV')\,dx = \int_a^b (UV)'\,dx = \Big[\,UV\Big]_a^b$$

[13]If an integrable p has discontinuities, then the result is still true, provided the incantation "almost everywhere" is not forgotten.

[14]Think about differentiating $\int_0^3 y^2\,dy = 9$ with respect to y.

$$\int_a^b uV\,dx = \left[\,UV\right]_a^b - \int_a^b UV'\,dx\,.$$

This is the formula for integrating by parts. It is useful whenever a product has to be integrated. You have to decide which of the terms of the product to be integrated should be u and which should be V. Usually you will want to make V whichever term is the more complicated, since it may become simpler when differentiated. You also get a choice about which primitive U for u to use. Usually it is best to choose a primitive that vanishes at one of the limits of integration. (See, for example, Exercise 11.10.17.)

11.4.4 Expectation

Section 2.2.2 explains how expected values are calculated by multiplying each possible value of the random variable by its probability and then summing. The equivalent definition for a continuous random variable X with a probability density function p is

$$\mathcal{E}X = \int xp(x)\,dx\,,$$

where the range of integration extends over all values taken by X. For example, your dollar expectation in the problem of Section 11.4.1 is \$4 because

$$\mathcal{E}X = \int_0^6 xp(x)\,dx = \int_0^6 \tfrac{1}{18}x^2\,dx = \tfrac{1}{18}\left[\,\tfrac{1}{3}x^3\right]_0^6 = 4\,.$$

This expectation is easy to calculate, but often one needs to know how to integrate by parts, as in Exercise 11.10.21.

11.5 Duopoly with Incomplete Information

Econ 11.6 ⟶

Some recapitulation of the Cournot duopoly model of Section 7.2.1 may be helpful. Recall that firm I and firm II are producers of widgets. Each simultaneously decides how many widgets to produce. If firm I produces q_1 widgets and firm II produces q_2 widgets, the price p at which widgets sell is determined by the demand equation $p = M - q_1 - q_2$. Each firm is assumed to seek to maximize its expected profit, where firm i's profit is given by

$$\pi_i(q_1, q_2) = (p - c_i)q_i = (M - c_i - q_1 - q_2)q_i\,.$$

Here c_i is firm i's unit cost. This is assumed to be constant, and so each widget costs c_i to manufacture.

If all this information is common knowledge, one may proceed as in Section 7.2.1 and compute a Nash equilibrium $(\tilde{q}_1, \tilde{q}_2)$. When $c_1 = c_2 = c$, we found a unique Nash equilibrium with $\tilde{q}_1 = \tilde{q}_2 = \frac{1}{3}(M - c)$.

11.5.1 Incomplete Information About Costs

In the story[15] that follows, it continues to be common knowledge that firm II's cost is c, but now only firm I knows its own unit cost for sure.

Harsanyi's theory tells us to begin by asking what actors we wish to consider. Let $\mathcal{M}$ be the set of all the possible unit costs that might characterize firm I. Each a in $\mathcal{M}$ will correspond to a possible actor whom Chance might select to run firm I. The preferences of Mr. a are specified by his profit function

$$\pi_a(q_1, q_2) = (M - a - q_1 - q_2)q_1 .$$

Recall, however, that an actor's type is determined not only by his preferences but also by his beliefs. It will therefore be necessary to return to Mr. a later to specify what he believes.

In the meantime, consider firm II. If Chance selects Ms. b to run firm II, her preferences are fixed by her profit function

$$\pi_b(q_1, q_2) = (M - c - q_1 - q_2)q_2 .$$

However, Ms. b's beliefs are not necessarily fixed. To make things interesting, it will be assumed that each b in the set $\mathcal{F}$ corresponds to a different piece of information about firm I's technology. Each Ms. b therefore has her own beliefs about firm I's unit cost. These will be summarized by a probability density function $m_b : \mathcal{M} \to \mathbb{R}_+$. In particular, Ms. b's expectation of firm I's unit cost is

$$\overline{a}(b) = \int_{\mathcal{M}} a m_b(a)\, da .$$

Now return to Mr. a. His beliefs were not specified. However, just as Ms. b's probability density function describes her beliefs about which Mr. a is running firm I, so Mr. a needs a probability density function to describe his beliefs about which Ms. b is running firm II. To keep things as simple as

[15] This is an elaboration of Exercise 7.9.15.

possible,[16] all Mr. a's will be assumed to have the same probability density function $f : \mathcal{F} \to \mathbb{R}_+$. In particular, any Mr. a will have the same expectation $\overline{\overline{a}}$ of what Ms. b's expectation of firm I's unit cost will be. In fact:

$$\overline{\overline{a}} = \int_{\mathcal{F}} \overline{a}(b) f(b)\, db\,.$$

If everything specified so far is common knowledge,[17] then the original incomplete information problem has been converted into a game of imperfect information. It is usual, in this context, to regard it as a two-player game. That is, in the language of Section 11.2.2, player I will be identified with Von Neumann who regards each Mr. a as one of his agents. Player II is identified with Morgenstern. He similarly regards each Ms. b as one of his agents.

Player I has to choose a *function* $Q_1 : \mathcal{M} \to \mathbb{R}_+$. If Mr. a is chosen to run firm I, he tells Von Neumann his type, and asks how much he should produce. Von Neumann's reply will be $Q_1(a)$. Similarly, player II chooses a function $Q_2 : \mathcal{F} \to \mathbb{R}_+$. If Ms. b is chosen to run firm II, her advice from Morgenstern will be $Q_2(b)$.

Finding a Nash Equilibrium. For a Nash equilibrium, each Q_1 and Q_2 must be a best reply to the other. Thus, player I's advice to each Mr. a must be optimal given that player II has chosen Q_2. Hence $q_1 = Q_1(a)$ must maximize Mr. a's expected profit:

$$\begin{aligned}\pi_a(q_1, Q_2) &= \mathcal{E}_b\,\{\pi_a(q_1, Q_2(b))\}\\ &= \int_{\mathcal{F}} (M - a - q_1 - Q_2(b))q_1 f(b)\, db\,.\end{aligned}$$

To find the maximizing q_1, differentiate[18] this expression

---

[16]If different actors who might be running firm I were allowed to have different beliefs, it would be necessary to expand the set $\mathcal{M}$. The type of an actor $\mathcal{M}$ would then specify, not only his unit cost a, but also what he believed about the actor running firm II.

[17]This is a *big* assumption here. To make Harsanyi's methodology work, one always has to cut off the chains that go "I believe that he believes that I believe ..." somewhere. How much sense it makes to do so depends on the circumstances.

[18]Do not be afraid to differentiate under the integral sign. This works for the same reason that the derivative of a sum is the sum of the derivatives. Only in pathological situations do difficulties arise. If you are still worried about differentiating under integral signs, you can integrate *before* differentiating in this case.

with respect to q_1, keeping everything else constant. Then set the derivative equal to zero. This yields

$$\begin{aligned} 0 &= \int_{\mathcal{F}} (M - a - 2q_1 - Q_2(b))f(b)\,db \\ &= (M - a - 2q_1) - \overline{Q}_2, \end{aligned}$$

where $\overline{Q}_2$ is Mr. a's expectation of firm II's output.[19] It follows that the function Q_1 that is a best reply to the function Q_2 is given by

$$Q_1(a) = \tfrac{1}{2}(M - a - \overline{Q}_2). \tag{11.2}$$

The advice that player II gives to Ms. b must also be optimal given that player I has chosen Q_1. Hence $q_2 = Q_2(b)$ must maximize Ms. b's expected profit:

$$\begin{aligned} \pi_b(Q_1, q_2) &= \mathcal{E}_a\{\pi_b(Q_1(a), q_2)\} \\ &= \int_{\mathcal{M}} (M - c - Q_1(a) - q_2)q_2\, m_b(a)\,da \\ &= \int_{\mathcal{M}} (M - c - \tfrac{1}{2}(M - a - \overline{Q}_2) - q_2)q_2\, m_b(a)\,da\,. \end{aligned}$$

Differentiate this expression with respect to q_2 keeping everything else constant, and then set the result equal to zero. This yields

$$0 = \tfrac{1}{2}M - c + \tfrac{1}{2}\overline{Q}_2 - 2q_2 + \tfrac{1}{2}\overline{a}(b)\,.$$

It follows that the function Q_2, which is a best reply to the function Q_1 that satisfies (11.2), is given by

$$Q_2(b) = \tfrac{1}{4}M - \tfrac{1}{2}c + \tfrac{1}{4}\overline{Q}_2 + \tfrac{1}{4}\overline{a}(b)\,. \tag{11.3}$$

So far, we have been working with $\overline{Q}_2$ without knowing what it is. However, since it is the expected value of Q_2, it can be computed from (11.3). In fact,

$$\begin{aligned} \overline{Q}_2 &= \tfrac{1}{4}M - \tfrac{1}{2}c + \tfrac{1}{4}\overline{Q}_2 + \tfrac{1}{4}\int_{\mathcal{F}} \overline{a}(b)f(b)\,db \\ \tfrac{3}{4}\overline{Q}_2 &= \tfrac{1}{4}M - \tfrac{1}{2}c + \tfrac{1}{4}\overline{\overline{a}} \\ \overline{Q}_2 &= \tfrac{1}{3}(M - 2c + \overline{\overline{a}})\,. \end{aligned}$$

[19]Given by $\overline{Q}_2 = \int_{\mathcal{F}} Q_2(b)f(b)\,db$. Keep in mind that $\int_{\mathcal{F}} f(b)\,db = 1$ because it is certain that b is in $\mathcal{F}$.

On substituting this conclusion in (11.3), we obtain formulas for the functions Q_1 and Q_2 that make (Q_1, Q_2) a Nash equilibrium. The formulas are

$$Q_1(a) = \tfrac{1}{6}(2M + 2c - 3a - \bar{\bar{a}}),$$
$$Q_2(b) = \tfrac{1}{12}(4M - 8c + 3\bar{a}(b) + \bar{\bar{a}}).$$

Discussion. Two points are worthy of note. The first is that, in the special case when it is common knowledge that firm I's unit cost is c, $a = \bar{a}(b) = \bar{\bar{a}} = c$, and hence the result collapses back to the situation studied in Section 7.2.1.

Secondly, it is worth noting how firm I's output depends on what the guy running the firm believes about what the guy running firm II believes about firm I's unit cost. This dependence is explicit in the term $\bar{\bar{a}}$. The same term also directly affects firm II's output.

To take an extreme case, suppose that the Mr. a running firm I actually has a very low unit cost. This would put him in a powerful position if his low unit cost were common knowledge. However, it may be that nearly all Ms. b's believe it very unlikely that firm I has low unit cost. If so, then $\bar{a}(b)$ and hence $\bar{\bar{a}}$ will be large. A kibitzer who knew nothing about who believes what might then be very puzzled about why firm I's production is so low and firm II's is so high.

11.6 Purification

Math 11.7 →

A recurring matter of concern in the latter part of this book has been the story to be told about Nash equilibria in mixed strategies (Sections 6.4.3, 7.1.4 and 9.3.3). The interpretation pursued here eliminates the need for players to be seen as actively randomizing their strategy choices. Each player makes a no-nonsense choice of a pure strategy without any spinning of roulette wheels or rattling of dice-boxes. However, the other players are uncertain about what this choice will be. They therefore attach subjective probabilities to the options open to their opponents, and then optimize given these beliefs. That is to say, each player chooses *as though* their opponents were using mixed strategies.

Such a story is said to *purify* the idea of a mixed Nash equilibrium. Insofar as any mixing occurs, it occurs inside the players' heads as they seek to predict what their

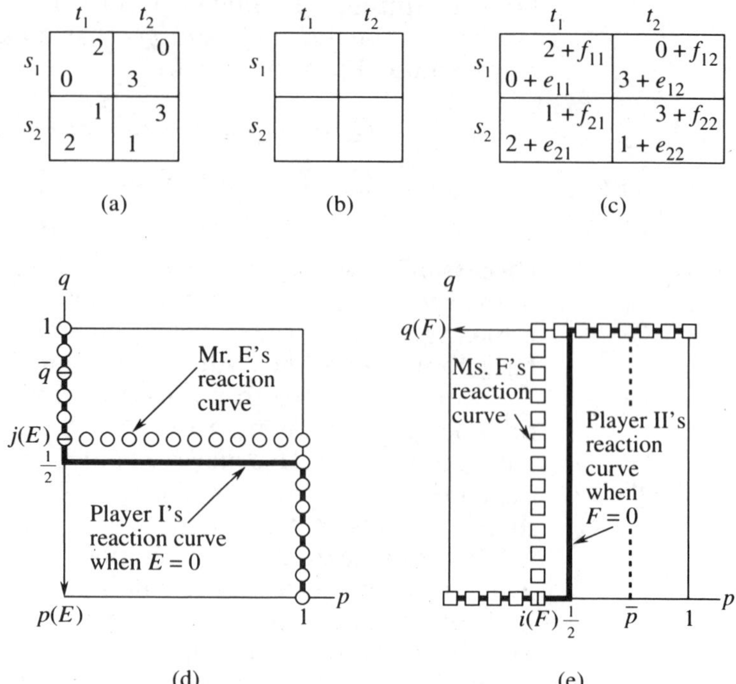

Figure 11.3 Purifying mixed strategies.

opponents will do. The equilibrium then becomes an equilibrium in *beliefs* rather than an equilibrium in *actions*.[20]

At first sight, a purification story does not seem to make sense. If nobody is randomizing, how come people are uncertain about what will happen? As an application of his theory of incomplete information, Harsanyi offered an elegant model that explains how this circle can be squared. His argument will be outlined here for the bimatrix game of Figures 7.7(a) and 9.5(a). The game is repeated yet again as Figure 11.3(a). Player I's payoff matrix in the game will be denoted by A, and player II's by B.

Figure 9.5(b) shows both players' reaction curves for the game. They cross just once, showing that the game has a unique Nash equilibrium. This Nash equilibrium would usually be described by saying that both players use each of their pure strategies with probability $\frac{1}{2}$. Our task is to formulate a purified alternative interpretation.

[20]This is an attractive idea but it should not be allowed to displace other interpretations altogether. In particular, Poker players will often be wise to randomize very actively.

Fluctuating Payoffs. Since the players are not to randomize, the random element that creates uncertainty in everybody's mind has got to come from somewhere else. Harsanyi supposes that there is some small uncertainty in each player's mind about what the other players' preferences are. This does not mean that there need be any doubt about whether the opponent prefers \$100 to a slap in the face. However, as noted in Section 11.1.2, there may perhaps be small uncertainties about how risk-averse an opponent is. Indeed, a person's attitude to risk may vary slightly from day to day. Such variations will be reflected in a player's Von Neumann and Morgenstern utility function, and hence in the payoffs to the game. Introducing such uncertainty creates an incomplete information situation. This will be studied using the first approach of Section 11.2.2.

The script with which the model begins is shown in Figure 11.3(b). The fact that the cells in this table are empty indicates that information is incomplete. An actor, Mr. E, in the set $\mathcal{M}$ of male actors will be identified with a 2×2 matrix E. The entries of E represent fluctuations from player I's payoffs in the basic game of Figure 11.3(a). An actor, Ms. F, in the set $\mathcal{F}$ of female actors will also be identified with a 2×2 matrix F representing fluctuations from player II's payoffs in the basic game of Figure 11.3(a). Thus, if it were common knowledge who had been cast in each role, then the game being played would be that of Figure 11.3(c). However, the actor, Mr. E, cast in role I knows only that his own payoff matrix is $A + E$. He is uncertain about the payoff matrix of his opponent. Similarly, the actor, Ms. F, cast in role II knows only that her own payoff matrix is $B + F$.

Specifying the actors' payoff matrices determines their preferences. As regards their beliefs, it is common knowledge that the casting director's selections of Mr. E and Ms. F are made independently. We shall not need to write down what the probability density functions are that govern this choice.[21]

Computing a Nash Equilibrium. Before the casting move, each Mr. E chooses a 2×1 column vector $P(E)$. Such column vectors represent his mixed strategies. The second coordinate of $P(E)$ will be denoted by $p(E)$. This is the probability with which $P(E)$ requires Mr. E's *second* pure strategy to be used. If our purification project is successful, the mixed strategy

[21] Looking back over Section 11.5.1, you will find that we did not really need to specify the probability density functions there either.

$P(E)$ will actually turn out to be a pure strategy and so $p(E)$ will be 0 or 1. Player II does not know what E is, but she can compute that the expected mixed strategy choice by player I is $\overline{P} = \mathcal{E}_E\{P(E)\}$. The second coordinate of this 2×1 column vector will be denoted by $\overline{p}$.

Similar notation is needed for Ms. F. She chooses a 2×1 $Q(F)$ that represents a mixed strategy for her. Its second coordinate is denoted by $q(F)$. Player I's calculation of the expected mixed strategy choice by player II yields that $\overline{Q} = \mathcal{E}_F\{Q(F)\}$. The second coordinate of this 2×1 column vector will be denoted by $\overline{q}$.

Recall from Section 6.4.4, that Mr. E's payoff when he is matched with Ms. F is given by $P(E)^\top(A+E)Q(F)$. Since he does not know who his opponent is, he calculates the expected value of this quantity:

$$\begin{aligned}\mathcal{E}_F\{P(E)^\top(A+E)Q(F)\} &= P(E)^\top(A+E)\mathcal{E}_F\{Q(F)\}\\ &= P(E)^\top(A+E)\overline{Q}\,. \qquad (11.4)\end{aligned}$$

Similarly, Ms. F's expected payoff is:

$$\begin{aligned}\mathcal{E}_E\{P(E)^\top(B+F)Q(F)\} &= \mathcal{E}_E\{P(E)^\top\}(B+F)Q(F)\\ &= \overline{P}^\top(B+F)Q(F)\,. \qquad (11.5)\end{aligned}$$

If each actor is making a best reply to the choices of the others, as required for a Nash equilibrium, then (11.4) tells us that $P(E)$ must be a best reply to $\overline{Q}$ in a game in which player I's payoff matrix is $A+E$. Figure 11.3(d) shows player I's reaction curve in such a game.[22] In seeking a best reply to $\overline{Q}$, Mr. E cares about whether $\overline{q} > j(E)$ or $\overline{q} < j(E)$. In the former case, he takes $p(E) = 0$; in the latter case he takes $p(E) = 1$. Only when $\overline{q} = j(E)$ is it possible that Mr. E might use a mixed strategy because it is only then that he is indifferent between his two pure strategies.

The corresponding situation for Ms. F is shown in Figure 11.3(e). She takes $q(F) = 0$ if $\overline{p} < i(F)$, and $q(F) = 1$ if $\overline{p} > i(F)$. Only when $\overline{p} = i(F)$ might she use a mixed strategy.

Small Fluctuations. So far no use has been made of the fact that the entries in E and F represent *small* fluctuations in the payoffs of the game of Figure 11.3(a). This requirement is needed so that the reaction curves of Figures 11.3(d) and 11.3(e) are close to the reaction curves for the case when E

[22]Recall that, in such diagrams, our convention is to graph the probabilities with which each player uses his or her *second* pure strategy.

and F are the zero matrix. In particular, both $i(F)$ and $j(E)$ will then both be close to $\frac{1}{2}$ for all E and F.[23]

It follows that $\overline{p}$ and $\overline{q}$ must be close to $\frac{1}{2}$. This conclusion is a consequence of the fact that the original game of Figure 11.3(a) has no pure strategy equilibria. Suppose, for example, that $\overline{p}$ were so much larger than $\frac{1}{2}$ that $i(F) < \frac{1}{2}$ for all F. Then $q(F) = 1$ for all F and so $\overline{q} = 1$. Hence $p(E) = 0$ for all E, and so $\overline{p} = 0$. But this is not consistent with the assumption that $\overline{p} > \frac{1}{2}$.

Taking Stock. What does the argument show?

1. All actors use a *pure* strategy.[24]
2. The beliefs of the actor in role I about what his opponent will do are summarized by $\overline{q}$. This is the probability with which it seems to player I that player II will use her second pure strategy. Similarly, $\overline{p}$ is the probability with which it seems to player II that player I will use his first pure strategy.
3. When the fluctuations become small, $\overline{p}$ and $\overline{q}$ approach $\frac{1}{2}$.

Thus, although the players actually use *pure* strategies, their *beliefs* about what the opponent will do approach the Nash equilibrium of the underlying game as the fluctuations in the payoffs become vanishingly small. This is the promised purification of the mixed Nash equilibrium.

11.7 Auctions and Mechanism Design

Econ 11.8 ⟶

It is traditional that those who seek revelation must first be purified. The previous section provided an initiation into what passes for a purification rite in game theory. The time has therefore come to unveil the mysteries of the revelation principle. However, first something needs to be said about the problem of *designing* games to meet a specific purpose.

11.7.1 Auctions

People with objects to sell usually want to sell them for the highest price they can get. Sometimes, they have no choice

[23]To be precise, let all entries of E and F be less than δ in absolute value. Then, given any $\varepsilon > 0$, there exists δ_0 such that $|i(F) - \frac{1}{2}| < \varepsilon$ and $|j(E) - \frac{1}{2}| < \varepsilon$ provided $0 < \delta < \delta_0$.

[24]Except possibly for the Mr. E for whom $\overline{q} = j(E)$ and the Ms. F for whom $\overline{p} = i(F)$. But the probability that either will be chosen at the casting move is zero.

but to bargain with prospective purchasers as discussed in Chapter 5. Often, there is an established market that takes the problem of price-setting out of their hands. However, in some cases, the seller can choose a set of rules that govern how her object will be sold. Such a set of rules is called a *mechanism* for selling the object. A risk-neutral seller with the power to commit herself to a specific selling mechanism will obviously want to choose whatever mechanism maximizes the expected selling-price. She will therefore be seeking an *optimal* mechanism.

Whenever the question of what is *optimal* arises, it is first necessary to consider what is *feasible.* What is the set of mechanisms from which the seller can choose? This is seldom an easy question to answer in precise terms. Indeed, the revelation principle is useful largely because it allows the question to be evaded for some purposes. However, it is not hard to give examples of some of the mechanisms a seller might consider. We call the mechanisms to be considered *auctions*, although they do not necessarily involve an auctioneer with a block and hammer. Where it matters, everybody will be assumed to be risk-neutral in an attempt to keep things simple.

The simplest kind of auction is perhaps that conducted by retail outlets. One might call this a *take-it-or-leave-it auction.* A price is written on the object and prospective buyers can take it or leave it.[25]

A *sealed-bid auction* is a little more complicated. Each potential buyer privately writes his or her bid on a piece of paper and seals it in an envelope. The seller commits herself to selling the object to whoever makes the highest bid. (She needs some means of breaking ties. Our assumption will always be that the winner is chosen at random from those who make the highest bid.)

The so-called[26] *English auction* is the most commonly used type of auction. An auctioneer invites oral bids. The bidding continues until no-one is willing to go above the last bid made. Whoever made the final bid then gets the object at the price bid.

Dutch auctions require the auctioneer to begin by announcing a high price. This is then lowered gradually until a buyer

---

[25]Although the customer ought not to be too ready to believe that the store is *really* committed to this mechanism. Even the most high-class stores will often resort to bargaining about their more valuable merchandise if pressed sufficiently firmly.

[26]I suspect it is called this only to distinguish it from a Dutch auction.

calls a halt. The first buyer to do so then acquires the object at the price outstanding when he or she intervened. Used furniture stores sometimes run a Dutch auction by reducing the price of unsold pieces by 10% each month.

Other more exotic auctions can also be considered. Instructors in game theory courses, for example, are fond of auctioning a dollar according to the following rules. The bidding is as in an English auction, with the highest bidder getting the dollar, but *everyone* pays their highest bid *including* those who do not win the dollar.[27]

In a *Vickrey auction*, the object is sold to the highest bidder, but at the highest price bid by a *loser*. This will be the *second*-highest price unless there is a tie for first place. (The winner is then chosen at random from the highest bidders.) Only the case when the bids are submitted using the sealed-bid mechanism will be considered. (If confusion is possible, one can always make clear what sort of sealed-bid auction is being considered by distinguishing between first-price and second-price auctions as in Section 0.1.2.)

At first sight it may seem crazy for a seller to choose a Vickrey auction. Why should she settle for the second-highest price? Why not use a first-price, sealed-bid auction and sell the object to the highest bidder at the the price he bid? This is one of those paradoxical questions that were considered in the Introduction. The reason is that the seller stands to get higher bids if a Vickrey auction is used. In fact, in a Vickrey auction, it is a weakly dominating strategy for each buyer to seal his true valuation[28] of the object into his envelope. You can never benefit from bidding *below* your true valuation, because, whatever bids the other buyers may have sealed in their envelopes, bidding below your own valuation can only lessen your probability of winning the auction without altering the amount you will pay if you win. Equally, you can never benefit from bidding *above* your true valuation because, if this is necessary in order to win, it must be because some other player has submitted a bid that is at least equal to your true valuation. In this case, you would have to pay at least your true valuation if you won, and perhaps you would have to pay more.

Using a Vickrey auction therefore guarantees the seller the second-highest valuation amongst the set of potential buyers,

---

[27]My experience is that American students will bid, sometimes quite fiercely. English students will not.

[28]This is the same as his *reservation price*—the price that makes him indifferent between acquiring the object and leaving it in the seller's hands.

provided that these can be counted on to use the weakly dominating strategy (Exercise 11.10.31). An English auction does no better. In fact, it generates exactly the same outcome. Nobody is going to stop bidding in an English auction if there is still an opportunity to buy the object for less than his valuation, and nobody is going to continue bidding once his last rival has stopped raising. Like Vickrey auctions, English auctions therefore result in the object being sold at the second-highest valuation among the potential buyers (Exercise 11.10.33). What is more surprising is that one cannot count on doing any better with a first-price sealed-bid auction (Section 0.1.2 and Exercise 11.10.39). Nor does a Dutch auction advance matters at all. Just as an English auction is essentially the same as a Vickrey auction, so a Dutch auction is essentially the same as a first-price, sealed-bid auction (Exercise 11.10.34).

Of course, if the seller *knew* all the buyers' true valuations, she could sell the object to the buyer with the highest valuation at his or her reservation price.[29] Economists would then say that she had extracted the entire surplus from the situation, and hence achieved a "first-best" outcome. However, the seller will seldom be well-informed about the buyers' true valuations. She will therefore have to settle for a "second-best" outcome. How much of the surplus she is able to extract will depend on how cleverly she chooses the selling mechanism. We have seen that a Vickrey auction guarantees her the second-highest valuation among the prospective buyers. But sometimes she may be able to do better.

11.7.2 Principals and Agents

How is the problem of mechanism design to be formulated in game-theoretic terms? The discussion is often couched in terms of a *principal* and one or more *agents*.[30] In Section 11.7.1, the principal is the seller and the potential buyers are the agents. However, the same setting will also suffice for numerous other related problems.

For example, the principal might be an employer and the agents might constitute the firm's work-force. The employer would like to maximize the effort that the workers exert but is unable to monitor them closely. The employer therefore

[29]Or perhaps at one penny less than the reservation price. As in the Ultimatum Game of Section 5.8.1, she would make a take-it-or-leave-it demand.

[30]These are not agents in the sense of Section 10.4.2. They are separate individuals who act on their own behalf.

needs to invent an *incentive scheme* that rewards the industrious and penalizes the idle. But how are these to be distinguished if their work habits cannot be directly observed? Such a principal-agent problem is often addressed under the heading of *moral hazard*. The reason for this terminology is that the principal will be taking a risk if she relies on the moral scruples of her workers to ensure that they will do what they promise after agreeing to an employment contract that is not compatible with their incentives.

Moral hazard problems are sometimes called *hidden action* problems because the principal cares about actions taken by the agents that she cannot observe. Although the methods of analysis for both types of problem are much the same, our focus will be on what one might call a *hidden type* problem, since Harsanyi's theory is already set up in such terms. Textbooks often introduce such principal-agent problems with examples of *adverse selection*. If an insurance company, for example, is not careful in how it designs the insurance contracts it sells, it might easily find that only high-risk types choose to buy them. Its clientele will then be self-selected in a manner that is adverse for the insurance company's profits. Economists who have studied Akerlof's "lemons model", in which only defective used cars get traded in equilibrium, will be familiar with the difficulties that can arise.

However, the principal-agent problem with hidden types appears in perhaps its purest form when the principal is a benevolent government seeking to redistribute wealth from the rich to the poor. The agents are then the nation's citizens. How does the government determine who is rich and who is poor? It would be unwise to rely on a questionnaire if everybody knows that the result of declaring oneself rich is a tax demand, and the result of declaring oneself poor is a benefit check!

It is possible to formulate the principal-agent problem in an abstract manner that encompasses a whole range of applications simultaneously. But nothing so ambitious will be attempted here. Instead, the ideas will be illustrated with a simplified version of the auctioning problem discussed in Section 11.7.1. This is a problem with hidden types because the seller does not know the valuations that the potential buyers place on the object that she has to sell. One advantage of working with an auctioning model is that things remain interesting when it is taken to be common knowledge that everybody is risk-neutral. Other variants of the principal-agent problem often hinge on the fact that the principal and the agents have different attitudes to taking risks.

Formulating a Principal-Agent Problem. Ms. Principal has a fancy house to sell that is worth nothing to her if it cannot be sold. There are two interested parties, agent I and agent II. An agent knows his or her own valuation of the house, but this information is unknown to anybody else. A problem of incomplete information therefore has to be faced.

The set $\mathcal{M}$ of actors who may be cast in the role of agent I will be assumed to consist of just two individuals, Mr. High and Mr. Low. Similarly, the set $\mathcal{F}$ of actors who may be cast in the role of agent II will consist of just Ms. High and Ms. Low. High actors value the house at \$4m. Low actors value the house at \$3m. It will be assumed to be common knowledge that the casting move selects male and female actors independently, and that the probability that the Low actor is chosen in each case is p.

Ms. Principal begins by choosing a mechanism. It is important that she be *committed* to her choice of mechanism. She *cannot* chose one mechanism, thereby tempting agents into revealing some information, and then turn around and announce that she has decided to use some other mechanism after all.[31]

Her choice of mechanism constitutes a *script* with two roles: one for agent I and one for agent II. Harsanyi's theory converts this script into a game of imperfect information. If the agents are rational, Ms. Principal will be able to predict how the game she has invented for them will be played. In particular, she will be able to predict her own expected gain. The final step is to postulate that she will choose the mechanism that *maximizes* this expected gain. She will then have designed an optimal mechanism for the problem.

The first-best outcome for Ms. Principal would be to sell the house for \$4m when one of the agents is a High, and to sell for \$3m when both agents are Lows. Since both agents are Lows with probability p^2, Ms. Principal's expected payoff with this first-best outcome is $3p^2 + 4(1 - p^2) = 4 - p^2$. However, Ms. Principal's ignorance of the agents' true valuations means that she will not be able to achieve this first-best result. It is instructive to see how close she can come by using some of the simple auctions discussed in Section 11.7.1.

Take-It-or-Leave-It. If Ms. Principal decides simply to post a take-it-or-leave-it price, she would be stupid to consider any prices except 3 or 4 (million dollars). If she sets the price at

[31] Which is one reason the theory is not always appropriate when the principal is a government.

3, the house will be sold at that price whoever the agents may be,[32] and her expected payoff will therefore be 3. This is a second-best result because $3 < 4 - p^2$ except when $p = 1$.

If she sets the price at 4, the house will be sold at that price unless both agents are Lows. If both are Lows, the house will not be sold at all. With this arrangement, her expected payoff is therefore $4(1 - p^2)$. This is also second-best, because $4(1 - p^2) < 4 - p^2$ except when $p = 0$.

If Ms. Principal were confined to using take-it-or-leave-it auctions, she would choose to post a price of 3 when $3 > 4(1 - p^2)$. This occurs if and only if $p > \frac{1}{2}$. If $p < \frac{1}{2}$, she would choose to post a price of 4.

Vickrey. We already know that it is a Nash equilibrium for each agent to bid his true valuation in a Vickrey auction. In this example, the highest price bid by a loser will therefore be 3 unless both agents are High. In the latter case, the highest losing bid is 4. (Recall that ties are broken at random.) With such an auction, Ms. Principal's expected payoff is $4(1 - p)^2 + 3(1 - (1 - p)^2) = 3 + (1 - p)^2$. This is a second-best, because $3 + (1 - p)^2 < 4 - p^2$ unless $p = 0$ or $p = 1$.

However, the Vickrey auction is better than posting a take-it-or-leave-it price of 3 unless $p = 1$. It is better than posting a take-it-or-leave-it price of 4 when $3 + (1 - p)^2 > 4(1 - p)^2$. This occurs when $\frac{2}{5} < p < 1$.

English. Looking at an English auction takes us nowhere new because an English auction and a Vickrey auction are essentially the same thing.

First-Price, Sealed-Bid. Here we get into deep waters, because agents with a high valuation will necessarily randomize their bids. Section 0.1.2 describes a Nash equilibrium in the case when $p = \frac{1}{2}$. Exercise 11.10.39 asks for the same to be done for the general case. It is remarkable that the expected selling-price when this Nash equilibrium is used is $3 + (1 - p)^2$, just as in a Vickrey auction. This is no accident, as Exercise 11.10.38 confirms.

Dutch. A Dutch auction is essentially the same as a first-price, sealed-bid auction. We are therefore still doing no better than in a Vickrey auction.

---

[32]Why will a Low actor buy although indifferent between buying and selling? Recall the discussion of Section 5.8.2.

Modified Vickrey. So far the Vickrey auction is looking good when $\frac{2}{5} < p < 1$. However, it is possible to improve on a Vickrey auction. Restrict the agents to bids of 3 or 4, and make the winner pay the *average* of the winning and losing bids.

It remains a Nash equilibrium for all actors to plan to bid their true valuations. To see this, consider Mr. Low first. If he bids 3, he gets nothing if he loses and nothing if he wins (because he has to pay his true valuation). If he bids 4, he gets nothing if he loses, and at most $3 - \frac{1}{2}(3+4) = -\frac{1}{2}$ if he wins. Thus he does best by bidding 3, and so does Ms. Low.

Now consider Mr. High. If he bids 4, he gets nothing when he wins and nothing when he loses on those occasions when his opponent is Ms. High. When his opponent is Ms. Low, he will win, and gain $4 - \frac{1}{2}(3+4) = \frac{1}{2}$. Thus his expected payoff from bidding 4 is $\frac{1}{2}p$. If he bids 3, he gets nothing when his opponent is Ms. High. When his opponent is Ms. Low, he will win with probability $\frac{1}{2}$. Thus his expected payoff from bidding 3 is $\frac{1}{2}(4-3)p = \frac{1}{2}p$. It follows that Mr. High has no incentive to switch from bidding 4 to bidding 3 because he is indifferent between the two bids. The same goes for Ms. High.

What does Ms. Principal get when this Nash equilibrium is used? Her expected payoff is $4(1-p)^2 + \frac{1}{2}(3+4)p(1-p) + \frac{1}{2}(3+4)(1-p)p + 3p^2 = 4 - p$. This is still second-best, because $4 - p < 4 - p^2$ except when $p = 0$. But it is better than the regular Vickrey auction unless $p = 0$ or $p = 1$. It is also better than posting a take-it-or-leave-it price of 4 provided $4 - p > 4(1 - p^2)$. This occurs when $\frac{1}{4} < p \leq 1$.

Summary. Of the auctions considered, posting a take-it-or-leave-it price of 4 does best when $0 \leq p \leq \frac{1}{4}$ and the modified Vickrey auction does best when $\frac{1}{4} \leq p \leq 1$. In fact, using these schemes is *optimal* for Ms. Principal. To see why, some more theory is necessary.

11.7.3 Revelation Principle

The time has come for the mountain to heave and bring forth a mouse. The mechanisms considered in Section 11.7.1 are *indirect* mechanisms. In a *direct* mechanism, the agents are asked straight out what their type is. The *revelation principle* says that, whatever can be done with an indirect mechanism can also be done with a direct mechanism.

This result is a mouse because no effort whatsoever is required to deduce it from a careful statement of what the principal-agent problem says. However, as we shall see, it is a very useful mouse, and so it is worth stating the principal-agent problem again to make sure all its wrinkles have been ironed out.

The principal commits herself to mechanism M with the aim of inducing one or more agents to behave in a manner favorable to her. She does not know the types of the agents. However, it is common knowledge how Chance selects the actors for the various agent roles. The principal's choice of M therefore serves as the script for a game G. The actors' behavior in G determines an outcome x. If the actors are rational, the principal will only be able to achieve those outcomes x that result when the actors use a Nash equilibrium in G. Such an x is *implementable* for the principal. She can get it if she wants it[33] by selecting the mechanism M.

The revelation principle simplifies the task of deciding whether or not an outcome is implementable. In precise terms, it says the following:

Theorem 11.7.1 (Gibbard) Any implementable x can also be implemented as a truth-telling Nash equilibrium of a game H derived from a direct mechanism D.

Proof. Since x is implementable, there is a mechanism M that implements it. To implement x with a direct mechanism, the principal need only announce that the mechanism M is to be used, but that she proposes to save the agents the trouble of thinking out what strategies to use in the game G that the choice of M forces them to play. She will play their strategies for them. They need only tell her their types, and, for each type of actor, she will use the strategy that such an actor would play in the Nash equilibrium of G that yields the outcome x.

No actor then has an incentive to do other than tell the truth about his or her type, provided all other actors also plan to tell the truth. Nothing can be gained from misleading the principal. The last thing you want her to do is to play a strategy on your behalf that you would not have chosen yourself if given the opportunity. □

Since it has so little content, one should not expect too much of the revelation principle. In particular, it does not

[33]Provided that, when multiple Nash equilibria exist in G, she can induce the actors to use the equilibrium she nominates. Sometimes this is a questionable assumption, but it is not questioned here. In particular, the merits of a truth-telling equilibrium in a direct mechanism are not compared with the merits of other possible equilibria.

provide a magical means of inducing people to report their true incomes so that they can be taxed fairly. It says only that, *if* something can be done, then it can be done just by asking people to reveal their true characteristics. However, this is a valuable insight for the optimal design of mechanisms, because it means that, in considering what outcomes are implementable, it is only necessary to consider outcomes that are implementable by *direct* mechanisms. To see how this works, it will be helpful to return to the example of Section 11.7.2.

11.7.4 Designing an Optimal Auction

Section 11.7.2 considered various auctioning schemes that the principal might use. There are many others. She might set entry fees to be paid by all bidders. She might designate minimum bids, or otherwise restrict the bids that can be made. She might even seed the auction room with shills primed to push the bidding up if things look slow. The possibilities are bewilderingly large. However, the revelation principle tells us that, in considering what outcomes can be achieved, all the possibilities that do not arise from a truth-telling equilibrium in a direct mechanism can be ignored. This fact will be exploited here to solve the auction-design problem raised in Section 11.7.2. To keep things simple, attention will be restricted to the case of symmetric equilibria of mechanisms that treat agents I and II symmetrically.[34] As always when auctions are under study, we assume it to be common knowledge that everybody is risk-neutral.

Characterizing Truth-Telling Equilibria. The direct mechanism chosen by Ms. Principal will be characterized by four numbers, h, l, H and L. They are defined as follows. Provided that the other actors tell the truth, an actor who announces "High" will win the auction with some probability and make some payment. Let the probability with which he wins the auction be h. How much he pays will depend on whether he wins the auction, and possibly on other things as well. The parameter H is therefore taken to be the *expected value* of the amount he will pay. An actor who announces "Low" in the same circumstances will win the auction with probability l and have an expectation of paying L. A High

[34]So-called "games of incomplete information" are often called "games of asymmetric information", presumably because, *after* the casting move, the actors occupying the roles of players I and II may be of different types. This has the unfortunate effect of making it necessary to describe a game like that being considered as a "symmetric game of asymmetric information".

actor who announces "High" will therefore get an overall expected payoff of $4h - H$ if cast as an agent. A High actor who announces "Low" will get $4l - L$. For truth-telling to be optimal for a High actor, it is therefore necessary that

$$4h - H \geq 4l - L. \tag{11.6}$$

Similarly, for truth-telling to be optimal for a Low actor,

$$3l - L \geq 3h - H. \tag{11.7}$$

The inequalities (11.6) and (11.7) are called *incentive-compatibility* constraints because they express the requirement that the principal must provide incentives that make it optimal for the agents to take the actions that the principal is designing the mechanism to induce. A simple consequence of the current incentive-compatibility conditions is that $h \geq l$ and $H \geq L$. Thus a High actor wins more often than a Low actor, but expects to pay more.

Ms. Principal's Optimization Problem. Ms. Principal does not know the agents' types. She therefore expects each agent to pay her

$$F = (1 - p)H + pL. \tag{11.8}$$

Her aim is to maximize the quantity F by choosing h, l, H and L suitably. However, she cannot choose these parameters freely. She cannot, for example, make H and L as large as she likes. If she makes them too big, no actor would be willing to play. To ensure the participation of both types of actor, it is necessary that

$$4h - H \geq 0, \tag{11.9}$$

$$3l - L \geq 0. \tag{11.10}$$

The inequalities (11.9) and (11.10) are called *individual rationality* constraints because, as in Section 5.4.2, they express the requirement that the mechanism that the principal is designing must offer the agents at least as much for their participation as their best outside option.

As for the probabilities h and l, Ms. Principal believes that the probability that agent I will win is $(1 - p)h + pl$. In a symmetric auction, this cannot exceed $\frac{1}{2}$. A bound must also be placed on h. In a symmetric auction, a High actor cannot do better than win all the time against a Low opponent and half the time against a High opponent. Thus

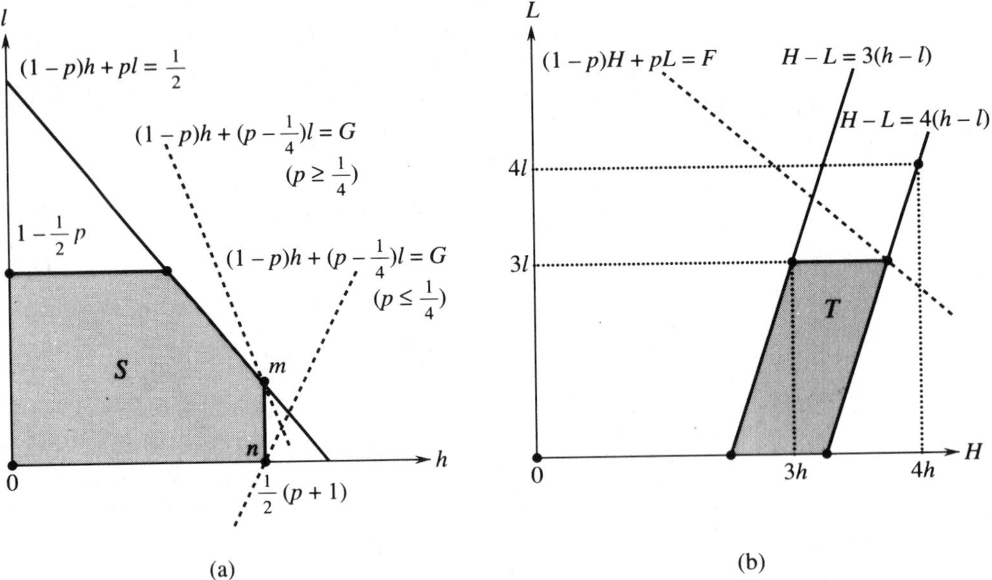

Figure 11.4 Designing an optimal auction.

$h \leq p + \frac{1}{2}(1-p) = \frac{1}{2}(p+1)$. Similarly, $l \leq 1 - \frac{1}{2}p$. The inequalities constraining h and l are therefore,

$$(1-p)h + pl \leq \tfrac{1}{2} \tag{11.11}$$

$$h \leq \tfrac{1}{2}(p+1) \tag{11.12}$$

$$l \leq 1 - \tfrac{1}{2}p\,. \tag{11.13}$$

Figure 11.4(a) shows the set S of pairs (h, l) that satisfy these inequalities.[35]

Perhaps more constraints on Ms. Principal's choice of h, l, H and L are necessary, but let us see what the solution of her optimization problem is with the constraints listed so far. She is, in fact, faced with a linear programming problem. Her objective is to maximize the "linear objective function" $(1-p)H + pL$ subject to the "linear inequalities" (11.6), (11.7), (11.9), (11.10), (11.11), (11.12) and (11.13). Such problems can be quite formidable unless one is willing to indulge in some judicious guesswork. The issue that matters is: which of the constraints are *active*?[36]

[35] Note that $\frac{1}{2}(p+1) \leq \frac{1}{2}(1-p)^{-1}$ and $\frac{1}{2}(1-p) \leq \frac{1}{2}p^{-1}$.

[36] For example, if the solution to the problem is $(\tilde{h}, \tilde{l}, \tilde{H}, \tilde{L})$, then (11.6) is *active* if $4\tilde{h} - \tilde{H} = 4\tilde{l} - \tilde{L}$. It is *inactive* if $4\tilde{h} - \tilde{H} < 4\tilde{l} - \tilde{L}$.

Simplifying the Problem. Here it is not hard to guess that the active constraints involving H and L must be (11.6) and (11.10). The intuition is that it is a High actor who will have the greater inducement to lie and the Low actor who will have the greater inducement not to participate. The intuition can be checked by examining Figure 11.4(b), which shows the set T of all feasible pairs (H, L) for a pair (h, l). Observe that, whenever $h \geq l$, the expression $F = (1-p)H + pL$ is maximized[37] at the point (H, L) satisfying

$$H - L = 4(h - l) \qquad (11.14)$$

$$L = 3l\,. \qquad (11.15)$$

This observation simplifies the problem immensely. Substitute $H = 4h - l$ and $L = 3l$ into (11.8). We then have to maximize

$$G = (1-p)h + (p - \tfrac{1}{4})l$$

subject to the constraints (11.11), (11.12) and (11.13). The location of the maximum depends on whether $p \geq \frac{1}{4}$ or $p \leq \frac{1}{4}$. Figure 11.4(a) shows that the maximum is achieved at m in the former case, and at n in the latter case.[38]

The case $p \geq \frac{1}{4}$. Since $m = (\frac{1}{2}(p+1), \frac{1}{2}p)$, optimal values for h and l in the case $p \geq \frac{1}{4}$ are $\tilde{h} = \frac{1}{2}(p+1)$ and $\tilde{l} = \frac{1}{2}p$. The corresponding values for $\tilde{H}$ and $\tilde{L}$ are $\tilde{H} = 4\tilde{h} - \tilde{l} = \frac{3}{2}p + 2$ and $\tilde{L} = 3\tilde{l} = \frac{3}{2}p$. Ms. Principal then gets an expected payoff of $2\tilde{F} = 2(1-p)\tilde{H} + 2p\tilde{L} = 4 - p$.

The case $p \leq \frac{1}{4}$. Since $n = (\frac{1}{2}(p+1), 0)$, optimal values for h and l in the case $p \leq \frac{1}{4}$ are $\tilde{h} = \frac{1}{2}(p+1)$ and $\tilde{l} = 0$. The corresponding values for $\tilde{H}$ and $\tilde{L}$ are $\tilde{H} = 4\tilde{h} - \tilde{l} = 2(p+1)$ and $\tilde{L} = 3\tilde{l} = 0$. Ms. Principal then gets an expected payoff of $2\tilde{F} = 2(1-p)\tilde{H} + 2p\tilde{L} = 4(1-p^2)$.

What Is Optimal? Recall the conclusion of Section 11.7.2. We learned there that Ms. Principal can get an expected payoff of $4(1-p^2)$ by using a take-it-or-leave-it auction with

[37]If the reason for this is not clear, see Section 3.2.1.

[38]If $p > \frac{1}{4}$, the line $G = (1-p)h + (p - \frac{1}{4})l$ slopes down more steeply than $(1-p)h + pl = \frac{1}{2}$. If $p < \frac{1}{4}$, the line $G = (1-p)h + (p - \frac{1}{4})l$ slopes upwards. If $p = \frac{1}{4}$, the line $G = (1-p)h + (p - \frac{1}{4})l$ is vertical, and any point on the line segment joining m and n is optimal.

the posted price of 4. Now we know that this outcome is optimal[39] when $0 \leq p \leq \frac{1}{4}$.

We also learned that Ms. Principal can get an expected payoff of $4 - p$ by using a modified Vickrey auction. Now we know that this outcome is optimal when $\frac{1}{4} \leq p \leq 1$.

Neither of these auctions is first-best unless $p = 0$ or $p = 1$. However, there is no way that Ms. Principal can extract all the surplus. Some of the surplus will inevitably be retained by the agents. She has to be satisfied with a second-best outcome. Our analysis tells her how to avoid making do with a third-best outcome.

11.8 Assessment Equilibrium

So far, this chapter has been concerned with the *Nash* equilibria of games of imperfect information obtained by completing incomplete informational structures. However, the previous chapters provide many examples of cases for which the idea of a Nash equilibrium is inadequate. Our major tool in such cases has been the idea of a subgame-perfect equilibrium. This often works very well in games of perfect information, but we shall see that it is much less successful when games of imperfect information need to be studied.

As is often the case, one needs to return to first principles in order to make some progress with this difficulty. Recall that a Bayesian-rational player always behaves as though maximizing expected utility with respect to a subjective probability distribution. This suggests that an equilibrium in a game between Bayesian-rational players should be defined not just in terms of what players *do*, as in a subgame-perfect equilibrium, but also in terms of what they *believe*.

What Players Do. As previously, this will be described by a *strategy profile s* consisting of one strategy for each player. In what follows, attention will be restricted to games of *perfect recall* (Section 10.4.1), and the strategies will be taken to be *behavioral strategies* (Section 10.4.3).

What Players Believe. When a player has to decide what action to take at an information set, he or she will be uncertain about which node within the information set h the game has

---

[39]Since we can actually point to an auction that achieves the outcome $4(1 - p^2)$, we need no longer worry about whether we succeeded in listing all the constraints in the optimization problem. Adding further constraints could only make the maximum smaller.

reached. A Bayesian-rational player will therefore attach subjective probabilities to each node in h. These probabilities represent the player's beliefs. They are summarized by a *belief profile* μ which assigns a probability measure μ_h to each information set h. It is to be understood that, if information set h is reached, then the player with the move at h will assign probability $\mu_h\{x\}$ to each node x in the information set h.

As an example, consider the game Quiche of Figure 10.6(b). A belief profile μ for Quiche consists of four probability measures μ_T, μ_W, μ_Q and μ_B corresponding to the four information sets TOUGH, WIMP, QUICHE and BEER. The probability measures for the information sets TOUGH and WIMP are easy. A player with the move at TOUGH or WIMP will know for sure the node the game has reached because each of these information sets contains only one node. This single node must therefore be assigned a probability of 1.

The information set QUICHE contains two nodes, e and f. The probability measure μ_Q must assign probabilities to these. It may be, for example, that $\mu_Q\{e\} = \frac{1}{4}$ and $\mu_Q\{f\} = \frac{3}{4}$. Similarly, μ_B must assign probabilities to the two nodes in the information set BEER.

Assessments. Following Kreps and Wilson, a pair (s, μ) is called an *assessment*. An assessment is therefore a profile of behavioral strategies together with a belief profile.

Assessment Equilibrium. An *assessment equilibrium*[40] will be an assessment (s, μ) for which two properties hold:

1. The first property requires that the players *always* plan to choose an optimal action. More precisely, a player with the move at an information set h assumes that after his or her move, play will be according to s. The action at h designated by s must then be optimal, given the player's beliefs μ_h about the node in h that the game has reached.
2. The second property is that the players' beliefs respect the laws of probability. More precisely, wherever beliefs can be deduced from other beliefs and the fact that s is in use,

---

[40]This is not a standard piece of terminology. What is being defined is a watered down version of what Kreps and Wilson call a *sequential equilibrium*. Kreps and Wilson call the first property that follows *sequential rationality*. The second property is part of what they call *consistency*. Fudenberg and Tirole propose less stringent consistency requirements than Kreps and Wilson, and call what results a *perfect Bayesian equilibrium*. Property 2 is substantially weaker than the consistency requirements in both of these equilibrium notions.

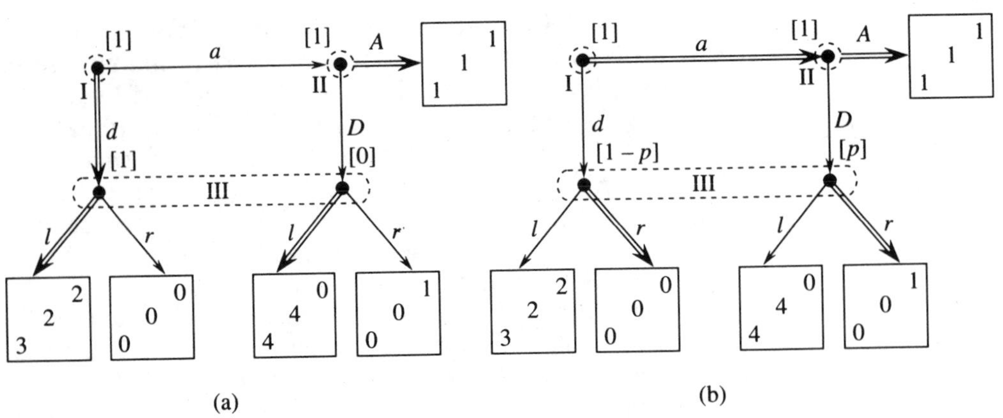

Figure 11.5 Selten's Horse.

then the beliefs actually held must be consistent with these deductions. This means that Bayesian updating (Section 10.5) must *always* be used wherever possible.

The reasons for formulating such a complicated definition will be apparent after the following discussion of Selten's Horse game.

11.8.1 Selten's Horse

Selten's Horse of Figure 11.5 has two Nash equilibria in pure strategies (and numerous others in mixed strategies). The first Nash equilibrium (d, A, l) is illustrated in Figure 11.5(a). The second Nash equilibrium (a, A, r) is illustrated in Figure 11.5(b).[41]

Incredible Plans. At first sight, the Nash equilibrium (d, A, l) seems more attractive than (a, A, r) because it leads to the outcome $(3, 2, 2)$ while (a, A, r) leads to $(1, 1, 1)$. In the terminology of Section 7.3.3, (d, A, l) Pareto-dominates (a, A, r). But consider player II's plan to play A in the equilibrium (d, A, l). If player I actually plays d, player II would never be called upon to carry out her plan. However, if she *were* called upon to make a decision, she would not want to play A. If player III does not deviate from the play of l specified in the equilibrium, then player II gets 4 from playing D and only 1 from playing A. In the language of Section 4.6.3, player

[41] It is worth checking that these are indeed Nash equilibria. For example, would player I gain if he deviated from (d, A, l) by playing a?

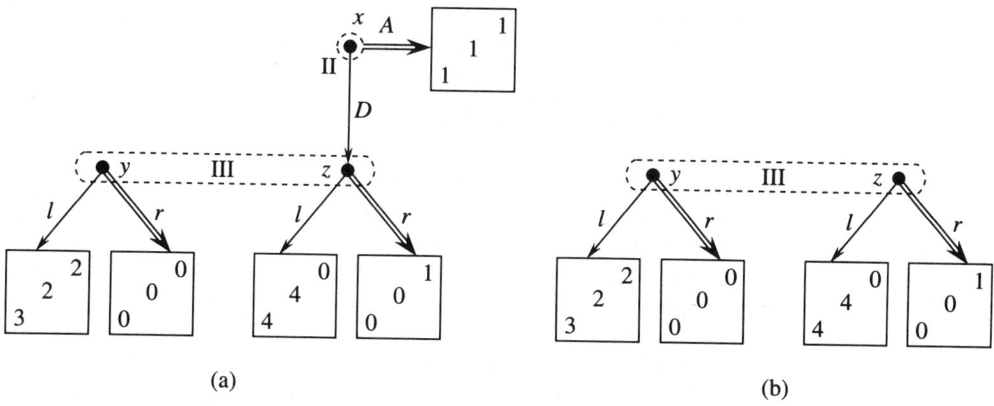

Figure 11.6 Horse play.

II's plan to play A in the equilibrium (d, A, l) is *incredible.* A game theory book that recommended (d, A, l) would not be taken seriously.[42]

Subgame-Perfect Equilibria. Section 4.6.3 was about subgame-perfect equilibria. This notion is at its most powerful for games of perfect information, because such games have many subgames. In a game of perfect information, any decision node is the root of a subgame. This is false for games of imperfect information. Indeed, Selten's Horse has no proper[43] subgames at all. The structure of Figure 11.6(a) that is obtained by deleting everything that precedes player II's information set is not a subgame. It does not have a root to represent its first move. If it were treated as a game, we would not know whether to start at node x or node y. The same goes for the structure of Figure 11.6(b) obtained by deleting everything that precedes player III's information set. In this case, we would not know whether to start at node y or node z.

A subgame-perfect equilibrium is a Nash equilibrium that induces Nash equilibrium play in all subgames. But Horse has no proper subgames. Hence, *any* Nash equilibrium for Horse is necessarily a subgame-perfect equilibrium. Subgame-perfection does not therefore serve to eliminate incredible plans in a game like Horse. Something with more bite is needed.

[42]If it claimed to be authoritative. However, the story need not be the same if different game theory books were in circulation, some advocating (d, A, l) and others (a, A, r).

[43]A game is always a subgame of itself. When the whole game is to be excluded, one speaks of a *proper* subgame.

Assessment Equilibrium. How does an assessment equilibrium deal with the problem of incredible plans? Consider the strategy profile $s = (d, A, l)$ for Horse. What belief profile μ can be twinned with this to produce an assessment (s, μ) that satisfies the two properties for an assessment equilibrium?

Refer to Figure 11.5(a). Player I and player II's information sets each contain only one node. Thus μ must assign probability 1 to the single node in each of these information sets. These assignments are shown in square brackets in Figure 11.5(a). The probabilities that μ must assign to the nodes in player III's information set are tied down by property 2 for an assessment equilibrium. Player III knows[44] that player I will use d. Hence, player III can deduce that he is at the left node of his information set when called upon to play. Thus μ must assign probability 1 to the left node and 0 to the right node.

But the assessment (s, μ) we have constructed does not satisfy property 1 for an assessment equilibrium. Players I and III are certainly optimizing given their beliefs, but player II is not. Although her information set will not be reached in equilibrium, if it were reached for some reason, she would play D and not A.

Having checked that $s = (d, A, l)$ cannot be part of an assessment equilibrium, we ought also to check that $s = (a, A, r)$ *is* part of an assessment equilibrium. As before, μ must assign probability 1 to the single node in each of player I and player II's information sets. However, property 2 for an assessment equilibrium does not help with player III's information set. This is not reached in the equilibrium under study, and hence Bayesian updating does not apply. However, property 1 does restrict the probabilities $1 - p$ and p that μ assigns to the left and right nodes of player III's information set. If r is to be optimal for player III given her beliefs, she must expect more from choosing r than from choosing l. Thus

$$0(1-p) + 1p \geq 2(1-p) + 0p$$

$$p \geq \tfrac{2}{3}\,.$$

As long as p satisfies $p \geq \frac{2}{3}$, it follows that (s, μ) is an assessment equilibrium for Horse.[45]

---

[44] Because it is written in the game theory book for all to see.

[45] One might ask: *Why* does player III believe that his right node is more likely that his left? However, Bayesianism does not offer answers to such questions.

11.8.2 Signaling

Econ 11.8.3 ⟶

When the game Quiche of Figure 11.1(f) was studied in Section 10.5.1, attention was restricted to the case $r = \frac{2}{3}$, so that there would always be a positive probability that every information set is reached in equilibrium. Problems about incredible plans off the equilibrium path were thereby evaded. But things are different if $r = \frac{1}{3}$. One then obtains a game that typifies the difficulties that arise in signaling problems.

In Section 10.5.1, the signaling issues were straightforward. A tough player I signalled his toughness by drinking beer. It was clear to player II that beer-drinking was the "right" signal for a tough guy, and so she bullied an opponent who ate quiche. A wimpish player I therefore found it in his best interests not to eat quiche all the time. Instead of always sending the "right" signal for his type, he bluffed by sending the "wrong" signal just enough of the time to keep player II guessing about the nature of a beer-drinking adversary.

In such discussions, it is useful to speak of beer and quiche, and of tough guys and wimps, because it is easy to lose track of what everybody's preferences are without the help of something to jog the memory where necessary. However, one has to be careful not to allow the meanings of the words used in describing the game to prejudice an equilibrium analysis of the game. In particular, if beer-drinking is the "right" signal for a tough guy to send, this conclusion should emerge *endogenously* from the analysis. *After* an equilibrium has been computed, it may make sense to ask how the players interpret the signals they receive while using the equilibrium strategies. However, *before* the equilibria are computed, one is not entitled to take for granted that any particular signal will be interpreted in any particular way.[46] When communicating in an ironic or satirical mode, for example, we play by different

[46]One must not confuse the problem of deciding what the equilibria of a game are with the problem of selecting an equilibrium from those available. In Section 7.3.2, we saw that the conventions used for selecting equilibria may very well depend on issues that are arbitrary from the game-theoretic point of view—like which letter comes first in the alphabet. Indeed, the mere fact that I have chosen to write this book in English is a recognition that a large part of the world has chosen to coordinate on an equilibrium in which certain signals have specific conventional meanings. However, the meanings are not intrinsic to the signals. Words mean what they mean only because a series of historical accidents has led society to coordinate on one equilibrium rather than another. If we wanted to know what the other possible equilibria might have been, we would need to separate the words we use from their familiar meanings in English and treat them as abstract signals.

rules than when simply communicating facts. We do not then expect the words we use to be taken literally. What we say is often the opposite of what we mean, and yet we would be astonished to be misunderstood.

Matters are usually less subtle in economic games, but the essential issues are just the same. What does it mean, for example, if the other firm lowers its price? Is it a sign of strength or weakness? Sometimes a study of the equilibria of the game allows an unambiguous interpretation of such signals to be made, as in the version of Quiche studied in Section 10.5.1. However, in the version of Quiche with $r = \frac{1}{3}$ that follows, we shall find that matters are much less simple.

Quiche-Eaters Are Wimps. Consider first the strategy profile s in which player I uses (*beer*, *beer*) and player II uses (*bully*, *defer*). Property 2 for an assessment equilibrium then requires that μ assign probability $\frac{2}{3}$ to the left node in the BEER information set, and $\frac{1}{3}$ to the right node. The reason is that the signal *beer* conveys no information. Player I will drink beer whatever his type may be. Thus Bayesian updating at BEER leaves the probabilities $1 - r = \frac{2}{3}$ and $r = \frac{1}{3}$ that player II assigns to the two possible types of player I unchanged.

Property 2 says nothing about how μ should assign probabilities to the nodes in QUICHE. The reason is that this information set will be reached with zero probability if player I plays according to s. Thus it is impossible to use Bayesian updating at QUICHE. We are therefore free to assign probability 0 to the left node and 1 to right node. Given the beliefs built into μ, everybody is then always planning to optimize. Thus (s, μ) satisfies both property 1 and property 2 for an assessment equilibrium.

In this assessment equilibrium, player II believes that a quiche-eater is necessarily a wimp. The result is that both wimps and tough guys drink beer, and player II defers to both.

In Section 10.5.1, a version of Quiche was studied in which player II was able to elicit *some* information about player I's type from the signal that he sent. Sometimes, signaling games have equilibria in which player II is able to deduce *everything* about player I's type from his signal. In such equilibria, the choice of whether to eat quiche or to drink beer might be said to "separate the men from the boys". It is therefore appropriate that economists refer to an equilibrium of this kind as a *separating equilibrium*. However, in the equilibrium just examined, both types of player I send the same signal, and hence player II can deduce *nothing* about player I's type from his signal. Economists call such an equilibrium a *pooling equilibrium.*

Beer-Drinkers Are Wimps. We have examined one pooling equilibrium for Quiche. But there is another. Consider next the strategy profile s in which player I uses $(quiche, quiche)$ and player II uses $(defer, bully)$. Property 2 tells us that μ must assign probability $\frac{2}{3}$ to the left node in QUICHE, and $\frac{1}{3}$ to the right node. Property 2 does not help with the BEER information set, and so we are free to assign 0 to its left node and 1 to its right node. The result is an assessment equilibrium in which player II believes that a beer-drinker is necessarily a wimp. Both wimps and tough guys therefore eat quiche and player II defers to both.

Kreps' Intuitive Criterion. The second of these assessment equilibria may seem very perverse. The signals have somehow reversed their "natural" meaning. However, such perversity is endemic in the signaling games of which Quiche is a typical example. My own attitude is that one must look to the circumstances in which the game is being played when seeking a justification for eliminating perverse equilibria—just as a mathematician looks at the circumstances under which a quadratic equation arose when seeking reasons for eliminating one of the roots. It may be, for example, that the players have the opportunity for an extended period of "cheap talk" before Quiche is played. If so, Kreps argues that a tough player I would "refute" a supposedly authoritative game theory book that recommends the perverse equilibrium by making the following speech.

> *Mr. Tough*: I am Mr. Tough. The game theory book says that both Mr. Wimp and I will eat quiche. However, I plan to drink beer anyway. I'm telling you this so you don't make the mistake of bullying me.
>
> *Ms. Nasty*: How do I know that you're not really Mr. Wimp trying to fool me?
>
> *Mr. Tough*: You can tell that I'm Mr. Tough from the fact that I'm trying to persuade you not to follow the book. I have a motive for doing so while Mr. Wimp does not. If I succeed in persuading you, I will get a payoff of 3 after drinking beer, whereas I would only get a payoff of 2 if we all follow the book. On the other hand, Mr. Wimp has no

incentive to drink beer whether you are persuaded or not by my argument. According to the book he gets 3, whereas the most he can get after drinking beer is 2.

Should Ms. Nasty be persuaded by this argument? If I were Ms. Nasty, I would not easily be convinced. My response would go like this:

Ms. Nasty: You argue that I should believe that you are Mr. Tough because Mr. Wimp would have no grounds for seeking to challenge the authority of the game theory book. However, I put it to you that, if it were correct for me to be persuaded not to follow the book every time it was challenged by an argument like yours, then the book would not be authoritative. Mr. Wimp would then have no sound reason for anticipating a payoff of 3. In any case, whatever he is expecting to get, he would certainly not remain silent when offered the opportunity to make a speech. He would see this as just another opportunity for sending a signal and so would be careful to make precisely the same speech as Mr. Tough would make. Any such speech is therefore meaningless.

This criticism of Kreps' intuitive criterion is not intended as a last word on the subject. It simply reflects my view that the labyrinthine twists and turns of game-theoretic reasoning require maintaining an attitude of healthy skepticism. Such an attitude is particularly valuable when evaluating the myriads of equilibrium selection criteria that have been proposed for signaling games like Quiche!

11.8.3 Refinements

Phil 11.9 ⟶

The preceding discussion of Quiche raises the issue of refinements of Nash equilibrium. For example, subgame-perfect equilibria are a refinement of Nash equilibria. Assessment equilibria are a refinement of subgame-perfect equilibria. It is natural to look for further refinements in an attempt to short-circuit the equilibrium selection problem. Kreps' intuitive criterion represents one possible attempt at such a refinement.

My intention in writing this book has been to avoid controversial matters except when it would be intellectually dishonest to do so. This means that little can be said about the subject of refinements of Nash equilibrium. It is the most controversial of subjects within game theory. Every game theorist has his own favorite recipe for refining Nash equilibria—and so, it sometimes seems, do all their uncles, brothers, cousins and aunts. It is true that this chapter is supposed to be about knowing whom to believe, but this is an area in which I recommend not believing *anyone* until the experts achieve some sort of consensus. Nothing whatever will therefore be said about particular refinements other than those already considered. It may be helpful, however, to say something about the general problem that the refinement literature seeks to address.

Property 2 for an assessment equilibrium (s, μ) tells us to use Bayesian updating in computing the belief profile μ whenever possible. The only time that Bayesian updating at an information set h will be impossible is when h cannot be reached if s is used. This is because one cannot condition on a zero probability event. Bayesian updating calls for the calculation of conditional probabilities of the form $\text{prob}(A|B) = \text{prob}(A \cap B)/\text{prob}(B)$. But this expression is undefined if $\text{prob}(B) = 0$.

Kolmogorov's famous book, *The Theory of Probability*, has a proposal for dealing with such difficulties. He recommends considering a sequence of events B_n such that $B_n \to B$ as $n \to \infty$, but for which $\text{prob}(B_n) > 0$. One can then seek to define $\text{prob}(A|B)$ as

$$\lim_{n \to \infty} \text{prob}(A|B_n) .$$

However, Kolmogorov warns against using the "wrong" events B_n by giving examples in which the derived values of $\text{prob}(A|B)$ do not make any sense. In the geometric problems that Kolmogorov considers, it is not hard to see what the "right" value of $\text{prob}(A|B)$ ought to be, but game theorists are not so fortunate. This makes it vital that no mistakes be made in choosing the events B_n.

It is tempting to shrug one's shoulders at these difficulties. Rational players will not stray from the equilibrium path. So why should we care about what they would believe if they were to stray? The reason is simple. Rational players do not stay on the equilibrium path just because a game theory book recommends doing so. They remain on the equilibrium path because of what they anticipate *would* happen if they *were* to deviate. It is therefore impossible to say anything sensible about what happens in equilibrium without considering out-of-equilibrium play simultaneously. But out-of-equilibrium play occurs with zero probability if the players are rational.

Philosophers speak of *counterfactuals* in such contexts. It is, for example, counterfactual that a rational player will do something irrational. It is therefore counterfactual that a rational player will stray from the equilibrium path. Reasoning with such counterfactuals is like negotiating a minefield, but game theory cannot evade the difficulties. They have to be faced squarely. Philosophers seek to do so by using the language of *possible worlds.*

The ideal world of the game theorist is only one of many possible worlds. A zero probability event B in the world of game theory may correspond to an event B_n that occurs with positive probability in some nearby possible world. One may then ask what people would believe in this nearby possible world if B_n were to occur, and use *these* beliefs as approximations to what they would believe if B were to occur in the world of game theory.

How successful this line of attack will be depends on which nearby possible world is employed. This choice will determine what refinement emerges. So far game theorists have chosen to study nearby possible worlds that are mathematically easy to handle.[47] My own view is that the choice of nearby possible worlds is not up for grabs. Games are abstracted from real-world situations. When the level of abstraction selected leaves matters unresolved that need resolution, one must then return to the real-world situation for more information. In particular, this is the place to look for insight into what nearby possible worlds are worthy of attention. It may be that the insight one gains is unwelcome because one is forced to consider models that one cannot analyze successfully. However, unwelcome facts are part of life's rich tapestry.

11.9 More Agreeing to Disagree

Phil 11.10 ⟶

This section explains how the notion of an assessment equilibrium fits into Harsanyi's theory of incomplete information. Particular attention will be paid to the question of whether the players have *consistent* beliefs.

[47] Section 1.8.3 considers the kind of nearby possible world subsumed in Selten's *trembling-hand perfect* equilibrium. In such a possible world, nobody ever fails to think things out correctly, but the players' hands tremble so that even very bad actions get used with some minimal positive probability. As observed in Section 1.8.3, this is not a very realistic setting for a game like Chess. However, it is a setting that admits a concise mathematical description.

Up to now in this chapter, the Harsanyi doctrine has been taken for granted. Recall from Section 10.7.3 that this asserts that it is common knowledge that the players have common priors. In particular, it is common knowledge that they all attach the same prior probabilities to the outcomes of Chance moves in the game. This assumption will continue to be maintained here, except in respect of the *casting move* that opens a game obtained by completing an incomplete information structure.

In fact, for the ideas that follow, we can dispense with a casting move altogether. Assessment equilibria make sense in *rootless games.*[48] By this is meant a structure that has all the properties of a game except that no first move is designated. Figure 11.6 provides two simple examples.[49]

As with most of the ideas in this chapter, the notion of an assessment equilibrium in a rootless game was anticipated earlier. In particular, Section 10.8.1 uses the idea. Recall that Section 10.8.1 is about the finitely repeated Prisoners' Dilemma when the players do not know for sure how many repetitions there are to be. In the language of Section 11.2, each nonnegative integer n corresponds to an actor who knows that, if he or she is chosen to play, then the Prisoners' Dilemma will be repeated either n or $n + 1$ times.[50] Actors who correspond to an odd integer are male and hence candidates for the role of player I. Actors corresponding to an even integer are female and hence candidates for the role of player II.

However, in the formulation of Section 10.8.1, no casting move appears. Instead, beliefs are attributed to the actors. Mr. n, for example, must assign probabilities to the two nodes in his information set $\{n, n + 1\}$. These probabilities may be expressed in the form $\text{prob}\{\text{II} = n - 1 \mid \text{I} = n\}$ and $\text{prob}\{\text{II} = n + 1 \mid \text{I} = n\}$, since they are the conditional probabilities that Mr. n assigns to the possible actors who might be filling the role of player II, given that he is filling the role of player I. Section 10.8.1 considers the case in which each actor with $n \geq 1$ attaches probability $\frac{1}{2}$ to each actor who might be filling the opposing role. After Section 11.8, the argument of Section 10.8.1 can be seen as demonstrating the

[48] Of course, something that doesn't have a root is not really a game, and so this is an abuse of our terminology.

[49] A complicated rootless game might involve histories that recede into the indefinite past, with each node having an infinite number of predecessors. The model of Section 8.5.1 is an example of such a structure.

[50] Except for Ms. Zero who knows that the Prisoners' Dilemma will be played exactly once if she is cast as player II.

existence of an assessment equilibrium with these beliefs in which the players cooperate until the last stage of the game.

11.9.1 Consistency

Although the preceding discussion shows that one can dispense with a casting move in using Harsanyi's theory of incomplete information, some caution is appropriate in doing so. The reason is that the device of the casting move ensures that the Harsanyi doctrine of Section 10.7.3 is satisfied. This requires that it be common knowledge that the players have common priors. In this context, the players' priors are determined by the subjective probabilities they assign to the Chance moves in the game. Under the standard assumptions for a game, it is common knowledge that all players agree on what probabilities should be attached to the actions available at a move made by Chance.

Without a casting move, there is therefore a possibility that the players' beliefs may involve some agreeing to disagree.[51] In some situations, the availability of a free lunch may best represent the realities of what has to be modeled. However, it is not an assumption that any modeler would wish to make without being fully aware of what he or she is doing.

Consider, for example, the repeated Prisoners' Dilemma model of Section 10.8.1. Suppose that this is modeled *with* a casting move in which Chance selects the number of stages to be n with probability $p_n > 0$. Mr. n can then calculate his beliefs at the information set $\{n, n+1\}$ using Bayesian updating. In fact,

$$\text{prob}\{\text{II} = n-1 \mid \text{I} = n\} = \frac{p_n}{p_n + p_{n+1}},$$

$$\text{prob}\{\text{II} = n+1 \mid \text{I} = n\} = \frac{p_{n+1}}{p_n + p_{n+1}}.$$

Section 10.8.1 assumes that both these conditional probabilities are $\frac{1}{2}$. Thus $p_n = p_{n+1}$. But, if this is true for all $n \geq 1$, the probabilities p_n cannot sum to 1. The reason is that, if

[51] With so much else to think about, it is easy forget that the common knowledge problems associated with a casting move do not vanish when one adopts the format of a rootless game. The problems just appear in a new guise as problems about who knows what about the *equilibrium* in use. In particular, when an assessment equilibrium (s, μ) is studied, it is implicitly assumed that it is common knowledge what (s, μ) is. Or, as it would have been expressed in earlier chapters, it is common knowledge what game theory book the players are using.

a positive number is added to itself sufficiently often, then the resulting sum can be made as large as we choose. This shows that there is *no* casting move that is consistent with the beliefs that Section 10.8.1 attributes to the actors.[52]

The beliefs that the actors hold are therefore *inconsistent* in the sense that they cannot be deduced from a common prior. As observed earlier, how worrying this is will depend on the context. It is certainly worrying in the context of Section 10.8.1, where the actors do not represent different people who might have historical reasons for agreeing to disagree. In Section 10.8.1, the male actors are all alter egos of Mr. Ten. They represent Mr. Ten as he might have been if he had received different information. One is certainly skating on thin ice if one argues that such alter egos might have beliefs inconsistent with that held by Mr. Ten, especially in a context in which the emphasis is on what is or is not rational.[53]

My own view is easy to predict after Section 10.8.2. Working with inconsistent beliefs pushes the Bayesian approach beyond its legitimate domain of application. Real people do, of course, have inconsistent beliefs about many things, but a good theory of this phenomenon will not follow Bayesianism in neglecting the question of where people get their beliefs from in the first place.

11.10 Exercises

1. Section 11.2.1 explains how Harsanyi's theory can be used to complete an incomplete informational structure. This exercise asks you to follow the same procedure with a simpler problem of the same general type.
   (a) The underlying rules are shown in Figure 11.7(a). In the terminology of Section 11.2.1, this figure shows a script for a game.
   (b) The actors who might be cast as player I are Mr. High and Mr. Low. The only actor available for the role of player II is Ms. Hoozat.
   (c) The actors' preferences are shown in Figures 11.7(b) and 11.7(c). As in Section 11.2.1, these diagrams show how the empty payoff boxes of Figure 11.7(a) would

[52]Recall Exercise 3.7.18(a).

[53]In fact, there is no way to rescue the cooperative conclusion of Section 10.8.1 if the actors are required to hold consistent beliefs. However, if slightly different payoffs are used in the Prisoners' Dilemma, the problem evaporates (Exercise 11.10.49).

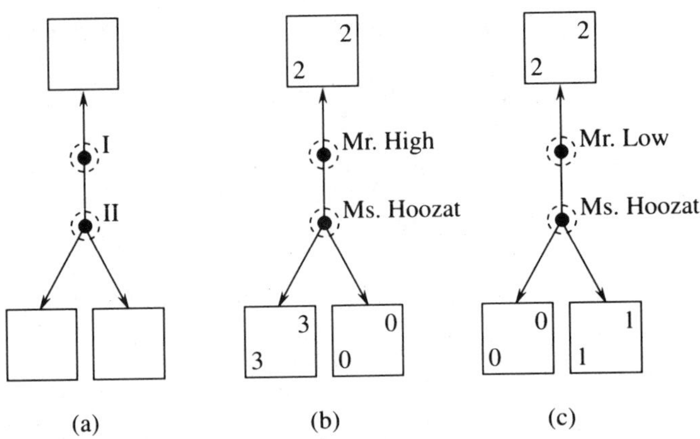

Figure 11.7 Information for Exercise 11.10.1.

be filled if it were common knowledge who was cast in the role of player I.

(d) For the actors' beliefs, it is enough to specify it to be common knowledge that Ms. Hoozat believes that each of Mr. High and Mr. Low is equally likely.

Draw extensive forms for *two* games of imperfect information to which Harsanyi's theory may lead. One should be a game with two players, and the other should be a game with three players.

2. Check that Figure 11.8(a) shows the correct strategic form for the two-player extensive form constructed in Exercise 11.10.1. (The pure strategy XY for player I means that Mr. High should use X if he gets to play, and that Mr. Low should use Y if he gets to play.) Also check that Figure 11.8(b) shows the correct strategic form for the three-player extensive form.
   (a) Confirm that (UU, R) and (DU, L) are the only Nash equilibria in pure strategies for the strategic form of Figure 11.8(a).
   (b) Confirm that (U, U, R) and (D, U, L) are the only Nash equilibria in pure strategies for the strategic form of Figure 11.8(b).
   (c) There are also mixed Nash equilibria for both strategic forms. Find all of these.
   (d) Find all the subgames for the extensive forms of Exercise 11.10.1, and hence explain why all the Nash equilibria you have found are subgame-perfect.
3. Review Section 4.6 on the successive deletion of dominated strategies.

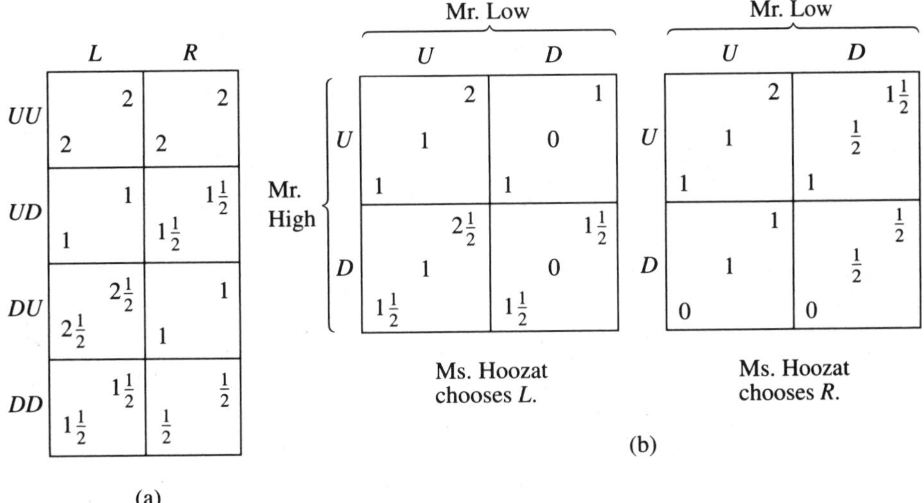

Figure 11.8 Strategic forms for Exercise 11.10.2.

(a) Which of the Nash equilibria of Exercise 11.10.2(a) and Exercise 11.10.2(b) survive the successive deletion of dominated strategies?

(b) For most purposes it does not matter whether one models the problem of Exercise 11.10.1 as a two-player or a three-player game of imperfect information, but occasionally subtle differences arise. Detect such a difference by considering how things change in part (a) when only *strongly* dominated strategies are deleted.

4. The game of Exercise 11.10.1 can be seen as a signaling game in which Mr. High seeks to communicate his identity to Ms. Hoozat so that she can select the outcome that he and she jointly prefer. Since the players in such *team games* (Section 1.9.1) have identical goals, the games often provide a particularly uncluttered arena for the study of signaling problems.

(a) Exercise 11.10.2 identifies two subgame-perfect equilibria in pure strategies. Reformulate these as assessment equilibria (Section 11.8).

(b) Which of the two equilibria is selected by Kreps' "intuitive criterion" (Section 11.8.2).

(c) Give an alternative selection criterion based on Exercise 11.10.3.

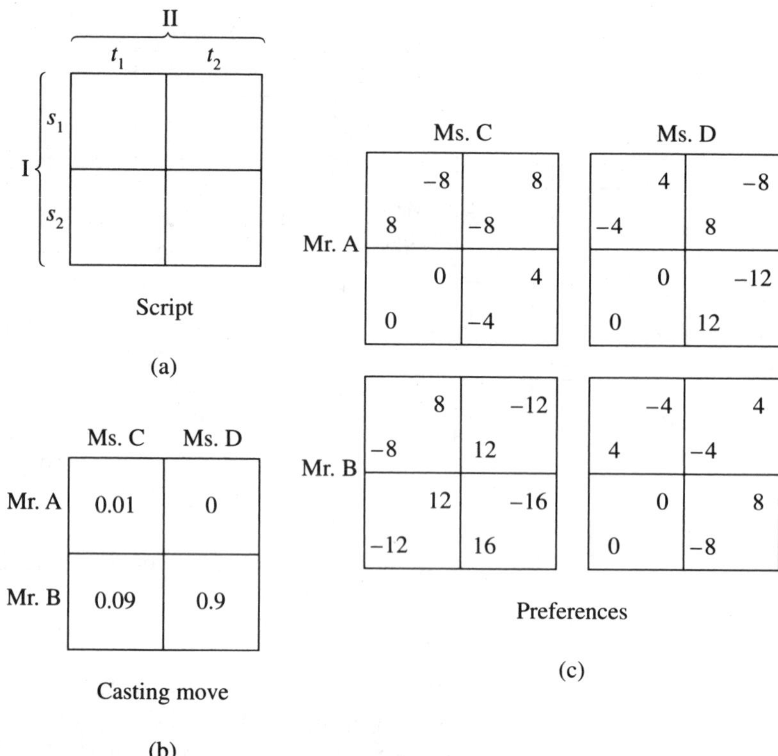

Figure 11.9 Information for Exercise 11.10.5.

5. This exercise requires Harsanyi's theory to be applied to a problem that is a little more distant from Section 11.2.1 than Exercise 11.10.1.
   (a) The underlying rules are shown in Figure 11.9(a). In the terminology of Section 11.2.1, this figure shows a script for a game.
   (b) The actors who might be cast as player I are Mr. A and Mr. B. The actors who might be cast in the role of player II are Ms. C and Ms. D.
   (c) Figure 11.9(b) shows how Chance casts the roles of player I and player II. For example, the probability that Mr. B and Ms. D are cast as player I and player II is 0.9.
   (d) The actors' preferences are shown in Figure 11.9(c). As in Section 11.2.1, these diagrams show how the empty payoff boxes of Figure 11.9(a) would be filled if it were common knowledge how the players had been cast. Notice that the payoffs always sum to zero.[54]

[54]As a consequence, the game of imperfect information obtained by completing the incomplete information structure will be zero-sum, although we would not be entitled to draw this conclusion if the actors had inconsistent beliefs (Exercise 11.10.10).

Explain why it is not true that Chance's choice of who is to be player I is independent of her choice of who is to be player II. Find the probability prob(B|C) that Ms. C will assign to the event that her opponent is Mr. B, conditional on Ms. C learning that she has been chosen to be player II. (Exercise 2.6.9.) Also find the other seven conditional probabilities of this type. (It may be convenient to list these in tables using the format illustrated in Figure 11.11.) Who are the actors who will know for sure who their opponent is should they be chosen to play?

6. This exercise continues Exercise 11.10.5.
   (a) Solve each of the four two-player, zero-sum games shown in Figure 11.9(c). Mark the cell in each payoff table that will result when the solution strategies are used. These four games show the four possible ways Figure 11.9(a) could be completed if it were common knowledge who was occupying what role.
   (b) Think of the game of imperfect information described in Exercise 11.10.5 as a four-player game whose players are Mr. A, Mr. B, Ms. C and Ms. D. Solve this four-player game by successively deleting strongly dominated strategies. (You will not need to calculate carefully. For example, if Ms. C gets to play, she believes it very likely that her opponent is Mr. B. Her second pure strategy in this eventuality is so adverse[55] that she will always play her first pure strategy.)
   (c) What did you assume to be common knowledge in part (b)?
   (d) Return to 11.9(c) and mark the cell in each payoff table that will result if the actors for that table are chosen to play, and each uses the pure strategy you calculated in part (b). (Your mark should not be the same as that used in part (a)!)
   (e) Comment on the difference between the cells marked in part (a) and part (d). Explain, in particular, how Mr. A is able to exploit Ms. C's ignorance.[56]

---

[55]The calculation that you are being recommended to evade goes like this. Ms. C's second pure strategy yields at most 8 if her opponent is Mr. A, and at most -12 if she is playing Mr. B. The former occurs with probability $\frac{1}{10}$ and the latter with probability $\frac{9}{10}$. Her expected payoff from her second pure strategy is therefore at most $(8 - 12 \times 9)/10$. A similar calculation shows that she gets at least $(-8 + 8 \times 9)/10$ from her first pure strategy.

[56]If he is chosen to play, then he knows, not only that his opponent is Ms. C, but that she is much less well-informed than he.

7. This exercise is a second approach to Exercise 11.10.5.
   (a) Section 11.2.2 suggests thinking of player I as being a reincarnation of Von Neumann who gives advice to Mr. A and Mr. B. Similarly, player II may be seen as a reincarnation of Morgenstern who gives advice to Ms. C and Ms. D. Figure 11.10 shows the shape of the extensive form of the game that Von Neumann and Morgenstern will then see themselves as playing. Fill in the payoff boxes.

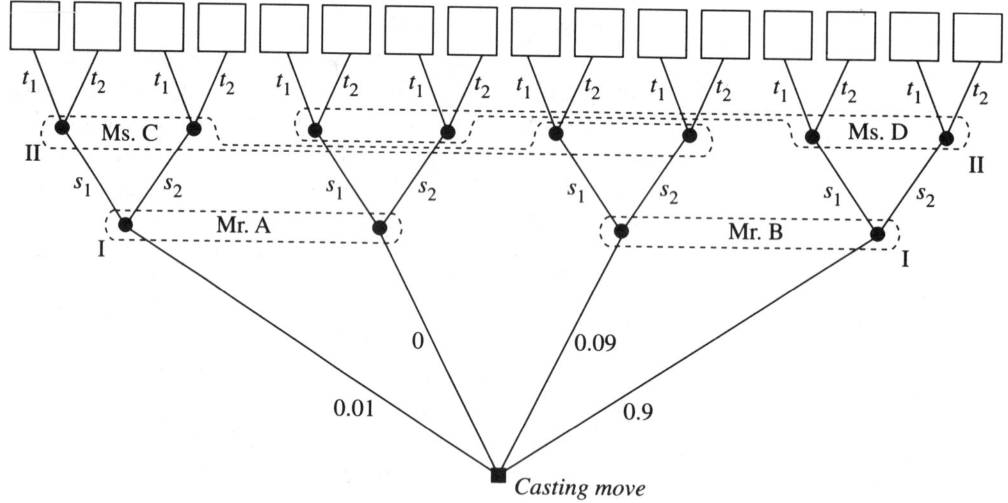

Figure 11.10 The skeleton game tree for Exercise 11.10.7.

   (b) Von Neumann and Morgenstern each have four pure strategies. What are they?
   (c) Find the strategic form of the game between Von Neumann and Morgenstern.[57] Confirm that the game is zero-sum. (See Exercise 11.10.10.)
   (d) Observe that Von Neumann's payoff matrix has a saddle point. Hence solve the game. Check that your solution coincides with that obtained in Exercise 11.10.6.
   (e) Check that the game can also be solved by the successive deletion of dominated strategies.

Phil

8. Von Neumann and Morgenstern will get the right answer in the two-player, zero-sum game constructed in Exercise 11.10.7 by selecting their strategies using the "maximin principle" (Section 6.5.7). Confirm that the same is not true of the actors in Exercise 11.10.6. Why is this?

[57] This is hard work!

Phil

9. This exercise asks yet more about the problem of Exercise 11.10.5.
   (a) How does the tree of Figure 11.10 need to be modified for it to represent the four-player game studied in Exercise 11.10.6?
   (b) If the players needed to randomize, explain why the approach of Exercise 11.10.6 would amount to using behavioral strategies where Exercise 11.10.7 would use mixed strategies.

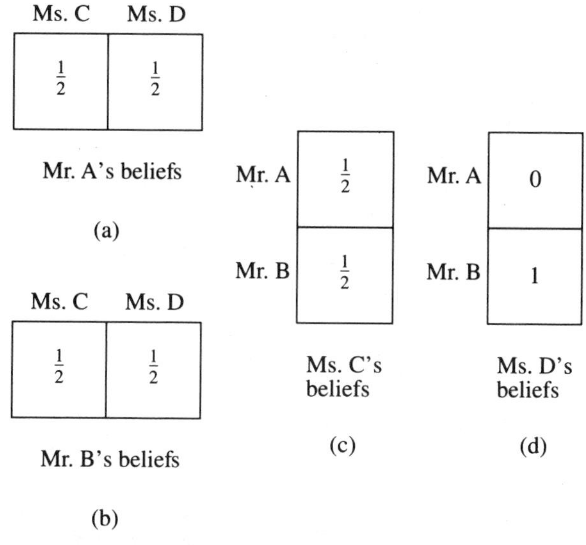

Figure 11.11 Tables for Exercise 11.10.10.

10. This is the final exercise based on the problem of Exercise 11.10.5. Suppose that it is no longer true that there is common knowledge of the probabilities with which a casting move selects the actors. Thus Figure 11.9(b) no longer applies. It is therefore necessary to consider a rootless game as described in Section 11.9. It is common knowledge that the actors' beliefs in this rootless game are those given in Figure 11.11.
    (a) Show that the specified beliefs are not consistent with the Harsanyi doctrine. That is, there is no casting move that would lead to the actors holding these beliefs after learning that they were to play. (It may help to review Exercise 11.10.5.)
    (b) Model the situation as a two-player game of imperfect information played between Von Neumann and Morgenstern.

(c) Compute enough of the strategic form to demonstrate that the game is *not* zero-sum, even though the payoffs in each cell of Figure 11.9(c) sum to zero.

Econ 11. Each of two agents simultaneously decides whether to pay for the provision of a *public good.* The good is said to be public because, if it is made available, an agent who free-rides by paying nothing gets just as much pleasure from its enjoyment as an agent who paid for it. Figure 11.12(a) shows what the payoffs would be if all costs and benefits were common knowledge. In this payoff table, c_i represents the cost to player i of ensuring that the public good is available.

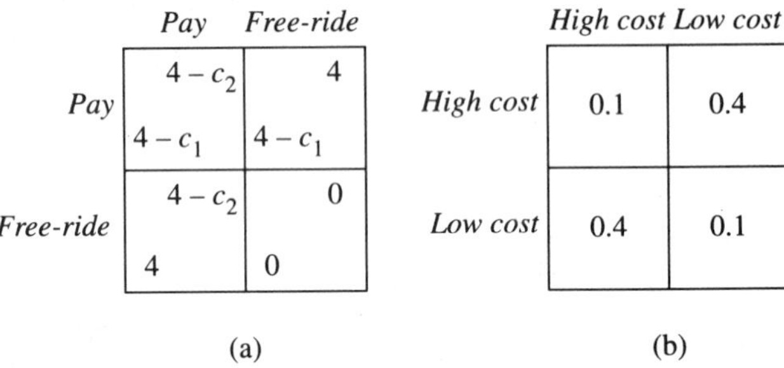

Figure 11.12 Information for Exercise 11.10.11.

(a) Explain why Figure 11.12(a) is a version of Chicken (Figure 7.3(c) and Figure 7.17(a)). Find its three Nash equilibria in the case when $0 < c_i < 4$. If $c_1 = c_2 = 1$ and the mixed Nash equilibrium is used, how often will the public good be provided? Answer the same question when $c_1 = c_2 = 3$.

(b) Now consider the case when the costs c_i are not common knowledge. Assume instead that each agent's cost can be "high" ($c_i = 3$) or "low" ($c_i = 1$). It is common knowledge that each cost is determined independently, and that the probability of an agent having a high cost is p. Use Harsanyi's theory to model this situation as a simultaneous-move game with four players. If $\frac{1}{4} \leq p \leq \frac{3}{4}$, show that the game has a Nash equilibrium in which low-cost agents pay up and high-cost agents ride free. How often will the public good be provided?

(c) What do symmetric Nash equilibria look like when p is not in the range $\frac{1}{4} \leq p \leq \frac{3}{4}$?

(d) Find a symmetric Nash equilibrium when the assumptions of part (b) about what is commonly known about the distribution of costs is replaced by the assumption that Chance selects (c_1, c_2) on the basis of the table of Figure 11.12(b). How often will the public good be provided?

Econ

12. In Exercise 11.10.11(b), a benevolent government steps in to ensure that the public good is *always* provided. However, it still insists that the cost of providing the good be borne by the players. This cost cannot be shared between the players, and so the government's task is to decide who should pay. It would prefer to assign the cost to a player whose cost is low, but only the players themselves know their true costs. However, civil servants are well-educated people who are aware that the revelation principle of Section 11.7.3 exists. An economist is therefore employed to design a direct mechanism that induces both players to report their true costs of providing the public good. Why will the government be disappointed with the scheme the economist designs?

Review

13. Let $I = [a, b]$ be an interval of length $l = b - a$. For values of x inside I, a function $p : \mathbb{R} \to \mathbb{R}_+$ is given by $p(x) = l^{-1}$. For values of x outside I, $p(x) = 0$. A random variable X that has p as its probability density function (Section 11.4.1) is said to be *uniformly distributed* on the interval I. Such a random variable never takes values outside I, and is "equally likely" to take any of the values inside I (Section 12.2.1). Show that the probability distribution function $P : \mathbb{R} \to [0, 1]$ for X satisfies $P(x) = 0$ when $x < a$, $P(x) = 1$ when $x > b$, and $P(x) = (x - a)/l$ when $a < x < b$.

Review

14. Calculate the probability that a random variable which is uniformly distributed on the interval $[3, 5]$ takes a value in the interval $[2, 4]$.

Review

15. A random variable is *exponentially distributed* on the interval $[0, \infty)$ if it has a probability density function $p : \mathbb{R} \to \mathbb{R}_+$ given by $p(x) = 0$ when $x < 0$ and $p(x) = ae^{-ax}$ when $x \geq 0$. The parameter a must be positive. What is the corresponding probability distribution function? Why would it not be admissible to seek to specify that $p(x) = 0$ for $x < 0$, and $p(x) = e^{-2x}$ for $x \geq 0$?

Review 16. Compute [58]

(a) $\frac{d}{dx}\left(\int_0^x (1+y^{10})^{-20}\right)$

(b) $\frac{d}{dx}\left(\int_{-23}^x (1+y^{10})^{-20}\,dy\right)$

(c) $\frac{d}{dx}\left(\int_x^{67} (1+y^{10})^{-20}\,dy\right)$

(d) $\frac{d}{dx}\left(\int_0^{x^2} (1+y^{10})^{-20}\,dy\right)$

Review 17. Let $f : [3,4] \to \mathbb{R}$ be continuous on $[3,4]$ and differentiable on $(3,4)$. Assume that $f(3) = 0$. Integrate by parts (Section 11.4.3) to show that

$$\int_3^4 f(v)\,dv = -\int_3^4 (v-4)f'(v)\,dv\,.$$

Review 18. Why is a probability distribution function $P : \mathbb{R} \to [0,1]$ increasing? Why does it follow that a continuous[59] probability density function $p : \mathbb{R} \to \mathbb{R}_+$ must be nonnegative? If $P(a) = P(b)$ and $a < b$, why must it be true that $p(x) = 0$ for $a < x < b$?

Review 19. Give an example of a random variable that has no probability density function. (Any random variable from an earlier chapter will suffice.) *Explain* why no probability density function exists.

Review 20. If the random variable X is uniformly distributed (Exercise 11.10.13) on the interval $[a,b]$, confirm that $\mathcal{E}X = \frac{1}{2}(a+b)$.

Review 21. If the random variable X is exponentially distributed as in Exercise 11.10.15, confirm that $\mathcal{E}X = 1/a$.

Econ 22. Answer Exercise 11.10.11(b) again, but with the assumption that the agents' costs are independent and uniformly distributed on the interval [0,4]. You will now need to formulate your own criterion for what number γ should constitute the dividing line between "high" and "low" cost, since you are still seeking an equilibrium in which low-cost agents pay and high-cost agents free-ride.

Econ 23. In the Cournot duopoly model of Section 11.5.1, take $\mathcal{M} = [0,c]$ and $\mathcal{F} = [\gamma, c]$, where $0 < \gamma < c < M$. For each

---

[58] Before trying to evaluate the integrals, recall the fundamental theorem of calculus (Section 11.4.2). For part (d), remember the rule for differentiating a "function of a function". In this case, you have to differentiate an expression of the form $F(x^2)$, and so the derivative will take the form $F'(x^2)2x$.

[59] Without this proviso it would be strictly necessary to qualify the statements that follow with the phrase "almost everywhere".

b in $\mathcal{F}$, assume that Ms. b's beliefs about the firm I's unit cost a are represented by a uniform probability distribution on $[0, b]$. Assume that the beliefs of each Mr. a (about the parameter b that describes firm II's beliefs about firm I's unit cost) are represented by a uniform probability distribution on $[\gamma, c]$. Using the notation of Section 11.5.1, show that $\overline{a}(b) = \frac{1}{2}b$ and $\overline{\overline{a}} = \frac{1}{4}(\gamma + c)$. Deduce that Mr. a's expected profit is $\{(8M + 7c - 12a - \gamma)/24\}^2$, and that Ms. b's expected profit is $\{(16M - 31c + 6b + \gamma)/48\}^2$.

Econon 24. Take $M = 10$, $c = 5$ and $\gamma = 0$ in Exercise 11.10.23. Assume it to be common knowledge that firm II must now pay a fixed cost of $F^2 = \frac{1}{16}$ to enter the industry, while firm I continues to face no fixed cost at all. If Ms. b plans to stay out when $b < b^* < c$ and to enter when $b > b^* > 0$, explain why her expected profit when she enters is $\{(5 + 6b + b^*)/48\}^2$. Deduce that the equilibrium value of b^* is 1.

Econ 25. Section 7.2.1 describes a Cournot Duopoly Game in which two firms with constant unit cost compete in the presence of the demand equation $p = M - q$. Section 11.5.1 introduced some incomplete information into the story. The current exercise studies a simpler problem of incomplete information based on the same duopoly problem. Each firm knows its own unit cost, but is uncertain about the other firm's unit cost. However, there is no uncertainty about what each firm believes about its opponent's unit cost. In fact, it is common knowledge that every firm's beliefs are described by the same probability density function. Show that the equilibrium ouput of a firm with unit cost c is $Q(c) = \frac{1}{2}(\frac{2}{3}M - c - \frac{1}{3}\overline{c})$, where $\overline{c}$ is the expected unit cost of the opponent.

Econ 26. This exercise is another incomplete information variant of the Cournot Duopoly Game. In this version, it is common knowledge that all firms have zero unit cost. However, the demand equation is unknown. It is common knowledge that the equation has the form $p = w - q$, but the precise value of $w > 0$ is uncertain. Different types of firm will have different beliefs about the probability density function for w. Each firm knows its own type but not the type of its opponent. It therefore needs a second probability density function to describe its beliefs about the type of the opponent. It is common knowledge that this second probability density function is the same whatever the other characteristics of a firm may be. In equilibrium, show that $3\overline{Q} = \overline{\overline{w}}$, where $\overline{Q}$ is what a firm expects the other's output to be, and $\overline{\overline{w}}$ is what a firm expects the other's expectation of w to be. (Assume that each firm's expected value of w is close to $\overline{\overline{w}}$.)

Econ 27. This exercise returns to the setting of Section 11.5.1 to pose a problem about entry deterrence with signaling. The industry is now to operate for *two* periods after which it will cease to exist. Each of two firms seeks to maximize its sum of profits over both periods. Firm I is an incumbent monopolist who produces in both periods. In the first period he is the only producer. The demand equation is $p = M - q$ and his unit cost is a. However, firm I does not necessarily produce the monopoly output of $\frac{1}{2}(M - a)$ in the first period because this may convey useful information about his costs to firm II, who is waiting in the wings with a view to entering the industry in the second period.

At the beginning of the first period, everybody's knowledge is as described for the Cournot model with incomplete information of Section 11.5.1. However, at the end of the first period, firm II will update her beliefs about firm I's unit cost a using any information he has revealed by his production decision in the first period. Using her updated beliefs, she now predicts what will happen if she were to enter the industry. If she stays out, firm I will be pleased, since he is then free to produce the monopoly output in the second period. However, firm II will enter if her expected profit exceeds the positive fixed cost F^2 of entry. Assume that F^2 is common knowledge.

Proceed on the assumption that a separating equilibrium (Section 11.8.2) exists. In a separating equilibrium, each Mr. a plans to produce a different amount. Firm I's output therefore fully reveals its unit cost to firm II. This trivializes the updating problem for each Ms. b.

(a) If firm II knows that firm I's cost is a, show that she will enter in the second period if $a > a^*$ and stay out if $a < a^*$, where $a^* = 3F + 2c - M$. To keep things simple, assume it to be common knowledge that every Ms. b has a probability density function that is positive on $(a^* - \delta, a^* + \delta)$ for some $\delta > 0$.

(b) In a separating equilibrium, no Mr. a will wish to mimic the behavior of a Mr. α with $a \neq \alpha$. In particular, no Mr. a with $a < a^*$ will wish to mimic a Mr. α with $\alpha < a^*$. Deduce that any Mr. a with $a^* - \delta < a < a^*$ must be producing his monopoly output in the first period.

(c) A Mr. a with $a^* < a < a^* + \delta$ decides to deviate from his separating equilibrium output in the first period. Instead, he copies the first-period output of a Mr. α with $a^* - \delta < \alpha < a^*$. Why does Mr. a gain

$$\{\tfrac{1}{2}(M-a)\}^2 - \{\tfrac{1}{3}(M+c-2a)\}^2$$

in the second period. Show that this quantity is positive when $a = a^*$. Given any $\varepsilon > 0$, explain why Mr. a's deviation in the first period can be guaranteed to cost less than ε by taking both a and α sufficiently close to a^*.

(d) Deduce that no separating equilibria can exist under the conditions considered in this exercise.

Econon

28. Show that a separating equilibrium can exist in Exercise 11.10.27 if the conditions are changed. Consider the case in which it is common knowledge that Mr. a can only be one of two types.

Econ

29. This exercise investigates pooling equilibria (Section 11.8.2) in the entry deterrence game of Exercise 11.10.27, but with the assumptions of Exercise 11.10.24. In a pooling equilibrium, each Mr. a plans to produce the *same* output in the first period. This trivializes the updating problem for Ms. b because what happens in the first period conveys no information to her.

(a) Consult Exercises 11.10.23 and 11.10.24, and so obtain an expression for Mr. a's expected second-period profit in a pooling equilibrium.

(b) Whether it is profitable for Mr. a to deviate depends on what firm II will believe if she should observe such out-of-equilibrium behavior. Show that there is an assessment equilibrium in which all Mr. a's produce the output of 5 in the first period that would be produced by a monopolist with zero unit cost. Let each Ms. b have the optimistic belief that, if firm I deviates from producing 5 in the first period, then its unit cost must be as large as it can possibly be. After such a deviation, Ms. b therefore enters and produces 5/3 in the second period, because this is optimal against an opponent with unit cost $a = 5$. The deviant Mr. a then produces his best reply to 5/3 in the second period.

(c) Why might a kibitzer who is unaware of the possibility of a rival appearing in the second period be puzzled while watching the production decisions of a firm I with unit cost 5 in those cases when firm II decides not to enter?

Phil

30. Explain why a principal who is confined to using a take-it-or-leave-it mechanism in auctioning her house can be seen as playing a kind of Ultimatum Game (Section 5.8) with the potential buyers. Use the analogy to discuss how reasonable it is in designing mechanisms to assume that ties should be broken in favor of the principal.

Econ

31. A painting is to be sold at a Vickrey auction. It is common knowledge that all the dollar valuations of the painting by potential buyers are different positive integers, but the valuations themselves are unknown. Section 11.7.1 explains why it is a weakly dominating strategy for each potential buyer to bid his true valuation. Explain why it is also an equilibrium for each potential buyer to bid one dollar less than his true valuation. Why is this lying equilibrium a Pareto-improvement on the truth-telling equilibrium? Explain why auction theory disregards such alternatives to the truth-telling equilibrium.

Econ

32. An antique Chess set is to be sold at a dealer's auction. One of the 32 pieces is slightly chipped, and so the set is worth only \$10,000. If it were perfect, it would be worth \$100,000. For reasons beyond anyone's control, each of the N dealers has time to inspect only 31 of the pieces carefully. Nearly all the dealers therefore find the damaged piece, but some may not. To a dealer who happens not to inspect the damaged piece, it will seem that good care has been taken of the Chess set, and so he assigns a probability of 0.9 to the event that the set is perfect.
   (a) What is the probability that all the dealers find the damaged piece? What is the probability that exactly one dealer fails to find the damaged piece?
   (b) Why is the probability that two or more dealers fail to find the damaged piece equal to

$$1 - \left(\tfrac{31}{32}\right)^N - \left(\tfrac{N}{32}\right)\left(\tfrac{31}{32}\right)^{N-1} ?$$

   Estimate this probability for the cases $N = 2$, $N = 10$ and $N = 100$.
   (c) The dealers are risk-neutral, and the Chess set is sold using the sealed-bid, Vickrey mechanism (Section 11.7.1). At what prices is it possible that the set might sell?
   (d) For each of the cases of part (b), determine the probability that the Chess set will be sold for \$100,000.
   (e) Guess what economists mean when they speak of the *winner's curse*!

Econ 33. Various auctioning mechanisms are described in Section 11.7.1. Model an English auction as a game of timing like Duel of Section 2.4.1. Insist that the initial bid is \$0, and that subsequent bids raise the previous bid by a fixed amount \$$m$. Why is it a dominating strategy to plan to continue raising until you win, unless this would require you to make a bid that exceeds your valuation? If players use these strategies, why is the seller's expected selling price the same as in a Vickrey auction for the limiting case when $m \to 0$? In Section 6.3.2, a "continuous time" strategic form for Duel is given. Offer a similar model for an English auction and hence pinpoint its essential equivalence to a Vickrey auction.

Econ 34. Why is a Dutch auction essentially equivalent to a (first-price) sealed-bid auction?

Econ 35. It is common knowledge that the valuations V_1 and V_2 of the two risk-neutral potential buyers at a Vickrey auction are independent and uniformly distributed on [3,4]. If $3 \leq v \leq 4$, explain why the probability that both valuations exceed v is $(4 - v)^2$. Assuming that the object is sold at a price equal to the smaller of the two valuations, it follows that the probability that it is sold for v or less is $P(v) = 1 - (4 - v)^2$. You can use this fact to find a probability density function p for the selling price. Use this to show that the expected selling price is $3\frac{1}{3}$. (Assume that the owner is willing to sell at any positive price.) Why is the expected selling price the same in an English auction?

Econ 36. With the same assumptions about buyers as in the preceding exercise, use the following method to show that there is an equilibrium in a (first-price) sealed-bid auction in which each potential buyer bids his expectation of the other buyer's valuation conditional on this being less than his own. A potential buyer with valuation v will then bid $\frac{1}{2}(v + 3)$. If all the actors who might be occupying the role of the other buyer behave this way but you bid w, you will win the auction with probability $2w - 6$ when $3 < w < 3\frac{1}{2}$. If your valuation for the object is v, your expected payoff will then be $(v - w)(2w - 6)$. In equilibrium, you will have chosen w to maximize this quantity.

Econ 37. Continuing the previous exercise, show that the expected selling price is $3\frac{1}{3}$ when the equilibrium strategies are used. (If you use the same method as Exercise 11.10.29, you will need to show that the probability that both buyers bid w or less is $P(w) = (2w - 6)^2$ when $3 < w < 3\frac{1}{2}$. When $w > 3\frac{1}{2}$, $P(w) = 1$.)

Econ

38. Under the assumptions about buyers of Exercise 11.10.35, the last few exercises have shown that the expected selling price will be the same for sealed-bid, English, Dutch and Vickrey auctions. Such a result is called a *revenue equivalence* theorem. Why will a risk-neutral principal who uses her optimal take-it-or-leave-it auction demand whatever value of w maximizes $w\{1-(w-3)^2\}$? Show that her expected selling price is then less than $3\frac{1}{3}$.

Econ

39. If $0 < p < 1$, find a formula for $Q : [3, B] \to [0, 1]$ which has $Q(3) = 0$ and $Q(B) = 1$, and which makes $\{p + (1-p)Q(b)\}(4-b)$ constant for $3 \leq b \leq B$. This will be helpful in adapting the technique of Section 0.1.2 to obtain a Nash equilibrium in the game that the agents play in Section 11.7.2 when the principal chooses the first-price, sealed-bid auctioning mechanism. Use a technique like that of Exercise 11.10.35 to show that the expected selling price is $3 + (1-p)^2$ when this equilibrium is used. Exercise 11.10.38 mentions a revenue equivalence theorem. What is the revenue equivalence theorem here?

Econ

40. Section 11.7.2 considered various auctioning mechanisms for selling a house. None of the mechanisms envisaged the possibility that the seller might charge the potential buyers a fee to participate in the auction. Is this possibility also neglected in Section 11.7.4, where the design of an optimal auctioning mechanism is discussed?

Econ

41. Exercises 11.10.35 through 11.10.38 are about auctions in which everybody is risk-neutral and the valuations of the two potential buyers are independent and uniformly distributed on $[3, 4]$. The next four exercises are concerned with designing an *optimal* symmetric auction when these facts are common knowledge. As in Section 11.7.4, the revelation principle tells us that it is only necessary to look at truth-telling Nash equilibria of *direct* mechanisms in which each potential buyer announces a valuation v. In Section 11.7.4, a valuation could only be 3 or 4, but here v may be any number in $[3, 4]$. After announcing v, a buyer expects to pay $f(v)$, and to win the auction with probability $p(v)$. (It will be assumed throughout that the functions f and p are continuous on $[3, 4]$ and differentiable on $(3, 4)$.)
(a) Explain why the *incentive-compatibility* constraints

$$vp(v) - f(v) \geq vp(w) - f(w) \qquad (11.16)$$

must be satisfied for all v and w in $[3, 4]$. (Recall

(11.6) and (11.7) of Section 11.7.4.) Deduce that $v(p(v) - f(v)$, $p(v)$ and $f(v)$ are all increasing.[60]

(b) Inequality (11.16) says that $vp(w) - f(w)$ is maximized when $w = v$. Deduce that a necessary condition for incentive-compatibility is that

$$vp'(v) = f'(v), \tag{11.17}$$

for each v in $(3, 4)$.

Econ

42. Continue the previous exercise by showing that the *individual rationality* constraints corresponding to (11.9) and (11.10) in Section 11.7.4 are

$$vp(v) - f(v) \geq 0, \tag{11.18}$$

for all v in $[3, 4]$. Explain why (11.18) is necessarily satisfied when the incentive-compatibility constraints (11.16) are satisfied, provided only that (11.18) holds for $v = 3$.

Why must the individual rationality constraint $3p(3) - f(3) = 0$ for a potential buyer with the lowest possible valuation be active for an optimal mechanism?[61] It turns out that $p(3) = f(3) = 0$, but $p(v) > 0$ for $v > 3$. To keep the algebra under control, these properties of the optimal mechanism will be assumed in the following exercises.[62]

Math

43. Following Section 11.7.4, the next step in continuing the optimal design problem of the preceding exercises is to consider the constraints corresponding to (11.11), (11.12) and (11.13) that govern the values that the probabilities $p(v)$ can assume. Write

$$P(v) = \int_3^v p(w)\, dw .$$

Suppose the principal is told that a particular agent has a valuation less than v, but is otherwise uninformed. Why does she assign a probability of $P(v)/(v - 3)$ to the event

[60]Remember that *increasing* does not mean the same as *strictly increasing*. The method by which you prove these "monotonicity" results is widely useful in mechanism design.

[61]Consider the result of replacing the function f by $f - \varepsilon$.

[62]Only a few extra calculations are entailed in replacing the assumption $p(3) = f(3) = 0$ by $3p(3) - f(3) = 0$. However, the final sentence of the next exercise depends on the fact that any buyer with a valuation above the minimum does sometimes win the auction. If it is not true that $p(v) > 0$ for $v > 3$, one can let m be the largest valuation for which $p(m) = 0$. The coming exercises can then be answered with $[m, 4]$ replacing $[3, 4]$ where appropriate. A final extra step is then needed to determine m.

that he will win the auction?[63] Recalling that only *symmetric* mechanisms are permitted, explain why $P(4) \leq \frac{1}{2}$ says that it is impossible that both agents can win. Explain why $P(v)/(v-3) \geq \frac{1}{2}(v-3)$ says that it is impossible that both agents will lose, given that both valuations are less than v.

Math

44. This exercise continues the optimal design problem of the preceding exercises by observing that the principal expects to collect

$$F = \int_3^4 f(v)\,dv$$

from each of the two agents (rather than (11.8) as in Section 11.7.4.) Integrate by parts (Exercise 11.10.17), and then use (11.17). Integrate what results *twice* by parts[64] to obtain that

$$F = 4P(4) - 2\int_3^4 P(v)\,dv\,.$$

Deduce from the previous exercise that $2F \leq 3\frac{1}{3}$. However, Exercise 11.10.35 tells us that an expected selling price of $3\frac{1}{3}$ can be achieved. Why does it follow that the sealed-bid, English, Dutch and Vickrey auctions are all optimal for the principal?

45. Find *all* Nash equilibria in Selten's Horse of Section 11.8.1, including those in mixed strategies. Which of the Nash equilibria can be twinned with a belief system to produce an assessment equilibrium? (Since each player has only one information set, mixed and behavioral strategies coincide in this game.)

Math

46. This exercise illustrates the problems raised by moral hazard. A risk-neutral manager is responsible for two workers who can operate at two effort levels: idle ($E = 0$) or busy ($E = 8$). Their effort levels cannot be directly monitored. The manager therefore constructs an incentive scheme based on a worker's output. Each worker can either output a satisfactory item worth \$10, or a reject item worth \$0. The manager pays the worker \$$X$ in the first instance, and \$$Y$ in the second. When a worker's wage is W and his effort level is E, his utility is $U(W,E) = 10\sqrt{W} - E$. Each worker has a reservation utility of 10.

---

[63]Section 12.2 explains how to compute conditional probabilities in such circumstances.

[64]It is amazing how often integrating by parts turns out to be a good idea!

		Idle		Busy	
		\$0	\$10	\$0	\$10
Idle	\$0	$\frac{8}{12}$	$\frac{1}{12}$	$\frac{3}{12}$	$\frac{5}{12}$
	\$10	$\frac{1}{12}$	$\frac{2}{12}$	$\frac{1}{12}$	$\frac{3}{12}$
Busy	\$0	$\frac{3}{12}$	$\frac{1}{12}$	$\frac{2}{12}$	$\frac{1}{12}$
	\$10	$\frac{5}{12}$	$\frac{3}{12}$	$\frac{1}{12}$	$\frac{8}{12}$

Figure 11.13 The table for Exercise 11.10.46.

Figure 11.13 shows how the workers' effort levels are related to their outputs. The entries are probabilities that reflect factors in the production process outside anyone's control. Find the principal's optimal values for $\$X$ and $\$Y$ given that her aim is to induce both workers to remain in her employ operating at the busy effort level.[65] Compare the principal's expected payoff from the use of the optimal scheme with the "first-best" payoff that she could obtain if she were able to monitor the workers' effort levels directly.

Econon

47. Akerlof's "Market for Lemons" is a celebrated example of the operation of adverse selection (Section 11.7.2). In the following simplified version, a used car is sold at a take-it-or-leave-it auction. The car may either be an orange or a lemon,[66] but you have to own the car before you can tell the difference. Everybody is risk-neutral. Working in units of a thousand dollars, sellers value oranges

[65] You are being invited to write down individual rationality and incentive compatibility constraints. The form of the workers' utility function also imposes the additional implicit constraints that $X \geq 0$ and $Y \geq 0$.

[66] For those whose native language is not English, "being left with a lemon" means ending up with something unexpectedly bad. Presumably, this is because a lemon can sometimes be mistaken for an orange until the first bite is taken. But why should "being sold a pup" mean the same thing?

at \$9 k and lemons at \$3 k. The many potential buyers all value oranges at \$12 k and lemons at \$6 k. All this is common knowledge.

(a) If it is common knowledge that there is a probability p of the car being a lemon, why does the car sell for $6(2-p)$?

(b) Why does a value of $\frac{1}{2} < p < 1$ deny the rationality of some participant?

(c) If the circumstances are such that more lemons are brought for sale to such auctions than oranges, what can be said about the number of oranges that will get auctioned this way?

Math

48. This exercise provides a more dramatic version of the "Market for Lemons" problem studied in Exercise 11.10.47. Everybody is still risk-neutral, and you still have to own a car to know its type. But now there are many types of car. At a take-it-or-leave-it auction, there are many potential buyers who would pay $\$(1+\varepsilon)x$ k for a car worth $\$x$ k to its current owner if they knew for sure what they were buying. To make things interesting, assume that $\varepsilon > 0$, and that nobody attributes a negative valuation to a car.

(a) If a car is offered at price $\$y$ k, write down a formula for the buyer's expected valuation of the car in terms of his probability density function f for the owner's valuation.

(b) Explain why the car will not be bought unless

$$(1+\varepsilon)\int_0^y xf(x)\,dx \geq y\int_0^y f(x)\,dx\,.$$

(c) Let $\varepsilon \to 0$ in this formula, and then integrate the left-hand side of the resulting formula by parts.

(d) If there is a positive probability that the owner values the car below $\$y$ k, show that the car will not be sold at price $\$y$ k when ε is sufficiently small.

(e) What can be said about the type of car that will be offered for auction, and the price at which it will sell in the case when ε is small? What does this have to do with lemons?

(f) What implicit assumptions have been made about what is common knowledge?

49. Section 10.8.1 studied the finitely repeated Prisoners' Dilemma of Figure 7.3(b) when the number of repetitions is not common knowledge. Section 11.9 explains why the model of Section 10.8.1 has the structure of a

rootless game. Section 11.9.1 explains why the actors' beliefs in the assessment equilibrium considered in Section 10.8.1 are not consistent with the Harsanyi doctrine. In this exercise, different beliefs are assigned to the actors. Let an actor whose information set is $\{n, n+1\}$ assign probability $1/(1+\delta)$ to the node n and probability $\delta/(1+\delta)$ to the node $n+1$.

(a) Why are these beliefs consistent when $0 < \delta < 1$? If a casting move were provided to give the game a root, with what probability would Chance choose Mr. n?

(b) Why does the cooperating equilibrium of Section 10.8.1 not survive this change in beliefs?

(c) Show that the same cooperating equilibrium is viable if the changed beliefs have $\delta \geq \frac{3}{4}$, provided that each 6 in the payoff table for the one-shot Prisoners' Dilemma of Figure 7.3(b) is replaced by a 5.

Phil

50. A novelty shop used to sell large decks of cards containing only Jokers and Knaves. It is common knowledge that the fraction p of Jokers in a deck was uniformly distributed on $[0, 1]$. Over the years, all but one of the decks is lost or destroyed. Current fashion now decrees that the remaining deck is valuable, but that its value is a function of the number of Jokers it contains. Before seeking to sell the deck, the owner visits all the collectors of such curiosities. Time allows each collector to inspect only a randomly chosen 10% of the cards in the deck. Each collector uses this information to update her prior for p. Why is the knowledge structure of this situation similar to that of Section 11.5.1? Use the analogy to comment on whether the model of Section 11.5.1 is consistent with the Harsanyi doctrine.

CHAPTER

12

Bluffing It Out

12.1 Poker

This last chapter contains no new ideas. It is a series of exercises on how to construct and analyze game-theoretic models.[1] The topic to be studied is Poker. There are several reasons for this choice. The first is sentimental. It was Von Neumann's second Poker model that led to my getting interested in game theory. I thought I knew that good Poker players had to bluff a lot, but I was amazed at the bluffing behavior that Von Neumann characterized as optimal.

The second reason for studying Poker is also sentimental to some extent. It provides an opportunity to pay tribute, not only to Von Neumann, but also to Borel, Nash and Shapley. The credit for creating game theory as a discipline has to go to Von Neumann, but the French mathematician Borel went some of the way before him. For example, Borel seems to have been the first to formulate the notion of a pure strategy.[2] Nash is, of course, an old friend, but little has been heard of Shapley because his best-known contributions are in cooperative game theory, about which this book has had little to say.

The third reason for studying Poker is not at all sentimental. Perhaps the most important thing that game theory has to offer is a language within which informational questions can be discussed sensibly. What people know and believe matters enormously to how they treat each other. This is particularly true in economics. But, until game theory came along, those who thought about such matters at all had nothing more solid to work with than their untutored intuition. And, as my own experience with Von Neumann's second Poker model bears witness, untutored intuition can be way off the mark in such matters. However, Poker presents at least some of the issues in a very pure form, unadulterated by the controversial empirical or policy questions that make it so hard to keep the logic straight in more complicated situations. It is not for nothing that a set of Poker-players is called a school. Once rational play in Poker has been mastered, it becomes impossible to make a certain class of errors in a broader context. This goes not only for Poker, but for numerous other parlor games also. It is particularly obvious in the case of toy games like Chicken and the Prisoners' Dilemma.

---

[1]Those who have been assiduously working the exercises in previous chapters will be relieved to learn that this chapter therefore requires no exercise section of its own.

[2]However, he thought that the minimax theorem was probably false. Fortunately, Von Neumann was unaware of Borel's work; otherwise he might have been discouraged.

People who do not understand how human knowledge is advanced are often scornful of such claims. What is the point, they say, of studying a silly parlor game like Poker if the aim is to gain insight into the broad sweep of human affairs? I like to characterize such folk as *naive positivists.* They have seldom received any serious mathematical training. Otherwise they would have learned that difficult problems do not commonly succumb to frontal attacks. One has to lay siege to them. In graduate school, mathematicians are taught to look at simpler versions of their problems first. Examples help to rid the mind of misconceptions and clarify what the difficulties are. They are also taught to look for analogies between the problem at hand and other problems that may have been solved, or perhaps are solvable. Such a search for insight may take one far afield. A political scientist may end up studying the Prisoners' Dilemma. Economists may look at the literature on Poker models. Naive positivists will think their labors ridiculous. But this is because naive positivists do not understand that nobody ever solved a difficult problem who had not learned to solve simple problems first.

12.1.1 How to Play Poker

Poker is a card game for which one needs about seven players for the variants normally played to be entertaining. Neighborhood games are often played for nickels and dimes, but there is really no point in playing Poker except for sums of money that it would really hurt to lose. Otherwise it is impossible to bluff effectively, and bluffing is what Poker is all about.

In Straight Poker, each player is dealt a *hand* consisting of five cards. For our purposes, it is only necessary to know that some hands are better than others. However, for the sake of completeness, the various types of hands are listed below in increasing order:

Bust (no distinguishing feature)
Pair
Two pair
Three of a kind
Straight (five cards of any suit in sequence)
Flush (five cards all of the same suit)
Full house (three of a kind plus a pair)
Four of a kind
Straight flush

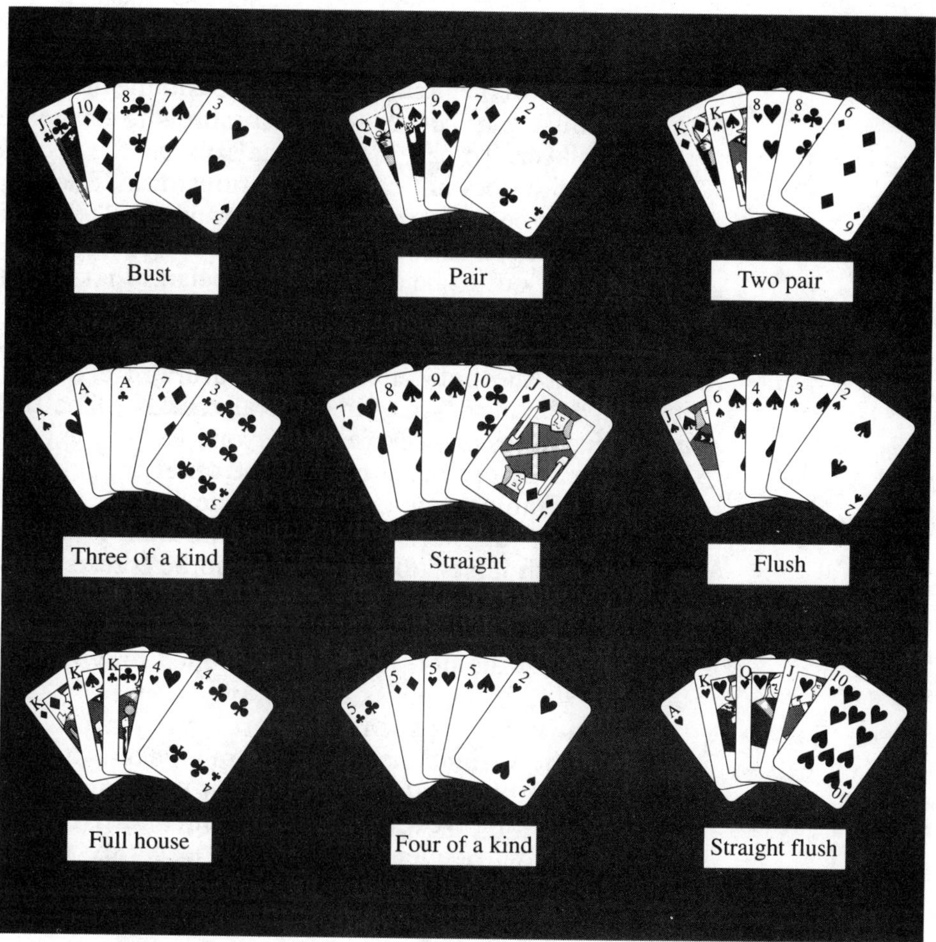

Figure 12.1 Poker hands.

Examples of the possible hands are shown in Figure 12.1. The hands are also ordered within each category. Thus, for example, a pair of Kings beats a pair of nines.[3] I have never been dealt a straight flush, and it is unlikely you will be any luckier. Often a pair is enough to win the pot in Straight Poker.

After the deal, the betting begins. Usually the players buy Poker *chips* to use instead of money. The chips that have been bet constitute the *pot*. In most Poker schools, each player is

[3]An Ace curiously counts as the highest card. Thus the sequence A,K,Q,J,10 is the best possible straight. However, the Ace is not allowed to forget its humble origins altogether, since the sequence A,2,3,4,5 is the lowest possible straight.

required to sweeten the pot by paying an amount called the *ante* before anything else happens. The player to the dealer's left then makes the first bet. After each bet, the next player on the left must *fold*, *call* or *raise*. To raise is to bet more than the last player. To call is to bet the same as the last player.[4] A player who does not call or raise, must fold. Such a player takes no further part in the game and loses all the chips he or she has staked so far. This is true even if a hand that was folded turns out to be better than the hand that finally wins the pot.

Once everyone who has not folded has the same number of chips in the pot, the betting is over. In a lively game, this may sometimes require several rounds of betting with numerous raises and reraises. Everyone still in the game now shows their cards, and the best hand takes the pot.

Usually limits are imposed on how much can be bet. With pot-limit betting, nobody can bet more than is currently in the pot. With table-stakes, nobody can be forced to play for more than the number of chips they choose to keep on the table. Limits of some sort are necessary to prevent rich players from "buying the pot", but, as mentioned previously, Poker becomes dull if the limits are too low.

Straight Poker, as such, is almost never played. However, innumerable variants flourish. In Draw Poker, there are two rounds of betting, with an opportunity to change some cards in between. In Five Card Stud, the first card is dealt face down. Each subsequent card is dealt face up, followed by a round of betting (making four rounds of betting in all). Seven Card Stud is similar in that some cards are dealt face up. Sometimes, the rules call for cards to be passed from one player to another. Sometimes wild cards[5] are designated. Nowadays, Hi-Lo games are very popular. In such games the high hand and the low hand split the pot.

Unlike Chess, Poker is not too complex to be analyzed with the help of a computer. However, detailed analyses of Poker variants that are actually played are of limited interest. They are of limited interest to those whose goal is to make a quick buck because game theory concerns itself with what to do when the opponents play optimally. But, with some exceptions—like the World Poker Championships—real Poker players seldom come anywhere near

---

[4]If nobody has bet anything previously, to call is to bet zero. This is known as *checking*.

[5]A wild card counts as anything that a player who holds it finds convenient.

optimizing. One makes money against such opponents by exploiting their mistakes, not by assuming that they don't make them.

Nor is a game-theoretic analysis of a Poker variant that is actually played of great interest to those, like us, who are seeking insight into how much bluffing and deceit one should anticipate from rational individuals. For this purpose, one wants to study *simple* models so that any insights that emerge are not hidden amongst a mass of detail.

One simplification will be to sweep away all the colorful but irrelevant labeling of Poker hands. Instead, each hand will be assigned a number, with the understanding that high numbers beat low numbers. A second simplification will be to look at Poker games played only by two or three players. The third simplification is to treat Poker as a zero-sum game. As observed in Section 6.5.1, this is not an assumption that can be taken for granted. It is true that whatever is won by one player must be lost by the others, but this will make the game zero-sum only if the players are risk-neutral and care only about money. However, real Poker players are often more concerned with finding opportunities for some macho posturing than with actually making money and, if the stakes are large, they are unlikely to be risk-neutral even if money is their major concern. However, it is the fourth simplification that is the most serious. The manner in which the players can bet will be restricted. Fortunately, this can be done in a way that leaves the essential strategic issues unaltered.

12.2 Conditional Probability Densities

Review 12.3 ⟶

Section 11.4 explains what it means to say that a random variable X has a probability distribution function $P : \mathbb{R} \to [0, 1]$ and a probability density function $p : \mathbb{R} \to \mathbb{R}_+$. If some new information about X is obtained, these functions have to be updated. Suppose the new information is that $a < X \leq b$. What will the new distribution function $Q : \mathbb{R} \to [0, 1]$ and the new density function $q : \mathbb{R} \to \mathbb{R}_+$ be, conditional on this new information?

Since one cannot condition on a zero probability event, it is necessary to assume that

$$c^{-1} = \text{prob}(a < X \leq b) = \int_a^b p(v)\,dv$$

is not zero. A formula for $Q(x) = \text{prob}(X \leq x \mid a < x \leq b)$

is then easy to obtain using the definition of a conditional probability from Section 2.1.4.

$$\begin{aligned} Q(x) &= \frac{\text{prob}(X \leq x \text{ and } a < X \leq b)}{\text{prob}(a < X \leq b)} \\ &= c\,\text{prob}(X \leq x \text{ and } a < X \leq b), \end{aligned}$$

and so

$$Q(x) = \begin{cases} 0, & \text{if } x \leq a \\ c\,\text{prob}(a < X \leq x), & \text{if } a < x \leq b \\ 1, & \text{if } x > b. \end{cases}$$

The interesting range is therefore $a < x \leq b$. For values of x in this range,

$$Q(x) = c \int_a^x p(u)\,du.$$

It is therefore an easy matter to write down a formula for the density of X conditional on the fact that $a < X \leq b$. We have that $q(x) = 0$ unless $a < x \leq b$. When $a < x \leq b$,

$$q(x) = cp(x) = p(x) \left\{ \int_a^b p(u)\,du \right\}^{-1}. \tag{12.1}$$

12.2.1 The Uniform Distribution

A random variable X is *uniformly distributed* on $[0, 1]$ if it has the probability density function $f : \mathbb{R} \to \mathbb{R}_+$ defined by

$$f(u) = \begin{cases} 1, & \text{if } 0 \leq u \leq 1 \\ 0, & \text{otherwise.} \end{cases}$$

If I is an interval in $[0, 1]$, then the fact that X is uniformly distributed on $[0, 1]$ implies that the probability that X lies in I is simply equal to the length l of the interval I. Thus, given any two intervals I of equal length in $[0, 1]$, it is just as likely that X lies in one as the other. This is what is meant when people say that X is "equally likely" to take all values in $[0, 1]$.[6]

What is the conditional probability density f_I for X when the conditioning information is that X lies in an interval I

[6] It does not mean that $\text{prob}(X = x) = \text{prob}(X = y)$ for all x and y in $[0, 1]$. This is true whenever X has a probability density function because the probability that X takes any particular value is then zero.

of length $l > 0$ inside [0, 1]? This can be read off from (12.1). We have that $f_I(u) = 0$ unless u is in I. If u is in I, then

$$f_I(u) = f(u)/l = 1/l. \qquad (12.2)$$

12.3 Borel's Poker Model

Borel modeled Poker as a two-player, zero-sum game with the very simple game tree shown in Figure 12.2(a). Figure 12.2(b) shows the game tree for the second of Von Neumann's Poker models. What these models have to tell us about bluffing is very instructive. However, comment is delayed until Section 12.5 when both models are considered together.

The Rules. Both players are assumed to be risk-neutral so that bets can be quoted in dollars. To begin with, each player pays an *ante* of $1. The cards are then dealt. One can tell that

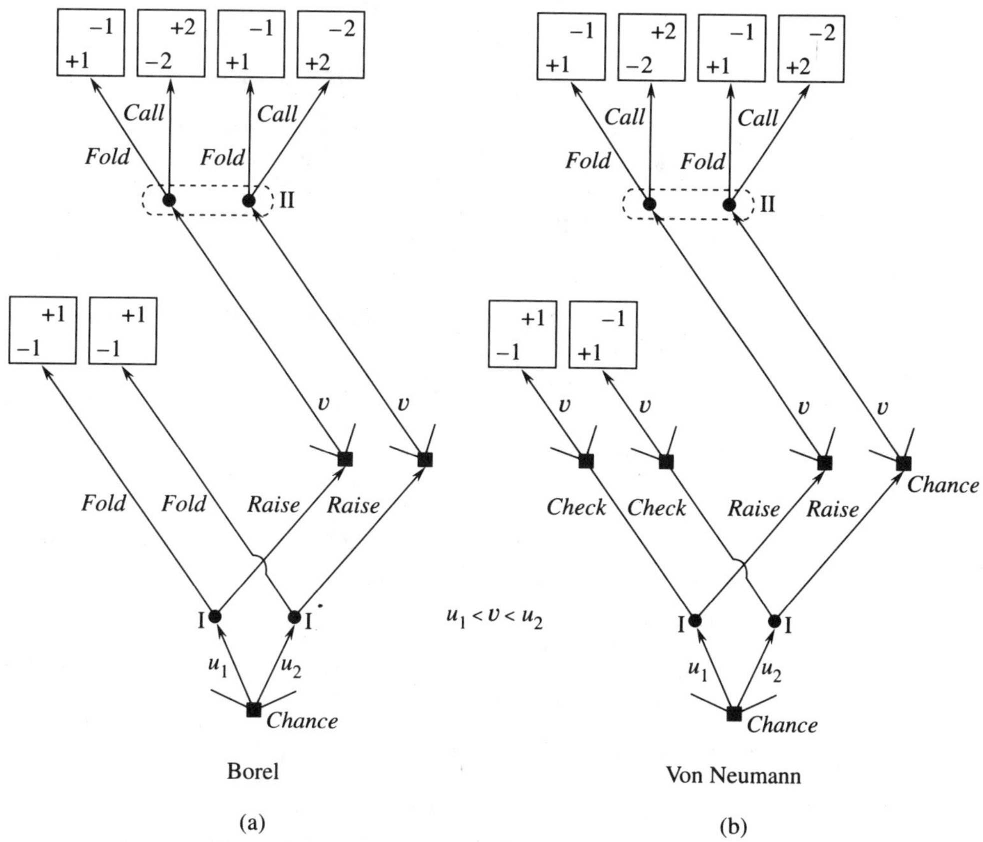

Figure 12.2 Some Poker models.

mathematicians constructed these models from the fact that a *hand* is simply a real number in the interval [0, 1]. Player I's hand is the value u of a random variable U, and player II's hand is the value v of a random variable V. The random variables U and V are *independent* and *uniformly distributed* on [0, 1].

In Figure 12.2, two possible hands, u_1 and u_2, for player I are shown. For convenience in drawing the game tree, player II is shown receiving her hand v after player I has decided how to bet. Notice that the hand v shown in Figure 12.2 satisfies $u_1 < v < u_2$.

In Borel's model, player I can only *fold* or *raise* after seeing his hand. If he folds, then he loses his[7] ante of \$1 to player II. A raise consists of betting a further \$1. After player II sees her hand, she can *fold* or *call*. If she folds, then she loses her ante of \$1 to player I. To call, she must put a further \$1 in the pot. The game is then over, and the players show their cards. Whoever has the better hand takes the whole pot.[8] The loser is then down by the \$2 that the winner gains.

12.3.1 First Approach to Borel's Model

This chapter is an extended exercise on the techniques of elementary game theory. *Two* analyses of Borel's model are therefore offered. Although one would not normally think of Poker in terms of "incomplete information", the two analyses are close cousins of the two approaches distinguished in Section 11.2.2.

In the first approach, one can imagine that a player waits until *after* he or she has been dealt a card before deciding what action to take. If it helps, one can therefore think of a player I holding hand u as Mr. u, and a player II holding hand v as Ms. v.

To keep things simple, we will look for an equilibrium in which the strategies used are those that Colonel Blotto would appreciate. They tell a player to bet high with a high hand and low with a low hand. More precisely, the plan is to look for

---

[7]The word *his* is tendentious here. A major source of error among novice Poker players is to suppose that the money you put in the pot is still somehow yours. It is not. It now belongs to whoever finally wins the pot, and this also goes for any further money that you may bet in "seeking to protect your investment". As economists say, any money you have bet is a *sunk cost*.

[8]If the hands are equal, assume that the pot is split equally. However, what one chooses to assume is irrelevant since the event occurs with zero probability.

values of x and y such that player I should raise if and only if $u > x$, and player II should call if and only if $v > y$.

Suppose that player I raises. If player II is holding v, should she call? The answer depends on her probability w of winning. If she folds, her payoff is -1. If she calls, her payoff is $2w - 2(1 - w)$. It is therefore optimal for her to call if and only if

$$w \geq \tfrac{1}{4}. \qquad (12.3)$$

To calculate w, player II consults a game theory book and discovers that player I raises if and only if $u > x$. The probability $w = \text{prob}\{U < v \mid x < U \leq 1\}$ can be found using (12.2). It is is given by

$$w = \int_x^v \frac{du}{1-x} = \frac{v-x}{1-x} \qquad (x \leq v \leq 1).$$

Substitute this result in (12.3) to give $4v \geq 3x + 1$ as the necessary and sufficient condition for it to be optimal for a player II holding v to call. It follows that y must be given by

$$4y = 3x + 1. \qquad (12.4)$$

Next, consider player I. If he is dealt $u \leq y$, then he knows that he will lose \$2 if he raises and player II calls. However, he will win \$1 if he raises and player II folds. Since she folds with probability y, his expected payoff from raising is $-2(1 - y) + y$. His payoff from folding is -1. Three cases need to be considered, depending on whether $-2(1 - y) + y$ is greater than, less than, or equal to -1.

Case 1: $y > \frac{1}{3}$. In this case, it is optimal for player I to raise whenever $u \leq y$. This implies that $x = 0$. But then (12.4) yields that $y = \frac{1}{4}$, which is incompatible with $y > \frac{1}{3}$.

Case 2: $y < \frac{1}{3}$. In this case, it is optimal for player II to fold whenever $u \leq y$. This implies that $x \geq y$. But then (12.4) yields that $y \geq 1$, which is incompatible with $y < \frac{1}{3}$.

Case 3: $y = \frac{1}{3}$. In this case, player I is always indifferent between raising and folding when $u \leq y$. Since the other cases have been eliminated, this is the case that must hold if our search for an equilibrium is not to fail.

The final step is to substitute $y = \frac{1}{3}$ into (12.4) to find x. This yields

$$x = \tfrac{1}{9}; \quad y = \tfrac{1}{3}. \qquad (12.5)$$

Notice that $0 < x < y$. Thus, although player I is indifferent between raising and folding when $u \leq y$, nevertheless he folds when $0 \leq u \leq x$ and raises when $x < u \leq y$ in this equilibrium.[9]

Comments. (1) The first comment is that the better hand sometimes gets folded. In fact, player I folds the better hand with probability $\frac{1}{18}$, and player II folds the better hand with probability $\frac{2}{27}$. There is an important moral. If you never fold a hand that would have been a winner, then you must be playing badly.

(2) The second comment is that nothing guarantees that all the Nash equilibria have been found. It is easy to see that player I's strategy can be modified without disturbing the equilibrium. He *must* raise when $u > \frac{1}{3}$, but he has a lot of freedom when $u \leq \frac{1}{3}$. The only constraint is that the probability with which he folds given that $u \leq \frac{1}{3}$ is equal to $\frac{1}{3}$. Section 12.4 describes one method of finding *all* Nash equilibria in such models.

12.3.2 Second Approach to Borel's Poker Model

In the preceding discussion, optimizing decisions were taken *after* the deal. One could therefore think of each different hand as specifying a particular type of actor, as in the first approach of Section 11.2.2. However, in what follows, optimizing decisions will be made *before* the deal. If it helps, one can therefore think of player I as Von Neumann and player II as Morgenstern in the story of Section 11.2.2. Or, more straightforwardly, one can observe that the plan is to look for Nash equilibria in the strategic form of Borel's model.

Strategic Form. To construct the strategic form, it is first necessary to specify the game's pure strategies. A pure strategy for player I is a function $g : [0, 1] \to \{fold, raise\}$. Such a function tells player I what he should do for each hand u that he might be dealt. If dealt u, he should fold if $g(u) = fold$ and he should raise if $g(u) = raise$. Similarly, a pure strategy for player II is a function $h : [0, 1] \to \{fold, call\}$.

[9] We ought to check that it is optimal for player I to raise when $u > y$, since only the case that $u \leq y$ is considered in the text. However, he must expect more from raising when $u > y$ than when $u \leq y$ because he will sometimes win the showdown in the former case.

As in Section 12.3.1, no attempt will be made to examine all pure strategies. Attention will be confined to Colonel Blotto strategies of the form

$$g(u) = \begin{cases} \textit{fold}, & \text{if } u \le x \\ \textit{raise}, & \text{if } u > x \end{cases} \qquad h(v) = \begin{cases} \textit{fold}, & \text{if } v \le y \\ \textit{call}, & \text{if } v > y . \end{cases}$$

Each of player I's pure strategies to be considered therefore corresponds to a real number x in $[0, 1]$. Similarly, each of player II's pure strategies corresponds to a real number y in $[0, 1]$. For the strategic form of the game, we need to determine player I's payoff function $\pi : [0, 1] \times [0, 1] \to \mathbb{R}$. Since the game is zero-sum, player II's payoff function will be determined simultaneously.

Figures 12.3(a) and 12.3(b) are designed to lighten the work involved in finding a formula for $\pi(x, y)$. Figure 12.3(a) applies when $y > x$. It shows how much player I wins when the pair (u, v) of cards dealt lies in various regions of the square $[0, 1] \times [0, 1]$. For example, if (u, v) lies inside the region S of Figure 12.3(a), then $u > x$ and $v > y$. Thus player I raises and player II calls. They then show their cards. Notice that the region S lies below the line $u = v$. Thus, when (u, v) lies in S, $u > v$ and so player I wins the showdown. The amount he wins is \$2.

Of course, before the cards are dealt nobody knows what the hands will be. Thus $\pi(x, y)$ must be calculated as an expectation over all the possibilities. Recall that Figure 12.3(a) applies when $y > x$. Calculating $\pi(x, y)$ when $x > y$ therefore requires multiplying each amount that player I might win in this figure by the probability with which that amount is won. The expectation $\pi(x, y)$ is then the sum of the resulting products.

Fortunately, it is fairly easy to find the necessary probabilities because U and V are independent and uniformly distributed on $[0, 1]$. Thus, the probability that (u, v) lies in any region R of $[0, 1] \times [0, 1]$ is simply the area of R. It follows that, for $y > x$,

$$\pi(x, y) = -x + (1 - x)y - 2(1 - y)(y - x) . \tag{12.6}$$

(Notice that it is not necessary to work out the areas of the triangular regions in Figure 12.3(a) because the contributions from these regions cancel out when the expectation is calculated.) Proceeding similarly with Figure 12.3(b), we obtain that, for $y < x$,

$$\pi(x, y) = -x + (1 - x)y + 2(1 - x)(x - y) . \tag{12.7}$$

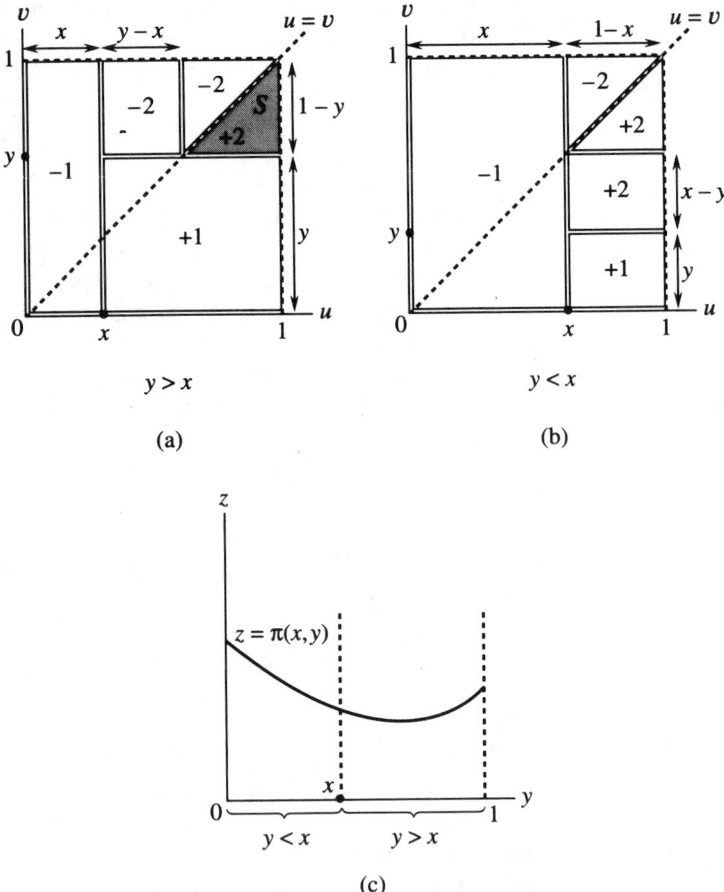

Figure 12.3 Payoffs in Borel's Poker model.

Maximin. As we know from Section 1.8.1, a Nash equilibrium in a finite, two-person, zero-sum game is a saddle point of player I's payoff matrix. We could therefore proceed[10] by looking for a pair $(\tilde{x}, \tilde{y})$ that makes $\pi(\tilde{x}, \tilde{y})$ largest in its "column" and smallest in its "row" (so that $\pi(x, \tilde{y}) \geq \pi(\tilde{x}, \tilde{y}) \geq \pi(\tilde{x}, y)$ for all x and y in $[0, 1]$). However, it is perhaps slightly easier to proceed by calculating player I's maximin value.

Figure 12.3(c) shows the graph[11] of $z = \pi(x, y)$ for a fixed

[10]As in Moulin's *Game Theory for the Social Sciences.* This book is a rich source of instructive examples.

[11]How do we know the graph looks like this? Differentiate (12.7) with respect to y, keeping x fixed. The result is $-(1 - x) \leq 0$. Thus $\pi(x, y)$ decreases for $0 \leq y \leq x$. We also need to know that y, as defined by (12.4),

value of x. Since its minimum occurs when $x < y < 1$, one finds the minimum by writing

$$\frac{\partial \pi}{\partial y} = 0, \tag{12.8}$$

using the formula (12.6) for π. This yields that $4y = 3x + 1$ as in (12.4). Let $y = y(x) = \frac{1}{4}(3x + 1)$ be the solution of this equation. Then we need to maximize $w = \pi(x, y(x))$ to find player I's maximin value.

Recalling (12.8), we have that

$$\begin{aligned} \frac{dw}{dx} &= \frac{\partial \pi}{\partial x} + \frac{\partial \pi}{\partial y}\frac{dy}{dx} = \frac{\partial \pi}{\partial x} \\ &= 1 - 3y(x) . \end{aligned}$$

The possibilities $x = 0$ and $x = 1$ for the point at which $w = \pi(x, y(x))$ is maximized can be eliminated because the fact that $4y(x) = 3x + 1$ tells us that dw/dx is positive at the former and negative at the latter. Since there are no corner solutions, $w = \pi(x, y(x))$ is maximized where $dw/dx = 0$. Thus, at the maximum, $y(x) = \frac{1}{3}$ and so the maximizing value of x is $\frac{1}{9}$. These conclusions confirm the results of (12.5).

The conclusions of Section 12.3.1 have therefore been confirmed by an alternative method. The formula (12.6) makes it easy to calculate the *value* of the game. In a two-person, zero-sum game, this is player I's security level (and what he actually gets if both players act optimally). Substituting the values of $x = \frac{1}{9}$ and $y = \frac{1}{3}$ from (12.5) in (12.6), we obtain that the value of the game is $-\frac{1}{9}$. Since the value is negative, player I would prefer not to play if he could avoid it.

12.4 Von Neumann's Poker Model

Math 12.5 ⟶ Von Neumann proposed two Poker models of which that to be described here is the second and more interesting. Its game tree is shown in Figure 12.2(b). It differs from Borel's model in being more realistic about the betting opportunities available to player I. In Borel's model, he must fold if he does not raise. However, in a real Poker game, to fold at the first betting opportunity is a weakly dominated strategy for player

---

lies between x and 1. If $x > y$, then it follows from (12.4) that $4x > 3x + 1$, and so $x > 1$, which is not allowed. If $1 < y$, then it follows from (12.4) that $4 < 3x + 1$, and so $x > 1$ again.

I because he can always check and fold later if necessary. To *check* is simply to bet zero chips.

Although player I's situation is made more realistic in Von Neumann's model, player II's situation continues to be artificially constrained. If player I checks, she is *forced* to call. If player I raises, she is not allowed to raise him back. She may only choose between calling and folding. In spite of these seemingly very tight restrictions, Von Neumann's model captures the essence of what bluffing is all about in Poker in a way that Borel's model does not.

Finding All Nash Equilibria. In the analysis of Borel's model in Section 12.3, only some of the possible pure strategies were considered. We called these Colonel Blotto strategies because their use does not call for much creative thinking. Mixed strategies were not considered at all. This section is more ambitious. The analysis goes most of the way to finding *all* Nash equilibria of the game.[12] Partly, this is because Colonel Blotto strategies will not suffice in Von Neumann's Poker model. But mostly, it is because the analysis provides an instructive exercise in the use of behavioral strategies.

Behavioral Strategies. Pure strategies for Von Neumann's Poker model are functions $g : [0,1] \to \{check, raise\}$ and $h : [0,1] \to \{fold, call\}$, pretty much as described in Section 12.3.2 for Borel's model. A mixed strategy is therefore a mathematical object of considerable complexity.[13] The reasons given in Section 10.4.3 for working with behavioral strategies rather than mixed strategies are therefore particularly cogent here.

A behavioral strategy for player I in Von Neumann's Poker model is a *function* $p : [0,1] \to [0,1]$, where $p(u)$ is the *probability* with which he plans to raise if dealt the hand u. Similarly, a behavioral strategy for player II is a function

[12] What *all* should mean here is open to some debate. We consider, for example, only behavioral strategies that are *measurable* functions of what a player is dealt. We also ignore the fact that what a player plans to do on a set of hands that is dealt with probability zero is irrelevant to his expected winnings. The functions $\tilde{p}$ and $\tilde{q}$ of Figure 12.4(c) and 12.4(d) can therefore be changed on a set of measure zero without altering the fact that $(\tilde{p}, \tilde{q})$ is a Nash equilibrium.

[13] However, often it is possible to get by in such situations by restricting attention to mixed strategies with *finite support*. Such a mixed strategy assigns positive probability only to a finite number of pure strategies.

$q : [0,1] \to [0,1]$, where $q(v)$ is the probability with which she plans to raise if dealt the hand v.

These are not mixed strategies. An example of a *mixed* strategy for player II would be for her to toss a coin, *before* the deal, and to use one Colonel Blotto pure strategy if it falls heads and a second Colonel Blotto pure strategy if it falls tails. Suppose that the first Blotto strategy required her to raise if and only if $v > \frac{1}{3}$, and the second to raise if and only if $v > \frac{2}{3}$. An equivalent *behavioral* strategy $Q : [0,1] \to [0,1]$ would then be given by

$$Q(v) = \begin{cases} 0, & \text{if } v \leq \frac{1}{3} \\ \frac{1}{2}, & \text{if } \frac{1}{3} < v \leq \frac{2}{3} \\ 1, & \text{if } v > \frac{2}{3}. \end{cases}$$

With such a behavioral strategy, player II waits until *after* the deal before deciding what to do. This signals that the first approach of Section 12.3 is to be adopted. In particular, one can think of the deal as a casting move that completes an incomplete information structure. The actor Mr. u is then player I holding hand u, and the actor Ms. v is player II holding hand v.

Expected Payoffs. Suppose that the players use the behavioral strategies p and q. After the deal, a kibitzer who can see both hands will then be able to compute player I's expected gain $z(u, v)$. What this is depends on who has the better hand.

Suppose first that $u > v$. Then player I has to be satisfied with winning player II's ante of \$1, unless he raises and she calls, when he will win \$2. The latter possibility occurs with probability $p(u)q(v)$, and so for $u > v$,

$$\begin{aligned} z(u, v) &= 1 - p(u)q(v) + 2p(u)q(v) \\ &= 1 + p(u)q(v). \end{aligned}$$

Next suppose that $u < v$. (We ignore the case $u = v$ since this occurs with zero probability.) Player I may then still win \$1 by raising, because player II will then fold with probability $1 - q(v)$. Otherwise, player I loses \$1 if he checks, and \$2 if he raises and player II calls. It follows that, for $u < v$,

$$\begin{aligned} z(u, v) &= p(u)(1 - q(v)) - 2p(u)q(v) - (1 - p(u)) \\ &= 2p(u) - 1 - 3p(u)q(v). \end{aligned}$$

Although a kibitzer can calculate $z(u, v)$, player I cannot because he does not know what player II is holding. He must therefore calculate the expectation

$$E_1(u) = \mathcal{E}_v\, z(u,v) = \int_{v<u} z(u,v)\,dv + \int_{v>u} z(u,v)\,dv$$
$$= \int_0^u (1+pq)\,dv + \int_u^1 (2p-1-3pq)\,dv\,,$$

in which p and q are *not* constant, but are abbreviations for $p(u)$ and $q(v)$. It follows that

$$E_1(u) = p(u)S_1(u) + T_1(u)\,, \tag{12.9}$$

where

$$S_1(u) = 2(1-u) + \int_0^u q(v)\,dv - 3\int_u^1 q(v)\,dv\,, \tag{12.10}$$
$$T_1(u) = 2u - 1\,.$$

The same sequence of steps for player II yields that

$$E_2(u) = -\mathcal{E}_u\, z(u,v) = -\int_{u<v} z(u,v)\,du - \int_{u>v} z(u,v)\,du$$
$$= -\int_0^v (2p-1-3pq)\,du - \int_v^1 (1+pq)\,du\,,$$

and thus

$$E_2(v) = q(v)S_2(v) + T_2(v)\,, \tag{12.11}$$

where

$$S_2(v) = 3\int_0^v p(u)du - \int_v^1 p(u)du\,, \tag{12.12}$$
$$T_2(v) = 2v - 1 - \int_v^1 p(u)\,du\,.$$

This is a daunting list of formulas. However, all that matters in looking for a Nash equilibrium $(\tilde{p},\tilde{q})$ are the *signs* of the functions $\tilde{S}_1$ and $\tilde{S}_2$ obtained by writing $q(v) = \tilde{q}(v)$ and $p(u) = \tilde{p}(u)$ in (12.10) and (12.12). Why is this?

First consider player I. He looks in a game theory book and observes that player II is advised to use the behavioral strategy $\tilde{q} : [0,1] \to [0,1]$. That is, she should raise with probability $\tilde{q}(v)$ when dealt v. From (12.9), it then follows that player I will get a payoff of $p(u)\tilde{S}_1(u) + \tilde{T}_1(u)$ if he raises with probability $p(u)$ when dealt u. After looking at his hand u, player I is free to make any choice of the number $p(u)$ in the interval $[0,1]$. If $\tilde{S}_1(u) > 0$, the choice $p(u) = 1$ is optimal. If

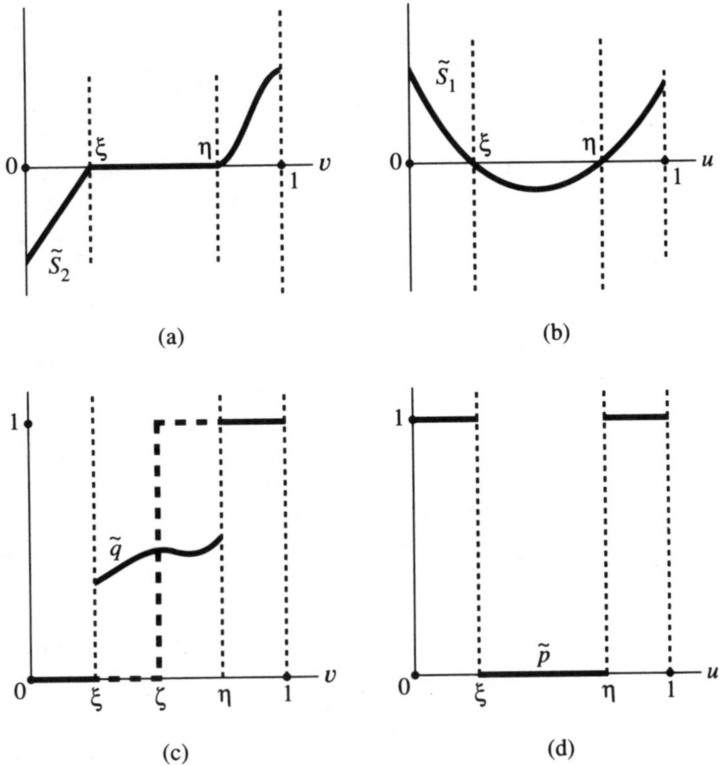

Figure 12.4 Finding $\tilde p$ and $\tilde q$ in Von Neumann's model.

$\tilde S_1(u) < 0$, the choice $p(u) = 0$ is optimal. Only if $\tilde S_1(u) = 0$ are other choices of $p(u)$ optimal.. Since similar considerations apply to player II, we obtain the following criteria for $\tilde p$ and $\tilde q$:

$$\begin{aligned} \tilde S_1(u) > 0 &\Rightarrow \tilde p(u)=1; & \tilde S_2(v) > 0 &\Rightarrow \tilde q(v)=1 \\ \tilde S_1(u) < 0 &\Rightarrow \tilde p(u)=0; & \tilde S_2(v) < 0 &\Rightarrow \tilde q(v)=0 \\ 0 < \tilde p(u) < 1 &\Rightarrow \tilde S_1(u)=0; & 0 < \tilde q(v) < 1 &\Rightarrow \tilde S_2(v)=0. \end{aligned}$$

Figure 12.4(a) shows what the graph $z = \tilde S_2(v)$ looks like. To check this, begin by differentiating (12.12), as explained in Section 11.4.2, to obtain that[14]

$$\tilde S_2'(v) = 4\tilde p(v). \tag{12.13}$$

Since the right-hand side is nonnegative, it follows that the function $\tilde S_2$ *increases*. Writing $v = 0$ in (12.13), we learn that $\tilde S_2(0) \leq 0$. Writing $v = 1$, we learn that $\tilde S_2(1) \geq 0$. Since $\tilde S_2$

[14]Here and elsewhere a careful account would add "almost everywhere".

is necessarily continuous on $[0,1]$, it follows that there is a smallest number ξ in $[0,1]$ for which $\tilde{S}_2(\xi)=0$, and a largest number η in $[0,1]$ for which $\tilde{S}_2(\eta)=0$. (Unless $\xi=\eta$, the function $\tilde{S}_2$ is therefore not *strictly* increasing.)

The information about $\tilde{S}_2$ summarized in Figure 12.4(a) tells us a great deal about the function $\tilde{q}$. What we now know about $\tilde{q}$ is summarized in Figure 12.4(c).

The identity (12.13) is informative about the function $\tilde{p}$. Since $\tilde{S}_2(v)=0$ for $\xi \le v \le \eta$, it follows that $\tilde{S}_2'(v)=0$ for $\xi < v < \eta$, and therefore that $\tilde{p}(v)=0$ on the interval (ξ,η). However, $\tilde{p}(v)$ cannot be zero on a larger *open* interval I, because (12.13) implies that $\tilde{S}_2(v)$ would then be constant on I. This constant would need to be zero because $\tilde{S}_2(v)=0$ on $[\xi,\eta]$. However, $[\xi,\eta]$ is the largest interval on which $\tilde{S}_2(v)=0$, and so a contradiction would arise.

What we have learned about $\tilde{p}$ tells us something about $\tilde{S}_1$. It cannot be that $\tilde{S}_1(u)<0$ immediately to the left of ξ because then $\tilde{p}(u)=0$ immediately to the left of ξ. Because $\tilde{S}_1$ is continuous, it follows that $\tilde{S}_1(\xi)\ge 0$. For similar reasons $\tilde{S}_1(\eta)\ge 0$. However, differentiating (12.10), we obtain that

$$\tilde{S}_1'(u) = -2 + 4\tilde{q}(u)\,. \tag{12.14}$$

But Figure 12.4(c) tells us that $\tilde{q}(u)=0$ for $0<u<\xi$, and $\tilde{q}(u)=1$ for $\eta<u<1$. Thus $\tilde{S}_1(u)<0$ for $0<u<\xi$, and $\tilde{S}_1(u)>0$ for $\eta<u<1$. Consequently, $\tilde{S}_1$ decreases on $[0,\xi]$ and increases on $[\eta,1]$ as indicated in Figure 12.4(b).

Figure 12.4(b) makes it possible to tie down $\tilde{p}$ completely. We already know that $\tilde{p}(u)=0$ for $\xi<u<\eta$. But now we know that $\tilde{S}_1(u)>0$ on $[0,\xi)$ and $(\eta,1]$. Thus, $\tilde{p}(u)=1$ on these intervals, as shown in Figure 12.4(d).

This completes the interesting part of the analysis. One can check that

$$\xi = \tfrac{1}{10}\,; \quad \eta = \tfrac{7}{10}$$

using the fact that $\tilde{S}_1(\xi)=\tilde{S}_1(\eta)=\tilde{S}_2(\xi)=\tilde{S}(\eta)=0$. Thus $\tilde{p}$ is determined uniquely. However, $\tilde{q}$ is not determined uniquely. For $\xi \le \eta$, $\tilde{q}(v)$ can be chosen freely, subject to the constraints

$$\frac{1}{\eta-\xi}\int_{\xi}^{\eta} \tilde{q}(v)\,dv = \tfrac{1}{2}\,; \quad \frac{1}{\eta-u}\int_{u}^{\eta} \tilde{q}(v)\,dv \ge \tfrac{1}{2}\,.$$

The simplest possibility for $\tilde{q}$ is the Blotto strategy indicated in Figure 12.4(c), where

$$\zeta = \tfrac{2}{5}\,.$$

Comments. The most interesting outcome of the preceding analysis is the light it casts on the nature of bluffing. Comment on this appears in Section 12.5. At this stage, only a secondary point will be made. Notice that *pure* strategy Nash equilibria exist, both in Borel's model and in Von Neumann's.[15] But Poker is all about keeping the other guy guessing. So how can it be that the use of *mixed* strategies can be evaded? The answer takes us back to the issue of "purification" last mentioned in Section 11.5. In brief, the deal in Poker is a "natural purification device". In the models studied, player I has no need to make life harder for player II by randomizing because her ignorance about the hand dealt to him is already enough to keep her guessing. However, this is not true in all Poker models. In particular, mixed strategies get used in the Poker model of Nash and Shapley described in Section 12.6.[16]

12.5 Why Bluff?

Von Neumann's Poker model is especially interesting because of the starkness of the behavior that a game-theoretic analysis requires of player I. As Figure 12.4(d) illustrates, Nash equilibrium play calls for player I to raise for certain *when his hand is sufficiently bad.* Such go-for-broke behavior is hard to get a feel for, but it is important to do so because the behavior is not a by-product of Von Neumann's simplification of the strategic realities of Poker. On the contrary, his model captures the essence of the situation. In particular, a computer analysis of two-person, pot-limit, Straight Poker shows that the opening player should *always* raise when dealt the worst possible hand.[17]

Most Poker players behave very differently in neighborhood games. They know they ought to bluff, but they bluff too cautiously. They are reluctant to bluff on really bad hands, and try instead to hedge their bets by "bluffing" on

[15]In both cases, Nash equilibria in which one of the players uses a mixed strategy exist also, but this is beside the point.

[16]And in Von Neumann's first Poker model, which is even simpler than the second model described here.

[17]Also as in Von Neumann's model, he should *always* call with a moderate hand (like a pair of twos), and fold if raised. There are also other surprises. Against a rational opponent, rational play with a really good hand like four of a kind seems incredibly cautious to the untutored intuition. Cutler, who carried out the analysis, remarks that Poker played rationally is about as interesting as watching paint dry!

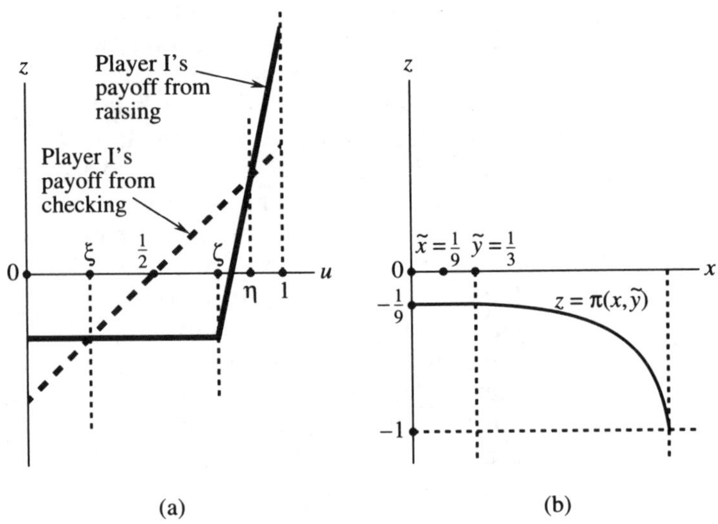

Figure 12.5 Poker payoffs.

middle-range hands because they figure that they might win on such a hand even if there is a showdown. Why is such thinking mistaken when it is common knowledge that the players are rational?

At one level, the answer to this question is very straightforward in Von Neumann's Poker model. Figure 12.5(a) shows player I's expected winnings for each possible hand that he might be dealt, and for each possible betting choice he can make. The assumption about player II in this diagram is that she uses the Blotto strategy of raising if and only if $v > \zeta$. As the diagram clearly shows, player I gets more by raising when dealt $u = 0$ than he gets by checking.

What Figure 12.5(a) illustrates is the crudest motivation for bluffing. This is the hope that a raise will induce the opponent to fold a good hand so that the bluffer's bad hand can win the pot.

However, it would be a major error to regard this motivation for bluffing as being the only reason that a rational player will bluff. A player bluffs not only because of the hope of winning money on a bad hand, but because bluffing on bad hands is necessary to ensure making money when dealt a good hand. Players who never raise on a bad hand might as well light up a neon sign advertising their strength on those occasions when they do raise. The other players will then fold except when holding a hand that is especially strong.

This point is easier to see in Borel's model than Von Neumann's. Figure 12.5(b) shows player I's payoff $z = \pi(x, \tilde{y})$

when player II uses her Nash equilibrium strategy $\tilde{y} = \frac{1}{3}$. The graph is horizontal for $0 \leq x \leq \tilde{y}$. Anything in this range is therefore a best reply to $\tilde{y}$. So why does player I select $\tilde{x} = \frac{1}{9}$ as specified in (12.5)? It is because of what *would* happen if he did not.[18] As we know from Section 12.3, player II's best reply $y(x)$ to player I's choice of x is given by $4y(x) = 3x + 1$. Thus, if player I were to bluff less than the Nash equilibrium level specified in $\tilde{x}$ by choosing $x > \tilde{x}$, then player II would respond by choosing $y > \tilde{y}$. That is, player II would use a more stringent criterion for calling a raise by player I. Player I would therefore win less on his good hands, since his raises would be called less often.

12.6 Nash and Shapley's Poker Model

Math 12.7 →

This is a three-player model in which the betting rules are very much more realistic than in the Poker models considered so far. However, to prevent the analysis becoming difficult, it is necessary to be less realistic about the hands that can be dealt.

In analyzing the model, a new type of deceit will be uncovered. *Bluffing* occurs when a player with a bad hand seeks to deceive the other players into thinking that the hand might be good by making a raise. *Sandbagging*[19] occurs when a player with a good hand seeks to deceive the other players into thinking that the hand might be bad by *not* making a raise.

The Rules. As previously, all players are assumed to be risk-neutral so that bets can be quoted in dollars. To begin with, each player pays an ante of \$2. The cards are then dealt. One must imagine that the deck contains only two types of card, H and L. Each player receives a hand consisting of one card. It is assumed that it is equally likely that any player will be dealt H or L, and that each player's hand is independent of what the other is holding.

The betting now begins. The opportunity to place a bet rotates, starting with player I. Each player can bet (B) or

[18]Of course, if Borel's model is played only once, then player II would not learn about player I's deviation. However, the story that follows implicitly assumes that the game is played repeatedly and that the players learn by trial-and-error as discussed in Chapter 9.

[19]In kinder times, muggers would lurk in dark alleys with a sock filled with sand. Such a weapon disables the victim without the risk of causing permanent injury.

	Betting sequences							
Deals	*BBB* *PBBB* *PPBBB*	*BBP* *PBPB*	*BPB* *PPBBP*	*BPP*	*PBBP* *PPBPB*	*PBPP*	*PPBPP*	*PPP*
HHH	0 0 0	−2 1 1	1 −2 1	−2 −2 4	1 1 −2	−2 4 −2	4 −2 −2	0 0 0
HHL	−10 5 5	−2 1 1	−10 −2 12	−2 −2 4	−10 12 −2	−2 4 −2	4 −2 −2	0 0 0
HLH	5 −10 5	−2 −10 12	1 −2 1	−2 −2 4	12 −10 −2	−2 4 −2	4 −2 −2	0 0 0
HLL	−10 −10 20	−2 −10 12	−10 −2 12	−2 −2 4	1 1 −2	−2 4 −2	4 −2 −2	0 0 0
LHH	5 5 −10	−2 12 −10	12 −2 −10	−2 −2 4	1 1 −2	−2 4 −2	4 −2 −2	0 0 0
LHL	−10 20 −10	−2 12 −10	1 −2 1	−2 −2 4	−10 12 −2	−2 4 −2	4 −2 −2	0 0 0
LLH	20 −10 −10	−2 1 1	12 −2 −10	−2 −2 4	12 −10 −2	−2 4 −2	4 −2 −2	0 0 0
LLL	0 0 0	−2 1 1	1 −2 1	−2 −2 4	1 1 −2	−2 4 −2	4 −2 −2	0 0 0

Figure 12.6 Payoffs in the Nash-Shapley Poker model.

pass (P). A bet consists of contributing \$8 to the pot. A pass consists of contributing nothing to the pot. Players are allowed to bet only once. However, having passed at the first opportunity does not prevent a player from betting later.

Figure 12.6 shows who wins what after each possible betting sequence. This is determined according to the usual rules of Poker except that, if everyone passes, there is no showdown and everyone gets their ante back. (Note that, if there is more than one winner at the showdown, the winners split the pot equally.)

Pure Strategies. Player I has eight information sets at which he might be called upon to make a decision. A pure strategy must specify whether he will select B or P at each of these

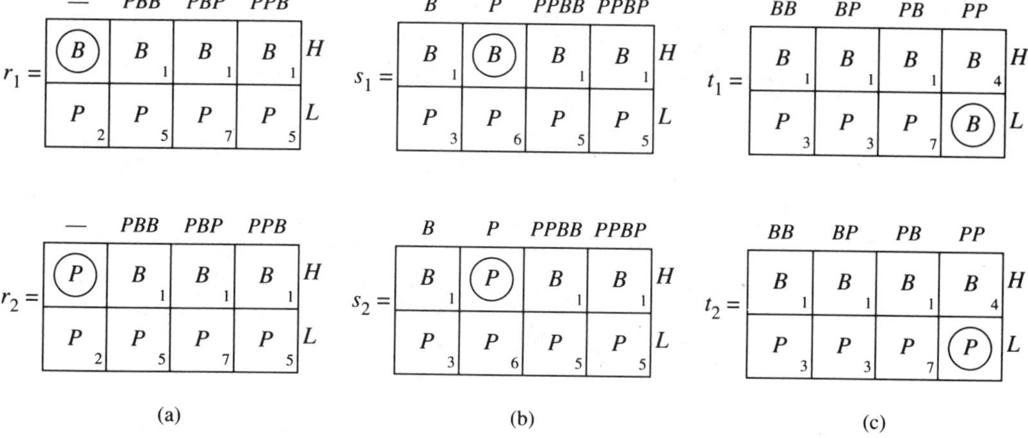

Figure 12.7 Two pure strategies for each player.

information sets. He therefore has $8 \times 2 = 16$ pure strategies. Figure 12.7(a) illustrates two of these pure strategies, r_1 and r_2. For example, at the information set where what player I knows is that he has been dealt H and that the betting so far has been PPB, then r_2 specifies that player I should choose B. Figures 12.7(b) and 12.7(c) similarly show two pure strategies each for players II and III.

The various embellishments of the tables in Figure 12.7 will be explained shortly. At this point, observe only that the circled actions indicate where the two pure strategies shown for each player differ.

Plan of Attack. The aim of the analysis is to locate the *Nash equilibria* in Nash and Shapley's model. It turns out, in fact, that there is a *unique* Nash equilibrium. However, we face some formidable technical problems because the strategic form is huge. Its dimensions are $16 \times 16 \times 16$.

However, we can use the method of successively deleting strongly dominated strategies as discussed in Section 4.6.1. This reduces the situation to a $2 \times 2 \times 2$ problem. Recall that no Nash equilibria will be lost along the way as long as the temptation to delete strategies that are only *weakly* dominated is resisted.

Deleting Dominated Strategies. The only pure strategies that survive the successive deletion of strongly dominated strategies are those shown in Figure 12.7. The small numbers in each cell of Figure 12.7 indicate the step in the process at which the alternative to the action shown is eliminated.

Step 1. Any pure strategy that calls on a player to fold when holding H is strongly dominated. A player who folds loses his ante. However, a player holding H who remains until the showdown always recovers his ante, and sometimes may win more.

After the deletion of these strongly dominated strategies, each player has $5 \times 2 = 10$ pure strategies left to consider.

Step 2. Suppose that player I is dealt L. The initial probability that both of the other players are holding L is $\frac{1}{2} \times \frac{1}{2} = \frac{1}{4}$. The probability that at least one of the opponents is holding H is therefore $1 - \frac{1}{4} = \frac{3}{4}$. Such an opponent will never fold because of Step 1. Hence the most that player I can get if he opens the betting by choosing B is

$$\tfrac{3}{4} \times -10 + \tfrac{1}{4} \times 4 = -6\tfrac{1}{2}\,.$$

(If he bets, and one of the opponents is holding H, player I loses $2 + 8 = 10$. If he bets and both opponents are holding L, then they may or may not fold. If player I is lucky and they both fold, he will win their antes and so get $2 + 2 = 4$.)

Since player I can get -2 by passing, it follows that any pure strategy that tells him to open with B when dealt L is strongly dominated. After such strategies have been eliminated, player I is left with $4 \times 2 = 8$ pure strategies.

Step 3. In view of Step 2, players II and III must update their beliefs about what player I is holding if he opens with B. They then know for certain that he was dealt H. An opponent holding L then has nothing to play for, because Step 1 establishes that player I will never fold. Hence, any pure strategy that tells player II or III to choose B when dealt L after player I has opened with B must be strongly dominated.

After such strategies have been eliminated, player II is left with $4 \times 2 = 8$ pure strategies, and player III is left with $3 \times 2 = 6$ pure strategies.

Step 4. Suppose that player III has been dealt H, and the previous betting has been PP. If player III chooses P, he gets 0 (because the hand is then passed out). However, if he chooses B he will have a positive probability of winning something provided that the betting sequence PP does not guarantee that players I and II are both holding H. This is admittedly a somewhat unlikely possibility, but it has to be ruled out to ensure that we eliminate only *strongly* dominated strategies. Fortunately, it was ruled out at Step 2, which shows that player I always opens with P when dealt L.

Step 5. Steps 1 through 4 establish that player III never bets when holding L. This fact tells the other players something about the probability prob$(H|B)$ that he is holding H when he plays B. Since prob(H) = prob$(L) = \frac{1}{2}$, Bayes' rule (Section 2.1.4) yields that

$$\text{prob}(H|B) = \frac{\text{prob}(B|H)\text{prob}(H)}{\text{prob}(B|H)\text{prob}(H) + \text{prob}(B|L)\text{prob}(L)}$$

$$= \frac{1}{1 + \text{prob}(B|L)} \geq \tfrac{1}{2}\,.$$

It follows that an opponent holding L who passed at the first opportunity can expect at most

$$\tfrac{1}{2} \times -10 + \tfrac{1}{2} \times 1 = -4\tfrac{1}{2}$$

by calling. On the other hand, folding guarantees a payoff of -2. Thus any strategy that tells a player holding L to choose B after player III has chosen B is strongly dominated.

After such strategies have been eliminated, players I and II are each left with $2 \times 2 = 4$ pure strategies.

Step 6. Suppose that player II is dealt L and that player I opens with P. The probability that both opponents have been dealt L then certainly satisfies $\pi \leq \frac{1}{2}$, since $\frac{1}{2}$ is the probability that player III is dealt L. The most that player II can then expect from choosing B is therefore

$$4\pi + (-10)(1 - \pi) = -10 + 14\pi \leq -3\,.$$

On the other hand, she guarantees -2 by checking and then folding if raised. Thus any strategy that tells player II to choose B when holding L after player I opens with P is strongly dominated.

After such strategies have been eliminated, player II is left with $1 \times 2 = 2$ pure strategies.

Step 7. It has been established that player II never chooses B when holding L. Hence, if she chooses B, she must be holding H. It follows that strategies that tell her opponents to follow the play of B by player II with a call when holding L are strongly dominated.

After the deletion of these strongly dominated strategies, players I and III are both left with $1 \times 2 = 2$ pure strategies.

Reduced Strategic Form. It is important that all the deletions that have been made are of *strongly* dominated strategies. As Section 4.6.1 explains, this guarantees that no Nash equilibria have been eliminated.

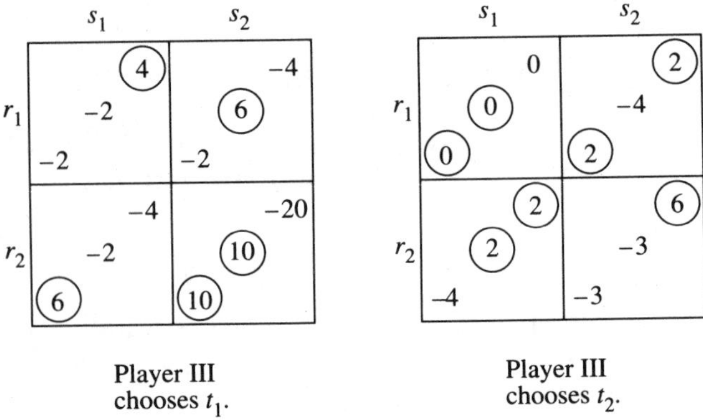

Figure 12.8 A reduced strategic form.

It remains to analyze the $2 \times 2 \times 2$ reduced strategic form of Figure 12.8. The payoffs in this strategic form are calculated using the table of Figure 12.9. The cells in the table indicate what each player gets for each possible strategy profile and for each possible deal. When the strategy profile (r, s, t) is used, a player's expected payoff before the deal is therefore obtained by summing his or her payoffs in the column corresponding to (r, s, t), and then multiplying the result by $\frac{1}{8}$. However, for the payoffs in Figure 12.8, the final multiplication by $\frac{1}{8}$ is omitted to avoid introducing fractions.

The circled payoffs in Figure 12.8 show best replies. Since no cell gets all its payoffs circled, it follows that the game has no pure strategy Nash equilibria. It is therefore necessary to look at mixed strategies.

Mixed Strategies. The next stage of the analysis of the Poker model of Nash and Shapley is to look for the Nash equilibria of the reduced strategic form of Figure 12.8 in which players I, II and III use their second pure strategies with probabilities a, b and c respectively. We shall be particularly interested in the probability a with which player I opens by checking when holding H.

Step 1. In a Nash equilibrium, player III must use a completely mixed strategy. This means that each pure strategy is used with positive probability, and so the claim is that $0 < c < 1$. Figure 12.8 helps to show this. If $c = 0$, so that player III uses t_1, then strong domination in the game that ensues between players I and II shows that they must then use r_2 and s_2 respectively. But (r_2, s_2, t_1) is not a Nash equilibrium. Similarly, if $c = 1$, so that player III uses t_2, then

	Strategy profiles							
Deals	(r_1,s_1,t_1)	(r_1,s_1,t_2)	(r_1,s_2,t_1)	(r_1,s_2,t_2)	(r_2,s_1,t_1)	(r_2,s_1,t_2)	(r_2,s_2,t_1)	(r_2,s_2,t_2)
HHH	*BBB* 0 0 0	*BBB* 0 0 0	*BBB* 0 0 0	*BBB* 0 0 0	*PBBB* 0 0 0	*PBBB* 0 0 0	*PPBBB* 0 0 0	*PPBBB* 0 0 0
HHL	*BBP* −2 1 1	*BBP* −2 1 1	*BBP* −2 1 1	*BBP* −2 1 1	*PBPB* −2 1 1	*PBPB* −2 1 1	*PPBBB* −10 5 5	*PPP* 0 0 0
HLH	*BPB* 1 −2 1	*BPB* 1 −2 1	*BPB* 1 −2 1	*BPB* 1 −2 1	*PPBBP* 1 −2 1	*PPBBP* 1 −2 1	*PPBBP* 1 −2 1	*PPBBP* 1 −2 1
HLL	*BPP* −2 −2 4	*BPP* −2 −2 4	*BPP* −2 −2 4	*BPP* −2 −2 4	*PPBBP* 10 −2 12	*PPP* 0 0 0	*PPBBP* 10 −2 12	*PPP* 0 0 0
LHH	*PBBP* 1 1 −2	*PBBP* 1 1 −2	*PPBPB* 1 1 −2	*PPBPB* 1 1 −2	*PBBP* 1 1 −2	*PBBP* 1 1 −2	*PPBPB* 1 1 −2	*PPBPB* 1 1 −2
LHL	*PBPP* −2 4 −2	*PBPP* −2 4 −2	*PPBPB* −10 12 −2	*PPP* 0 0 0	*PBPP* −2 4 −2	*PBPP* −2 4 −2	*PPBPB* −10 12 −2	*PPP* 0 0 0
LLH	*PPBPP* 4 −2 −2	*PPBPP* 4 −2 −2	*PPBPP* 4 −2 −2	*PPBPP* 4 −2 −2	*PPBPP* 4 −2 −2	*PPBPP* 4 −2 −2	*PPBPP* 4 −2 −2	*PPBPP* 4 −2 −2
LLL	*PPBPP* 4 −2 −2	*PPP* 0 0 0	*PPBPP* 4 −2 −2	*PPP* 0 0 0	*PPBPP* 4 −2 −2	*PPP* 0 0 0	*PPBPP* 4 −2 −2	*PPP* 0 0 0
Expected payoff ×8	4 −2 −2	0 0 0	−4 6 −2	2 −4 2	−4 −2 6	2 2 −4	−20 10 10	6 −3 −3

Figure 12.9 Computing payoffs for the reduced strategic form.

players I and II must use r_1 and s_1 respectively. But (r_1, s_1, t_2) is not a Nash equilibrium.

Step 2. Since player III uses a completely mixed strategy, he must be indifferent between t_1 and t_2 (Section 7.1.2). Thus

$$[1-a \quad a]\begin{bmatrix} 4 & -4 \\ -4 & -20 \end{bmatrix}\begin{bmatrix} 1-b \\ b \end{bmatrix}$$

$$= [1-a \quad a]\begin{bmatrix} 0 & 2 \\ 2 & 6 \end{bmatrix}\begin{bmatrix} 1-b \\ b \end{bmatrix},$$

because the left-hand side is what he gets from using t_1 and the right-hand side from using t_2. It follows that

$$[1-a \quad a]\begin{bmatrix} 4 & -6 \\ -6 & -26 \end{bmatrix}\begin{bmatrix} 1-b \\ b \end{bmatrix} = 0. \qquad (12.15)$$

Step 3. We have some way to go before we are ready to claim that players I and II also use completely mixed strategies. However, when this is established, we shall know that

$$[1-a \quad a]\begin{bmatrix} -8 & 4 \\ -12 & 5 \end{bmatrix}\begin{bmatrix} 1-c \\ c \end{bmatrix} = 0, \qquad (12.16)$$

because player II is indifferent between s_1 and s_2. Since Figure 12.8 treats players I and II symmetrically, (12.16) will also be true when a is replaced by b.

Step 4. It is not possible that $a = 1$ because this would make the left-hand side of (12.15) negative. Can it be possible that $a = 0$? If so, then (12.15) implies that $b = \frac{3}{5}$. Thus player II is using a completely mixed strategy, and so (12.16) applies. Since $a = 0$, it follows that $c = \frac{2}{3}$. However, the best reply[20] for player I to the choice of $b = \frac{3}{5}$ by player II and $c = \frac{2}{3}$ by player III is $a = 1$.

This argument establishes that $0 < a < 1$. By symmetry, it follows that $0 < b < 1$ also.

Step 5. It has now been shown that a Nash equilibrium for the reduced strategic form of Figure 12.8 requires each player to use a completely mixed strategy.[21] Thus (12.16) holds, and so does the same equation with b replacing a. It follows that $a = b$. The quadratic equation

$$5a^2 + 10a - 2 = 0$$

is obtained by writing $a = b$ in (12.15). Its solutions are $a = -1 \pm \sqrt{7/5}$. Of these, only $a = -1 + \sqrt{7/5} \approx 0.18$ is acceptable as a probability. It then only remains to write this value in (12.16) to obtain that

$$c = \frac{4a+8}{5a+12} \approx 0.68\,.$$

[20]No calculating is necessary. It is apparent from Figure 12.8 that, if player III uses t_1 more frequently than t_2, then r_2 is optimal for player I whatever player II may do.

[21]One may deduce immediately from Exercise 7.9.9 that the game has a unique Nash equilibrium. It then follows via Exercise 7.9.8 that $a = b$. However, the text ignores such short cuts.

Summary. It has been shown that the Poker model of Nash and Shapley has a unique Nash equilibrium that requires all three players to use mixed strategies. These mixed strategies assign zero probability to all pure strategies except those listed in Figure 12.7. Player I uses r_2 with probability $a \approx 0.18$. Player II uses s_2 with probability $b \approx 0.18$. Player III uses t_2 with probability $c \approx 0.68$. Our final task is to consider what moral should be drawn from these conclusions.

12.6.1 Sandbagging

Notice first that player III has an advantage in the Poker model of Nash and Shapley. (In equilibrium, he expects to win about 80 cents, and his opponents expect to lose about 40 cents each.) Player III has this advantage because he bets last. He exploits this advantage by sometimes *bluffing* after his opponents have both passed and therefore apparently advertised that they are weak. As we have seen, he bluffs a lot in this situation. When holding L, he raises about two-thirds of the time after the betting sequence PP. At real Poker tables, such behavior is sometimes contemptuously referred to as an attempt to "buy the pot".

However, player III does not have things all his own way. Players I and II have read the game theory book also, and so they know that player III often raises with a bad hand after the sequence PP. Both player I and player II therefore have an incentive to set a trap for player III. Sometimes each opens by checking when holding H. This is *sandbagging*. If players I or II were always to raise when holding H, player III would never call the raise when holding L.

How often does player III get sandbagged? The probability $\text{prob}(L|P)$ that player I is holding L when he opens with P can be calculated using Bayes' Rule (Section 2.1.4). Since the prior probabilities for H and L are $\text{prob}(H) = \text{prob}(L) = \frac{1}{2}$,

$$\text{prob}(L|P) = \frac{\text{prob}(P|L)\text{prob}(L)}{\text{prob}(P|L)\text{prob}(L) + \text{prob}(P|H)\text{prob}(H)}$$

$$\approx \frac{1}{1+0.18} \approx 0.85\,.$$

An identical calculation shows that, after I has opened with P, the probability that player II is holding L if he follows with P also, is 0.85 as well. Thus, after the betting sequence PP, the probability that either player I or player II is sandbagging is $1 - (0.85)^2 = 0.28$. When player III bluffs, he expects to get his knuckles wrapped more than a quarter of the time.

12.7 Conclusion

As promised in Section 12.1, this chapter has no exercise section. The time has therefore come for me to say farewell, and to apologize to anyone who had got this far for sandbagging you so mercilessly. You were tempted in with promises of fun and games, but what you got was sweat and tears. I hope it now seems worthwhile. Game theory is currently in its infancy, but if we ever get a handle on the bounded rationality issues raised in Chapter 9, it may well revolutionize the way we run our societies one of these days. Perhaps it is optimistic to look forward to a time when the stupidity, ignorance and prejudice with which we currently run our affairs withers away under the cool light of reason. If so, then I don't mind admitting to be an optimist.

Answers

Selected Exercises

This chapter contains Bruce Linster's outline answers to ten exercises selected from each of Chapters 1 through 11. The exercises to which answers are provided are listed in the table below. The questions from the earlier chapters to which answers are given are mostly of the type that one might reasonably ask undergraduates to attempt. These mainstream answers are supplemented with a few hints on how to solve the occasional brain-teaser with which the exercises have been salted. There is no overlap between the questions to which answers are provided and those that appear as suggested assignments in the Teaching Guide. Teachers can obtain a full set of answers from the publisher.

Exercise section	Exercises									
1.10	1	4	5	8	9	11	12	14	17	18
2.6	1	3	6	8	10	12	18	22	25	26
3.7	1	2	3	7	10	17	18	19	20	21
4.8	1	4	8	9	17	18	19	20	29	30
5.9	2	4	6	7	8	11	12	18	20	26
6.10	5	6	17	20	21	22	28	37	38	40
7.9	2	3	5	6	10	15	17	26	37	41
8.6	1	4	6	9	13	14	19	20	22	28
9.8	5	8	10	12	14	20	22	24	25	26
10.9	7	9	13	14	18	28	29	32	33	36
11.10	5	6	7	8	9	10	26	35	39	46

Exercises 1.10

Exercise 1.10.1

(a) Player I has $3 \times 2 \times 2 = 12$ pure strategies. Player II has $3 \times 3 = 9$ pure strategies.

(b)

lll	llr	lrl	lrr		LL	LL	LR
mll	mlr	mrl	mrr		ML	MM	MR
rll	rlr	rrl	rrr		RL	RM	RR

(c) $[rM]$

(d) (rll, LR), (rrl, LR), (rll, MR), (rrl, MR), (rll, RR), (rrl, RR)

(e) See Figure A.1.

	LL	LL	LR	ML	MM	MR	RL	RM	RR
lll	D	D	D	D	D	D	L	L	L
llr	D	D	D	D	D	D	L	L	L
lrl	L	L	L	D	D	D	L	L	L
lrr	L	L	L	D	D	D	L	L	L
mll	D	D	D	D	D	D	D	D	D
mlr	D	D	D	D	D	D	D	D	D
mrl	D	D	D	D	D	D	D	D	D
mrr	D	D	D	D	D	D	D	D	D
rll	W	D	W	W	D	W	W	D	W
rlr	W	D	D	W	D	D	W	D	D
rrl	W	D	W	W	D	W	W	D	W
rrr	W	D	D	W	D	D	W	D	D

Figure A.1 The strategic form for the game G of Exercise 1.10.1(e).

(f) The saddle points are of the form (mxy, XM), where x and y are in the set $\{l, r\}$ and X is in the set $\{L, R, M\}$.

Exercise 1.10.4 See Figure A.2. The complete play shown is called Fool's Mate.

Exercise 1.10.5 See Figure A.3.

Exercise 1.10.8 Player I always has a winning strategy because the game is unbalanced. With $n = 3$, player I begins by taking a match from the largest pile. Play then continues as in Section 1.5.

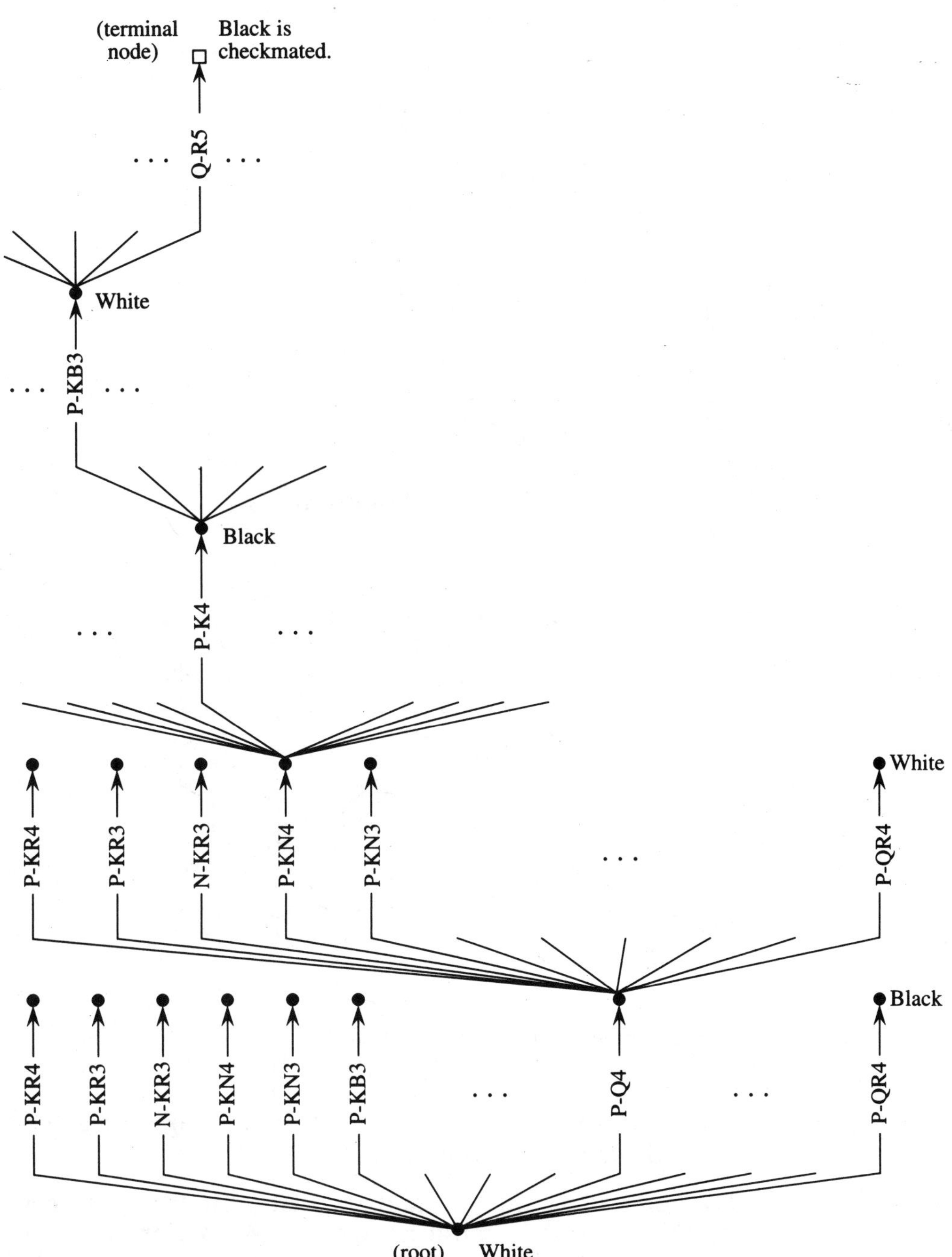

Figure A.2 Beginning the game tree for Chess.

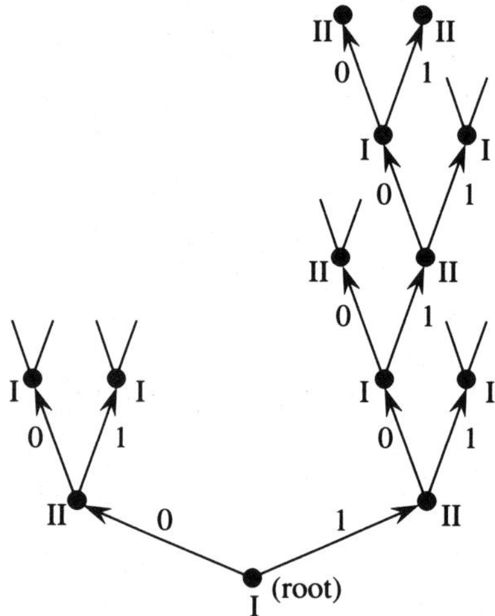

Figure A.3 The game tree for Exercise 1.10.5.

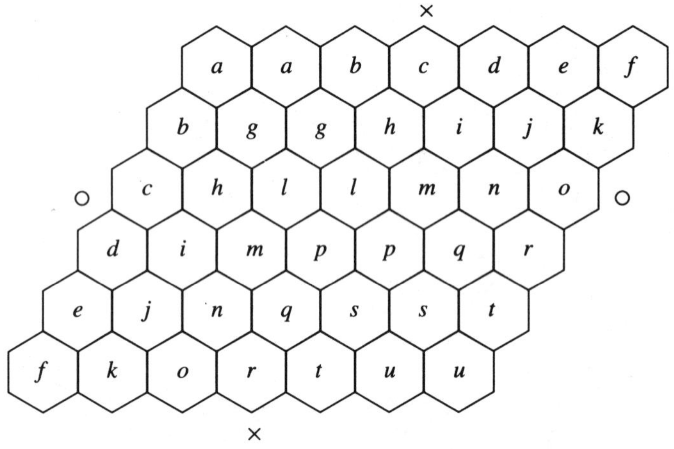

Figure A.4 An asymmetric Hex board.

Exercise 1.10.9 Player II always has a winning strategy because the game is balanced.

Exercise 1.10.11 In 3×3 and 5×5 Hex, Circle should open by playing in the central hexagon. In 4×4 Hex, with the board orientated as in Figure 1.2(a), he should play in the topmost hexagon not on the boundary.

Exercise 1.10.12 Cross should always reply to Circle by occupying the hexagon labeled with the same letter in Figure

A.4 as that just occupied by Circle. Such a blocking strategy makes it impossible for Circle to win, and so Cross must win.[1]

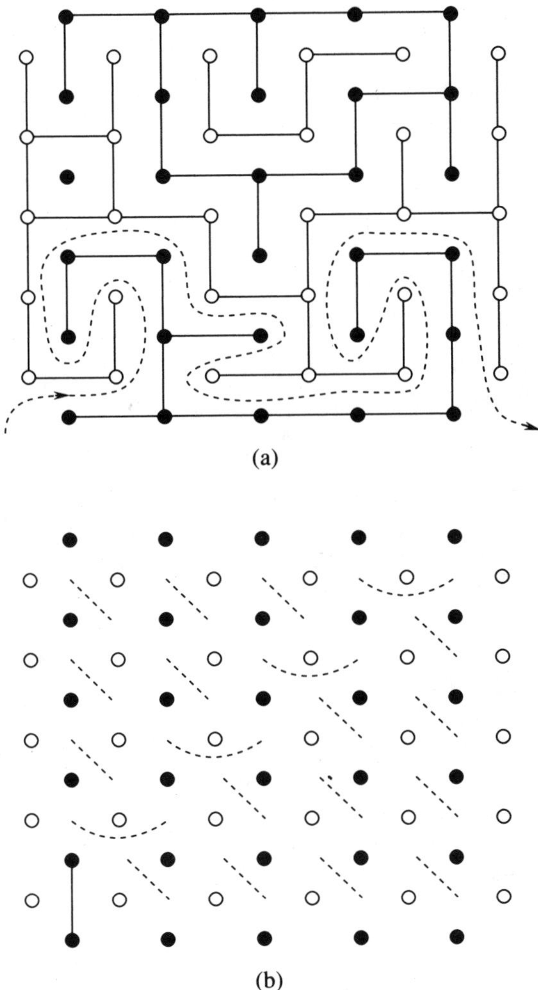

Figure A.5 Diagrams for Bridgit.

Exercise 1.10.14

(a) Figure A.5(a) shows a Bridgit board on which no further linkages can be made without violating the rules. The result is a sort of maze. Someone who entered the maze at the

[1]This solution and the next are borrowed from Martin Gardner's now sadly defunct puzzle column in *Scientific American*.

bottom-left would finally exit at the bottom-right, having kept White's linkages always on his left. Thus White must have won.

(b) Since the outcome $\mathcal{D}$ is impossible, the value of Bridgit must be either $\mathcal{W}$ or $\mathcal{L}$.

(c) A strategy-stealing argument just like that given for Hex applies.

(d) If Black moves first, he should begin by moving as shown in Figure A.5(b). It is pointless for either player to link two nodes that lie on the edge of the board. If White avoids such pointless moves, her linkages will always touch an end of one of the broken lines shown in Figure A.5(b). Black should always reply by making a linkage that touches the other end of this broken line.

Exercise 1.10.17 Player I can ensure victory when $E = \{x : x > \frac{1}{2}\}$ by choosing 1 at both the first and the second opportunity. To win when $E = \{x : x \geq \frac{2}{3}\}$, player I must choose 1 at *every* opportunity. Player II can ensure victory when $E = \{x : x > \frac{2}{3}\}$ by choosing 0 at every opportunity. The decimal expansion of a rational number is one that is eventually periodic, and the same is true for binary expansions. To win when E is the set of all rational numbers, player II therefore merely needs to destroy any periodicity that looks as though it might be getting established. If she is satisfied to win with probability 1, she can do this simply by playing at random.

Exercise 1.10.18 Since (s,t) is a saddle point, $v(a,t) \succeq_1 v(s,t) \succeq_1 v(s,b)$, for all a in S and all b in T. Similarly, $v(c,t') \succeq_1 v(s',t') \succeq_1 v(s',d)$, for all c in S and all d in T. To prove that (s,t') is a saddle point, take $a = s'$ and $d = t$. Then $v(c,t') \succeq_1 v(s',t') \succeq_1 v(s',t) \succeq_1 v(s,t) \succeq_1 v(s,b)$.

Exercises 2.6

Exercise 2.6.1 The first card in your hand can be chosen in 52 ways. This leaves 51 choices for your second card, 50 for your third card, and so on. The number of ways in which you can be dealt a hand is therefore $52 \times 51 \times 50 \times 49 \times 48$. But this calculation takes into account the *order* in which the cards are dealt. To find the answer to the question, it is therefore necessary to divide by the number of ways that the five cards you are dealt can be reshuffled into a different order. There are 5 places to which the first card you are dealt may be relocated. This leaves 4 places to which the second card may be relocated, 3 places for the third, and so on. The number of ways of reshuffling your hand is therefore $5 \times 4 \times 3 \times 2 \times 1$. The total number of possible hands is therefore $N = 52 \times 51 \times 50 \times 49 \times 48/5 \times 4 \times 3 \times 2 \times 1$. There are only 4 royal flushes, one for each suit. Thus the probability of being dealt a royal flush in a fair deal is $4/N$.

Exercise 2.6.3 No. Since he is prepared to bet on Punter's Folly, he believes that the probability that Punter's Folly will win is at least $\frac{1}{3}$. Similarly, he believes that the probability that Gambler's Ruin will win is at least $\frac{1}{4}$. Therefore, he must believe that the probability that both will win is at least $\frac{1}{12}$.[2]

Exercise 2.6.6 $\frac{1}{2}(-2) + \frac{1}{12}(12) + \frac{1}{4}(3) = \frac{3}{4}$.

Exercise 2.6.8 Accept the bet only if the man offers you odds of 1 : 2 or better against the unseen coin drawn from the box being gold. This means that you believe the probability of the coin being gold is $\frac{2}{3}$. The fact that he has shown you a silver coin does not raise the probability that the second coin is gold. The man will show you a silver coin *whatever* pair of coins are drawn. Things are different if the coin you get to see is chosen at random from the drawn pair. Bayes' Rule then tells you to accept the bet if offered odds of 1 : 1 or better.

Exercise 2.6.10 No calculation is necessary to see that the answer is $\text{prob}(1|L) = L_1/L$, where $L = L_1 + \cdots + L_n$. To check this using Bayes' Rule, note that

$$\text{prob}(1|L)\text{prob}(L) = \text{prob}(L|1)\text{prob}(1) = \frac{L_1}{M_1} \times \frac{M_1}{M} = \frac{L_1}{M},$$

where $M = M_1 + \cdots + M_n$. But

$$\begin{aligned}\text{prob}(L) &= \text{prob}(L|1)\text{prob}(1) + \cdots + \text{prob}(L|n)\text{prob}(n)\\ &= \frac{L_1}{M} + \cdots + \frac{L_n}{M} = \frac{L}{M}.\end{aligned}$$

Exercise 2.6.12 Since each player always has an equal chance of being put into a winning position, $v = \frac{1}{2}$.

Exercise 2.6.18 $\frac{5}{32}$

Exercise 2.6.22 $\frac{49}{78}$

[2]A more careful answer would be qualified by some discussion of risk-averse or risk-loving preferences (Section 3.4.3). In brief, one then needs the utility functions to be smooth, and to confine attention to small bets.

Exercise 2.6.25

(a) There are 16 ways the wheels can stop. Player I wins outright when the wheels stop showing $(2, 1)$, $(4, 1)$, $(6, 1)$, $(6, 5)$, $(9, 1)$, $(9, 5)$, $(9, 6)$ or $(9, 8)$. He therefore wins outright with probability $\frac{1}{2}$. However, with probability $\frac{1}{16}$, the wheels stop showing $(6, 6)$. If so, they are spun again, so that player I wins with probability p. It follows that $p = \frac{1}{2} + \frac{1}{16}p$, and so $p = \frac{8}{15}$.

(b) Player I should choose wheel 1, in which case he wins with probability $\frac{8}{15}$.

Exercise 2.6.26

(a) Open a door that does not conceal a prize.

(b) The prize is equally likely to be behind any of the three doors. She knew that the quizmaster would show her an empty box *before* she made her choice, and so she has no reason to update her probability of winning with the box she has chosen after being shown an empty box. After an empty box has been opened, a naive person might argue that there was an equal chance of the prize being in either of the two remaining boxes.

(c) Since her probability of winning if she sticks with the original box is $\frac{1}{3}$, her probability of winning if she switches is necessarily $\frac{2}{3}$. A naive person would argue as in part (b).

(d) If the contestant knows that the quizmaster opens any of the three doors at random, then her probability of winning after an empty box has been opened is $\frac{1}{2}$ whether she switches or not.

Exercises 3.7

Exercise 3.7.1 Totality says that $a \preceq b$ or $b \preceq a$. When mathematicians write "P or Q", they mean that one and only one of "P and Q", "P and (not Q)", "(not P) and Q" is true. The first of these possibilities yields the definition of $a \sim b$, the second yields $a \prec b$, and the third $a \succ b$.

Exercise 3.7.2 Take $a = b$ in the totality formula $a \preceq b$ or $b \preceq a$.

Exercise 3.7.3 Since totality and transitivity apply to both $\preceq$ and $\succeq$, they must also apply to $\sim$. If $a \prec b$ and $b \prec c$, then $a \preceq c$ by the transitivity of $\preceq$. But it cannot also be that $c \preceq a$, since we could then use transitivity to show that $b \preceq a$. To show that $\prec$ does not satisfy totality, apply Exercise 3.7.1 with $a = b$.

Exercise 3.7.7

x	a	b	c	d	e	f
$U(x)$	0	0	$\frac{1}{2}$	$\frac{3}{4}$	1	1
$V(x)$	−100	−100	20	21	1,000	1,000

Exercise 3.7.10 With $a < 0$, the person prefers less money to more money. With $a = 0$, the person doesn't care how much money he or she has. When $0 \le a \le 1$, $u''(x) \le 0$, and so the person is risk-averse. When $a \ge 1$, $u''(x) \ge 0$, and so the person is risk-loving. If $a = 2$, $\mathcal{E}u(\mathbf{K}) = 0.01 \times 0^2 + 0.89 \times 1^2 + 0.1 \times 5^2 = 3.39$, where money is counted in units of one million. This has to be compared with the utility $u(1) = 1^2 = 1$ of getting \$1m for certain. Since $3.39 > 1$, the person would prefer participating in the lottery to owning \$1m. The dollar equivalent X of the lottery $\mathbf{K}$ is found by solving the equation $u(X) = \mathcal{E}u(\mathbf{K})$. Thus $X = \sqrt{3.39}$.

Exercise 3.7.17 The organizer's utility function u is strictly increasing when $u'(x) > 0$ for all x. It is strictly concave when $u''(x) < 0$ for all x. The function u' is strictly decreasing because its derivative is u''.

(a) $M - p(y - z)$. "Actuarially fair" means that the insurance company gets zero expected profit.

(b) Her utility is $u(y - Mf)$ if it is sunny, and $u(z + (y - z)f - Mf)$ if it rains. Differentiating her expected utility yields

$$\begin{aligned} E = &-M(1 - p)u'(y - Mf) \\ &+p(y - z - M)u'(z + (y - z)f - Mf) . \end{aligned}$$

(c) and (d) If $f = 1$, then $E = 0$ if and only if $M = p(y - z)$.[3]

(e) If $f \ge 1$, then $s = y - Mf \le z + (y - z)f - Mf = r$. Hence $u'(s) \ge u'(r)$, and so $E \le u'(r)\{-M(1 - p) + p(y - z - M)\} = u'(r)\{-M + p(y - z)\} < 0$.

Exercise 3.7.18

(a) No.

(b) She will necessarily regret whatever choice she makes.

(c) Yes.

[3]The concavity of u implies that one need not be concerned with second order conditions.

(d) The billionaire has arranged that an integer j be chosen with probability p_j. When Pandora opens her box and finds $\$2^k$, she knows that j is either $k-1$ or k. The event $B = \{k-1, k\}$ has therefore occurred. The event that the other box contains $\$2^{k+1}$ is $A = \{k\}$. The conditional probability we need is therefore $\text{prob}(A|B) = \text{prob}(A \cap B)/\text{prob}(B) = \text{prob}(A)/\text{prob}(B) = p_k/(p_{k-1} + p_k)$.

(e) If the billionaire were right, then $p_k/(p_{k-1} + p_k) = \frac{1}{2}$ for all k. But then all the probabilities p_j are all equal, and so they cannot sum to 1.

Exercise 3.7.19 If Pandora opens her box and finds $\$M_1$ inside, she will certainly regret her choice because $M_1 < M_2$. If she finds $\$M_k$ with $k \geq 2$, she will assign probability $p_{k-1}/(p_{k-1} + p_k)$ to the event that the other box contains $\$M_{k-1}$ and $p_k/(p_{k-1} + p_k)$ to the event that it contains $\$M_{k+1}$. Her expected value for the contents of the other box is therefore $\$(M_{k-1}p_{k-1} + M_{k+1}p_k)/(p_{k-1} + p_k)$. If she regrets her choice, this must exceed $\$M_k$. For the last sentence of the question, simply substitute the values given for M_k and p_k into the inequality.

Exercise 3.7.20 The formula is justified by computing the probability that Pandora will get M_k. When $k \geq 2$, she can get M_k only when the billionaire selects k or $k-1$. Her probability of getting M_k conditional on his choosing k is $\frac{1}{2}$, and it is also $\frac{1}{2}$ conditional on his choosing $k-1$. The total probability of her getting M_k is therefore $\frac{1}{2}(p_k + p_{k-1})$.

If her initial expected utility is finite, it makes sense to sum both sides of the formula of Exercise 3.7.19 between K and infinity, and then to cancel identical terms on each side.[4] This leaves $M_{K-1}p_{K-1} > M_K p_{K-1}$. However, the billionaire needs $M_2 > M_1$ to work his trick. The exercise shows that the Von Neumann and Morgenstern theory does not eliminate all problems of the type exposed by the St. Petersburg paradox.

Exercise 3.7.21 Let probabilities $p_k > 0$ be given. Having chosen $M_1, M_2, \ldots, M_k$ suitably, the billionaire needs to choose M_{k+1} to satisfy the formula of Exercise 3.7.19 if he is to be able to play his trick. If Pandora's Von Neumann and Morgenstern utility function $u : \mathbb{R}_+ \to \mathbb{R}$ is unbounded, his task is easy since he need only find a sum of money $\$X$ that makes $M_{k+1} = u(X)$ sufficiently large. Pandora cannot

[4]The sums need to add up to something finite for this canceling to be legitimate. One cannot, for example, deduce that $1 = 0$ from the fact that $1 + 1 + 1 + \cdots = 0 + 1 + 1 + \cdots$.

always be risk-loving because u cannot be strictly increasing and bounded if it is convex.

Exercises 4.8

Exercise 4.8.1 See Figure A.6.

	d_9	d_7	d_5	d_3	d_1
d_{10}	0.0, 1.0	0.0, 1.0	0.0, 1.0	0.0, 1.0	0.0, 1.0
d_8	0.81, 0.19	0.36, 0.64	0.36, 0.64	0.36, 0.64	0.36, 0.64
d_6	0.81, 0.19	0.49, 0.51	0.64, 0.36	0.64, 0.36	0.64, 0.36
d_4	0.81, 0.19	0.49, 0.51	0.25, 0.75	0.84, 0.16	0.84, 0.16
d_2	0.81, 0.19	0.49, 0.51	0.25, 0.75	0.09, 0.81	0.96, 0.04
d_0	0.81, 0.19	0.49, 0.51	0.25, 0.75	0.09, 0.81	0.01, 0.99

Figure A.6 The strategic form for Exercise 4.8.1.

Exercise 4.8.4

(a) If MN is to be meaningful, the matrix M must have the same number of columns as N has rows.

$$AB = \begin{pmatrix} 4 & 0 \\ 2 & 4 \\ 6 & 0 \end{pmatrix}$$

(b) BC and CB are meaningful because B and C are both 2×2 matrices. $BC \neq CB$.

(c) $(AB)C = \begin{pmatrix} 4 & 8 \\ 10 & 8 \\ 6 & 12 \end{pmatrix} = A(BC)$

(d) $(BC)^\top = \begin{pmatrix} 2 & 2 \\ 1 & 4 \end{pmatrix} = C^\top B^\top$

Exercise 4.8.8

(a) $x^\top x = 14$ (b) $x^\top y = -9$ (c) $x^\top z = -1$

(d) $y^\top z = 0$ (e) $\|x\| = \sqrt{15}$ (f) $\|x - y\| = \sqrt{46}$

Exercise 4.8.9

(a) $\sqrt{14}$ (b) $\sqrt{46}$ (c) y and z

Exercise 4.8.17 The strategy profile (d_6, d_7) is a subgame-perfect equilibrium because it is what remains after dominated strategies are deleted in the same order that they would be deleted when Zermelo's algorithm is used.

Exercise 4.8.18 The two subgame-perfect equilibria are (l, L) and (r, R). Nothing can be eliminated by deleting dominated strategies in this game.

Exercise 4.8.19 The Nash equilibrium outcome $(100, 100)$ is eliminated when weakly dominated strategies are deleted. Yes.

Exercise 4.8.20 If the row player's weakly dominated strategy is deleted first, we are left with the bottom row. If the column player's weakly dominated strategy is deleted first, we are left with the right column.

Exercise 4.8.29

(a) The subgame-perfect equilibrium is $(DDDDD, DDDDD)$. This would also be the result of successively deleting weakly dominated strategies.
(b) No. If the president of Yaleton is offered \$100,000, he may believe he is playing an irrational player and move across.

Exercise 4.8.30

(a) Just double edges in Figure 4.23 in the familiar way.
(b) At every stage, I's optimal choice is l whatever the other players may do.
(c) The potential entrant would probably predict that the incumbent was irrationally aggressive, and hence decide not to enter. However, in a subgame-perfect equilibrium, the potential entrant would enter.
(d) I would resist for the first few stages in the hope of convincing the potential entrants that I am irrational. It is irrational not to play according to the subgame-perfect equilibrium only if nobody can ever be persuaded that the

other players might play irrationally in the future no matter what they have done in the past.

Exercises 5.9

Exercise 5.9.2 See Figure A.7(a).

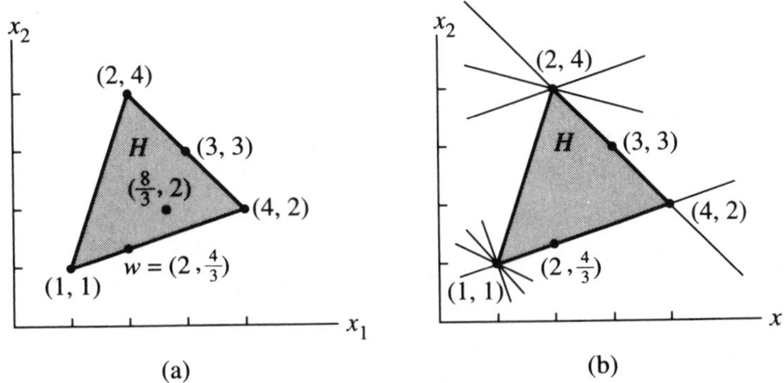

Figure A.7 The diagrams for Exercises 5.9.2 and 5.9.4.

Exercise 5.9.4 See Figure A.7(b).

Exercise 5.9.6 See Figure A.8(a).

Exercise 5.9.7 See Figure A.8(b).

Exercise 5.9.8 See Figure A.8(c).

Exercise 5.9.11 The set of Pareto-efficient points of Y is the straight line segment joining $(1,3)$ and $(3,0)$. The bargaining set for Y when the disagreement point is $e = (1,0)$ is the same. When the disagreement point is $d = (0,1)$, the bargaining set is the straight line segment joining $(1,3)$ and $(2\frac{1}{3},1)$. The set of Pareto-efficient points of Z is the whole of the line with equation $x_1 + x_2 = 4$. The bargaining set for Z when the disagreement point is $d = (0,1)$ is the line segment joining $(3,1)$ and $(0,4)$. When the disagreement point is $e = (1,0)$, the bargaining set is the line segment joining $(1,3)$ and $(4,0)$.

Exercise 5.9.12 $(1\frac{2}{3},2)$, $(1\frac{1}{2},2\frac{1}{2})$, $(2,1\frac{1}{2})$, $(2\frac{1}{2},1\frac{1}{2})$

Exercise 5.9.18 See Figure A.9 for the first sentence. No.

Exercise 5.9.20 The Kalai-Smorodinsky bargaining solution fails to satisfy Axiom 5.3. For an example, (X,d) can be

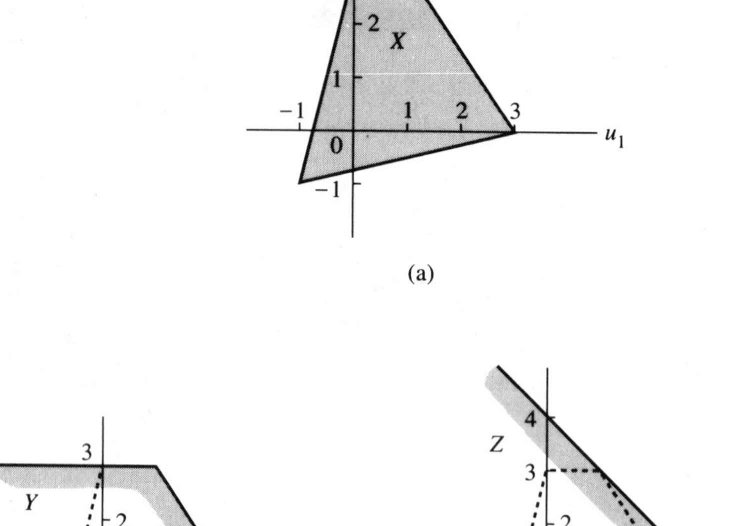

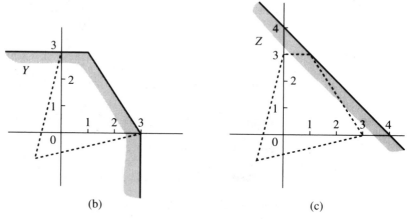

Figure A.8 The diagrams for Exercises 5.9.6, 5.9.7 and 5.9.8.

almost anything, and Y can be the set obtained by deleting everything in X to the right of the Kalai-Smorodinsky solution.

Exercise 5.9.26

(a) John always plans to demand the whole dollar and to refuse unless offered the whole dollar. Mary always plans to offer the whole dollar to John and to accept if offered nothing.

(b) Here John and Mary swap the stategies from part (a). John's planned behavior is always optimal given Mary's strategy because he will get nothing whatever he does. Why does the same argument not apply in Section 5.8.6?

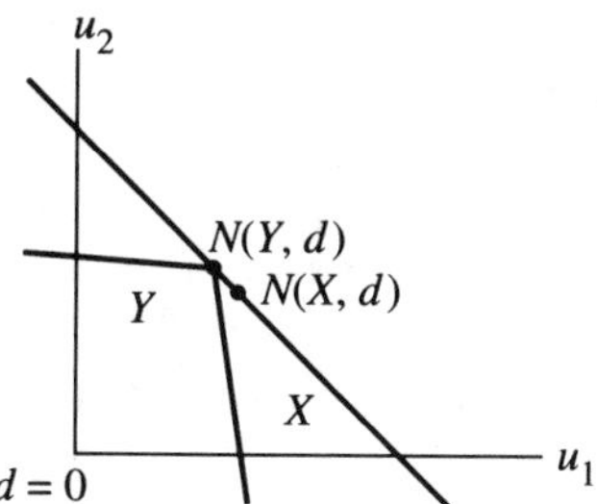

Figure A.9 The Nash bargaining solution is not monotone.

Exercises 6.10

Exercise 6.10.5 Here is a formal argument:

$$\begin{aligned}&\text{maximin}(-A^\top)\\&\quad= \max\{\min\{-a_{11},\ldots,-a_{1n}\},\ldots,\{\min\{-a_{m1},\ldots,-a_{mn}\}\}\\&\quad= \max\{-\max\{a_{11},\ldots,a_{1n}\},\ldots,\{-\max\{a_{m1},\ldots,a_{mn}\}\}\\&\quad= -\min\{\max\{a_{11},\ldots,a_{1n}\},\ldots,\{\max\{a_{m1},\ldots,a_{mn}\}\}\\&\quad= -\text{minimax}(A)\end{aligned}$$

Exercise 6.10.6 A: (s_2, t_2); B and C: no saddle point; D: (s_3, t_4).

Exercise 6.10.17 If player II uses t_1, t_2 or t_3, then player I gets an expected payoff of 4 by using p. If player II uses t_4, player I is certain to get 3 whatever he does. Player I's security level is 3, and p is a security strategy.

Exercise 6.10.20 The formal statement just says that, for some q, $\tilde{p}$ is at least as good for player I as any p. The statement $\forall p\ (\tilde{p}^\top Aq \geq p^\top Aq)$ is equivalent to $\forall p\ ((p - \tilde{p})^\top Aq \leq 0)$. This is equivalent to $\max_p (p - \tilde{p})^\top Aq \leq 0$. Now prefix the last formula by $\exists q$ and express what results in terms of $\min_q$.

Exercise 6.10.21 The first formal statement says that some p is better for player I than $\tilde{p}$ whatever q player II may choose. The second formal statement is equivalent for the reason given in footnote 33 of Chapter 6. The final statement is derived using the methodology of Exercise 6.10.20.

Exercise 6.10.22 The minimax that concludes Exercise 6.10.20 is equal to the maximin that concludes Exercise 6.10.21.

Exercise 6.10.28

(a) $v = 1$, $\tilde{p} = (0, 1)^\top$, $\tilde{q} = (0, 1, 0)^\top$
(b) $v = 1$, $\tilde{p} = (\frac{1}{2}, \frac{1}{2})^\top$, $\tilde{q} = (a, b, a)^\top$
(c) $v = -2$, $\tilde{p} = (a, b, 0)^\top$, $\tilde{q} = (1, 0)^\top$

Exercise 6.10.37 Proceed as in Section 6.8 but with Figure 6.19 modified so that its top-right cell is v_{n-1} and its bottom-right cell is u_{n-1}. Then $E_1(r) = 1 - 2r$ and $E_2(r) = (1-r)v_{n-1} + ru_{n-1}$. Player I's security strategy $\tilde{r}$ is found by setting these equal. The formula for u_n then follows by writing $u_n = E_1(\tilde{r})$. Since $u_2 = 1$, it follows that $u_3 = \frac{1}{3}$ and therefore that $u_4 = 0$. The agency should inspect with probability $\frac{1}{2}$ on the first day.

Exercise 6.10.38 The optimal strategies are for Colonel Blotto to send 1 or 2 companies each with probability $\frac{1}{2}$. Count Baloney sends 0 or 1 companies each with probability $\frac{1}{2}$. Colonel Blotto's expected payoff is v_n, where $v_n = \frac{1}{2}(1 + v_{n-1})$. Since $v_0 = 0$, it follows that $v_n = 1 - (\frac{1}{2})^n$.

Exercise 6.10.40 The only security strategy is to choose *heads* and *tails* with equal probability. It is a Nash equilibrium if all players choose *heads*. For a two-player zero-sum game, a strategy profile is a Nash equilibrium if and only if each player uses one of his or her security strategies.

Exercises 7.9

Exercise 7.9.2 See Figure A.10.

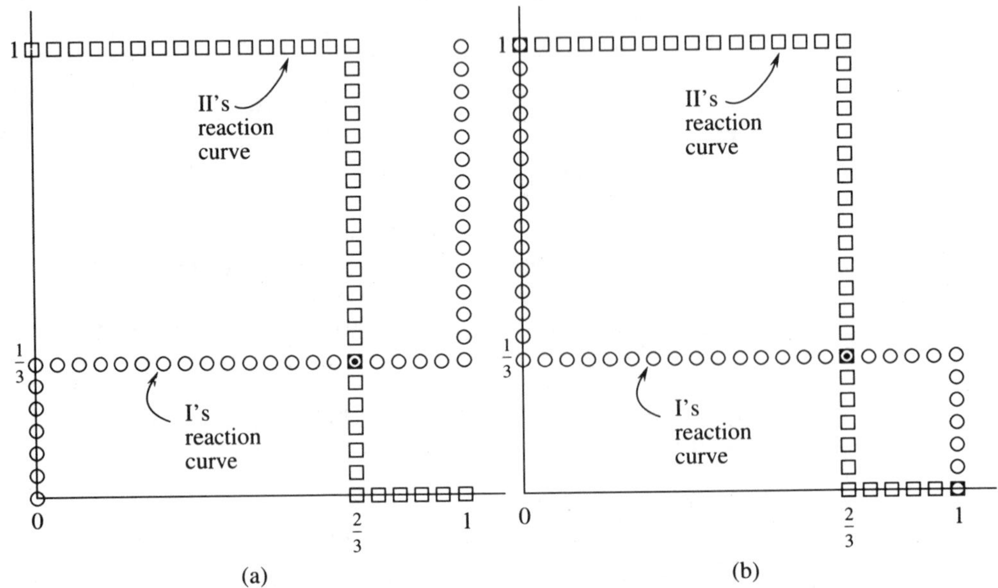

Figure A.10 Reaction curves for Exercise 7.9.2.

Exercise 7.9.3 Let E_i be a matrix with 1s in its ith column and 0s elswhere. Then $p^{\top}(A + kE_i)q = p^{\top}Aq + kq_i$. Since the term kq_i does not depend on p, it follows that the same p maximizes both $p^{\top}(A + kE_i)q$ and $p^{\top}Aq$.

The second version of Chicken (Figure 7.17(a)) is obtained from the first (Figure 7.3(c)) by adding 1 to player I's payoffs in the first column and 1 to player II's payoffs in the first row. The two versions therefore have the same best reply correspondences, and hence the same Nash equilibria.

Exercise 7.9.5

(a) See Figure A.11(a).
(b) See Figure A.11(b).

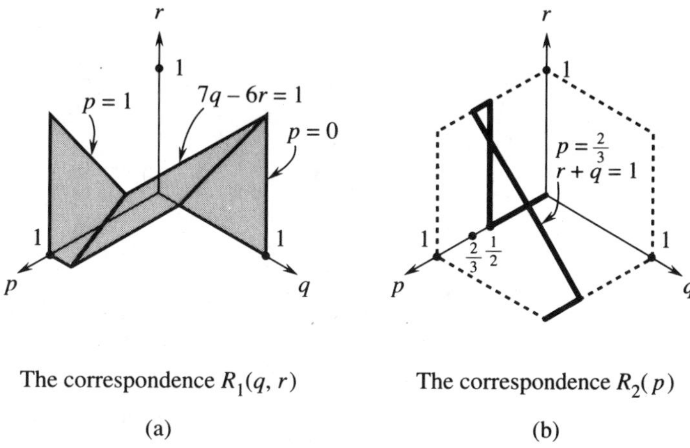

The correspondence $R_1(q, r)$

(a)

The correspondence $R_2(p)$

(b)

Figure A.11 A reaction surface and a reaction curve for Exercise 7.9.5.

(c) The Nash equilibrium is $(\frac{2}{3}, \frac{7}{13}, \frac{6}{13})$. The equilibrium values of q and r are obtained by solving the equations $q + r = 1$ and $7q - 6r = 1$ simultaneously. The equilibrium outcome is $(\frac{96}{13}, \frac{4}{3})$.
(d) $(9.03, 2.97)$

Exercise 7.9.6

(a) (A, A, A); (B, B, B)
(b) $(\frac{1}{2}, \frac{1}{2}, \frac{3}{4})$
(c) They should agree to play (A, A). It would not be in player II's interest to back out of the agreement. Players I and II should switch to (B, B) if they are sure that player III believes that they will play (A, A).

Exercise 7.9.10 If $(\tilde{p}, \tilde{q})$ is a Nash equilibrium, then $\tilde{p}$ is a best reply to $\tilde{q}$. It follows that $\Pi_1(\tilde{p}, \tilde{q}) = \max_p \Pi_1(p, \tilde{q}) \geq \min_q \max_p \Pi_1(p, q)$. The rest of the inequality comes from Theorem 6.4.1. The corresponding inequality for player II is $\max_q \min_p \Pi_2(p, q) \leq \min_p \max_q \Pi_2(p, q) \leq \Pi(\tilde{p}, \tilde{q})$. The left-hand side of the last inequality is player II's security level. She therefore gets at least this much in a Nash equilibrium. Similarly for player I. No calculations are really necessary to see this because players can guarantee their security levels independently of what the opponent may do. They must therefore get at least as much by making a best reply to whatever strategy the other player actually does use.

Exercise 7.9.15

(a) See Figure A.12.

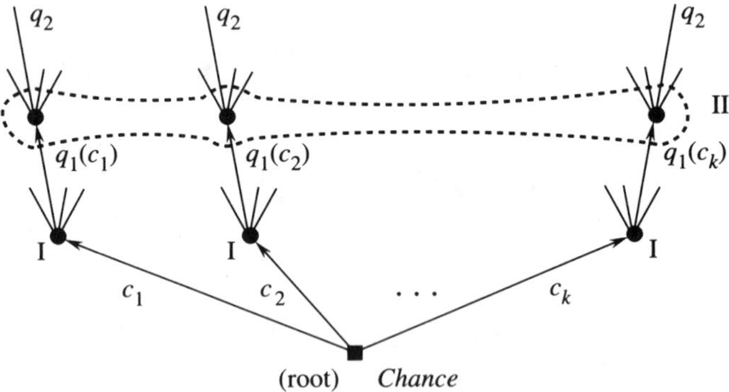

Figure A.12 A schematic game tree for Exercise 7.9.15.

(b) The quantity that player I produces depends on the unit cost with which he is endowed by Chance. However, player II's unit cost is given.
(c) Player II's expected profit is $\mathcal{E}\pi_1 = (M - c - \bar{q}_1 - q_2)q_2$, where $\bar{q}_1 = \mathcal{E}q_1 = r_1 q_1(c_1) + r_2 q_1(c_2) + \cdots + r_k q_1(c_k)$. Her best reply to q_1 is $q_2 = \frac{1}{2}(M - c - \bar{q}_1)$.
(d) If player II produces q_2, then player I should produce $\frac{1}{2}(M - c_i - q_2)$. Thus, the pure strategy that is a best reply for player I to player II's choice of q_2 is the function $q_1 : C \to [0, M]$ defined by $q_1(c_i) = \frac{1}{2}(M - c_i - q_2)$. Player I's expected output when he uses this best reply strategy is $\bar{q}_1 = \frac{1}{2}(M - \bar{c} - q_2)$, where $\bar{c} = \mathcal{E}c_i = r_1 c_1 + r_2 c_2 + \cdots + r_k c_k$.
(e) To find a Nash equilibrium, solve the equations $q_2 = \frac{1}{2}(M - c - \bar{q}_1)$ and $\bar{q}_1 = \frac{1}{2}(M - \bar{c} - q_2)$ for q_2. Then

substitute this value in $q_1(c_i) = \frac{1}{2}(M - c_i - q_2)$. The equilibrium outputs are $q_1(c_i) = \frac{1}{6}(M - 3c_i + 2c - \bar{c})$ and $q_2 = \frac{1}{3}(M - 2c + \bar{c})$.

Exercise 7.9.17 Suppose that $p_1 > c$. Then player II can profitably capture the whole market by choosing p_2 to be slightly less than p_1. Similarly, player I can profitably capture the whole market by taking p_1 slightly less than p_2 if $p_2 > c$. Thus, for a Nash equilibrium with two firms in the market producing positive amounts, it must be the case that $p_1 = p_2 = c$. Each will then make zero profit—as in the case of perfect competition. If the firms do not have the same unit cost, the firm with the lower unit cost can profitably capture the whole market by setting a price slightly below the unit cost of its rival. There are no Nash equilibria in which both firms produce positive amounts. The high-cost firm will be forced out of the market, and the low-cost firm will set a price equal to its potential rival's cost to ensure that it is not worthwhile for it to reenter.

Exercise 7.9.26

(a) The kth farmer's profit is $\pi_k = e^{-W} W_k$. This has a strict maximum at $W_k = 1$ whatever the outputs of the other farmers. If all farmers produce 1 unit, then $W = n$, and so $\pi_k = e^{-n}$.

(b) A monopolist controlling all wheat production would maximize profit by taking $W = 1$. If the farmers form a cartel and jointly produce the same output as a monopolist would produce, each individual's output will be $1/n$. The cartel agreement would need to be binding because it is strictly dominating for each individual farmer to produce 1, whatever the other farmers may do.

(c) If each farmer produces 1, then each gets profit e^{-n}. If each produces $1/n$, each gets profit e^{-1}/n. The latter exceeds the former if and only if $ne^{-n} < 1e^{-1}$.

(d) If all farmers use their strictly dominating strategies, the result is Pareto-inferior.

Exercise 7.9.37

(a) $\tilde{\pi}_1 = \frac{1}{2}(\pi_1 + \tilde{\pi} - \pi_2)$, $\tilde{\pi}_2 = \frac{1}{2}(\pi_2 + \tilde{\pi} - \pi_1)$, where $\tilde{\pi} = \frac{1}{4}(M - c)^2$.

(b) $\tilde{\pi}_1 + \tilde{\pi}_2 = \tilde{\pi}$. The game is therefore constant-sum, and so strategically equivalent to a zero-sum game. $\pi_1 - \pi_2 = 2\pi_1 - \tilde{\pi}$.

(c) $\pi_1 - \pi_2 = (M - c - q_1 - q_2)(q_1 - q_2)$. Player I's security level is 0.

(d) Each player's security strategy is to produce the output that a monopolist would choose.

Exercise 7.9.41 The answers to the parenthetical questions are:

1. y_k maximizes profit at prices p_k.
2. The function $f : \mathbb{R}_+^{2n} \to \mathbb{R}$ defined by $f(p, y) = p^\top y$ is continuous.
3. y maximizes profit at prices p.

The flaw in the argument is that nothing ensures the convergence of the sequence y_k. To patch up the proof, we need to invoke the fact that Y is compact. It is then guaranteed that y_k has a convergent *subsequence*. We can then continue as before using this subsequence instead of the original sequence.

Exercises 8.6

Exercise 8.6.1 See Figure A.13.

(a)

	t_1t_1	t_1t_2	t_2t_1	t_2t_2
s_1s_1	$\frac{3}{2}$	1	$\frac{1}{2}$	0
s_1s_2	1	$\frac{3}{2}$	0	$\frac{1}{2}$
s_2s_1	$\frac{1}{2}$	0	$\frac{3}{2}$	1
s_2s_2	0	$\frac{1}{2}$	1	$\frac{3}{2}$

(b)

	t_1t_1	t_1t_2	t_2t_1	t_2t_2
s_1s_1	1	0	0	0
s_1s_2	0	1	0	0
s_2s_1	0	0	0	1
s_2s_2	0	0	0	1

Figure A.13 Strategic forms for Exercise 8.6.1.

Exercise 8.6.4 Zermelo's algorithm requires that the unique Nash equilibrium be played at the last stage. Now consider the penultimate stage, and reason as in Section 8.3.

Exercise 8.6.6 Consider a pure strategy profile s whose use leads to a play P of the repeated game. Let j be the last stage on the play P at which someone does not play *hawk*. Then a player who chose *dove* at stage j can improve his or her payoff in the repeated game by choosing *hawk* at stage j and thereafter. Thus s cannot be a Nash equilibrium unless no such stage j exists.[5] Consider a pure strategy e for the twice-repeated Prisoners' Dilemma in which each player plans to play *hawk* at the first stage, and *hawk* at the second stage if the opponent plays *hawk* at the first stage. If something other than (*hawk, hawk*) were to occur at the first stage, let the strategy specify the play of *dove* at the second stage. Then (e, e) is a Nash equilibrium that is not subgame-perfect.

Exercise 8.6.9 If each player uses GRIM, then each will get an average payoff of 3. A player who deviates from GRIM does best by playing *dove* up to the last stage and only then switching to *hawk*. If the deviant's opponent sticks to GRIM, the deviant will get an average payoff of $(3(n-1)+6)/n = 3 + 3/n$. For (GRIM, GRIM) to be an approximate Nash equilibrium, the requirement is therefore that $3/n \leq \varepsilon$. For the version of the Prisoners' Dilemma of Figure 8.13(a), the condition is $1/n \leq \varepsilon$.

Exercise 8.6.13 A Moore machine with 100 states cannot count to 101 because it needs a new state for each number that it counts. If player I uses GRIM, player II can only improve on playing GRIM herself by using *dove* up to the last stage and then using *hawk*. But this improvement is unavailable to her if she must use a machine with only 100 states because such a machine cannot count up to 101, and hence it is unable to identify the last stage.

Exercise 8.6.14 TIT-FOR-TAT.

Exercise 8.6.19 $U_2(a,b) = (6+\delta+\delta^2)/(1-\delta^4)$. But $1-\delta^4 = (1-\delta)(1+\delta+\delta^2+\delta^3)$, and so $(1-\delta)U_2(a,b) = (6+\delta+\delta^2)/(1+\delta+\delta^2+\delta^3) \to \frac{1}{4}(6+1+1) = 2$ as $\delta \to 1$.

Exercise 8.6.20 Figure A.14 shows the required strategic form. The cells corresponding to Nash equilibria have both their payoffs circled.

Exercise 8.6.22

(a) and (b) See Figure A.15.

(c) The Nash equilibrium outcomes in pure strategies are dense in the set of all (r_1, r_2) such that $r_1 + r_2 \leq 10$, $r_1 \geq x$ and $r_2 \geq x$. This set is empty if $x > 5$.

(d) If $x > 10$, then only (x, x) is a Nash equilibrium outcome. If $x < 0$, only $(10, 10)$ is a Nash equilibrium outcome.

[5] If mixed strategies are to be considered, define j as the last stage at which someone plays *dove* with positive probability.

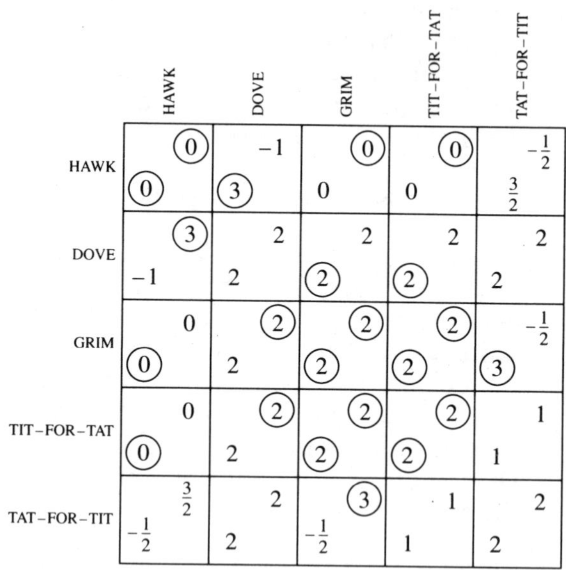

	HAWK	DOVE	GRIM	TIT–FOR–TAT	TAT–FOR–TIT
HAWK	(0), (0)	(3), −1	0, (0)	0, (0)	$\frac{3}{2}$, $-\frac{1}{2}$
DOVE	−1, (3)	2, 2	(2), 2	(2), 2	2, 2
GRIM	(0), 0	2, (2)	(2), (2)	(2), (2)	(3), $-\frac{1}{2}$
TIT–FOR–TAT	(0), 0	2, (2)	(2), (2)	(2), (2)	1, 1
TAT–FOR–TIT	$-\frac{1}{2}$, $\frac{3}{2}$	2, 2	$-\frac{1}{2}$, (3)	1, 1	2, 2

Figure A.14 The reduced strategic form for Exercise 8.6.20.

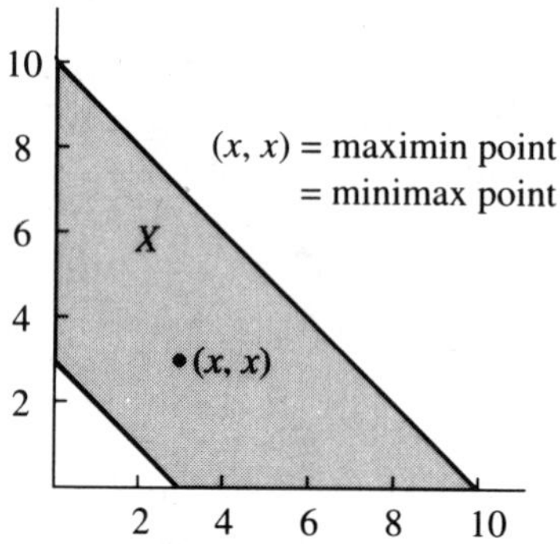

Figure A.15 Using the folk theorem in Exercise 8.6.22.

Exercise 8.6.28

(a) It is not profitable to deviate for the first time at the last stage because choosing *dove* and *hawk* with equal probability is a Nash equilibrium for the one-shot game. Nor is it profitable to deviate at an earlier stage because the first person to deviate gets punished at all subsequent stages.

(b) Subgames of the repeated game are reached in three possible ways. If (*dove, hawk*) or (*hawk, dove*) have never been played at a preceding stage, then (s, s) calls for Nash equilibrium play in the ensuing subgame by part (a). Otherwise, one of (*dove, hawk*) and (*dove, hawk*) was played first. In the former case, the Nash equilibrium (*hawk, dove*) of the one-shot game is played thereafter. In the latter case, the Nash equilibrium (*dove, hawk*) of the one-shot game is played thereafter.

(c) 3, 0, 2, 3, 0, 2, ..., 3, 0, 2, 1

(d) Chicken has multiple Nash equilibria so that deviants can be punished by switching to a Nash equilibrium of the one-shot game that the deviant doesn't like.

Exercises 9.8

Exercise 9.8.5 Yes. See Figure A.16.

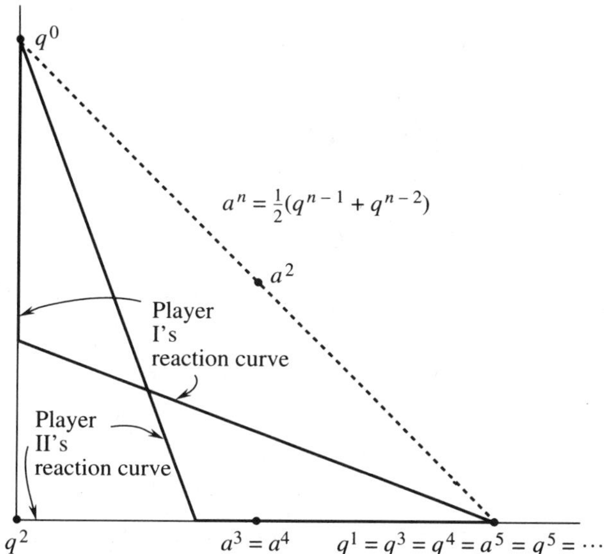

Figure A.16 Convergence to equilibrium in Exercise 9.8.5.

Exercise 9.8.8 See Figure A.17(a).

Exercise 9.8.10 $p' = p(3 - 2p)(1 - p)$. The rest points are $p = 0$ and $p = 1$. If $p(0) = 0$, then $p' = 0$. Otherwise $p' > 0$ and p increases to the limit 1.

Exercise 9.8.12

(a) If only one strategy is present, the population cannot change its composition. Thus $(1, 0)$ is a rest point. If $a > c$ then there exists a p close to 1 such that $p' > 0$. If $a = c$ and $b > d$ then $p' > 0$ for all $p \in (0, 1]$.

(b) The argument is similar to part (a).

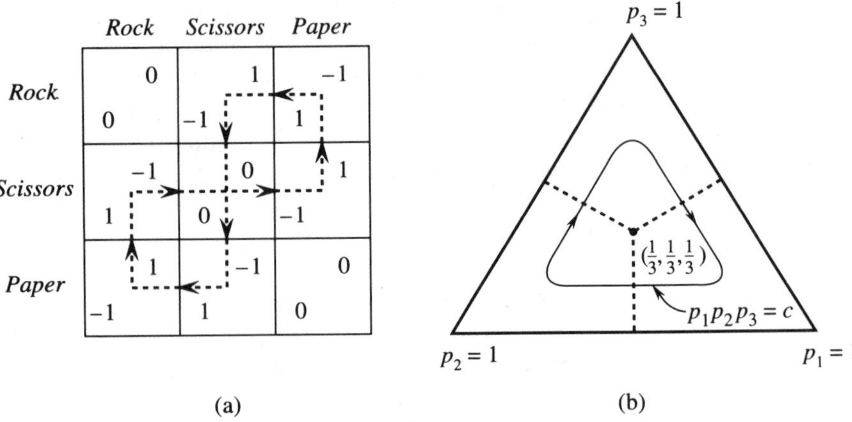

Figure A.17 Diagrams for Exercises 9.8.8 and 9.8.24(c).

(c) In this case the population does not move from its initial point. Thus, any point is a rest point, but no point is an asymptotic attractor.
(d) Write $p_1 = \tilde{p}_1$ and $p_2 = \tilde{p}_2$ in the right-hand side of the replicator equations.
(e) If $p_1 > \tilde{p}_1$, then $p_1' < 0$. Similarly, if $p_1 < \tilde{p}_1$, then $p_1' > 0$.
(f) If these strict inequalities hold, p_1' will be negative if p_1 is greater than $\tilde{p}_1$ and positive if it is less.

Exercise 9.8.14 We can deduce these conclusions from Exercises 9.8.12(a), 9.8.12(b) and Exercise 9.8.12(f) using Lemma 9.6.1, but it is just as easy to use the definition of an evolutionarily stable strategy directly.

Exercise 9.8.20 Simply replace the expected payoff to player i by $(Ap)_i$ and the average expected payoff by $p^\top Ap$.

Exercise 9.8.22

(a) If $\tilde{p}$ is an evolutionarily stable strategy, then $(\tilde{p}, \tilde{p})$ is a Nash equilibrium. Thus each pure strategy to which $\tilde{p}$ assigns positive probability must be a best reply to the choice of $\tilde{p}$ by the opponent. But, since $\tilde{p}$ is completely mixed, it assigns positive probability to all pure strategies. Thus $(Ap)_i$ is the same for all i.
(b) Any p is an alternative best reply because all replies yield the same payoff.
(c) Lemma 9.6.1.
(d) Since $A^\top = -A$ we have $-p^\top A\tilde{p} > -p^\top Ap$ by taking transposes. Thus, $p^\top A\tilde{p} < p^\top Ap$. But $\tilde{p}^\top A\tilde{p} = p^\top A\tilde{p} = w$. Hence $\tilde{p}^\top A\tilde{p} < p^\top Ap$, which contradicts the hypothesis that $\tilde{p}$ is evolutionarily stable.

Exercise 9.8.24 On adding the three equations, we obtain $d(p_1p_2p_3)/dt = 0$. This differential equation has the immediate solution $p_1p_2p_3 = c$.

(a) A cute method for the maximization uses the inequality of the arithmetic and geometric means: $\sqrt[3]{p_1p_2p_3} \leq \frac{1}{3}(p_1 + p_2 + p_3)$, with equality if and only if $p_1 = p_2 = p_3$. An asymptotic attractor would need to be $\tilde{p}$ because this is the only rest point. But no trajectories approach $\tilde{p}$.
(b) Since $p_1(c)$, $p_2(c)$ and $p_3(c)$ are all close to $\tilde{p}$ when c is close to $\frac{1}{27}$, it follows that the whole trajectory $p_1p_2p_3 = c$ must also be close to $\tilde{p}$.
(c) See Figure A.17(b).

Exercise 9.8.25 $\Pi(s_1, s_1) = 0 > \Pi(s_2, s_1) = -3$ and $\Pi(s_1, s_1) = 0 > \Pi(s_3, s_1) = -1$. The strategy profile $(\tilde{p}, \tilde{p})$ is a Nash equilibrium because anything is a best reply to the opponent's choice of $\tilde{p}$. However, $\Pi(\tilde{p}, s_1) = -4/3 < \Pi(s_1, s_1)$, and so $\tilde{p}$ is not an evolutionarily stable strategy.

Exercise 9.8.26

(a) $(A\tilde{p})_i = \tilde{p}^\top A\tilde{p} = \frac{2}{3}$
(b) After eliminating quadratic terms from the replicator equation, $q_i' \approx \frac{1}{3}\{(Aq)_i - \tilde{p}^\top Aq - q^\top A\tilde{p}\}$.
(c) This is easy if you know what an eigenvalue is.
(d) $e^{\lambda t} \to 0$ as $t \to \infty$ if $\Re\lambda < 0$. Thus $q \to \tilde{p}$ as $t \to \infty$, provided that $q(0)$ is close enough to $\tilde{p}$.

Exercises 10.9

Exercise 10.9.7

(a) By (K3), $\mathcal{K}E \subseteq \mathcal{K}(\mathcal{K}E)$. Thus $\mathcal{K}E$ is a truism.
(b) Show that $\sim\mathcal{K}F$ is a truism by writing $E = \sim F$ in (K4) and recalling the definition of $\mathcal{P}$.
(c) Use (K4).
(d) Put $F = \sim E$, and use the fact that $\sim\mathcal{K}F$ is a truism by part (b).

Exercise 10.9.9 The first inclusion is implied by (K2). The second follows from the fact that the set of all E is larger than the set of those E of the form $E = \mathcal{K}F$. The next identity follows from Exercise 10.9.2(b). For the final part, one uses the earlier parts to show that

$$\mathcal{P}\{\omega\} = \bigcap_{\omega \in T} T = \bigcap_{\omega \in \mathcal{K}(\mathcal{K}E)} \mathcal{K}E = \bigcap_{\omega \in \mathcal{K}E} \mathcal{K}E$$

by the first part of the exercise.

Exercise 10.9.13 Nobody blushes until the third second, at which time everybody blushes simultaneously. See Figure A.18.

Exercise 10.9.14 Let Alice have the first opportunity to blush, and then let Bob and Nanny have the opportunity to blush *simultaneously* one second later. Then let Alice have the opportunity to blush, and so on.

Exercise 10.9.18

(a) The pure strategies lL, lR, rL and rR should be used with probabilities $(1-p)(1-P)$, $(1-p)P$, $p(1-P)$ and pP.
(b) The given mixed strategy assigns probability $\frac{1}{4}$ to each of the plays $[Hl]$, $[HrR]$, $[Tr]$ and $[TlL]$. A behavioral strategy in which action r is chosen with probability p and action R with probability P assigns probabilities $\frac{1}{2}(1-p)$, $\frac{1}{2}pP$, $\frac{1}{2}P$ and $\frac{1}{2}(1-p)(1-P)$ to these plays. No values of p and P make each of these probabilities equal to $\frac{1}{4}$.
(c) Kuhn's theorem does not apply because the game has imperfect recall.

Exercise 10.9.28 Only the case of Exercise 10.9.13 is considered. See Figure A.18 for the communal possibility sets. The event that both Bob and Nanny have dirty faces is $D_{B,N} = \{7, 8\}$. If this event occurs, then either the true state is $\omega = 7$ or $\omega = 8$. Eventually, $\mathcal{M}(7) = \{7\}$ and $\mathcal{M}(8) = \{8\}$. In both cases, $\mathcal{M}(\omega) \subseteq D_{B,N}$.

Exercise 10.9.29 In the general case, $d(S)$ may be a *set* of actions because there need not be a unique optimum. Let $\mathcal{E}u(x|S)$ denote the expected utility of x given that event S has occurred. When E and F are disjoint, $\mathcal{E}u(x|E \cup F) = p\mathcal{E}u(x|E) + q\mathcal{E}u(x|F)$, where $p = \text{prob}(E|E \cup F)$ and $q = \text{prob}(F|E \cup F)$. Hence, $\mathcal{E}u(x|E \cup F) \leq p\mathcal{E}u(y|E) + q\mathcal{E}u(y|F) = \mathcal{E}u(y|E \cup F)$, for each y in the set $d(E) = d(F)$. We may deduce that $y \in d(E) \Rightarrow y \in d(E \cup F)$ when $d(E) = d(F)$. One can similarly show that $y \notin d(E) \Rightarrow y \notin d(E \cup F)$.

Exercise 10.9.32

(a) See Figure A.19(a).
(b) See Figure A.19(b).
(c) The same as in Figure A.19(b).
(d) 2
(e) See Figure A.20.
(f) No.
(g) After the first announcement.

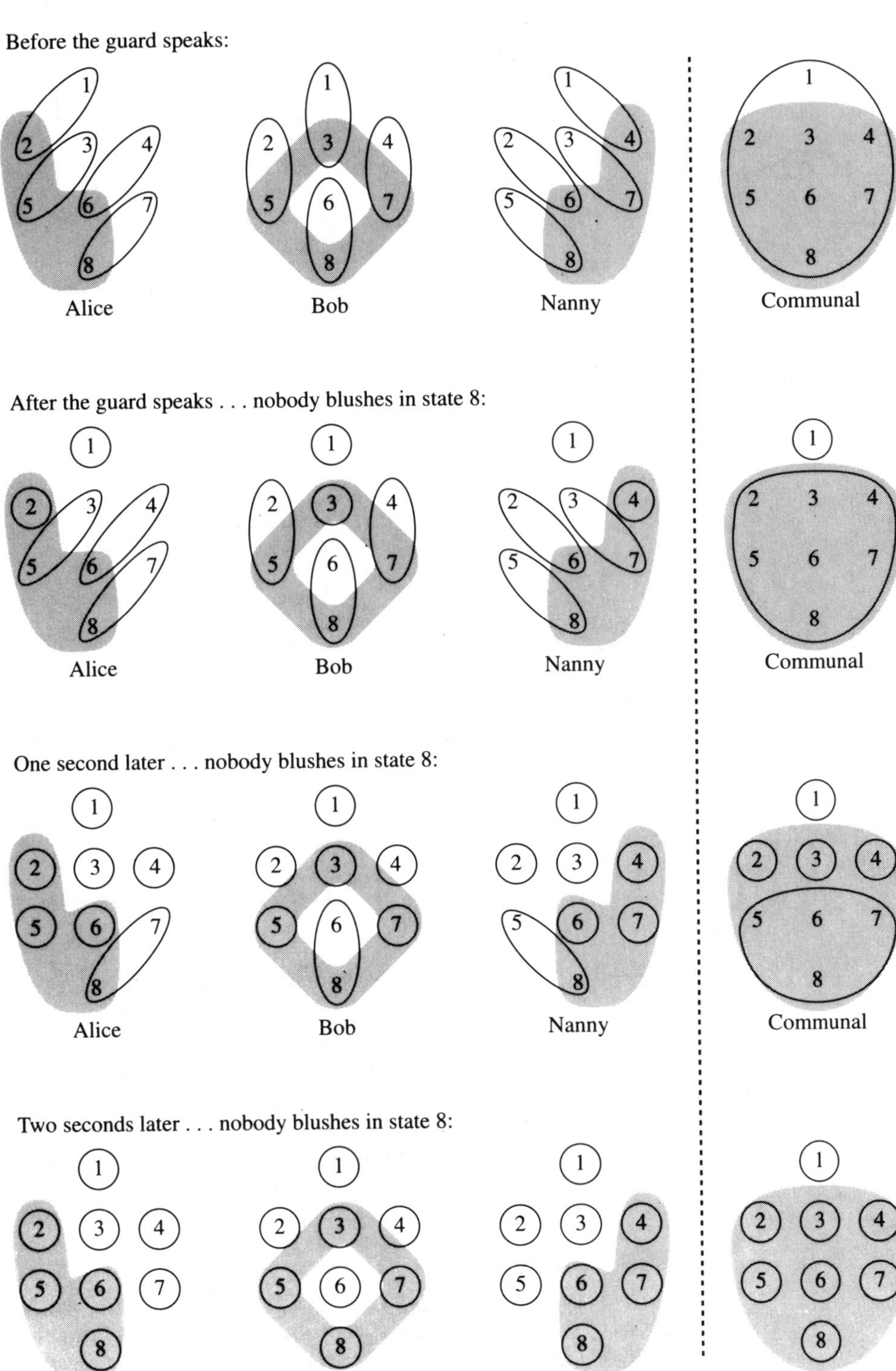

Figure A.18 Simultaneous blushing for Exercise 10.9.13.

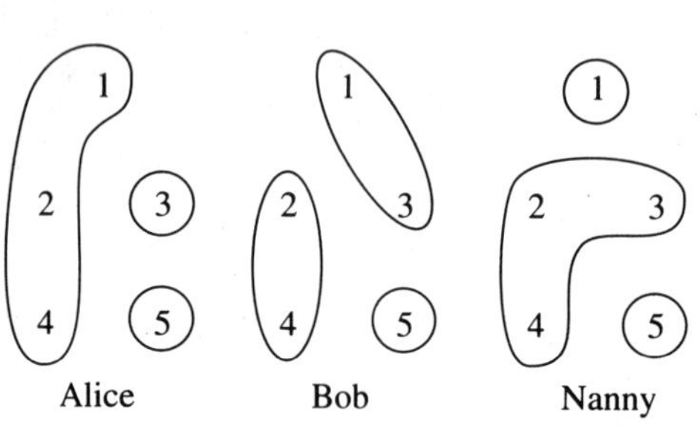

State	Alice	Bob	Nanny	Average
1	$\frac{2}{3}$	1	1	$\frac{8}{9}$
2	$\frac{2}{3}$	$\frac{1}{2}$	$\frac{2}{3}$	$\frac{11}{18}$
3	1	1	$\frac{2}{3}$	$\frac{8}{9}$
4	$\frac{2}{3}$	$\frac{1}{2}$	$\frac{2}{3}$	$\frac{11}{18}$
5	0	0	0	0

(a)

State	Alice	Bob	Nanny	Average
1	1	1	1	1
2	$\frac{1}{2}$	$\frac{1}{2}$	$\frac{1}{2}$	$\frac{1}{2}$
3	1	1	1	1
4	$\frac{1}{2}$	$\frac{1}{2}$	$\frac{1}{2}$	$\frac{1}{2}$
5	0	0	0	0

(b)

Figure A.19 Diagrams for Exercise 10.9.32(a) and (b).

(h) After the second announcement.
(i) Everybody's posterior probabilities will equal the average.

Exercise 10.9.33 Bayesian-rational players optimize given their information. If each knows the strategy choice of the other, each will therefore make a best reply to the strategy chosen by the other.

Exercise 10.9.36

(a) The second derivative of $\pi_1(q_1, q_2)$ with respect to q_1 is -2. If firm 1 chooses output a with probability α and output b with probability β, his expected profit is $\alpha\pi_1(a, q_2) + \beta\pi_1(b, q_2) < \pi_1(\alpha a + \beta b, q_2)$ because π_1 is strictly concave.

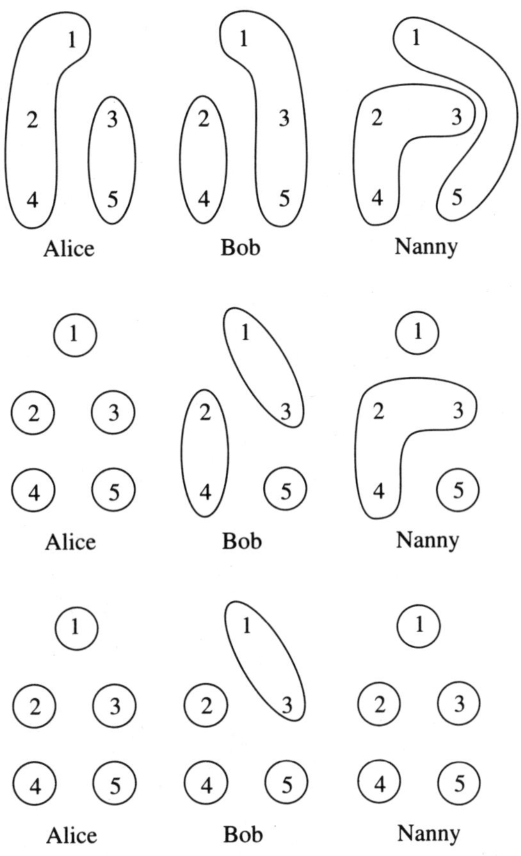

Figure A.20 Possibility sets for Exercise 10.9.32(e).

(b) See Figure A.21(a).
(c) The function R is continuous.
(d) Player i's reaction curve never gets above the line $q_i = x_1$. See Figure A.21(b).
(e) For the same reason as part (d). See Figure A.21(c).
(f) Delete the shaded part of Figure A.21(c).
(g) The sequence x_{2n} increases and the sequence x_{2n+1} decreases.
(h) This follows from part (g) and part (c).

Exercises 11.10

Exercise 11.10.5 Since $\text{prob}(A \cap C) = 0.01$, $\text{prob}(A) = 0.01$, and $\text{prob}(C) = 0.1$, $\text{prob}(A \cap C) \neq \text{prob}(A)\text{prob}(C)$. See Figure A.22. Mr. A and Ms. D will know who their opponent is for sure.

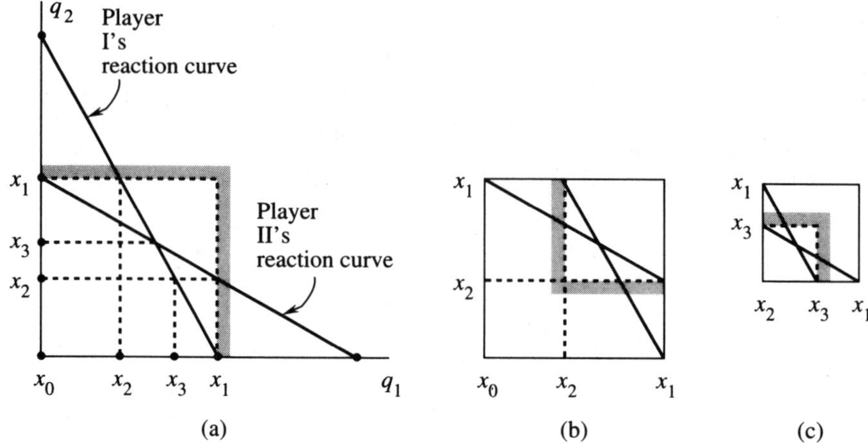

Figure A.21 Diagrams for Exercise 10.9.36(b), (d), (e) and (f).

Ms. C	Ms. D
1	0

Mr. A's beliefs
(a)

Ms. C	Ms. D
$\frac{1}{11}$	$\frac{10}{11}$

Mr. B's beliefs
(b)

Mr. A	Mr. B
$\frac{1}{10}$	$\frac{9}{10}$

Ms. C's beliefs
(c)

Mr. A	Mr. B
1	0

Ms. D's beliefs
(d)

Figure A.22 Beliefs in Exercise 11.10.5.

Exercise 11.10.6

(a) Mr. A against Ms. C: bottom-right. Mr. A against Ms. D: bottom-left. Mr. B against Ms. C: top-left. Mr. B against Ms. D: top-right.
(b) (a_1, b_1, d_2, c_1)
(c) The payoffs and the probabilities for the casting move are assumed to be common knowledge.
(e) Mr. A knows that if he is chosen to play he is playing Ms. C, but she thinks she is most likely playing Mr. B.

Exercise 11.10.7

(a) See Figure A.23.

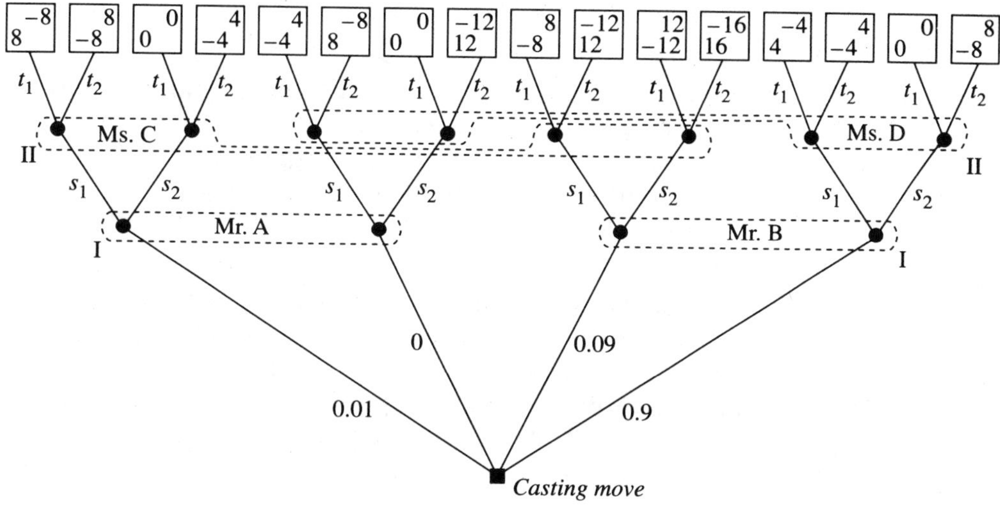

Figure A.23 The game tree for Exercise 11.10.7(a).

(b) Von Neumann: s_1s_1, s_1s_2, s_2s_1 and s_2s_2. Morgenstern: t_1t_1, t_1t_2, t_2t_1 and t_2t_2.

(c) See Figure A.24.

	c_1d_1	c_1d_2	c_2d_1	c_2d_2
a_1b_1	2.91	4.6	−4.24	−2.6
a_1b_2	2.88	4.64	−4.32	−2.56
a_2b_1	−1	1.46	−8.2	−5.74
a_2b_2	−1.08	1.5	−8.28	−8.7

Figure A.24 The strategic form for Exercise 11.10.7(c).

Exercise 11.10.8 Only in two-player zero-sum games is it necessarily true that a Nash equilibrium calls for a player to use a security strategy. But the game of Exercise 11.10.6 is a four-player game.

Exercise 11.10.9

(a) Erase the references to players I and II.
(b) One can think of Mr. A and Mr. B as being Von Neumann's agents (as explained in Section 10.4.2).

Exercise 11.10.10

(a) Ms. D believes that he can only be playing Mr. B, and so the casting director would have to put 0 in the top-right cell when constructing the table corresponding to Figure 11.9(b). But then Mr. A would have to believe that he is playing against Ms. C for sure, which is not consistent with his beliefs.
(b) and (c) Proceed as in Exercise 11.10.7(c).

Exercise 11.10.26 Let $\overline{w}_t$ be the expected value for w used by a firm of type t. If firm 1 is of type t, then its expected profit is $q_1(\overline{w}_t - q_1 - \overline{Q}_2)$, where $\overline{Q}_2$ is the expected output of firm 2. Firm 1 therefore optimizes by taking $q_1 = Q_1(t) = \frac{1}{2}(\overline{w}_t - \overline{Q}_2)$. Thus, $\overline{Q}_1 = \frac{1}{2}(\overline{\overline{w}} - Q_2)$. For the same reason, $\overline{Q}_2 = \frac{1}{2}(\overline{\overline{w}} - Q_1)$. Hence, $\overline{Q}_1 = \overline{Q}_2 = \frac{1}{3}\overline{\overline{w}}$.

Exercise 11.10.35 $\text{prob}(V_i > v) = 4 - v$. Thus, $\text{prob}(V_i > v$ and $V_2 > v) = (4 - v)^2$. The probability density function is $p(v) = P'(v) = 2(4 - v)$. The expected selling price is $E(P) = \int_3^4 2t(4 - t)dt = 3\frac{1}{3}$. Section 11.7.1 explains why the expected selling price is the same in Vickrey and English auctions.

Exercise 11.10.39 $Q(b) = p(b - 3)/(1 - p)(4 - b)$ $(3 \leq b \leq B)$, where $B = 4 - p$. As in Section 0.1.2, Low buyers bid their true valuation of \$3m and High buyers randomize by making bids between 3 and B so that the probability of bidding less than b is precisely $Q(b)$. If both buyers turn out to be High, the probability that the higher bid will be less than b is $R(b) = Q^2(b)$. The expected selling price for this equilibrium is:

$$3(1 - p)^2 + 2p(1 - p)\int_3^B bQ'(b)\,db + p^2\int_3^B bR'(b)\,db\,.$$

This expected selling price is the same as for English, Dutch and Vickrey auctions.

Exercise 11.10.46 If both workers are busy, the manager's expected profit is $\frac{2}{12}(0 - 2Y) + \frac{2}{12}(10 - Y - X) + \frac{8}{12}(20 - 2X)$. To maximize this is to minimize $3x^2 + y^2$, where $x = 10\sqrt{X}$ and $y = 10\sqrt{Y}$. However, the workers will not remain busy unless their incentives are adequate.Their incentive compatibility constraint is $\frac{9}{12}(10\sqrt{X} - 8) + \frac{3}{12}(10\sqrt{Y} - 8) \geq \frac{4}{12}(10\sqrt{X} - 0) + \frac{8}{12}(10\sqrt{Y} - 0)$, which simplifies to $5x - 5y \geq$

96. Their individual rationality constraint is $\frac{9}{12}(10\sqrt{X} - 8) + \frac{3}{12}(10\sqrt{Y} - 8) \geq 10$, which simplifies to $3x + y \geq 8$. These constraints on the manager's maximization problem need to be supplemented with $x \geq 0$ and $y \geq 0$. The active constraints are the first and the last, so that the optimizing values of x and y are 19.2 and 0. Thus the manager will pay $3.69 for a good article and nothing for a bad article.

Index